The Hutchinson

Concise Dictionary

of

Quotes

The Hutchinson

Concise Dictionary

of

Quotes

Helicon

First published 1995

Copyright © Helicon Publishing Ltd 1995

All rights reserved

Helicon Publishing Ltd
42 Hythe Bridge Street
Oxford OX1 2EP

Printed and bound in Great Britain by
Cox & Wyman Ltd, Reading, Berkshire

ISBN 1-85986-066-4

British Cataloguing in Publication Data

A catalogue record of this book is available from the British Library

ABELARD Peter 1079–1142
French scholastic philosopher.

1 Insofar as reason is hidden, let us be content with authority. [Quoted in Gordon Leff *Medieval Thought: St Augustine to Ockham*]

2 All acts are in themselves indifferent and only become good or evil according to the intention of their author. [Quoted in J P Migne (ed) *Patrologiae Latina* 178, 644a]

ACHESON Dean 1893–1971
US Democratic politician.

1 The first requirement of a statesman is that he be dull. This is not always easy to achieve. [*Observer* 21 June 1970]

2 Great Britain has lost an empire and has not yet found a role. [Speech at the Military Academy, West Point 5 Dec 1962]

ACTON John, Lord 1834–1902
English historian and Liberal politician.

Power tends to corrupt and absolute power corrupts absolutely. [Letter to Mandell Creighton April 1887]

ADAMS Henry Brooks 1838–1918
US historian and novelist.

1 Politics, as a practice, whatever its professions, has always been the systematic organization of hatreds. [*Education of Henry Adams* ch 1]

2 A friend in power is a friend lost. [*Education of Henry Adams* ch 7]

3 One friend in a lifetime is much; two are many; three are hardly possible. [*Education of Henry Adams* ch 20]

ADAMS John Quincy 1767–1848
US Federalist president.

Think of your forefathers! Think of your posterity! [Speech 22 Dec 1802]

ADDISON Joseph 1672–1719
English poet, playwright and essayist.

1 There is nothing more requisite in business than dispatch. [*Ancient Medals*]

2 'Tis not in mortals to command success, / But we'll do more, Sempronius; we'll deserve it. [*Cato* I. ii]

3 Beauty soon grows familiar to the lover, / Fades in his eye, and palls upon the sense. [*Cato* I. iv]

4 When love's well-tim'd, 'tis not a fault to love; / The strong, the brave, the virtuous, and the wise, / Sink in the soft captivity together. [*Cato* III. i]

5 The woman that deliberates is lost. [*Cato* IV. i]

6 Content thyself to be obscurely good. / When vice prevails, and impious men bear sway, / The post of honour is a private station. [*Cato* IV. iv]

7 Why shrinks the soul / Back on herself, and startles at destruction? / 'Tis the divinity that stirs within us; / 'Tis heaven itself, that points out an hereafter, / And intimates eternity to man. / Eternity! thou pleasing, dreadful thought! [*Cato* V. i]

8 From hence, let fierce contending nations know / What dire effects from civil discord flow. [*Cato* V. iv]

9 I should think my self a very bad Woman, if I had done what I do, for a Farthing less. [*The Drummer* I]

10 He more had pleas'd us, had he pleas'd us less. [On Abraham Cowley, *English Poets*]

11 Music, the greatest good that mortals know, / And all of heaven we have below. ['Song for St Cecilia's Day']

12 Thus I live in the world rather as a spectator of mankind than as one of the species. [*Spectator* no. 1]

13 A perfect Tragedy is the noblest Production of human Nature. [*Spectator* no. 39]

14 We have in England a particular bashfulness in every thing that regards religion. [*Spectator* no. 458]

15 A woman seldom asks advice before she has bought her wedding clothes. [*Spectator* no. 475]

16 I value my garden more for being full of blackbirds than of cherries, and very frankly give them fruit for their songs. [*Spectator* no. 477]

17 See in what peace a Christian can die. [Last words]

ADENAUER Konrad 1876–1967
German Christian Democrat politician.

A thick skin is a gift from God. [*New York Times* 30 Dec 1959]

ADLER Alfred 1870–1937
Austrian psychologist.

Whenever a child lies you will always find a severe parent. A lie would have no sense unless the truth were felt to be dangerous. [*New York Times* 1949]

ADLER Larry 1914–
US musician.

Vasectomy means never having to say you're sorry. [Attributed remark]

AESCHYLUS c. 525–c. 456 BC
Athenian dramatist.

Every ruler is harsh whose rule is new. [*Prometheus Bound*]

AGAR Herbert 1897–1980
US writer.

The truth which makes men free is for the most part the truth which men prefer not to hear. [*Time for Greatness*]

AGATE James Evershed 1877–1947
English essayist and theatre critic.

I am not interested in what anybody else thinks. My mind is not a bed to be made and remade. [*Ego*]

AÏDÉ Hamilton 1830–1906
English poet and novelist.

I sit beside my lonely fire, / And pray for wisdom yet – / For calmness to remember / Or courage to forget. ['Remember or Forget']

AIKEN Conrad 1889–1973
US poet and novelist.

Rock meeting rock can know love better / Than eyes that stare or lips that touch. / All that we know in love is bitter, / And it is not much. ['Annihilation']

AIMÉE Anouk 1932–
French actress.

You can only perceive real beauty in a person as they get older. [Quoted in *Guardian* 24 Aug 1988]

AKHMATOVA Anna 1889–1966
Russian poet.

In human intimacy there is a secret boundary, / Neither the experience of being in love nor passion can cross it, / Though lips be joined together in awful silence, / And the heart break asunder with love. ['In Human Intimacy']

ALBEE Edward 1928–
US playwright.

I have a fine sense of the ridiculous, but no sense of humour. [*Who's Afraid of Virginia Woolf?*]

ALCUIN 735–804
English scholar.

> The voice of the people is the voice of God. [Letter to the Emperor Charlemagne AD 800]

ALDINGTON Richard 1892–1962
English poet, novelist, and critic.

> Patriotism is a lively sense of collective responsibility. Nationalism is a silly cock crowing on its own dunghill. [*Colonel's Daughter*]

ALDISS Brian 1925–
English science-fiction writer.

> Whatever creativity is, it is in part a solution to a problem. [*Bury My Heart at W. H. Smith's*, 'Apéritif']

ALDRICH Henry 1648–1710
English scholar.

> If all be true that I do think, / There are five reasons we should drink; / Good wine – a friend – or being dry / Or lest we should be by and by / Or any other reason why. ['Reasons for Drinking']

ALEXANDER Cecil Frances 1818–1895
English hymn writer.

> All things bright and beautiful, / All creatures great and small, / All things wise and wonderful, / The Lord God made them all. ['All Things Bright and Beautiful']

ALEXANDER II 1818–1881
Tsar of Russia.

> It is better to abolish serfdom from above than to wait for it to abolish itself from below. [Speech to the Moscow nobility March 1856]

ALEXANDER THE GREAT 356–323 BC
King of Macedonia.

> I will not steal a victory. [Remark on refusing to attack the Persian army before the Battle of Gaugamela 331 BC, quoted in Plutarch *Life of Alexander*]

Statue of Alexander the Great by Moustakas, in Thessaloniki, Greece. A brilliant military tactician with a highly professional army, Alexander the Great established an empire that stretched from Greece to India. His conquests spread Greek culture throughout the Mediterranean and brought about the distinctive blending of Western and Eastern ideas that characterized the Hellenistic period.

ALFONSO XIII 1885–1941
King of Spain.

> Assassination – an accident of my trade. [Remark after an attempt on his life May 1906]

ALI Muhammad 1942–
US boxer.

> 1 It's just a job. Grass grows, birds fly, waves pound the sand. I beat people up. [*New York Times* 6 April 1977]
>
> 2 Float like a butterfly, sting like a bee. [Catch-phrase]

ALISON Richard c. 1596–1616
English poet.

> There cherries grow, that none can buy / Till cherry ripe themselves do cry. ['An Hour's Recreation in Music']

ALLEN Woody 1935–
US film writer, director, and actor.

1 A relationship, I think, is like a shark, you know? It has to constantly move forward or it dies. And I think what we got on our hands is a dead shark. [*Annie Hall* 1977]

2 It's not that I'm afraid to die. I just don't want to be there when it happens. [*Death*]

3 My wife was an immature woman...I would be home in the bathroom, taking a bath, and [she] would walk in whenever she felt like and sink my boats. ['I Had a Rough Marriage']

4 I should've known something was wrong with my first wife when I brought her home to meet my parents–they approved of her but my dog died. [*Illustrated Woody Allen Reader*, 'Monologue']

5 Man consists of two parts, his mind and his body, only the body has more fun. [*Love and Death* 1975]

6 To love is to suffer. To avoid suffering, one must not love. But, then one suffers from not loving. Therefore, to love is to suffer, not to love is to suffer, to suffer is to suffer. To be happy is to love, to be happy then, is to suffer, but, suffering makes one unhappy, therefore, to be unhappy one must love, or love to suffer, or suffer from too much happiness. I hope you're getting this down. [*Love and Death* 1975]

7 I'm old-fashioned. I don't believe in extramarital relationships. I think people should mate for life, like pigeons or Catholics. [*Manhattan* 1979]

8 If only God would give me some clear sign! Like making a large deposit in my name at a Swiss bank. [*New Yorker* 5 Nov 1973]

9 Bisexuality immediately doubles your chances of a date on Saturday night. [*New York Herald Tribune* 1975]

10 Marrying for love is a very recent idea. In the old country, they didn't marry for love. A man married a woman because he needed an extra mule. [*Radio Days* 1987]

11 For a while we pondered whether to take a vacation or get a divorce. We decided that a trip to Bermuda is over in two weeks but a divorce is something you always have. [Quoted in *Time Magazine* 3 July 1972]

12 My wife got the house, the car, the bank account, and if I marry again and have children, she gets them too. [Quoted in B Chieger *Was It Good for You Too?*]

13 The chief problem about death, incidentally, is the fear that there may be no afterlife – a depressing thought, particularly for those who have bothered to shave. Also, there is the fear that there is an afterlife but no one will know where it is being held. [*Without Feathers*]

14 Money is better than poverty, if only for financial reasons. [*Without Feathers*]

15 For the first year of marriage I had a basically bad attitude. I tended to place my wife underneath a pedestal. [From his nightclub act 1964]

ALLSTON Washington 1779–1843
US painter.

The love of gain has never made a painter, but it has marred many. [*Lectures on Art*]

ALVA or Alba Ferdinand, Duke of
1508–1582
Spanish politician and general.

I have tamed men of iron and why then shall I not be able to tame these men of butter? [Reply to King Philip II of Spain on being appointed governor general of the Netherlands 1567]

ALVAREZ Alfred 1929–
English poet and writer.

> Divorce and suicide have many characteristics in common and one crucial difference: although both are devastatingly public admissions of failure, divorce, unlike suicide, has to be lived through. [*Life After Marriage*]

AMIEL Henri-Frédéric 1821–1881
Swiss philosopher and poet.

> 1 Our systems, perhaps, are nothing more than an unconscious apology for our faults – a gigantic scaffolding whose object is to hide from us our favourite sin. [*Journal Intime*]

> 2 Truth is not only violated by falsehood; it may be outraged by silence. [*Journal Intime*]

AMIS Kingsley 1922–
English novelist and poet.

> 1 It was no wonder that people were so horrible when they started life as children. [*Lucky Jim*]

> 2 I was never an Angry Young Man. I am angry only when I hit my thumb with a hammer. [On the labelling of authors as 'Angry Young Men', *Eton College Chronicle*]

ANARCHARSIS LIVED 6TH CENTURY BC
Scythian sage, prince, and inventor.

> Granted that my country is a disgrace to me, you are a disgrace to your country. [Reply to an Athenian who reproached him for being a Scythian, quoted in Diogenes Laertius *Lives of the Philosophers*]

ANDERSON John 1893–1962
Australian philosopher.

> The adoption of an adult and independent outlook is marked by a refusal to be protected for one's own good; and, in harmony with this position, we should refuse to protect others for their good. [*Education and Politics*]

ANDERSON Lindsay 1923–1994
British film director.

> Art is an experience, not the formulation of a problem. [*The Times* 29 March 1989]

ANDERSON Sherwood 1876–1941
US writer.

> 1 I've never been able to work without a woman to love. Perhaps I'm cruel. They are earth and sky and warmth and light to me. I'm like an Irish peasant, taking potatoes out of the ground. I live by the woman loved. I take from her. [*Letters of Sherwood Anderson*]

> 2 I found it impossible to work with security staring me in the face. [Remark to his publisher, on declining a weekly cheque.]

ANDREWES Lancelot 1555–1626
Church of England bishop.

> The nearer the Church the further from God. ['Sermon on the Nativity' 1622]

ANGELOU Maya 1928–
US writer.

> 1 The sadness of the women's movement is that they don't allow the necessity of love. See, I don't personally trust any revolution where love isn't allowed. [*California Living* 14 May 1975]

> 2 Children's talent to endure stems from their ignorance of alternatives. [*I Know Why the Caged Bird Sings* ch 17]

> 3 Africa to me ... is more than a glamorous fact. It is a historical truth. No man can know where he is going unless he knows exactly where he has been and exactly how he arrived at his present place. ['Involvement in Black and White', interview in *Oregonian* 17 Feb 1951]

ANONYMOUS

> 1 Know thyself. [Saying written on the wall of the ancient temple of Delphi]

> 2 Before you advise anyone 'Be yourself!' reassess his character.

ANOUILH Jean 1910–1987
French dramatist.

1 Tragedy is restful and the reason is that hope, that foul, deceitful thing, has no part in it. [*Antigone*]

2 There is, of course, love. And then there's life, its enemy. [*Ardèle*]

3 Beauty is one of the rare things that do not lead to doubt of God. [*Becket* I]

4 Until the day of his death, no man can be sure of his courage. [*Becket* I]

ANSTEY Christopher 1724–1805
English poet.

1 How he welcomes at once all the world and his wife, / And how civil to folk he ne'er saw in his life. [*New Bath Guide*]

2 If ever I ate a good supper at night, / I dream'd of the devil, and wak'd in a fright. [*New Bath Guide* Letter 4]

ANTHONY Susan B 1820–1906
US campaigner for women's rights.

1 The true Republic: men, their rights and nothing more; women, their rights and nothing less. [Motto of her newspaper *Revolution*]

2 Marriage, to women as to men, must be a luxury, not a necessity; an incident of life, not all of it. [Speech on Social Purity, Spring 1875]

ANTIPHANES LIVED 4TH CENTURY BC
Greek comic poet.

Idly inquisitive tribe of grammarians, / who dig up the poetry of others / by the roots ... Get away, bugs, / that bite secretly at the eloquent. [*Greek Anthology*]

APOCRYPHA
Appendix to Old Testament of the Bible.

1 He that toucheth pitch shall be defiled therewith. [Ecclesiasticus 13:1]

2 Let us now praise famous men, and our fathers that begat us. [Ecclesiasticus 44:1]

3 Their bodies are buried in peace: but their name liveth for evermore. [Ecclesiasticus 44:14]

APPLETON Thomas 1812–1884
US writer.

1 Good Americans, when they die, go to Paris. [Quoted in O W Holmes *Autocrat of the Breakfast Table* ch 6]

2 A Boston man is the east wind made flesh. [Attributed remark]

AQUINAS St Thomas c. 1226–1274
Italian philosopher and theologian.

1 All I have written seems to me like so much straw ... compared with what has been revealed to me. [Quoted in F C Copleston *Aquinas*]

2 It sometimes happens that someone is a good citizen who has not the quality according to which someone is also a good man. [Quoted in Walter Ullmann *A History of Political Thought: The Middle Ages*]

3 Grace does not abolish nature, but perfects it. [Quoted in Gordon Leff *Medieval Thought: St Augustine to Ockham*]

ARAB PROVERB

He who eats alone chokes alone.

ARAFAT Yassir 1929–
Leader of the PLO.

The PLO recognizes the right of the State of Israel to exist in peace and security. [On signing peace agreement with Israel, Sept 1993]

ARAGON Louis 1897–1982
French poet and novelist.

The function of genius is to furnish cretins with ideas twenty years later. [*Traité du Style*, 'Le Porte-Plume']

ARBUTHNOT John 1667–1735
Scottish writer and physician.

Law is a bottomless pit. [*The History of John Bull*]

ARCHILOCHUS 7TH CENTURY BC
Greek poet.

> The fox knows many things – the hedgehog one *big* one. [Attributed remark]

ARCHIMEDES c. 287–212 BC
Greek mathematician.

> **1** Eureka! I have found it! [Remark, quoted in Vitruvius Pollio *De Architectura* IX]
>
> **2** Give me but one firm place on which to stand, and I will move the earth. [On the lever, quoted in *Pappus Alexander*]

ARISTOTLE 384–322 BC
Greek philosopher.

> **1** When devoid of virtue, man is the most unscrupulous and savage of animals, and the worst in regard to sexual indulgence and gluttony. [*Politics* bk 1, 1235a 36–38]
>
> **2** Man by nature is a political animal. [*Politics* bk 1, 1253a 2–3]
>
> **3** Accordingly we conclude that the appropriate age for marriage is about the eighteenth year for girls and for men the thirty-seventh plus or minus. [*Politics*]

ARMISTEAD Lewis Addison 1817–1863
US army officer.

> Give them the cold steel, boys! [Attributed remark during American Civil War]

ARMSTRONG Louis 1901–1971
US jazz musician and singer.

> **1** Making money ain't nothing exciting to me. You might be able to buy a little better booze than the wino on the corner. But you get sick just like the next cat and when you die you're just as graveyard dead. [Quoted in *Observer* 5 July 1970]
>
> **2** A lot of cats copy the Mona Lisa, but people still line up to see the original. [Reply when asked whether he objected to people copying his style]

ARNOLD Edwin 1832–1904
English poet and journalist.

> Somewhere there waiteth in this world of ours / For one lone soul another lonely soul, / Each choosing each through all the weary hours, / And meeting strangely at one sudden goal. ['Somewhere There Waiteth']

ARNOLD Matthew 1828–1888
English poet and critic.

> **1** The same heart beats in every human breast. ['The Buried Life']
>
> **2** The men of culture are the true apostles of equality. [*Culture and Anarchy*]
>
> **3** The pursuit of perfection, then, is the pursuit of sweetness and light. [*Culture and Anarchy*]
>
> **4** And we are here as on a darkling plain / Swept with confused alarms of struggle and flight, / Where ignorant armies clash by night. ['Dover Beach']
>
> **5** The sea of faith / Was once, too, at the full, and round earth's shore / Lay like the folds of a bright girdle furl'd; / But now I only hear / Its melancholy, long, withdrawing roar. ['Dover Beach']

US jazz musician Louis Armstrong, whose virtuoso trumpet playing and gravelly singing voice made him known worldwide.

6 Home of lost causes, and forsaken beliefs, and unpopular names, and impossible loyalties! [*Essays in Criticism* 1st Series, preface]

7 What helps it now, that Byron bore, / With haughty scorn which mock'd the smart, / Through Europe to the Aetolian shore / The pageant of his bleeding heart? ['The Grande Chartreuse']

8 The unplumb'd, salt, estranging sea. ['Isolation, or To Marguerite']

9 Culture, the acquainting ourselves with the best that has been known and said in the world, and thus with the history of the human spirit. [*Literature and Dogma*, preface to 1873 edn]

10 Miracles do not happen. [*Literature and Dogma*, preface to 1883 edn, last words]

11 The East bow'd low before the blast, / In patient, deep disdain. / She let the legions thunder past, / And plunged in thought again. ['Obermann Once More']

12 Eternal Passion! / Eternal Pain! ['Philomela']

13 Strew on her roses, roses, / And never a spray of yew. / In quiet she reposes: / Ah! would that I did too. ['Requiescat']

14 Ye fill up the gaps in our files, / Strengthen the wavering line, / Stablish, continue our march, / On, to the bound of the waste, / On, to the City of God. ['Rugby Chapel']

15 All the live murmur of a summer's day. [*The Scholar-Gipsy*]

16 This strange disease of modern life. [*The Scholar-Gipsy*]

17 Others abide our question. Thou art free. ['Sonnet, Shakespeare']

18 Who saw life steadily, and saw it whole: / The mellow glory of the Attic stage. ['Sonnet to a Friend']

19 And that sweet City with her dreaming spires, / She needs not June for beauty's heightening. [*Thyrsis*]

20 Too quick despairer, wherefore wilt thou go? [*Thyrsis*]

ARNOLD Thomas 1795–1842
English schoolmaster.

My object will be, if possible, to form Christian men, for Christian boys I can scarcely hope to make. [Letter, on appointment to headmastership of Rugby 1828]

ARTAUD Antonin 1896–1948
French theatre actor, director, and theorist.

1 So long as we have failed to eliminate any of the causes of human despair, we do not have the right to try to eliminate those means by which man tries to cleanse himself of despair. [*General Security: The Liquidation of Opium*]

2 Where there is a stink of shit / there is a smell of being. [*To Have Done with the Judgment of God*, 'The Pursuit of Fecality']

3 No one has ever written, painted, sculpted, modeled, built, or invented except literally to get out of hell. [*Van Gogh, the Man Suicided by Society*]

ASAF George 1880–1951
English songwriter.

What's the use of worrying? / It never was worth while, / So, pack up your troubles in your old kit-bag, / And smile, smile, smile. ['Pack Up Your Troubles In Your Old Kit-Bag']

ASCHAM Roger c. 1515–1568
English scholar and royal tutor.

He that will write well in any tongue must follow the counsel of Aristotle: to speak as the common people do, to think as wise men do. [*Toxophilus*]

ASHFORD Daisy 1881–1972
English author, aged nine years.

1 I am not quite a gentleman but you would hardly notice it but can't be helped anyhow. [*The Young Visiters* ch 1]

2 Oh I see said the Earl but my own idear is that these things are as piffle before the wind. [*The Young Visiters* ch 5]

3 My life will be sour grapes and ashes without you. [*The Young Visiters* ch 8]

ASHMORE Edward Bailey 1872–1953
British general in World War I.

The fact that I was exchanging the comparative safety of the front for the probability of being hanged in the streets of London did not worry me. [Remark on being sent to command the London air defences]

ASIMOV Isaac 1920–1992
Russian-born US writer.

If my doctor told me I only had six months to live, I wouldn't brood. I'd type a little faster. [*Life*]

ASQUITH Herbert, Earl of 1852–1928
British Liberal politician and prime minister.

1 Youth would be an ideal state if it came a little later in life. [*Observer* 15 Apr 1923]

2 One to mislead the public, another to mislead the Cabinet, and the third to mislead itself. [On the War Office's sets of figures, quoted in Alistair Horne *Price of Glory* .]

ASQUITH Margot 1865–1945
Second wife of Herbert Asquith.

1 He can't see a belt without hitting below it. [On Lloyd George, quoted in *Listener* 11 June 1953.]

2 Lord Birkenhead is very clever but sometimes his brains go to his head. [*Listener* 11 June 1953]

ASTAIRE Fred 1899–1987
US dancer, actor, singer, and choreographer.

I have no desire to prove anything by dancing ... I just dance. [Remark]

US dancer, singer, and film star Fred Astaire with his dancing partner Ginger Rogers in *Flying Down to Rio* 1933, the first of the ten films they made together. The sophisticated and intimate style of dancing, its grace and technical excellence, and the integration of plot and music in the Rogers–Astaire films revolutionized the musical comedy. Astaire's later co-stars included Judy Garland, Leslie Caron, and Audrey Hepburn.

ASTLEY Sir Jacob 1579–1652
English Royalist general.

> O Lord! thou knowest how busy I must be this day: / if I forget thee, do not thou forget me. [Prayer before the Battle of Edgehill, quoted in Sir Philip Warwick *Memoires*]

ASTOR Nancy, Lady 1879–1964
US-born British politician; first female British MP.

> 1 One reason why I don't drink is because I wish to know when I am having a good time. [*Christian Herald* June 1960]

> 2 I married beneath me, all women do. [Quoted in *Dictionary of National Biography 1961–1970*]

ATATÜRK Kemal 1881–1938
Turkish president.

> I don't act for public opinion. I act for the nation and for my own satisfaction. [Quoted in Lord Kinross *Atatürk*]

ATKINSON Brooks 1894–1984
US journalist.

> After each war there is a little less democracy to save. [*Once Around the Sun*]

ATTENBOROUGH David 1926–
English broadcaster and zoologist.

> Anyone who spends any time watching animals has to conclude that the overriding purpose of an individual's existence is to pass on some part of it to the next generation. [*The Trials of Life*]

ATTLEE Clement 1883–1967
British Labour prime minister.

> 1 I should be a sad subject for any publicity expert. I have none of the qualities which create publicity. [Quoted in Harold Nicolson *Diary* 14 Jan 1949]

> 2 I think the British have the distinction above all other nations of being able to put new wine into old bottles without bursting them. [*Hansard* 24 Oct 1950]

> 3 I must remind the Right Honourable Gentleman that a monologue is not a decision. [Remark to Winston Churchill, quoted in F Williams *Prime Minister Remembers*]

> 4 Democracy means government by discussion, but it is only effective if you can stop people talking. [Speech at Oxford 14 June 1957]

AUBREY John 1626–1697
English antiquary and folklorist.

> When he killed a calf he would do it in a high style, and make a speech. [*Brief Lives*, 'William Shakespeare']

AUDEN W H 1907–1973
English-born US poet.

> 1 I'll love you till the ocean / Is folded and hung up to dry / And the seven stars go squawking / Like geese about the sky. ['As I Walked Out One Evening']

> 2 A poet's hope: to be, / like some valley cheese, / local, but prized elsewhere. [*Collected Poems*]

> 3 Almost all of our relationships begin and most of them continue as forms of mutual exploitation, a mental or physical barter, to be terminated when one or both parties run out of goods. [*Dyer's Hand*, 'Hic et Ille']

> 4 Every autobiography is concerned with two characters, a Don Quixote, the Ego, and a Sancho Panza, the Self. [*Dyer's Hand*, 'Hic et Ille']

> 5 One cannot review a bad book without showing off. [*Dyer's Hand*, 'Reading']

> 6 Some books are undeservedly forgotten; none are undeservedly remembered. [*Dyer's Hand*, 'Reading']

> 7 When he laughed, respectable senators burst with laughter, / And

when he cried the little children died in the streets. ['Epitaph on a Tyrant']

8 He was my North, my South, my East and West, / My working week and my Sunday rest, / My noon, my midnight, my talk, my song; / I thought that love would last for ever; I was wrong. ['Funeral Blues']

9 Evil is unspectacular and always human, / And shares our bed and eats at our own table. [*Herman Melville* 4]

10 To us he is no more a person / Now but a whole climate of opinion. ['In Memory of Sigmund Freud']

11 O but he was as fair as a garden in flower, / As slender and tall as the great Eiffel Tower, / When the waltz throbbed out on the long promenade / O his eyes and his smile they went straight to my heart; / 'O marry me, Johnny, I'll love and obey': / But he frowned like thunder and he went away. ['Johnny']

12 Lay your sleeping head, my love, / Human on my faithless arm. ['Lay Your Sleeping Head My Love']

13 She survived whatever happened; she forgave; she became. ['The Model']

14 To the man-in-the-street, who, I'm sorry to say, / Is a keen observer of life, / The word 'Intellectual' suggests straight away / A man who's untrue to his wife. [*New Year Letter*]

15 The girl whose boy-friend starts writing her love poems should be on her guard. [*Poets at Work*, 'Squares and Oblongs']

16 My Dear One is mine as mirrors are lonely. [*The Sea and the Mirror*]

17 We must love one another or die. ['September 1, 1939']

18 When it comes, will it come without warning / Just as I'm picking my nose? / Will it knock on my door in the morning, / Or tread in the bus on my toes? / Will it come like a change in the weather? / Will its greeting be courteous and rough? / Will it alter my life altogether? / O tell me the truth about love. [*Twelve Songs* XII]

19 Was he free? Was he happy? The question is absurd: / Had anything been wrong, we should certainly have heard. ['The Unknown Citizen']

20 My face looks like a wedding-cake left out in the rain. [Quoted in H Carpenter *W H Auden* pt 2, ch 6]

AUGIER Émile 1820–1889
French dramatist.

Nostalgia for the gutter. [*Le Mariage d'Olympe* I. i]

AUGUSTINE OF HIPPO St 354–430
Christian theologian.

1 Give me chastity and continency, but do not give it yet. [*Confessions*]

2 Rome has spoken; the argument is at an end. [Sermon on the Pelagian Controversy]

3 Love and do what you will. [Treatise on the Joannine Epistles.]

AUGUSTUS 63 BC–14 AD
First of the Roman emperors.

Make haste slowly [Quoted in Suetonius *Divus Augustus* 25]

AUSTEN Jane 1775–1817
English novelist.

1 Human nature is so well disposed towards those who are in interesting situations, that a young person, who either marries or dies, is sure to be kindly spoken of. [*Emma* ch 22]

2 One half of the world cannot understand the pleasures of the other. [*Emma*]

Jane Austen's work appeared anonymously in her lifetime, and she received very little recognition or payment for it, but she has since become one of the most popular English novelists.

3 There certainly are not so many men of large fortune in the world, as there are pretty women to deserve them. [*Mansfield Park* ch 1]

4 There is not one in a hundred of either sex who is not taken in when they marry. Look where I will, I see that it *is* so; and I feel that it *must* be so, when I consider that it is, of all transactions, the one in which people expect most from others, and are least honest themselves. [*Mansfield Park* ch 5]

5 Let other pens dwell on guilt and misery. [*Mansfield Park* ch 48]

6 Being now in her twenty-first year, Maria Bertram was beginning to think matrimony a duty. [*Mansfield Park*]

7 She had been forced into prudence in her youth, she learned romance as she grew older–the natural sequel to an unnatural beginning. [*Persuasion* ch 4]

8 All the privilege I claim for my own sex . . . is that of loving longest, when existence or when hope is gone. [*Persuasion* ch 23]

9 It is a truth universally acknowledged, that a single man in possession of a good fortune, must be in want of a wife. [*Pride and Prejudice* ch 1]

10 Happiness in marriage is entirely a matter of chance. [*Pride and Prejudice* ch 6]

11 A lady's imagination is very rapid; it jumps from admiration to love, from love to matrimony in a moment. [*Pride and Prejudice* ch 6]

12 From this day you must be a stranger to one of your parents. – Your mother will never see you again if you do *not* marry Mr Collins, and I will never see you again if you *do*. [*Pride and Prejudice* ch 20]

13 Without thinking highly either of men or of matrimony, marriage had always been her object, it was the only honourable provision for well-educated young women of small fortune, and however uncertain of giving happiness, must be their pleasant preservative from want. [*Pride and Prejudice* ch 22]

14 Next to being married, a girl likes to be crossed in love a little now and then. [*Pride and Prejudice* ch 24]

15 What is the difference in matrimonial affairs, between the mercenary and the prudent move? Where does discretion end, and avarice begin? [*Pride and Prejudice* ch 27]

16 'Jane will be quite an old maid soon, I declare. She is almost three and twenty! Lord, how ashamed I should be of not being married before three and twenty!' [*Pride and Prejudice* ch 39]

17 For what do we live, but to make sport for our neighbours, and laugh at them in our turn? [*Pride and Prejudice* ch 57]

18 Mrs Hall of Sherbourne was brought to bed yesterday of a dead child, some weeks before she expected, owing to a fright. I suppose she happened unawares to look at her husband. [Letter 27 Oct 1798]

19 Single women have a dreadful propensity for being poor–which is one very strong argument in favour of matrimony. [Letter to Fanny Knight 13 March 1817]

AUSTIN Alfred 1835–1913
English poet.

I dare not alter these things, they come to me from above. [Remark rejecting the accusation of writing ungrammatical verse]

AVERROËS 1126–1198
Arabian philosopher.

1 Philosophy is the friend and milk-sister of the Law. [*The Decisive Treatise*]

2 This man (Aristotle) is ... an example which nature has devised to demonstrate supreme human perfection. [Quoted in Gordon Leff *Medieval Thought: St Augustine to Ockham*]

AVICENNA 979–1037
Arabian philosopher and physician.

A horse is simply a horse. [Quoted in Gordon Leff *Medieval Thought: St Augustine to Ockham*]

AYCKBOURN Alan 1939–
English dramatist.

1 You must come to our house next time. Absolute peace. Neither of us ever says a word to each other. That's the secret of a successful union. [*Absent Friends*]

2 Few women care to be laughed at and men not at all, except for large sums of money. [*Norman Conquests*]

AYER A J 1910–1989
English philosopher.

1 No morality can be founded on authority, even if the authority were divine. [*Essay on Humanism*]

2 To say that authority, whether secular or religious, supplies no ground for morality is not to deny the obvious fact that it supplies a sanction. [*Meaning of Life and Other Essays*, title essay]

3 If I had been someone not very clever, I would have done an easier job like publishing. That's the easiest job I can think of. [Remark]

AYTOUN Robert 1570–1638
Scottish poet.

I loved thee once, I'll love no more, / Thine be the grief, as is the blame; / Thou art not what thou wast before, / What reason I should be the same? ['To an Inconstant Mistress']

AYTOUN William Edmondstoune 1813–1865
Scottish poet.

The earth is all the home I have, / The heavens my wide roof-tree. [*Wandering Jew*]

B

BACH Richard
US writer.

> Don't believe what your eyes are telling you, all they show is limitation. Look with your understanding, find out what you already know, and you'll see the way to fly.
> [*Jonathan Livingstone Seagull*]

BACHELARD Gaston 1884–1962
French philosopher and scientist.

1 Even a minor event in the life of a child is an event of that child's world and thus a world event. [*Fragments of a Poetics of Fire* ch 1]

2 There is no original truth, only original error. [*Fragments of a Poetics of Fire*, 'A Retrospective Glance at the Lifework of a Master of Books']

3 The subconscious is ceaselessly murmuring, and it is by listening to these murmurs that one hears the truth. [*Poetics of Reverie* ch 2]

4 Man is a creation of desire, not a creation of need. [*Psychoanalysis of Fire* ch 2]

BACKUS Jim 1913–
US comedian and actor.

> Many a man owes his success to his first wife, and his second wife to his success. [Attributed remark]

BACON Sir Francis 1561–1626
English politician, philosopher, and essayist.

1 If a man will begin with certainties, he shall end in doubts; but if he will be content to begin with doubts, he shall end in certainties. [*Advancement of Learning* bk 1]

English philosopher, politician and author Sir Francis Bacon. A pioneer of the empirical scientific method, it is said that he died as a result of one his experiments. In an attempt to prove that cold temperatures preserve flesh, he collected snow to stuff a chicken. As a result he caught a chill and died soon after.

2 Time, which is the author of authors. [*Advancement of Learning* bk 1]

3 Antiquities are history defaced, or some remnants of history which have casually escaped the shipwreck of time. [*Advancement of Learning* bk 2]

4 A man must make his opportunity, as oft as find it. [*Advancement of Learning* bk 2]

5 Man seeketh in society comfort, use, and protection. [*Advancement of Learning* bk 2]

6 They are ill discoverers that think there is no land, when they

can see nothing but sea. [*Advancement of Learning* bk 2]

7 Hope is a good breakfast, but it is a bad supper. [*Apothegms*]

8 Envy never makes holiday. [*De Augmentis Scientiarum*]

9 Silence is the virtue of fools. [*De Augmentis Scientiarum*]

10 Prosperity is not without many fears and distastes; and adversity is not without comforts and hopes. [*Essays*, 'Of Adversity']

11 A little philosophy inclineth man's mind to atheism, but depth in philosophy bringeth men's minds about to religion. [*Essays*, 'Of Atheism']

12 Virtue is like a rich stone, best plain set. [*Essays*, 'Of Beauty']

13 Nothing doth more hurt in a state than that cunning men pass for wise. [*Essays*, 'Of Cunning']

14 I do not believe that any man fears to be dead, but only the stroke of death. [*Essays*, 'Of Death']

15 Men fear death as children fear to go in the dark. [*Essays*, 'Of Death']

16 Riches are for spending. [*Essays*, 'Of Expense']

17 There is little friendship in the world, and least of all between equals. [*Essays*, 'Of Followers and Friends']

18 A crowd is not company, and faces are but a gallery of pictures, and talk but a tinkling cymbal, where there is no love. [*Essays*, 'Of Friendship']

19 God Almighty first planted a garden; and, indeed, it is the purest of human pleasures. [*Essays*, 'Of Gardens']

20 If a man be gracious and courteous to strangers, it shows he is a citizen of the world. [*Essays*, 'Of Goodness, and Goodness of Nature']

21 All rising to great place is by a winding stair. [*Essays*, 'Of Great Place']

22 Men in great place are thrice servants: servants of the sovereign or state, servants of fame, and servants of business. [*Essays*, 'Of Great Place']

23 Love can find entrance, not only into an open heart, but also into a heart well fortified, if watch be not well kept. [*Essays*, 'Of Love']

24 Nuptial love maketh mankind; friendly love perfecteth it; but wanton love corrupteth and embaseth it. [*Essays*, 'Of Love']

25 He that hath wife and children hath given hostages to fortune. [*Essays*, 'Of Marriage and the Single Life']

26 He was reputed one of the wise men, that made answer to the question, when a man should marry? A young man not yet, an elder man not at all. [*Essays*, 'Of Marriage and the Single Life']

27 Wives are young men's mistresses, companions for middle age, and old men's nurses. [*Essays*, 'Of Marriage and the Single Life']

28 It is a reverend thing to see an ancient castle or building not in decay. [*Essays*, 'Of Nobility']

29 Children sweeten labours, but they make misfortunes more bitter. [*Essays*, 'Of Parents and Children']

30 Fame is like a river, that beareth up things light and swollen, and drowns things weighty and solid. [*Essays*, 'Of Praise']

31 Revenge is a kind of wild justice. [*Essays*, 'Of Revenge']

32 Money is like muck, not good except it be spread. [*Essays*, 'Of Seditions and Troubles']

33 The remedy is worse than the disease. [*Essays*, 'Of Seditions and Troubles']

34 Reading maketh a full man; conference a ready man and writing an exact man. [*Essays*, 'Of Studies']

35 Some books are to be tasted, others to be swallowed, and some few to be chewed and digested. [*Essays*, 'Of Studies']

36 Studies serve for delight, for ornament, and for ability. [*Essays*, 'Of Studies']

37 Suspicions amongst thoughts are like bats amongst birds, they ever fly by twilight. [*Essays*, 'Of Suspicion']

38 There is a superstition in avoiding superstition. [*Essays*, 'Of Superstition']

39 There is nothing makes a man suspect much, more than to know little. [*Essays*, 'Of Suspicion']

40 A mixture of a lie doth ever add pleasure. [*Essays*, 'Of Truth']

41 What is truth? said jesting Pilate; and would not stay for an answer. [*Essays*, 'Of Truth']

42 Books must follow sciences, and not sciences books. [*Proposition Touching Amendment of Laws*]

43 I have taken all knowledge to be my province. [Letter to Lord Burleigh 1592]

44 Opportunity makes a thief. [Letter to the Earl of Essex 1598]

BADEN-POWELL Robert 1857–1941
British general and founder of the Boy Scout movement.

A Scout smiles and whistles under all circumstances. [*Scouting for Boys*]

BAEZ Joan 1941–
US folk singer.

I've never had a humble opinion. If you've got an opinion, why be humble about it? [Remark]

BAGEHOT Walter 1826–1877
English writer and economist.

1 Royalty is a government in which the attention of the nation is concentrated on one person doing interesting actions. A Republic is a government in which that attention is divided between many, who are all doing uninteresting actions. [*English Constitution* ch 2]

2 Women – one half of the human race at least – care fifty times more for a marriage than a ministry. [*English Constitution*, 'The Monarchy']

3 The most melancholy of human reflections, perhaps, is that, on the whole, it is a question whether the benevolence of mankind does most good or harm. [*Physics and Politics*]

4 One of the greatest pains to human nature is the pain of a new idea. [*Physics and Politics*]

BAIRNSFATHER Bruce 1888–1959
English artist and cartoonist.

Well, if you knows of a better 'ole, go to it. [*Fragments from France* 1]

BAKATIN Vadim 1937–
Candidate in first Russian presidential election.

Making capitalism out of socialism is like making eggs out of an omelette. [Speech May 1991]

BAKER Janet 1933–
English opera singer.

Singing lieder is like putting a piece of music under a microscope. [*Opera News* July 1977]

BAKER Sidney John 1912–1976
Australian writer.

Visitors to Australia rarely fail to feel ... that, although we are hospitable outdoor types, we live in what is tantamount to a cultural concentration camp. [*The Drum*]

BAKUNIN Mikhail 1814–1876
Russian political theorist.

Does it follow that I reject all authority? Perish the thought. In the matter of boots, I defer to the authority of the bootmaker. [*God and the State*]

BALDWIN James 1924–1987
US writer and civil-rights activist.

1 Money, it turned out, was exactly like sex, you thought of nothing else if you didn't have it and thought of other things if you did. ['Black Boy looks at the White Boy']

2 Anyone who has ever struggled with poverty knows how extremely expensive it is to be poor. [*Nobody Knows My Name*, 'Fifth Avenue, Uptown: a letter from Harlem']

3 Freedom is not something that anybody can be given; freedom is something people take and people are as free as they want to be. [*Nobody Knows My Name*, 'Notes for a Hypothetical Novel']

4 Children have never been very good at listening to their elders, but they have never failed to imitate them. ['The Precarious Vogue of Ingmar Bergman', *Esquire* April 1960]

5 Confronted with the impossibility of remaining faithful to one's beliefs, and the equal impossibility of becoming free of them, one can be driven to the most inhuman excesses. ['Stranger in the Village', *Harper's* Oct 1953]

6 Rage cannot be hidden, it can only be dissembled. This dissembling deludes the thoughtless, and strengthens rage and adds, to rage, contempt. ['Stranger in the Village', *Harper's* Oct 1953]

7 To be a Negro in this country and to be relatively conscious is to be in a rage almost all the time. [*Time* Aug 1965]

8 It comes as a great shock to see Gary Cooper killing off the Indians and, although you are rooting for Gary Cooper, that the Indians are you. [Speech at Cambridge University 17 Feb 1965]

BALDWIN Stanley 1867–1947
British Conservative prime minister.

1 A platitude is simply a truth repeated until people get tired of hearing it. [*Hansard* 29 May 1924]

2 I think it is well also for the man in the street to realize that there is no power on earth that can protect him from being bombed. Whatever people may tell him, the bomber will always get through. The only defence is in offence, which means that you have to kill more women and children more quickly than the enemy if you want to save yourselves. [*Hansard* 10 Nov 1932]

3 The gift of rhetoric has been responsible for more bloodshed on this earth than all the guns and explosives that were ever invented. [Quoted in *Observer* 16 March 1924]

4 The intelligent are to the intelligentsia what a gentleman is to a gent. [Quoted in G M Young *Stanley Baldwin* ch 13]

5 'Safety first' does not mean a smug self-satisfaction with every-

Arthur Balfour, British statesman, formulated the Balfour Declaration - he delivered the Gifford Lecture on *Atheism and Humanism* - he was sometimes considered too detached to excel in politics.

thing as it is. It is a warning to all persons who are going to cross a road in dangerous circumstances. [*The Times* 21 May 1929]

BALFOUR Arthur 1848–1930
British Conservative prime minister.

1 I never forgive but I always forget. [Quoted in R Blake *Conservative Party* ch 7]

2 Biography should be written by an acute enemy. [*Observer* 30 Jan 1927]

3 It is unfortunate, considering that enthusiasm moves the world, that so few enthusiasts can be trusted to speak the truth. [Letter to Mrs Drew May 1891]

BALLOU Sullivan D. 1861
US major in the Union army.

O Sarah! If the dead can come back to this earth and flit unseen around those they loved, I shall always be near you; in the gladdest days and in the darkest nights ... *always, always*, and if there be a soft breeze upon your cheek, it shall be my breath, as the cool air fans your throbbing temple, it shall be my spirit passing by. Sarah do not mourn me dead; think I am gone and wait for thee, for we shall meet again ... . [Letter to his wife 14 July 1861 before the Battle of Bull Run, at which he was killed]

BALZAC Honoré de 1799–1850
French novelist.

1 Equality may be perhaps a right, but no power on earth can turn it into a fact. [*La Duchesse de Langeais*]

2 The majority of husbands remind me of an orangutan trying to play the violin. [*Physiology of Marriage*]

3 No man should marry until he has studied anatomy and dissected at least one woman. [*Physiology of Marriage*]

4 It is easier to be a lover than a husband, for the same reason that it

is more difficult to show a ready wit all day long than to produce an occasional *bon mot*. [Attributed remark]

BANGS Lester 1948–1982
US rock journalist.

The first mistake of Art is to assume that it's serious. [*Who put the Bomp* Winter/Spring 1971]

BANKHEAD Tallulah 1903–1968
US actress.

1 I'm as pure as the driven slush. [*Saturday Evening Post* 12 Apr 1947]

2 There is less in this than meets the eye.
[Remark on Maeterlinck's play *Aglavaine and Selysette*, quoted in Alexander Woollcott *Shouts and Murmurs*]

BANNISTER Roger Gilbert 1929–
English athlete.

I felt like an exploded flashlight ... There is a certain oblivion at that point. [On crossing the finishing line 6 May 1954 at Oxford, after running the mile in under four minutes]

BARA Theda 1890–1955
US silent-film actress.

The reason good women like me and flock to my pictures is that there is a little bit of vampire instinct in every woman. [Attributed remark]

BARAKA Amiri 1934–
US poet, dramatist, and black activist.

1 A rich man told me recently that a liberal is a man who tells other people what to do with their money. [*Kulchur* Spring 1962, 'Tokenism']

2 God has been replaced, as he has all over the West, with respectability and air conditioning. [*Midstream*]

BARBELLION W N P 1889–1919
English diarist.

Give me the man who will surrender the whole world for a moss or a caterpillar, and impracticable visions for a simple human delight. [*Enjoying Life and Other Literary Remains*, 'Crying for the Moon']

BARDOT Brigitte 1934–
French film actress.

1   In marriage you are chained, it is an obligation; living with someone is a mutual agreement that is renegotiated and re-endorsed every day. [Quoted in *News of the World* 1974]

2   It is better to be unfaithful than faithful without wanting to be. [Quoted in *Observer* 18 Feb 1968]

3   I gave my beauty and my youth to men. I am going to give my wisdom and experience to animals. [Describing her animal rights campaign 1987]

BARKER Ronnie 1929–
English comic actor and writer.

The marvellous thing about a joke with a double meaning is that it can only mean one thing. [*Sauce*, 'Daddie's Sauce']

BARNES Clive 1927–
US writer and critic.

The kind of show to give pornography a dirty name. [Of *Oh, Calcutta!*, *New York Times* 18 June 1969]

BARNES Julian 1946–
English novelist.

1   Do not imagine that Art is something which is designed to give gentle uplift and self-confidence. Art is not a *brassière*. At least, not in the English sense. But do not forget that *brassière* is the French for life-jacket. [*Flaubert's Parrot* ch 10]

2   Women were brought up to believe that men were the answer. They weren't. They weren't even one of the questions. ['Staring at the Sun pt 2]

3   Love is just a system for getting someone to call you darling after sex. [*Talking It Over* ch 16]

BARNUM Phineas T 1810–1891
US showman.

How were the receipts today in Madison Square Garden? [Last words]

BARRIE J M 1860–1937
Scottish dramatist and novelist.

1   His lordship may compel us to be equal upstairs, but there will never be equality in the servants' hall. [*Admirable Crichton* I]

2   I'm a second eleven sort of chap. [*Admirable Crichton* III]

3   It's grand, and you canna expect to be baith grand and comfortable. [*Little Minister* vol 1, ch 10]

4   Every time a child says 'I don't believe in fairies' there is a little fairy somewhere that falls down dead. [*Peter Pan* I]

5   To die will be an awfully big adventure. [*Peter Pan* III]

6   Do you believe in fairies? ... If you believe, clap your hands! [*Peter Pan* IV]

7   That is ever the way. 'Tis all jealousy to the bride and good wishes to the corpse. [*Quality Street*]

8   The printing press is either the greatest blessing or the greatest curse of modern times, one sometimes forgets which. [*Sentimental Tommy* ch 5]

9   There are few more impressive sights in the world than a Scotsman on the make. [*What Every Woman Knows* II]

10   You've forgotten the grandest moral attribute of a Scotsman, Maggie, that he'll do nothing which might damage his career. [*What Every Woman Knows* II]

11   Every man who is high up loves to think he has done it all himself; and the wife smiles, and lets it go at that. It's our only joke. Every woman knows that. [*What Every Woman Knows* IV]

12 Never ascribe to an opponent motives meaner than your own. [Address at St Andrew's 3 May 1922]

13 A loving wife is better than making 50 at cricket or even 99; beyond that I will not go. [*Observer* 7 June 1925]

BARRYMORE John 1882–1942
US film actor.

Love ... the delightful interval between meeting a beautiful girl and discovering that she looks like a haddock. [Attributed remark]

BARUCH Bernard 1870–1965
US financier.

1 To me old age is always fifteen years older than I am. [*Newsweek* 29 Aug 1955]

2 Let us not be deceived – we are today in the midst of a cold war. [Speech to South Carolina Legislature 16 Apr 1947]

BASHKIRTSEFF Marie 1860–1884
Russian diarist and painter.

If I had been born a man, I would have conquered Europe. As I was born a woman, I exhausted my energy in tirades against fate, and in eccentricities. [*Journal* June 1884]

BASIL St *c.* 330–379
Cappadocian monk.

Teaching a Christian how he ought to live does not call so much for words as for daily example. [*Oration*]

BATAILLE Georges 1897–1962
French novelist and critic.

Intellectual despair results neither in weakness nor dreams, but in violence ... . It is only a matter of knowing how to give vent to one's rage; whether one only wants to wander like madmen around prisons, or whether one wants to overturn them. [*Documents* no. 7, 'The Lugubrious Game']

BATEMAN Edgar 19TH CENTURY
English songwriter.

Wiv a ladder and some glasses, / You could see to 'Ackney Marshes, / If it wasn't for the 'ouses in between. [*If It Wasn't For The 'Ouses In Between*]

BATT Neil Leonard Charles 1937–
Australian politician.

Politics is just like being mixed up with a bad woman. You know it's not a good idea, but you just can't let it go. [Responding to a question from the chairman of the parliamentary salaries' tribunal, Tasmania, *c.* 1970]

French poet Charles Baudelaire. Perhaps the first great poet of the modern city, celebrating its contrasts of richness and poverty, beauty and ugliness, Baudelaire spent almost all his adult life in Paris. The publication of his book of verse *Les Fleurs du mal/ Flowers of Evil* 1857 led to a conviction for obscenity.

BAUDELAIRE Charles 1821–1867
French Symbolist poet.

1 There are as many kinds of beauty as there are habitual ways of seeking happiness. [*Curiosités Esthétiques*, 'Salon of 1846' 2]

2 But the real travellers are only those who leave / For the sake of leaving. ['The Voyage']

BAUDRILLARD Jean 1929–
French semiologist.

1 A negative judgment gives you more satisfaction than praise, provided it smacks of jealousy. [*Cool Memories* ch 5]

2 Terror is as much a part of the concept of truth as runniness is of the concept of jam ... . We wouldn't like truth if it wasn't sticky, if, from time to time, it didn't ooze blood. [*Cool Memories* ch 5]

BAUM L Frank 1856–1919
US writer, children's author.

'The road to the City of Emeralds is paved with yellow brick,' said the Witch, 'so you cannot miss it.' [*Wonderful Wizard of Oz*]

BAUM Vicki 1888–1960
Austrian-born US novelist.

Marriage always demands the finest arts of insincerity possible between two human beings. [*Results of an Accident*]

BAYLY Thomas Haynes 1797–1839
English writer.

Absence makes the heart grow fonder. [*Isle of Beauty*]

BEATTY David 1871–1936
British admiral.

There's something wrong with our bloody ships today, Chatfield. [Remark during the Battle of Jutland 1916]

BEAUMONT Francis 1584–1616
English dramatist.

Those have most power to hurt us that we love. [*Maid's Tragedy* V. vi]

BEAUMONT AND FLETCHER Francis Beaumont 1584–1616 and John Fletcher 1579–1625
English dramatists.

1 You are no better than you should be. [*Coxcomb*]

2 Death hath so many doors to let out life. [*Custom of the Country*]

3 But what is past my help, is past my care. [*Double Marriage*]

4 It is always good / When a man has two irons in the fire. [*Faithful Friends*]

5 Let's meet, and either do, or die. [*Island Princess*]

6 I find the medicine worse than the malady. [*Lover's Progress*]

7 I'll put a spoke among your wheels. [*Mad Lover*]

8 'Tis virtue, and not birth that makes us noble: / Great actions speak great minds. [*Prophetess*]

9 Kiss till the cows come home. [*Scornful Lady*]

10 Whistle and she'll come to you. [*Wit Without Money*]

BEAUVOIR Simone de 1908–1986
French socialist, feminist, and writer.

One is not born a woman. One becomes one. [*Second Sex*]

BEAVERBROOK Max, Lord 1879–1964
Canadian-born British financier, newspaper proprietor, and politician.

1 The Daily Express declares that Great Britain will not be involved in a European war this year or next year either. [*Daily Express* 19 Sept 1938]

2 He did not seem to care which way he travelled providing he was in the driver's seat. With the publication of his Private Papers in 1952, he committed suicide 25 years after his death. [Of Earl Haig *Men and Power* 1956]

French writer and feminist Simone de Beauvoir. A close collaborator with the philosopher Jean-Paul Sartre, de Beauvoir applied existentialism to postwar moral and political issues. In *The Second Sex* 1949 – which became a feminist classic – she analyzed the role of women in a male- dominated society. Her novels and her series of autobiographies give a vivid account of French intellectual life from the 1940s to the 1980s

BECKETT Samuel 1906–1989
Irish dramatist and writer.

1 To find a form that accommodates the mess, that is the task of the artist now. [Quoted in Bair, *Samuel Beckett, a Biography* ch 21]

2 Vladimir: 'That passed the time.' Estragon: 'It would have passed in any case.' Vladimir: 'Yes, but not so rapidly.' [*Waiting for Godot*]

3 The expression that there is nothing to express, nothing with which to express, nothing from which to express, no power to express, no desire to express, together with the obligation to express. [Explaining the paradox he faced as a writer]

BECON 1512–1567
English Protestant divine.

For when the wine is in, the wit is out. [*Catechism*]

BEDDOES Thomas Lovell 1798–1851
English poet and physiologist.

If there were dreams to sell, / What would you buy? / Some cost a passing bell; / Some a light sigh. ['Dream-Pedlary']

BEE Barnard Elliott 1824–1861
US soldier.

Let us determine to die here, and we will conquer. There is Jackson standing like a stone wall. Rally behind the Virginians. [At the first Battle of Bull Run]

BEECHAM Thomas 1879–1961
English orchestral conductor.

1 There are two golden rules for an orchestra: start together and finish together. The public doesn't give a damn what goes on in between. [*Beecham Stories*]

2 The English may not like music, but they absolutely love the noise it makes. [*New York Herald Tribune* 1961]

3 At a rehearsal I let the orchestra play as they like. At the concert I make them play as I like. [Quoted in N Cardus *Sir Thomas Beecham*]

BEERBOHM Max 1872–1956
English caricaturist and author.

1 I have known no man of genius who had not to pay, in some affliction or defect either physical or spiritual, for what the gods had given him. [*And Even Now*]

2 There is always something rather absurd about the past. [*1880*]

3 To give an accurate and exhaustive account of that period would need a far less brilliant pen than mine. [*1880*]

4 Mankind is divisible into two great classes: hosts and guests. [*Hosts and Guests*]

5 The dullard's envy of brilliant men is always assuaged by the suspicion that they will come to a bad end. [*Zuleika Dobson*]

6 Women who love the same man have a kind of bitter freemasonry. [*Zuleika Dobson* ch 4]

7 You will find that the woman who is really kind to dogs is always one who has failed to inspire sympathy in men. [*Zuleika Dobson* ch 6]

BEERS Ethel Lynn 1827–1879
US poet.

All quiet along the Potomac tonight. [*Picket Guard*]

BEHAN Brendan 1923–1964
Irish dramatist.

1 He was born an Englishman and remained one for years. [*The Hostage*]

2 I'm a secret policeman, and I don't care who knows it! [*The Hostage*]

3 There's no such thing as bad publicity except your own obituary. [Quoted in Dominic Behan *My Brother Brendan*]

4 New York is my Lourdes, where I go for spiritual refreshment – a place where you're least likely to be bitten by a wild goat. [*New York Post* 22 March 1964]

5 Other people have a nationality. The Irish and the Jews have a psychosis. [*Richard's Cork Leg* I]

6 The most important things to do in this world are to get something to eat, something to drink and somebody to love you. [Quoted in *Weekend* 1968]

BEHN Aphra 1640–1689
English novelist and dramatist.

1 Oh, what a dear ravishing thing is the beginning of an Amour! [*Emperor of the Moon* I. i]

Brendan Behan, Irish playwright, best known for *The Quare Fellow* (1954), which was also made into a film. This reflected his experience of prison life, following a 14 year sentence for attempted murder in 1942. As a youth his involvement with the IRA had already led to three years in a reform school, a period he wrote about in *The Borstal Boy* (1958). Behan's personal life-style, often described as 'flamboyant', received widespread press coverage in the 1950s.

2 Love ceases to be a pleasure, when it ceases to be a secret. [*Lover's Watch*, 'Four o'clock']

3 Faith, Sir, we are here today, and gone tomorrow. [*Lucky Chance* IV]

4 Variety is the soul of pleasure. [*Rover* pt II, I]

5 Come away; poverty's catching. [*Rover* pt II, III.i]

6 Money speaks sense in a language all nations understand. [*Rover* pt II, III. i]

BEHRENS Peter 1868–1940
German architect.

Architecture comprises two ideas: the mastery of the practical, and the art of the beautiful. [*Architectural Press* 1981]

BÉJART Maurice 1927–
French ballet director and choreographer.

> The last refuge in our world where a man can discover the exact measure of his own soul. [Of the stage, in *Ballet and Modern Dance*, 'Dynamic Tradition']

BELAFONTE Harry 1927–
US singer and civil rights activist.

> You can cage the singer but not the song. [*International Herald Tribune* 3 Oct 1988]

BELL Alexander Graham 1847–1922
Scottish-born US scientist.

> Mr Watson, come here; I want you. [First complete sentence spoken over the telephone March 1876]

BELLOC Hilaire 1870–1953
French-born English writer and politician.

> **1** Child! do not throw this book about; / Refrain from the unholy pleasure / Of cutting all the pictures out! / Preserve it as your chiefest treasure. [*Bad Child's Book of Beasts*, dedication]

> **2** Your little hands were made to take / The better things and leave the worse ones: / They also may be used to shake / The massive paws of elder persons. [*Bad Child's Book of Beasts*, dedication]

> **3** I shoot the Hippopotamus / With bullets made of platinum, / Because if I use leaden ones / His hide is sure to flatten 'em. [*Bad Child's Book of Beasts*, 'Hippopotamus']

> **4** Godolphin Horne was nobly born; / He held the human race in scorn. [*Cautionary Tales*, 'Godolphin Horne']

> **5** The chief defect of Henry King / Was chewing little bits of string. [*Cautionary Tales,,* 'Henry King']

> **6** Physicians of the Utmost Fame / Were called at once; but when they came / They answered, as they took their Fees, / 'There is no Cure for this Disease.' [*Cautionary Tales*, 'Henry King']

> **7** And always keep a-hold of Nurse / For fear of finding something worse. [*Cautionary Tales*, 'Jim']

> **8** In my opinion, Butlers ought / To know their place, and not to play / The Old Retainer night and day. [*Cautionary Tales*, 'Lord Lundy']

> **9** Lord Lundy from his earliest years / Was far too freely moved to tears. [*Cautionary Tales*, 'Lord Lundy']

> **10** Matilda told such Dreadful Lies, / It made one Gasp and Stretch one's Eyes; / Her Aunt, who, from her Earliest Youth, / Had kept a Strict Regard for Truth, / Attempted to Believe Matilda: / The effort very nearly killed her. [*Cautionary Tales*, 'Matilda']

> **11** Of Courtesy, it is much less / Than Courage of Heart or Holiness, / Yet in my Walks it seems to me / That the Grace of God is in Courtesy. ['Courtesy']

> **12** Carthage had not desired to create, but only to enjoy: therefore she left us nothing. [*Esto Perpetua*]

> **13** I'm tired of Love: I'm still more tired of Rhyme. / But Money gives me pleasure all the time. ['Fatigued']

> **14** Whatever happens we have got / The Maxim Gun, and they have not. [*Modern Traveller*]

> **15** The accursed power which stands on Privilege / (And goes with Women, and Champagne, and Bridge) / Broke – and Democracy resumed her reign: / (Which goes with Bridge, and Women and Champagne). ['On a Great Election']

> **16** I am a sundial, and I make a botch / Of what is done much better by a watch. ['On a Sundial']

17 When I am dead, I hope it may be said: / 'His sins were scarlet, but his books were read.' ['On His Books']

18 Gentlemen, I am a Catholic. As far as possible, I go to Mass every day. This is a rosary. As far as possible, I kneel down and tell these beads every day. If you reject me on account of my religion, I shall thank God that He has spared me the indignity of being your representative. [Speech to voters of South Salford 1906]

BELLOW Saul 1915–
Canadian-born US novelist.

Death is the dark backing a mirror needs if we are to see anything. [*Observer* Dec 1983]

BELMONDO Jean-Paul 1933–
French film actor.

Women over thirty are at their best, but men over thirty are too old to recognize it. [Attributed remark]

BENCHLEY Robert 1889–1945
US humorist, actor, and drama critic.

1 My only solution for the problem of habitual accidents and, so far, nobody has asked me for my solution, is to stay in bed all day. Even then, there is always the chance that you will fall out. [*Chips off the Old Benchley*, 'Safety Second']

2 The surest way to make a monkey of a man is to quote him. [*My Ten Years in a Quandary*]

3 In America there are two classes of travel – first class, and with children. [*Pluck and Luck*]

BENDA Julien 1867–1956
French writer and philosopher.

The Treason of the Intellectuals. [Book title]

BENÉT Stephen Vincent 1898–1943
US writer.

Bury my heart at Wounded Knee.

The works of US novelist Saul Bellow combine cultural sophistication with the wisdom of the streets. Mainly set in Chicago and New York, they present characterizations of modern urban life and contain a sense of moral and social alarm. His many literary awards include the National Book Award 1965 and 1971, the Pulitzer Prize 1976, and the Nobel prize 1976.

[*Yale Review* (1927) vol 17, 'American Names']

BEN-GURION David 1886–1973
Israeli prime minister.

Ours is a country built more on people than on territory. The Jews will come from everywhere: from France, from Russia, from America, from Yemen ... Their faith is their passport. [Recalled by Shimon Peres *New York Times* 5 Oct 1986]

BENJAMIN Walter 1892–1940
German critic and philosopher.

1 To be happy is to be able to become aware of oneself without fright. [*One-Way Street*, 'Fancy Goods']

2 The killing of a criminal can be moral – but never its legitimation. [*One-Way Street*, 'Hardware']

3 Like ultraviolet rays memory shows to each man in the book of life a script that invisibly and prophetically glosses the text. [*One-Way Street*, 'Madame Ariane – Second Courtyard on the Left']

BENN Tony 1925–
British Labour politician.

A faith is something you die for, a doctrine is something you kill for. There is all the difference in the world. [BBC TV 11 April 1989]

BENNETT Alan 1934–
English dramatist, screenwriter, and actor.

1 Life is rather like a tin of sardines – we're all of us looking for the key. [*Beyond the Fringe*]

2 I have never understood this liking for war. It panders to instincts already catered for within the scope of any respectable domestic establishment. [*Forty Years On* I]

3 We started off trying to set up a small anarchist community, but people wouldn't obey the rules. [*Getting On* I]

4 Definition of a classic: a book everyone is assumed to have read and often thinks they have. [*Independent on Sunday* 27 Jan 1991]

5 We were put to Dickens as children but it never quite took. That unremitting humanity soon had me cheesed off. [*Old Country* II]

BENNETT Arnold 1867–1931
English novelist.

1 At twenty a man is rash in love, and again, perhaps, at fifty; a man of middle-age enamoured of a young girl is capable of sublime follies. But the man of thirty who loves for the first time is usually the embodiment of cautious discretion. He does not fall in love with a vio-

lent descent, but rather lets himself gently down, continually testing the rope. [*Anna of the Five Towns*]

2 Ye can call it influenza if ye like ... There was no influenza in my young days. We called a cold a cold. [*The Card* ch 8]

3 'And yet, ... what's he done? Has he ever done a day's work in his life? What great cause is he identified with?' 'He's identified ... with the great cause of cheering us all up.' [*The Card* ch 12]

4 The price of justice is eternal publicity. [*Things That Have Interested Me*, 'Secret Trials']

5 Pessimism, when you get used to it, is just as agreeable as optimism. [*Things That Have Interested Me*, 'Slump in Pessimism']

6 Being a husband is a whole-time job. [*The Title* I]

7 Journalists say a thing that they know isn't true, in the hope that if they keep on saying it long enough it will be true. [*The Title* II]

BENNETT Jill 1931–1990
English actress.

Never marry a man who hates his mother, because he'll end up hating you. [Referring to her ex-husband John Osborne, *Observer* 12 Sept 1982]

BENSON A C 1862–1925
English writer.

1 Land of Hope and Glory, Mother of the Free, / How shall we extol thee, who are born of thee? ['Land of Hope and Glory']

2 I don't like authority, at least I don't like other people's authority. [*Excerpts from Letters to M. E. A.*]

BENTHAM Jeremy 1748–1832
English philosopher and legal reformer.

1 All punishment is mischief: all punishment in itself is evil. [*Principles of Morals and Legislation*]

2 The greatest happiness of the greatest number is the foundation of morals and legislation. [*Works* x. 142]

BENTLEY Edmund Clerihew 1875–1956
English author.

1 The Art of Biography / Is different from Geography. / Geography is about Maps, / But Biography is about Chaps. [*Biography for Beginners*, introduction]

2 What I like about Clive / Is that he is no longer alive. / There's a great deal to be said / For being dead. [*Biography for Beginners*, 'Clive']

3 Sir Christopher Wren / Said, 'I am going to dine with some men. / If anybody calls / Say I am designing St Paul's.' [*Biography for Beginners*, 'Sir Christopher Wren']

4 Sir Humphrey Davy / Abominated gravy. / He lived in the odium / Of having discovered Sodium. [*Biography for Beginners*, 'Sir Humphrey Davy']

5 George the Third / Ought never to have occurred. / One can only wonder / At so grotesque a blunder. [*More Biography*, 'George the Third']

BERGER John 1926–
English art critic and novelist.

1 In the sky of the cinema people learn what they might have been and discover what belongs to them apart from their single lives. ['Ev'ry Time We Say Goodbye', in *Expressen* Stockholm, 3 Nov 1990]

2 A man's death makes everything certain about him. [*A Fortunate Man* 160]

3 Nothing in the nature around us is evil. This needs to be repeated since one of the human ways of *talking oneself into* evil acts is to cite the supposed cruelty of nature. [*Harper's* May 1989]

Swedish film actress Ingrid Bergman. She established herself as a Hollywood star with films such as *Casablanca* 1942, starring with Humphrey Bogart, and the two Hitchcock films *Spellbound* 1945 and *Notorious* 1946. In 1948 her romance with Italian director Roberto Rossellini took her to Italy but she returned to Hollywood 1956. Her last film was *Autumn Sonata* 1978, directed by Ingmar Bergman (no relation).

4 All weddings are similar but every marriage is different. Death comes to everyone but one mourns alone. [*White Bird*, 'Storyteller']

BERGMAN Ingrid 1917–1982
Swedish-born US actress.

Keep it simple. Make a blank face and the music and the story will fill it in. [Advice on film-acting, TV interview 1956]

BERGSON Henri 1859–1941
French philosopher.

The essential function of the universe, which is a machine for making gods. [*Les deux sources de la morale et de la religion*]

BERKELEY George 1684–1753
Irish philosopher and cleric.

1 Westward the course of empire takes its way. [*On the Prospect of Planting Arts and Learning in America*]

2 Truth is the cry of all, but the game of few. [*Siris 368*]

3 I do know that I, who am a spirit or thinking substance, exist as certainly as I know my ideas exist. [*Three Dialogues between Hylas and Philonous*]

BERLIN Irving 1888–1989
Russian-born US songwriter.

1 They say that falling in love is wonderful, / It's wonderful, so they say. ['Falling in Love']

2 God bless America, Land that I love. ['God Bless America']

3 Oh! how I hate to get up in the morning, / Oh! how I'd love to remain in bed. ['Oh! How I Hate to Get Up in the Morning']

4 I'm dreaming of a white Christmas, / Just like the ones I used to know, / Where the tree-tops glisten / And children listen / To hear sleigh bells in the snow. ['White Christmas']

5 The song is ended (but the melody lingers on). [Song title]

6 There's no business like show business. [Song title]

BERLIN Sir Isaiah 1906–
Latvian-born British philosopher.

1 Rousseau was the first militant low-brow. [*Observer* 9 Nov 1952]

2 Liberty is liberty, not equality or fairness or justice or human happiness or a quiet conscience. [*Two Concepts of Liberty*]

BERLIOZ Hector 1803–1869
French romantic composer.

Time is a great teacher, but unfortunately it kills all its pupils. [*Almanach des lettres françaises*]

US songwriter Irving Berlin. Beginning with ragtime at the turn of the century, he wrote successful songs over a period of nearly 50 years, many of them becoming familiar worldwide. Bing Crosby's version of Irving Berlin's *White Christmas* is the world's biggest selling record, and *God Bless America* is considered as the unofficial US anthem.

BERNANOS Georges 1888–1948
French author.

1 Hell, ... is to love no more. [*Diary of a Country Priest*]

2 The wish for prayer is itself a prayer. [*Diary of a Country Priest*]

3 The first sign of corruption in a society that is still alive is that the end justifies the means. [*Last Essays of Georges Bernanos*, 'Why Freedom?']

BERNE Eric 1910–1970
US psychiatrist.

Games People Play. [Book title]

BETJEMAN John 1906–1984
English poet and essayist.

1 Phone for the fish-knives, Norman / As Cook is a little unnerved; / You kiddies have crumpled the serviettes / And I must have things daintily served. ['How to get on in Society']

2 Think of what our Nation stands for, / Books from Boots' and country lanes, / Free speech, free passes, class distinction. ['In Westminster Abbey']

3 One cannot assess in terms of cash or exports and imports an imponderable thing like the turn of a lane or an inn or a church tower or a familiar skyline. [*Observer* 1969]

4 Come, friendly bombs, and fall on Slough! / It isn't fit for humans now, / There isn't grass to graze a cow. ['Slough']

5 Ghastly Good Taste, or a depressing story of the rise and fall of English architecture. [Book title]

BEVAN Aneurin (Nye) 1897–1960
British Labour politician.

1 Damn it all, you can't have the crown of thorns and the thirty pieces of silver. [Quoted in Michael Foot *Aneurin Bevan*]

2 Freedom is the by-product of economic surplus. [Quoted in Michael Foot *Aneurin Bevan*]

3 If we complain about the tune, there is no reason to attack the monkey when the organ grinder is present. [*Hansard* 16 May 1957]

4 We know what happens to people who stay in the middle of the road. They get run down. [*Observer* 6 Dec 1953]

5 This island is made mainly of coal and surrounded by fish. Only an organizing genius could produce a shortage of coal and fish at the same time. [Speech at Blackpool 24 May 1945]

BEVIN Ernest 1881–1951
British Labour politician.

My [foreign] policy is to be able to take a ticket at Victoria Station and go anywhere I damn well please. [*Spectator* April 1951]

BIBLE The sacred book of the Jewish and Christian religions.

1 In the beginning God created the heaven and the earth. [Genesis 1:1]

2 And God saw that it was good. [Genesis 1:10]

3 Male and female created he them. [Genesis 1:27]

4 And the Lord God planted a garden eastward in Eden. [Genesis 2:7]

5 But of the tree of the knowledge of good and evil, thou shalt not eat of it. [Genesis 2:17]

6 Now the serpent was more subtil than any beast of the field. [Genesis 3:1]

7 For dust thou art, and unto dust thou shalt return. [Genesis 3:19]

8 Am I my brother's keeper? [Genesis 4:1]

9 His hand will be against every man, and every man's hand against him. [Genesis 16:12]

10 Old and well stricken in age. [Genesis 18:11]

11 Mizpah; for he said, The Lord watch between me and thee, when we are absent one from another. [Genesis 31:49]

12 I will not let thee go, except thou bless me. [Genesis 32:26]

13 A coat of many colours. [Genesis 37:3]

14 Bring down my grey hairs with sorrow to the grave. [Genesis 42:38]

15 A land flowing with milk and honey. [On the land of Canaan, Exodus 3:8]

16 I am that I am. [Exodus 3:14]

17 Eye for eye, tooth for tooth, hand for hand, foot for foot. [Exodus 21:23]

18 A stiff-necked people [Exodus 33:3]

19 The Lord bless thee, and keep thee: / The Lord make his face to shine upon thee, and be gracious unto thee: / The Lord lift up his countenance upon thee, and give thee peace. [Numbers 6:24]

20 Man doth not live by bread only, but by every word that proceedeth out of the mouth of the Lord doth man live. [Deuteronomy 8:3]

21 Underneath are the everlasting arms. [Deuteronomy 33:27]

22 Hewers of wood and drawers of water. [Joshua 9:21]

23 The stars in their courses fought against Sisera. [Judges 5:20]

24 She brought forth butter in a lordly dish. [Judges 5:25]

25 Intreat me not to leave thee, or to return from following after thee: for whither thou goest, I will go; and where thou lodgest, I will lodge: thy people shall be my people, and thy God my God. [Ruth 1:16]

26 Saul and Jonathan were lovely and pleasant in their lives, and in their death they were not divided. [2 Samuel 1:23]

27 How the mighty are fallen in the midst of the battle! [2 Samuel 1:25]

28 The half was not told me. [1 Kings 10:7]

29 There ariseth a little cloud out of the sea, like a man's hand. [1 Kings 18:44]

30 After the fire a still small voice. [1 Kings 19:11]

31 Let not him that girdeth on his harness boast himself as he that putteth it off. [1 Kings 20:11]

32 And a certain man drew a bow at a venture. [1 Kings 22:34]

33 The driving is like the driving of Jehu, the son of Nimshi: for he driveth furiously. [2 Kings 9:20]

34 The Lord gave, and the Lord hath taken away; blessed be the name of the Lord. [Job 1:21]

35 Curse God, and die. [Job 2:9]

36 Man is born unto trouble, as the sparks fly upward. [Job 5:7]

37 I know that my redeemer liveth, and that he shall stand at the latter day upon the earth: / And though after my skin worms destroy this body, yet in my flesh shall I see God. [Job 19:25]

38 The price of wisdom is above rubies. [Job 28:18]

39 Who is this that darkeneth counsel by words without knowledge? [Job 38:2]

40 Wisdom is the principal thing; therefore get wisdom; and with all thy getting get understanding. [Proverbs 4:7]

41 Go to the ant, thou sluggard; consider her ways, and be wise. [Proverbs 6:6]

42 Yet a little sleep, a little slumber, a little folding of the hands to sleep. [Proverbs 6:10]

43 So shall thy poverty come as one that travelleth, and thy want as an armed man. [Proverbs 6:11]

44 A wise son maketh a glad father: but a foolish son is the heaviness of his mother. [Proverbs 10:1]

45 In the multitude of counsellors there is safety. [Proverbs 11:14]

46 As a jewel of gold in a swine's

snout, so is a fair woman which is without discretion. [Proverbs 11:22]

47 Hope deferred maketh the heart sick. [Proverbs 13:12]

48 He that spareth his rod hateth his son. [Proverbs 13:24]

49 A soft answer turneth away wrath. [Proverbs 15:1]

50 There is a friend that sticketh closer than a brother. [Proverbs 18:24]

51 Wine is a mocker, strong drink is raging. [Proverbs 20:1]

52 Confidence in an unfaithful man in time of trouble is like a broken tooth, and a foot out of joint. [Proverbs 25:19]

53 As a dog returneth to his vomit, so a fool returneth to his folly. [Proverbs 26:11]

54 He that rebuketh a man afterwards shall find more favour than he that flattereth with the tongue. [Proverbs 28: 23]

55 Who can find a virtuous woman? for her price is above rubies. [Proverbs 31:10]

56 Vanity of vanities, saith the Preacher, vanity of vanities; all is vanity. [Ecclesiastes 1:2]

57 To every thing there is a season, and a time to every purpose under the heaven: / A time to be born, and a time to die. [Ecclesiastes 3:1]

58 The race is not to the swift, nor the battle to the strong. [Ecclesiastes 9:11]

59 Cast thy bread upon the water: for thou shalt find it after many days. [Ecclesiastes 11:1]

60 Man goeth to his long home, and the mourners go about the streets: / Or ever the silver cord be loosed, or the golden bowl be broken, or pitcher be broken at the fountain, or the wheel broken at the cistern. / Then shall the dust return to the earth as it was: and the spirit shall return unto God who gave it. [Ecclesiastes 12:5]

61 Let him kiss me with the kisses of his mouth: for thy love is better than wine. [Song of Solomon 1:2]

62 Stay me with flagons, comfort me with apples: for I am sick of love. [Song of Solomon 2:5]

63 Rise up, my love, my fair one, and come away. / For, lo! the winter is past, the rain is over and gone; / The flowers appear on the earth: the time of the singing of birds is come, and the voice of the turtle is heard in our land. [Song of Solomon 2:10]

64 Set me as a seal upon thine heart, as a seal upon thine arm: for love is strong as death; jealousy is cruel as the grave. [Song of Solomon 8:6]

65 Many waters cannot quench love. [Song of Solomon 8:7]

66 A garden inclosed is my sister, my spouse. [Song of Solomon 12:4]

67 They shall beat their swords into plowshares, and their spears into pruninghooks. [Isaiah 2:4]

68 The people that walked in darkness have seen a great light: they that dwell in the land of the shadow of death, upon them hath the light shined. [Isaiah 9:2]

69 The wolf also shall dwell with the lamb, and the leopard shall lie down with the kid. [Isaiah 11:7]

70 Watchman, what of the night? [Isaiah 21:11]

71 The voice of him that crieth in the wilderness, Prepare ye the way of the Lord, make straight in the desert a highway for our God. Every valley shall be exalted, and every mountain and hill shall be made low: and the crooked shall be made straight, and the rough places plain. [Isaiah 43:3]

72 There is no peace, saith the Lord, unto the wicked. [Isaiah 48:22]

73 Man of sorrows, and acquainted with grief. [Isaiah 53:2]

74 Peace to him that is far off, and to him that is near. [Isaiah 57:19]

75 Saying, Peace, peace; when there is no peace. [Jeremiah 6:14]

76 Can the Ethiopian change his skin, or the leopard his spots? [Jeremiah 13:23]

77 Your old men shall dream dreams, your young men shall see visions. [Joel 2:28]

78 Blessed are the meek: for they shall inherit the earth. [Matthew 5:5]

79 Ye are the salt of the earth. [Matthew 5:13]

80 Let your light so shine before men, that they may see your good works. [Matthew 5:16]

81 Agree with thine adversary quickly, whiles thou art in the way with him. [Matthew 5:25]

82 Where your treasure is, there will your heart be also. [Matthew 6:21]

83 No man can serve two masters ... Ye cannot serve God and mammon. [Matthew 6:24]

84 Consider the lilies of the field, how they grow; they toil not, neither do they spin. [Matthew 6:28]

85 Neither cast ye your pearls before swine. [Matthew 6:34]

86 Sufficient unto the day is the evil thereof. [Matthew 6:34]

87 By their fruits ye shall know them. [Matthew 7:20]

88 Be ye therefore wise as serpents, and harmless as doves. [Matthew 10:16]

89 He that is not with me is against me. [Matthew 12:30]

90 A prophet is not without honour, save in his own country and in his own house. [Matthew 13:57]

91 If the blind lead the blind, both shall fall into the ditch. [Matthew 15:14]

92 Get thee behind me, Satan. [Matthew 16:23]

93 What is a man profited, if he shall gain the whole world, and lose his own soul. [Matthew 16:26]

94 For this cause shall a man leave father and mother, and shall cleave to his wife: and they twain shall be one flesh. [Matthew 19:5]

95 Thou shalt love thy neighbour as thyself. [Matthew 19:19]

96 Render therefore unto Caesar the things which are Caesar's. [Matthew 22:21]

97 The spirit indeed is willing, but the flesh is weak. [Matthew 26:41]

98 All they that take the sword shall perish with the sword. [Matthew 26:52]

99 The sabbath was made for man, and not man for the sabbath. [Mark 2:27]

100 If a house be divided against itself, that house cannot stand. [Mark 3:25]

101 He that hath ears to hear, let him hear. [Mark 4:9]

102 Had suffered many things of many physicians, and had spent all that she had, and was nothing better but rather grew worse. [Mark 5:26]

103 Suffer the little children to come unto me. [Mark 10:14]

104 To give light to them that sit in darkness and in the shadow of death, to guide our feet into the way of peace. [Luke 1:79]

105 Lord, now lettest thou thy servant depart in peace, according to thy word. [Luke 2:29]

106 Physician, heal thyself. [Luke 4:23]

107 For the labourer is worthy of his hire. [Luke 10:7]

108 But Martha was cumbered about much serving. [Luke 10:40]

109 Wasted his substance with riotous living. [Luke 15:13]

110 Bring hither the fatted calf, and kill it. [Luke 15:23]

111 In the beginning was the Word, and the Word was with God, and the Word was God. [John 1:1]

112 There is no truth in him. [John 8:44]

113 The poor always ye have with you. [John 12:8]

114 Greater love hath no man than this, that a man lay down his life for his friends. [John 15:13]

115 Silver and gold have I none; but such as I have give I thee. [Acts 3:6]

116 It is more blessed to give than to receive. [Acts 20:35]

117 A citizen of no mean city. [Acts 21:39]

118 Much learning, doth make thee mad. [Acts 26:24]

119 The wages of sin is death. [Romans 6:23]

120 Vengeance is mine; I will repay, saith the Lord. [Romans 12:19]

121 Let the husband render unto the wife due benevolence; and likewise also the wife unto the husband. [1 Corinthians 7:3]

122 It is better to marry than to burn. [1 Corinthians 7:9]

123 But he that is married careth for the things that are of the world, how he may please his wife. [1 Corinthians 7:33]

124 Though I speak with tongues of men and of angels, and have not charity, I am become as sounding brass, or a tinkling cymbal. [1 Corinthians 13:1]

125 Charity never faileth. [1 Corinthians 13:8]

126 When I was a child, I spake as a child, I understood as a child, I thought as a child; but when I became a man, I put away childish things. [1 Corinthians 13:11]

127 And now abideth faith, hope, charity, these three; but the greatest of these is charity. [1 Corinthians 13:13]

128 The last enemy that shall be destroyed is death. [1 Corinthians 15:26]

129 Behold, I shew you a mystery; We shall not all sleep but we shall all be changed, / In a moment, in the twinkling of an eye, at the last trump. [1 Corinthians 15:51]

130 O death, where is thy sting? O grave, where is thy victory. [1 Corinthians 15:55]

131 God loveth a cheerful giver. [2 Corinthians 9:7]

132 Let not the sun go down upon your wrath. [Ephesians 4:26]

133 Husbands, love your wives, and be not bitter against them. [Colossians 3:19]

134 The love of money is the root of all evil. [1 Timothy 6:10]

135 Be not forgetful to entertain strangers: for thereby some have entertained angels unawares. [Hebrews 13:1]

136 All flesh is as grass, and all the glory of man as the flower of grass. The grass withereth, and the flower thereof falleth away. [1 Peter 1:24]

137 Giving honour unto the wife, as unto the weaker vessel. [1 Peter 3:7]

138 Charity shall cover the multitude of sins. [1 Peter 4:8]

139 I am Alpha and Omega, the beginning and the ending, saith the Lord. [Revelation 1:7]

140 And I looked, and behold a pale horse: and his name that sat on him was Death. [Revelation 6:8]

141 And I saw a new heaven and a new earth: for the first time heaven and the first earth were passed away; and there was no more sea. [Revelation 21:1]

BIDAULT Georges 1899–1983
French prime minister.

1 Freedom is when one hears the bell at 7 o'clock in the morning and knows it is the milkman and not the Gestapo. [Quoted in *Observer* 23 April 1950]

2 The weak have one weapon: the errors of those who think they are strong. [*Observer* July 1962]

BIERCE Ambrose 1842–c. 1914
US author.

1 *Admiration* Our polite recognition of another's resemblance to ourselves. [*Cynic's Word Book*]

2 *Bore* A person who talks when you wish him to listen. [*Cynic's Word Book*]

3 *Cynic* A blackguard whose faulty vision sees things as they are, not as they ought to be. [*Cynic's Word Book*]

4 *Education* That which discloses to the wise and disguises from the foolish their lack of understanding. [*Cynic's Word Book*]

5 *History* An account, mostly false, of events, mostly unimportant, which are brought about by rulers, mostly knaves, and soldiers, mostly fools. [*Cynic's Word Book*]

6 *Abdication* The act whereby a sovereign attests his sense of the high temperature of the throne. [*Devil's Dictionary*]

7 *Marriage,* The state or condition of a community consisting of a master, a mistress and two slaves, making in all two. [*Devil's Dictionary*]

8 *Noise* A stench in the ear ... The chief product and authenticating sign of civilization. [*Devil's Dictionary*]

9 *Patience* A minor form of despair, disguised as a virtue. [*Devil's Dictionary*]

BIKO Steve 1946–1977
South African political leader.

The power of a movement lies in the fact that it can indeed change the habits of people. This change is not the result of force but of dedication, of moral persuasion. [Interview July 1976]

BINYON Laurence 1869–1943
English poet.

They shall grow not old, as we that are left grow old: / Age shall not weary them, nor the years condemn. / At the going down of the sun and in the morning / We will remember them. ['Poem For the Fallen']

BIRRELL Augustine 1850–1933
English politician and writer.

That great dust-heap called 'history'. [*Obiter Dicta*, 'Carlyle']

BISMARCK Otto, Prince von 1815–1898
Prussian prime minister.

1 Politics is not an exact science. [Speech in Prussian Chamber 18 Dec 1863]

2 Blood and iron. [Speech in Prussian House of Deputies 28 Jan 1886]

BISSET Jacqueline 1946–
English-born US film actress.

Character ... fortifies a woman as her youth fades. A mode of conduct, a standard of courage, discipline, fortitude and integrity can do a great deal to make a woman beautiful. [Quoted in *Los Angeles Times* 16 May 1974]

Prusso-German politician Prince Otto von Bismark, known as the Iron Chancellor, came to prominence after the collapse of the revolution of 1848.

BLACKSTONE William 1723–1780
English jurist.

1 The king never dies. [*Commentaries*]

2 Mankind will not be reasoned out of the feelings of humanity. [*Commentaries*]

3 That the king can do no wrong, is a necessary and fundamental principle of the English constitution.

[*Commentaries* bk 3]

BLAKE William 1757–1827
English poet, artist, engraver, and visionary.

1 Ah, Sun-flower! weary of time, / Who countest the steps of the Sun. ['Ah, Sun-Flower!']

2 A Robin Redbreast in a Cage / Puts all Heaven in a Rage. [*Auguries of Innocence*]

3 The strongest poison ever known / Came from Cæsar's laurel crown. [*Auguries of Innocence*]

4 To see a World in a Grain of Sand, / And a Heaven in a Wild Flower, Hold Infinity in the palm of your hand, / And Eternity in an hour. [*Auguries of Innocence*]

5 Everything that lives, / Lives not alone, nor for itself. [*Book of Thel* 2]

6 Love seeketh not itself to please, / Nor for itself hath any care, / But for another gives its ease, / And builds a Heaven in Hell's despair. ['The Clod and the Pebble']

7 For Mercy has a human heart, / Pity a human face, / And Love, the human form divine, / And Peace, the human dress. ['Divine Image']

8 To Mercy, Pity, Peace, and Love / All pray in their distress. ['Divine Image']

9 Great things are done when men and mountains meet. [*Gnomic Verses* 1]

10 What is it men in women do require? / The lineaments of gratified desire. / What is it women do in men require? / The lineaments of gratified desire. [*Gnomic Verses* 17]

11 Little Lamb, who made thee? / Dost thou know who made thee? ['The Lamb']

12 Always be ready to speak your mind, and a base man will avoid you. [*Marriage of Heaven and Hell*, 'Proverbs of Hell' plate 8]

13 The road of excess leads to the palace of wisdom. [*Marriage of Heaven and Hell: The Voice of the Devil*, 'Proverbs of Hell']

14 The tigers of wrath are wiser than the horses of instruction. [*Marriage of Heaven and Hell: The Voice of the Devil*, 'Proverbs of Hell']

15 And did those feet in ancient time / Walk upon England's mountains green? / And was the holy Lamb of God / On England's pleasant pastures seen? [*Milton*, preface]

16 Never seek to tell thy love, / Love that never told can be. ['Never Seek to Tell Thy Love']

17 I was angry with my friend / I told my wrath, my wrath did end. / I was angry with my foe: / I told it not, my wrath did grow. ['Poison Tree']

18 The look of love alarms / Because 'tis filled with fire; / But the look of soft deceit / Shall win the lover's hire. ['Several Questions Answered']

19 Tiger! Tiger! burning bright / In the forests of the night, / What immortal hand or eye / Could frame thy fearful symmetry? ['Tiger']

BLAMEY Field Marshal Thomas Albert 1884–1951
Australian field marshal.

The rabbit that runs away is the rabbit that gets shot. [Address to his troops]

BLANCH Lesley 1907–
English writer.

She was an Amazon. Her whole life was spent riding at breakneck speed towards the wilder shores of love. [*Wilder Shores of Love* pt 2, ch 1]

BLESSINGTON Marguerite 1789–1849
Irish novelist, poet and conversationalist.

Love-matches are made by people who are content, for a month of honey, to condemn themselves to a life of vinegar. [*Commonplace Book*]

BLOOMER Amelia Jenks 1818–1894
US campaigner for women's rights.

The costume of woman ... should conduce at once to her health, comfort, and usefulness ... while it should not fail also to conduce to her personal adornment, it should make that end of secondary importance. [Letter June 1857]

BLUNDEN Edmund 1896–1974
English poet.

1 I am for the woods against the world, / But are the woods for me? ['The Kiss']

2 Cricket to us, like you, was more than play, / It was a worship in the summer sun. [*Pride of the Village*]

BLYTHE Ronald 1922–
English writer.

As for the British churchman, he goes to church as he goes to the bathroom, with the minimum of fuss and with no explanation if he can help it. [*Age of Illusion*]

BOETHIUS Anicius Manilius Severinus 480–524 AD
Roman philosopher and Christian theologian.

It is the nature of human affairs to be fraught with anxiety. [*The Consolation of Philosophy* II. iv]

BOHR Niels 1885–1962
Danish physicist.

An expert is a man who has made all the mistakes which can be made in a very narrow field. [Quoted in Mackay *Harvest of a Quiet Eye*]

BOLINGBROKE Henry St John, Viscount 1678–1751
English Tory politician and political philosopher.

Nations, like men, have their infancy. [*On the Study of History*]

BOLÍVAR Simón 1783–1830
S. American nationalist and revolutionary.

A people that loves freedom will in the end be free. [*Letter from Jamaica*]

BOND Edward 1935–
English dramatist.

We have only one thing to keep us sane, pity; and the man without pity is mad. [*Lear*]

BOORMAN John 1933–
English film director.

> What is passion? It is surely the becoming of a person ... . In passion, the body and spirit seek expression outside of self. [*Projections* (co-edited with W Donohoe) 16 May 1991]

BOORSTIN Daniel J 1914–
US writer.

> The celebrity is a person who is known for his well-knownness. [*The Image*]

BOOTH John Wilkes 1839–1865
US assassin of President Abraham Lincoln.

> Tell mother – tell mother – I died for my country. [Remark after having assassinated President Lincoln 1865]

BORGES Jorge Luis 1899–1986
Argentine poet and writer.

> **1** Writing is nothing more than a guided dream. [*Dr Brodie's Report*]
>
> **2** The Falklands thing was a fight between two bald men over a comb. [Of the Falklands War 1982, *Time* 14 Feb 1983]

BORGIA Lucrezia 1480–1519
Illegitimate daughter of Pope Alexander VI.

> My husbands have been very unlucky. [On the murder of her second husband. Quoted in R Erlanger *Lucrezia Borgia*]

BORROW George Henry 1803–1881
English author and traveller.

> **1** My favourite, I might say, my only study, is man. [*The Bible in Spain* ch 5]
>
> **2** A losing trade, I assure you, sir: literature is a drug. [*Lavengro* ch 30]
>
> **3** Good ale, the true and proper drink of Englishmen. [*Lavengro* ch 48]
>
> **4** Youth will be served, every dog has his day, and mine has been a fine one. [*Lavengro* ch 92]

BOSQUET Maréchal 1810–1861
French marshal.

> It is magnificent, but it is not war. [Remark on the Charge of the Light Brigade 1854]

BOSSIDY John Collins 1860–1928
US writer.

> And this is good old Boston, / The home of the bean and the cod, / Where the Lowells talk to the Cabots, And the Cabots talk only to God. [*On the Aristocracy of Harvard*]

BOTHA P W 1916–
South African politician and prime minister 1978–89.

> After all, Moses had a mixed marriage. [Speech 4 Sept 1980]

BOTTOMLEY Gordon 1874–1948
English poet and dramatist.

> When you destroy a blade of grass / You poison England at her roots: / Remember no man's foot can pass / Where evermore no green life shoots. ['To Ironfounders and Others']

BOTTOMLEY Horatio 1860–1933
English newspaper editor.

> I have not had your advantages. What poor education I have received has been gained in the University of Life. [Speech at Oxford Union 2 Dec 1920]

BOURDILLON Francis William 1852–1921
English poet.

> The mind has a thousand eyes, / And the heart but one; / Yet the light of a whole life dies / When love is done. [*Among the Flowers*, 'Light']

BOURNE W St Hill 1846–1929

> The sower went forth sowing, / The seed in secret slept. [*Church Bells*, 'The Sower Went Forth Sowing']

BOWEN Edward Ernest 1836–1901
English writer.

> Forty years on, when afar and asunder / Parted are those who are singing to-day. ['Harrow School Song', *Forty Years On*]

BOWEN Elizabeth 1899–1973
Irish novelist.

> **1** Experience isn't interesting till it begins to repeat itself – in fact, till it does that, it hardly is experience. [*Death of the Heart*]

> **2** There is no end to the violations committed by children on children, quietly talking alone. [*House in Paris* pt 1, ch 2]

> **3** Jealousy is no more than feeling alone against smiling enemies. [*House in Paris* pt 2, ch 8]

> **4** No, it is not only our fate but our business to lose innocence, and once we have lost that, it is futile to attempt a picnic in Eden. ['Out of a Book']

> **5** When you're young, you think of marriage as a train you simply have to catch. You run and run until you've caught it, and then you sit back and look out of the window and realize you're bored. [Interview *Sunday Times* 11 Sep 1988]

BOWEN George Ferguson 1821–1899
British colonial governor.

> The rain it raineth on the just / And also on the unjust fella: / But chiefly on the just, because / The unjust steals the just's umbrella. [*Sichel, Sands of Time*]

BOWRA Sir Maurice 1898–1971
English scholar.

> I'm a man more dined against than dining. [Quoted in John Betjeman *Summoned by Bells*]

BOYD Martin a'Beckett 1893–1972
Australian writer.

> Our minds are like those maps at the entrance to the Metro stations in Paris. They are full of unilluminated directions. [*Outbreak of Love* ch 1]

BRADBURY Malcolm 1932–
British novelist and critic.

> **1** Marriage is the most advanced form of warfare in the modern world. [*History Man*]

> **2** 'We stay together, but we distrust one another.''Ah, yes ... but isn't that a definition of marriage?' [*History Man* ch 3]

BRADLEY Omar 1893–1981
US general in World War II.

> In war there is no second prize for the runner up. [*Military Review* Sept 1951]

BRADMAN Sir Donald George 1908–
Australian cricketer.

> The game of cricket existed long before I was born. It will be played centuries after my demise. During my career I was privileged to give the public my interpretation of its character in the same way that a pianist might interpret the works of Beethoven. [*Farewell to Cricket*]

BRADSTREET Anne c. 1616–1672
English-born US poet.

> If ever two were one, then surely we. / If ever man were loved by wife, then thee; / If ever wife was happy in a man, / Compare with me ye women if you can. [*To My Dear and Loving Husband*]

BRAHAM John c. 1774–1856
English tenor singer.

> England, home and beauty. [*The Americans*, 'The Death of Nelson']

BRAISTED Harry 1834–1881
US songwriter.

> If you want to win her hand, / Let the maiden understand / That she's not the only pebble on the beach. ['You're Not the Only Pebble on the Beach']

BRANDO Marlon 1924–
US actor.

> An actor is a guy who, if you aren't talking about him, isn't listening. [*Observer* Jan 1956]

BRANSON Richard 1950–
English entrepreneur.

> Borrow fivers off everyone you meet. [Answer on being asked what is the quickest way to become a millionaire]

BRAQUE Georges 1882–1963
French painter.

> 1 Truth exists; only lies are invented. [*Day and Night: Notebooks 1917–52*]

> 2 Art is meant to disturb, science reassures. [*Pensées sur l'Art*]

BRECHT Bertolt 1898–1956
German dramatist and poet.

> 1 Unhappy the land that is in need of heroes. [*Leben des Galilei* (Life of Galileo)]

> 2 War always finds a way. [*Mother Courage*]

> 3 War is like love, it always finds a way. [*Mother Courage*]

> 4 What's breaking into a bank compared with founding a bank? [*Threepenny Opera*]

> 5 Food comes first, then morals. [*Threepenny Opera*)]

BRENAN Gerald 1894–1987
British writer.

> 1 Absence and letters are the forcing ground of love. What renews it and confirms it is presence and bed. [*Thoughts in a Dry Season*]

> 2 In a happy marriage it is the wife who provides the climate, the husband the landscape. [*Thoughts in a Dry Season*, 'Marriage']

> 3 Marriage is an arrangement by which two people start by getting the best out of each other and often end by getting the worst. [*Thoughts in a Dry Season*]

> 4 Those who have some means think that the most important thing in the world is love. The poor know that it is money. [*Thoughts in a Dry Season*]

BRENNER Sidney 1927–
South African scientist.

> Progress in science depends on new techniques, new discoveries and new ideas, probably in that order. [*Nature* May 1980]

BRESSON Robert 1907–1958
French film director.

> Make visible what, without you, might perhaps never have been seen. [*Notes on the Cinematographer*, '1950']

BRETON André 1896–1966
French surrealist.

> 1 It is living and ceasing to live that are imaginary solutions. Existence is elsewhere. [*Manifesto of Surrealism*]

> 2 In the world we live in ... everything militates in favor of things that have not yet happened, of things that will never happen again. [*Surrealism and Painting*]

> 3 To recognize ... means everything. Between what I do recognize and what I do not recognize there stands myself. And what I do not recognize I shall continue not to recognize. [*Surrealism and Painting*]

BRETON Nicholas c. 1545–c. 1626
English poet.

> 1 We rise with the lark and go to bed with the lamb. [*The Court and Country*]

> 2 A Mad World, My Masters. [Dialogue title]

BRICE Fanny 1891–1951
US entertainer.

> Let the world know you as you are, not as you think you should be, because sooner or later, if you are posing, you will forget the pose, and then where are you? [Quoted in Norman Katkov, *Fabulous Fanny* ch 24]

BRIDGES Robert 1844–1930
English poet and critic.

> 1 I love all beauteous things, / I seek and adore them; / God hath no better praise, / And man in his hasty days / Is honoured for them. ['I Love All Beauteous Things']

> 2 I will not let thee go. / Ends all our month-long love in this? ['I Will Not Let Thee Go']

> 3 Whither, O splendid ship, thy white sails crowding, / Leaning across the bosom of the urgent West. ['A Passer-by']

> 4 So sweet love seemed that April morn, / When first we kissed beside the thorn, / So strangely sweet, it was not strange / We thought that love could never change. [*Shorter Poems* bk 5, no 5]

John Bright, British Victorian politician and humanitarian campaigner against the Corn Laws and the Crimean War. A stirring orator, he said of the Crimean War: 'The angel of death has been abroad throughout the land; you may almost hear the beating of his wings'.

BRIEN Alan 1925–
English journalist and writer.

> My theory is that mature woman is physically polygamous but emotionally monogamous, while man is emotionally polygamous but physically monogamous. [Quoted in *New Statesman*, 6 Dec 1968]

BRIGHT John 1811–1889
English radical Liberal politician.

> 1 England is the mother of Parliaments. [Speech in House of Commons 1865]

> 2 Force is not a remedy. [Speech in Birmingham 1880]

BRODSKY Joseph 1940–
Russian-born US poet and critic.

> 1 The real history of consciousness starts with one's first lie. [*Less Than One*, title essay]

> 2 For aesthetics is the mother of ethics ... . Were we to choose our leaders on the basis of their reading experience and not their political programs, there would be much less grief on earth. [In his Nobel prize acceptance speech, 1987]

BROME Richard c. 1590–1652
English dramatist.

> I am a gentleman, though spoiled i' the breeding. ... We came in with the Conqueror. [*English Moor*]

BRONOWSKI Jacob 1908–1974
Polish-born US historian and mathematician.

> 1 That is the essence of science: ask an impertinent question, and you are on the way to a pertinent answer. [*Ascent of Man*].

2 The wish to hurt, the momentary intoxication with pain, is the loophole through which the pervert climbs into the minds of ordinary men. [*Face of Violence* ch 5]

3 The world is made of people who never quite get into the first team and who just miss the prizes at the flower show. [*Face of Violence* ch 6]

BRONTË Anne 1820–1849
English novelist.

Because the road is rough and long, / Shall we despise the skylark's song? [*Views of Life*]

BRONTË Charlotte 1816–1855
English novelist.

Reader, I married him. [*Jane Eyre*]

BRONTË Emily 1818–1848
English novelist and poet.

1 No coward soul is mine. [*Last Lines*]

2 Vain are the thousand creeds / That move men's hearts: unutterably vain. [*Last Lines*]

3 My love for Linton is like the foliage in the woods: time will change it, I'm well aware, as winter changes the trees. My love for Heathcliff resembles the eternal rocks beneath: a source of little visible delight, but necessary. Nelly I *am* Heathcliff! [*Wuthering Heights* ch 9]

BROOKE Rupert 1887–1915
English poet.

1 Blow out, you bugles, over the rich Dead! ['The Dead']

2 Stands the Church clock at ten to three? / And is there honey still for tea? [*Old Vicarage, Grantchester*]

3 Unkempt about those hedges blows / An English unofficial rose. [*Old Vicarage, Grantchester*]

4 Now, God be thanked Who has matched us with His hour, / And caught our youth, and wakened us from sleeping. ['Peace']

5 The worst friend and enemy is but Death. ['Peace']

6 If I should die, think only this of me ... That there's some corner of a foreign field / That is forever England. ['The Soldier']

BROOKNER Anita 1938–
English writer and art historian.

1 No blame should attach to telling the truth. But it does, it does. [*Friend from England* ch 10]

2 Good women always think it is their fault when someone else is being offensive. Bad women never take the blame for anything. [*Hotel du Lac*]

3 There are moments when you feel free, moments when you have energy, moments when you have hope, but you can't rely on any of these things to see you through. Circumstances do that. [Quoted in Haffenden *Novelists in Interview*]

4 Eventually he asked her to marry him. In this he showed sense; it is best to marry for purely selfish reasons. [*Start in Life* ch 22]

BROOKS Mel 1926–
US film director and comedian.

That's it baby, when you got it, flaunt it. [*The Producers* 1968]

BROOKS Thomas 1608–1680
English theologian.

For (magna est veritas et prævalebit) great is truth, and shall prevail. [*Crown and Glory of Christianity*]

BROOKS Van Wyck 1886–1963
US author and critic.

His wife not only edited his works but edited him. [*Ordeal of Mark Twain* ch 5]

BROWN Helen Gurley 1922–
US founding editor of *Cosmopolitan* magazine.

> Sex and the Single Girl. [Book title]

BROWN John Mason 1900–1969
US journalist.

> Tallulah Bankhead barged down the Nile last night as Cleopatra – and sank. [*New York Post* 11 Nov 1937]

BROWN Norman O 1913–
US philosopher.

> The human body is an energy system ... which is never a complete structure; never static; is in perpetual inner self-construction and self-destruction; we destroy in order to make it new. [*Love's Body* ch 8]

BROWN T E 1830–1897
English poet.

> A garden is a lovesome thing, God wot! [*My Garden*]

BROWN Thomas 1663–1704
English satirist.

> I do not love you Dr. Fell, / But why I cannot tell; / But this I know, and know full well, / I do not love you, Dr. Fell. [*Works of Mr Thomas Brown*]

BROWNE Charles Farrar 1834–1867
US humorist.

> He is dreadfully married. He's the most married man I ever saw in my life. [On the Mormon leader Brigham Young, who had 17 wives, *Moses, the Sassy*]

BROWNE Thomas 1605–1682
English author and physician.

> **1** He who discommendeth others obliquely commendeth himself. [*Christian Morals* pt 1]

> **2** All places, all airs make unto me one country; I am in England, everywhere, and under any meridian. [*Religio Medici*]

> **3** For the world, I count it not an inn, but an hospital, and a place, not to live, but to die in. [*Religio Medici*]

> **4** I could never divide my self from any man upon the difference of an opinion, or be angry with his judgment for not agreeing with me in that, from which perhaps within a few days I should dissent my self. [*Religio Medici*]

> **5** Many ... have too rashly charged the troops of error, and remain as trophies unto the enemies of truth. [*Religio Medici*]

> **6** No man can justly censure or condemn another, because indeed no man truly knows another. [*Religio Medici*]

> **7** Persecution is a bad and indirect way to plant religion. [*Religio Medici*]

> **8** We all labour against our own cure; for death is the cure of all diseases. [*Religio Medici*]

> **9** We carry within us the wonders we seek without us. There is all Africa, and her prodigies in us. [*Religio Medici*]

> **10** The long habit of living indisposeth us for dying. [*Urn Burial*]

> **11** Man is a noble animal, splendid in ashes, and pompous in the grave. [*Urn Burial*]

> **12** Old families last not three oaks. [*Urn Burial*]

> **13** What song the Syrens sang, or what name Achilles assumed when he hid himself among women. [*Urn Burial*]

BROWNING Elizabeth Barrett 1806–1861
English poet.

> **1** 'Guess now who holds thee?'– 'Death', I said, but there / The silver answer rang, ... 'Not Death, but Love.' [*Sonnets from the Portuguese*]

> **2** How do I love thee? Let me count the ways. [*Sonnets from the Portuguese* XLIII]

3 I love thee with a love I seemed to lose / With my lost saints – I love thee with the breath, / Smiles, tears, of all my life! – and, if God choose, / I shall but love thee better after death. [*Sonnets from the Portuguese* XLIII]

BROWNING Robert 1812–1889
English poet.

1 He said true things, but called them by wrong names. ['Bishop Blougram's Apology']

2 Just when we're safest, there's a sunset-touch, / A fancy from a flower-bell, some one's death, / A chorus-ending from Euripides, / And that's enough for fifty hopes and fears, – / The grand Perhaps. [*Bishop Blougram's Apology*]

3 My own, see where the years conduct! / At first, 'twas something our souls / should mix as mists do; each is sucked / In each now. ['By the Fireside']

4 Boot, saddle, to horse, and away! [*Cavalier Tunes*, 'Boot and Saddle']

5 Dauntless the slug-horn to my lips I set, / And blew. ['Childe Roland to the Dark Tower came']

6 The sprinkled isles, / Lily on lily, that o'erlace the sea. / And laugh their pride when the light wave lisps 'Greece'. ['Cleon']

7 We loved, sir – used to meet: / How sad and bad and mad it was– / But then, how it was sweet! ['Confessions']

8 Progress, man's distinctive mark alone, / Not God's, and not the beasts': God is, they are, / Man partly is and wholly hopes to be. ['Death in the Desert']

9 Such ever was love's way; to rise, it stoops. ['Death in the Desert']

10 Oh, to be in England / Now that April's there. ['Home Thoughts from Abroad']

Robert Browning's works have influenced poets as disparate as Robert Frost and Ezra Pound. During Browning's lifetime, critical recognition came rapidly after 1864, and although his books never sold as well as his wife's or Tennyson's, he acquired a considerable and enthusiastic public.

11 That's the wise thrush; he sings each song twice over, / Lest you should think he never could recapture / The first fine careless rapture! ['Home Thoughts from Abroad']

12 'Tis an awkward thing to play with souls, / And matter enough to save one's own. ['Light Woman']

13 Just for a handful of silver he left us, / Just for a riband to stick in his coat. ['Lost Leader']

14 Never glad confident morning again! ['Lost Leader']

15 We that had loved him so, followed him, honoured him, / Lived in his mild and magnificent eye, / Learned his great language, caught his clear accents, / Made him our pattern to live and to die! ['Lost Leader']

16 Ah, did you once see Shelley plain, / And did he stop and speak to you / And did you speak to him again? ['Memorabilia']

17 Dante, who loved well because he hated, / Hated wickedness that hinders loving. ['One Word More']

18 Truth is within ourselves. ['Paracelsus']

19 It was roses, roses, all the way. ['The Patriot']

20 The year's at the spring, / And day's at the morn; / Morning's at seven; / The hill-side's dew-pearled; / The lark's on the wing; / The snail's on the thorn: / God's in his heaven – / All's right with the world! ['Pippa Passes']

21 Grow old along with me! / The best is yet to be, / The last of life, for which the first was made. [*Rabbi ben Ezra*]

22 O lyric Love, half angel and half bird. [*The Ring and the Book* bk 1]

23 How good is man's life, the mere living! how fit to employ / All the heart and the soul and the senses, for ever in joy! ['Saul']

24 One who never turned his back but marched breast forward, / Never doubted clouds would break, / Never dreamed, though right were worsted, wrong would triumph. ['Summum Bonum']

25 Only I discern – / Infinite passion, and the pain / Of finite hearts that yearn. ['Two in the Campagna']

26 What's become of Waring / Since he gave us all the slip? ['Waring']

BRUMMELL Beau 1778–1840
English dandy.

Who's your fat friend? [Referring to the Prince Regent, in Gronow *Reminiscences*]

BRUNO Frank 1961–
English boxer.

Boxing is just show business with blood. [*Guardian* 19 Nov 1991]

BRYAN William Jennings 1860–1925
US lawyer and politician.

You shall not press down upon the brow of labour this crown of thorns, you shall not crucify mankind upon a cross of gold. [Speech at the National Democratic Convention, Chicago 1896]

BRYANT Anita 1940–
Former Miss America.

If homosexuality were the normal way, God would have made Adam and Bruce. [*New York Times* 5 June 1977]

BUCHAN John, Baron Tweedsmuir
1875–1940
Scottish politician and author.

1 To live for a time close to great minds is the best kind of education. [*Memory Hold-the-Door*]

2 It's a great life if you don't weaken. [*Mr Standfast*]

BUCHANAN Robert Williams 1841–1901
English poet, playwright, and novelist.

The Fleshly School of Poetry. [Article title]

BUCK Pearl 1892–1973
US novelist.

1 It is better to be first with an ugly woman than the hundredth with a beauty. [*Good Earth* ch 1]

2 The bitterest creature under heaven is the wife who discovers that her husband's bravery is only bravado, that his strength is only a uniform, that his power is but a gun in the hands of a fool. [*To My Daughter, With Love*]

3 None who have always been free can understand the terrible fascinating power of the hope of freedom to those who are not free. [*What America Means to me* ch 4]

BUFFON Georges-Louis Leclerc, Comte de 1707–1778
French naturalist.

> **1** Style is the man himself. [*Discourse on Style*]

> **2** Genius is only a great aptitude for patience. [Attributed remark]

BUKHARIN Nikolai Ivanovich 1888–1938
Soviet politician and theorist.

> We might have a two-party system, but one of the two parties would be in office and the other in prison. [Attributed remark]

BUNN Alfred c. 1796–1860
English poet and theatre manager.

> I dreamt that I dwelt in marble halls. ['I Dreamt That I Dwelt']

BUÑUEL Luis 1900–1983
Spanish film director.

> **1** Our memory is our coherence, our reason, our feeling, even our action. Without it, we are nothing. [*My Last Sigh* ch 1]

> **2** This rage to understand, to fill in the blanks, only makes life more banal. If we could only find the courage to leave our destiny to chance, to accept the fundamental mystery of our lives, then we might be closer to the sort of happiness that comes with innocence. [*My Last Sigh* ch 15]

> **3** The Discreet Charm of the Bourgeoisie. [Film title]

BUNYAN John 1628–1688
English author.

> **1** A castle, called Doubting-Castle, the owner whereof was Giant Despair. [*Pilgrim's Progress*]

> **2** He that is down needs fear no fall, / He that is low no pride. [*Pilgrim's Progress*]

> **3** It beareth the name of Vanity-Fair, because the town where 'tis kept, is lighter than vanity. [*Pilgrim's Progress*]

> **4** The name of the slough was Despond. [*Pilgrim's Progress*]

> **5** An ornament to her profession. [*Pilgrim's Progress*]

> **6** Sleep is sweet to the labouring man. [*Pilgrim's Progress*]

> **7** So he passed over, and all the trumpets sounded for him on the other side. [*Pilgrim's Progress*]

> **8** Who would true valour see, / Let him come hither; / One here will constant be, / Come wind, come weather. / There's no discouragement / Shall make him once relent / His first avow'd intent / To be a pilgrim. [*Pilgrim's Progress*]

BURGESS Anthony 1917–1993
English novelist and literary critic.

> A work of fiction should be, for its author, a journey into the unknown, and the prose should convey the difficulties of the journey. [*Homage to Qwert Yuiop*]

BURGON John William 1813–1888
English divine.

> A rose-red city – half as old as Time! [*Petra*]

BURKE Edmund 1729–1797
Anglo-Irish political theorist and Whig politician.

> **1** It is a general popular error to imagine the loudest complainers for the public to be the most anxious for its welfare. [*Observation on a Publication, 'The present state of the nation'*]

> **2** Custom reconciles us to everything. [*On the Sublime and Beautiful*]

> **3** I am convinced that we have a degree of delight, and that no small one, in the real misfortunes and pains of others. [*On the Sublime and Beautiful*]

4 The age of chivalry is gone. That of sophisters, economists, and calculators, has succeeded; and the glory of Europe is extinguished for ever. [*Reflections on the Revolution in France*]

5 Better to be despised for too anxious apprehensions, than ruined by too confident a security. [*Reflections on the Revolution in France*]

6 Man is by his constitution a religious animal. [*Reflections on the Revolution of France*]

7 People will not look forward to posterity, who never look backward to their ancestors. [*Reflections on the Revolution in France*]

8 Rage and frenzy will pull down more in half an hour, than prudence, deliberation, and foresight can build up in a hundred years. [*Reflections on the Revolution in France*]

9 A state without the means of some change is without the means of its conservation. [*Reflections on the Revolution in France*]

10 Superstition is the religion of feeble minds. [*Reflections on the Revolution in France*]

11 Whenever our neighbour's house is on fire, it cannot be amiss for the engines to play a little on our own. [*Reflections on the Revolution in France*]

12 The greater the power, the more dangerous the abuse. [Speech on the Middlesex Election 1771]

13 Great men are the guide-posts and landmarks in the state. [Speech on American Taxation 1774]

14 It is the nature of all greatness not to be exact. [Speech on American Taxation 1774]

15 To tax and to please, no more than to love and to be wise, is not given to men. [Speech on American Taxation 1774]

16 Would twenty shillings have ruined Mr Hampden's fortune? No! but the payment of half twenty shillings, on the principle it was demanded, would have made him a slave. [Speech on American Taxation 1774]

17 I do not know the method of drawing up an indictment against an whole people. [Speech on Conciliation with America 1775]

18 Magnanimity in politics is not seldom the truest wisdom; and a great empire and little minds go ill together. [Speech on Conciliation with America 1775]

19 The use of force alone is but *temporary*. It may subdue for a moment; but it does not remove the necessity of subduing again: and a nation is not governed, which is perpetually to be conquered. [Speech on Conciliation with America 1775]

20 The people are the masters. [Speech on the Economical Reform 1780]

21 An event has happened, upon which it is difficult to speak, and impossible to be silent. [Speech on the Impeachment of Warren Hastings 1789]

22 Lastly, in the name of human nature itself, in the name of both sexes, in the name of every age, in the name of every rank, I impeach the common enemy and oppressor of all! [Speech on the Impeachment of Warren Hastings 1789]

23 Nothing is so fatal to religion as indifference, which is, at least, half infidelity. [Letter to William Smith 29 Jan 1795]

24 Liberty, too, must be limited in order to be possessed. [Letter to the Sheriffs of Bristol]

25 Not merely a chip off the old 'block', but the old block itself. [Remark on Pitt the younger's first speech]

BURKE Johnny 1908–1964
US songwriter.

Every time it rains, it rains / Pennies from heaven. ['Pennies from Heaven']

BURNEY Fanny 1752–1840
English novelist and diarist.

1 No man is in love when he marries. He may have loved before; I
have even heard that he has loved
after: but at the time never. There is
something in the formalities of the
matrimonial preparations that drive
away all the little cupidons. [*Camilla*
bk 6, ch 10]

2 Travelling is the ruin of all happiness! There's no looking at a
building here after seeing Italy.
[*Cecilia*]

BURNS George 1896–
US comedian.

Too bad all the people who know
how to run the country are busy driving cabs and cutting hair. [Quoted
in Michael Shea *Influence* ch 27]

BURNS Robert 1759–1796
Scottish poet.

1 But to see her was to love her, /
Love but her, and love for ever. ['Ae
Fond Kiss']

2 Should auld acquaintance be forgot, / And never brought to mind?
['Auld Lang Syne']

3 We'll tak a cup o' kindness yet,
/ For auld lang syne. ['Auld Lang
Syne']

4 Gin a body meet a body /
Coming through the rye; / Gin a
body kiss a body. / Need a body
cry? ['Coming through the Rye']

5 Farewell dear, deluding Woman,
/ The joy of joys! ['Epistle to James
Smith']

6 Flow gently, sweet Afton, among
thy green braes, / Flow gently, I'll
sing thee a song in thy praise. ['Flow
Gently, Sweet Afton']

7 A man's a man for a' that. ['For
a' That and a' That']

8 Green grow the rashes, O! ['Green
Grow the Rashes']

9 Man's inhumanity to man /
Makes countless thousands mourn!
['Man Was Made to Mourn']

10 O Death, the poor man's dearest friend, / The kindest and the
best! ['Man Was Made to Mourn']

11 My heart's in the Highlands,
my heart is not here; / My heart's
in the Highlands a-chasing the deer;
/ Chasing the wild deer, and following the roe, / My heart's in the
Highlands, wherever I go. ['My
Heart's in the Highlands']

12 O, my Luve's like a red red rose
/ That's newly sprung in June. ['My
Love is like a Red Red Rose']

13 Liberty's in every blow! / Let
us do or die! ['Scots, Wha Hae']

14 Some hae meat, and canna eat,
/ And some wad eat that want it; /
But we hae meat and we can eat, /
And sae the Lord be thankit. ['The
Selkirk Grace, as attributed to Burns']

15 The best laid schemes o' mice
an' men / Gang aft a-gley. ['To a
Mouse']

16 Wee, sleekit, cow'rin, tim'rous
beastie, / O what a panic's in thy
breastie! ['To a Mouse']

17 What can a young lassie do wi'
an auld man? ['What can a Young
Lassie']

18 O whistle, and I'll come to you,
my lad. ['Whistle, and I'll Come to You,
my Lad']

19 Ye banks and braes o' bonny
Doon, / How can ye bloom sae
fresh and fair? ['Ye Banks and Braes o'
Bonny Doon']

BURROUGHS Edgar Rice 1875–1950
US novelist.

Me Tarzan, you Jane. [*Tarzan of the
Apes*]

BURROUGHS William 1914–
US writer.

After one look at this planet any

visitor from outer space would say 'I WANT TO SEE THE MANAGER.' [*Adding Machine*, 'Women: A Biological Mistake?']

BURT Benjamin Hapgood 1880–1950
US lyricist and composer.

When you're all dressed up and no place to go. [Song title]

BURTON Richard 1925–1984
Welsh actor.

This diamond has so many carats, it's almost a turnip. [On his gift to Elizabeth Taylor, quoted in *Observer* 5 March 1972]

BURTON Robert 1577–1640
English philosopher and clergyman.

1 All poets are mad. [*Anatomy of Melancholy*, 'Democritus to the Reader']

2 They lard their lean books with the fat of others' works. [*Anatomy of Melancholy*, 'Democritus to the Reader']

3 Cookery is become an art, a noble science. [*Anatomy of Melancholy* pt 1]

4 One was never married, and that's his hell; another is, and that's his plague. [*Anatomy of Melancholy* pt 1]

5 England is a paradise for women, and hell for horses: Italy a paradise for horses, hell for women. [*Anatomy of Melancholy* pt 3]

6 Love indeed (I may not deny) first united provinces, built cities, and by a perpetual generation makes and preserves mankind; but if it rage it is no more love, but burning lust, a disease, frenzy, madness, hell. [*Anatomy of Melancholy* pt 3]

7 Marriage and hanging go by destiny; matches are made in heaven. [*Anatomy of Melancholy* pt 3]

8 The miller sees not all the water that goes by his mill. [*Anatomy of Melancholy* pt 3]

9 No cord nor cable can so forcibly draw, or hold so fast, as love can do with a twined thread. [*Anatomy of Melancholy* pt 3]

10 One religion is as true as another. [*Anatomy of Melancholy* pt 3]

11 'Tis a hazard both ways I confess, to live single or to marry. ... It may be bad, it may be good, as it is a cross and calamity on the one side, so 'tis a sweet delight, an incomparable happiness, a blessed estate, a most unspeakable benefit, a sole content, on the other, 'tis all in the proof. [*Anatomy of Melancholy*]

BUSH George 1924–
US Republican president.

Read my lips – no new taxes. [Promise made during 1988 US presidential campaign]

BUSSY-RAMBUTIN Comte de 1618–1693
French poet and soldier.

Absence is to love what wind is to fire; / It extinguishes the small, it kindles the great. [*Histoire Amoureuse des Gaules: maximes d'amour* pt 2]

BUTLER Samuel 1612–1680
English poet.

1 All love at first, like generous wine, / Ferments and frets, until 'tis fine; / But when 'tis setttled on the lee, / And from th' impurer matter free, / Becomes the richer still, the older, / And proves the pleasanter, the colder. [*Genuine Remains*, 'Miscellaneous Thoughts']

2 She that with poetry is won, / Is but a desk to write upon. [*Hudibras* pt 2]

3 Through perils both of wind and limb, / Through thick and thin she follow'd him. [*Hudibras* pt 2]

4 For money has a power above / The stars and fate, to manage love. [*Hudibras* pt 3]

BUTLER Samuel 1835–1902
English writer.

1 It has been said that that though God cannot alter the past, historians can; it is perhaps because they can be useful to Him in this respect that He tolerates their existence. [*Erewhon Revisited*]

2 Conscience is thoroughly well-bred and soon leaves off talking to those who do not wish to hear it. [*Further Extracts from Notebooks*]

3 The three most important things a man has are, briefly, his private parts, his money, and his religious opinions. [*Further Extracts from Notebooks*]

4 An apology for the Devil: It must be remembered that we have only heard one side of the case. God has written all the books. [*Notebooks* ch 14]

5 God is love – I dare say. But what a mischievous devil love is! [*Notebooks* ch 14]

6 The great pleasure of a dog is that you may make a fool of yourself with him and not only will he not scold you, but he will make a fool of himself too. [*Notebooks* ch 14]

7 To live is like love, all reason is against it, and all healthy instinct for it. [*Notebooks* ch 15]

8 The history of art is the history of revivals. [*Notebooks*, 'Handel and Music']

9 All progress is based upon a universal innate desire on the part of every organism to live beyond its income. [*Notebooks*, 'Life']

10 The world will, in the end, follow only those who have despised as well as served it. [*Notebooks*, 'Life of the World to Come. The World']

11 Belief like any other moving body follows the path of least resistance. [*Notebooks* 220]

12 Oh God! Oh Montreal! ['Psalm of Montreal']

13 It is our less conscious thoughts and our less conscious actions which mainly mould our lives and the lives of those who spring from us. [*Way of All Flesh* ch 5]

14 They would have been equally horrified at hearing the Christian religion doubted, and at seeing it practised. [*Way of All Flesh* ch 15]

15 All animals, except man, know that the principal business of life is to enjoy it – and they do enjoy it as much as man and other circumstances will allow. [*Way of All Flesh* ch 19]

16 The advantage of doing one's praising for oneself is that one can lay it on so thick and exactly in the right places. [*Way of All Flesh* ch 34]

17 His instinct told him that the best liar is he who makes the smallest amount of lying go the longest way. [*Way of All Flesh* ch 39]

18 A man's friendships are, like his will, invalidated by marriage – but they are also no less invalidated by the marriage of his friends. [*Way of All Flesh* ch 75]

19 'Tis better to have loved and lost, than never to have loved at all. [*Way of All Flesh* ch 77]

20 It was very good of God to let Carlyle and Mrs Carlyle marry one another and so make only two people miserable instead of four. [Letter to Miss E M Savage 21 Nov 1884]

21 Life is like playing a violin solo in public and learning the instrument as one goes on. [Speech at the Somerville Club 27 Feb 1895]

22 Brigands demand your money or your life; women require both. [Attributed remark]

BUTLER William 1535–1618
English physician.

Doubtless God could have made a better berry but doubtless God never did. [Of the strawberry, quoted in Izaak Walton *Compleat Angler*]

BYROM John 1692–1763
English poet and stenographer.

God bless the King, I mean the Faith's Defender; / God bless - - no harm in blessing – the Pretender; / But who Pretender is, or who is King, / God bless us all – that's quite another thing. ['To an Officer in the Army']

BYRON George, Lord 1788–1824
English poet.

1 His heart was one of those which most enamour us, / Wax to receive, and marble to retain. ['Beppo']

2 Mark! where his carnage and his conquests cease! / He makes a solitude, and calls it – peace! [*Bride of Abydos* II. 22]

3 The self-torturing sophist, wild Rousseau. [*Childe Harold* II. 77]

4 Where'er we tread 'tis haunted, holy ground. [*Childe Harold* II. 88]

5 Years steal / Fire from the mind as vigour from the limb; / And life's enchanted cup but sparkles near the brim. [*Childe Harold* III. 8]

6 And all went merry as a marriage bell. [*Childe Harold* III. 21]

7 There was a sound of revelry by night, / And Belgium's capital had gather'd then / Her beauty and her chivalry, and bright / The lamps shone o'er fair women and brave men; [*Childe Harold* III. 21]

8 On with the dance! let joy be unconfined; / No sleep till morn, when Youth and Pleasure meet / To chase the glowing Hours with flying feet. [*Childe Harold* III. 22]

9 Battle's magnificently stern array! [*Childe Harold* III. 28]

10 Rider and horse, – friend, foe, – in one red burial blent! [*Childe Harold* III. 28]

11 His love was passion's essence:– as a tree / On fire by lightning, with ethereal flame / Kindled he was, and blasted. [*Childe Harold* III. 78]

George Gordon Byron in Albanian dress. The poetry and personality of Byron captured the imagination of Europe. After his death he became the symbol of disinterested patriotism and a Greek national hero.

12 Butcher'd to make a Roman holiday. [*Childe Harold* IV. 141]

13 I love not man the less, but Nature more. [*Childe Harold* IV. 178]

14 The glory and the nothing of a name. ['Churchill's Grave']

15 For a man to become a poet ... he must be in love or miserable. [*Conversations*]

16 I never wrote anything worth mentioning till I was in love. [*Conversations*]

17 The Assyrian came down like a wolf on the fold, / And his cohorts were gleaming in purple and gold; / And the sheen of their spears was like stars on the sea, When the blue wave rolls nightly on deep Galilee. [*Destruction of Sennacherib*]

18 I wish he would explain his explanation. [*Don Juan* I. 2]

19 What men call gallantry, and gods adultery, / Is much more common where the climate's sultry. [*Don Juan* I. 63]

20 Pleasure's a sin and sometimes sin's a pleasure. [*Don Juan* I. 133]

21 A little she strove and much repented, / And whispering 'I will ne'er consent'–consented. [*Don Juan* I. 194]

22 Man's love is of man's life a thing apart, / 'Tis woman's whole existence. [*Don Juan* I. 194]

23 There's nought, no doubt, so much the spirit calms / As rum and true religion. [*Don Juan* II. 34]

24 Alas! the love of women! it is known / To be a lovely and a fearful thing! [*Don Juan* II. 199]

25 In her first passion woman loves her lover, / In all the others all she loves is love. [*Don Juan* III. 3]

26 'Tis melancholy, and a fearful sign / Of human frailty, folly, also crime, / That love and marriage rarely can combine, / Although they both are born in the same clime; / Marriage from love, like vinegar from wine– / A sad, sour, sober beverage–by time / Is sharpened from its high celestial flavour, / Down to a very homely household savour. [*Don Juan* III. 5]

27 Think you, if Laura had been Petrarch's wife, / He would have written sonnets all his life? [*Don Juan* III. 8]

28 All tragedies are finished by a death, / All comedies are ended by a marriage; / The future states of both are left to faith. [*Don Juan* III. 9]

29 The isles of Greece, the isles of Greece! / Where burning Sappho loved and sung, / Where grew the arts of war and peace, / Where Delos rose, and Phœbus sprung! [*Don Juan* III. 86]

30 The mountains look on Marathon – / And Marathon looks on the sea; / And musing there an hour alone, / I dream'd that Greece might still be free. [*Don Juan* III. 86]

31 And if I laugh at any mortal thing, / 'Tis that I may not weep. [*Don Juan* IV. 4]

32 Thus in the East they are extremely strict, / And wedlock and a padlock mean the same; ... / But then their own polygamy's to blame; / Why don't they knead two virtuous souls for life / Into that moral centaur, man and wife? [*Don Juan* V. 158]

33 There is a tide in the affairs of women, / Which, taken at the flood, leads – God knows where. [*Don Juan* VI. 2]

34 For talk six times with the same single lady, / And you may get the wedding dresses ready. [*Don Juan* XII. 59]

35 Now hatred is by far the longest pleasure; / Men love in haste, but they detest at leisure. [*Don Juan* XIII. 6]

36 Cervantes smiled Spain's chivalry away. [*Don Juan* XIII, 11]

37 Friendship is Love without his wings! [*Hours of Idleness*, 'L'Amitié']

38 Though women are angels, yet wedlock's the devil. [*Hours of Idleness*, 'To Eliza']

39 Who killed John Keats? / 'I,' says the Quarterly, / So savage and Tartarly; / 'Twas one of my feats.' ['John Keats']

40 I awoke one morning and found myself famous. [Remark quoted in T Moore *Life of Byron* referring to the instantaneous success of *Childe Harold*]

41 Eternal spirit of the chainless mind! ['Sonnet on Chillon']

42 So, we'll go no more a roving / So late into the night, / Though the heart be still as loving, / And the moon be still as bright. ['So, We'll Go No More a Roving']

44 When we two parted / In silence and tears, / Half broken-hearted / To sever for years, / Pale grew thy cheek and cold, / Colder thy kiss. ['When We Two Parted']

45 There is no such thing as a life of passion any more than a continuous earthquake, or an eternal fever. Besides, who would ever *shave* themselves in such a state? [Letter to Thomas Moore 5 July 1821]

CABELL James Branch 1879–1958
US novelist and journalist.

> The optimist proclaims that we live
> in the best of all possible worlds;
> and the pessimist fears this is true.
> [*Silver Stallion*]

CAEDMON Earliest known English poet.

> Light was first / Through the Lord's
> word / Named day: / Beauteous,
> bright creation.
> ['Creation. The First Day']

CAESAR Augustus 63 BC–AD 14
Roman emperor.

> **1** He so improved the city that he
> justly boasted that he found it brick
> and left it marble. [Suetonius *Life of
> Augustus*]

> **2** Varus, give me back my legions.
> [Suetonius *Life of Augustus*]

CAESAR Julius 100–40 BC
Roman statesman and general.

> **1** The die is cast. [Attributed remark
> on crossing the Rubicon, quoted in
> Suetonius *Lives of the Caesars*, 'Divus
> Julius']

> **2** I came, I saw, I conquered.
> [On his campaign in Pontus, quoted in
> Suetonius *Lives of the Caesars*, 'Divus
> Julius']

> **3** You also, Brutus?
> [Attributed remark on seeing his protégé
> Brutus among the assassins attacking
> him]

CAHN Sammy 1913–1993
US songwriter.

> Love and marriage, love and mar-
> riage, / Go together like a horse and
> carriage, / This I tell ya, brother, /
> Ya can't have one without the other.
> ['Love and Marriage']

CALDERÓN DE LA BARCA Pedro
1600–1681
Spanish dramatist.

> Even in dreams good works are not
> wasted. [*La Vida es Sueño*]

CALIGULA AD 12–41
Roman emperor.

> Would that the Roman people had
> but one neck! [Suetonius *Life of Caligula*]

CALVINO Italo 1923–1985
Italian writer and critic.

> **1** The unconscious is the ocean of
> the unsayable, of what has been
> expelled from the land of language,
> removed as a result of ancient pro-
> hibitions. ['Cybernetics and Ghosts', lec-
> ture, Turin Nov 1969; published in *The
> Literature Machine*]

> **2** A classic is a book that has never
> finished saying what it has to say.
> ['Why Read the Classics?', *L'Espresso* 28
> June 1981]

CAMBRONNE Pierre-Jacques 1770–1842
French general

> The Guards die but do not surren-
> der. [Attributed remark, when called
> upon to surrender]

CAMDEN William 1551–1623
English antiquary.

> Betwixt the stirrup and the ground
> / Mercy I asked, mercy I found.
> [*Remains*, 'Epitaph for a Man Killed by
> Falling from His Horse']

CAMPBELL Beatrix 1947–
British journalist.

> A society in which adults are
> estranged from the world of chil-
> dren, and often from their own
> childhood, tends to hear children's
> speech only as a foreign language,
> or as a lie. [*Unofficial Secrets* ch 2]

CAMPBELL David Gordon 1915–1979
Australian poet.

> Mountain and brilliant bird, / The ram and the wren, / For each there is a word; / In every grain of sand / Stands a singer in white. / What's matter but a hardening of the light? ['Hear the Bird of Day']

CAMPBELL Jane Montgomery 1817–1878
English writer.

> We plough the fields, and scatter / The good seed on the land. ['We Plough the Fields']

CAMPBELL Kim 1947–
Canadian politician and prime minister.

> Don't mess with me, I got tanks. [Remark while defence minister]

CAMPBELL Mrs Patrick 1865–1940
English actress.

Mrs Patrick Campbell. Making her stage debut 1888, English actress Mrs Patrick Campbell quickly gained fame as a temperamental yet highly talented leading lady. Her early successes were in the plays of Pinero and Ibsen and she later became well known in the roles of Ophelia, Lady Teazle, Lady Macbeth and Juliet.

1 It doesn't matter what you do in the bedroom as long as you don't do it in the street and frighten the horses. [Quoted in D Fielding *Duchess of Jermyn Street*]

2 The deep, deep peace of the double-bed after the hurly-burly of the chaise-longue. [On her recent marriage. Quoted in A Woollcott *While Rome Burns*]

CAMPBELL Roy 1901–1957
South African poet.

> Translations (like wives) are seldom strictly faithful if they are in the least attractive. [Quoted in *Poetry Review* June–July 1949]

CAMPBELL Thomas 1777–1844
Scottish poet.

1 O leave this barren spot to me! / Spare, woodman, spare the beechen tree. [*Beech-Tree's Petition*]

2 Gentlemen, you must not mistake me. I admit that he is the sworn foe of our nation, and, if you will, of the whole human race. But, gentlemen, we must be just to our enemy. We must not forget that he once shot a bookseller. [Of Napoleon, quoted in G O Trevelyan *The Life and Letters of Lord Macaulay*]

3 'Tis the sunset of life gives me mystical lore, / And coming events cast their shadows before. ['Lochiel's Warning']

CAMPION Thomas 1567–1620
English poet and musician.

1 There is a garden in her face, / Where roses and white lilies grow; ... / There cherries grow, which none may buy / Till 'Cherry ripe' themselves do cry. [*Book of Airs*, 'There is a Garden in her Face']

2 The Summer hath his joys, / And Winter his delights. / Though Love and all his pleasures are but toys, / They shorten tedious nights. ['Now Winter Nights Enlarge']

CAMUS Albert 1913–1960
Algerian/French philosopher and writer.

1 Without freedom, no art; art lives only on the restraints it imposes on itself, and dies of all others. [*Demain* 21 Feb 1957]

2 You know what charm is: a way of getting the answer yes without having asked any clear question. [*The Fall*]

3 A sub-clerk in the post-office is the equal of a conqueror if consciousness is common to them. [*Myth of Sisyphus*, 'The Absurd Man']

4 As a remedy to life in society I would suggest the big city. Nowadays it is the only desert within our means. [*Notebooks*]

5 An intellectual is someone whose mind watches itself. [*Notebooks*]

6 Every revolutionary ends as an oppressor or a heretic. [*The Rebel*]

7 What is a rebel? A man who says no. [*The Rebel*]

Albert Camus in 1957. His writings often brought him into conflict with other existentialist thinkers, such as Jean-Paul Sartre, but won him the Nobel Prize for Literature in 1957.

CANETTI Elias 1905–1985
Austrian novelist and philosopher.

1 History portrays everything as if it could not have come otherwise. History is on the side of what happened. [*Human Province*]

2 When you write down your life, every page should contain something no one has ever heard about. [*Secret Heart of the Clock*, 'Notes, Aphorisms, Fragments, 1973']

3 Adults find pleasure in deceiving a child. They consider it necessary, but they also enjoy it. The children very quickly figure it out and then practise deception themselves. [*Secret Heart of the Clock*, '1980']

CANNING George 1770–1827
British Tory prime minister.

1 Save me, oh, save me from the candid friend. [*New Morality*]

2 A sudden thought strikes me, let us swear an eternal friendship. [*The Rovers*]

ČAPEK Karel 1890–1938
Czech writer.

Man will never be enslaved by machinery if the man tending the machine be paid enough. [*News Chronicle*]

CAPONE Al *Scarface* 1898–1947
US gangster.

I've been accused of every death except the casualty list of the World War. [Newspaper interview.]

CAPP Al 1909–1979
US cartoonist.

A product of the untalented, sold by the unprincipled to the utterly bewildered. [On abstract art, *National Observer* 1 July 1963]

CARDUCCI Giosuè 1835–1907
Italian poet.

> Far better in one's work to forget than to seek to solve the vast riddles of the universe. [*Idillio Maremmano*]

CAREW Thomas c. 1595–1640
English poet and courtier.

> Then fly betimes for only they / Conquer love, that run away. ['Conquest by Flight']

CARLYLE Jane 1801–1866
Wife of historian Thomas Carlyle.

> 1 It is sad and wrong to be so dependent for the life of my life on any human being as I am on you; but I cannot by any force of logic cure myself at this date, when it has become second nature. If I have to lead another life in any of the planets, I shall take precious good care not to hang myself round any man's neck, either as a locket or a millstone. [Quoted in E Drew *Literature of Gossip*]

> 2 A positive engagement to marry a certain person at a certain time, at all haps and hazards, I have always considered the most ridiculous thing on earth. [Letter to Thomas Carlyle Jan 1825]

> 3 The triumphal procession air which, in our manners and customs, is given to marriage at the outset–that singing of *Te Deum* before the battle has begun. [Letter to Miss Barnes 24 Aug 1859]

CARLYLE Thomas 1795–1881
Scottish essayist and social historian.

> 1 A well-written Life is almost as rare as a well-spent one. [*Critical and Miscellaneous Essays* vol 1]

> 2 'Genius' (which means transcendent capacity of taking trouble, first of all). [*Frederick the Great* bk 4, ch 3]

> 3 Happy the people whose annals are blank in history-books! [*Frederick the Great* bk 16, ch 1]

Scottish historian and essayist Thomas Carlyle. Carlyle's works greatly influenced contemporary religious and political thought and established him as one of the great sages of his era.

> 4 The history of the world is but the biography of great men. [*Heroes and Hero-Worship*]

> 5 The seagreen Incorruptible. [Of Robespierre, *History of the French Revolution* bk 4, ch 4]

> 6 A whiff of grapeshot. [*History of the French Revolution* bk 5, ch 3]

> 7 Captains of industry. [*Past and Present* bk 4, ch 4]

> 8 Man is a tool-using animal ... Without tools he is nothing, with tools he is all. [*Sartor Resartus* bk 1, ch 5]

> 9 The everlasting no. [*Sartor Resartus* bk 2, title of ch 7]

CARNEGIE Dale 1888–1955
US author and teacher.

> How to Win Friends and Influence People. [Book title]

CARROLL Lewis 1832–1898
English author.

1 'Curiouser and curiouser!' cried Alice. [*Alice's Adventures in Wonderland* ch 2]

2 'I'll be judge, I'll be jury,' said cunning old Fury; 'I'll try the whole cause, and condemn you to death.' [*Alice's Adventures in Wonderland* ch 3]

3 'You are old, Father William,' the young man said, / 'And your hair has become very white; / And yet you incessantly stand on your head / – Do you think, at your age, it is right?' [*Alice's Adventures in Wonderland* ch 5]

4 If everybody minded their own business, ... the world would go round a deal faster than it does. [*Alice's Adventures in Wonderland* ch 6]

5 A cat may look at a king. [*Alice's Adventures in Wonderland* ch 8]

6 Soup of the evening, beautiful Soup! [*Alice's Adventures in Wonderland* ch 10]

7 Will you, won't you, will you, won't you, will you join the dance? [*Alice's Adventures in Wonderland* ch 10]

8 'That's not a regular rule: you invented it just now.' 'It's the oldest rule in the book,' said the King. 'Then it ought to be Number One,' said Alice. [*Alice's Adventures in Wonderland* ch 12]

9 Beware the Jabberwock, my son! [*Alice Through the Looking-Glass* ch 1]

10 Curtsey while you're thinking what to say. It saves time. [*Alice Through the Looking-Glass* ch 2]

11 'If seven maids with seven mops / Swept it for half a year, / Do you suppose,' the Walrus said, / 'That they could get it clear?' / 'I doubt it,' said the Carpenter, / And shed a bitter tear. [*Alice Through the Looking-Glass* ch 4]

12 'Let's fight till six, and then have dinner,' said Tweediedum. [*Alice Through the Looking-Glass* ch 4]

13 The rule is, jam to-morrow and jam yesterday – but never jam to-day. [*Alice Through the Looking-Glass* ch 5]

14 Why, sometimes I've believed as many as six impossible things before breakfast. [*Alice Through the Looking-Glass* ch 5]

15 It's as large as life, and twice as natural! [*Alice Through the Looking-Glass* ch 7]

16 What I tell you three times is true. [*Hunting of the Snark* Fit 1, 'The Landing']

17 But oh, beamish nephew, beware of the day, / If your Snark be a Boojum! For then / You will softly and suddenly vanish away, / And never be met with again! [*Hunting of the Snark* Fit 3, 'The Baker's Tale']

18 They sought it with thimbles, they sought it with care; / They pursued it with forks and hope; / They threatened its life with a railway-share; / They charmed it with smiles and soap. [*Hunting of the Snark* Fit 5, 'The Beaver's Lesson']

CARTER Angela 1940–1992
English novelist and essayist.

1 What is marriage but prostitution to one man instead of many? [*Nights at the Circus*, 'London 2']

2 Comedy is tragedy that happens to *other* people. [*Wise Children* ch 4]

CARTER Jimmy 1924–
US Democratic president.

1 I've looked on a lot of women with lust. I've committed adultery in my heart many times. This is something God recognizes I will do – and I have done it – and God forgives me for it. [Interview in *Playboy*, Nov 1976]

2 We should live our lives as though Christ were coming this afternoon. [Speech to Bible class in Plains, Georgia March 1976]

3 If you fear making anyone mad [= angry], then you ultimately probe for the lowest common denominator of human achievement. [Speech in Kansas City 9 Nov 1978]

CARY Joyce 1888–1957
English novelist.

1 Sara could commit adultery at one end and weep for her sins at the other, and enjoy both operations at once. [*Horse's Mouth* ch 8]

2 The will is never free – it is always attached to an object, a purpose. It is simply the engine in the car – it can't steer. [Interview in Cowley *Writers at Work*, 1st Series]

CASALS Pablo 1876–1973
Catalan cellist, composer, and conductor.

1 To make divine things human, and human things divine; such is Bach, the greatest and purest moment in music of all times. [Speech at Prades Bach Festival 1950]

2 I was aware at the time that some people noted a certain discrepancy in our ages – a bridegroom is not usually thirty years *older* than his father-in-law. [On his marriage in 1957]

CASSON Sir Hugh 1910–
English architect.

The British love permanence more than they love beauty. [*Observer* 1964]

CASTRO Fidel 1927–
Cuban communist president.

1 History will absolve me. [After an unsuccessful assault on army barracks July 1953]

2 A revolution is not a bed of roses. A revolution is a struggle to the death between the future and the past. [Speech given on the second anniversary of the revolution, Havana Jan 1961]

3 When you interviewed the Pope, did you ask him why it is that he

The Cuban revolutionary leader Fidel Castro. After his overthrow of the right-wing Batista regime in 1959, Castro maintained his leadership of Cuba despite the enmity of his powerful neighbour, the USA. From 1990 events in E Europe and the USSR left Castro increasingly isolated.

always wears that white outfit? [When asked why he always wears uniform, Dec 1993]

CATHER Willa 1873–1947
US novelist and short-story writer.

1 Religion and art spring from the same root and are close kin. Economics and art are strangers. [*Commonweal* 17 Apr 1936]

2 When kindness has left people, even for a few moments, we become afraid of them as if their reason has left them. [*My Mortal Enemy*]

3 I like trees because they seem more resigned to the way they have to live than other things do. [*O Pioneers!*]

4 Artistic growth is ... a refining of the sense of truthfulness. The stupid believe that to be truthful is easy; only the artist, the great artist, knows how difficult that is. [*Song of the Lark* pt 6, ch 11]

CATHERINE II (the Great) 1729–1796
Empress of Russia.

I shall be an autocrat: that's my trade. And the good Lord will forgive me: that's his. [Attributed remark]

CATHERINE OF ARAGON 1485–1536
Queen of England.

The hour of my death approaching ... I cannot choose, but out of love I bear you, advise you of your soul's health which you ought to prefer before all considerations of the world or flesh whatsoever. For which yet you have cast me into many calamities, and yourself into many troubles ... Lastly, I make this vow, that mine eyes desire you above all things. Farewell. [Letter to Henry VIII, written on her deathbed 5 Jan 1536]

CATO Marcus Porcius *the Elder*
234–149 BC
Roman consul and reformer.

Carthage must be destroyed. [Plutarch *Life of Cato*]

CATULLUS Gaius Valerius c. 87–54 BC
Roman lyric poet.

1 Kiss me a thousand times. [*Carmina* 5]

2 Let us live, my Lesbia, and let us love. [*Carmina* 5]

3 It is difficult suddenly to lay aside a long-cherished love. [*Carmina* 76]

4 I hate, I love. [*Carmina* 85]

5 And so, my brother, forever, hail, and farewell! [*Carmina* 101]

6 What a woman says to her ardent lover should be written in wind and running water. [*Odes* no. 70]

CAVAFY Constantine 1863–1933
Greek poet.

Body, remember not only how much you were loved, / not only the beds you lay on, / but also those desires glowing openly / in eyes that looked at you, / trembling for you in voices. ['Body, Remember']

CAVELL Edith 1865–1915
English hospital matron in World War I.

I realize that patriotism is not enough. I must have no hatred or bitterness towards any one. [Last words 12 Oct 1915, quoted in *The Times* 23 Oct 1915]

CÉLINE Louis-Ferdinand 1894–1961
French writer.

1 Almost every desire a poor man has is a punishable offence. [*Journey to the End of the Night* 176]

2 If you aren't rich you should always look useful. [*Journey to the End of the Night*]

3 Experience is a dim lamp, which only lights the one who bears it. [Interview in Plimpton *Writers at Work*, 3rd Series]

CELLINI Benvenuto 1500–1571
Italian sculptor and goldsmith.

The difference between a painting and a sculpture is the difference between a shadow and the thing that casts it. [Letter to Benedetto Varchi 1547]

CENTILEVRE Susannah c. 1669–1723
Irish-born English dramatist and actress.

1 When the glowing of passion's over, and pinching winter comes, will amorous sighs supply the want of fire, or kind looks and kisses keep off hunger? [*Artifice*]

2 The real Simon Pure. [*Bold Stroke for a Wife* V. i]

CERVANTES Miguel de 1547–1616
Spanish novelist and dramatist.

1 The eyes those silent tongues of Love. [*Don Quixote* pt 1, bk 2]

2 Absence, that common cure of love. [*Don Quixote* pt 1, bk 3]

3 Love and War are the same thing, and stratagems and policy are as allowable in the one as in the other. [*Don Quixote* pt 2, bk 3]

4 There are only two families in the world ... : the Haves and the Have-nots. [*Don Quixote* pt 2, ch 20]

5 Marriage is a noose. [*Don Quixote* pt 3, ch 19]

CHAMBERLAIN Joseph 1836–1914
British Conservative politician.

The day of small nations has long passed away. The day of Empires has come. [Speech in Birmingham 12 May 1904]

CHAMBERLAIN Neville 1869–1940
British Conservative politician.

1 In war, whichever side may call itself the victor, there are no winners, but all are losers. [Speech at Kettering 3 July 1938]

2 Peace with honour. I believe it is peace for our time. [Speech from 10 Downing Street 30 Sept 1938]

CHAMFORT Nicolas-Sébastien 1741–1794
French writer.

Love, in the form in which it exists in society, is nothing but the exchange of two fantasies and the superficial contact of two bodies. [*Maximes et Pensées* ch 6]

CHANDLER Raymond 1888–1959
English-born US novelist.

1 It was a blonde. A blonde to make a bishop kick a hole in a stained glass window. [*Farewell, My Lovely* ch 13]

2 She gave me a smile I could feel in my hip pocket. [*Farewell, My Lovely* ch 18]

3 Alcohol is like love: the first kiss is magic, the second is intimate, the third is routine. After that you just take the girl's clothes off. [*Long Goodbye*]

4 Down these mean streets a man must go who is not himself mean, who is neither tarnished nor afraid. ['Simple Art of Murder']

5 If my books had been any worse, I should not have been invited to Hollywood, and if they had been any better, I should not have come. [Letter to Charles W Morton 12 Dec 1945]

6 When I split an infinitive, God damn it, I split it so it will stay split. [Letter to Edward Weeks 18 Jan 1947]

CHAPLIN Charlie 1889–1977
English comic actor and filmmaker.

1 Life is a tragedy when seen in close-up, but a comedy in long-shot. [Quoted in his obituary, *Guardian* 28 Dec 1977]

2 All I need to make a comedy is a park, a policeman and a pretty girl. [*My Autobiography*]

CHAPMAN John Jay 1862–1933
US author.

You can get assent to almost any proposition as long as you are not going to do anything about it. [*Practical Agitation* ch 7]

CHARLES Prince of Wales 1948–
Heir to the throne of Great Britain and Northern Ireland.

1 I wish I had been Bob Geldof. [Quoted in *Observer* 21 Feb 1988]

2 Conservation must come before recreation. [*The Times* 5 July 1989]

3 A monstrous carbuncle on the face of a much-loved and elegant friend. [On a 1984 proposal for an extension to the National Gallery, London]

CHARLES II 1630–1685
King of Great Britain and Ireland, 1660–85.

He had been, he said, an unconscionable time dying; but he hoped that they would excuse it. [T B Macaulay *History of England*]

1 Let not poor Nelly starve. [Quoted in Gilbert Burnet *History of My Own Time*]

2 That is very true: for my words are my own, and my actions are my ministers. [Reply to Lord Rochester's epitaph on him]

CHATEAUBRIAND François René 1768–1848
French writer and politician.

The original writer is not he who refrains from imitating others, but he who can be imitated by none. [*Le Génie du Christianisme*]

CHATTERTON Thomas 1752–1770
English poet.

What is love? 'tis nature's treasure, / 'Tis the storehouse of her joys; / 'Tis the highest heaven of pleasure, / 'Tis a bliss which never cloys. [*Revenge* I. ii]

CHAUCER Geoffrey c. 1340–1400
English poet.

1 A Clerk ther was of Oxenford also. [*Canterbury Tales*, Prologue]

2 He was a verray parfit gentil knight. [*Canterbury Tales*, Prologue]

3 She was a worthy womman al hir lyve, / Housbondes at chirchedore she hadde fyve, / Withouten other companye in youthe. [*Canterbury Tales*, Prologue]

4 Whanne that Aprille with his shoures sote / The droghte of Marche hath perced to the rote. [*Canterbury Tales*, Prologue]

5 Love is noght oold as whan that it is newe. [*Canterbury Tales*, 'Clerk's Tale']

Posthumous portrait of English poet Geoffrey Chaucer by an unknown artist, National Portrait Gallery, London. Chaucer's work has been admired from his own time to the present day. It confirmed the domination of southern English as the language of literature throughout England.

6 Servant in love, and lord in marriage. [*Canterbury Tales*, 'Franklin's Tale']

7 For pitee renneth sone in gentil herte. [*Canterbury Tales*, 'Knightes Tale']

8 So was hir joly whistle wel y-wet. [*Canterbury Tales*, 'Reve's Tale']

9 Whan that the month of May. / Is comen, and that I here the foules singe, / And that the floures ginnen for to springe, / Farwel my book and my devocion. [*Legend of Good Women*, Prologue]

10 The lyf so short, the craft so long to lerne, / Th' assay so hard, so sharp the conquering. [*Parlement of Fowls* translation of an aphorism of Hippocrates]

11 For ever it was, and ever it shall befal, / That Love is he that alle thing may bind. [*Troilus and Criseyde* bk 1]

12 Go, litel book, go litel myn tragedie. [*Troilus and Criseyde* bk 5]

CHEKHOV Anton 1860–1904
Russian dramatist and writer.

1 *Medvedenko*: Why do you wear black all the time? *Masha*: I'm in mourning for my life, I'm unhappy. [*The Seagull*]

2 A woman can become a man's friend only in the following stages – first an acquaintance, next a mistress, and only then a friend. [*Uncle Vanya* II]

CHER 1946–
US singer and actress.

The trouble with some women is they get all excited about nothing – and then marry him. [Quoted in M Brown and A O'Connor *Hammer and Tongues*]

CHESTERFIELD Philip, Lord 1694–1773
English politician and writer.

1 The knowledge of the world is only to be acquired in the world, and not in a closet. [*Letters to his Son* 4 Oct 1746]

2 I recommend you to take care of the minutes; for hours will take care of themselves. [*Letters to his Son* 6 Nov 1747]

3 Advice is seldom welcome; and those who want it the most always like it the least. [*Letters to his Son* 29 Jan 1748]

4 A man of sense only trifles with them [women], plays with them, humours and flatters them, as he does with a sprightly and forward child; but he neither consults them

about, nor trusts them with, serious matters. [*Letters to his Son* 5 Sept 1748]

5 To have frequent recourse to narrative betrays great want of imagination. [*Letters to his Son* 19 Oct 1748]

6 No man tastes pleasures truly, who does not earn them by previous business; and few people do business well, who do nothing else. [*Letters to his Son* 7 Aug 1749]

7 Every woman is infallibly to be gained by every sort of flattery, and every man by one sort or other. [*Letters to his Son* 16 Mar 1752]

8 In matters of religion and matrimony I never give any advice; because I will not have anybody's torments in this world or the next laid to my charge. [*Letters to his Son* 12 Oct 1765]

9 Religion is by no means a proper subject of conversation in a mixed company. [*Letter to his Godson* no. 112]

10 Tyrawley and I have been dead these two years; but we don't choose to have it known. [Quoted in Boswell's *Life of Johnson* 3 Apr 1773]

CHESTERTON G K 1874–1936
English novelist, essayist, and poet.

1 Talk about the pews and steeples / And the cash that goes therewith! / But the souls of Christian people ... / Chuck it, Smith! ['Antichrist, or the Reunion of Christendom']

2 I tell you naught for your comfort, / Yea, naught for your desire, / Save that the sky grows darker yet / And the sea rises higher. [*Ballad of the White Horse*]

3 A stiff apology is a second insult ... The injured party does not want to be compensated because he has been wronged; he wants to be healed because he has been hurt. [*Common Man*, 'The Real Dr. Johnson']

4 There is a road from the eye to the heart that does not go through the intellect. [*Defendant*]

English journalist, novelist, and broadcaster G K Chesterton.

5 The devil's walking parody / Of all four-footed things. [*The Donkey*]

6 One bears great things from the valley, only small things from the peak. [*Hammer of God*]

7 Don John of Austria is going to the war. [*Lepanto*]

8 And they think we're burning witches when we're only burning weeds. ['Me Heart']

9 For I come from Castlepatrick, and me heart is on me sleeve, / But a lady stole it from me on St. Gallowglass's Eve. ['Me Heart']

10 Every advance in science leaves morality in its ancient balance; and it depends still on the inscrutable soul of man whether any discovery is mainly a benefit or mainly a calamity. [Quoted in *Observer* 2 April 1922]

11 From all the easy speeches / That comfort cruel men. [*O God of Earth and Altar*]

12 The cosmos is about the smallest hole that a man can hide his head in. [*Orthodoxy* ch 1]

13 A man's friend likes him but leaves him as he is: his wife loves him and is always trying to turn him into somebody else. [*Orthodoxy* ch 5]

14 'What of vile dust?' the preacher said. ['Praise of Dust']

15 Before the Roman came to Rye or out to Severn strode, / The rolling English drunkard made the rolling English road. [*Rolling English Road*]

16 That night we went to Birmingham by way of Beachy Head. [*Rolling English Road*]

17 And a few men talked of freedom, while England talked of ale. [*Secret People*]

18 Smile at us, pay us, pass us; but do not quite forget. / For we are the people of England, that never have spoken yet. [*Secret People*]

19 And Noah he often said to his wife when he sat down to dine, / 'I don't care where the water goes if it doesn't get into the wine.' [*Wine and Water*]

CHEVALIER Albert 1861–1972
English music-hall performer.

There ain't a lady livin' in the land / As I'd swap for my dear old Dutch! ['My Old Dutch']

CHEVALIER Maurice 1888–1972
French actor and singer

Many a man has fallen in love with a girl in a light so dim he would not have chosen a suit by it. [Attributed remark 1955]

CHIANG KAI-SHEK 1887–1975
Chinese nationalist politician, head of state 1928–49.

We shall not talk lightly about sacrifice until we are driven to the last extremity which makes sacrifice inevitable. [Speech to Fifth Congress of the Guomindang]

CHINESE APHORISM

Man is the head of the family,
woman the neck that turns the head.

CHINESE PROVERB

Do not use a hatchet to remove a fly
from your friend's forehead.

CHOMSKY Noam 1928–
US linguist and political analyst.

1 If we don't believe in freedom of
expression for people we despise,
we don't believe in it at all. [BBC TV
'Late Show' 25 Nov 1992]

2 Colourless green ideas sleep furiously. [Example of a meaningless sentence, in *Syntactic Structures*]

CHRISTIE Agatha 1891–1975
English writer.

An archaeologist is the best husband
any woman can have: the older she
gets, the more interested he is in her.
[Attributed remark 1954]

CHURCHILL Charles 1731–1764
English satirical poet.

1 Just to the windward of the law.
[*The Ghost* bk 3]

2 A joke's a very serious thing. [*The
Ghost* bk 4]

3 Keep up appearances; there lies
the test; / The world will give thee
credit for the rest. [*Night*]

4 A heart to pity, and a hand to
bless. ['Prophecy of Famine']

5 Fashion! – a word which knaves
and fools may use, / Their knavery
and folly to excuse. ['Rosciad']

6 Genius is of no country.
['Rosciad']

CHURCHILL Randolph 1849–1894
British Conservative politician.

1 The duty of an Opposition is to
oppose. [Quoted in W S Churchill *Lord
Randolph Churchill* vol 1, ch 5]

2 Ulster will fight; Ulster will be
right. [Letter 1886]

CHURCHILL Winston 1874–1965
British Conservative prime minister.

1 In defeat unbeatable: in victory
unbearable. [Of Viscount Montgomery,
quoted in Marsh *Ambrosia and Small Beer*]

2 A modest man who has a good
deal to be modest about. [Of Clement
Attlee, *Chicago Sunday Tribune Magazine of
Books* 27 June 1954]

3 Don't talk to me about naval tradition. It's nothing but rum, sodomy
and the lash. [Quoted in Peter Gretton
Former Naval Person]

4 It cannot be classified as slavery
in the extreme acceptance of the
word without some risk of termino-
logical inexactitude. [*Hansard* 22 Feb
1906]

5 We shall go on to the end. We
shall fight in France, we shall fight
on the seas and oceans, we shall
fight with growing confidence and
growing strength in the air, we shall
defend our island, whatever the cost
may be. We shall fight on the
beaches, we shall fight on the landing grounds, we shall fight in the
fields and in the streets, we shall
fight in the hills; we shall never surrender. [*Hansard* 4 June 1940]

6 This was their finest hour.
[*Hansard* 18 June 1940]

7 Never in the field of human conflict was so much owed by so many
to so few. [Of the British airmen at the
Battle of Britain, *Hansard* 20 Aug 1940]

8 In war: resolution. In defeat:
defiance. In victory: magnanimity.
In peace: goodwill. [*Second World War*,
'Moral of the Work']

9 It may almost be said, 'Before
Alamein we never had a victory.
After Alamein we never had a
defeat.' [*Second World War* vol 4, ch 33]

10 The British people have taken
for themselves this motto –

'Business carried on as usual during alterations on the map of Europe'. [Speech at the Guildhall 9 Nov 1914]

11 The belief that security can be obtained by throwing a small state to the wolves is a fatal delusion. [On Czechoslovakia 21 Sept 1938]

12 I cannot forecast to you the action of Russia. It is a riddle wrapped in a mystery inside an enigma. [Radio broadcast 1 Oct 1939]

13 We are waiting for the long-promised invasion. So are the fishes. [Radio broadcast to the French people 21 Oct 1940]

14 Give us the tools and we will finish the job. [Speech on radio 9 Feb 1942]

15 The people of London with one voice would say to Hitler: ... You do your worst – and we will do our best.' [Speech at County Hall, London 14 July 1942]

16 I have not become the King's First Minister in order to preside over the liquidation of the British Empire. [Speech in London 10 Nov 1942]

17 Some chicken! Some neck! [Reply to the French assertion in World War II that 'In three weeks England will have her neck wrung like a chicken', speech to Canadian Parliament 30 Dec 1942]

18 There is no finer investment for any community than putting milk into babies. Healthy citizens are the greatest asset any country can have. [Speech on radio 21 Mar 1943]

19 From Stettin in the Baltic to Trieste in the Adriatic, an iron curtain has descended across the Continent. [Speech at Westminster College, Fulton, Missouri 5 Mar 1946]

20 To jaw-jaw is always better than to war-war. [Speech at White House 26 June 1954]

21 It was the nation and the race dwelling all around the globe that had the lion's heart. I had the luck to be called upon to give the roar. [On World War II; 80th birthday address to Parliament 30 Nov 1954]

22 I am prepared to meet my Maker. Whether my Maker is prepared for the great ordeal of meeting me is another matter. [News conference, Washington 1954]

CIBBER Colley 1671–1757
English dramatist.

Oh, how many torments lie in the small circle of a wedding Ring! [*Double Gallant* I. ii]

CICERO 106–43 BC
Roman orator, writer, and politician.

1 The good of the people is the chief law. [*De Legibus*]

2 The highest good. [*De Officiis* I. 2]

3 Let wars yield to peace. [*De Officiis* I. 22]

4 What times, what customs! [*In Catilinam* I. 1]

5 Let them hate so long as they fear. [*Philippic* I. 14 (quoting the tragedian Accius)]

6 To whose profit? [*Pro Milone* XII. 32]

CIMINO Michael 1943–
US film director.

A film lives, becomes alive, because of its shadows, its spaces. [*Variety* July 1980]

CIORAN E M 1911–
Romanian-born French philosopher.

1 ... Since freedom ... is no more than a *sensation*, what difference is there between being free and believing ourselves free? [*New Gods* 3]

2 There is no means of *proving* it is preferable to be than not to be. [*New Gods*, 'Strangled Thoughts' 1]

3 As soon as they consent to live, the unbeliever and the man of faith are fundamentally the same, since both have made the only decision that defines a *being* [*Temptation to Exist*, title essay]

4 Consciousness is much more than the thorn, it is the *dagger* in the flesh. [*Trouble with Being Born* ch 3]

5 Every thought derives from a thwarted sensation. [*Trouble with Being Born* ch 5]

CLARE John 1793–1864
English poet.

He could not die when trees were green, / For he loved the time too well. ['Dying Child']

CLARK Kenneth 1903–1983
English art historian and writer.

Medieval marriages were entirely a matter of property, and, as everyone knows, marriage without love means love without marriage. [*Civilization* ch 3]

CLARKE Arthur C 1917–
English science fiction writer.

Any sufficiently advanced technology is indistinguishable from magic. [*Lost Worlds of 2001*]

CLAY Henry 1777–1852
US politician.

I had rather be right than be President. [Remark to Senator Preston of South Carolina 1839]

CLEESE John 1939–
English actor and comedian.

This parrot is no more. It's ceased to be. It has expired. The parrot has gone to meet its maker. This is a late parrot ... If you had't nailed it to the perch, it would be pushin' up the daisies. ['Monty Python's Flying Circus' 1969]

CLEMENCEAU Georges 1841–1929
French politician and journalist.

It is easier to make war than to make peace. [Speech at Verdun 20 July 1919]

Bill Clinton who defeated George Bush in the US presidential election of November 1992 to become the first Democratic president for twelve years. He had been governor of Arkansas since 1983.

CLEMENT OF ALEXANDRIA c. 150–c. 215 AD
Greek theologian and philosopher.

For lust is not easily restrained, when it has no fear. [*Exhortation to the Greeks* ch iv. 43P]

CLINTON Bill 1946–
US Democratic president.

There is nothing wrong with America that cannot be cured by what is right with America. [Inaugural speech as US president 1993]

CLIVE Robert, Lord 1725–1774
British soldier and administrator.

1 By God, Mr. Chairman, at this moment I stand astonished at my own moderation! [Reply during Parliamentary cross-examination 1773]

2 I feel that I am reserved for some end or other. [Comment after failed suicide attempt]

CLOUGH Arthur 1819–1861
English poet.

> **1** Grace is given of God, but knowledge is bought in the market. [*Bothie of Tober-na-Vuolich*]

> **2** Do not adultery commit; / Advantage rarely comes of it. ['Latest Decalogue']

> **3** Thou shalt not kill; but need'st not strive / Officiously to keep alive. ['Latest Decalogue']

> **4** Say not, the struggle naught availeth, / The labour and the wounds are vain. ['Say Not, the Struggle Naught Availeth']

COBBETT William 1763–1835
English Radical politician and journalist.

> **1** From a very early age, I had imbibed the opinion, that it was every man's duty to do all that lay in his power to leave his country as good as he had found it. [*Political Register* 22 Dec 1832]

> **2** Give me, Lord, neither poverty nor riches. [*Political Register* 22 Dec 1832]

COBORN Charles 1852–1945
English actor.

> Two lovely black eyes, / Oh! what a surprise! / Only for telling a man he was wrong, / Two lovely black eyes! ['Two Lovely Black Eyes']

COCHRAN C B 1872–1951
British impresario.

> I am interested in everything so long as it is well done. I would rather see a good juggler than a bad Hamlet. [*Secrets of a Showman*]

COCTEAU Jean 1889–1963
French writer, artist, and filmmaker.

> **1** A film is a petrified fountain of thought. [*Esquire* Feb 1961]

> **2** A car can massage organs which no masseur can reach. It is the one remedy for the disorders of the great sympathetic nervous system. [*Opium*]

> **3** Life is a horizontal fall. [*Opium*]

> **4** If it has to choose who is to be crucified, the crowd will always save Barabbas. [*Recall to Order*, 'The Cock and the Harlequin']

> **5** What the public criticizes in you, cultivate. It is you. [*Recall to Order*, 'The Cock and the Harlequin']

> **6** The worst tragedy for a poet is to be admired through being misunderstood. [*Recall to Order*, 'The Cock and the Harlequin']

COHEN Leonard 1934–
Canadian singer-songwriter, poet, and novelist.

> **1** What is most original in a man's nature is often that which is most desperate. Thus new systems are forced upon the world by men who simply cannot bear the pain of living with what is. [*Beautiful Losers* 61]

> **2** Seven to eleven is a huge chunk of life, full of dulling and forgetting ... As our eyes grow accustomed to sight they arm themselves against wonder. [*Favourite Game* bk 1, ch 17]

> **3** A woman watches her body uneasily, as though it were an unreliable ally in the battle for love. [*Favourite Game* bk 3, ch 8]

COKE Edward 1552–1634
English Lord Chief Justice.

> For a man's house is his castle. [*Institutes, Commentary upon Littleton* Third Institute, ch 73]

COLERIDGE Hartley 1796–1849
English poet and essayist.

> **1** But what is Freedom? Rightly understood, / A universal licence to be good. ['Liberty']

> **2** She is not fair to outward view / As many maidens be; / Her loveliness I never knew / Until she smiled on me. ['She is not Fair']

COLERIDGE Samuel Taylor 1772–1834
English Romantic poet.

1 'God save thee, ancient Mariner! / From the fiends that plague thee thus! – / Why look'st thou so?' – With my cross-bow / I shot the Albatross. [*Ancient Mariner* pt 1]

2 It is an ancient Mariner, / And he stoppeth one of three. / 'By thy long grey beard and glittering eye, / Now wherefore stopp'st thou me?' [*Ancient Mariner* pt 1]

3 As idle as a painted ship / Upon a painted ocean. [*Ancient Mariner* pt 2]

4 Water, water, everywhere, / Nor any drop to drink. [*Ancient Mariner* pt 2]

5 Alone, alone, all, all alone, / Alone on a wide wide sea! / And never a saint took pity on / My soul in agony. [*Ancient Mariner* pt 4]

6 A spring of love gushed from my heart, / And I blessed them unaware. [*Ancient Mariner* pt 4]

7 Oh Sleep! it is a gentle thing, / Beloved from pole to pole! [*Ancient Mariner* pt 5]

8 He prayeth well, who loveth well / Both man and bird and beast. / He prayeth best, who loveth best / All things both great and small. [*Ancient Mariner* pt 7]

9 A sadder and a wiser man, / He rose the morrow morn. [*Ancient Mariner* pt 7]

10 That willing suspension of disbelief for the moment, which constitutes poetic faith. [*Biographia Literaria* ch 14]

11 No man was ever yet a great poet, without being at the same time a profound philosopher. [*Biographia Literaria* ch 15]

12 And the Devil did grin, for his darling sin / Is pride that apes humility. ['Devil's Thoughts']

13 Swans sing before they die – / 'twere no bad thing / Did certain persons die before they sing. [Epigram on a Volunteer Singer]

14 The frost performs its secret ministry, / Unhelped by any wind. ['Frost at Midnight']

15 Five miles meandering with a mazy motion / Through wood and dale the sacred river ran, / Then reached the caverns measureless to man, / And sank in tumult to a lifeless ocean: / It was a miracle of rare device, / A sunny pleasure-dome with caves of ice! [*Kubla Khan*]

16 In Xanadu did Kubla Khan / A stately pleasure-dome decree. ['Kubla Khan']

17 All thoughts, all passions, all delights, / Whatever stirs this mortal frame, / All are but ministers of Love, / And feed his sacred flame. ['Love']

18 In many ways doth the full heart reveal / The presence of the love it would conceal. [*Poems Written in Later Life*, motto]

19 The most happy marriage I can picture or imagine to myself would be the union of a deaf man to a blind woman. [*Recollections*, 'Allsop']

20 The man's desire is for the woman; but the woman's desire is rarely other than for the desire of the man. [*Table Talk*]

21 Marriage, has, as you say, no *natural* relation to love. Marriage belongs to society; it is a social contract. [*Table Talk*]

22 I wish our clever young poets would remember my homely definitions of prose and poetry; that is, prose = words in their best order; – poetry = the best words in the best order. [*Table Talk* 12 July 1827]

COLETTE 1873–1954
French writer.

1 Don't ever wear artistic jewellery, it wrecks a woman's reputation. [*Gigi*]

2 If we want to be sincere, we must admit that there is a well-nourished love and an ill-nourished love. And the rest is literature. [*Last of Chéri*]

3 The day after that wedding night I found that a distance of a thousand miles, abyss and discovery and irremediable metamorphosis, separated me from the day before. ['Wedding Night']

COLLINGWOOD Robin George 1889–1943
English philosopher.

Perfect freedom is reserved for the man who lives by his own work, and in that work does what he wants to do. [*Speculum Mentis*]

COLLINS John Churton 1848–1908
English scholar and critic.

To ask advice is in nine cases out of ten to tout for flattery. [L C Collins *Life of John Churton Collins*]

COLLINS Mortimer 1827–1876
English poet and novelist.

A man is as old as he's feeling, / A woman as old as she looks. [*Unknown Quantity*]

COLLINS Wilkie 1824–1889
English novelist.

I am not against hasty marriages, where a mutual flame is fanned by an adequate income. [*No Name* bk 4, ch 8]

COLLINS William 1721–1759
English poet.

1 How sleep the brave, who sink to rest, / By all their country's wishes blest! ['Ode Written in the Year 1746']

2 Too nicely Jonson knew the critic's part, / Nature in him was almost lost in Art. [*Verses to Sir Thomas Hanmer*]

COLMAN George 1762–1836
English dramatist.

1 What a recreation it is to be in love! It sets the heart aching so delicately, there's no taking a wink of sleep for the pleasure of the pain. [*Mountaineers* I. i]

2 His heart runs away with his head. [*Who Wants a Guinea?* I. i]

COLMAN AND GARRICK George Colman *the Elder* 1732–1794 and David Garrick 1717–1779
English dramatists.

Love and a cottage! Eh, Fanny! Ah, give me indifference and a coach and six. [*Clandestine Marriage* I. ii]

COLTON Charles Caleb 1780–1832
English epigrammatic writer.

1 Imitation is the sincerest of flattery. [*Lacon* vol 1, 217]

2 If you would be known, and not know, vegetate in a village; if you would know, and not be known, live in a city. [*Lacon* vol 1, 334]

COMMON PRAYER, BOOK OF service book of the Church of England.

1 Grant that the old Adam in this Child may be so buried, that the new man may be raised up in him. [Baptism Invocation of Blessing on the Child]

2 In the midst of life we are in death. [Burial of the Dead. First Anthem]

3 To keep my hands from picking and stealing, and my tongue from evil speaking, lying and slandering. [Catechism]

4 The author of peace and lover of concord, in knowledge of whom standeth our eternal life, whose service is perfect freedom. [Collect for Peace]

5 Hear them, read, mark, learn, and inwardly digest them. [Collect for 2nd Sunday in Advent]

6 Lighten our darkness, we beseech thee, O Lord. [Evening Prayer, Third Collect]

7 That peace which the world cannot give. [Evening Prayer, Second Collect]

8 We have left undone those things which we ought to have done; / And we have done those things which we ought not to have done; / And there is no health in us. [General Confession]

9 All the changes and chances of this mortal life. [Holy Communion, Collect after the Offertory]

10 All sorts and conditions of men. [Prayer for All Conditions of Men]

11 A happy issue out of all their afflictions. [Prayer for All Conditions of Men]

12 Out of the mouth of very babes and sucklings hast thou ordained strength. [Psalm 8]

13 What is man, that thou art mindful of him. [Psalm 8]

14 The fool hath said in his heart: there is no God. [Psalm 14]

15 The lot is fallen unto me in a fair ground: yea, I have a goodly heritage. [Psalm 16]

16 Keep me as the apple of an eye: hide me under the shadow of thy wings. [Psalm 17]

17 The heavens declare the glory of God: and the firmament showeth his handiwork. [Psalm 19]

18 The Lord is my shepherd: therefore can I lack nothing. / He shall feed me in a green pasture: and lead me forth beside the waters of comfort. [Psalm 23]

19 Heaviness may endure for a night, but joy cometh in the morning. [Psalm 30]

20 I have been young, and now am old: and yet never saw I the righteous forsaken, nor his seed begging their bread. [Psalm 37]

21 For man walketh in a vain shadow, and disquieteth himself in vain: he heapeth up riches, and cannot tell who shall gather them. [Psalm 39]

22 God is our hope and strength: a very present help in trouble. [Psalm 46]

23 They are as venomous as the poison of a serpent: even like the deaf adder that stoppeth her ears. / Which refuseth to hear the voice of the charmer: charm he never so wisely. [Psalm 58]

24 They grin like a dog, and run about through the city. [Psalm 59 (Cranmer's Prayer Book)]

25 I had rather be a doorkeeper in the house of my God: than to dwell in the tents of ungodliness. [Psalm 84]

26 Mercy and truth are met together: righteousness and peace have kissed each other. [Psalm 85]

27 The days of our age are threescore years and ten. [Psalm 90]

28 Thou shalt not be afraid for any terror by night: nor for the arrow that flieth by day. For the pestilence that walketh in darkness: nor for the sickness that destroyeth in the noonday. [Psalm 91]

29 Wine that maketh glad the heart of man: and oil to make him a cheerful countenance, and bread to strengthen man's heart. [Psalm 104]

30 They that go down to the sea in ships: and occupy their business in great waters; / These men see the works of the Lord: and his wonders in the deep. [Psalm 107]

31 The fear of the Lord is the beginning of wisdom. [Psalm 111]

32 The same stone which the builders refused: is become the head-stone in the corner. [Psalm 118]

33 I will lift up mine eyes unto the hills: from whence cometh my help. [Psalm 121]

34 The Lord shall preserve thy going out, and thy coming in: from this time forth for evermore. [Psalm 121]

35 O pray for the peace of Jerusalem: they shall prosper that love thee. [Psalm 122]

36 Except the Lord build the house: their labour is but lost that build it. / Except the Lord keep the city: the watchman waketh but in vain. [Psalm 127]

37 Like as the arrows in the hand of the giant: even so are the young children. / Happy is the man that hath his quiver full of them. [Psalm 127]

38 By the waters of Babylon we sat down and wept: when we remembered thee, O Sion. [Psalm 137]

39 How shall we sing the Lord's song: in a strange land? / If I forget thee, O Jerusalem: let my right hand forget her cunning. [Psalm 137]

40 O put not your trust in princes, nor in any child of man: for there is no help in them. [Psalm 146]

41 If any of you know cause, or just impediment, why these two persons should not be joined in holy Matrimony, ye are to declare it. [Solemnization of Matrimony, Banns]

42 To have and to hold from this day forward, for better for worse, for richer for poorer, in sickness and in health, to love and to cherish, till death us do part. [Solemnization of Matrimony]

COMPTON-BURNETT Ivy 1892–1969
English novelist.

As regards plots I find real life no help at all. Real life seems to have no plots. [R Lehmann *et al. Orion I*]

COMTE Auguste 1798–1857
French philosopher.

Men are not allowed to think freely about chemistry and biology, why should they be allowed to think freely about political philosophy? [*Positive Philosophy*]

CONDILLAC Étienne Bonnot de
1715–1780
French philosopher.

We cannot recollect the ignorance in which we were born. [*Traités des sensations*]

CONGREVE William 1670–1729
English dramatist and poet.

1 Though marriage makes man and wife one flesh, it leaves 'em still two fools. [*Double Dealer* II. iii]

2 If I marry, Sir Sampson, I'm for a good estate with any man, and for any man with a good estate. [*Double Dealer* III. v]

3 She lays it on with a trowel. [*Double Dealer* III. x]

4 Oh fie Miss, you must not kiss and tell. [*Love for Love*]

5 Musick has charms to sooth a savage breast. [*Mourning Bride* I. i]

6 Heav'n has no rage, like love to hatred turn'd, / Nor Hell a fury, like a woman scorn'd. [*Mourning Bride* I. viii]

7 Thus grief still treads upon the heels of pleasure; / Marry'd in haste, we may repent at leisure. [*Old Bachelor* V. viii]

8 Courtship to marriage, is a very witty prologue to a very dull Play. [*Old Bachelor* V. x]

9 Say what you will, 'tis better to be left than never to have been loved. [*Way of the World* II. i]

10 Lord, what is a lover, that it can give? Why, one makes lovers as fast as one pleases, and they live as long as one pleases, and they die as soon as one pleases: and then if one pleases one makes more. [*Way of the World* II. v]

11 I nauseate walking; 'tis a country diversion, I loathe the country. [*Way of the World* IV. iv]

12 Let us never visit together, nor go to a play together, but let us be very strange and wellbred: let us be as strange as if we had been married a great while; and as wellbred as if we were not married at all. [*Way of the World* IV. v]

13 These articles subscribed, if I continue to endure you a little longer, I may by degrees dwindle into a wife. [*Way of the World* IV. v]

14 Wife, spouse, my dear, joy, jewel, love, sweet-heart and the rest of that nauseous cant, in which men and their wives are so fulsomely familiar. [*Way of the World* IV. v]

CONNOLLY Billy 1942–
Scottish comedian.

Marriage is a wonderful invention; but, then again, so is a bicycle repair kit. [Quoted in D Campbell *Billy Connolly*]

CONNOLLY Cyril 1903–1974
English critic and author.

1 As repressed sadists are supposed to become policemen or butchers so those with irrational fear of life become publishers. [*Enemies of Promise* ch 3]

2 Whom the gods wish to destroy they first call promising. [*Enemies of Promise* ch 13]

3 There is no more sombre enemy of good art than the pram in the hall. [*Enemies of Promise* ch 14]

4 All charming people have something to conceal, usually their total dependence on the appreciation of others. [*Enemies of Promise* ch 16]

5 If, as Dr Johnson said, a man who is not married is only half a man, so a man who is very much married is only half a writer. [*Enemies of Promise*]

6 It is closing time in the gardens of the West and from now on an artist will be judged only by the resonance of his solitude or the quality of his despair. [*Horizon* Dec 1949]

7 Better to write for yourself and have no public, than to write for the public and have no self. [*New Statesman* 25 Feb 1933]

8 As bees their sting, so the promiscuous leave behind them in each encounter something of themselves by which they are made to suffer. [*Unquiet Grave*]

9 In the sex-war thoughtlessness is the weapon of the male, vindictiveness of the female. [*Unquiet Grave*]

10 Our memories are card indexes consulted and then returned in disorder by authorities whom we do not control. [*Unquiet Grave*]

11 There are two great moments in a woman's life: when first she finds herself to be deeply in love with her man, and when she leaves him ... Women are different from men, and to break with the past and mangle their mate in the process fulfills a dark need of theirs. [*Unquiet Grave*]

12 There is no fury like an ex-wife searching for a new lover. [*Unquiet Grave*]

13 We are all serving a life-sentence in the dungeon of self. [*Unquiet Grave*]

CONNOLLY James 1870–1916
Irish Labour leader.

The worker is the slave of capitalist society, the female worker is the slave of that slave. [*Re-conquest of Ireland*]

CONRAD Joseph 1857–1924
Polish-born English novelist.

1 The conquest of the earth, which mostly means the taking it away from those who have a different complexion or slightly flatter noses than ourselves, is not a pretty thing when you look into it. [*Heart of Darkness* ch 1]

2 He [Kurtz] cried in a whisper at some image, at some vision, – he cried out twice, a cry that was no more than a breath – 'The horror! The horror!'. [*Heart of Darkness* ch. 3]

3 A man that is born falls into a dream, like a man that falls into the sea. [*Lord Jim* ch 20]

4 Any work that aspires, however humbly, to the condition of art should carry its justification in every line. [*Nigger of the Narcissus*, author's note]

5 The terrorist and the policeman both come from the same basket. [*Secret Agent*]

6 All ambitions are lawful except those which climb upwards on the miseries or credulities of mankind. [*Some Reminiscences*]

7 A belief in a supernatural source of evil is not necessary; men alone are quite capable of every wickedness. [*Under Western Eyes*]

8 They talk of a man betraying his country, his friends, his sweetheart. There must be a moral bond first. All a man can betray is his conscience. [*Under Western Eyes* pt 1, ch 2]

CONRAN Shirley 1932–
English writer.

Life is too short to stuff a mushroom. [*Superwoman*]

COOK James, Captain 1728–1779
British naval explorer.

Was this country settled by an Industrus people they would very soon be suppl'd not only with the necessarys but many of the luxuries of life. [Of New Zealand, *Journal* March 1770]

COOLEY Charles Horton 1864–1929
US sociologist.

No matter what a man does, he is not fully sane or human unless there is a spirit of freedom in him, a soul unconfined by purpose and larger than the practicable world. [*Human Nature and the Social Order* ch 5]

COOLIDGE Calvin 1872–1933
US Republican president.

1 Civilization and profits go hand in hand. [Speech 27 Nov 1920]

2 The chief business of the American people is business. [Speech 17 Jan 1925]

The Republican Calvin Coolidge, 30th president of the United States of America 1923–1929. A taciturn man, he was widely admired and would in all probability have been re-elected if he had run for a second term.

3 There is no right to strike against the public safety by anybody, anywhere, any time. [Telegram to Samuel Gompers]

COOPER Jilly 1937–
English journalist and novelist.

The male is a domestic animal which, if treated with firmness and kindness, can be trained to do most things. [*Cosmopolitan* 1972]

COPE Wendy 1945–
English poet.

1 When you're a spinster of forty, / You're reduced to considering bids / From husbands inclined to be naughty / And divorcés obsessed with their kids. So perhaps you should wed in a hurry, / But that has its drawbacks as well. / The answer? There's no need to worry – / Whatever you do, life is hell. ['Advice to Young Women']

2 There are so many kinds of awful men – / One can't avoid them all. She often said / She'd never make the same mistake again: / She always made a new mistake instead. ['Rondeau Redoublé']

3 Bloody men are like bloody buses – / You wait for about a year / And as soon as one approaches your stop / Two or three others appear. [*Serious Concerns*, 'Bloody Men']

4 At Christmas little children sing and merry bells jingle, / The cold winter air makes our hands and faces tingle / And happy families go to church and cheerily they mingle / And the whole business is unbelievably dreadful, if you're single. [*Serious Concerns*, 'Christmas Poem']

5 The day he moved out was terrible – / That evening she went through hell. / His absence wasn't a problem / But the corkscrew had gone as well. [*Serious Concerns*, 'Loss']

6 I spell it out on this fridge door / you are so wonderful / i even like th way you snor [*Serious Concerns*, 'Magnetic']

7 I hardly ever tire of love or rhyme – / That's why I'm poor and have a rotten time. [*Serious Concerns*, 'Variation on Belloc's 'Fatigue'']

8 Love, love, love, / Love, love, love, / Love, love, love, / Dooby doo dooby doo, / All you need is love, / Dooby dooby do, / All you need is love, / Dooby dooby do, / All you need is love, love / Or, failing that, alcohol. [*Serious Concerns*, 'Variation on a Lennon and McCartney Song']

CORDAY Charlotte 1768–1793
French Girondin.

I have done my task, let others do theirs. [Remark on being interrogated for the murder of Marat July 1793]

CORNEILLE Pierre 1606–1684
French dramatist.

When there is no peril in the fight, there is no glory in the triumph. [*Le Cid*]

CORNFORD Frances 1886–1960
US poet.

O fat white woman whom nobody loves, / Why do you walk through the fields in gloves, ... / Missing so much and so much? [*To a Fat Lady Seen from a Train*]

CORNFORD Francis 1874–1943
English philosopher.

Every public action, which is not customary, either is wrong, or, if it is right, is a dangerous precedent. It follows that nothing should ever be done for the first time. [*Microcosmographia Academica*]

CORNFORTH John Warcup 1917–
Australian chemist.

For him [the scientist], truth is so seldom the sudden light that shows new order and beauty; more often, truth is the uncharted rock that sinks his ship in the dark. [Nobel prize address 1975]

CORNUEL Anne Bigot de 1614–1694
French wit and woman of letters.

> No man is a hero to his valet. [*Lettres de Mlle Aissé*]

CORTÉS Hernán 1485–1547
Spanish conqueror of Mexico.

> I and my companions suffer from a disease of the heart that can be cured only with gold. [Message sent to Montezuma 1519]

COUBERTIN Pierre de 1863–1937
French scholar and educator.

> The important thing in life is not the victory but the contest; the essential thing is not to have won but to have run the race. [Speech 24 July 1908]

COUÉ Émile 1857–1926
French chemist and psychotherapist.

> Every day, in every way, I am getting better and better. [Slogan that Coué advised his patients to repeat, quoted in *De la suggestion et de ses applications*]

COURBET Gustave 1819–1877
French artist.

> I deny that art can be taught. [Letter to prospective students 1861]

COWARD Noël 1899–1973
English dramatist and composer.

> **1** Don't let's be beastly to the Germans / When our Victory is ultimately won. ['Don't Let's Be Beastly to the Germans']
>
> **2** I believe that since my life began / The most I've had is just / A talent to amuse. ['If Love Were All']
>
> **3** Mad dogs and Englishmen / Go out in the midday sun. ['Mad Dogs and Englishmen']
>
> **4** Don't put your daughter on the stage, Mrs Worthington. ['Mrs Worthington']
>
> **5** Poor little rich girl / You're a bewitched girl, / Better beware! ['Poor Little Rich Girl']
>
> **6** Extraordinary how potent cheap music is. [*Private Lives*]
>
> **7** Someday I'll find you, / Moonlight behind you, / True to the dream I am dreaming. ['Someday I'll Find You']
>
> **8** The Stately Homes of England, / How beautiful they stand, / To prove the upper classes / Have still the upper hand. ['Stately Homes of England']
>
> **9** I never realized before that Albert married beneath him. [On seeing a certain actress playing the part of Queen Victoria, quoted in K Tynan *Tribute to Mr Coward*]

English playwright, director, and songwriter Noël Coward in 1966. Coward evolved his distinct brand of satirical humour between the wars in a series of successful revues and plays, before turning to film scripts and, after World War II, becoming a successful performer of his own songs.

10 Dear 338171 (May I call you 338?) [Letter to T E Lawrence 25 Aug 1930]

11 Mad About the Boy. [Song title]

COWLEY Abraham 1618–1667
English poet.

1 God the first garden made, and the first city Cain. ['The Garden']

2 Ye fields of Cambridge, our dear Cambridge, say, / Have ye not seen us walking every day? / Was there a tree about which did not know / The love betwixt us two? ['On the Death of Mr William Hervey']

3 Life is an incurable disease. ['To Dr. Scarborough']

COWPER William 1731–1800
English poet.

1 John Gilpin was a citizen / Of credit and renown, / A train-band captain eke was he / Of famous London town. [*John Gilpin*]

2 Tomorrow is our wedding day / And we will then repair / Unto the Bell at Edmonton / All in a chaise and pair. ['John Gilpin']

3 Toll for the brave – ['Loss of the Royal George']

4 Misses! the tale that I relate / This lesson seems to carry– / Choose not alone a proper mate, / But proper time to marry. ['Pairing Time Anticipated: Moral']

5 The poplars are fell'd, farewell to the shade / And the whispering sound of the cool colonnade. ['The Poplar-Field']

6 Talks of darkness at noon-day. ['Progress of Error']

7 God made the country, and man made the town. [*The Task* bk 1]

8 There is a public mischief in your mirth. [*The Task* bk 1]

9 England, with all thy faults, I love thee still – / My country! [*The Task* bk 2]

English poet William Cowper. Despite being plagued by melancholia, he wrote the long poem *The Task*, the amusing narrative *John Gilpin*, and such hymns as *God moves in a mysterious way*. His letters to friends are graceful and personal models of letter-writing.

10 Slaves cannot breathe in England; if their lungs / Receive our air, that moment they are free. [*The Task* bk 2]

11 Variety's the very spice of life, / That gives it all its flavour. [*The Task* bk 2]

12 Detested sport, / That owes its pleasures to another's pain. [*The Task* bk 3]

13 I was a stricken deer, that left the herd / Long since. [*The Task* bk 3]

14 The parson knows enough who knows a duke. ['Tirocinium']

15 I am monarch of all I survey. [*Verses Supposed to be Written by Alexander Selkirk*]

CRABBE George 1754–1832
English poet.

> The ring so worn, as you behold, /
> So thin, so pale, is yet of gold: / The
> passion such it was to prove; /
> Worn with life's cares, love yet was
> love. ['His Late Wife's Wedding-Ring']

CRAIK Mrs 1826–1887
English novelist and essayist.

> Oh, my son's my son till he gets him
> a wife, / But my daughter's my
> daughter all her life. ['Young and Old']

CRASHAW Richard c. 1612–1649
English religious poet.

> 1   Love, thou art absolute sole Lord
> / Of life and death. ['Hymn to the
> Name & Honour of the Admirable Saint
> Teresa']

> 2   I would be married but I'd have
> no wife, / I would be married to a
> single life. ['On Marriage']

CRISP Quentin 1908–
English writer and conversationalist.

> 1   It is explained that all relation-
> ships require a little give and take.
> This is untrue. Any partnership
> demands that we give and give and
> give and at the last, as we flop into
> our graves exhausted, we are told
> that we didn't give enough. [*How to
> Become a Virgin*]

> 2   Whenever we confront an unbri-
> dled desire we are surely in the
> presence of a tragedy-in-the-mak-
> ing. [*Manners from Heaven*]

> 3   There was no need to do any
> housework at all. After the first four
> years the dirt doesn't get any worse.
> [*Naked Civil Servant* ch 15]

> 4   An autobiography is an obituary
> in serial form with the last instalment
> missing. [*Naked Civil Servant* ch 29]

> 5   Though intelligence is powerless
> to modify character, it is a dab hand
> at finding euphemisms for its weak-
> nesses. [*Naked Civil Servant* ch 29]

> 6   As we all know from witnessing
> the consuming jealousy of husbands
> who are never faithful, people do
> not confine themselves to the emo-
> tions to which they are entitled.
> [*Naked Civil Servant*]

> 7   The *vie de bohème* is a way of life
> that has two formidable enemies—
> time and marriage. Even hooligans
> marry, though they know that mar-
> riage is but for a little while. It is
> alimony that is for ever ... [*Naked Civil
> Servant*]

CRITCHLEY Julian 1930–
British Conservative politician.

> The only safe pleasure for a parlia-
> mentarian is a bag of boiled sweets.
> [*Listener* 10 June 1982]

CROMWELL Oliver 1599–1658
English general and politician.

> 1   A few honest men are better than
> numbers. [Letter to W Spring Sept 1643]

> 2   I beseech you, in the bowels of
> Christ, think it possible you may be
> mistaken.   [Letter   to   the   General
> Assembly of the Church of Scotland 3
> Aug 1650]

> 3   Take away these baubles. [Remark
> referring to the symbols of parliamentary
> power when he dismissed parliament
> 1653]

CRONENBERG David 1943–
Canadian filmmaker.

> 1   Censors tend to do what only
> psychotics do: they confuse reality
> with illusion. [*Cronenberg on Cronenberg*
> ch 5]

> 2   I don't think that the flesh is nec-
> essarily treacherous, evil, bad. It is
> cantankerous, and it is independent.
> The idea of independence is the key
> ... Ultimately, it can be seen as the
> separation of a partner that could be
> very valuable as an equal rather
> than as something you dominate.
> [*Cronenberg on Cronenberg* ch 5]

CUMBERLAND Richard 1631–1718
English philosopher.

> It is better to wear out than to rust out. ['Duty of Contending for the Faith']

CUMMINGS e e 1894–1962
US poet.

> Listen: there's a hell of a good universe next door: let's go. [*Pity this busy monster, manunkind*]

CUMMINGS William Thomas 1903–1945
US chaplain.

> There are no atheists in the foxholes. [Quoted in C P Romulo *I Saw the Fall of the Philippines* ch 15]

DACRE Harry LIVED 19TH CENTURY
English song writer.

Daisy, Daisy, give me your answer, do! / I'm half crazy, all for the love of you! / It won't be a stylish marriage, / I can't afford a carriage, / But you'll look sweet upon the seat / Of a bicycle made for two. ['Daisy Bell']

DAHLBERG Edward 1900–1977
US writer and critic.

Everything ultimately fails, for we die, and that is either the penultimate failure or our most enigmatical achievement. [*Alms for Oblivion*, 'Our Vanishing Cooperative Colonies']

DALI Salvador 1904–1989
Spanish painter and designer.

1 There is only one difference between a madman and me. I am not mad. [*The American* July 1956]

2 Surrealism is destructive, but it destroys only what it considers to be shackles limiting our vision. [Declaration]

3 Mistakes are almost always of a sacred nature. Never try to correct them. [*Diary of a Genius* 30 June 1952]

4 Since man's highest mission on earth is to spiritualize everything, it is his excrement in particular that needs it most. [*Diary of a Genius* 2 Sept 1952]

5 The difference between false memories and true ones is the same as for jewels; it is always the false ones that look the most real, the most brilliant. [*Secret Life of Salvador Dali* ch 3]

DALY Mary 1928–
US writer and theologian.

We will look upon the earth and her sister planets as being *with* us, not *for* us. One does not rape a sister. [*Beyond God the Father* ch 6]

DANA Charles Anderson 1819–1897
US journalist.

When a dog bites a man that is not news, but when a man bites a dog that is news. ['What is News?' in *New York Sun* 1882]

DANIEL Samuel 1563–1619
English poet and dramatist.

1 Love is a sickness full of woes, / All remedies refusing; / A plant that with most cutting grows, / Most barren with best using. [*Hymen's Triumph* I]

2 This is the thing that I was born to do. ['Musophilus']

3 Princes in this case / Do hate the traitor, though they love the treason. [*Tragedy of Cleopatra* IV. i]

DANTE ALIGHIERI 1265–1321
Italian poet.

1 In the middle of the road of our life. [*Divine Comedy*, Inferno I]

2 All hope abandon, ye who enter here. [*Divine Comedy*, 'Inferno' III]

3 The love that moves the sun and the other stars. [*Divine Comedy* 'Paradiso' XXXIII]

DARLING Charles 1849–1936
English judge.

If a man stays away from his wife for seven years, the law presumes the separation to have killed him; yet according to our daily experience, it might well prolong his life. [*Scintillae Juris*]

DAVIES John 1569–1626
English poet.

1 This wondrous miracle did Love devise, / For dancing is love's proper exercise. ['Orchestra, or a Poem of Dancing']

2 Judge not the play before the play be done. [*Respice Finem*]

DAVIES W H 1871–1940
Welsh poet.

1 A rainbow and a cuckoo's song / May never come together again; / May never come / This side the tomb. ['Great Time']

2 What is this life if, full of care, / We have no time to stand and stare? ['Leisure']

DA VINCI Leonardo 1425–1519
Italian artist and scientist.

The function of muscle is to pull and not to push, except in the case of the genitals and the tongue. [*Notebooks of Leonardo da Vinci* vol 1, ch 3]

DAY-LEWIS Cecil 1904–1972
English poet.

Now the peak of summer's past, the sky is overcast / And the love we swore would last for an age seems deceit. ['Hornpipe']

DEBS Eugene V 1855–1926
US labour leader and socialist.

I said then, I say now, that while there is a lower class, I am in it; while there is a criminal element, I am of it; while there is a soul in prison, I am not free. [Speech at his trial 14 Sept 1918]

DECATUR Stephen 1779–1820
US naval hero.

Our country, right or wrong. [A S Mackenzie *Life of Decatur* ch 14]

DE CHAMFORT Sébastien-Roch Nicolas 1741–1794
French writer and wit.

Conviction is the conscience of intellect. [*Maxims and Considerations* vol 1, no. 151]

DE GAULLE Charles 1890–1970
President of France.

1 Patriotism is when love of your own people comes first; nationalism, when hate for people other than your own comes first. [*Life* 9 May 1969]

2 How can you govern a country which has 246 varieties of cheese? [Quoted in E Mignon *Les Mots du Général*]

3 Since a politician never believes what he says, he is quite surprised to be taken at his word. [Quoted in E Mignon *Les Mots du Général*]

4 No country without an atom bomb could properly consider itself independent. [*New York Times* 1968]

5 To govern is always to choose among disadvantages. [*New York Times* 14 Nov 1965]

6 France has lost a battle. But France has not lost the war! [*Proclamation* 18 June 1940]

7 A great country worthy of the name does not have any friends. [*Time* 28 May 1965]

8 If I am not France, what am I doing in your office? [Making claim to Winston Churchill to lead the Free French 1940]

DEIGHTON Len 1929–
English novelist.

Divorce is a system whereby two people make a mistake and one of them goes on paying for it. [Quoted in A Alvarez *Life after Marriage*]

DEKKER Thomas c. 1572–c. 1632
English dramatist and pamphleteer.

1 Art thou poor, yet hast thou golden slumbers: / Oh sweet content! / Honest labour bears a lovely face. [*Patient Grissill* I. i]

2 Golden slumbers kiss your eyes, / Smiles awake you when you rise. [*Patient Grissill* IV. ii]

DE KOONING Willem 1904–
Dutch-born US artist.

1 As soon as an artist fills a certain area on the canvas or circumscribes it, he becomes historical. He acts from or upon other artists. ['Desperate View', paper delivered New York 18 Feb 1949]

2 My interest in desperation lies only in that sometimes I find myself having become desperate. Very seldom do I start out that way. I can see of course that, in the abstract, thinking and all activity is rather desperate. ['Desperate View', paper delivered New York 18 Feb 1949]

DE LA MARE Walter 1873–1956
English poet.

1 Oh, no man knows / Through what wild centuries / Roves back the rose. ['All That's Past']

2 Look thy last on all things lovely, / Every hour. ['Fare Well']

3 'Is there anybody there?' said the traveller, / Knocking on the moonlit door. ['The Listeners']

4 It's a very odd thing – / As odd as can be – / That whatever Miss T eats / Turns into Miss T. ['Miss T']

DEMOSTHENES c. 384–322 BC
Greek orator.

A man is his own easiest dupe, for what he wishes to be true he generally believes to be true. [*Third Olynthiac* 19]

DEMPSEY Jack 1895–1983
US heavyweight boxer.

Honey, I just forgot to duck. [Remark to his wife after losing his World Heavyweight title 23 Sept 1926]

DENNIS John 1657–1734
English poet, dramatist, and critic.

1 A man who could make so vile a pun would not scruple to pick a pocket. [*Gentleman's Magazine*, 1781]

2 Damn them! They will not let my play run, but they steal my thunder! [Quoted in W S Walsh *Handy-book of Literary Curiosities*]

3 Oh! what a snug little Island, / A right little, tight little Island! ['Snug Little Island']

DEPARDIEU Gérard 1948–
French actor.

At 20 you have many desires that hide the truth, but beyond 40 there are only real and fragile truths – your abilities and your failings. [*Observer* March 1991]

DE SADE Marquis 1740–1814
French writer.

Your body is the church where Nature asks to be reverenced. [*L'Histoire de Juliette* pt 1]

DESBORDES-VALMORE Marceline 1786–1859
French actress and poet.

It is certainly true that housekeeping cares bring with them a thousand endearing compensations. They are a woman's peculiar joy, and women are apt to be light-hearted. [Letter to her children 1 Nov 1840]

DESCARTES René 1596–1650
French philosopher and mathematician.

1 Commonsense is the most widely distributed commodity in the world, for everyone thinks himself so well endowed with it. [*Le discours de la méthode*]

2 I think, therefore I am. [*Le discours de la méthode*]

3 It is not enough to have a good mind. The main thing is to use it well. [*Le discours de la méthode*]

DEVLIN (MCALISKEY) Bernadette 1947–
Northern Irish politician.

To gain that which is worth having, it may be necessary to lose everything else. [*Price of my Soul*, Preface]

DE VRIES Peter 1910–1993
US novelist and short story writer.

1 Marriage is to courtship as humming is to singing. [*Consenting Adults* ch 6]

2 We must love one another, yes, yes, that's all true enough, but nothing says we have to like each other. [*Glory of the Hummingbird* ch 1]

3 It is the final proof of God's omnipotence that he need not exist in order to save us. [*Mackerel Plaza* ch 1]

4 The value of marriage is not that adults produce children but that children produce adults. [*Tunnel of Love* ch 8]

DEWEY John 1859–1952
US philosopher.

For one man who thanks God that he is not as other men there are a few thousand to offer thanks that they are as other men, sufficiently as others to escape attention. [*Human Nature and Conflict*]

DÍAZ Porfirio 1830–1915
Mexican president.

Poor Mexico, so far from God, and so close to the United States! [Attributed remark]

DIBDIN Charles 1745–1814
English songwriter and dramatist.

1 Did you ever hear of Captain Wattle? / He was all for love, and a little for the bottle. ['Captain Wattle and Miss Roe']

2 In every mess I finds a friend, / In every port a wife. ['Jack in his Element']

DICKENS Charles 1812–1870
English novelist.

1 Something will come of this. I hope it mayn't be human gore. [Simon Tappertit in *Barnaby Rudge* ch 4]

Born into s family on the fringes of gentility, Charles Dickens was always acutely conscious of the social and economic abysses of Victorian society. His immence creative energy made him the most popular novelist of his age; his death at the age of 58 was largely due to overwork.

2 Polly put the kettle on, we'll all have tea. [Grip in *Barnaby Rudge* ch 17]

3 'There are strings', said Mr Tappertit, 'in the human heart that had better not be wibrated'. [*Barnaby Rudge* ch 22]

4 This is a London particular. ... A fog, miss. [*Bleak House* ch 3]

5 Discipline must be maintained. [*Bleak House* ch 27]

6 It is a melancholy truth that even great men have their poor relations. [*Bleak House* ch 28]

7 'God bless us every one!' said Tiny Tim, the last of all. [*Christmas Carol*]

8 'I am a lone lorn creetur,' were Mrs. Gummidge's words, / ... 'and everythink goes contrary with me.' [*David Copperfield* ch 3]

9 Barkis is willin'. [*David Copperfield* ch 5]

10 Annual income twenty pounds, annual expenditure nineteen nineteen six, result happiness. Annual income twenty pounds, annual expenditure twenty pounds ought and six, result misery. [Mr Micawber in *David Copperfield* ch 12]

11 I will never desert Mr. Micawber. [*David Copperfield* ch 12]

12 We are so very 'umble. [Uriah Heep in *David Copperfield* ch 12]

13 Accidents will occur in the best-regulated families. [Mr Micawber in *David Copperfield* ch 28]

14 It's only my child-wife. [Of Dora in *David Copperfield* ch 44]

15 There can be no disparity in marriage like unsuitability of mind and purpose. [*David Copperfield* ch 44]

16 I positively adore Miss Dombey; – I – I am perfectly sore with loving her. [*Dombey and Son* ch 30]

17 England, Home, and Beauty! [Captain Cuttle in *Dombey and Son* ch 48]

18 Now, what I want is, Facts ... Facts alone are wanted in life. [Mr Gradgrind in *Hard Times* bk 1, ch 1]

19 As to marriage on the part of a man, my dear. Society requires that he should retrieve his fortunes by marriage. Society requires that he should gain by marriage. Society requires that he should found a handsome establishment by marriage. Society does not see, otherwise, what he has to do with marriage. [*Little Dorrit* bk 1, ch 33]

20 Charity begins at home, and justice begins next door. [*Martin Chuzzlewit* ch 27]

21 All is gas and gaiters. [*Nicholas Nickleby*]

22 Oliver Twist has asked for more! [*Oliver Twist* ch 2]

23 Known by the *sobriquet* of 'The artful Dodger.' [*Oliver Twist* ch 8]

24 'If the law supposes that,' said Mr. Bumble ... 'the law is a ass – a idiot.' [*Oliver Twist* ch 51]

25 I wants to make your flesh creep. [*Pickwick Papers* ch 8]

26 Take example by your father, my boy, and be wery careful o' widders all you life, specially if they've kept a public house, Sammy. [*Pickwick Papers* ch 19]

27 Ven you're a married man, Samivel, you'll understand a good many things as you don't understand now; but vether it's worth while goin' through so much to learn so little, as the charity-boy said ven he got to the end of the alphabet, is a matter o' taste. [*Pickwick Papers* ch 27]

28 Anythin' for a quiet life, as the man said wen he took the sitivation at the lighthouse. [Sam Weller in *Pickwick Papers* ch 43]

29 It is a far, far better thing that I do, than I have ever done; it is a far, far better rest that I go to, than I have ever known. [*Tale of Two Cities*]

DICKINSON Emily 1830–1886
US poet.

1 Parting is all we know of heaven, / And all we need of hell. ['Parting']

2 That Love is all there is, / Is all we know of Love; / It is enough, the freight should be / Proportioned to the groove. [Poem no 1765]

3 Unto a broken heart / No other one may go / Without the high prerogative / Itself hath suffered too. ['Unto a Broken Heart']

DICKINSON John 1732–1808
US lawyer and statesman.

Our cause is just. Our union is perfect. [*Declaration on Taking Up Arms* 1775]

DIDEROT Denis 1713–1784
French writer and philosopher.

1 To men, love is an incident; to women a vocation. They live by and for their emotions. [*Celibate's Apology*]

2 It is said that desire is a product of the will, but the converse is in fact true: will is a product of desire. [*Elements of Physiology*, 'Will, Freedom']

3 There is only one passion, the passion for happiness. [*Elements of Physiology*, 'Will, Freedom']

4 It has been said that love robs those who have it of their wit, and gives it to those who have none. [*Paradoxe sur le comédien*]

DIETRICH Sepp 1892–1976
German SS officer.

All I had to do was cross the river, capture Brussels, and then go on to take the port of Antwerp. The snow was waist-deep and there wasn't room to deploy four tanks abreast, let alone six Panzer divisions. It didn't get light till eight and was dark again at four and my tanks can't fight at night. And all this at Christmas time! [Remark on the Battle of the Bulge]

DILLON Wentworth c. 1633–1685
English poet and translator.

1 But words once spoke can never be recall'd. [*Art of Poetry*]

2 Choose an author as you choose a friend. [*Essay on Translated Verse*]

DIMNET Ernest 1869–1954
French churchman and writer.

Architecture, of all the arts, is the one which acts the most slowly, but the most surely, on the soul. [*What We Live By* pt 2, ch 12]

DIOGENES c. 412–323 BC
Greek philosopher of the Cynic school.

1 Sell me to him. He needs a master. [Remark on being put up for sale at a slave auction, quoted in M I Finley *Aspects of Antiquity*]

2 Stand out of my sun a little. [Response to Alexander the Great when he asked him if he wanted anything, quoted in Plutarch *Life of Alexander*]

DIOR Christian 1905–1957
French couturier.

My dream is to save [women] from nature. [Quoted in *Collier's* 1955]

DIRAC Paul 1902–1984
British physicist.

A theory with mathematical beauty is more likely to be correct than an ugly one that fits some experimental data. God is a mathematician of a very high order, and He used very advanced mathematics in constructing the universe. [*Scientific American* May 1963]

DISRAELI Benjamin 1804–1881
British Conservative prime minister and novelist.

1 Read no history: nothing but biography, for that is life without theory. [*Contarini Fleming*]

2 His Christianity was muscular. [*Endymion*]

3 The magic of first love is our ignorance that it can ever end. [*Henrietta Temple* bk 4, ch 1]

4 Damn your principles! Stick to your party. [Quoted in Latham *Famous Sayings*]

5 When a man fell into his anecdotage it was a sign for him to retire from the world. [*Lothair* ch 28]

6 Every woman should marry – and no man. [*Lothair* ch 30]

7 You know who the critics are? The men who have failed in literature and art. [*Lothair* ch 35]

8 To do nothing and get something, formed a boy's ideal of a manly career. [*Sybil* bk 1, ch 5]

9 Little things affect little minds. [*Sybil* bk 3, ch 2]

10 'Frank and explicit' – that is the right line to take when you wish to conceal your own mind and to confuse the minds of others. [*Sybil* bk 6, ch 1]

11 A majority is always the best repartee. [*Tancred* ch 14]

12 Experience is the child of Thought, and Thought is the child of Action. We cannot learn men from books. [*Vivian Grey* bk 5, ch 1]

13 There is moderation even in excess. [*Vivian Grey* bk 6, ch 1]

14 The Continent will not suffer England to be the workshop of the world. [Speech in House of Commons 15 March 1838]

15 The right hon. Gentleman caught the Whigs bathing, and walked away with their clothes. [Of Sir Robert Peel, speech in House of Commons 28 Feb 1845]

16 Justice is truth in action. [Speech in House of Commons 11 Feb 1851]

17 Finality is not the language of politics. [Speech in House of Commons 28 Feb 1859]

18 Is man an ape or an angel? Now I am on the side of the angels. [Speech in Oxford 25 Nov 1864]

19 Increased means and increased leisure are the two civilizers of man. [Speech in Manchester 3 April 1872]

20 All those institutions and all those principles ... in due time will become great and 'burning' questions. [Speech in Manchester 20 March 1873]

DIX Dorothy 1861–1951
US journalist.

So many persons think divorce a panacea for every ill, who find out, when they try it, that the remedy is worse than the disease. [*Dorothy Dix, Her Book* ch 13]

DOCTOROW E L 1931–
US writer.

It's like driving a car at night. You never see further than your headlights, but you can make the whole trip that way. [On his writing technique, interviewed in ed. Plimpton *Writers at Work*, 8th Series]

DONNE John 1571–1631
English metaphysical poet.

1 Twice or thrice had I loved thee, / Before I knew thy face or name. / So in a voice, so in a shapeless flame, / Angels affect us oft, and worshipped be. ['Air and Angels']

2 Come live with me, and be my love, / And we will some new pleasures prove / Of golden sands, and crystal brooks, / With silken lines, and silver hooks. ['Bait']

3 For God's sake hold your tongue, and let me love. ['The Canonization']

4 Love built on beauty, soon as beauty, dies. [*Elegies*, 'The Anagram']

5 No Spring, nor Summer beauty hath such grace, / As I have seen in one Autumnal face. [*Elegies* no. 9, 'The Autumnal']

6 Licence my roving hands, and let them go, / Behind, before, above, between, below. / O my America, my new found land, / My kingdom, safeliest when with one man manned. [*Elegies*, 'Going to Bed']

7 Whoever loves, if he do not propose / The right true end of love, he's one that goes / To sea for nothing but to make him sick. [*Elegies*, 'Love's Progress']

8 O my America! my new-found-land. [*Elegies* no. 19, 'To his Mistress Going to Bed']

9 And now good morrow to our waking souls, / Which watch not one another out of fear. ['The Good-Morrow']

10 I wonder by my troth, what thou, and I / Did, till we lov'd? were we not wean'd till then? ['The Good-Morrow']

11 Death be not proud, though some have called thee / Mighty and dreadful, for, thou art not so. [*Holy Sonnets* no. 10, 'Death be not Proud']

12 Take me to you, imprison me, for I / Except you enthral me, never shall be free, / Nor ever chaste, except you ravish me. [*Holy Sonnets* no. 10, 'Death be not Proud']

13 Go, and catch a falling star, / Get with child a mandrake root, / Tell me, where all past years are, / Or who cleft the Devil's foot. ['Song, Go and Catch a Falling Star']

14 All other things, to their destruction draw, / Only our love hath no decay; / This, no tomorrow hath, nor yesterday, / Running it never runs from us away, / But truly keeps his first, last, everlasting day. [*Songs and Sonnets*, 'The Anniversary']

15 When I died last, and, dear, I die / As often as from thee I go, / Though it be but an hour ago, / And lovers' hours be full eternity. [*Songs and Sonnets*, 'Legacy']

16 Busy old fool, unruly Sun, / Why dost thou thus, / Through windows, and through curtains call on us? [*Songs and Sonnets*, 'The Sun Rising']

17 Love, all alike, no season knows, nor clime, / Nor hours, days, months, which are the rags of time. [*Songs and Sonnets*, 'The Sun Rising']

18 Sweetest love, I do not go, / For weariness of thee, / Nor in hope the world can show / A fitter Love for me. [*Songs and Sonnets* 'Sweetest love, I do not go']

19 I am two fools, I know, / For loving, and for saying so / In whining Poetry. [*Songs and Sonnets* 'The Triple Fool']

DORMAN-SMITH 1899–1977
British politician.

Let 'Dig for Victory' be the motto of every one with a garden and of every able-bodied man and woman capable of digging an allotment in their spare time. [Radio broadcast 3 Oct 1939]

DOUGLAS Alfred 1870–1945
English writer and poet.

I am the Love that dare not speak its name. ['Two Loves']

DOUGLAS Norman 1868–1952
English diplomat and travel writer.

1 To find a friend one must close one eye. To keep him – two. [*Almanac*]

2 You can tell the ideals of a nation by its advertisements. [*South Wind* ch 6]

DOUGLAS-HOME William 1912–1992
Scottish playwright.

Every morning I read the obits in *The Times*. If I'm not there, I carry on. [Quoted in *Observer* 16 Aug 1987]

DOWELL Coleman 1925–1985
US writer.

Being is a fiction invented by those who suffer from becoming. [*Mrs. October Was Here* pt 3]

DOWSON Ernest 1867–1900
English poet.

1 And I was desolate and sick of an old passion. ['Non Sum Qualis Eram']

2 I have been faithful to thee, Cynara! in my fashion. ['Non Sum Qualis Eram']

3 They are not long, the weeping and the laughter, / Love and desire and hate; / I think they have no portion in us after / We pass the gate. ['Vitae Summa Brevis']

DOYLE Arthur Conan 1859–1930
English writer.

1 It has long been an axiom of mine that the little things are infinitely the most important. [*Adventures of Sherlock Holmes*, 'A Case of Identity']

2 Circumstantial evidence is occasionally very convincing, as when you find a trout in the milk, to quote Thoreau's example. [*Adventures of Sherlock Holmes*, 'The Noble Bachelor']

3 The giant rat of Sumatra, a story for which the world is not yet prepared. [*Case Book*, 'Sussex Vampire']

4 The husband was a teetotaller, there was no other woman, and the conduct complained of was that he had drifted into the habit of winding up every meal by taking out his false teeth and hurling them at his wife. [*Case of Identity*]

5 All other men are specialists, but his specialism is omniscience. [*His Last Bow*, 'Bruce-Partington Plans']

6 You know my methods, Watson. [*Memoirs of Sherlock Holmes*, 'The Crooked Man']

7 'It is my duty to warn you that it will be used against you,' cried the Inspector, with the magnificent fair play of the British criminal law. [*Memoirs of Sherlock Holmes*, 'Dancing Men']

8 A long shot, Watson; a very long shot! [*Memoirs of Sherlock Holmes*, 'The Silver Blaze']

9 The Baker Street irregulars. [*Sign of Four*]

10 How often have I said to you that when you have eliminated the impossible, whatever remains, however improbable, must be the truth? [*Sign of Four*]

11 'I am inclined to think' said I. 'I should do so,' Sherlock Holmes remarked impatiently. [*Valley of Fear*]

12 Mediocrity knows nothing higher than itself, but talent instantly recognizes genius. [*Valley of Fear*]

DRAYTON Michael 1563–1631
English poet.

1 How many paltry, foolish, painted things, / That now in coaches trouble ev'ry street, / Shall be forgotten, whom no poet sings, / Ere they be well wrapped in their winding sheet? [*Idea*, Sonnet 6]

2 Since there's no help, come let us kiss and part. [*Idea*, Sonnet 61]

3 Fair stood the wind for France. [*To the Cambro-Britans*, 'Agincourt']

4 For that fine madness still he did retain / Which rightly should possess a poet's brain. [*To Henry Reynolds, of Poets and Poesy*]

5 Had in him those brave translunary things, / That the first poets had. [Of Marlowe, in *To Henry Reynolds, of Poets and Poesy*]

DRINKWATER John 1882–1937
English poet and dramatist.

1 Those book-learned fools who miss the world. [*From Generation to Generation*]

2 Age with the best of all his seasons done, / Youth with his face towards the upland hill. [*Olton Pools*, Dedication]

DRYDEN John 1631–1700
English poet and dramatist.

1 Better one suffer, than a nation grieve. [*Absalom and Achitophel*]

2 Beware the fury of a patient man. [*Absalom and Achitophel*]

3 During his office treason was no crime, / The sons of Belial had a glorious time. [*Absalom and Achitophel*]

4 Great wits are sure to madness near alli'd. [*Absalom and Achitophel*]

5 In pious times, ere priestcraft did begin, / Before polygamy was made a sin. [*Absalom and Achitophel*]

6 Resolv'd to ruin or to rule the state. [*Absalom and Achitophel*]

7 Youth, beauty, graceful action seldom fail: / But common interest always will prevail. [*Absalom and Achitophel*]

8 Lovely Thais sits beside thee, / Take the good the gods provide thee. [*Alexander's Feast*]

9 None but the brave deserves the fair. [*Alexander's Feast*]

10 Men are but children of a larger growth; / Our appetites as apt to change as theirs. [*All For Love*]

11 My love's a noble madness. [*All for Love* II: i]

12 A knock-down argument; 'tis but a word and a blow. [*Amphitryon*]

13 A thing well said will be wit in all languages. [*Essay of Dramatic Poesy*]

14 Learn to write well, or not to write at all. [*Essay on Satire*]

15 'Tis sufficient to say, according to the proverb, that here is God's plenty. [Of Chaucer, *Fables*, Preface]

16 And love's the noblest frailty of the mind. [*Indian Emperor* II:ii]

17 All human things are subject to decay, / And, when fate summons, monarchs must obey. [*Mac Flecknoe*]

18 I am to be married within these three days; married past redemption. [*Marriage à la Mode* I]

19 For, Heaven be thanked, we live in such an age, / When no man dies for love, but on the stage. [*Mithridates*, Epilogue]

20 Fool, not to know that love endures no tie, / And Jove but laughs at lovers' perjury. [*Palamon and Arcite* bk 2]

21 From harmony, from heavenly harmony / This universal frame began: / From harmony to harmony / Through all the compass of the notes it ran, / The diapason closing full in Man. [*St. Cecilia's Day*]

22 Joy rul'd the day, and Love the night. [*Secular Masque*]

23 And, dying, bless the hand that gave the blow. [*Spanish Friar*]

24 Pains of love be sweeter far / Than all other pleasures are. [*Tyrannic Love* IV. i]

25 Here lies my wife: here let her lie! / Now she's at rest, and so am I. [Epitaph intended for Dryden's wife]

DUHAMEL Georges 1884–1966
French novelist.

I have too much respect for the idea of God to make it responsible for such an absurd world. [*Chronique des Pasquier*, 'Le Désert de Bièvres']

DUNBAR William c. 1465–1530
Scottish poet.

Fear of death throws me into confusion. [*Lament for the Makaris*]

DÜRER Albrecht 1471–1528
German artist and engraver.

If a man devotes himself to art, much evil is avoided that happens otherwise if one is idle. [*Outline of a General Treatise on Painting*]

DURRELL Lawrence 1912–1990
English novelist, poet and travel writer.

If you really worship women they'll forgive you almost everything, even if your balls are dropping off. [Attributed remark 1973]

DWORKIN Andrea 1946–
US feminist critic.

All feminist arguments, however radical in intent or consequence, are with or against or premises implicit in the male system, which is made credible or authentic by the power of men to name. [*Pornography* ch 1]

DYER Sir Edward D. 1607
English poet.

My Mind to Me a Kingdom Is [Title of poem]

DYLAN Bob 1941–
US singer and songwriter.

1 How many roads must a man walk down / Before you can call him a man? ... / The answer, my friend, is blowin' in the wind, / The answer is blowin' in the wind. ['Blowin' in the Wind']

2 Money doesn't talk, it swears. ['It's Alright, Ma']

EARHART Amelia 1898–1937
US aviation pioneer and author.

Failure must be but a challenge to others. [*Last Fight*]

EASTERN PROVERB

Experience is a comb which nature gives to men when they are bald.

EASTMAN George 1854–1932
US entrepreneur and inventor.

My work is done. Why wait? [Suicide note]

EBAN Abba 1915–
Israeli diplomat and politician.

History teaches us that men and nations behave wisely once they have exhausted other alternatives. [Speech 16 Dec 1970]

EBBINGHAUS Hermann 1850–1909
German psychologist.

Psychology has a long past, but only a short history. [*Summary of Psychology*]

EDGEWORTH Maria 1767–1849
Irish novelist.

Some people talk of morality, and some of religion, but give me a little snug property. [*The Absentee*]

EDISON Thomas Alva 1847–1931
US scientist and inventor.

Genius is one per cent inspiration and ninety-nine per cent perspiration. [*Life* ch 24]

EDWARD III 1312–1377
King of England 1327–77.

Let the boy win his spurs. [Of the Black Prince at Crécy 1345]

EDWARD VIII known as the *Duke of Windsor* 1894–1972
King of Great Britain and Northern Ireland 1936.

1 The thing that impresses me most about America is the way parents obey their children. [*Look* 5 Mar 1957]

2 I have found it impossible to discharge my duties as King as I would wish to do without the help and support of the woman I love. [Abdication speech, broadcast on radio 11 Dec 1936]

EDWARDS Jonathan 1703–1758
US theologian and philosopher.

The bodies of those that made such a noise and tumult when alive, when dead, lie as quietly among the graves of their neighbours as any others. [*Procrastination*]

EDWARDS Oliver 1711–1791
English lawyer.

I have tried too in my time to be a philosopher; but, I don't know how, cheerfulness was always breaking in. [Quoted in Boswell's *Life of Johnson* 17 Apr 1778]

EINSTEIN Albert 1879–1955
German-born US physicist.

1 Nationalism is an infantile sickness. It is the measles of the human race. [Quoted in H Dukas and B Hoffman *Albert Einstein, the Human Side*]

2 Peace cannot be kept by force. It can only be achieved by understanding. [*Notes on Pacificism*]

3 If A is a success in life, then A equals x plus y plus z. Work is x; y is play; and z is keeping your mouth shut. [*Observer* 15 Jan 1950]

Physicist Albert Einstein, 1944. He developed his theories by using simple 'thought experiments', but the full flowering of his ideas required very complex mathematics.

4 God is subtle but he is not malicious. [Remark made at Princeton University in 1921, later carved above the fireplace of the Common Room of Fine Hall (the Mathematical Institute)]

5 At any rate, I am convinced that He [God] does not play dice. [Letter to Max Born 4 Dec 1926]

6 If my theory of relativity is proven correct, Germany will claim me as a German and France will declare that I am a citizen of the world. Should my theory prove untrue, France will say that I am a German and Germany will declare that I am a Jew. [Address at the Sorbonne, Paris Dec 1929]

7 The unleashed power of the atom has changed everything save our modes of thinking and we thus drift toward unparalleled catastrophe. [Telegram sent to prominent Americans 24 May 1946]

EISENHOWER Dwight ('Ike') 1890–1969
US Republican president and general.

1 Every gun that is made, every warship launched, every rocket fired signifies, in the final sense, a theft from those who hunger and are not fed, those who are cold and are not clothed. [Speech in Washington 16 Apr 1953]

2 Your business is to put me out of business. [Addressing a graduating class at a university]

EKLAND Britt 1942–
Swedish film actress.

I say I don't sleep with married men, but what I mean is that I don't sleep with happily married men. [Remark 1980s]

ELIOT George 1819–1880
English novelist.

1 It's them as take advantage that get advantage i' this world. [*Adam Bede* ch 32]

2 I'm not denyin' the women are foolish: God Almighty made 'em to match the men. [*Adam Bede* ch 53]

3 A woman dictates before marriage in order that she may have an appetite for submission afterwards. [*Middlemarch* bk 1, ch 9]

4 Great feelings will often take the aspect of error, and great faith the aspect of illusion. [*Middlemarch* bk 8, 'Finale']

5 I've never any pity for conceited people, because I think they carry their comfort about with them. [*Mill on the Floss* bk 5, ch 4]

6 The happiest women, like the happiest nations, have no history. [*Mill on the Floss* bk 6, ch 3]

7 I should like to know what is the proper function of women, if it is not to make reasons for husbands to stay at home, and still stronger reasons for bachelors to go out. [*Mill on the Floss* bk 6, ch 6]

8 In every parting there is an image of death. [*Scenes of Clerical Life*, 'Amos Barton']

9 Nothing is so good as it seems beforehand. [*Silas Marner*]

ELIOT T S 1888–1965
US poet and playwright.

> **1** I grow old ... I grow old ... / I shall wear the bottoms of my trousers rolled. [*Love Song of J. Alfred Prufrock*]

US poet, critic and dramatist T S Eliot, one of the major figures of 20th-century literature. Born in the USA, Eliot embraced British nationality, culture, and religious traditions. His early and most influential poems, *Prufrock* 1917 and *The Waste Land* 1922, portrayed the disillusionment engendered by World War I in the radically modernist style.

2 April is the cruellest month, breeding / Lilacs out of the dead land, mixing / Memory and desire. [*Waste Land*]

3 I will show you fear in a handful of dust. [*Waste Land*]

4 When lovely woman stoops to folly and / Paces about her room again, alone, / She smoothes her hair with automatic hand, / And puts a record on the gramophone. [*Waste Land*]

2 Webster was much possessed by death. ['Whispers of Immortality']

3 I must say, Bernard Shaw is greatly improved by music. [On the opening night of *My Fair Lady* 1956]

ELIZABETH *the Queen Mother* 1900–
Wife of King George VI of Great Britain and Northern Ireland

> I'm glad we've been bombed. It makes me feel I can look the East End in the face. [Remark to a policeman 13 Sept 1940 following German bombing of Buckingham Palace]

ELIZABETH I 1533–1603
Queen of England.

> **1** Madam I may not call you; mistress I am ashamed to call you; and so I know not what to call you; but howsoever, I thank you. [Quoted in Harington *Brief View of the State of the Church*]
>
> **2** God may forgive you, but I never can. [To the Countess of Nottingham, quoted in Hume *History of England under the House of Tudor* vol 2, ch 7]
>
> **3** Though God hath raised me high, yet this I count the glory of my crown: that I have reigned with your loves. [The Golden Speech 1601, D'Ewes *Journal*]
>
> **4** I know I have the body of a weak and feeble woman, but I have the heart and stomach of a king, and of a king of England too. [Speech to the troops at Tilbury on the approach of the Armada 1588]

5 Anger makes dull men witty, but it keeps them poor. [Attributed remark]

ELLIOT Jane 1727–1805
Scottish lyricist.

The flowers of the forest are a' wede awae. ['Flowers of the Forest']

ELLIS Havelock 1859–1939
British psychologist.

The sun, the moon and the stars would have disappeared long ago ... had they happened to be within the reach of predatory human hands. [*Dance of Life* ch 7]

ELLISON Ralph 1914–
US novelist.

I am an invisible man. I am invisible, understand, because people refuse to see me. [*Invisible Man*]

ELTON Ben 1959–
English writer and comedian.

The earth only has so much bounty to offer and inventing ever larger and more notional prices for that bounty does not change its real value. [*Stark*, 'Dinner in Los Angeles']

EMERSON Ralph Waldo 1803–1882
US philosopher, essayist, and poet.

1 The shot heard round the world. ['Concord Hymn']

2 Passion, though a bad regulator, is a powerful spring. [*Conduct of Life*, 'Considerations by the Way']

3 Fate, then, is a name for facts not yet passed under the fire of thought; for causes which are unpenetrated. [*Conduct of Life*, 'Fate']

4 Art is a jealous mistress. [*Conduct of Life*, 'Wealth']

5 Belief consists in accepting the affirmations of the soul; unbelief, in denying them. [*Conduct of Life*, 'Worship']

Ralph Waldo Emerson, poet and essayist. His lucid style and clarity of thought made his writings eminently quotable, although he claimed to 'hate quotations'.

6 The louder he talked of his honour, the faster we counted our spoons. [*Conduct of Life*, 'Worship']

7 The silence that accepts merit as the most natural thing in the world is the highest applause. ['Divinity School Address' 15 July 1838, Harvard University]

8 The moment we indulge our affections, the earth is metamorphosed; there is no winter and no night; all tragedies, all ennuis, vanish – all duties even. [*Essays*, 'Friendship']

9 There is properly no history; only biography. [*Essays*, 'History']

10 All mankind loves a lover. [*Essays*, 'Love']

11 In skating over thin ice, our safety is in our speed. [*Essays*, 'Prudence']

12 A foolish consistency is the hobgoblin of little minds, adored by little statesmen and philosophers and divines. [*Essays*, 'Self-Reliance']

13 Give all to love; / Obey thy heart; / Friends, kindred, days, / Estate, good fame, / Plans, credit, and the Muse,– / Nothing refuse. ['Give All to Love']

14 By necessity, by proclivity, and by delight, we all quote. [*Letters and Social Aims*, 'Quotation and Originality']

15 Is not marriage an open question, when it is alleged, from the beginning of the world, that such as are in the institution wish to get out, and such as are out wish to get in? [*Representative Men*, 'Montaigne; or, The Skeptic']

16 Every hero becomes a bore at last. [*Representative Men*, 'Uses of Great Men']

17 Hitch your wagon to a star. [*Society and Solitude*, 'Civilization']

18 If a man write a better book, preach a better sermon, or make a better mouse-trap than his neighbour, tho' he build his house in the woods, the world will make a beaten path to his door. [Attributed remark]

ENGLISH PROVERB 18TH CENTURY

Some have been thought brave because they were afraid to run away.

EPHELIA LIVED 17TH CENTURY
English poet.

And yet I love this false, this worthless man, / With all the passion that a woman can; / Dote on his imperfections, though I spy / Nothing to love; I love, and know not why. ['To one that asked me why I loved J.G.']

EPHRON Nora 1941–
US writer.

1 Beware of men who cry. It's true that men who cry are sensitive to and in touch with feelings, but the only feelings they tend to be sensitive to and in touch with are their own. [*Heartburn* 1986]

2 If you're looking for monogamy, you'd better marry a swan. [*Heartburn* 1986]

ERASMUS Desiderius c. 1469–1536
Dutch scholar and humanist.

How a man must hug, and dandle, and kittle, and play a hundred little tricks with his bedfellow when he is disposed to make that use of her that nature designed for her. [*Praise of Folly*]

ERHARD Ludwig 1897–1977
West German politician.

A compromise is the art of dividing a cake in such a way that everyone believes that he has got the biggest piece. [Quoted in *Observer* 28 Dec 1958]

ERSKINE Ralph 1914–
British architect.

The job of buildings is to improve human relations; architecture must ease them, not make them worse. [*The Times* 16 Sept 1992]

ESCHENBACH Marie Ebner von 1830–1916
Austrian writer.

We don't believe in rheumatism and true love until after the first attack. [Attributed remark]

ESSEX Robert Devereux, Earl of 1566–1601
English soldier and politician.

Reasons are not like garments, the worse for wearing. [To Lord Willoughby 1598 or 1599]

ESTIENNE Henri 1531–1598
French classical scholar.

If youth knew; if age could. [*Les Prémices*]

EURIPEDES c. 485–406 BC
Greek dramatist.

1 Never say that marriage has more of joy than pain. [*Alcestis* 238]

2 Love distills desire upon the eyes, / love brings bewitching grace into the heart of those he would destroy. / I pray that love may never come to me with murderous intent. [*Hippolytus* 525]

EVANS Abel 1679–1737
English poet.

Under this stone, Reader, survey / Dead Sir John Vanbrugh's house of clay. / Lie heavy on him, Earth! for he / Laid many heavy loads on thee! [Epitaph on John Vanbrugh, architect of Blenheim Palace]

EVANS Dame Edith 1888–1976
English actress.

When a woman behaves like a man, why doesn't she behave like a nice man? [*Observer* 30 Sept 1956]

FANON Frantz 1925–1961
Martiniquan psychiatrist, philosopher, and political activist.

> However painful it may be for me to accept this conclusion, I am obliged to state it: for the black man there is only one destiny. And it is white. [*Black Skins, White Masks,* Introduction]

FAROUK 1920–1965
King of Egypt 1936–52.

> The whole world is in revolt. Soon there will be only five Kings left – the King of England, the King of Spades, the King of Clubs, the King of Hearts and the King of Diamonds. [Remark at a conference in Cairo 1948]

FARQUHAR George 1677–1707
Irish dramatist.

> **1** My Lady Bountiful. [*Beaux Stratagem* I. i]

> **2** No woman can be a beauty without a fortune. [*Beaux Stratagem* II. ii]

> **3** I believe they talked of me, for they laughed consumedly. [*Beaux Stratagem* III. i]

> **4** How a little love and good company improves a woman! [*Beaux Stratagem* IV. i]

> **5** Spare all I have, and take my life. [*Beaux Stratagem* V. ii]

> **6** Money is the sinews of love, as of war. [*Love and a Bottle* II. i]

> **7** Hanging and marriage, you know, go by Destiny. [*Recruiting Officer* III. ii]

FAULKNER William 1897–1962
US novelist.

> **1** If a writer has to rob his mother, he will not hesitate; the Ode on a Grecian Urn is worth any number of old ladies. [*Paris Review* Spring 1956]

> **2** Between twenty and forty the will of the child to do gets stronger, more dangerous, but it has not begun to learn to know yet. Since his capacity to do is forced into channels of evil through environment and pressures, man is strong before he is moral. The world's anguish is caused by people between twenty and forty. [Interview in Malcolm Cowley *Writers at Work*, 1st Series]

> **3** William [A man's] moral conscience is the curse he had to accept from the gods in order to gain from them the right to dream. [Interview in Cowley *Writers at Work*, 1st Series]

> **4** I believe man will not merely endure, he will prevail. He is immortal, not because he, alone among creatures, has an inexhaustible voice but because he has a soul, a spirit capable of compassion and sacrifice and endurance. [Nobel Prize speech 1950]

FEATHER Vic 1908–1976
British trade-unionist.

> Industrial relations are like sexual relations. It's better between two consenting parties. [*Guardian Weekly* 8 Aug 1976]

FELLINI Federico 1920–1994
Italian film director.

> What is an artist? A provincial who finds himself somewhere between a physical reality and a metaphysical one ... It's this in-between that I'm calling a province, this frontier

country between the tangible world and the intangible one – which is really the realm of the artist. [Quoted by John Berger in 'Every Time We Say Goodbye', in *Sight and Sound* June 1991]

FERBER Edna 1887–1968
US novelist and dramatist.

Being an old maid is like death by drowning, a really delightful sensation after you cease to struggle. [R E Drennan *Wit's End*]

FERMI Enrico 1901–1954
Italian-born US physicist.

Whatever Nature has in store for mankind, unpleasant as it may be, man must accept, for ignorance is never better than knowledge. [*Atoms in the Family*]

FEUERBACH Ludwig 1804–1872
German philosopher.

It is with books as with young girls. It is often the best, the worthiest that are left the longest on the shelf. Yet eventually someone comes who recognizes them and draws them from the darkness of seclusion into the light of a fine sphere of activity. [*Writer and Man*]

FEYERABEND Paul K 1924–1994
US philosopher of science.

Variety of opinion is necessary for objective knowledge. [*Against Method*]

FEYNMAN Richard P 1918–1988
US physicist.

One does not, by knowing all the physical laws as we know them today, immediately obtain an understanding of anything much. [*Character of Physical Law*]

FFRANGCON-DAVIES Dame Gwen 1891–1992
Actress.

My dear, I am always nervous about doing something for the first time. [Referring to death, aged 101, Feb 1992]

FIELDING Henry 1707–1754
English novelist and dramatist.

1 When widows exclaim loudly against second marriage, I would always lay a wager that the man, if not the wedding-day, is absolutely fixed on. [*Amelia* bk 6, ch 10]

2 Public schools are the nurseries of all vice and immorality. [*Joseph Andrews*]

3 Love and scandal are the best sweeteners of tea. [*Love in Several Masques* IV. xi]

4 His designs were strictly honourable, as the phrase is; that is, to rob a lady of her fortune by way of marriage. [*Tom Jones* bk 2, ch 4]

5 What is commonly called love, namely the desire of satisfying a voracious appetite with a certain quantity of delicate white human flesh. [*Tom Jones* bk 6, ch 1]

6 That monstrous animal, a husband and wife. [*Tom Jones* bk 15, ch 9]

FIELDS Dorothy 1905–1974
US songwriter.

A fine romance with no kisses. / A fine romance, my friend, this is. / We should be like a couple of hot tomatoes, / But you're as cold as yesterday's mashed potatoes. ['Fine Romance']

FIELDS W C 1880–1946
US film actor and screenwriter.

1 I was in love with a beautiful blonde once, dear. She drove me to drink. That's the one thing I'm indebted to her for. [Quoted in R J Anobile *Flask of Fields*]

2 I always keep a supply of stimulant handy in case I see a snake – which I also keep handy. [Quoted in C Ford *Time of Laughter*]

3 Here lies W. C. Fields. I would rather be living in Philadelphia. [Suggested epitaph for himself]

US comedian WC Fields. His misanthropic nature and his suspicion of reverent institutions such as banks and the family were typical of his recent character, both on and off screen.

4 Never give a sucker an even break. [Catch-phrase]

FITZGERALD Edward 1809–1883
English poet and translator.

1 Awake! for Morning in the Bowl of Night / Has flung the Stone that puts the Stars to Flight: / And Lo! the Hunter of the East has caught / The Sultan's Turret in a Noose of Light. [*Omar Khayyám* 1]

2 Come, fill the Cup, and in the Fire of Spring / The Winter Garment of Repentance fling. [*Omar Khayyám* 7]

3 Here with a Loaf of Bread beneath the bough, / A Flask of Wine, a Book of Verse – and Thou / Beside me singing in the Wilderness – / And Wilderness is Paradise enow. [*Omar Khayyám* 11]

4 Ah, take the Cash in hand and waive the Rest; / Oh, the brave Music of a distant Drum! [*Omar Khayyám* 12]

5 I sometimes think that never blows so red / The Rose as where some buried Caesar bled. [*Omar Khayyám* 18]

6 The Moving Finger writes; and, having writ / Moves on: nor all thy Piety nor Wit / Shall lure it back to cancel half a Line, / Nor all thy Tears wash out a Word of it. [*Omar Khayyám* 51]

7 Who is the Potter, pray, and who the Pot? [*Omar Khayyám* 60]

8 Alas, that Spring should vanish with the Rose! [*Omar Khayyám* 72]

9 Sans Wine, sans Song, sans Singer, and – sans End! [*Omar Khayyám* 23]

10 Myself when young did eagerly frequent / Doctor and Saint, and heard great argument / About it and about: but evermore / Came out by the same door as in I went. [Omar Khayyám 27]

11 I wonder often what the Vintners buy / One half so precious as the Goods they sell. [Omar Khayyám 71]

FITZGERALD F Scott 1896–1940
US novelist.

1 Let me tell you about the very rich. They are different from you and me. [*All the Sad Young Men* 'Rich Boy']

2 In a real dark night of the soul it is always three o'clock in the morning, day after day. [*The Crack-Up*]

3 You can stroke people with words. [*The Crack-up*]

4 A big man has no time really to do anything but just sit and be big. [*This Side of Paradise*]

FLATMAN Thomas 1637–1688
English poet.

How happy a thing were a wedding / And a bedding, / If a man might purchase a wife / For a twelve month, and a day; / But to live with her all a man's life, / For ever and for ay, / 'Till she grow as grey as a Cat, / Good faith, Mr Parson, I thank you for that. ['Bachelor's Song']

FLAUBERT Gustave 1821–1880
French novelist.

Of all the icy blasts that blow on love, a request for money is the most chilling and havoc-wreaking. [*Madame Bovary* ch 8]

FLECKER James Elroy 1884–1915
English poet.

1 And some to Mecca turn to pray, and I toward thy bed, Yasmin. [*Hassan* I. ii]

2 We take the Golden Road to Samarkand. [*Hassan* V. ii]

3 It was so old a ship – who knows, who knows? / And yet so beautiful, I watched in vain / To see the mast burst open with a rose, / And the whole deck put on its leaves again. [*The Old Ships*]

FLEMING Ian 1908–1964
English novelist.

Most marriages don't add two people together. They subtract one from the other. [*Diamonds are Forever*]

FLETCHER John 1579–1625
English dramatist.

Of all the paths lead to a woman's love / Pity's the straightest. [*Knight of Malta* I]

FLETCHER Phineas 1582–1650
English poet and clergyman.

1 Love's tongue is in the eyes. [*Piscatory Eclogues* no. 5]

2 Love is like linen, often chang'd, the sweeter. [*Sicelides* III. v]

FLORIAN Jean-Pierre Claris de 1755–1794
French poet and writer.

Love's pleasure lasts but a moment; love's sorrow lasts all through life. [*Célestine*]

FOCH Ferdinand 1851–1929
French marshal.

1 My centre is giving way, my right is in retreat; situation excellent. I am attacking. [Attributed remark quoted in Aston *Biography of Foch*]

2 What a marvellous place to drop one's mother-in-law! [Attributed remark on being shown the Grand Canyon]

FOOT Isaac 1880–1960
British Liberal politician.

Men of power have no time to read; yet men who do not read are unfit for power. [*Debts of Honour*]

FORD Ford Madox 1873–1939
English author.

In all matrimonial associations there is, I believe, one constant factor – a desire to deceive the person with whom one lives as to some weak spot in one's character or in one's career. For it is intolerable to live constantly with one human being who perceives one's small meannesses. It is really death to do so – that is why so many marriages turn out unhappily. [*Good Soldier*]

FORD Henry 1863–1947
US automobile manufacturer.

1 People can have the Model T in any colour – so long as it's black. [A Nevins *Ford*]

2 History is bunk. [Remark]

FORD John 1586–c. 1640
English poet and dramatist.

1   The joys of marriage are the heaven on earth, / Life's paradise, great princess, the soul's quiet, / Sinews of concord, earthly immortality, / Eternity of pleasures; no restoratives / Like to a constant woman. [*Broken Heart* II. ii]

2   Love is the tyrant of the heart; it darkens / Reason, confounds discretion; deaf to counsel, / It runs headlong course to desperate madness. [*Lover's Melancholy* III. iii]

3   'Tis Pity She's a Whore. [Play title]

FORD Lena Gilbert 1870–1916
English poet.

Keep the home fires burning. [Poem title]

FORD Thomas 1580–1648
English composer and musician.

There is a lady sweet and kind, / Was never face so pleased my mind; / I did but see her passing by, / And yet I love her till I die. [*Music of Sundry Kinds*]

FORMAN Milos 1932–
Czech film director.

The Czechs voted for the jungle, while the Slovaks voted for the zoo. It is clear that a compromise is impossible. [Remark on the division of Czechoslovakia 1992]

FORMBY George 1905–1961
English singer and comedian.

I'm leaning on a lamp-post at the corner of the street / In case a certain little lady comes by. ['Leaning on a Lamp-post']

FORSTER E M 1879–1970
English novelist and critic.

1   The historian must have some conception of how men who are not historians behave. Otherwise he will move in a world of the dead. [*Abinger Harvest*, 'Captain Edward Gibbon']

2   It is not that the Englishman can't feel – it is that he is afraid to feel. He has been taught at his public school that feeling is bad form. [*Abinger Harvest*, 'Notes on English Character']

3   Personal relations are the important thing for ever and ever, and not this outer life of telegrams and anger. [*Howards End* ch 19]

4   Only connect! [*Howards End* ch 22]

5   Spoon feeding in the long run teaches us nothing but the shape of the spoon. [*Observer* 7 Oct 1951]

6   The so-called white races are really pinko-grey. [*Passage to India* ch 7]

7   The huge city which the West had built and abandoned with a gesture of despair. [On Bombay in *Passage to India*]

8   She ... joined the vast armies of the benighted, who follow neither the heart nor the brain, and march to their destiny by catchwords. [*Room with a View*]

9   I suggest that the only books that influence us are those for which we are ready, and which have gone a little farther down our particular path than we have yet got ourselves. [*Two Cheers for Democracy*, 'Books That Influenced Me']

10   Faith, to my mind, is a stiffening process, a sort of mental starch, which should be applied as sparingly as possible. [*Two Cheers for Democracy*, 'What I Believe']

11   I hate the idea of causes, and if I had to choose between betraying my country and betraying my friend, I hope I should have the guts to betray my country. [*Two Cheers for Democracy*, 'What I Believe']

FOUCAULT Michel 1926–1984
French philosopher.

> 1 Man is neither the oldest nor the most constant problem that has been posed for human knowledge. [*Order of Things*]

> 2 Freedom of conscience entails more dangers than authority and despotism. [*Madness and Civilization* ch 7]

FOX Henry, 3rd Baron Holland
1773–1840
English Liberal statesman.

> If Mr. Selwyn calls again, shew him up; if I am alive I shall be delighted to see him; and if I am dead he would like to see me. [Last words]

FRANCE Anatole 1844–1924
French writer.

> 1 Christianity has done a great deal for love by making a sin of it. [*Garden of Epicurus*]

> 2 The good critic is he who relates the adventures of his soul among masterpieces. [*Literary Life*, dedicatory letter]

> 3 They [the poor] have to labour in the face of the majestic equality of the law, which forbids the rich as well as the poor to sleep under bridges, to beg in the streets, and to steal bread. [*Red Lily* ch 7]

> 4 A tale without love is like beef without mustard: insipid. [*Revolt of the Angels* ch 8]

FRANCIS I 1494–1547
King of France 1515–47.

> Out of all I had, only honour remains, and my life, which is safe. [Letter to his mother after losing Battle of Pavia 1525]

FRANCIS DE SALES, ST 1567–1622
French churchman and writer.

> Make friends with the angels, who though invisible are always with you. [*Introduction to the Devout Life* pt 2, ch 16]

FRANKLIN Benjamin 1706–1790
US author, scientist, and statesman.

> 1 Remember, that time is money. ['Advice to Young Tradesman']

> 2 Keep your eyes wide open before marriage, half shut afterwards. [*Poor Richard's Almanack*]

> 3 No nation was ever ruined by trade. ['Thoughts on Commercial Subjects']

> 3 We must indeed all hang together, or, most assuredly, we shall all hang separately. [Remark to John Hancock, at Signing of the Declaration of Independence 4 July 1776]

> 4 There never was a good war, or a bad peace. [Letter to Quincey 11 Sept 1783]

> 5 But in this world nothing can be said to be certain, except death and taxes. [Letter to Jean Baptiste Le Roy 13 Nov 1789]

FRANKS Oliver Shewell 1905–1992
English college principal.

> A secret in the Oxford sense: you may tell it to only one person at a time. [Quoted by K Rose in the *Sunday Telegraph* 30 Jan 1977]

FRAZER Sir J G 1854–1941
Scottish anthropologist.

> The awe and dread with which the untutored savage contemplates his mother-in-law are amongst the most familiar facts of anthropology. [*Golden Bough* vol I

FRENCH Marilyn 1929–
US writer and critic.

> 'I hate discussions of feminism that end up with who does the dishes,' she said. So do I. But at the end, there are always the damned dishes. [*Women's Room* ch 1]

FREUD Clement 1924–
English journalist.

> If you resolve to give up smoking, drinking and loving, you don't actually live longer; it just seems longer. [*Observer* Dec 1964]

FREUD Sigmund 1856–1939
Austrian founder of psychoanalysis.

> **1** Civilization is a process in the service of Eros, whose purpose is to combine single human individuals, and after that families, then races, peoples and nations, into one great unity, the unity of mankind. Why this has to happen, we do not know; the work of Eros is precisely this. [*Civilization and its Discontents* ch 6]

> **2** We are never so defenceless against suffering as when we love, never so forlornly unhappy as when we have lost our love-object or its love. [*Civilization and Its Discontents*]

> **3** Anatomy is destiny. [*Collected Writings*]

> **4** Devout believers are safeguarded in a high degree against the risk of certain neurotic illnesses; their acceptance of the universal neurosis spares them the task of constructing a personal one. [*Future of an Illusion* ch 8]

> **5** The act of birth is the first experience of anxiety, and thus the source and prototype of the affect of anxiety. [*Interpretation of Dreams* ch 6]

> **6** A strong egotism is a protection against disease, but in the last resort we must begin to love in order that we may not fall ill, and must fall ill, if in consequence of frustration, we cannot love. [Quoted in N O Brown *Life Against Death*]

> **7** Analogies decide nothing, that is true, but they can make one feel more at home. [*New Introductory Lectures on Psychoanalysis*]

> **8** All that matters is love and work. [Attributed remark]

The Austrian psychiatrist and pioneer of psychanalysis, Sigmund Freud. His insights into the human psyche grew in part from his interest in literature, mythology, and comparative religion, and he was a keen collector of archaeological artefacts such as ancient Egyptian statuettes.

> **9** The great question that has never been answered ... is 'What does a woman want?' [Letter to Marie Bonaparte]

FROMM Erich 1900–1980
US psychologist.

> Man is the only animal for whom his own existence is a problem which he has to solve. [*Man for Himself* ch 3]

FROST Robert 1874–1963
US poet.

> **1** Most of the change we think we see in life / Is due to truths being in or out of favour. ['Black Cottage']

2 Love is an irresistible desire to be irresistibly desired. ['Comment']

3 Home is the place where, when you have to go there, / They have to take you in. ['Death of the Hired Man']

4 I never dared be radical when young / For fear it would make me conservative when old. [*Further Range*, 'Precaution']

5 I've given offence by saying that I'd as soon write free verse as play tennis with the net down. [E Lathem *Interviews with Robert Frost*]

6 I would have written of me on my stone: / I had a lover's quarrel with the world. ['Lesson for Today']

7 Something there is that doesn't love a wall. ['Mending Wall']

8 Poetry is what is lost in translation. It is also what is lost in interpretation. [Quoted in L Untermeyer *Robert Frost: a Backward Look*]

9 Poetry is a way of taking life by the throat. [Quoted in E S Sergeant *Robert Frost: the Trial by Existence* ch 18]

10 We dance round in a ring and suppose, / But the Secret sits in the middle and knows. ['The Secret Sits']

11 Thinking isn't agreeing or disagreeing. That's voting. [Interview in Plimpton, *Writers at Work* 2nd Series]

FRY Christopher 1907–
English dramatist.

1 I travel light; as light, / That is, as a man can travel who will / Still carry his body around because / Of its sentimental value. [*Lady's Not for Burning*]

2 Try thinking of love, or something. / *Amor vincit insomnia*. [*Sleep of Prisoners*]

3 I tell you, / Miss, I knows an undesirable character / When I see one; I've been one myself for years. [*Venus Observed*]

4 Comedy is an escape, not from truth but from despair; a narrow escape into faith. [*Time* 20 Nov 1950]

FRY Roger 1866–1934
English artist and art critic.

Bach almost persuades me to be a Christian. [Virginia Woolf *Roger Fry*]

FRYE Northrop 1912–1991
Canadian literary critic.

Nature is inside art as its content, not outside as its model. [*Fables of Identity*]

FULLER R Buckminster 1895–1983
US architect and engineer.

Now there is one outstandingly important fact regarding Spaceship Earth, and that is that no instruction book came with it. [*Operating Manual for Spaceship Earth*]

FULLER Thomas 1608–1661
English preacher and historian.

1 Anger is one of the sinews of the soul; he that wants it hath a maimed mind. [*Holy State and the Profane State* bk 3, 'Of Anger']

2 Light, God's eldest daughter, is a principal beauty in a building. [*Holy State and the Profane State* bk 3, 'Of Building']

3 Deceive not thyself by overexpecting happiness in the married estate. Remember the nightingales which sing only some months in the spring, but commonly are silent when they have hatched their eggs. [*Holy State and the Profane State*, 'Of Marriage']

4 They that marry ancient people merely in expectation to bury them, hang themselves, in hope that one will come and cut the halter. [*Holy State and the Profane State*, 'Of Marriage']

5 They that marry where they do not love, will love where they do not marry. [*Holy State and the Profane State*, 'Of Marriage']

6 A book that is shut is but a block. [*Gnomologia* no. 23]

GABOR Dennis 1900–1979
Hungarian-born British physicist.

Till now man has been up against Nature, from now on he will be up against his own nature. [*Inventing the Future*]

GABOR Zsa Zsa 1919–
Hungarian-born US film actress.

1 I haven't known many open marriages, though quite a few have been ajar. [Quoted in M Brown and A O'Connor *Hammer and Tongues*]

2 Husbands are like fires–they go out when unattended. [Quoted in *Newsweek* 1960]

3 A man in love is incomplete until he has married. Then he's finished. [Quoted in *Newsweek* 28 March 1960]

4 I never hated a man enough to give him diamonds back. [*Observer* 25 Aug 1957]

5 Personally I know nothing about sex because I've always been married. [*Observer* 'Sayings of the Week' 16 Aug 1987]

6 I am a marvellous housekeeper. Every time I leave a man, I keep his house. [Quoted in B Chieger *Was It Good For You Too?*]

GAINSBOROUGH Thomas 1727–1788
English painter.

We are all going to heaven, and Vandyke is of the company. [Last words]

GALBRAITH J K 1908–
Canadian-born US economist.

1 The enemy of the conventional wisdom is not ideas but the march of events. [Quoted in *Affluent Society*]

2 In the affluent society no useful distinction can be made between luxuries and necessaries. [Quoted in *Affluent Society*]

3 When people put their ballots in the boxes, they are, by that act, inoculated against the feeling that the government is not theirs. [*Age of Uncertainty* ch 12]

4 There is certainly no absolute standard of beauty. That precisely is what makes its pursuit so interesting. [Quoted in *New York Times Magazine* 9 Oct 1960]

5 Politics is not the art of the possible. It consists in choosing between the disastrous and the unpalatable. [Letter to President Kennedy 2 March 1962]

GALSWORTHY John 1867–1933
English novelist and dramatist.

I am probably the most happily married man in England. ... I know ... the value and beauty of a perfect union. [Quoted in H V Marrot *Life and Letters of John Galsworthy*]

GANDHI Indira 1917–1984
Indian prime minister.

Politics is the art of acquiring, holding and wielding power. [Quoted in *Observer* 4 May 1975]

GANDHI Mahatma 1869–1948
Indian spiritual and nationalist leader.

1 Capital as such is not evil; it is its wrong use that is evil. Capital in some form or other will always be needed. [*Harijan* 28 July 1940]

2 What difference does it make to the dead, the orphans and the homeless, whether the mad destruction is wrought under the name of totalitarianism or the holy name of liberty or democracy? [*Non-Violence in Peace and War* vol 1, ch 142]

3 The moment the slave resolves that he will no longer be a slave, his

fetters fall. He frees himself and shows the way to others. Freedom and slavery are mental states. [*Non-Violence in Peace and War* vol 2, ch 5]

4 Truth never damages a cause that is just. [*Non-Violence in Peace and War* vol 2, ch 162]

5 Rights that do not flow from duty well performed are not worth having. [*Non-Violence in Peace and War* vol 2, ch 269]

GARCÍA MÁRQUEZ Gabriel 1928–
Colombian writer.

She discovered with great delight that one does not love one's children just because they are one's children, but because of the friendship formed while raising them. [*Love in the Time of Cholera* 207]

GARNER James 1928–
US film actor.

Marriage is a lot like the army; everyone complains, but you'd be surprised at the large number that re-enlist. [Attributed remark 1980]

GARRICK David 1717–1779
English actor and theatre manager.

1 Heart of oak are our ships. ['Heart of Oak']

2 A fellow-feeling makes one wond'rous kind. ['An Occasional Prologue on Quitting the Theatre' 10 June 1776]

GASKELL Elizabeth 1810–1865
English novelist.

1 A man ... is *so* in the way in the house! [*Cranford* ch 1]

2 'It is very pleasant dining with a bachelor, ' said Miss Matty, softly, as we settled ourselves in the counting-house, 'I only hope it is not improper; so many pleasant things are!' [*Cranford* ch 4]

Portrait of the English actor David Garrick by William Hogarth.

3 A little credulity helps one on through life very smoothly. [*Cranford* ch 11]

GAUGUIN Paul 1848–1903
French artist.

Art is either plagiarism or revolution. [Quoted in Huneker *Pathos of Distance* 128]

GAY John 1685–1732
English poet and dramatist.

1 Do you think your mother and I should have liv'd comfortably so long together, if ever we had been married? [*Beggar's Opera* I. viii]

2 How happy could I be with either, / Were t'other dear charmer away! [*Beggar's Opera* I. xiii]

3 If with me you'd fondly stray / Over the hills and far away. [*Beggar's Opera* I. xiii]

4 Do like other widows – buy yourself weeds, and be cheerful. [*Beggar's Opera* II. xi]

5 One wife is too much for most husbands to hear, / But two at a time there's no mortal can bear. [*Beggar's Opera* III. xi]

6 Life is a jest; and all things show it. / I thought so once; but now I know it. ['My Own Epitaph']

7 We only part to meet again. / Change, as ye list, ye winds; my heart shall be / The faithful compass that still points to thee. ['Sweet William's Farewell to Black-Eyed Susan']

8 A miss for pleasure, and a wife for breed. ['The Toilette']

GELDOF Bob 1954–
Irish rock singer.

1 Most people get into bands for three very simple rock and roll reasons: to get laid, to get fame, and to get rich. [*Melody Maker* 27 Aug 1977]

2 I don't think that the possible death of 120 million people is a matter for charity. It is a matter of moral imperative. [To Prime Minister Thatcher on the threatened famine in Africa 1985]

GENET Jean 1910–1986
French dramatist and novelist.

1 Anyone who hasn't experienced the ecstasy of betrayal knows nothing about ecstasy at all. [*Prisoner of Love* pt 1]

2 Anyone who knows a strange fact shares in its singularity. [*Prisoner of Love* pt 1]

GEORGE I 1660–1727
King of Great Britain and Ireland, 1714–27.

I hate all Boets and Bainters. [Quoted in J Campbell *Lives of the Chief Justices* ch 30]

GEORGE II 1683–1760
King of Great Britain and Ireland, 1727–60.

Oh! he is mad, is he? Then I wish he would bite some other of my generals. [Reply to a complaint that General James Wolfe was a madman]

GEORGE Henry 1839–1897
US economist.

Capital is a result of labor, and is used by labor to assist it in further production. Labor is the active and initial force, and labor is therefore the employer of capital. [*Progress and Poverty* bk 3, ch 1]

GERSHWIN Ira 1896–1983
US lyricist.

1 You like potato and I like po-tah-to, / You like tomato and I like to-mah-to; / Potato, po-tah-to, tomato, to-mah-to- / Let's call the whole thing off! ['Let's Call the Whole Thing Off']

2 Holding hands at midnight / 'Neath a starry sky, / Nice work if you can get it, / And you can get it if you try. ['Nice Work If You Can Get It']

GETTY J Paul 1892–1976
US oil billionaire.

If you can actually count your money, then you are not really a rich man. [Quoted in Observer 3 Nov 1957]

GIACOMO Count Leopardi 1798–1837
Italian romantic poet.

No one is so completely disenchanted with the world, or knows it so thoroughly, or is so utterly disgusted with it, that when it begins to smile upon him he does not become partially reconciled to it. [*Pensieri*]

GIBBON Edward 1737–1794
English historian.

1 [Antoninus Pius's] reign is marked by the rare advantage of furnishing very few materials for history; which is, indeed, little more than the register of the crimes, follies, and misfortunes of mankind. [*Decline and Fall of the Roman Empire* ch 3]

2 All taxes must, at last, fall upon agriculture. [*Decline and Fall of the Roman Empire* ch 8]

3 Corruption, the most infallible symptom of constitutional liberty. [*Decline and Fall of the Roman Empire* ch 21]

4 Dr. – well remembered that he had a salary to receive, and only forgot that he had a duty to perform. [*Memoirs of My Life*]

5 I sighed as a lover, I obeyed as a son. [*Memoirs of My Life*]

6 It was at Rome, on the 15th of October, 1764, as I sat musing amidst the ruins of the Capitol, while the barefooted friars were singing vespers in the Temple of Jupiter, that the idea of writing the decline and fall of the city first started to my mind. [*Memoirs of My Life*]

7 I was never less alone than when by myself. [*Memoirs of My Life*]

8 My early and invincible love of reading, which I would not exchange for the treasures of India. [*Memoirs of My Life*]

9 Their dull and deep potations excused the brisk intemperance of youth. [*Memoirs of My Life*]

GIBBONS Stella 1902–1989
English journalist.

1 There are some things (like first love and one's reviews) at which a woman in her middle years does not care to look too closely. [*Cold Comfort Farm*, Foreword]

2 The dark flame of his male pride was a little suspicious of having its leg pulled. [*Cold Comfort Farm* ch 7]

3 When you were very small ... you had seen something nasty in the woodshed. [*Cold Comfort Farm* ch 10]

GIBRAN Kahlil 1883–1931
Lebanese-born US writer and illustrator.

1 Everyone has experienced that truth: that love, like a running brook, is disregarded, taken for granted; but when the brook freezes over, then people begin to remember how it was when it ran, and they want it to run again. [*Beloved Prophet*]

2 No human relation gives one possession in another – every two souls are absolutely different. In friendship or in love, the two side by side raise hands together to find what one cannot reach alone. [*Beloved Prophet*]

3 Love gives naught but itself and takes naught but from itself. / Love possesses not nor would it be possessed; / For love is sufficient unto love. [*The Prophet*, 'On Love']

4 Love one another, but make not a bond of love: / Let it rather be a moving sea between the shores of your souls. [*The Prophet*, 'On Love']

5 When love beckons to you, follow him, / Though his ways are hard and steep. / And when his wings enfold you yield to him, / Though the sword hidden among his pinions may wound you. / And when he speaks to you believe in him, / Though his voice may shatter your dreams as the north wind lays waste the garden. [*The Prophet*, 'On Love']

6 Work is love made visible. And if you cannot work with love but only with distaste, it is better that you should leave your work and sit at the gate of the temple and take alms of those who work with joy. [*The Prophet* 'On Work']

GIDE André 1869–1951
French novelist.

1 It is the special quality of love not to be able to remain stationary, to be obliged to increase under pain of diminishing. [*Counterfeiters* pt 3, ch 5]

2 Sadness is almost never anything but a form of fatigue. [*Journal*]

GILBERT Humphrey c. 1539–1583
English soldier and navigator.

We are as near to heaven by sea as by land! [*Hakluyt's Voyages*]

GILBERT W S 1836–1911
English humorist and dramatist.

1 Down went the owners – greedy men whom hope of gain allured: / Oh, dry the starting tear, for they were heavily insured. [*Etiquette*]

2 The padre said, 'Whatever have you been and gone and done?' ['Gentle Alice Brown']

3 He led his regiment from behind / He found it less exciting. [*Gondoliers*]

4 Take a pair of sparkling eyes. [*Gondoliers*]

5 That celebrated, / Cultivated, / Underrated / Nobleman, / The Duke of Plaza Toro! [*Gondoliers*]

6 When every one is somebodee, / Then no one's anybody! [*Gondoliers*]

7 And so do his sisters and his cousins and his aunts! [*H.M.S. Pinafore*]

8 But in spite of all temptations / To belong to other nations, / He remains an Englishman! [*H.M.S. Pinafore*]

9 I never use a big, big D. [*H.M.S. Pinafore*]

10 Now I am the Ruler of the Queen's Navee! [*H.M.S. Pinafore*]

11 Things are seldom what they seem, / Skim milk masquerades as cream. [*H.M.S. Pinafore*]

12 Faint heart never won fair lady! / Nothing venture, nothing win– / Blood is thick, but water's thin, / In for a penny, in for a pound– / It's Love that makes the world go round. [*Iolanthe* I]

13 Hearts just as pure and fair / May beat in Belgrave Square / As in the lowly air / Of Seven Dials. [*Iolanthe*]

14 A pleasant occupation for / A rather susceptible Chancellor! [*Iolanthe*]

15 Awaiting the sensation of a short, sharp shock, / From a cheap and chippy chopper on a big black block. [*Mikado*]

16 The flowers that bloom in the spring, Tra la, / Have nothing to do with the case. [*Mikado*]

17 The idiot who praises, with enthusiastic tone, / All centuries but this, and every country but his own. [*Mikado*]

18 I've got a little list – I've got a little list / Of social offenders who might well be under ground / And who never would be missed – who never would be missed! [*Mikado*]

19 Matrimonial devotion / Doesn't seem to suit her notion. [*Mikado*]

20 Merely corroborative detail, intended to give artistic verisimilitude to an otherwise bald and unconvincing narrative. [*Mikado*]

21 Modified rapture! [*Mikado*]

22 My object all sublime / I shall achieve in time / To make the punishment fit the crime – / The punishment fit the crime. [*Mikado*]

23 A source of innocent merriment! / Of innocent merriment. [*Mikado*]

24 Three little maids who, all unwary, / Come from a ladies' seminary. [*Mikado*]

25 A wandering minstrel I / A thing of shreds and patches. [*Mikado*]

26 The meaning doesn't matter if it's only idle chatter of a transcendental kind. [*Patience*]

27 Why, what a very singularly deep young man this deep young man must be! [*Patience*]

28 I am the very model of a modern Major-General. [*Pirates of Penzance*]

29 The policeman's lot is not a happy one. [*Pirates of Penzance*]

30 I was a pale young curate then. [*Sorcerer*]

31 And many a burglar I've restored / To his friends and his relations. [*Trial by Jury*]

32 She may very well pass for forty-three / In the dusk with a light behind her! [*Trial by Jury*]

GILMAN Charlotte Perkins 1860–1935
US feminist poet, novelist, and historian.

1 The people people have for friends / Your common sense appall, / But the people people marry / Are the queerest folk of all. ['Queer People']

2 There is no female mind. The brain is not an organ of sex. As well speak of a female liver. [*Woman and Economics*]

3 Where young boys plan for what they will achieve and attain, young girls plan for whom they will achieve and attain. [*Women and Economics*]

GINSBERG Allen 1926–
US poet and political activist.

What if someone gave a war & Nobody came? ['Graffiti']

GIOVANNI Nikki 1943–
US poet.

Mistakes are a fact of life / It is the response to error that counts. [*Black Feeling / Black Talk / Black Judgment*, 'Of Liberation' st 16]

GIRAUDOUX Jean 1882–1944
French writer.

1 Faithful women are all alike, they think only of their fidelity, never of their husbands. [*Amphitryon 38*]

2 The life of a wife and husband who love each other is never at rest. Whether the marriage is true or false, the marriage portion is the same: elemental discord. [*Tiger at the Gates* II]

GLADSTONE William Ewart 1809–1898
British Liberal politician and prime minister.

All the world over, I will back the masses against the classes. [Speech in Liverpool 28 June 1886]

19th-century British Liberal prime minister William Gladstone. Queen Victoria disliked his pomposity, and many members of the upper classes feared him as the representative of a dangerous liberalism, but probably no other British minister has left behind so long and so successful a record of practical legislation.

GLENDINNING Victoria 1937–
English biographer and novelist.

Why are women – most women – more interested in a man after he has made love to them than before? Why are men – most men – more interested in a woman before they have made love to her than after? ... Men have to *unload*, he thought, rubbish doesn't care about the feelings of the skip. [*Grown-ups* ch 11]

GODARD Jean-Luc 1930–
French filmmaker and writer.

1 The truth is that there is no terror untempered by some great moral idea. [*Cahiers du Cinéma* 10 March 1952]

2 The cinema is not an art which films life: the cinema is something *between* art and life. Unlike painting and literature, the cinema both gives life and takes from it. [Quoted in Roud *Godard*, Introduction]

3 Photography is truth. The cinema is truth 24 times per second. [*Le Petit Soldat*]

4 Stereo is more democratic, mono more totalitarian. [Opening a cinema in Dolby stereo in Moscow, Feb 1992]

GODOLPHIN Sidney 1610–1643
English poet.

Or love me less or love me more / And play not with my liberty; / Either take all, or all restore, / Bind me at least, or set me free. ['Song']

GOEBBELS Joseph 1897–1945
German Nazi leader.

We can manage without butter but not, for example, without guns. If we are attacked we can only defend ourselves with guns not with butter. [Speech in Berlin 17 Jan 1936]

GOERING Hermann 1893–1946
Nazi leader, German field marshal from 1938.

Guns will make us powerful; butter will only make us fat. [Radio broadcast 1936]

GOETHE Johann Wolfgang von
1749–1832
German poet, novelist, and dramatist.

1 The sum which two married people owe to one another defies calculation. It is an infinite debt, which can only be discharged through all eternity. [*Elective Affinities* bk 1, ch 9]

2 He who seizes the right moment, / Is the right man. [*Faust*]

GOGOL Nicolai Vasilyevich 1809–1852
Russian writer.

Gambling is the great leveller. All men are equal – at cards. [*Gamblers*]

GOLDMAN Emma 1869–1940
Russian-born US anarchist.

The history of progress is written in the blood of men and women who have dared to espouse an unpopular cause, as, for instance, the black man's right to his body, or woman's right to her soul. ['What I Believe', *New York World* 1908]

GOLDSMITH Oliver 1728–1774
Anglo-Irish writer, poet and dramatist.

1 As writers become more numerous, it is natural for readers to become more indolent. [*The Bee*]

2 And still they gaz'd, and still the wonder grew, / That one small head could carry all he knew. [*Deserted Village*]

3 Ill fares the land, to hast'ning ills a prey, / Where wealth accumulates, and men decay. [*Deserted Village*]

4 Sweet Auburn! loveliest village of the plain. [*Deserted Village*]

5 Truth from his lips prevail'd with double sway, / And fools, who came to scoff, remain'd to pray. [*Deserted Village*]

6 The man recover'd of the bite, / The dog it was that died. ['Elegy on the Death of a Mad Dog']

7 Friendship is a disinterested commerce between equals; love, an abject intercourse between tyrants and slaves. [*Good Natured Man* I]

8 You, that are going to be married, think things can never be done too fast; but we, that are old, and know what we are about, must elope methodically, madam. [*Good-Natured Man* II]

9 There is no arguing with Johnson; for when his pistol misses fire, he knocks you down with the butt end of it. [Remark quoted in James Boswell's *Life of Johnson*]

10 Why, Dr. Johnson, ... if you were to make little fishes talk, they would talk like whales. [Quoted in James Boswell's *Life of Johnson* 27 Apr 1773]

11 This is Liberty-Hall, gentlemen. [*She Stoops to Conquer*]

12 The very pink of perfection. [*She Stoops to Conquer*]

13 And learn the luxury of doing good. [*The Traveller*]

14 As writers become more numerous, it is natural for readers to become more indolent. ['Upon Unfortunate Merit']

15 I ... chose my wife, as she did her wedding gown, not for a fine glossy surface, but such qualities as would wear well. [*Vicar of Wakefield* ch 1]

16 I was ever of opinion, that the honest man who married and brought up a large family, did more service than he who continued single and only talked of population. [*Vicar of Wakefield* ch 1]

17 It seemed to me pretty plain, that they had more of love than matrimony in them. [*Vicar of Wakefield* ch 16]

18 When lovely woman stoops to folly / And finds too late that men betray, / What charm can soothe her melancholy, / What art can wash her guilt away? [*Vicar of Wakefield* ch 29]

19 She Stoops to Conquer. [Play title]

GOLDWYN Samuel 1882–1974
US film producer.

1 Pictures are for entertainment, messages should be delivered by Western Union. [Quoted in A Marx *Goldwyn*]

US film producer Sam Goldwyn became one of the most powerful figures in Hollywood during its golden age. Many stars, including Gary Cooper, Danny Kaye, and David Niven, began their screen careers in Goldwyn's studios.

2 Gentlemen, include me out. [*Goldwyn Touch*]

3 A verbal contract isn't worth the paper it is written on. [Quoted in A Johnston *Great Goldwyn*]

4 Any man who goes to a psychiatrist should have his head examined. [Quoted in N Zierold *Moguls*]

GONCOURT Edmond de 1822–1896 and Jules Huot de 1830–1870
French writers.

1 As a general truth, it is safe to say that any picture that produces a moral impression is a bad picture. [*Goncourt Journals* 7 Dec 1860]

2 Man is a mind betrayed, not served, by his organs. [*Goncourt Journals* 30 July 1861]

3 A book is never a masterpiece: it becomes one. Genius is the talent of a dead man. [*Goncourt Journals* 23 July 1864]

GONNE Maud 1865–1953
Irish actress and feminist.

Poets should never marry. The world should thank me for not marrying you. [On her refusal to marry W B Yeats. Quoted in N Cardozo *Maud Gonne*]

GORBACHEV Mikhail 1931–
Soviet president.

1 No party has a monopoly over what is right. [Quoted in *Observer* March 2 1986]

2 Sometimes ... when you stand face to face with someone, you cannot see his face. [Press conference after summit meeting with US president Reagan, Iceland, 12 Oct 1986]

3 The market came with the dawn of civilization and is not the invention of capitalism. If the market leads to the improvement of people's daily lives, then there is no contradiction with socialism. [Rebutting the complaints of his conservative rivals that he was attempting to restore capitalism in the Soviet Union, June 1990]

GORDIMER Nadine 1923–
South African writer.

Censorship ... is a brand on the imagination that affects the individual who has suffered it, forever. [Address to Writer's day conference, London, June 1990: 'Censorship and its Aftermath']

GORDON Adam Lindsay 1833–1870
Australian poet.

1 Life is mostly froth and bubble, / Two things stand like stone, / Kindness in another's trouble, / Courage in your own. [*Ye Wearie Wayfarer*]

2 Yet if once we efface the joys of the chase / From the land, and outroot the Stud, / Goodbye to the Anglo-Saxon race! / Farewell to the Norman blood! [Ye Wearie Wayfarer]

GORER Geoffrey 1905–1985
English writer and anthropologist.

The trouble with my wife is that she is a whore in the kitchen and a cook in bed. [*Exploring the British Character*]

GORKY Maxim 1868–1936
Russian dramatist and writer.

When a woman gets married it is like jumping into a hole in the ice in the middle of winter; you do it once and you remember it the rest of your days. [*Lower Depths*]

GOULD Stephen Jay 1941–
US palaeontologist and author.

Science is all those things which are confirmed to such a degree that it would be unreasonable to withhold one's provisional consent. [*Lecture on Evolution*]

GOURMONT Rémy de 1858–1915
French poet, novelist and critic.

1 Aesthetic emotion puts man in a state favourable to the reception of erotic emotion. Art is the accomplice of love. Take love away and there is no longer art. [*Decadence*]

2 All existence is a theft paid for by other existences; no life flowers except on a cemetery. ['Dissociation of Ideas']

GOWER John c. 1330–1408
English poet.

It hath and schal ben evermor / That love is maister wher he wile. [*Confessio Amantis*, prologue]

GRAHAM Harry 1874–1936
English writer and journalist.

1 'There's been an accident,' they said, / 'Your servant's cut in half; he's dead!' / 'Indeed!' said Mr Jones, 'and please, / Send me the half that's got my keys.' ['Mr Jones']

2 Billy, in one of his nice new sashes, / Fell in the fire and was burnt to ashes; / Now, although the room grows chilly, / I haven't the heart to poke poor Billy. ['Tender-Heartedness']

3 Last night I slew my wife, / Stretched her on the parquet flooring: / I was loth to take her life, / But I *had* to stop her snoring. [*When Grandma Fell off the Boat*, 'Necessity']

GRAHAM Martha 1894–1991
US dancer and choreographer.

No artist is ahead of his time. He *is* his time; it is just that others are behind the times. [*Observer Magazine* 8 July 1979]

GRAHAME Kenneth 1859–1932
Scottish author.

1 Believe me, my young friend, there is *nothing* – absolutely nothing – half so much worth doing as simply messing about in boats. [*Wind in the Willows* ch 2]

2 The clever men at Oxford / Know all that there is to be knowed. / But they none of them know one half as much / As intelligent Mr Toad! [*Wind in the Willows* ch 10]

GRANT Ulysses S 1822–1885
US Republican president.

I know no method to secure the repeal of bad or obnoxious laws so effective as their stringent execution. [Inaugural Address 4 March 1869]

GRANVILLE George, Baron Lansdowne 1666–1735
English poet and dramatist.

Of all pains, the greatest pain / Is to love, and love in vain. ['Happiest mortals once we were']

GRASS Günther 1927–
German writer.

Art is so wonderfully irrational, exuberantly pointless, but necessary all the same. Pointless and yet nec-essary, that's hard for a puritan to understand. [Interview in *New Statesman and Society* 22 June 1990]

2 Believing: it means believing in our own lies. And I can say that I am grateful that I got this lesson very early. ['Omnibus', BBC TV, 3 Nov 1992]

GRAVES Robert 1895–1985
English poet and author.

1 In love as in sport, the amateur status must be strictly maintained. [*Occupation: Writer*]

2 As you are woman, so be lovely: / As you are lovely, so be various, / Merciful as constant, constant as various, / So be mine, as I yours for ever. ['Pygmalion to Galatea']

3 Why have such scores of lovely, gifted girls / Married impossible men? ['Slice of the Wedding Cake']

4 Love is a universal migraine, / A bright stain on the vision / Blotting out reason. ['Symptoms of Love']

5 Goodbye to All That. [Title of autobiography]

GRAY Thomas 1716–1771
English poet.

1 Youth on the prow, and Pleasure at the helm. ['The Bard']

2 The curfew tolls the knell of parting day, / The lowing herd winds slowly o'er the lea, / The ploughman homeward plods his weary way, / And leaves the world to darkness and to me. ['Elegy Written in a Country Churchyard' 1]

3 Each in his narrow cell for ever laid, / The rude forefathers of the hamlet sleep. ['Elegy Written in a Country Churchyard' 4]

4 The short and simple annals of the poor. ['Elegy Written in a Country Churchyard' 8]

5 The paths of glory lead but to the grave. ['Elegy Written in a Country Churchyard' 9]

6 Full many a flower is born to blush unseen, / And waste its sweetness on the desert air. / Some village-Hampden, that with dauntless breast / The little tyrant of his fields withstood; / Some mute inglorious Milton here may rest, / Some Cromwell guiltless of his country's blood. ['Elegy Written in a Country Churchyard' 14–15]

7 Far from the madding crowd's ignoble strife, / Their sober wishes never learn'd to stray; / Along the cool sequester'd vale of life / They kept the noiseless tenor of their way. ['Elegy Written in a Country Churchyard' 19]

8 A youth to fortune and to fame unknown. ['Elegy Written in a Country Churchyard' 30]

9 And weep the more because I weep in vain. ['Sonnet on the Death of Richard West']

GREELEY Horace 1811–1872
US editor, publisher, and politician.

Go West, young man, and grow up with the country. [*Hints toward Reform*]

GREENE Graham 1904–1991
English novelist.

1 Those who marry God ... can become domesticated too – it's just as humdrum a marriage as all the others. [*Burnt-Out Case* ch 1]

2 Against the beautiful and the clever and the successful, one can wage a pitiless war, but not against the unattractive. [*Heart of the Matter* bk 1, pt 1, ch 2]

3 In human relations, kindness and lies are worth a thousand truths. [*Heart of the Matter* bk 1, pt 2, ch 2]

4 He felt the loyalty we all feel to unhappiness – the sense that that is where we really belong. [*Heart of the Matter* bk 3, pt 2, ch 2]

5 Have you seen a room from which faith has gone? ... Like a marriage from which love has gone ... And patience, patience everywhere like a fog. [*Potting Shed*]

6 If only it were possible to love without injury – fidelity isn't enough ... The hurt is in the act of possession: we are too small in mind and body to possess another person without pride or to be possessed without humiliation. [*Quiet American* pt 2, ch 3]

7 God ... created a number of possibilities in case some of his prototypes failed – that is the meaning of evolution. [*Travels With My Aunt* pt 2, ch 7]

GREENE Robert c. 1560–1592
English poet and dramatist.

Ah! what is love! It is a pretty thing, / As sweet unto a shepherd as a king. ['Shepherd's Wife's Song']

GREER Germaine 1939–
Australian-born British feminist and writer.

1 *Love* is the drug which makes sexuality palatable in popular mythology. [*Female Eunuch*]

2 Love, love, love–all the wretched cant of it, masking egotism, lust, masochism, fantasy under a mythology of sentimental postures, a welter of self-induced miseries and joys, blinding and masking the essential personalities in the frozen gestures of courtship, in the kissing and the dating and the desire, the compliments and the quarrels which vivify its barrenness. [*Female Eunuch*]

3 Mother is the dead heart of the family, spending father's earnings on consumer goods to enhance the environment in which he eats, sleeps, and watches the television. [*Female Eunuch*, 'Obsession']

4 I love men like some people like good food or wine. [Quoted in *Observer* 18 Feb 1979]

The Australian feminist Germaine Greer came to prominence in the 1970s with her polemical study *The Female Eunuch*, which argues that women have to determine their own social and sexual identity 1984, in which she argued that sexual liberation was often to women's detriment. Greer has also written on Shakespeare and on the nature of ageing.

5 Human beings have an inalienable right to invent themselves; when that right is pre-empted it is called brain-washing. [*The Times* 1 Feb 1986]

GRENFELL Joyce 1910–1975
English entertainer.

George – don't do that. [Catch-phrase]

GREY Sir Edward 1862–1933
British Liberal politician.

The lamps are going out all over Europe; we shall not see them lit again in our lifetime. [On the impending war 3 Aug 1914 *Twenty-Five Years*]

GROPIUS Walter Adolf 1883–1969
German architect who lived in the USA from 1937.

The human mind is like an umbrella – it functions best when open. [*Observer* 1965]

GROSSMITH George *the Younger* 1874–1935
English actor, singer and songwriter.

If you were the only girl in the world, / And I were the only boy. ['If you were the Only Girl']

GROSSMITH George 1847–1912 and Weedon 1854–1919
English writers and entertainers.

1 What's the good of a home if you are never in it? [*Diary of a Nobody* ch 1]

2 I left the room with silent dignity, but caught my foot in the mat. [*Diary of a Nobody* ch 12]

GROTIUS Hugo 1583–1645
Dutch jurist and politician.

Not to know something is a great part of wisdom. [*Doctu Ignorantia*]

GUDMUNDSDOTTIR Björk 1966–
Icelandic pop singer.

I think I was lucky – I was loved but not brought up. [Remark on her unconventional childhood]

GUEDALLA Philip 1889–1944
English writer and historian.

1 The work of Henry James has always seemed divisible by a simple dynastic arrangement into three reigns; James I, James II, and the Old Pretender. [*Supers and Supermen*, 'Some Critics']

2 History repeats itself. Historians repeat each other. [*Supers and Supermen*, 'Some Historians']

GUITRY Sacha 1885–1957
French actor and dramatist.

1 When a man steals your wife,

there is no better revenge than to let him keep her. [*Elles et toi*]

2 The others were only my wives. But you, my dear, will be my widow. [To his fifth wife. Attributed remark *c.* 1950]

GULBENKIAN Nubar 1896–1972
British-born Turkish oil magnate.

The best number for a dinner party is two – myself and a dam' good head waiter. [*Daily Telegraph* 14 Jan 1965]

GUMILEV Nikolai 1886–1921
Russian poet.

Fine is the wine that is in love with us, and the goodly bread that goes into the oven for our sake, and the woman whom we enjoy, after she has tormented us to the full. ['Tram that Lost its Way']

GURDJIEFF George *c.* 1877–1949
Greek-Armenian mystic and teacher.

1 A considerable percentage of the people we meet on the street are people who are empty inside, that is, they are actually *already dead* ... . If we knew what a number of people are already dead and what a number of these dead people govern our lives, we should go mad with horror. [Quoted in P D Ouspensky *In Search of the Miraculous* ch 8]

2 A man may be born, but in order to be born he must first die, and in order to die he must first awake. [Quoted in P D Ouspensky, *In Search of the Miraculous* ch 11]

HÂFIZ 1326–1390
Persian lyric poet.

> There is an ambush everywhere from the army of accidents; therefore the rider of life runs with loosened reins. [*Diwan*]

HAGGARD Rider 1856–1925
English writer.

> She who must be obeyed. [*She* ch 6. Catchphrase used by John Mortimer's 'Rumpole of the Bailey' to describe his wife]

HAIG Douglas, 1st Earl Haig 1861–1928
British army officer.

> D. is a very weak-minded fellow I am afraid, and, like the feather pillow, bears the marks of the last person who has sat on him! [Of the 17th Earl of Derby in a letter to Lady Haig 14 Jan 1918]

HALDEMAN H R 1926–
US politician.

> Once the toothpaste is out of the tube, it is awfully hard to get it back in. [Comment on the Watergate affair 1973]

HALL Jerry 1956–
US model and actress.

> My mother said it was simple to keep a man, you must be a maid in the living room, a cook in the kitchen and a whore in the bedroom. I said I'd hire the other two and take care of the bedroom bit. [Remark 1985]

HALL Peter 1930–
English theatre, opera, and film director.

> We do not necessarily improve with age: for better or worse we become more like ourselves. [*Observer* Jan 1988]

HALSEY Margaret 1910–
US writer.

> Englishwomen's shoes look as if they had been made by someone who had often heard shoes described but had never seen any. [*With Malice Toward Some*]

HAMERTON Philip Gilbert 1834–1894
English writer on art.

> The art of reading is to skip judiciously. [*Intellectual Life* pt 4]

HAMMARSKJÖLD Dag 1905–1961
Swedish UN Secretary-General.

> **1** A task becomes a duty from the moment you suspect it to be an essential part of that integrity which alone entitles a man to assume responsibility. [*Markings*, 'Night is Drawing Nigh']

> **2** We are not permitted to choose the frame of our destiny. But what we put into it is ours. [*Markings*, 'Night is Drawing Nigh']

> **3** The only kind of dignity which is genuine is that which is not diminished by the indifference of others. [*Markings*]

> **4** Perhaps a great love is never returned. [*Markings*]

HAMMERSTEIN Oscar 1895–1960
US songwriter.

> **1** You are the promised kiss of springtime that makes / the lonely winter seem long. / You are the breathless hush of evening that trembles / on the brink of a lovely song. ['All the Things You Are']

> **2** Some enchanted evening, / You may see a stranger, / You may see a stranger, / Across a crowded room. ['Some Enchanted Evening']

As secretary general 1953–61, Dag Hammarskjöld greatly increased the power and prestige of the UN, having the courage and determination to play a leading role in such major conflicts as the Korean War, the Suez Crisis, and the war in the Congo. His book of reflections, *Markings*, was published 1964.

3 Hello, Young Lovers, Wherever You Are. [Song title]

HANDS Terry 1941–
English stage director.

We may pretend that we're basically moral people who make mistakes, but the whole of history proves otherwise. [Remark]

HARBACH Otto 1873–1963
US songwriter.

When a lovely flame dies; smoke gets in your eyes. ['Smoke Gets in your Eyes']

HARBURG E Y (Yip) 1898–1981
US songwriter.

When I'm not near the girl I love, / I love the girl I'm near. ['When I'm Not Near the Girl I Love']

HARDING Warren G 1865–1923
US Republican president.

America's present need is not heroics, but healing; not nostrums but normalcy; not revolution, but restoration. [Speech at Boston 14 May 1920]

HARDY Thomas 1840–1928
English novelist and poet.

1 When the Present has latched its postern behind my tremulous stay, / And the May month flaps its glad green leaves like wings, / Delicate-filmed as new-spun silk, will the neighbours say, / 'He was a man who used to notice such things'? ['Afterwards']

2 Ah! stirring, times we live in – stirring times. [*Far From the Madding Crowd*]

3 It may be said that married men of forty are usually ready and generous enough to fling passing glances at any specimen of moderate beauty they may discern by the way. [*Far From the Madding Crowd*]

4 We two kept house, the Past and I. [*Ghost of the Past*]

5 Yonder a maid and her wight / Come whispering by: / War's annals will cloud into night / Ere their story die. ['In Time of 'The Breaking of Nations'']

6 The President of the Immortals (in Aschylean phrase) had ended his sport with Tess. [*Tess of the D'Urbervilles*]

7 'Good, but not religious-good.' [*Under the Greenwood Tree*]

8 Silent? Ah, he is silent! He can keep silence well. That man's silence is wonderful to listen to. [*Under the Greenwood Tree*]

9 This is the weather the cuckoo likes, / And so do I. ['Weathers']

HARINGTON John 1561–1612
English translator and author.

Treason doth never prosper: what's the reason? / For if it prosper, none dare call it treason. ['Of Treason']

HARRIS Joel Chandler 1848–1908
US author.

1 Tar-baby ain't sayin' nuthin', en Brer Fox, he lay low. [*Uncle Remus. Legends of the Old Plantation* ch 2]

2 Bred en bawn in a brier-patch! [*Uncle Remus. Legends of the Old Plantation* ch 4]

3 Hit look lak sparrer-grass, hit feel like sparrer-grass, hit tas'e lak sparrer-grass, en I bless ef 'taint sparrer-grass. [*Nights with Uncle Remus* ch 27]

HARRISON Paul 1936–
US dramatist and director.

The higher our income, the more resources we control and the more havoc we wreak. [*Guardian* 1 May 1992]

HART Lorenz 1895–1943
US songwriter.

When love congeals / It soon reveals / The faint aroma of performing seals, / The double crossing of a pair of heels. / I wish I were in love again. ['I Wish I Were in Love Again']

HARTLEY L P 1895–1972
English author.

The past is a foreign country: they do things differently there. [*Go-Between*, prologue]

HARVEY F W 1835–1901
English poet.

From troubles of the world / I turn to ducks / Beautiful comical things. ['Ducks']

HASSAN II 1930–
King of Morocco.

Morocco is like a tree nourished by roots deep in the soil of Africa which breathes through foliage rustling to the winds of Europe. [*The Challenge* 1979]

HAWES Stephen LIVED 1502–1521
English poet.

For though the day be never so longe, / At last the belles ringeth to evensonge. [*Passetyme of Pleasure*]

HAWKER Robert Stephen 1803–1875
English poet.

And have they fixed the where and when? / And shall Trelawny die? / Here's twenty thousand Cornish men / Will know the reason why! ['Song of the Western Men']

HAWKING Stephen 1942–
English physicist.

How can the complexity of the universe and all its trivial details be determined by a simple set of equations? Alternatively, can one really believe that God chose all the trivial details, like who should be on the cover of *Cosmospolitan*? [*Black Holes and Baby Universes*]

HAY Ian 1876–1952
Scottish novelist and dramatist.

In half an hour nothing is left and we take off our helmets, sniffing the morning air dubiously. But all we smell is the old mixture – corpses and chloride of lime. [*First Hundred Thousand*]

HAYLEY William 1745–1820
English poet.

She draws, she engraves, & sings delightfully & is so truly the Half of her good Man, that they seem animated by one Soul, & that a soul of indefatigable Industry & Benevolence. [Describing Kate Blake, wife of the poet and artist William Blake. Quoted in A Gilchrist *Life of William Blake*]

HAZLITT William 1778–1830
English essayist and critic.

1 It is well that there is no one without a fault; for he would not have a friend in the world. [*Characteristics: In the Manner of Rochefoucault's Maxims* no. 66]

2 His sayings are generally like women's letters; all the pith is in the postscript. [On Charles Lamb in *Conversations of Northcote*]

3 He talked on for ever; and you wished him to talk on for ever. [On Coleridge in *Lectures on the English Poets*]

4 A nickname is the heaviest stone that the devil can throw at a man. [*Sketches and Essays*, 'Nicknames']

5 We can scarcely hate any one that we know. [*Table Talk*, 'On Criticism']

6 When I am in the country I wish to vegetate like the country. [*Table Talk*, 'On Going a Journey']

HEATH Edward 1916–
British Conservative politician and prime minister.

It is the unpleasant and unacceptable face of capitalism. [On the Lonrho Scandal, *Hansard* 15 May 1973]

HECHT Ben 1893–1964
US writer and screenwriter.

I discovered early in my movie work that a movie is never any better than the stupidest man connected with it. [*Child of the Century* bk 5, 'Illustrations by Doré']

HEGEL Georg Wilhelm Friedrich 1770–1831
German philosopher.

The English have undertaken the weighty responsibility of being the missionaries of civilisation to the world ... [*Philosophy of History*]

HEISENBERG Werner Carl 1901–1976
German physicist.

An expert is someone who knows some of the worst mistakes that can be made in his subject and how to avoid them. [*Part and the Whole*]

HELLER Joseph 1923–
US novelist.

1 I'd like to see the government get out of war altogether and leave the whole field to private industry. [*Catch 22*]

2 Some men are born mediocre, some men achieve mediocrity, and some men have mediocrity thrust

US novelist Joseph Heller, best known for his anti-war novel *Catch 22* 1961. His later novels, often as bleakly pessimistic as *Catch 22*, include *God Knows* 1984, a lively retelling of the Old Testament story of King David, for which he was awarded the French Prix Medici Etranger 1985.

upon them. With Major Major it had been all three. [*Catch-22*]

3 There was only one catch and that was Catch-22, which specified that a concern for one's own safety in the face of dangers that were real and immediate was the process of a rational mind. [*Catch-22*]

HELLMAN Lillian 1907–1984
US dramatist.

1 Cynicism is an unpleasant way of saying the truth. [*Little Foxes*]

2 I cannot and will not cut my conscience to fit this year's fashions. [Letter to the House Un-American Activities Committee May 1952]

HEMANS Felicia Dorothea 1793–1835
English poet.

1 The boy stood on the burning deck / Whence all but he had fled. [*Casabianca*]

2 The stately homes of England, / How beautiful they stand! [*Homes of England*]

HEMINGWAY Ernest 1899–1961
US writer.

1 All good books are alike in that they are truer than if they had really happened and after you are finished reading one you will feel that all that happened to you and afterwards it all belongs to you. ['Old Newsman Writes: a Letter from Cuba', *Esquire* Dec 1934]

2 But did thee feel the earth move? [*For Whom the Bell Tolls* ch 13]

3 Cowardice, as distinguished from panic, is almost always simply a lack of ability to suspend the functioning of the imagination. [*Men at War*]

4 If you are lucky enough to have lived in Paris as a young man, then wherever you go for the rest of your life, it stays with you, for Paris is a movable feast. [*Movable Feast*]

5 Grace under pressure. [Defining 'guts' in interview with Dorothy Parker, *New Yorker* 30 Nov 1929]

6 A man can be destroyed but not defeated. [*Old Man and the Sea*]

7 The most essential gift for a good writer is a built-in, shock-proof shit detector. This is the writer's radar and all great writers have had it. [*Paris Review* Spring 1958]

HENLEY W E 1849–1903
English poet.

1 My head is bloody, but unbowed. ['Invictus']

2 Out of the night that covers me, / Black as the Pit from pole to pole, / I thank whatever gods may be / For my unconquerable soul. ['Invictus']

3 I am the master of my fate: / I am the captain of my soul. ['Invictus']

HENRI IV 1553–1610
King of France.

1 Hang yourself, brave Crillon; we fought at Arques and you were not there. [Traditional wording by Voltaire of a letter of Henri to Crillon]

2 Paris is well worth a mass. [Attributed remark on his conversion to Catholicism]

HENRI Adrian 1932–
English poet.

Love is a fanclub with only two fans. ['Love is ...']

HENRY VIII 1491–1547
King of England 1509–47.

My Lord, if it were not to satisfy the world, and my Realm, I would not do that I must do this day for none earthly thing. [Remark to Thomas Cromwell, on the day of his wedding to Anne of Cleves, 5 Jan 1540]

HENRY O 1862–1910
US writer.

1 If men knew how women pass the time when they are alone, they'd never marry. ['Memoirs of a Yellow Dog']

2 It was beautiful and simple as all truly great swindles are. ['Octopus Marooned']

3 Turn up the lights; I don't want to go home in the dark. [Last words]

HENRY Patrick 1736–1799
US politician.

1 Cæsar had his Brutus – Charles the First, his Cromwell – and George the Third – ('Treason,' cried the Speaker) ... may profit by their example. If this be treason, make the most of it. [Speech in the Virginia Convention 23 Mar 1765]

2 I know not what course others may take; but as for me, give me liberty, or give me death! [Speech in the Virginia Convention 23 Mar 1775]

HENRY William 1743–1805
English chemist.

Another damned, thick, square book! Always scribble, scribble, scribble! Eh! Mr. Gibbon? [*Best's Literary Memorials*]

HERACLITUS c. 544–483 BC
Greek philosopher.

1 All is flux, nothing is stationary. [Quoted in Aristotle *De Caelo*]

2 Change alone is unchanging. [*Herakleitos and Diogenes* pt 1, 23]

3 To do the same thing over and over again is not only boredom: it is to be controlled by rather than to control what you do. [*Herakleitos and Diogenes* pt 1, 89]

4 You could not step twice into the same river; for other waters are ever flowing on to you. [Quoted in Hippocrates, *On the Universe* 41]

HERBERT A P 1890–1971
English writer and politician.

1 The Farmer will never be happy again; / He carries his heart in his boots; / For either the rain is destroying his grain / Or the drought is destroying his roots. ['The Farmer']

2 The critical period in matrimony is breakfast-time. ['Is Marriage Lawful?']

3 Let's find out what everyone is doing, / And then stop everyone from doing it. ['Let's Stop Somebody']

4 Let's stop somebody from doing something! [*Let's Stop Somebody*]

5 The concept of two people living together for 25 years without having a cross word suggests a lack of spirit only to be admired in sheep. [Quoted in *News Chronicle* 1940]

6 Other people's babies – / That's my life! / Mother to dozens, / And nobody's wife. ['Other People's Babies']

7 This high official, all allow, / Is grossly overpaid. / There wasn't any Board; and now / There isn't any trade. ['President of the Board of Trade']

8 The Common Law of England has been laboriously built about a mythical figure – the figure of 'The Reasonable Man'. ['Reasonable Man']

9 Well, fancy giving money to the Government! / Might as well have put it down the drain. / Fancy giving money to the Government! / Nobody will see the stuff again. ['Too Much!']

10 Holy Deadlock. [Title of novel]

HERBERT Edward, Lord 1583–1648
English soldier, statesman, and philosopher.

Now that the April of your youth adorns / The garden of your face. ['Ditty: Now That the April']

HERBERT George 1593–1633
English poet.

1 Let all the world in ev'ry corner sing / My God and King. ['Antiphon']

2 Be calm in arguing; for fierceness makes Error a fault and truth discourtesy. [*Church Porch*]

3 Drink not the third glass, which thou canst not tame, / When once it is within thee. [*Church Porch* 5]

4 Love is swift of foot; / Love's a man of war, / And can shoot, / And can hit from far. ['Discipline']

5 Teach me, my God and King, / In all things Thee to see. ['Elixir']

6 Marry your son when you will; your daughter when you can. [*Jacula Prudentum* 149]

7 Love bade me welcome; yet my soul drew back, / Guilty of dust and sin. ['Love']

8 King of glory, King of peace, / I will love Thee. ['Praise']

9 Wit's an unruly engine, wildly striking / Sometimes a friend, sometimes the engineer. ['Temple: The Church Porch']

10 Sweet spring, full of sweet days and roses, / A box where sweets compacted lie. ['Virtue']

HERRICK Robert 1591–1674
English poet and cleric.

1 Cherry ripe, ripe, ripe, I cry, / Full and fair ones; come and buy. ['Cherry Ripe']

2 So when or you or I are made / A fable, song, or fleeting shade, / All love, all liking, all delight / Lies drowned with us in endless night. ['Corinna's Going A-Maying']

3 Fair daffodils, we weep to see / You haste away so soon. ['Daffodils']

4 A sweet disorder in the dress / Kindles in clothes a wantonness. ['Delight in Disorder']

5 It is the end that crowns us, not the fight. ['The End']

6 What is a kiss? Why this, as some approve: / The sure, sweet cement, glue and lime of love. ['Kiss']

7 Love is a circle that doth restless move / In the same sweet eternity of love. ['Love What It Is']

8 Bid me to live, and I will live / Thy Protestant to be: / Or bid me love, and I will give / A loving heart to thee. ['To Anthea, Who May Command Him Anything']

9 Sweet, be not proud of those two eyes, / Which star-like sparkle in their skies. ['To Dianeme']

10 Gather ye rosebuds while ye may, / Old Time is still a-flying: / And this same flower that smiles today, / To-morrow will be dying. ['To the Virgins, to Make Much of Time']

11 Then be not coy, but use your time; / And while ye may, go marry: / For having lost but once your prime, / You may for ever tarry. ['To the Virgins, to make much of Time']

12 When as in silks my Julia goes, / Then, then (methinks) how sweetly flows / That liquefaction of her clothes. ['Upon Julia's Clothes']

HEWART Gordon 1870–1943
English lawyer and politician.

It is not merely of some importance, but is of fundamental importance that justice should not only be done, but should manifestly and undoubtedly be seen to be done. [Rex v Sussex Justices 9 Nov 1923]

HICKSON William Edward 1803–1870
English educationalist.

If at first you don't succeed, / Try, try again. ['Try and Try Again']

HILL Christopher 1912–
English historian.

> Only very slowly and late have men come to realize that unless freedom is universal it is only extended privilege. [*Century of Revolution* ch 20]

HILL Rowland 1795–1879
English cleric.

> He did not see any reason why the devil should have all the good tunes. [E W Broome *Rev. Rowland Hill*]

HILLINGDON Lady Alice 1857–1940
Wife of 2nd Baron Hillingdon.

> I am happy now that Charles calls on my bedchamber less frequently than of old. As it is, I now endure but two calls a week and when I hear his steps outside my door I lie down on my bed, close my eyes, open my legs and think of England. [*Journal* 1912]

HILTON James 1900–1954
English novelist.

> Nothing really wrong with him – only anno domini, but that's the most fatal complaint of all, in the end. [*Goodbye, Mr Chips*]

HIPPONAX c. 570–520 BC
Greek poet.

> There are two days when a woman is a pleasure: the day one marries her and the day one buries her. [Fragment]

HITCHCOCK Alfred 1899–1980
English-born US film director.

> Television has brought back murder into the home – where it belongs. [*Observer* 19 Dec 1965]

HOAGLAND Edward 1932–
US writer.

> Like a kick in the butt, the force of events wakens slumberous talents. [*Guardian* 11 Aug 1990]

HOBBES Thomas 1588–1679
English political philosopher.

> **1** I am about to take my last voyage, a great leap in the dark. [Last words, quoted in Watkins *Anecdotes of Men of Learning*]

> **2** They that approve a private opinion, call it opinion; but they that mislike it, heresy: and yet heresy signifies no more than private opinion. [*Leviathan* pt 1, ch 11]

> **3** No arts; no letters; no society; and which is worst of all, continual fear and danger of violent death; and the life of man, solitary, poor, nasty, brutish, and short. [*Leviathan* pt 1, ch 13]

Suspense, melodrama, and fleeting personal appearances are the hallmarks of Alfred Hitchcock's films. A meticulous director, a supreme technician and visual artist, Hitchcock contributed significantly to the growth of cinema as an art form.

4 The Papacy is not other than the Ghost of the deceased Roman Empire, sitting crowned upon the grave thereof. [*Leviathan* pt 4, ch 47]

HOCKNEY David 1937–
English artist.

If we are to change our world view, images have to change. The artist now has a very important job to do. He's not just a little peripheral figure entertaining rich people, he's really needed. [*Hockney on Photography*, 'New York: September 1986']

HODGSON Ralph 1871–1962
English poet.

1 'Twould ring the bells of Heaven / The wildest peal for years, / If Parson lost his senses / And people came to theirs, / And he and they together / Knelt down with angry prayers / For tamed and shabby tigers / And dancing dogs and bears, / And wretched, blind, pit ponies, / And little hunted hares. ['Bells of Heaven']

2 Time, you old gypsy man, / Will you not stay, / Put up your caravan / Just for one day? ['Time, You Old Gypsy Man']

HOFFA Jimmy 1913–c. 1975
US labour leader.

An ego is just imagination. And if a man doesn't have imagination he'll be working for someone else for the rest of his life. [*Esquire*]

HOFFER Eric 1902–1983
US philosopher.

1 The individual who has to justify his existence by his own efforts is in eternal bondage to himself. [*Ordeal of Change* ch 5]

2 It is the awareness of unfulfilled desires which gives a nation the feeling that it has a mission and a destiny. [*Passionate State of Mind* 24]

3 We do not really feel grateful toward those who make our dreams come true; they ruin our dreams. [*Passionate State of Mind* 232]

4 The world leans on us. When we sag, the whole world seems to droop. [*Passionate State of Mind* 237]

5 Absolute faith corrupts as absolutely as absolute power. [*Reflections on the Human Condition* 13]

6 There are no chaste minds. Minds copulate whenever they meet. [*Reflections on the Human Condition* 142]

HOFFMAN Heinrich 1809–1874
German writer.

1 Anything to me is sweeter / Than to see Shock-headed Peter. ['*Shock-Headed Peter*']

2 But fidgety Phil, / He won't sit still; / He wriggles / And giggles, / And then, I declare, / Swings backwards and forwards, / And tilts up his chair. ['Fidgety Philip']

3 Look at little Johnny there, / Little Johnny Head-In-Air! ['Johnny Head-in-Air']

HOGG James 1770–1835
Scottish novelist and poet.

1 Will you no come back again? ['Will You No Come Back Again']

2 And Charlie he's my darling, / My darling, my darling. ['The Young Chevalier']

HOLIDAY Billie 1915–1959
US jazz singer.

Mom and Pop were just a couple of kids when they got married. He was eighteen, she was sixteen, and I was three. [*Lady Sings the Blues*]

HOLMES John Oliver 1867–1906
English novelist.

> A woman would no doubt need a great deal of imagination to love a man for his virtue. [*Sinner's Comedy*]

HOLMES Oliver Wendell 1809–1894
US writer and physician.

> **1** Put not your trust in money, but put your money in trust. [*Autocrat of the Breakfast Table* ch 2]
>
> **2** To be seventy years young is sometimes far more cheerful and hopeful than to be forty years old. ['On the Seventieth Birthday of Julia Ward Howe']
>
> **3** It is the province of knowledge to speak and it is the privilege of wisdom to listen. [*Poet at the Breakfast Table*]
>
> **4** A moment's insight is sometimes worth a life's experience. [*Poet at the Breakfast Table*]
>
> **5** And, when you stick on conversation's burrs, / Don't strew your pathway with those dreadful urs. ['Rhymed Lesson']

HOMER LIVED 8TH CENTURY BC
Greek poet.

> May the gods grant you all things which your heart desires, and may they give you a husband and a home and gracious concord, for there is nothing greater and better than this – when a husband and wife keep a household in oneness of mind, a great woe to their enemies. [*Odyssey* bk VI]

HONEGGER Arthur 1892–1955
French composer.

> There is no doubt that the first requirement for a composer is to be dead. [*I Am a Composer*]

HOOD Thomas 1799–1845
English poet and humorist.

> **1** There are three things which the public will always clamour for, sooner or later: namely, Novelty, novelty, novelty. [*Announcement of Comic Annual for 1836*]
>
> **2** They went and told the sexton, and / The sexton toll'd the bell. ['Faithless Sally Brown']
>
> **3** I remember, I remember, / The house where I was born. ['I Remember']
>
> **4** It was the time of roses, / We plucked them as we passed! ['It Was Not in the Winter']
>
> **5** For that old enemy the gout / Had taken him in toe! ['Lieutenant Luff']
>
> **6** When Eve upon the first of Men / The apple press'd with specious cant / Oh! What a thousand pities then / That Adam was not adamant. ['Reflection']
>
> **7** Oh! God! that bread should be so dear, / And flesh and blood so cheap! ['Song of the Shirt']

HOOVER Herbert 1874–1964
US Republican president.

> **1** When there is a lack of honour in government, the morals of the whole people are poisoned. [*New York Times* 9 Aug 1964]
>
> **2** The American system of rugged individualism. [Campaign speech 1928]

HOPE Anthony 1863–1933
English novelist.

> **1** 'Boys will be boys ' / 'And even that ... wouldn't matter if we could only prevent girls from being girls.' [*Dolly Dialogues*]
>
> **2** He is very fond of making things which he doesn't want, and then giving them to people who have no use for them. [*Dolly Dialogues*]
>
> **3** 'I wish you would read a little poetry sometimes. Your ignorance cramps my conversation.' [*Dolly Dialogues*]

4 'You oughtn't to yield to temptation.' / 'Well, somebody must, or the thing becomes absurd.' [*Dolly Dialogues*]

HOPKINS Gerard Manley 1844–1889
English poet and Jesuit priest.

1 Not, I'll not, carrion comfort, Despair, not feast on thee. ['Carrion Comfort']

2 The world is charged with the grandeur of God. ['God's Grandeur']

3 I have desired to go / Where springs not fail, / To fields where flies no sharp and sided hail / And a few lilies blow. / And I have asked to be / Where no storms come, / Where the green swell is in the havens dumb, / And out of the swing of the sea. ['Heaven-Haven']

4 What would the world be, once bereft / Of wet and of wildness? Let them be left, / O let them be left, wildness and wet; / Long live the weeds and the wilderness yet. ['Inversnaid']

5 Glory be to God for dappled things. ['Pied Beauty']

HORACE 65–8 BC
Roman lyric poet and satirist.

1 But if worthy Homer nods for a moment, I think it a disgrace. [*Ars Poetica*]

2 Mountains will be in labour, the birth will be a ridiculous mouse. [*Ars Poetica*]

3 Anger is a short madness. [*Epistles* I. 2]

4 Dare to be wise. [*Epistles* I. 2]

5 If you drive out nature with a pitchfork, she will soon find a way back. [*Epistles* I. 10]

6 Life's short span forbids us to embark on far-reaching hopes. [*Odes* I. 4]

7 Seize the day. [*Odes* I. 11]

8 Happy, thrice happy and more, are they whom an unbroken bond unites and whose love shall know no sundering quarrels so long as they shall live. [*Odes* I. 13]

9 Alas, Postumus, the fleeting years slip by. [*Odes* II. 14]

10 I hate the profane crowd. [*Odes* III. 1]

11 It is a sweet and becoming thing to die for one's country. [*Odes* III. 2]

12 I have raised a memorial more enduring than brass. [*Odes* III. 30]

HORROCKS Sir Brian Gwynne 1895–1985
British general in World War II.

1 The British Army always fights uphill, in the rain, at the junction of two maps. [*Lieutenant-General Sir Brian Horrocks*]

2 There was no room for manoeuvre and no scope for cleverness; I had to blast my way through three defensive systems, the centre of which was the Siegfried Line. [Remark on his tactics in the battle for the Reichswald forest 1945]

HOUSMAN A E 1859–1936
English scholar and poet.

1 What God abandoned, these defended, / And saved the sum of things for pay. ['Epitaph on an Army of Mercenaries']

2 I know not if it rains, my love, / In the land where you do lie; / And oh, so sound you sleep, my love, / You know no more than I. ['Half-Moon Westers Low']

3 We'll to the woods no more, / The laurels all are cut. [*Last Poems* introductory]

4 The troubles of our proud and angry dust / Are from eternity, and shall not fail. [*Last Poems* 9]

5 I, a stranger and afraid / In a world I never made. [*Last Poems* 12]

127

6 Loveliest of trees, the cherry now / Is hung with bloom along the bough, / And stands about the woodland ride / Wearing white for Eastertide. [*Shropshire Lad* 2]

7 When I was one-and-twenty / I heard a wise man say, / 'Give crowns and pounds and guineas / But not your heart away.' [*Shropshire Lad* 13]

8 Oh, when I was in love with you, / Then I was clean and brave, / And miles around the wonder grew / How well did I behave. And now the fancy passes by, / And nothing will remain, / And miles around they'll say that I / Am quite myself again. [*Shropshire Lad* 18]

9 Here of a Sunday morning / My love and I would lie, / And see the coloured counties, / And hear the larks so high / About us in the sky. [*Shropshire Lad* 21]

10 The lads that will die in their glory and never be old. [*Shropshire Lad* 23]

11 Is my team ploughing, / That I was used to drive? [*Shropshire Lad* 27]

12 That is the land of lost content, / I see it shining plain, / The happy highways where I went / And cannot come again. [*Shropshire Lad* 40]

13 Malt does more than Milton can, / To justify God's ways to man. [*Shropshire Lad* 62]

14 This great College, of this ancient University, has seen some strange sights. It has seen Wordsworth drunk and Porson sober. And here am I, a better poet than Porson, and a better scholar than Wordsworth, betwixt and between. [Speech at Trinity College, Cambridge]

HOWARD Sidney 1891–1939
US dramatist and screenwriter.

Frankly, my dear, I don't give a damn. [*Gone With the Wind* 1939. Words spoken by Clark Gable as Rhett Butler]

HOWE Julia Ward 1819–1910
US feminist and antislavery campaigner.

Mine eyes have seen the glory of the coming of the Lord: / He is trampling out the vintage where the grapes of wrath are stored. ['Battle Hymn of the American Republic']

HOWITT Mary 1799–1888
English writer.

'Will you walk into my parlour?' said a spider to a fly. ['Spider and the Fly']

English astronomer Fred Hoyle. Together with Hermann Bondi and Thomas Gold, in 1948 Hoyle proposed the steady state theory of the universe as an alternative to the Big Bang theory, arguing that the large scale universe is unchanging. The theory avoided the problem of explaining how the universe began, but is now generally regarded as incorrect.

HOYLE Fred 1915–
English astronomer and writer.

> Space isn't remote at all. It's only an hour's drive away if your car could go straight upwards. [*Observer* Sept 1979]

HUBBARD Elbert 1856–1915
US writer.

> **1** Never explain – your friends do not need it and your enemies will not believe you anyway. [*Motto Book*]
>
> **2** Little minds are interested in the extraordinary; great minds in the commonplace. [*Thousand and One Epigrams*]
>
> **3** Life is just one damned thing after another. [*Thousand and One Epigrams*]
>
> **4** One machine can do the work of fifty ordinary men. No machine can do the work of one extraordinary man. [*Thousand and One Epigrams*]

HUGHES Thomas 1822–1896
English writer.

> Life isn't all beer and skittles. [*Tom Brown's Schooldays* pt 1, ch 2]

HUME David 1711–1776
Scottish philosopher.

> **1** The usual propensity of mankind towards the marvellous. [*Enquiry Concerning Human Understanding*, 'On Miracles']
>
> **2** Custom, then, is the great guide of human life. [*Enquiry Concerning Human Understanding* sec 5, pt I]
>
> **3** Avarice, the spur of industry. [*Essays: Moral and Political*, 'Of Civil Liberty']
>
> **4** The Christian religion not only was at first attended with miracles, but even at this day cannot be believed by any reasonable person without one. [*Essays: Moral and Political*, 'Of Civil Liberty']

HUMPHREY Hubert 1911–1978
US Democratic vice president.

> **1** Freedom is the most contagious virus known to man. [Speech, New York City, 29 Oct 1964]
>
> **2** As we begin to comprehend that the earth itself is a kind of manned spaceship hurtling through the infinity of space – it will seem increasingly absurd that we have not better organized the life of the human family. [Speech at San Fernando State College 26 Sept 1966]

HUMPHRIES Barry *Dame Edna Everidge* 1934–
Australian entertainer.

> Those extraordinary euphemisms for vomiting - parking the tiger, yodelling on the lawn, the technicolour yawn, the liquid laugh. [*From Fringe to Flying Circus*]

HUNT G W 1829–1904
English writer.

> We don't want to fight, but, by jingo if we do, / We've got the ships, we've got the men, we've got the money too. [Music hall song]

HUPFELD Herman 1894–1951
US songwriter.

> It's still the same old story, / A fight for love and glory, / A case of do or die! / The world will always welcome lovers / As time goes by. ['As Time Goes By']

HUSS John 1373–1415
Bohemian reformer.

> O holy simplicity! [Attributed remark at the stake, on an old peasant who was bringing wood to throw on the pile]

HUXLEY Aldous 1894–1963
English novelist.

> **1** There are few who would not rather be taken in adultery than in provincialism. [*Antic Hay*]

English writer Aldous Huxley. He began by writing social satires such as *Antic Hay* 1923 and then moved on to novels of ideas, the best known of which, *Brave New World* 1932, is a futuristic novel about a world made inhuman by science. His later writings are concerned increasingly with mysticism and include accounts of his experiences with hallucinogenic drugs.

5 Consistency is contrary to nature, contrary to life. The only completely consistent people are the dead. [*Do What You Will*, 'Wordsworth in the Tropics']

6 Man approaches the unattainable truth through a series of errors. [*Do What You Will*, 'Wordsworth in the Tropics']

7 So long as men worship the Caesars and Napoleons, Caesars and Napoleons will duly arise and make them miserable. [*Ends and Means*]

8 Specialized meaninglessness has come to be regarded, in certain circles, as a kind of hallmark of true science. [*Ends and Means* ch 14]

9 What we feel and think and are is to a great extent determined by the state of our ductless glands and viscera. [*Music at Night*, 'Meditation on El Greco']

10 A bad book is as much of a labour to write as a good one; it comes as sincerely from the author's soul. [*Point Counter Point* ch 13]

11 There is no substitute for talent. Industry and all the virtues are of no avail. [*Point Counter Point* ch 13]

12 Brought up in an epoch when ladies apparently rolled along on wheels, Mr Quarles was peculiarly susceptible to calves. [*Point Counter Point* ch 20]

13 Facts do not cease to exist because they are ignored. [*Proper Studies*, 'Note on Dogma']

14 I'm afraid of losing my obscurity. Genius only thrives in the dark. Like celery. [*Those Barren Leaves* pt 1, ch 1]

2 If the world had any ends British Honduras would certainly be one of them. [On Belize (formerly British Honduras) in *Beyond the Mexique Bay*]

3 Official dignity tends to increase in inverse ratio to the importance of the country in which the office is held. [*Beyond the Mexique Bay*]

4 That men do not learn very much from the lessons of history is the most important of all the lessons that history has to teach. [*Collected Essays*, 'Case of Voluntary Ignorance']

HUXLEY Julian 1887–1975
English biologist.

Operationally, God is beginning to resemble not a ruler but the last fading smile of a cosmic Cheshire cat. [*Religion without Revelation*]

Huxley Thomas Henry 1825–1895
English scientist and humanist.

1 Irrationally held truths may be more harmful than reasoned errors. [*Science and Culture,* 'The Coming of Age of the Origin of Species']

2 It is the customary fate of new truths to begin as heresies and to end as superstitions. [*Science and Culture,* 'The Coming of Age of the Origin of Species']

3 Logical consequences are the scarecrows of fools and the beacons of wise men. [*Science and Culture,* 'On the Hypothesis that Animals are Automata']

I

IBARRURI Dolores *La Pasionaria*
1895–1989
Spanish Basque politician, journalist, and orator.

It is better to die on your feet than to live on your knees. [Speech in Paris 3 Sept 1936]

IBSEN Henrik 1828–1906
Norwegian dramatist and poet.

1 Our house has never been anything but a playroom. I have been your doll wife, just as at home I was father's doll child. And the children in turn have been my dolls. I thought it was fun when you came and played with me, just as they thought it was fun when I went and played with them. That's been our marriage, Torvald. [*A Doll's House* III]

2 The minority is always right. [*Enemy of the People* IV]

3 One should never put on one's best trousers to go out to battle for freedom and truth. [*Enemy of the People* V]

4 Castles in the air – they are so easy to take refuge in. And so easy to build, too. [*Master Builder*]

5 What ought a man to be? Well, my short answer is "himself". [*Peer Gynt* IV]

ILLICH Ivan 1926–
Austrian-born US radical philosopher and activist.

In a consumer society there are inevitably two kinds of slaves: the prisoners of addiction and the prisoners of envy. [*Tools for Conviviality* ch 3]

INGE William 1860–1954
English dean.

1 The effect of boredom on a large scale in history is underestimated. It is a main cause of revolutions, and would soon bring to an end all the static Utopias and the farmyard civilization of the Fabians. [*End of an Age*]

2 To become a popular religion, it is only necessary for a superstition to enslave a philosophy. [*Idea of Progress*]

3 Many people believe that they are attracted by God, or by Nature, when they are only repelled by man. [*More Lay Thoughts of a Dean*]

4 It takes in reality only one to make a quarrel. It is useless for the sheep to pass resolutions in favour of vegetarianism, while the wolf remains of a different opinion. [*Outspoken Essays: First Series*, 'Patriotism']

5 A man may build himself a throne of bayonets, but he cannot sit on it. [Quoted in Marchant *Wit and Wisdom of Dean Inge*]

INGERSOLL Robert G 1833–1899
US lawyer and agnostic.

1 An honest God is the noblest work of man. [*Gods* pt I]

2 In nature there are neither rewards nor punishments – there are consequences. [*Lectures and Essays*, 'Some Reasons Why']

3 I had rather live and love where death is king, than have eternal life where love is not. [*Oration at a Child's Grave*]

INNOCENT III 1161–1216
Pope from 1198.

Greediness closed Paradise; it beheaded John the Baptist. [*De Contemptu Mundi*]

IONESCO Eugène 1912–1994
Romanian-born French dramatist.

1 Suffering and fear are born from the repression of the death wish. [*Fragments of a Journal* 56]

2 A work of art is above all an adventure of the mind. [*Notes and Counter-Notes* pt 2, 'An Address Delivered to a Gathering of French and German Writers']

3 There is no religion in which everyday life is not considered a prison; there is no philosophy or ideology that does not think that we live in alienation. [*Present Past – Past Present* ch 5]

IRISH PROVERB

Twenty years a child; twenty years running wild; twenty years a mature man – and after that, praying.

IRVING Washington 1783–1859
US essayist and short-story writer.

1 A woman's whole history is a history of the affections. [*Sketch Book*, 'Broken Heart']

2 I am always at a loss to know how much to believe of my own stories. [*Tales of a Traveller*]

3 The almighty dollar, that great object of universal devotion throughout our land, seems to have no genuine devotees in these peculiar villages. [*Wolfert's Roost*, 'The Creole Village']

IVAN IV *the Terrible* 1530–1584
Tsar of Russia..

Did I ascend the throne by robbery or armed bloodshed? I was born to rule by the grace of God ... I grew up upon the throne. [Letter to Prince Kurbsky Sept 1577]

J

JACKSON Holbrook 1874–1948
English bibliophile and literary historian.

> Pedantry is the dotage of knowledge. [*Anatomy of Bibliomania*]

JACKSON Jesse 1941–
US clergyman, politician, and civil rights leader.

> We've removed the ceiling above our dreams. There are no more impossible dreams. [*Independent* 9 June 1988]

JACKSON Robert 1892–1954
US judge.

> It is not the function of our Government to keep the citizen from falling into error; it is the function of the citizen to keep the Government from falling into error. [*American Communications Association v. Douds* May 1950]

JACOBS Joe 1896–1940
US boxing manager

> We was robbed! [Remark following Max Schmeling's defeat in the heavyweight title fight 21 June 1932]

JACOBSON Howard 1942–
English broadcaster and writer.

> She was no different from all other mothers, (how could she be?) in that while she wanted men, in a general way, to be married, she didn't want me, in a specific way, to have a wife. [*Peeping Tom* pt 1 ch 7]

JAMES Clive 1939–
Australian writer and critic.

> All television ever did was shrink the demand for ordinary movies. The demand for extraordinary movies increased. If any one thing is wrong with the movie industry today, it is the unrelenting effort to astonish. [*Observer* 16 June 1979]

JAMES Henry 1843–1916
US novelist, naturalized British 1915.

> 1   The deep well of unconscious cerebration. [*The American*, preface]

> 2   Experience … is an immense sensibility, a kind of huge spiderweb of the finest silken threads suspended in the chamber of consciousness, and catching every air-borne particle in its tissue. [*Art of Fiction*]

> 3   What is character but the determination of incident? What is incident but the illustration of character? [*Art of Fiction*]

> 4   The historian, essentially, wants more documents than he can really use; the dramatist only wants more liberties than he can really take. [*Aspern Papers*, preface]

> 5   It takes a great deal of history to produce a little literature. [*Life of Nathaniel Hawthorne*]

> 6   Cats and monkeys – monkeys and cats – all human life is there! [*Madonna of the Future*]

> 7   The only reason for the existence of a novel is that it does attempt to represent life. [*Partial Portraits*, 'Art of Fiction']

> 8   We work in the dark – we do what we can – we give what we have. Our doubt is our passion and our passion is our task. The rest is the madness of art. [*Scribner's* May 1893, 'The Middle Years']

JAMES P D 1920–
English novelist.

> **1** God gives every bird his worm, but He does not throw it into the nest. [*Devices and Desires* ch 40]

JAMES William 1842–1910
US psychologist and philosopher.

> **1** Man, biologically considered, and whatever else he may be into the bargain, is simply the most formidable of all the beasts of prey, and, indeed, the only one that preys systematically on its own species. [*Atlantic Monthly* Dec 1904]
>
> **2** Our faith is faith in someone else's faith, and in the greatest matters this is most the case. [*New World* June 1986]
>
> **3** Hogamus, higamous / Man is polygamous / Higamous, hogamous/ Woman monogamous. [Quoted in *Oxford Book of Marriage*]
>
> **4** The art of being wise is the art of knowing what to overlook. [*Principles of Psychology*]
>
> **5** There is no more miserable human being than one in whom nothing is habitual but indecision. [*Principles of Psychology*]
>
> **6** An idea, to be suggestive, must come to the individual with the force of a revelation. [*Varieties of Religious Experience*]
>
> **7** If merely 'feeling good' could decide, drunkenness would be the supremely valid human experience. [*Varieties of Religious Experience*, 'Religion and Neurology']
>
> **8** There is no worse lie than a truth misunderstood by those who hear it. [*Varieties of Religious Experience*]

JARRY Alfred 1873–1907
French dramatist and writer.

> We believe ... that the applause of silence is the only kind that counts. ['Twelve Theatrical Topics' Topic 12]

JEANS James Hopwood 1877–1946
English mathematician and scientist.

> Life exists in the universe only because the carbon atom possesses certain exceptional properties. [*Mysterious Universe*]

JEFFERSON Thomas 1743–1826
US Republican president.

> **1** When angry, count ten, before you speak; if very angry, an hundred. [*Decalogue of Canons for Observation in Practical Life* 10]
>
> **2** A little rebellion now and then is a good thing. [Letter to James Madison 30 Jan 1787]

3rd US president and great liberal statesman, Thomas Jefferson. He was the first president to be inaugurated in Washington (a city he helped to plan). Among the important events of his presidency were the Lousiana Purchase 1803 of the French territories in the Mississippi Basin, and the abolition of the slave trade 1808.

3 The tree of liberty must be refreshed from time to time with the blood of patriots and tyrants. It is its natural manure. [Letter to W S Smith 13 Nov 1787]

4 No government ought to be without censors, and where the press is free, no one ever will. [Letter to George Washington 9 Sept 1792]

5 Advertisements contain the only truths to be relied on in a newspaper. [Letter 1819]

6 When a man assumes a public trust, he should consider himself as public property. [Remark]

JENKINS David 1925–
English theologian; Bishop of Durham.

In institutions – including religious institutions – when people talk about unity, they're talking about keeping quiet. [Remark]

JEROME St c. 342–420
Christian monk and scholar.

Love is not to be purchased, and affection has no price. [Letter no. 3]

JEROME Jerome K 1859–1927
English journalist and writer.

1 It is always the best policy to speak the truth – unless, of course, you are an exceptionally good liar. [Idler Feb 1892]

2 It is impossible to enjoy idling thoroughly unless one has plenty of work to do. [Idle Thoughts of an Idle Fellow, 'On Being Idle']

3 Love is like the measles; we all have to go through it. [Idle Thoughts of an Idle Fellow, 'On Being in Love']

4 Nothing, so it seems to me ... is more beautiful than the love that has weathered the storms of life. ... The love of the young for the young, that is the beginning of life. But the love of the old for the old, that is the beginning of – of things longer. ['Passing of the Third Floor Back']

5 I want a house that has got over all its troubles; I don't want to spend the rest of my life bringing up a young and inexperienced house. [They and I]

6 But there, everything has its drawbacks, as the man said when his mother-in-law died, and they came down upon him for the funeral expenses. [Three Men in a Boat ch 3]

7 I like work: it fascinates me. I can sit and look at it for hours. I love to keep it by me: the idea of getting rid of it nearly breaks my heart. [Three Men in a Boat ch 15]

JERROLD Douglas 1803–1857
English dramatist.

1 Honest bread is very well – it's the butter that makes the temptation. [The Catspaw III]

2 Earth is here so kind that just tickle her with a hoe and she laughs with a harvest. [On Australia, in A Man Made of Money]

3 Some people are so fond of ill-luck that they run half-way to meet it. ['Meeting Troubles Half-way']

4 We love peace, as we abhor pusillanimity; but not peace at any price. ['Peace']

5 Love's like the measles – all the worse when it comes late in life. ['A Philanthropist']

6 He is one of those wise philanthropists who, in a time of famine, would vote for nothing but a supply of toothpicks. [Wit and Opinions of Douglas Jerrold, 'A Philanthropist']

JOHN PAUL II 1920–
Pope from 1978.

Adultery in your heart is committed not only when you look with excessive sexual desire at a woman who is not your wife, but also if you look in the same manner at your wife. [Speech at Vatican Synod Oct 1980]

JOHNSON Lyndon Baines 1908–1973
US Republican president.

1 It's probably better to have him inside the tent pissing out, than outside pissing in. [Of J Edgar Hoover, quoted in D Halberstam *Best and Brightest*]

2 We hope that the world will not narrow into a neighbourhood before it has broadened into a brotherhood. [Speech at lighting of the nation's Christmas Tree 22 Dec 1963]

3 I'd rather give my life than be afraid to give it. [On his decision to walk in President Kennedy's funeral procession 25 Nov 1963]

4 In your time we have the opportunity to move not only toward the rich society and the powerful society, but upward to the Great Society. [Speech at University of Michigan 22 May 1964]

JOHNSON Philip 1906–
US architect.

Architecture is the art of how to waste space. [*New York Times* 27 Dec 1964]

JOHNSON Samuel, *Dr Johnson*
1709–1784
English lexicographer, author, critic, and conversationalist.

1 The chief glory of every people arises from its authors. [*Dictionary of the English Language*]

2 *Dull* To make dictionaries is dull work. [*Dictionary of the English Language*]

3 Every quotation contributes something to the stability or enlargement of the language. [*Dictionary of the English Language*]

4 *Lexicographer* A writer of dictionaries, a harmless drudge. [*Dictionary of the English Language.*]

5 *Oats* A grain, which in England is generally given to horses, but in Scotland supports the people. [*Dictionary of the English Language*]

6 *Patron* Commonly a wretch who supports with insolence, and is paid with flattery. [*Dictionary of the English Language*]

7 The joy of life is variety; the tenderest love requires to be renewed by intervals of absence. [*Idler* no. 39 (1758–60)]

8 It is very strange, and very melancholy, that the paucity of human pleasures should persuade us ever to call hunting one of them. [G B Hill *Johnsonian Miscellanies* vol i]

9 Love is the wisdom of the fool and the folly of the wise. [G B Hill *Johnsonian Miscellanies* vol ii]

10 A man is in general better pleased when he has a good dinner upon his table, than when his wife talks Greek. [G B Hill *Johnsonian Miscellanies* vol ii]

11 The booksellers are generous liberal-minded men. [Boswell's *Life of Johnson* vol i]

12 He did not love clean linen; and I have no passion for it. [Boswell's *Life of Johnson* vol i]

13 If you call a dog Hervey, I shall love him. [Boswell's *Life of Johnson* vol i]

14 Ignorance, Madam, pure ignorance. [On being asked how he came to define a word incorrectly in his *Dictionary*, in Boswell's *Life of Johnson* vol i]

15 I had done all I could; and no man is well pleased to have his all neglected, be it ever so little. [Letter to Lord Chesterfield in Boswell's *Life of Johnson* vol i]

16 I'll come no more behind your scenes, David; for the silk stockings and white bosoms of your actresses excite my amorous propensities. [To the actor-manager David Garrick, in Boswell's *Life of Johnson* vol i]

17 Is not a Patron, my Lord, one who looks with unconcern on a man struggling for life in the water, and, when he has reached ground,

encumbers him with help? [Letter to Lord Chesterfield in Boswell's *Life of Johnson* vol i]

18 A man, Sir, should keep his friendship in constant repair. [Boswell's *Life of Johnson* vol i]

19 Sir, let me tell you, the noblest prospect which a Scotchman ever sees, is the high road that leads him to England! [Boswell's *Life of Johnson* vol i]

20 Sir, we are a nest of singing birds. [Boswell's *Life of Johnson* vol i]

21 Sir, a woman's preaching is like a dog's walking on his hinder legs. It is not done well; but you are surprised to find it done at all. [Boswell's *Life of Johnson* vol i]

22 They [Lord Chesterfield's Letters] teach the morals of a whore, and the manners of a dancing master. [Boswell's *Life of Johnson* vol i]

23 Your levellers wish to level down as far as themselves; but they cannot bear levelling up to themselves. [Boswell's *Life of Johnson* vol i]

24 In lapidary inscriptions a man is not upon oath. [Boswell's *Life of Johnson* vol ii]

25 I think the full tide of human existence is at Charing-Cross. [Boswell's *Life of Johnson* vol ii]

26 It was the triumph of hope over experience. [Boswell's *Life of Johnson* vol ii, referring to the second marriage of a man whose first marriage had been unhappy]

27 Marriages would in general be as happy, and often more so, if they were all made by the Lord Chancellor, upon a due consideration of characters and circumstances, without the parties having any choice in the matter. [Boswell's *Life of Johnson* vol ii]

28 Patriotism is the last refuge of a scoundrel. [Boswell's *Life of Johnson* vol ii]

29 Read over your compositions, and where ever you meet with a passage which you think is particularly fine, strike it out. [Boswell's *Life of Johnson* vol ii]

30 There is, indeed, nothing that so much seduces reason from vigilance, as the thought of passing life with an amiable woman. [Boswell's *Life of Johnson* vol ii]

31 Claret is the liquor for boys; port for men; but he who aspires to be a hero must drink brandy. [Boswell's *Life of Johnson* vol iii]

32 Depend upon it, Sir, when a man knows he is to be hanged in a fortnight, it concentrates his mind wonderfully. [Boswell's *Life of Johnson* vol iii]

33 If I had no duties, and no reference to futurity, I would spend my life in driving briskly in a postchaise with a pretty woman. [Boswell's *Life of Johnson* vol iii]

34 No man but a blockhead ever wrote, except for money. [Boswell's *Life of Johnson* vol iii]

35 Were it not for imagination, Sir, a man would be as happy in the arms of a chambermaid as of a Duchess. [Boswell's *Life of Johnson* vol iii]

36 When a man is tired of London, he is tired of life; for there is in London all that life can afford. [Boswell's *Life of Johnson* vol iii]

37 Worth seeing? yes; but not worth going to see. [Boswell's *Life of Johnson* vol iii]

38 Milton ... was a genius that could cut a Colossus from a rock; but could not carve heads upon cherry-stones. [Boswell's *Life of Johnson* vol iv]

39 No man is a hypocrite in his pleasures. [Boswell's *Life of Johnson* vol iv]

40 No man was more foolish when he had not a pen in his hand, or

more wise when he had. [Boswell's *Life of Johnson* vol iv]

41 Sir, I look upon every day to be lost, in which I do not make a new acquaintance. [Boswell's *Life of Johnson* vol iv]

42 Sir, there is no settling the point of precedency between a louse and a flea. [Boswell's *Life of Johnson* vol iv]

43 We are not here to sell a parcel of boilers and vats, but the potentiality of growing rich, beyond the dreams of avarice. [Boswell's *Life of Johnson* vol iv]

44 Language is the dress of thought. [*Lives of the English Poets,* 'Cowley']

45 I am disappointed by that stroke of death, which has eclipsed the gaiety of nations and impoverished the public stock of harmless pleasure. [Of Garrick's death, in *Lives of the English Poets* 'Edmund Smith']

46 Slow rises worth by poverty depress'd. [*London*]

47 Notes are often necessary, but they are necessary evils. [*Plays of William Shakespeare, with Notes* Preface]

48 Human life is everywhere a state in which much is to be endured, and little to be enjoyed. [*Rasselas* ch 11]

49 Marriage has many pains, but celibacy few pleasures. [*Rasselas*]

50 How small, of all that human hearts endure, / That part which laws or kings can cause or cure! [Lines added to Goldsmith's *Traveller*]

51 He left the name, at which the world grew pale, / To point a moral, or adorn a tale. [*Vanity of Human Wishes* l. 221]

52 Let observation with extensive view, / Survey mankind, from China to Peru. [*Vanity of Human Wishes* l. 1]

53 A wise Tory and a wise Whig, I believe, will agree. Their principles are the same, though their modes of thinking are different. [Written statement given to Boswell May 1781]

54 Fly fishing may be a very pleasant amusement; but angling or float fishing I can only compare to a stick and a string, with a worm at one end and a fool at the other. [Attributed remark]

55 You could not stand five minutes with that man [Edmund Burke] beneath a shed while it rained, but you must be convinced you had been standing with the greatest man you had ever yet seen. [*Attributed remark*]

JOLSON Al 1886–1950
Russian-born US singer.

'You ain't heard nuttin' yet!' [Martin Abramson *Real Story of Al Jolson*]

JONES John Paul 1747–1792
Scottish-born American naval officer.

I have not yet begun to fight. [On being asked during a sea battle 1779, if he would surrender, as his ship was sinking]

JONG Erica 1942–
US writer.

In every woman's heart there is a god of the woods, and this god is not available for marriage or for home improvement or for parenthood. [*Fear of Fifty*]

JONSON Ben 1572–1637
English dramatist, poet, and critic.

1 I remember the players have often mentioned it as an honour to Shakespeare that in his writing (whatsoever he penned) he never blotted out a line. My answer hath been 'Would he had blotted a thousand'. [*Discoveries*, 'De Shakespeare Nostrati']

2 It is not growing like a tree / In bulk, doth make men better be. ['Pindaric Ode on the Death of Sir H. Morison']

3 Follow a shadow, it still flies you, / Seem to fly it, it will pursue. / So court a mistress, she denies you; / Let her alone, she will court you. / Say, are not women truly, then, / Styled but the shadows of us men? ['That Women are but Men's Shadows']

4 Drink to me only with thine eyes, / And I will pledge with mine; / Or leave a kiss but in the cup, / And I'll not look for wine. ['To Celia']

5 He was not of an age, but for all time! [*To the Memory of My Beloved, the Author, Mr William Shakespeare*]

6 Small Latin, and less Greek. [*To the Memory of My Beloved, the Author, Mr William Shakespeare*]

7 Sweet Swan of Avon! [*To the Memory of My Beloved, the Author, Mr William Shakespeare*]

8 Come, my Celia, let us prove, / While we can, the sports of love, / Time will not be ours for ever, / He, at length, our good will sever. [*Volpone* III. v]

9 Suns, that set, may rise again; / But if once we lose this light, / 'Tis with us perpetual night. [*Volpone* III. v]

JOYCE James 1882–1941
Irish writer.

1 That ideal reader suffering from an ideal insomnia. [*Finnegans Wake* pt 1]

2 All moanday, tearsday, wailsday, thumpsday, frightday, shatterday till the fear of the Law. [*Finnegans Wake* pt 2]

3 Ireland is the old sow that eats her farrow. [*Portrait of the Artist as a Young Man*]

4 There is no heresy or no philosophy which is so abhorrent to the church as a human being. [Letter 22 Nov 1902, in which Joyce stated his intention of leaving Ireland]

5 A Portrait of the Artist as a Young Man. [Book title]

JULIAN c. 331–363
Roman emperor.

Thou hast conquered, O Galilean. [Last words]

JUNG Carl 1875–1961
Swiss psychiatrist.

1 In all chaos there is a cosmos, in all disorder a secret order. ['Archetypes of the Collective Unconscious' pt 1]

2 I don't *believe*. I must have a reason for a certain hypothesis. Either I *know* a thing, and then I know it – I don't need to believe it. [In BBC TV

Swiss psychiatrist and pioneer psychoanalyst Carl Jung. He argued that the unconscious contains two basic elements: personal experience and the inherited experience of mankind (the collective unconscious). His studies of personality types (introvert and extrovert), dreams, and religion were all influential.

'Face to Face' interview with John
Freeman]

3 The images of the unconscious
place a great responsibility upon a
man. Failure to understand them, or
a shirking of ethical responsibility,
deprives him of his wholeness and
imposes a painful fragmentariness
on his life. [*Memories, Dreams, and
Reflections* ch 6]

4 A man who has not passed
through the inferno of his passions
has never overcome them. [*Memories,
Dreams, Reflections* ch 9]

5 As far as we can discern, the sole
purpose of human existence is to
kindle a light in the darkness of
mere being. [*Memories, Dreams,
Reflections* ch 11]

6 Every form of addiction is bad,
no matter whether the narcotic be
alcohol or morphine or idealism.
[*Memories, Dreams, Reflections* ch 12]

7 Show me a sane man and I will
cure him for you. [*Observer* 19 July
1975]

8 Where love rules, there is no will
to power, and where power pre-
dominates, love is lacking. The one
is the shadow of the other. [*On the
Psychology of the Unconscious*]

JUSTER Norton 1929–
US writer.

Did you know that if a beaver two
feet long with a tail a foot and a half
long can build a dam twelve feet
high and six feet wide in two days,
all you would need to build the
Kariba Dam is a beaver sixty-eight
feet long with a fifty-one foot tail?
[*Phantom Tollbooth* ch 14]

JUVENAL c. 60 AD–140 AD
Roman satirist and poet.

1 No one ever became extremely
wicked suddenly. [*Satires* II. 83]

2 But who will guard the guards
themselves? [*Satires* VI. 347]

3 An inveterate itch of writing.
[*Satires* VII. 51]

4 Your prayer must be that you
may have a sound mind in a sound
body. [*Satires* X. 356]

KABIR LIVED 15TH CENTURY
Indian mystic poet.

1 Between the conscious and the unconscious, the mind has put up a swing: / all earth creatures, even the supernovas, sway between these two trees, / and it never winds down. ['The Fish in the Sea is not Thirsty', *Kabir Book*, translated by Robert Bly]

2 Go over and over your beads, paint weird designs on your forehead, / wear your hair matted, long, and ostentatious, / but when deep inside you there is a loaded gun, how can you have God? ['The Fish in the Sea is not Thirsty', *Kabir Book*, translated by Robert Bly]

3 Listen to the secret sound, the real sound, which is inside you. / The one no one talks of speaks the secret sound to himself, / and he is the one who has made it all. ['The Fish in the Sea is not Thirsty', *Kabir Book*, translated by Robert Bly]

4 Surely the Holy One is not deaf. / He hears the delicate anklets that ring on the feet of an insect as it walks. ['The Fish in the Sea is not Thirsty', *Kabir Book*, translated by Robert Bly]

KAEL Pauline 1919–
US film critic.

Irresponsibility is part of the pleasure of all art; it is the part the schools cannot recognize. [*Going Steady*, 'Movies as Opera']

KAFKA Franz 1883–1924
Czech/German novelist and short-story writer.

1 My 'fear' is my substance, and probably the best part of me. [Letter to Milena Jesenka, quoted in Buber-Neumann *Milena*

2 You may object that it is not a trial at all; you are quite right, for it is only a trial if I recognize it as such. [*The Trial* ch 2]

3 It's often better to be in chains than to be free. [*The Trial* ch 8]

KANT Immanuel 1724–1804
German philosopher.

1 Two things fill the mind with ever-increasing wonder and awe ... the starry heavens above me and the moral law within me. [*Critique of Practical Reason*, conclusion]

2 Who wills the end, wills also (so far as reason has a decisive influence on his actions) the means ... [*Moral Law*]

KAPUSCINSKI Ryszard 1932–
Polish journalist.

When is a crisis reached? When questions arise that can't be answered. [*Warsaw Diary*, in *Granta* no. 15, 1985]

KARR Alphonse 1808–1890
French writer.

The more things change, the more they remain the same. [*Les Guêpes*]

KAUFMAN Gerald 1930–
British Labour politician.

The longest suicide note in history. [Of the Labour Party's 1983 election manifesto, quoted in D Healey *Time of My Life*]

KAUNDA Kenneth 1924–
Zambian president.

1 The moment you have protected an individual you have protected society. [Quoted in *Observer* 6 May 1962]

2 The inability of those in power to still the voices of their own consciences is the great force leading to change. [*Observer* July 1965]

KEARNEY Denis 1847–1907
US labour leader.

> Horny-handed sons of toil. [Speech in San Francisco *c.* 1878]

KEATS John 1795–1821
English Romantic poet.

1 Bright star, would I were steadfast as thou art – ['Bright Star']

2 A thing of beauty is a joy for ever: / Its loveliness increases. [*Endymion*]

3 St. Agnes' Eve – Ah, bitter chill it was! / The owl, for all his feathers, was a-cold. [*Eve of St. Agnes*]

4 Soft adorings from their loves receive / Upon the honey'd middle of the night. [*Eve of St Agnes*]

5 Fanatics have their dreams, wherewith they weave / A paradise for a sect. ['Fall of Hyperion']

6 Ever let the fancy roam, / Pleasure never is at home. ['Fancy']

7 Oh what can ail thee, Knight at arms / Alone and palely loitering; / The sedge is wither'd from the lake, / And no birds sing. ['La Belle Dame Sans Merci']

8 Do not all charms fly / At the mere touch of cold philosophy? [*Lamia* pt 2]

9 Love in a hut, with water and a crust, / Is – Love, forgive us! – cinders, ashes, dust; / Love in a palace is perhaps at last / More grievous torment than a hermit's fast. [*Lamia* pt 2]

10 'Beauty is truth, truth beauty,' – that is all / Ye know on earth, and all ye need to know. ['Ode on a Grecian Urn']

11 For ever wilt thou love, and she be fair! ['Ode on a Grecian Urn']

12 Heard melodies are sweet, but those unheard / Are sweeter. ['Ode on a Grecian Urn']

13 Thou still unravish'd bride of quietness, / Thou foster-child of silence and slow time. ['Ode on a Grecian Urn']

14 My heart aches, and a drowsy numbness pains / My sense. ['Ode to a Nightingale']

15 Now more than ever seems it rich to die, / To cease upon the midnight with no pain. ['Ode to a Nightingale']

16 O for a beaker full of the warm South, / Full of the true, the blushful Hippocrene, / With beaded bubbles winking at the brim, / And purple-stained mouth. ['Ode to a Nightingale']

17 Was it a vision, or a waking dream? ['Ode to a Nightingale']

18 A bright torch, and a casement ope at night, / To let the warm Love in! ['Ode to Psyche']

19 Much have I travell'd in the realms of gold, / And many goodly states and kingdoms seen. ['On First Looking into Chapman's Homer']

20 Season of mists and mellow fruitfulness, / Close bosom-friend of the maturing sun. ['To Autumn']

21 O soft embalmer of the still midnight. ['To Sleep']

22 I am certain of nothing but of the holiness of the heart's affections and the truth of imagination. [Letter to Benjamin Bailey 22 Nov 1817]

23 Negative Capability, that is, when man is capable of being in uncertainties, mysteries, doubts, without any irritable reaching after fact and reason. [Letter to G and T Keats 21 Dec 1817]

24 We hate poetry that has a palpable design upon us ... Poetry should be great and unobtrusive, a thing which enters into one's soul, and does not startle or amaze it with itself, but with its subject. [Letter to J H Reynolds 3 Feb 1818]

25 If poetry comes not as naturally as leaves to a tree it had better not come at all. [Letter to John Taylor 27 Feb 1818]

26 I think I shall be among the English Poets after my death. [Letter to Richard Woodhouse 14 Oct 1818]

27 I have met with women whom I really think would like to be married to a poem, and to be given away by a novel. [Letter to Fanny Brawne 8 July 1819]

28 I equally dislike the favour of the public with the love of a woman – they are both a cloying treacle to the wings of independence. [Letter to John Taylor 24 Aug 1819]

29 You have ravish'd me away by a Power I cannot resist; and yet I could resist till I saw you; and even since I have seen you I have endeavoured often 'to reason against the reasons of my Love.' [Letter to Fanny Brawne 13 Oct 1819]

30 Here lies one whose name was writ in water. [His own epitaph]

KELLER Helen Adams 1880–1968
US deaf-blind author and campaigner.

Science may have found a cure for most evils; but it has found no remedy for the worst of them all – the apathy of human beings. [*My Religion*]

KELLY Hugh 1739–1777
Irish dramatist.

Of all the stages in a woman's life, none is so dangerous as the period between her acknowledgement of a passion for a man, and the day set apart for her nuptials. [*Memoirs of a Magdalen*]

KEMP Penny 1951–   and Derek Wall 1965–
English ecologists.

We are unravelling nature like an old jumper. [*Green Manifesto for the 1990s* ch 4]

KEMPIS Thomas à c. 1380–1471
German monk and writer.

Oh how quickly the glory of the world passes away! [*Imitatio Christi*]

KEMPTON Sally 1943–
US writer.

I became a feminist as an alternative to becoming a masochist. [*Esquire* July 1970]

KENNEDY John F 1917–1963
US Democratic president.

1 Probably the greatest concentration of talent and genius in this house except for perhaps those times when Thomas Jefferson ate alone. [Of a White House dinner for Nobel Prizewinners, in *New York Times* 30 Apr 1962]

The 35th president of the United States of America, John F Kennedy, the youngest person to be elected to the office. He was assassinated after less than three years in power.

2 It was involuntary. They sank my boat. [Answer to question about how he became a war hero, in A M Schlesinger Jr *A Thousand Days*]

3 When written in Chinese the word crisis is composed of two characters. One represents danger and the other represents opportunity. [Speech, Indianapolis 12 April 1959]

4 Conformity is the jailer of freedom and the enemy of growth. [Address to UN General Assembly 25 Sept 1961]

5 And so, my fellow Americans: ask not what your country can do for you – ask what you can do for your country. [Inaugural address 20 Jan 1962]

6 Those who make peaceful revolution impossible will make violent revolution inevitable. [Speech at White House 13 Mar 1962]

7 When we got into office, the thing that surprised me most was to find that things were just as bad as we'd been saying they were. [Speech at White House 27 May 1962]

8 Ich bin ein Berliner. [Speech in West Berlin 26 June 1963]

9 In free society art is not a weapon ... Artists are not engineers of the soul. [Speech 26 Oct 1963, Amherst College, Massachusetts]

KENNEDY Joseph P 1888–1969
US industrialist and diplomat.

When the going gets tough, the tough get going. [J H Cutler *Honey Fitz*]

KENNEDY Robert 1925–1968
US Democratic politician.

The free way of life proposes ends, but it does not prescribe means. [*Pursuit of Justice* pt 5]

KENT Corita 1918–
US artist.

Women's liberation is the liberation of the feminine in the man and the masculine in the woman. [Quoted in *Los Angeles Times* 11 July 1974]

KEROUAC Jack 1923–1969
US 'Beat Generation' novelist.

I had nothing to offer anybody except my own confusion. [*On the Road*]

KEY Ellen 1849–1926
Swedish writer.

1 Love is moral even without legal marriage, but marriage is immoral without love. [*Morality of Woman and Other Essays*, title essay]

2 Art, that great undogmatized church. [*Renaissance of Motherhood* pt 2, ch 1]

KEY Francis Scott 1779–1843
US lawyer and poet.

'Tis the star-spangled banner; O long may it wave / O'er the land of the free, and the home of the brave! ['Star-Spangled Banner']

KEYNES John Maynard 1883–1946
English economist.

1 The important thing for Government is not to do things which individuals are doing already, and to do them a little better or a little worse; but to do those things which at present are not done at all. [*End of Laissez-Faire* pt 4]

2 I think that Capitalism, wisely managed, can probably be made more efficient for attaining economic ends than any alternative system yet in sight, but that in itself it is in many ways extremely objectionable. [*End of Laissez-Faire* pt 5]

3 It is better that a man should tyrannize over his bank balance than over his fellow-citizens. [*General Theory of Employment*]

4 But this *long run* is a misleading guide to current affairs. *In the long run* we are all dead. [*Tract on Monetary Reform*]

KHRUSHCHEV Nikita 1894–1971
Soviet premier.

1 We are in favour of a détente, but if anybody thinks that for this reason we shall forget about Marx, Engels, and Lenin, he is mistaken. This will happen when shrimps learn to whistle. [July 1955, at Geneva conference]

2 Comrades! We must abolish the cult of the individual decisively, once and for all. [Speech to the secret session of 20th Congress of the Communist Party 25 Feb 1956]

3 Whether you like it or not, history is on our side. We will bury you. [Speech to Western diplomats at reception in Moscow 18 Nov 1956]

KILMER Joyce 1886–1918
US poet.

I think that I shall never see / A poem lovely as a tree. ['Trees']

KING Florence 1936–
US writer.

1 Democracy is the fig leaf of elitism. [*Reflections in a Jaundiced Eye*, 'Democracy']

2 The confidence and security of a people can be measured by their attitude towards laxatives. [*Reflections in a Jaundiced Eye*, 'Nice Guyism']

KING Henry 1592–1669
English bishop and poet.

But hark! My pulse like a soft drum / Beats my approach, tells thee I come; / And slow howe'er my marches be, / I shall at last sit down by thee. [*Exequy upon His Wife*]

KING Martin Luther 1929–1968
US civil-rights campaigner and Baptist minister.

1 I want to be the white man's brother, not his brother-in-law. [*New York Journal-American* 10 Sept 1962]

2 Nothing in all the world is more dangerous than sincere ignorance and conscientious stupidity. [*Strength to Love* ch 4]

3 The means by which we live have outdistanced the ends for which we live. Our scientific power has outrun our spiritual power. We have guided missiles and misguided men. [*Strength to Love* ch 7]

US civil-rights campaigner Martin Luther King. An advocate of non-violent protest, King organized many campaigns. In 1963 he led 200,000 protesters on a march to Washington DC, and in 1965 he and several hundred marchers attempted to walk from Salem to Montgomery in Alabama. On the latter occasion, the highly publicized violence used against the protesters by the police led to the rapid passing of the Voting Rights Act 1965, which ended all attempts to restrict black people's right to vote.

4 There can be no deep disappointment where there is not deep love. ['Letter from Birmingham Jail', in *Why We Can't Wait*]

5 Injustice anywhere is a threat to justice everywhere. [Letter from Birmingham jail, Alabama 16 Apr 1963]

6 I submit to you that if a man hasn't discovered something he will die for, he isn't fit to live. [Speech in Detroit 23 June 1963]

7 I have a dream that my four little children will one day live in a nation where they will not be judged by the colour of their skin but by the content of their character. [Speech at civil-rights march in Washington 28 Aug 1963]

8 Now, I say to you today my friends, even though we face the difficulties of today and tomorrow, I still have a dream. It is a dream deeply rooted in the American dream. I have a dream that one day this nation will rise up and live out the true meaning of its creed: – 'We hold these truths to be self-evident, that all men are created equal.' [Speech at civil-rights march in Washington 28 Aug 1963]

9 We must learn to live together as brothers or perish together as fools. [Speech at St Louis 22 Mar 1964]

10 I've been to the mountaintop and I've seen the promised land ... I may not get there with you, but I want you to know tonight that we as a people will get to the promised land. [Addressing a rally the night before his murder, 1968]

KING Stoddard 1889–1933
US songwriter.

There's a long, long trail a-winding / Into the land of my dreams, / Where the nightingales are singing / And a white moon beams. ['Long, Long Trail']

KINGSLEY Charles 1819–1875
English author and clergyman.

1 Be good, sweet maid, and let who will be clever. ['A Farewell']

2 As thorough an Englishman as ever coveted his neighbour's goods. [*Water Babies*]

KINGSLEY Mary Henrietta 1862–1900
British ethnologist.

For men must work, and women must weep, / And there's little to earn, and many to keep. ['Three Fishers']

KINGSMILL Hugh 1889–1949
English writer.

Friends ... are God's apology for relations. [M Holroyd *Best of Hugh Kingsmill*]

KINGTON Miles 1941–
English journalist and broadcaster.

It is better to have loved a short man, than never to have loved a tall. [*Independent* 27 Dec 1991]

KINNOCK Neil 1942–
British Labour politician.

1 If Margaret Thatcher wins on Thursday, I warn you not to be ordinary, I warn you not to be young, I warn you not to fall ill, and I warn you not to grow old. [Speech at Bridgend 7 June 1983]

2 Mr Shultz went off his pram. [Comment after meeting US Secretary of State.]

KIPLING Rudyard 1865–1936
Indian-born English writer.

1 He's an absent-minded beggar, and his weaknesses are great – ['Absent-Minded Beggar']

2 Oh, East is East, and West is West, and never the twain shall meet. ['Ballad of East and West']

English author Rudyard Kipling. The reputation of Kipling – who once had an international standing – suffered badly when he became closely identified with imperialism and racism. Recently, with more sympathetic and penetrating interpretation, his reputation has, to a certain extent, been restored.

3 And a woman is only a woman, but a good cigar is a smoke. ['Betrothed']

4 Take of English earth as much / As either hand may rightly clutch. / In the taking of it breathe / Prayer for all who lie beneath. ['A Charm']

5 Land of our birth, we pledge to thee / Our love and toil in the years to be. ['Children's Song']

6 It's clever, but is it Art? ['Conundrum of the Workshops']

7 When the Himalayan peasant meets the he-bear in his pride, / He shouts to scare the monster, who will often turn aside. / But the she-bear thus accosted rends the peasant tooth and nail / For the female of the species is more deadly than the male. ['Female of the Species']

8 For to admire an' for to see, / For to be'old this world so wide / It never done no good to me, / But I can't drop it if I tried! ['For to Admire']

9 Gentlemen-rankers out on the spree, / Damned from here to Eternity. ['Gentlemen Rankers']

10 And the Glory of the Garden it shall never pass away! ['Glory of the Garden']

11 You're a better man than I am, Gunga Din! ['Gunga Din']

12 If you can dream – and not make dreams your master; / If you can think – and not make thoughts your aim; / If you can meet with Triumph and Disaster / And treat those two imposters just the same. ['If']

13 If you can keep your head when all about you / Are losing theirs and blaming it on you. ['If']

14 If you can talk with crowds and keep your virtue, / Or walk with Kings – nor lose the common touch. ['If']

15 Then ye contended your souls / With the flannelled fools at the wicket or the muddied oafs at the goals. ['The Islanders']

16 The Cat. He walked by himself, and all places were alike to him. [*Just-So Stories*, 'The Cat That Walked By Himself']

17 An Elephant's Child – who was full of 'satiable curtiosity. [*Just-So Stories*, 'The Elephant's Child']

18 The great greygreen, greasy Limpopo River, all set about with fever trees. [*Just-So Stories* 'The Elephant's Child']

19 A man of infinite-resource-and-sagacity. [*Just-So Stories*, 'How the Whale Got His Throat']

20 'Nice,' said the small 'stute Fish. 'Nice but nubbly.' [*Just-So Stories*, 'How the Whale Got His Throat']

21 Old Man Kangaroo first, Yellow-Dog Dingo behind. [*Just-So Stories*, 'Sing-Song of Old Man Kangaroo']

22 And the ships shall go abroad / To the Glory of the Lord / Who heard the silly sailor-folk and gave them back their sea! ['Last Chantey']

23 There's a whisper down the field where the year has shot her yield, / And the ricks stand grey to the sun, / Singing: 'Over then, come over, for the bee has quit the clover, / And your English summer's done.' ['Long Trail']

24 On the road to Mandalay, / Where the flyin'-fishes play, / An' the dawn comes up like thunder outer China 'crost the / Bay! [*Mandalay*]

25 I'm sick of the hired women. I'll kiss my girl on her lips! ['Mary Gloster']

26 'Tisn't beauty, so to speak, nor good talk necessarily. It's just It. Some women'll stay in a man's memory if they once walked down a street. [*Mrs Bathurst*]

27 'Have you news of my boy Jack?' / Not this tide. / 'When d'you think that he'll come back?' / Not with this wind blowing, and this tide. ['My Boy Jack']

28 It is enough that, through Thy Grace, / I saw nought common on Thy Earth. ['My New-cut Ashlar']

29 'A Fool lies here who tried to hustle the East.' [*Naulahka* heading of ch 5]

30 It takes a great deal of Christianity to wipe out uncivilized Eastern instincts, such as falling in love at first sight. [*Plain Tales from the Hills*, 'Lispeth']

31 But that is another story. [*Plain Tales from the Hills*, 'Three and – an Extra']

32 Take my word for it, the silliest woman can manage a clever man; but it needs a very clever woman to manage a fool. [*Plain Tales from the Hills*, 'Three and – an Extra']

33 Brothers and Sisters, I bid you beware / Of giving your heart to a dog to tear. ['Power of the Dog']

34 God of our fathers, known of old, / Lord of our far-flung battle-line, / Beneath whose awful Hand we hold / Dominion over palm and pine – / Lord God of Hosts, be with us yet, / Lest we forget – lest we forget! ['Recessional']

35 Brother, thy tail hangs down behind! ['Road Song of the Bandar-Log']

36 Shillin' a day, / Bloomin' good pay – / Lucky to touch it, a shillin' a day! ['Shillin' a Day']

37 Them that asks no questions isn't told a lie. / Watch the wall, my darling, while the Gentlemen go by! ['Smuggler's Song']

38 The Sons of Mary seldom bother, for they have inherited that good part; / But the Sons of Martha favour their Mother of the careful soul and the troubled heart. / And because she lost her temper once, and because she was rude to the Lord her Guest, / Her Sons must wait upon Mary's Sons, world without end, reprieve, or rest. ['Sons of Martha']

39 I gloat! Hear me gloat! [*Stalky and Co.*]

40 You may carve it on his tombstone, you may cut it on his card, / That a young man married is a young man marred. ['Story of the Gadsbys']

41 God gives all men all earth to love, / But, since man's heart is small / Ordains for each one spot shall prove / Beloved over all. / Each to his choice, and I rejoice / The lot has fallen to me / In a fair ground – in a fair ground – / Yea, Sussex by the sea! ['Sussex']

As US secretary of state, Henry Kissinger attempted to maintain US control over world affairs by 'shuttle diplomacy', continually flying to trouble spots to negotiate face-to-face with world leaders. Since retiring from international politics, he has given lectures at Harvard University and has written two books of memoirs: *White House Years* 1979 and *Years of Upheaval* 1982.

42 'For the sin ye do by two and two ye must pay for one by one!' ['Tomlinson']

43 Of all the trees that grow so fair, / Old England to adorn, / Greater are none beneath the Sun, / Than Oak, and Ash, and Thorn. ['Tree Song']

44 It's boy; only boy. ['Unsavoury Interlude']

45 Take up the White Man's burden ['White Man's Burden']

46 Down to Gehenna or up to the Throne, / He travels the fastest who travels alone. ['The Winners']

47 Words are, of course, the most powerful drug used by mankind. [Speech 14 Feb 1923]

48 The Light that Failed. [Book title]

KISSINGER Henry 1923–
German-born US diplomat.

1 Power is the ultimate aphrodisiac. [*Guardian* 28 Nov 1976]

2 There cannot be a crisis next week. My schedule is already full. [*New York Times Magazine* 1 June 1969]

3 A little uncertainty is good for everyone. [Quoted in *Observer* 12 Dec 1976]

4 It is, after all, the responsibility of the expert to operate the familiar and that of the leader to transcend it. [*Years of Upheaval* ch 10]

KLEE Paul 1879–1940
Swiss artist.

1 A single day is enough to make us a little larger, or, another time, a little smaller. [*Diaries of Paul Klee 1898–1918* Jan 1908]

2 Standing at his appointed place, at the trunk of the tree, he does nothing other than gather and pass on what comes to him from the depths. He neither serves nor rules – he transmits ... . And the beauty at the crown is not his own. He is merely a channel. [*On Modern Art*]

KNOX John *c.* 1505–1572
Founder of the Church of Scotland.

The First Blast of the Trumpet Against the Monstrous Regiment of Women. [Pamphlet title]

KNOX Ronald Arbuthnott 1888–1957
English Roman Catholic scholar.

1 There once was a man who said, 'God / Must think it exceedingly odd / If he finds that this tree /

Continues to be / When there's no one about in the Quad.' [Langford Reed *Complete Limerick Book*]

2 It is stupid of modern civilization to have given up believing in the devil, when he is the only explanation of it. [*Let Dons Delight*]

KOESTLER Arthur 1905–1983
Hungarian-born British writer.

1 True creativity often starts where language ends. [*Act of Creation* bk 1, pt 2, ch 7]

2 God seems to have left the receiver off the hook, and time is running out. [*Ghost in the Machine* ch 18]

3 The most persistent sound which reverberates through man's history is the beating of war drums. [*Janus*, prologue]

KORAN Sacred book of Islam.

1 You are allowed on the night of the fast (Ramadan) to approach your wives: they are your garment and ye are their garment ... . Eat and drink until ye can discern a white thread from a black thread by the daybreak: afterwards fast strictly till night, and go not in unto them, but pass time in the Mosques. [2:183]

2 The Messiah Isa (Jesus), son of Maryam (Mary), is only an apostle of Allah, and his word which he conveyed unto Maryam. [4:169]

3 And do not say, regarding anything, 'I am going to do that tomorrow', but only, 'if God will'. [18:23–24]

4 If ye make reprisals, then make them to the same extent that ye were injured: but if ye can endure patiently, best will it surely be for the patiently enduring. [26:127]

5 ... the mischief of the stealthily withdrawing whisper (Satan) Who hides himself at the Name of Allah, Who whispereth in man's breast against Jinn and men. [94:16]

6 On that day shall men come forth in bands to behold their works. And whosoever shall have wrought an atom's weight of good shall behold it. And whosoever shall have wrought an atom's weight of evil shall behold it. [99:1-6]

7 O ye Unbelievers, I worship not what ye worship! to you your religion; and to me my religion. [109:1, 2, 6]

KRAUS Karl 1874–1936
Austrian dramatist and critic.

1 There is no unhappier creature on earth than a fetishist who yearns for a woman's shoe and has to embrace the whole woman. [*Aphorisms and More Aphorisms*]

2 Democracy means the opportunity to be everyone's slave. [*Die Fackel* 16 Oct 1911]

3 The esthete stands in the same relation to beauty as the pornographer stands to love, and the politician stands to life. [*Die Fackel* no. 406/12 (Vienna, 5 Oct 1915)]

4 My unconscious knows more about the consciousness of the psychologist than his consciousness knows about my unconscious. [*Die Fackel* 18 Jan 1917]

KUNDERA Milan 1929–
Czech author and critic.

Mankind's true moral test, its fundamental test ... consists of its attitude towards those who are at its mercy: animals. And in this respect mankind has suffered ... a debacle so fundamental that all others stem from it. [*Unbearable Lightness of Being* pt 7, ch 2]

KUNITZ Stanley 1905–
US poet.

In every house of marriage, / there's room for an interpreter. ['Route Six']

KUROSAWA Akira 1929–
Japanese cinema director.

To be an artist means never to look away. [*Guardian* 1980]

L

LA BRUYÈRE Jean de 1645–1696
French writer.

1 Time, which strengthens friendship, weakens love. [*Characters*, 'Of the Heart']

2 A man may deceive a woman by a pretence of love, provided he is not really in love with someone else. [*Characters*, 'Of Women']

3 Party loyalty lowers the greatest of men to the petty level of the masses. [*Characters*]

LACLOS Pierre Choderlos de 1741–1803
French novelist.

Have you not as yet observed that pleasure, which is undeniably the sole motive force behind the union of the sexes, is nevertheless not enough to form a bond between them? And that, if it is preceded by desire which impels, it is succeeded by disgust which repels? That is a law of nature which love alone can alter. [*Les Liaisons Dangereuses*, letter 131]

LAING R D 1927–1989
Scottish psychoanalyst.

1 Alienation as our present destiny is achieved only by outrageous violence perpetrated by human beings on human beings. [*Politics of Experience*, Introduction]

2 We are bemused and crazed creatures, strangers to our true selves, to one another, and to the spiritual and material world – mad, even, from an ideal standpoint we can glimpse but not adopt. [*Politics of Experience*, Introduction]

3 We are effectively destroying ourselves by violence masquerading as love. [*Politics of Experience*]

LAMARTINE Alphonse de 1790–1869
French poet.

To love for the sake of being loved is human, but to love for the sake of loving is angelic. [*Graziella* pt 4 ch 5]

LAMB Charles 1775–1834
English essayist and critic.

1 If ever I marry a wife, / I'll marry a landlord's daughter, / For then I may sit in the bar, / And drink cold brandy and water. ['Written in a copy of *Coelebs in Search of a Wife* '

Charles Lamb, the humane and humorous English essayist and critic. He was the friend of such contemporaries as the Romantics Wordsworth and Coleridge. His *Tales from Shakespeare*, in collaboration with his sister Mary, provide a simple and attractive means of access to the stories of Shakespeare's plays.

2 Nothing is to me more distasteful than that entire complacency and satisfaction which beam in the countenances of a new-married couple. [*Essays of Elia*, 'Bachelor's Complaint of Married People']

3 I am, in plainer words, a bundle of prejudices – made up of likings and dislikings. [*Essays of Elia*, 'Imperfect Sympathies']

4 I have been trying all my life to like Scotchmen, and am obliged to desist from the experiment in despair. [*Essays of Elia*, 'Imperfect Sympathies']

5 I love to lose myself in other men's minds. When I am not walking, I am reading; I cannot sit and think. Books think for me. [*Last Essays of Elia*, 'Detached Thoughts on Books and Reading']

6 The greatest pleasure I know, is to do a good action by stealth, and to have it found out by accident. ['Table Talk by the late Elia']

7 What a liberal confounding of those pedantic distinctions of *meum* and *tuum*! ['Two Races of Men']

LAMB Lady Caroline 1785–1828
English novelist.

Mad, bad, and dangerous to know. [On meeting Lord Byron, her future lover. Journal 1812]

LAMBERT Constant 1905–1951
English composer.

The whole trouble with a folk song is that once you have played it through there is nothing much you can do except play it over again and play it rather louder. [*Music Ho!*]

LAMPEDUSA Guiseppe di 1896–1957
Sicilian writer.

If we want everything to remain as it is, it will be necessary for everything to change. [*The Leopard* ch 1]

LANDOR Walter Savage 1775–1864
English poet and essayist.

1 George the First was always reckoned / Vile, but viler George the Second; / And what mortal ever heard / Any good of George the Third? / When from earth the Fourth descended / God be praised, the Georges ended! ['Epigram']

2 I strove with none; for none was worth my strife; / Nature I loved, and next to Nature, Art; / I warmed both hands before the fire of life; / It sinks, and I am ready to depart. ['Finis']

3 States, like men, have their growth, their manhood, their decrepitude, their decay. [*Imaginary Conversations*, 'Leonora di Este and Panigarola']

LANG Andrew 1844–1912
Scottish poet, historian, and folklorist.

The surge and thunder of the Odyssey. [Sonnet 'The Odyssey']

LANGER Suzanne 1895–1985
US philosopher.

Art is the objectification of feeling. [*Mind, an Essay on Human Feeling* vol 1, pt 2, ch 4]

LANGLAND William *c.* 1332–*c.* 1400
English poet.

1 A glotoun of wordes. [*Piers Plowman*, prologue]

2 In a somer seson whan soft was the sonne. [*Piers Plowman*, prologue]

LAO ZI or Lao Tzu *c.* 604–*c.* 531BC
Chinese philosopher.

A journey of a thousand miles must begin with a single step. [*Tao Tê Ching*]

LAPPÉ Frances Moore 1944–
US ecologist.

The act of putting into your mouth what the earth has grown is perhaps your most direct interaction with the earth. [*Diet for a Small Planet* pt 1]

LARKIN Philip 1922–1985
English poet.

1 Sexual intercourse began / In nineteen sixty-three / (Which was rather late for me). ['Annus Mirabilis']

2 'My wife and I – we're *pals*. Marriage is *fun*.' / Yes: two can live as stupidly as one. ['Marriage']

3 Far too many relied on the classic formula of a beginning, a muddle, and an end. [Of books entered for the 1977 Booker Prize in *New Fiction* Jan 1978]

4 Deprivation is for me what daffodils were for Wordsworth. [*Observer* 1979]

LASCH Christopher
US critic.

Nothing succeeds like the appearance of success. [*Culture of Narcissism*]

LAUDER Harry 1870–1950
Scottish comedian and singer.

1 Keep right on to the end of the road / Keep right on to the end. ['End of the Road']

2 O! it's nice to get up in the mornin' / But it's nicer to lie in bed. ['It's Nice to Get Up in the Mornin'']

3 I Love a Lassie. [Song title]

4 Roamin' in the Gloamin'. [Song title]

LAWRENCE D H 1885–1930
English poet, essayist and novelist.

1 Sex is the one thing you cannot really swindle; and it is the centre of the worst swindling of all, emotional swindling. ['A Propos of Lady Chatterley's Lover']

2 To the Puritan all things are impure, as somebody says. ['Cerveteri']

3 How beastly the bourgeois is / Especially the male of the species. ['How Beastly the Bourgeois Is']

4 A woman unsatisfied must have luxuries. But a woman who loves a man would sleep on a board. [Quoted in *Ladies' Home Journal* Feb 1949]

5 Men! The only animal in the world to fear! ['Mountain Lion']

6 Pornography is the attempt to insult sex, to do dirt on it. [*Phoenix*, 'Pornography and Obscenity']

7 I never saw a wild thing / Sorry for itself. ['Self-Pity']

8 Between her breasts is my home, between her breasts. / Three sides set on me space and fear, but the fourth side rests / Sure and a tower of strength, 'twixt the walls of her breasts. ['Song of a Man Who is Loved']

9 You love me so much, you want to put me in your pocket. And I should die there smothered. [*Sons and Lovers* ch 15]

10 Men are freest when they are most unconscious of freedom. [*Studies in Classic American Literature* ch 1]

11 'Be a good animal, true to your instincts,' was his motto. [*White Peacock*]

12 Don't you find it a beautiful clean thought, a world empty of people, just uninterrupted grass, and a hare sitting up? [*Women in Love*]

13 The pain of loving you / Is almost more than I can bear. I walk in fear of you. / The darkness starts up where / You stand, and the night comes through / Your eyes when you look at me. ['Young Wife']

14 I like to write when I feel spiteful; it's like having a good sneeze. [Letter to Lady Cynthia Asquith 1913]

15 It is so much more difficult to live with one's body than with one's soul. One's body is so much more exacting: what it won't have it won't have, and nothing can make bitter into sweet. [Letter 31 Oct 1913]

16 The dead don't die. They look on and help. [Letter to J Middleton Murry 2 Feb 1923]

17 I'm not sure if a mental relation with a woman doesn't make it impossible to love her. To know the *mind* of a woman is to end in hating her. Love means the pre-cognitive flow ... it is the honest state before the apple. [Letter to Dr Trigant Burrow 3 Aug 1927]

LAYTON Irving 1912–
Canadian poet.

Conscience: self-esteem with a halo. [*The Whole Bloody Bird*, 'Aphs']

LEACH Edmund 1910–1989
English social anthropologist.

Far from being the basis of the good society, the family, with its narrow privacy and tawdry secrets, is the source of all our discontents. [Reith Lecture 1967]

LEACOCK Stephen 1869–1944
Canadian political scientist, historian, and humorist.

1 Advertising may be described as the science of arresting human intelligence long enough to get money from it. [*Garden of Folly*, 'The Perfect Salesman']

2 Lord Ronald ... flung himself from the room, flung himself upon his horse and rode madly off in all directions. ['Gertrude the Governess']

3 The North alone is silent and at peace. Give man time and he will spoil that too. [*My Discovery of the West*]

LEAR Edward 1812–1888
English writer of comic verse.

1 'How pleasant to know Mr. Lear!' / Who has written such volumes of stuff! / Some think him ill-tempered and queer, / But a few think him pleasant enough. [*Nonsense Songs*, preface]

2 Far and few, far and few, / Are the lands where the Jumblies live; / Their heads are green, and their hands are blue, / And they went to sea in a Sieve. [*Nonsense Songs*, 'The Jumblies']

3 The Owl and the Pussy-Cat went to sea / In a beautiful pea-green boat. [*Nonsense Songs*, 'The Owl and the Pussy-Cat']

4 They dined on mince, and slices of quince, / Which they ate with a runcible spoon; / And hand in hand, on the edge of the sand, / They danced by the light of the moon. [*Nonsense Songs*, 'The Owl and the Pussy-Cat']

LEARY Timothy 1920–
US psychologist who popularized LSD.

Turn on, tune in and drop out. [*Politics of Ecstasy*]

LEASE Mary 1853–1933
US writer and lecturer.

Kansas had better stop raising corn and begin raising hell. [Attributed remark]

LE CARRÉ John 1931–
English novelist.

A committee is an animal with four back legs. [*Tinker, Tailor, Soldier, Spy*]

LEE Harper 1926–
US writer.

The one thing that doesn't abide by majority rule is a person's conscience. [*To Kill a Mockingbird* pt 1, ch 11]

LEE Nathaniel 1653–1692
English dramatist.

See the conquering hero comes, / Sound the trumpets, beat the drums. [*Rival Queens*]

LEHMANN Rosamond 1901–1990
English novelist.

One can present people with opportunities. One cannot make them equal to them. [*Ballad and the Source*]

LEHRER Tom 1928–
US mathematician and songwriter.

> Life is like a sewer. What you get out of it depends on what you put into it. [Preamble to song 'We Will All Go Together When We Go']

LEIGH Fred d. 1924
English songwriter.

> **1** There was I, waiting at the church, / Waiting at the church, waiting at the church, / When I found he'd left me in the lurch, / Lor, how it did upset me! / All at once he sent me round a note, / Here's the very note, / This is what he wrote – / 'Can't get away to marry you today, / My wife won't let me!' ['Waiting at the Church']

> **2** Why am I always the bridesmaid, / Never the blushing bride? ['Why Am I Always the Bridesmaid?']

LENIN Vladimir Ilyich 1870–1924
Russian revolutionary leader.

> **1** Authority poisons everybody who takes authority on himself. [To Kropotkin May 1919; quoted in T Deutsche, *Not by Politics Alone* ch 2]

> **2** It is true that liberty is precious – so precious that it must be rationed. [Quoted in S and B Webb *Soviet Communism*]

> **3** Communism is Soviet power plus the electrification of the whole country. [Report to 8th Congress of the Communist Party 1920]

LENNON John 1940–1980
English rock musician.

> **1** We're more popular than Jesus now; I don't know which will go first – rock 'n' roll or Christianity. [Of the Beatles *Evening Standard* 4 March 1966]

> **2** Will the people in the cheaper seats clap your hands? All the rest of you, if you'll just rattle your jewellery. [Royal Variety Performance 4 Nov 1963]

> **3** Give Peace a Chance. [Song title]

LENNON AND McCARTNEY John Lennon 1940–1980 and Paul McCartney 1942–
British musicians, members of the Beatles.

> **1** For I don't care too much for money, / Money can't buy me love. ['Can't Buy Me Love']

> **2** It's been a hard day's night, / And I've been working like a dog. ['Hard Day's Night']

> **3** Will you still need me, will you still feed me, / When I'm sixty four? ['When I'm Sixty Four']

> **4** Oh I get by with a little help from my friends. ['With a Little Help from My Friends']

> **5** All You Need Is Love. [Song title]

> **6** Magical Mystery Tour. [Title of song and TV film]

LENTHALL William 1591–1662
Speaker of the House of Commons.

> I have neither eye to see, nor tongue to speak here, but as the House is pleased to direct me. [Refusing to answer King Charles I's demand concerning the five MPs whom the king wished to arrest 4 Jan 1642]

LEON Henry Cecil 1902–1976
English judge.

> I think that a judge should be looked on rather as a sphinx than as a person – you shouldn't be able to imagine a judge having a bath. [Quoted in *Observer* 21 Dec 1975]

LE PEN Jean-Marie 1928–
French extreme right-wing politician.

> The left doesn't have a monopoly on ecology. We at the National Front respect life and love animals. I myself have a white rat whom I kiss every day on the mouth. [On environmentalism November 1991]

LERMONTOV Mikhail 1814–1841
Russian poet and writer.

1 The love of savages isn't much better than the love of noble ladies; ignorance and simple-heartedness can be as tiresome as coquetry. [*Hero of Our Time*, 'Bella']

2 I never sacrificed anything for those I loved. I loved for my own sake, for my own pleasure. [*Hero of Our Time*, 'Princess Mary']

LERNER Alan Jay 1918–1986
US lyricist.

1 Don't let it be forgot / That once there was a spot / For one brief shining moment that was known / As Camelot. [*Camelot* (invoked by Jacqueline Kennedy to describe her husband's presidency)]

2 I'm getting married in the morning, / Ding! dong! the bells are gonna chime. / Pull out the stopper; / Let's have a whopper; / But get me to the church on time. ['Get Me to the Church on Time']

3 Why can't a woman be more like a man? ['Hymn to Him']

4 On a clear day (you can see forever). [Song from musical *On a Clear Day*]

LESSING Gotthold 1729–1781
German dramatist and critic.

1 A man who does not lose his reason over certain things has none to lose. [*Emilia Galotti*]

2 Yesterday I loved, today I suffer, tomorrow I die: but I still think fondly, today and tomorrow, of yesterday. ['Lied aus dem Spanischen']

LEVANT Oscar 1906–1972
US pianist and composer.

1 Marriage is a triumph of habit over hate. [*Memoirs of an Amnesiac*]

2 Underneath this flabby exterior is an enormous lack of character. [*Memoirs of an Amnesiac*]

LEVERHULME Viscount 1851–1925
English industrialist.

Half the money I spend on advertising is wasted, and the trouble is I don't know which half. [Quoted in D Ogilvy *Confessions of an Advertising Man*.]

LÉVI-STRAUSS Claude 1908–
French anthropologist.

The world began without man, and it will end without him. [*Tristes Tropiques* pt 9, ch 40]

LEWIS C S 1898–1963
English theologian and novelist.

1 For this is one of the miracles of love; it gives – to both, but perhaps especially to the woman – a power

Lewis in 1950. He was the author of the popular children's books *The Chronicles of Narnia*. He was a committed Christian and wrote essays in popular theology such as *The Screwtape Letters* 1942 and the autobiographical *Surprised by Joy* 1955.

of seeing through its own enchantments and yet not being disenchanted. [*Grief Observed*]

2 My daughter and my mother, my pupil and my teacher, my subject and my sovereign; and always holding all these in solution, my trusty comrade, friend, shipmate, fellow-soldier. My mistress; but at the same time all that any man friend (and I have had good ones) has ever been to me. Perhaps more. [Of his wife, the US poet Joy Davidman in *Grief Observed*]

3 There is, hidden or flaunted, a sword between the sexes till an entire marriage reconciles them. [*Grief Observed*]

4 The safest road to Hell is the gradual one. [*Screwtape Letters*]

5 She's the sort of woman who lives for others – you can always tell the others by their hunted expression. [*Screwtape Letters*]

6 Courage is not simply *one* of the virtues but the form of every virtue at the testing point, which means at the point of highest reality. [Quoted in C Connolly *Unquiet Grave* pt 3]

LEWIS Sinclair 1885–1951
US novelist.

Our American professors like their literature clear and cold and pure and very dead. [*American Fear of Literature* (Nobel Prize Address 12 Dec 1930)]

LICHTENBERG G C 1742–1799
German physicist and philosopher.

1 Food probably has a very great influence on the condition of men ... Who knows if a well-prepared soup was not responsible for the pneumatic pump or a poor one for a war? [*Aphorisms*, 'Notebook A' 14]

2 If an angel were ever to tell us anything of his philosophy I believe many propositions would sound like 2 times 2 equals 13. [*Aphorisms*, 'Notebook B' 44]

3 Once we know our weaknesses they cease to do us any harm. [*Aphorisms*, 'Notebook D' 5]

4 Many things about our bodies would not seem so filthy and obscene if we did not have the idea of nobility in our heads. [*Aphorisms*, 'Notebook D' 6]

5 Man is to be found in reason, God in the passions. [*Aphorisms*, 'Notebook K' 21]

6 To receive applause for works which do not demand all our powers hinders our advance towards a perfecting of our spirit. [*Aphorisms*, 'Notebook K' 42]

LIDDELL HART Basil 1895–1970
British military strategist.

Fifty years were spent in the process of making Europe explosive. Five days were enough to detonate it. [*Real War, 1914–1918*]

LINCOLN Abraham 1809–1865
US Republican president.

1 No man is good enough to govern another man without that other's consent. [Speech 1854]

2 The ballot is stronger than the bullet. [Speech 19 May 1856]

3 You can fool all the people some of the time, and some of the people all the time, but you can not fool all the people all of the time. [Attributed words in a speech at Clinton 8 Sept 1858]

4 I intend no modification of my oft-expressed personal wish that all men everywhere could be free. [Letter to H Greeley 22 Aug 1862]

5 In giving freedom to the slave, we assure freedom to the free, – honourable alike in what we give and what we preserve. [Annual message to Congress 1 Dec 1862]

6 Fourscore and seven years ago our fathers brought forth upon this continent a new nation, conceived in liberty, and dedicated to the proposition that all men are created equal. ['Gettysburg Address' 19 Nov 1863]

President of the USA during the Civil War, Abraham Lincoln. His main aim was to preserve the union and prevent the secession of the southern States.

7 That we here highly resolved that the dead shall not have died in vain, that this nation, under God, shall have a new birth of freedom; and that government of the people, by the people, and for the people, shall not perish from the earth. [Gettysburg Address 19 Nov 1863]

8 With malice toward none; with charity for all; with firmness in the right, as God gives us to see the right. [Second Inaugural Address 4 March 1865]

9 People who like this sort of thing will find this the sort of thing they like. [Comment on a book]

LINKLATER Eric 1889–1974
Scottish novelist.

1 I've been married six months. She looks like a million dollars, but she only knows a hundred and twenty words and she's only got two ideas in her head. The other one's hats. [*Juan in America* ch 5]

2 Helen discovered that she was almost alone, among all her other friends, in never having been married or never having written a book. She decided that the second choice would probably have less permanent consequences. [*Magnus Merriman*]

LINKLETTER Art 1912–
US writer and broadcaster.

The four stages of man are infancy, childhood, adolescence and obsolescence. [*Child's Garden of Misinformation*]

LINNAEUS Carolus 1707–1778
Swedish naturalist and physician.

Nature does not make jumps. [*Philosophia Botanica*]

LIPPMANN Walter 1889–1974
US liberal political commentator.

1 The final test of a leader is that he leaves behind him in other men the conviction and the will to carry on. [*New York Herald Tribune* 14 Apr 1945]

2 Our conscience is not the vessel of eternal verities. It grows with our social life, and a new social condition means a radical change in conscience. [*Preface to Politics* ch 12]

LITVINOV Maxim 1876–1951
Soviet politician.

Peace is indivisible. [Speech to League of Nations July 1936]

LIVERMORE Mary c. 1820–1905
US writer and social reformer.

Above the titles of wife and mother, which, although dear, are transitory and accidental, there is the title human being, which precedes and out-ranks every other. [*What Shall We Do with Our Daughter* ch 7]

LIVINGSTONE David 1813–1873
Scottish physician, missionary, and explorer.

Men are immortal until their work is done. [Letter describing the death of Bishop Mackenzie March 1862]

LIVINGSTONE Ken 1945–
British left-wing Labour politician.

Part of the problem is that many MPs never see the London that exists beyond the wine bars and brothels of Westminster. [Quoted in *Observer* 22 Feb 1987]

LIVY 59 BC–AD 17
Roman historian.

Woe to the vanquished. [*History* V. 48]

LLEWELLYN Richard 1907–1983
Welsh writer.

How Green Was My Valley. [Book title]

LLOYD GEORGE David 1863–1945
British Liberal prime minister.

1 He had sufficient conscience to bother him, but not sufficient to keep him straight. [Of Ramsay MacDonald, quoted in A. J. Sylvester *Life with Lloyd George*]

2 A fully-equipped duke costs as much to keep up as two Dreadnoughts; and dukes are just as great a terror and they last longer. [Speech at Newcastle 9 Oct 1909]

3 What is our task? To make Britain a fit country for heroes to live in. [Speech at Wolverhampton 23 Nov 1918]

4 The finest eloquence is that which gets things done; the worst is that which delays them. [Speech at Paris Peace Conference Jan 1919]

LOCKE John 1632–1704
English philosopher.

1 It is one thing to show a man that he is in error, and another to put him in possession of the truth. [*Essay Concerning Human Understanding*]

2 Nothing was made by God for man to spoil or destroy. [*Second Treatise on Government* IV.31]

LODGE David 1935–
English academic, writer and critic.

Literature is mostly about having sex and not much about having children. Life is the other way round. [*British Museum is Falling Down*]

LODGE Thomas 1558–1625
English writer.

Love in my bosom like a bee / Doth suck his sweet; / Now with his wings he plays with me, / Now with his feet. / Within mine eyes he makes his nest, / His bed amidst my tender breast; / My kisses are his daily feast, / And yet he robs me of my rest. / Ah, wanton, will ye? ['Love in my bosom like a bee']

LOESSER Frank 1910–1969
US songwriter.

1 See what the boys in the back room will have / And tell them I'm having the same. ['Boys in the Back Room']

2 I'd love to get you / On a slow boat to China. ['Slow Boat to China']

LONGFELLOW Henry Wadsworth 1807–1882
US poet.

1 I shot an arrow into the air, / It fell to earth, I knew not where. ['Arrow and the Song']

2 A banner with the strange device, / Excelsior! ['Excelsior']

3 O, there is nothing holier, in this life of ours, than the first consciousness of love, – the first fluttering of its silken wings. [*Hyperion* bk 3 ch 6]

4 The men that women marry, / And why they marry them, will always be / A marvel and a mystery to the world. [*Michael Angelo*]

US poet Henry Wadsworth Longfellow. He was the most famous American poet of the 19th century and the first to be commemorated in Poets' Corner, Westminster Abbey, London. His best-known works are his long narrative poems such as *The Song of Hiawatha*.

5 Life is real! Life is earnest! ['Psalm of Life']

6 Though the mills of God grind slowly, yet they grind exceeding small. ['Retribution']

7 There's nothing in this world so sweet as love, / And next to love the sweetest thing is hate. [*Spanish Student* II. v]

8 Ships that pass in the night, and speak each other in passing. [*Tales of a Wayside Inn*, 'Theologian's Tale']

9 It was the schooner Hesperus, / That sailed the wintry sea. ['Wreck of the Hesperus']

LOOS Anita 1893–1981
US humorous writer.

So this gentleman said a girl with brains ought to do something with them besides think. [*Gentlemen Prefer Blondes*]

LORENZ Konrad 1903–1989
Austrian zoologist.

It is a good morning exercise for a research scientist to discard a pet hypothesis every day before breakfast. It keeps him young. [*So-Called Evil*]

LOUIS Joe 1914–1981
US boxer.

He can run, but he can't hide. [Of his opponent Billy Conn, in *New York Herald Tribune* 9 June 1946]

LOUIS XIV *the Sun King* 1638–1715
French monarch.

1 I am the State. [Attributed remark before the Parlement of Paris 13 April 1655]

2 The Pyrenees have ceased to exist. [Attributed remark on the accession of his grandson to the throne of Spain 1700]

LOVELACE Richard 1618–1658
English poet.

1 Stone walls do not a prison make / Nor iron bars a cage. ['To Althea, From Prison']

2 I could not love thee (Dear) so much, / Lov'd I not honour more. ['To Lucasta, Going to the Wars']

LOVELL Maria 1803–1877
English actress and dramatist.

Two souls with but a single thought, / Two hearts that beat as one. [*Ingomar the Barbarian* II]

LOWELL James Russell 1819–1891
US poet and critic.

1 A wise scepticism is the first attribute of a good critic. [*Among My Books*]

2 There is no good in arguing with the inevitable. The only argument available with an east wind is to put on your overcoat. [*Democracy and Addresses*]

LOWELL Robert 1917–1977
US poet.

1 After loving you so much, can I forget / you for eternity, and have no other choice? ['Obit']

2 The Lord survives the rainbow of His will. ['Quaker Graveyard in Nantucket']

3 If we see light at the end of the tunnel, / It's the light of the oncoming train. ['Since 1939']

LUCAS George 1944–
US cinema director and producer.

May the force be with you. [*Star Wars: from the Adventures of Luke Skywalker*]

LUCE Clare Boothe 1903–1987
US journalist, playwright, and politician.

1 But if God had wanted us to think just with our wombs, why did He give us a brain? [*Life* 16 Oct 1970]

2 There's nothing like a good dose of another woman to make a man appreciate his wife. [Quoted in L and M Cown *Wit of Women*]

3 You know, that's the only good thing about divorce; you get to sleep with your mother. [*The Women* I]

LUCRETIUS c. 99–c. 55 BC
Roman poet and Epicurean philosopher.

1 And like runners they hand on the torch of life. [*De Rerum Natura*]

2 Nothing can be created out of nothing. [*De Rerum Natura*]

LUDENDORFF Erich von 1965–1937
German general in World War I.

The Army had been fought to a standstill and was utterly worn out. [On the Battle of the Somme]

LUTHER Martin 1483–1546
German Christian church reformer, founder of Protestantism.

1 There is no more lovely, friendly and charming relationship, communion or company than a good marriage. [*Table Talk* 292]

2 Item: Man does not exist for the sake of woman, but woman exists for the sake of man and hence there shall be this difference that a man shall love his wife, but never be subject to her, but the wife shall honour and fear the husband. [*Vindication of Married Life*]

Rosa Luxemburg, German political activist and co-founder of the radical Spartacists, a group that subsequently became the German Communist Party. An effective orator and writer, she wrote *Sozialreform oder Revolution /Social Reform or Revolution* 1889.

3 My conscience is taken captive by God's word, I cannot and will not recant anything. ... Here I stand. I can do no other. God help me. Amen. [Speech at the Diet of Worms 18 Apr 1521]

4 Who loves not wine, woman and song, / Remains a fool his whole life long. [Attributed remark]

LUXEMBURG Rosa 1870–1919
Polish-born German communist.

Freedom is always and exclusively freedom for the one who thinks differently. [*Russian Revolution*]

LYDGATE John *c.* 1370–*c.* 1451
English poet.

Love is more than gold or gret richesse. [*Story of Thebes* pt 3]

LYLY John *c.* 1553–1606
English dramatist.

1 Cupid and my Campaspe play'd / At cards for kisses, Cupid paid. [*Campaspe* III. v]

2 O ye Gods, have ye ordained for every malady a medicine, for every sore a salve, for every pain a plaster, leaving only love remedyless? [*Euphues*]

3 Night hath a thousand eyes. [*Maides Metamorphose*]

LYTE Henry Francis 1793–1847
English cleric and hymn writer.

1 Abide with me; fast falls the eventide; / The darkness deepens; Lord, with me abide. ['Abide with Me']

2 Where is death's sting? Where, Grave, thy victory? ['Abide with Me']

MACAULAY Thomas, Lord 1800–1859
English historian.

1 Lues Boswelliana, or disease of admiration. [*Historical Essays* 'Earl of Chatham']

2 The business of everybody is the business of nobody. [*Historical Essays*, 'Hallam's Constitutional History']

3 He knew that the essence of war is violence, and that moderation in war is imbecility. [Of John Hampden in *Historical Essays*, 'Lord Nugent's Memorials of Hampden']

4 The Chief Justice was rich, quiet, and infamous. [*Historical Essays*, 'Warren Hastings']

5 The great Proconsul. [*Historical Essays*, 'Warren Hastings']

6 Persecution produced its natural effect on them. It found them a sect; it made them a faction. [*History of England*]

7 The Puritan hated bear-baiting, not because it gave pain to the bear, but because it gave pleasure to the spectators. [*History of England*]

8 Lars Porsena of Clusium / By the nine gods he swore / That the great house of Tarquin / Should suffer wrong no more. [*Lays of Ancient Rome*, 'Horatius' 1]

9 Now who will stand on either hand, / And keep the bridge with me? [*Lays of Ancient Rome*, 'Horatius' 29]

10 Was none who would be foremost / To lead such dire attack; / But those behind cried 'Forward!' / And those before cried 'Back!' [*Lays of Ancient Rome*, 'Horatius' 50]

11 And even the ranks of Tuscany / Could scarce forbear to cheer. [*Lays of Ancient Rome*, 'Horatius' 60]

12 As civilization advances, poetry almost necessarily declines. [*Literary Essays*, 'Milton']

13 We know no spectacle so ridiculous as the British public in one of its periodical fits of morality. [*Literary Essays*, Moore's 'Life of Lord Byron']

McAULIFFE Anthony 1898–1975
US brigadier general in World War II.

Nuts! [Reply to a German demand that he surrender in the Battle of the Bulge]

McCARTHY Joseph 1885–1943
US songwriter.

You made me love you, / I didn't want to do it. ['You made me Love You']

McCARTHY Joseph 1908–1957
US Republican politician.

McCarthyism is Americanism with its sleeves rolled. [Speech in Wisconsin 1952]

McCARTHY Mary 1912–1989
US novelist and critic.

1 If someone tells you he is going to make a 'realistic decision', you immediately understand that he has resolved to do something bad. ['American Realist Playwrights']

2 Every age has a keyhole to which its eye is pasted. [*On the Contrary* pt 1, 'My Confession']

McCOY Horace 1897–1955
US novelist and screenwriter.

They Shoot Horses Don't They. [Title of novel]

McCRAE John 1872–1918
Canadian poet.

Take up our quarrel with the foe; / To you from falling hands we throw / The torch; be yours to hold it high. / If ye break faith with us who die / We shall not sleep, though poppies grow / In Flanders fields. ['In Flanders Fields']

MCCULLERS Carson 1917–1967
US author.

1 There's nothing that makes you so aware of the improvisation of human existence as a song unfinished. [*Ballad of the Sad Café*, 'The Sojourner']

2 The Heart Is a Lonely Hunter. [Title of novel]

MACDONALD George 1824–1905
Scottish novelist and children's writer.

Here lie I, Martin Elginbrodde: / Hae mercy o' my soul, Lord God; / As I wad do, were I Lord God, / And ye were Martin Elginbrodde. [*David Elginbrod*]

MCGOOHAN Patrick 1928–
English-born US actor.

The greatest evil that one has to fight constantly, every minute of the day until one dies, is the worse part of oneself. [Quoted in Rogers *The Prisoner and Danger Man*, 'I Am Not a Number, I Am a Free Man']

MACKAY Charles 1814–1849
English songwriter.

There's a good time coming, boys, / A good time coming. ['Good Time Coming']

MACKENZIE Compton 1883–1972
Scottish author.

1 I asked him about the landing at Gallipoli, but he could tell me nothing about it. All he knew was that he had jumped out of a bloody boat in the dark and before he had walked five bloody yards he had a bloody bullet in his foot and he had been pushed back to Alexandria almost before he bloody well knew he had left it. [*Gallipoli Memories*]

2 Women do not find it difficult nowadays to behave like men, but they often find it extremely difficult to behave like gentlemen. [*Literature in My Time*]

MACKINTOSH James 1765–1832
Scottish lawyer, philosopher, and historian.

1 Men are never so good or so bad as their opinions. [*Ethical Philosophy*]

2 The Commons, faithful to their system, remained in a wise and masterly inactivity. [*Vindiciæ Gallicæ*]

MCLAUGHLIN Mignon c. 1915–
US writer and editor.

Every society honors its live conformists and its dead troublemakers. [*Neurotic's Notebook*]

MCLEOD Fiona 1855–1905
Scottish writer.

My heart is a lonely hunter that hunts on a lonely hill. ['Lonely Hunter']

MCLUHAN Marshall 1911–1980
Canadian communications theorist.

1 The new electronic interdependence recreates the world in the image of a global village. [*Gutenberg Galaxy*]

2 For tribal man space was the uncontrollable mystery. For technological man it is time that occupies the same role. [*Mechanical Bride*]

3 The mark of our time is its revulsion against imposed patterns. [*Understanding Media*, Introduction]

4 The medium is the message. [*Understanding Media* ch 1]

5 The car has become the carapace, the protective and aggressive shell, of urban and suburban man. [*Understanding Media* ch 22]

MACMILLAN Harold 1894–1986
British Conservative prime minister.

1 We have not overthrown the divine right of kings to fall down for the divine right of experts. [Speech in Strasbourg 16 Aug 1950]

2 Most of our people have never had it so good. [Speech in Bedford 20 July 1957]

3 The wind of change is blowing through this continent. [Speech in Cape Town 3 Feb 1960]

4 As usual the Liberals offer a mixture of sound and original ideas. Unfortunately none of the sound ideas is original and none of the original ideas is sound. [Speech to London Conservatives 7 March 1962]

MACNEICE Louis 1907–1963
Irish-born English poet.

1 Better authentic mammon than a bogus god. [*Autumn Journal*]

2 Time was away and somewhere else. ['Meeting Point']

3 The sunlight on the garden / Hardens and grows cold, / We cannot cage the minute / Within its net of gold, / When all is told / We cannot beg for pardon. ['Sunlight on the Garden']

4 So they were married – to be the more together – / And found they were never again so much together, / Divided by the morning tea, / By the evening paper, / By children and tradesmen's bills. ['Les Sylphides]

MADONNA 1959–
US pop star.

1 Catholicism is not a soothing religion. It's a painful religion. We're all gluttons for punishment. [Interview in *Rolling Stone* 23 March 1989]

2 Without you, I'm nothing ... without Elvis, you're nothing. [To her stage cast and crew]

MAETERLINCK Maurice, Count Maeterlinck
1862–1949
Belgian poet and dramatist.

We possess only the happiness we are able to understand. [*Wisdom and Destiny*]

MAHLER Gustav
1860–1911
Czechoslovakian-born Austrian composer.

Both my marriages were failures! Number one departed and number two stayed. [Attributed remark]

US singer and actress Madonna, one of the most successful and controversial pop icons of the 1980s and 1990s. For some, the frank eroticism of her songs and stage acts is a spirited refusal to pander to the prevalent submissive image of female sexuality. For others, it is a cynical manipulation of sexual stereotypes.

MAILER Norman 1923–
US novelist and journalist.

1 There are four stages to a marriage. First there's the affair, then the marriage, then children and finally the fourth stage, without which you cannot know a woman, the divorce. [Quoted in *Nova* 1969]

2 Women think of being a man as a gift. It is a duty. Even making love can be a duty. A man has always got to get it up and love isn't always enough. [Quoted in *Nova* 1969]

3 A modern democracy is a tyranny whose borders are undefined; one discovers how far one can go only by traveling in a straight line until one is stopped. [*Presidential Papers*, Preface]

4 Alimony is the curse of the writing classes. [Attributed remark 1980]

MAISTRE Joseph de 1753–1821
French monarchist.

Every country has the government it deserves. [*Lettres et opuscules inédits*]

MALAMUD Bernard 1914–1986
US novelist and short-story writer.

The past exudes legend: one can't make pure clay of time's mud. [*Dubin's Lives*]

MALCOLM X 1926–1965
US black nationalist leader.

1 If someone puts his hand on you, send him to the cemetery. [*Malcolm X Speaks*]

2 You can't separate peace from freedom because no one can be at peace unless he has his freedom. [Speech, New York City, 7 Jan 1965]

MALLORY George Leigh 1886–1924
English mountaineer.

Because it's there. [Response to question 'Why do you want to climb Mount Everest?']

MALORY Sir Thomas D. 1471
English writer.

The joy of love is too short, and the sorrow thereof, and what cometh thereof, dureth over long. [*Le Morte d'Arthur* bk 10 ch 56]

MANCROFT Lord 1917–1987
English businessman and writer.

Cricket – a game which the English, not being a spiritual people, have invented in order to give themselves some conception of eternity. [*Bees in Some Bonnets*]

MANDELA Nelson 1918–
South African president.

Never, never and never again shall it be that this beautiful land will again experience the oppression of one by another. [Inaugural speech as president of South Africa May 1994]

MANGIN Charles Marie Emmanuel 1866–1925
French general in World War I.

Whatever you do, you lose a lot of men. [Remark on comparing casualty figures from each division at Verdun 1916]

MANN Thomas 1875–1955
German writer and critic.

Logically considered, freedom and equality are mutually exclusive, just as society and the individual are mutually exclusive. [*Order of the Day*, 'The War and the Future']

MAO ZEDONG or *Mao Tse-tung* 1893–1976
Chinese Marxist leader and theoretician.

1 Communism is not love. Communism is a hammer which we use to crush the enemy. [*Time* 18 Dec 1950]

2 Letting a hundred flowers blossom and a hundred schools of thought contend is the policy for promoting progress in the arts and the sciences and a flourishing socialist culture in our land. [Speech in Peking 27 Feb 1957]

MARADONA Diego 1960–
Argentine footballer.

> The goal was scored a little bit by
> the hand of God, another bit by the
> head of Maradona.
> [After scoring a doubtful goal in the
> World Cup 1986]

MARCUS 121–180
Roman emperor and stoic philosopher.

> **1** Adapt thyself to the things
> amidst which thy lot has been cast
> and love in sincerity the fellow-crea-
> tures with whom destiny has
> ordained thou shalt live. [*Meditations*]

> **2** Let thy every action, word and
> thought be that of one who is pre-
> pared at any moment to quit this
> life. [*Meditations*]

> **3** Men exist for the sake of one
> another. Either teach them or bear
> with them. [*Meditations*]

> **4** Waste no more time arguing
> what a good man should be. Be one.
> [*Meditations*]

MARIE ANTOINETTE 1755–1793
Queen of France.

> Let them eat cake. [Attributed remark,
> on being told that the poor had no bread]

MARITAIN Jacques 1882–1973
French philosopher.

> We don't love qualities, we love per-
> sons; sometimes by reason of their
> defects as well as of their qualities.
> [*Reflections on America* ch 3]

MARLBOROUGH Sarah 1660–1744
Wife of the first Duke of Marlborough.

> The Duke returned from the wars
> today and did pleasure me in his
> top-boots. [Attributed remark]

MARLOWE Christopher 1564–1593
English poet and dramatist.

> **1** Unhappy spirits that fell with
> Lucifer, / Conspired against our
> God with Lucifer, / And are for ever

Marie Antoinette. Queen of France, consort of Louis XVI; daughter of Emperor Francis I and Maria Theresa. Unpopular because of her Austrian origin and extravagant life-style, she was eventually executed after sadistic treatment in prison. Her proud bearing in the face of adversity earned her belated respect.

> damned with Lucifer. [*Doctor Faustus*
> I. iii]

> **2** Why this is hell, nor am I out of
> it: / Thinkst thou that I who saw the
> face of God, / And tasted the eter-
> nal joys of heaven, / Am not tor-
> mented with ten thousand hells / In
> being deprived of everlasting bliss?
> [*Doctor Faustus* I. iii]

> **3** Was this the face that launch'd a
> thousand ships, / And burnt the
> topless towers of Ilium? [*Doctor
> Faustus* V. i]

4 Stand still you ever-moving spheres of heaven, / That time may cease, and midnight never come. [*Doctor Faustus* V. ii]

5 Cut is the branch that might have grown full straight, / And burnèd is Apollo's laurel bough, / That sometime grew within this learned man. [*Doctor Faustus*, epilogue]

6 My men, like satyrs grazing on the lawns, / Shall with their goat feet dance an antic hay. [*Edward II* I. i]

7 It lies not in our power to love, or hate, / For will in us is over-rul'd by fate. [*Hero and Leander* I]

8 Who ever loved that loved not at first sight? [*Hero and Leander* I]

9 I count religion but a childish toy, / And hold there is no sin but ignorance. [*Jew of Malta*, prologue]

10 Infinite riches in a little room. [*Jew of Malta* I. i]

11 Come live with me and be my love; / And we will all the pleasures prove / That hills and valleys, dales and fields, / Woods or steepy mountain yields. ['Passionate Shepherd to his Love']

12 Is it not passing brave to be a King, / And ride in triumph through Persepolis? [*Tamburlaine* I]

13 Jigging veins of rhyming mother wits. [*Tamburlaine* I]

14 That perfect bliss and sole felicity, / The sweet fruition of an earthly crown. [*Tamburlaine* I]

15 Holla, ye pampered Jades of Asia: / What, can ye draw but twenty miles a day? [*Tamburlaine* II]

MARQUIS Don 1878–1937
US writer.

1 Procrastination is the / art of keeping / up with yesterday. [*archy and mehitabel* XII, 'certain maxims of archy']

2 Honesty is a good thing but it is not profitable to its possessor unless it is kept under control. ['archygrams']

3 Now and then there is a person born who is so unlucky that he runs into accidents which started to happen to somebody else. ['archy says']

4 An optimist is a guy that has never had much experience. ['certain maxims of archy']

5 Writing a book of poetry is like dropping a rose petal down the Grand Canyon and waiting for the echo. [Quoted in E Anthony *O Rare Don Marquis*]

6 There's a dance in the old dame yet toujours gai toujours gai. ['song of mehitabel']

MARRYAT Frederick (Captain) 1792–1848
English naval officer and writer.

1 As savage as a bear with a sore head. [*King's Own*]

2 If you please, ma'am, it was a very little one. [*Midshipman Easy* (servant's excuse for her illegitimate baby)]

3 I think it much better that ... every man paddle his own canoe. [*Settlers in Canada*]

MARTIAL AD 41–104
Latin poet and epigrammatist.

The country in town. [*Epigrammata*]

MARTINEAU Harriet 1802–1876
English writer.

1 Any one must see at a glance that if men and women marry those whom they do not love, they must love those whom they do not marry. [*Society in America* vol III 'Marriage']

2 The early marriages of silly children ... where ... every woman is married before she well knows how serious a matter human life is. [*Society in America* vol III 'Marriage']

MARVELL Andrew 1620–1678
English metaphysical poet and satirist.

1 Where the remote Bermudas ride / In th' ocean's bosom unespied. ['The Garden']

2 Annihilating all that's made / To a green thought in a green shade. ['The Garden']

3 The Gods, that mortal beauty chase, / Still in a tree did end their race. ['The Garden']

4 How vainly men themselves amaze / To win the palm, the oak, or bays; / And their uncessant labours see / Crown'd from some single herb or tree. ['The Garden']

5 Society is all but rude, / To this delicious solitude. ['The Garden']

6 Two Paradises 'twere in one / To live in Paradise alone. ['The Garden']

7 He nothing common did or mean / Upon that memorable scene: / But with his keener eye / The axe's edge did try. ['Horatian Ode']

8 He is Translation's thief that addeth more, / As much as he that taketh from the store / Of the first author. ['To Dr. Witty']

9 But at my back I always hear / Time's wingèd chariot hurrying near. / And yonder all before us lie / Deserts of vast eternity. ['To His Coy Mistress']

10 The grave's a fine and private place, / But none I think do there embrace. ['To His Coy Mistress']

11 Had we but world enough, and time, / This coyness Lady were no crime. / We would sit down, and think which way / To walk, and pass our long love's day. ['To His Coy Mistress']

12 Thrice happy he who, not mistook, / Hath read in Nature's mystic book. ['Upon Appleton House']

MARX Groucho 1890–1977
US film comedian.

I never forget a face but in your case I'll be glad to make an exception. [Leo Rosten *People I have loved, known or admired*]

MARX Karl 1818–1883
German social theorist and economic historian.

Religion is the sigh of the oppressed creature, the sentiment of the heartless world, and the soul of soulless conditions. It is the opium of the people. [Quoted in Ernst Fischer *Marx in His Own Words*]

MARY I 1516–1558
Queen of England.

When I am dead and opened, you shall find 'Calais' lying in my heart. [Attributed remark in Holished's *Chronicles*]

MASEFIELD John 1878–1967
English poet and novelist.

1 But the loveliest things of beauty God ever has showed to me, / Are her voice, and her hair, and eyes, and the dear red curve of her lips. ['Beauty']

2 Dirty British coaster with a salt-caked smoke stack, / Butting through the Channel in the mad March days, / With a cargo of Tyne coal, / Road-rail, pig-lead, / Firewood, iron-ware, and cheap tin trays. ['Cargoes']

3 Quinquireme of Nineveh from distant Ophir / Rowing home to haven in sunny Palestine, / With a cargo of ivory, / And apes and peacocks, / Sandalwood, cedarwood, and sweet white wine. ['Cargoes']

4 I must go down to the seas again, to the lonely sea and the sky, / And all I ask is a tall ship and a star to steer her by. ['Sea Fever']

MASON Jackie 1931–
US humorist.

I have enough money to last me the rest of my life unless I buy something. [*Jackie Mason's America*]

MASSINGER Philip 1583–1640
English dramatist.

> **1** He that would govern others, first should be / The master of himself. [*The Bondman*]

> **2** A New Way to Pay Old Debts. [Play title]

MATISSE Henri 1869–1954
French painter.

> **1** I wouldn't mind turning into a vermilion goldfish. [F Gilot and C Lake 'Life with Picasso' (when asked about the afterlife, aged 80)]

> **2** There is nothing more difficult for a truly creative painter than to paint a rose, because before he can do so he has first to forget all the roses that were ever painted. [Remark recalled in obituaries after his death 5 Nov 1954]

MAUGHAM W Somerset 1874–1965
English novelist.

> **1** You know, of course, that the Tasmanians, who never committed adultery, are now extinct. [*The Breadwinner* III]

> **2** Beauty is an ecstasy ... There is really nothing to be said about it. It is like the perfume of a rose: you can smell it and that is all. [*Cakes and Ale* ch 11]

> **3** A woman will always sacrifice herself if you give her the opportunity. It is her favourite form of self-indulgence. [*The Circle* III]

> **4** It's not the seven deadly virtues that make a man a good husband, but the three hundred pleasing amiabilities. [*Constant Wife* I]

> **5** We have long passed the Victorian Era when asterisks were followed after a certain interval by a baby. [*Constant Wife*]

> **6** No married man's ever made up his mind till he's heard what his wife has got to say about it. [*Lady Frederick*]

> **7** Like all weak men he laid an exaggerated stress on not changing one's mind. [*Of Human Bondage* ch 39]

> **8** Money is like a sixth sense without which you cannot make a complete use of the other five. [*Of Human Bondage* ch 51]

> **9** It is not true that suffering ennobles the character; happiness does that sometimes, but suffering, for the most part, makes men petty and vindictive. [*Moon and Sixpence* ch 17]

> **10** Because women can do nothing except love, they've given it a ridiculous importance. [*Moon and Sixpence*]

> **11** There is no explanation for evil. It must be looked upon as a necessary part of the order of the universe. [*Summing Up* ch 73]

> **12** The tragedy of love is indifference. [*Trembling of a Leaf* ch 4]

> **13** Love is the only dirty trick played on us to achieve continuation of the species. [*Writer's Notebook*]

MAUPASSANT Guy de 1850–1893
French novelist.

> It is love that is sacred. ... Marriage and love have nothing in common. ... We marry only once ... but we may love twenty times. ... Marriage is law, and love is instinct. ['Love of Long Ago']

MAURIAC François 1885–1970
French novelist.

> Let us be wary of ready-made ideas about courage and cowardice: the same burden weighs infinitely more heavily on some shoulders than on others. [*Second Thoughts*]

MAUROIS André 1885–1967
French novelist.

> **1** A marriage without conflicts is almost as inconceivable as a nation without crises. [*Art of Living*]

2 A successful marriage is an edifice that must be rebuilt every day. [*Art of Living*]

3 A woman does not want her love affairs talked about. Yet she wants everybody to know that someone loves her. [Quoted in *Ladies' Home Journal* April 1942]

MAXTON James 1885–1946
British politician.

All I say is, if you cannot ride two horses you have no right in the circus. [On being told that he could not be in two political parties, in *Daily Herald* 12 Jan 1932]

MAYAKOVSKY Vladimir 1893–1930
Russian poet.

1 If you wish – / ... I'll be irreproachably tender; / not a man, but–a cloud in trousers. ['Cloud in Trousers']

2 Love / for us / is no arboured paradise – / to us / love / says humming, / that the heart's / stalled motor / has begun working again. ['Letter from Paris to Comrade Kostrov on the Nature of Love'

3 The love boat has crashed against the everyday. You and I, we are quits, and there is no point in listing mutual pains, sorrows, and hurts. [Unfinished poem written at the time of his suicide 1930.]

MAYO Charles H 1865–1939
US physician.

The definition of a specialist as one who 'knows more and more about less and less' is good and true. [*Modern Hospital* Sept 1938]

MEAD Margaret 1901–1978
US anthropologist.

Human beings do not carry civilization in their genes. [*New York Times Magazine* April 1964]

MEDAWAR Peter 1915–1987
Brazilian-born English immunologist.

If politics is the art of the possible, research is surely the art of the soluble. [*Art of the Soluble*]

MEHTA Gita 1943–
Indian writer.

The art of dialling has replaced the art of dialogue. [*Karma Cola* VIII 2]

MELBOURNE William, Lord 1779–1848
British Whig prime minister.

1 I wish I was as cocksure of anything as Tom Macaulay is of everything. [Remark]

English Whig politician William Melbourne, a supporter of Parliamentary reform. He was prime minister when Queen Victoria came to the throne and showed tact and benevolence in guiding her through her early years of rule.

2 Things have come to a pretty pass when religion is allowed to invade the sphere of private life. [Remark after listening to an evangelical sermon]

MELVILLE Herman 1819–1891
US novelist and short-story writer.

Call me Ishmael. [*Moby Dick*]

MENANDER c. 342 BC–291 BC
Greek comic dramatist.

1 Evil communications corrupt good manners. [*Oxford Book of Greek Verse*]

2 Marriage, if one will face the truth, is an evil, but a necessary evil. [Unidentified fragment 545]

MENCKEN H L 1880–1956
US essayist and critic.

1 Nineteen suburbs in search of a metropolis. [On Los Angeles, *Americana*]

2 The saddest life is that of a political aspirant under democracy. His failure is ignominious and his success is disgraceful. [*Baltimore Evening Sun* 9 Dec 1929]

3 No one in this world, so far as I know – has ever lost money by underestimating the intelligence of the great masses of the plain people. [*Chicago Tribune* 19 Sept 1926]

4 Archbishop – A Christian ecclesiastic of a rank superior to that attained by Christ. [*Chrestomathy*, 'Sententiae: Arcana Clestia']

5 A celebrity is one who is known to many persons he is glad he doesn't know. [*Chrestomathy*, 'Sententiae: The Mind of Men']

6 Conscience is the inner voice which warns us that someone may be looking. [*Chrestomathy*, 'Sententiae: the Mind of Men']

7 Love is the delusion that one woman differs from another. [*Chrestomathy* ch 30]

8 Puritanism. The haunting fear that someone, somewhere, may be happy. [*Chrestomathy*]

9 Democracy is the theory that the common people know what they want, and deserve to get it good and hard. [*Little Book in C major*]

10 Injustice is relatively easy to bear; what stings is justice. [*Prejudices*]

11 A man full of faith is simply one who has lost (or never had) the capacity for clear and realistic thought. [*Prejudices* ch 14]

12 To be in love is merely to be in a state of perceptual anesthesia – to mistake an ordinary young man for a Greek god or an ordinary young woman for a goddess. [*Prejudices*, 'First Series']

13 No man is genuinely happy, married, who has to drink worse gin than he used to drink when he was single. [*Prejudices*, 'Reflections on Monogamy']

14 If, after I depart this vale, you ever remember me and have thought to please my ghost, forgive some sinner and wink your eye at some homely girl. [*Smart Set* Dec 1922]

15 Love is based on a view of women that is impossible to those who have had any experience with them. [Attributed remark 1956]

MEREDITH George 1828–1909
English novelist and poet.

1 She whom I love is hard to catch and conquer, / Hard, but O the glory of the winning were she won! ['Love in the Valley']

2 The army of unalterable law. ['Lucifer in Starlight']

3 I expect that Woman will be the last thing civilized by Man. [*Ordeal of Richard Feverel* ch 1]

4 Kissing don't last: cookery do! [*Ordeal of Richard Feverel* ch 28]

5 Speech is the small change of silence. [*Ordeal of Richard Feverel* ch 34]

MEREDITH Owen 1831–1891
English statesman and poet.

Genius does what it must, and Talent does what it can. ['Last Words of a Sensitive Second-Rate Poet']

MERRITT Dixon Lanier 1879–1954
US writer.

Oh, a wondrous bird is the pelican! / His beak holds more than his belican. / He takes in his beak / Food enough for a week. / But I'll be darned if I know how the helican. [*Nashville Banner* 22 Apr 1913]

MIDDLETON Thomas c. 1580–1627
English dramatist.

You'll say the gentleman is somewhat simple– / The better for a husband, were you wise, / For those that marry fools live ladies' lives. [*Women Beware Women*]

MIKES George 1912–1987
Hungarian-born US humorist and writer.

1 Continental people have sex life; the English have hot-water bottles. [*How to be an Alien*]

2 An Englishman, even if he is alone, forms an orderly queue of one. [*How To Be an Alien*]

MILL John Stuart 1806–1873
English liberal philosopher and economist.

1 Ask yourself whether you are happy, and you cease to be so. [*Autobiography* ch 5]

2 No great improvements in the lot of mankind are possible, until a great change takes place in the fundamental constitution of their modes of thought. [*Autobiography* ch 7]

3 If all mankind minus one, were of one opinion, and only one person were of the contrary opinion, mankind would be no more justified in silencing that one person, than he, if he had the power, would be justified in silencing mankind. [*On Liberty* ch 2]

4 We can never be sure that the opinion we are endeavouring to stifle is a false opinion; and if we were sure, stifling it would be an evil still. [*On Liberty* ch 2]

5 The liberty of the individual must be thus far limited; he must not make himself a nuisance to other people. [*On Liberty* ch 3]

6 The worth of a State, in the long run, is the worth of the individuals composing it. [*On Liberty* ch 5]

7 If married life were all that it might be expected to be, looking to the laws alone, society would be a hell upon earth. [*Subjection of Women*]

8 There remain no legal slaves–except for the woman in every man's home. [*Subjection of Women*]

9 The true virtue of human beings is fitness to live together as equals; claiming nothing for themselves but what they as freely concede to everyone else; regarding command of any kind as an exceptional necessity, and in all cases a temporary one. [*Subjection of Women*]

MILLAY Edna St Vincent 1892–1950
US poet.

1 My candle burns at both ends; / It will not last the night; / But ah, my foes, and oh, my friends – / It gives a lovely light. ['First Fig']

2 I only know that summer sang in me / A little while, that in me sings no more. [*Harp-Weaver and Other Poems* sonnet 19]

3 Love is not all: it is not meat nor drink / Nor slumber nor a roof against the rain; / Nor yet a floating spar to men that sink. ['Love is Not All']

MILLER Arthur 1915–
US dramatist.

1 A salesman is got to dream, boy. It comes with the territory. [*Death of a Salesman,* 'Requiem']

2 Without alienation, there can be no politics. [*Marxism Today* Jan 1988]

3 A good newspaper, I suppose, is a nation talking to itself. [*Observer* 26 Nov 1962]

MILLER Henry 1891–1980
US writer.

1 Real antagonism is based on love, a love which has not recognized itself. [*Air-Conditioned Nightmare,* 'Stieglitz and Marin']

2 Back of every creation, supporting it like an arch, is faith. Enthusiasm is nothing; it comes and goes. But if one *believes,* then miracles occur. [*Air-Conditioned Nightmare,* 'With Edgar Varèse in the Gobi Desert']

3 Instead of asking – 'How much damage will the work in question bring about?' why not ask – 'How much good? How much joy?' [*Air-Conditioned Nightmare,* 'With Edgar Varèse in the Gobi Desert']

4 Our own physical body possesses a wisdom which we who inhabit the body lack. We give it orders which make no sense. [*Big Sur and the Oranges of Hieronymus Bosch* pt 3, 'Paradise Lost']

5 Confusion is a word we have invented for an order which is not understood. [*Tropic of Capricorn,* 'On the Ovarian Trolley: an Interlude']

6 The aim of life is to live, and to live means to be aware, joyously, drunkenly, serenely, divinely aware. [*Wisdom of the Heart,* 'Creative Death']

7 The world dies over and over again, but the skeleton always gets up and walks. [*Wisdom of the Heart,* 'Uterine Hunger']

Arthur Miller One of the most acclaimed US playwrights of the 20th Century, Arthur Miller has sought to find an authentic form of modern tragedy – an engaged and committed drama which does justice both to social themes and to the moral and psychological complexity of the individual.

8 The world itself is pregnant with failure, is the perfect manifestation of imperfection, of the consciousness of failure. [*Wisdom of the Heart,* 'Reflections of Writing']

9 In the beginning was the Word. Man acts it out. He is the act, not the actor. [*World of Sex* 119]

10 Civilization is the arteriosclerosis of culture. [Interview in Plimpton *Writers at Work* 2nd Series]

11 The waking mind ... is the least serviceable in the arts. [Interview in Plimpton *Writers at Work* 2nd Series]

MILLER Max 1895–1963
English music hall comedian.

I like the girls who do, / I like the girls who don't; / I hate the girl who says she will / And then she says she won't. / But the girl that I like best of all / And I think you'll say I'm right– / Is the one who says she never has / But looks as though she ... / 'Ere listen .... ['Girls who Do']

MILLIGAN Spike 1918–
English comic and humorist.

Money couldn't buy friends but you got a better class of enemy. [*Puckoon*]

MILNE A A 1882–1956
English children's writer.

1 King John was not a good man – / He had his little ways. ['King John's Christmas']

2 You must never go down to the end of the town if you don't go down with me. [*When We Were Very Young*, 'Disobedience']

3 I do like a little bit of butter to my bread! [*When We Were Very Young*, 'The King's Breakfast']

4 Isn't it funny / How a bear likes honey? / Buzz! Buzz! Buzz! / I wonder why he does? [*Winnie-the-Pooh* ch 2]

5 I am a Bear of Very Little Brain, and long words Bother me. [*Winnie-the-Pooh* ch 4]

6 Time for a little something. [*Winnie-the-Pooh* ch 6]

MILTON John 1608–1674
English poet.

1 Meadows trim with daisies pied, / Shallow brooks and rivers wide. ['L'Allegro']

2 Mirth, admit me of thy crew, / To live with her, and live with thee, / In unreproved pleasures free. ['L'Allegro']

3 Sport that wrinkled Care derides, / And Laughter holding both his sides. ['L'Allegro']

4 As good almost kill a man as kill a good book; who kills a man kills

The 17th-century English epic and lyric poet John Milton, whose Paradise Lost, 12 books in blank verse loosely based on the Biblical narrative of the Fall, was written to 'justify the works of God to men'. He also wrote pamphlets, in favour of divorce and freedom of the press.

a reasonable creature, God's image; but he who destroys a good book, kills reason itself, kills the image of God, as it were in the eye. [*Areopagitica*]

5 Books are not absolutely dead things, but do contain a potency of life in them to be as active as that soul was whose progeny they are. [*Areopagitica*]

6 A good book is the precious life-blood of a master spirit, embalmed and treasured up on purpose to a life beyond life. [*Areopagitica*]

7 I cannot praise a fugitive and cloistered virtue, unexercised and

unbreathed, that never sallies out and sees her adversary, but slinks out of the race, where that immortal garland is to be run for, not without dust and heat. [*Areopagitica*]

8 Blest pair of Sirens, pledges of Heaven's joy, / Sphere-born harmonious sisters, Voice and Verse. ['At a Solemn Music']

9 What hath night to do with sleep? [*Comus* 122]

10 Come, knit hands, and beat the ground, / In a light fantastic round. [*Comus* 143]

11 Virtue could see to do what virtue would / By her own radiant light, though sun and moon / Were in the flat sea sunk. [*Comus* 373]

12 How charming is divine philosophy! / Not harsh, and crabbed as dull fools suppose, / But musical as is Apollo's lute. [*Comus* 476]

13 That power / Which erring men call Chance. [*Comus* 587]

14 For such kind of borrowing as this, if it be not bettered by the borrower, among good authors is accounted plagiary. [*Iconoclastes* ch 23]

15 Hence, vain deluding joys, / The brood of Folly without father bred. [*Il Penseroso*]

16 Till old experience do attain / To something like prophetic strain. [*Il Penseroso*]

17 He knew / Himself to sing, and build the lofty rhyme. [*Lycidas* l. 10]

18 Whom universal Nature did lament. [*Lycidas* l. 60]

19 Fame is the spur that the clear spirit doth raise / (That last infirmity of noble mind) / To scorn delights, and live laborious days. [*Lycidas* 70]

20 Fame is no plant that grows on mortal soil. [*Lycidas* 78]

21 That strain I heard was of a higher mood. [*Lycidas* l. 87]

22 The hungry sheep look up, and are not fed. [*Lycidas* 123]

23 At last he rose, and twitch'd his mantle blue; / To-morrow to fresh woods, and pastures new. [*Lycidas* l. 192]

24 Brave men, and worthy patriots, dear to God, and famous to all ages. ['Of Education']

25 I call therefore a complete and generous education that which fits a man to perform justly, skilfully and magnanimously all the offices both private and public of peace and war. ['Of Education']

26 They also serve who only stand and wait. ['On his Blindness']

27 Bright-harnest Angels sit in order serviceable. [*On the Morning of Christ's Nativity*]

28 Perhaps their loves, or else their sheep, / Was all that did their silly thoughts so busy keep. [*On the Morning of Christ's Nativity*]

29 Time will run back, and fetch the age of gold, / And speckled Vanity / Will sicken soon and die. [*On the Morning of Christ's Nativity*]

30 Of Man's first disobedience, and the fruit / Of that forbidden tree, whose mortal taste / Brought death into the world, and all our woe, / With loss of Eden. [*Paradise Lost* I. 1]

31 Things unattempted yet in prose or rhyme. [*Paradise Lost* I. 16]

32 I may assert eternal Providence, / And justify the ways of God to Men. [*Paradise Lost* I. 25]

33 But O how fall'n! how changed / From him who, in the happy realms of light, / Clothed with transcendent brightness didst outshine / Myriads though bright. [*Paradise Lost* I. 84]

34 What though the field be lost? / All is not lost. [*Paradise Lost* I. 105]

35 Fall'n Cherub, to be weak is miserable / Doing or suffering: but of this be sure, / To do ought good never will be our task, / But ever to do ill our sole delight. [*Paradise Lost* I. 157]

36 And out of good still to find means of evil. [*Paradise Lost* I. 165]

37 The mind is its own place, and in it self / Can make a Heav'n of Hell, a Hell of Heav'n. [*Paradise Lost* I. 254]

38 Better to reign in hell, than serve in heav'n. [*Paradise Lost* I. 263]

39 Awake, arise, or be for ever fall'n! [*Paradise Lost* I. 330]

40 The sons / Of Belial, flown with insolence and wine. [*Paradise Lost* I. 501]

41 His form had yet not lost / All her original brightness, nor appeared / Less than archangel ruined, and th' excess / Of glory obscur'd. [*Paradise Lost* I. 591]

42 Who overcomes / By force, hath overcome but half his foe. [*Paradise Lost* I. 648]

43 My sentence is for open war: of wiles / More unexpert, I boast not. [*Paradise Lost* II. 44]

44 For who would lose, / Though full of pain, this intellectual being. [*Paradise Lost* II. 146]

45 And princely counsel in his face yet shone, / Majestic though in ruin. [*Paradise Lost* II. 304]

46 To sit in darkness here / Hatching vain empires. [*Paradise Lost* II. 377]

47 O shame to men! devil with devil damn'd / Firm concord holds, men only disagree / Of creatures rational. [*Paradise Lost* II. 496]

48 Vain wisdom all, and false philosophy. [*Paradise Lost* II. 565]

49 Their fatal hands / No second stroke intend. [*Paradise Lost* II. 712]

50 To compare / Great things with small. [*Paradise Lost* II. 921]

51 With ruin upon ruin, rout on rout, / Confusion worse confounded. [*Paradise Lost* II. 995]

52 Freely they stood who stood, and fell who fell. [*Paradise Lost* III. 102]

53 Evil be thou my Good. [*Paradise Lost* IV. 108]

54 Two of far nobler shape erect and tall, / Godlike erect, with native honour clad / In naked majesty seemed lords of all. [*Paradise Lost* IV. 288]

55 For contemplation he and valour formed; / For softness she and sweet attractive grace, / He for God only, she for God in him. [*Paradise Lost* IV. 297]

56 With thee conversing I forget all time. [*Paradise Lost* IV. 639]

57 Millions of spiritual creatures walk the earth / Unseen, both when we wake, and when we sleep. [*Paradise Lost* IV. 676]

58 Hail, wedded Love, mysterious law, true source / Of human offspring. [*Paradise Lost* IV. 750]

59 Abash'd the Devil stood, / And felt how awful goodness is, and saw / Virtue in her shape how lovely. [*Paradise Lost* IV. 846]

60 Necessity and chance / Approach not me, and what I will is fate. [*Paradise Lost* VII. 172]

61 Be lowly wise: / Think only what concerns thee and thy being. [*Paradise Lost* VIII. 173]

62 Pleas'd me long choosing, and beginning late. [*Paradise Lost* IX. 26]

63 The serpent subtlest beast of all the field. [*Paradise Lost* IX. 86]

64 So dear I love him, that with him all deaths / I could endure, without him live no life. [*Paradise Lost* IX. 832]

65 A Paradise within thee, happier far. [*Paradise Lost* XII. 587]

66 The world was all before them, where to choose / Their place of rest, and Providence their guide: / They hand in hand with wandering steps and slow, / Through Eden took their solitary way. [*Paradise Lost* XII. 646]

67 Of whom to be dispraised were no small praise. [*Paradise Regained* III. 56]

68 The childhood shows the man, / As morning shows the day. Be famous then / By wisdom; as thy empire must extend, / So let extend thy mind o'er all the world. [*Paradise Regained* IV. 220]

69 Deep versed in books and shallow in himself. [*Paradise Regained* IV. 327]

70 O dark, dark, dark, amid the blaze of noon, / Irrecoverably dark, total eclipse / Without all hope of day! [*Samson Agonistes* 80]

71 Love-quarrels oft in pleasing concord end. [*Samson Agonistes* 1008]

72 Nothing is here for tears, nothing to wail / Or knock the breast; no weakness, no contempt, / Dispraise or blame; nothing but well and fair, / And what may quiet us in a death so noble. [*Samson Agonistes* 1721]

73 And calm of mind all passion spent. [*Samson Agonistes* 1745]

74 None can love freedom heartily, but good men; the rest love not freedom, but licence. [*Tenure of Kings and Magistrates*]

75 O nightingale, that on yon bloomy spray / Warblest at eve, when all the woods are still. ['To the Nightingale']

76 They also serve who only stand and wait. ['When I Consider How My Light Is Spent']

MITCHELL Margaret 1900–1949
US novelist.

1 Death and taxes and childbirth! There's never any convenient time for any of them. [*Gone with the Wind* ch 38]

2 My dear, I don't give a damn. [*Gone with the Wind* ch 57]

MITFORD Nancy 1904–1973
English writer.

An aristocracy in a republic is like a chicken whose head has been cut off: it may run about in a lively way, but in fact it is dead. [*Noblesse Oblige*]

MITTERRAND François 1916–
President of France.

A man loses contact with reality if he is not surrounded by his books. [On why he remained in his former home, using the Elysée Palace only for official functions; *The Times* 10 May 1982]

MOLIÈRE pen name of *Jean Baptiste Poquelin* 1622–1673
French satirical playwright.

I assure you that a learned fool is more foolish than an ignorant fool.

MONKHOUSE William Cosmo 1840–1901
English poet and critic.

There once was an old man of Lyme / Who married three wives at a time, / When asked 'Why a third?' / He replied, 'One's absurd! / And bigamy, Sir, is a crime!' [*Nonsense Rhymes*]

MONMOUTH James, Duke of 1649–1685
Claimant to the English crown.

Do not hack me as you did my Lord Russell. [To his executioner]

MONTAGUE C E 1867–1928
English writer and journalist.

There is no limit to what a man can do so long as he does not care a straw who gets the credit for it. [*Disenchantment* ch 15, 3]

MONTAIGNE Michel de 1533–1592
French essayist.

1 How many things served us but yesterday as articles of faith, which today we deem but fables? [*Essays* bk 1, ch 26]

2 If you press me to say why I loved him, I feel that it can only be expressed by replying 'Because it was him; because it was me'. [Explaining his friendship with Etienne de La Boëtie, *Essays* bk I]

3 Love is nothing else but an insatiate thirst of enjoying a greedily desired object. [*Essays* III. v]

4 Marriage is like a cage; one sees the birds outside desperate to get in, and those inside equally desperate to get out. [*Essays* III. v]

MONTESQUIEU Charles 1689–1755
French philosophical historian.

An empire founded by war has to maintain itself by war. [*Considérations sur les causes de la grandeur des Romains et de leur décadence* ch 8]

MONTESSORI Maria 1870–1952
Italian educator.

1 If help and salvation are to come, they can only come from the children, for the children are the makers of men. [*Absorbent Mind* ch 1]

2 What is the use of transmitting knowledge if the individual's total development lags behind? [*Absorbent Mind* ch 1]

MONTHERLANT Henri de 1896–1972
French novelist.

1 The man who marries always makes the woman a present because she needs marriage and he does not ... woman is made for man, man is made for life. [*Girls*]

2 Beauty is still supposed to arouse desire. This is not the case. Beauty has nothing to do with the physical jerks under the coverlet. Ugliness is one of the most reliable stimulants. ['Goddess Cypris']

MOODIE Susanna 1803–1885
Canadian writer and poet.

I have no wish for a second husband. I had enough of the first. I like to have my own way – to lie down mistress, and get up master. [*Roughing It in the Bush* ch 12]

MOORE Edward 1712–1757
English dramatist and poet.

I am rich beyond the dreams of avarice. [*The Gamester* II. ii]

MOORE G E 1873–1958
English philosopher.

I ... use the word 'beautiful' to denote that of which the admiring contemplation is good in itself. [*Principia Ethica* ch 6]

MOORE George 1852–1933
Irish novelist.

1 A man travels the world in search of what he needs and returns home to find it. [*Brook Kerith*]

2 Art must be parochial in the beginning to become cosmopolitan in the end. [*Hail and Farewell*]

MOORE Thomas 1779–1852
Irish poet.

1 No, the heart that has truly loved never forgets, / But as truly loves on to the close, / As the sun-flower turns on her god, when he sets, / The same look which she turned when he rose. ['Believe me, if all those endearing young charms']

2 The harp that once through Tara's halls / The soul of music shed, / Now hangs as mute on Tara's walls / As if that soul were fled. – ['Harp that Once']

3 I never nurs'd a dear gazelle, / To glad me with its soft black eye, / But when it came to know me well, / And love me, it was sure to die! ['Lalla Rookh. The Fire-worshippers']

4 The light that lies / In women's eyes, / Has been my heart's undoing. ['Time I've Lost in Wooing']

5 'Tis the last rose of summer / Left blooming alone; / All her lovely companions / Are faded and gone. ['''Tis the Last Rose']

MORDAUNT Thomas 1730–1809
English poet.

Sound, sound the clarion, fill the fife, / Throughout the sensual world proclaim, / One crowded hour of glorious life / Is worth an age without a name. ['Verses Written During the War']

MORE Thomas 1478–1535
English politician and author.

I pray you, master Lieutenant, see me safe up, and my coming down let me shift for my self. [Ascending the scaffold. Quoted in W Roper *Life of Sir Thomas Moore*]

MORGAN Augustus de 1806–1871
English mathematician.

Great fleas have little fleas upon their backs to bite 'em, / And little fleas have lesser fleas, and so ad infinitum. [*Budget of Paradoxes*]

MORLEY Christopher 1890–1957
English writer.

Life is a foreign language; all men mispronounce it. [*Thunder on the Left* ch 14]

MORRIS Desmond 1928–
English anthropologist.

1 The city is not a concrete jungle, it is a human zoo. [*Human Zoo*, Introduction]

2 Every question we answer leads on to another question. This has become the greatest survival trick of our species. [*Naked Ape* ch 5]

MORRIS William 1834–1896
English writer and designer.

1 Dreamer of dreams, born out of my due time, / Why should I strive to set the crooked straight? [*Earthly Paradise*, 'An Apology']

2 The idle singer of an empty day. [*Earthly Paradise*, 'An Apology']

3 Have nothing in your houses that you do not know to be useful, or believe to be beautiful. [*Hopes and Fears for Art*]

William Morris with the Pre-Raphaelite artist Edward Burne-Jones. As a founder of the Arts and Crafts movement, Morris did much to raise British craft standards. He also published several volumes of verse.

4 Love is enough: though the world be a-waning, / And the woods have no voice but the voice of complaining. ['Love is Enough']

MORRISSEY 1959–
English rock singer and lyricist.

1 I was looking for a job, and then I found a job / And heaven knows I'm miserable now. ['Heaven Knows I'm Miserable Now']

2 I don't think black people and white people will ever really get on. The English will never like the French. That tunnel will collapse. [Remark on the Channel Tunnel]

MORTIMER John 1923–
English novelist, TV dramatist and barrister.

Matrimony and murder both carry a mandatory life sentence. [*Rumpole for the Defence*, 'Rumpole and the Boat People']

MOSER Sir Claus 1922–
German-born British academic.

Education costs money, but then so does ignorance. [*Daily Telegraph* 21 Aug 1990]

MOSS Stirling 1929–
English racing driver.

There are only two things no man will admit he can't do well: drive and make love. [Remark 1963]

MOTLEY John Lothrop 1814–1877
US historian and diplomat.

1 As long as he lived, he was the guiding-star of a brave nation, and when he died the little children cried in the streets. [*Rise of the Dutch Republic*, of William of Orange]

2 Give us the luxuries of life, and we will dispense with its necessities. [Attributed remark]

MOUNTBATTEN Louis, Lord 1900–1979
British admiral and administrator.

I can't think of a more wonderful thanksgiving for the life I have had than that everyone should be jolly at my funeral. [Quoted in R Hough *Mountbatten*]

MOZART Wolfgang Amadeus 1756–1791
Austrian composer.

Neither a lofty degree of intelligence nor imagination nor both together go to the making of genius. Love, love, love, that is the soul of genius. [Attributed remark]

MUGGERIDGE Malcolm 1903–1990
English journalist and author.

1 An orgy looks particularly alluring seen through the mists of righteous indignation. ['Dolce Vita in a Cold Climate']

2 As has truly been said in his days as an active politician, he was not only a bore; he bored for England. [Of Anthony Eden in *Tread Softly*,]

3 The world is so overflowing with absurdity that it is difficult for the humorist to compete. [On becoming editor of *Punch*]

MUIR Frank 1920–
English writer and broadcaster.

It has been said that a bride's attitude towards her betrothed can be summed up in three words: Aisle. Altar. Hymn. [*Upon My Word*, 'Jug of Wine']

MUMFORD Lewis 1895–1990
US urban planner and social critic.

1 Every generation revolts against its fathers and makes friends with its grandfathers. [*Brown Decade*]

2 The chief function of the city is to convert power into form, energy into culture, dead matter into the living symbols of art, biological reproduction into social creativity. [*City in History* ch 18]

MURASAKI Shikibu c. 978–c. 1015
Japanese writer, a lady at court.

> There are those who do not dislike wrong rumours if they are about the right men. [*Tale of Genji*]

MURDOCH Iris 1919–
English novelist.

> 1 Art is the final cunning of the human soul which would do anything rather than face the gods. [*Acastos: Two Platonic Dialogues*, 'Art and Eros']

> 2 Dora Greenfield left her husband because she was afraid of him. She decided six months later to return to him for the same reason. [*The Bell* ch 1]

> 3 Writing is like getting married. One should never commit oneself until one is amazed at one's luck. [*Black Prince*]

> 4 One doesn't have to get anywhere in a marriage. It's not a public conveyance. [*Severed Head* ch 3]

Irish-born English novelist and philosopher Iris Murdoch. Her novels are noted for their complex plots adroitly handled and the subtle, ever changing relationships of the characters. Though their incidents are often comic and bizarre, their underlying concern is how love, freedom, and goodness can survive moral and intellectual blindness. These themes are analysed formally in her philosophical works, which include studies of Sartre and Plato.

NABOKOV Vladimir 1899–1977
Russian novelist.

1 Adultery [is] ... a most conventional way to rise above the conventional. [*Lectures on Literature* 'Madame Bovary']

2 I am sufficiently proud of my knowing something to be modest about my not knowing all. [*Lolita*]

3 Lolita, light of my life, fire of my loins. My sin, my Soul. [*Lolita* ch 1]

4 Life is a great surprise. I do not see why death should not be an even greater one. [*Pale Fire*]

5 The cradle rocks above an abyss, and common sense tells us that our existence is but a brief crack of light between two eternities of darkness. [*Speak, Memory* ch 1, 1]

NAIPAUL V S 1932–
Trinidadian-born British writer.

I'm the kind of writer that people think other people are reading. [*Radio Times* 1979]

NAIRNE Carolina, Lady 1766–1845
Scottish songwriter.

1 Will ye no come back again? ['Bonnie Charlie's now awa"]

2 Wi' a hundred pipers an' a', an' a' ['Hundred Pipers']

3 I'm wearin' awa' / To the land o' the leal. ['Land o' the Leal']

NAPOLÉON I 1769–1821
Emperor of France.

1 Every French soldier carries in his cartridge-pouch the baton of a

Novelist Vladimir Nabokov spent all his adult life in exile. Born to a noble and wealthy family in Russia, he moved to Germany after the Russian Revolution, then, fleeing the Nazis, to the USA, and finally to Switzerland. Themes of estrangement and social isolation or, in the case of *Lolita*, perversity are integral to his finely styled novels.

marshal of France. [Quoted in Blaze *La Vie militaire sous l'empire*]

2 Soldiers! From the summit of these pyramids, forty centuries look down upon you. [Exhortation to his troops before the Battle of the Pyramids 1798]

3 There is only one step from the sublime to the ridiculous. [Remark to the Polish ambassador, after the retreat from Moscow]

4 England is a nation of shopkeepers. [Attributed remark]

5 Not tonight, Josephine. [Attributed remark]

NASH Ogden 1902–1971
US poet.

1 The turtle lives 'twixt plated decks / Which practically conceal its sex. / I think it clever of the turtle / In such a fix to be so fertile. ['Autres Bêtes, Autres Moeurs']

2 Oh, what a tangled web do parents weave / When they think that their children are naïve. ['Baby, What Makes the Sky Blue']

3 The camel has a single hump; / The dromedary, two; / Or else the other way around, / I'm never sure. Are you? ['The Camel']

4 The bronx? No thonx. [*New Yorker* 1931]

5 Candy / Is dandy / But liquor / Is quicker. ['Reflections on Ice-breaking']

6 I sit in an office at 244 Madison Avenue, / And say to myself You have a responsible job, havenue? [*Spring Comes to Murray Hill*]

NASHE Thomas 1567–1601
English poet and satirist.

Brightness falls from the air; / Queens have died young and fair; / Dust hath closed Helen's eye. ['In Time of Pestilence']

NATHAN George Jean 1882–1958
US critic.

To speak of morals in art is to speak of legislature in sex. Art is the sex of the imagination. [*American Mercury* July 1929, 'Art']

NELLIST David 1952–
British Labour politician.

The quickest way to become a left-winger in the Labour Party today is to stand still for six months. [Remark]

NELSON Horatio, Lord 1758–1805
British admiral.

1 Before this time to-morrow I shall have gained a peerage, or Westminster Abbey. [At the Battle of the Nile 1798]

2 I have only one eye, I have a right to be blind sometimes: ... I really do not see the signal! [At the Battle of Copenhagen 1801]

3 England expects every man will do his duty. [At the Battle of Trafalgar 1805]

4 Kiss me, Hardy. [Last words]

NERO AD 37–68
Roman emperor.

What an artist dies with me! [On his deathbed, quoted in Suetonius *Life of Nero*]

NEWBOLT Henry 1862–1938
English poet and naval historian.

1 Capten, art tha sleepin' there below? ['Drake's Drum']

2 'Ye have robb'd', said he, 'ye have slaughter'd and made an end, / Take your ill-got plunder, and bury the dead.' ['He Fell Among Thieves']

3 But cared greatly to serve God and the King, / And keep the Nelson touch. ['Minora Sidera']

4 Play up! play up! and play the game! ['Vitaï Lampada']

5 There's a breathless hush in the Close to-night – / Ten to make and the match to win. ['Vitaï Lampada']

NEWMAN John Henry 1801–1890
English Roman Catholic theologian.

1 Growth [is] the only evidence of life. ['Apologia pro Vita Sua']

2 May He support us all the day long, till the shades lengthen, and the evening comes, and the busy world is hushed, and the fever of life is over, and our work is done! [Sermon, 'Wisdom and Innocence' 1834]

NEWMAN Paul 1925–
US film actor.

> Why have hamburger out when you've got steak at home? That doesn't mean it's always tender. [Remark on marriage, Mar 1984]

NEWTON Isaac 1642–1727
English physicist and mathematician.

> I do not know what I may appear to the world, but to myself I seem to have been only a boy playing on the sea-shore, and diverting myself in now and then finding a smoother pebble or a prettier shell than ordinary, whilst the great ocean of truth lay all undiscovered before me. [Quoted in L T More *Isaac Newton*]

NICHOLSON Jack 1937–
US film actor.

> If there's any realistic deterrent to marriage, it's the fact that you can't afford divorce. [Quoted in *Playboy* 1972]

NIEBUHR Reinhold 1892–1971
US theologian and historian.

> **1** Man's capacity for justice makes democracy possible, but man's inclination to injustice makes democracy necessary. [*Children of Light and the Children of Darkness*]

> **2** God, give us the serenity to accept what cannot be changed; Give us the courage to change what should be changed; Give us the wisdom to distinguish one from the other. [Quoted in Richard Wightman Fox *Reinhold Niebuhr*]

NIETZSCHE Friedrich 1844–1900
German philosopher.

> **1** The anarchist and the Christian have a common origin. [*The Antichrist* 57]

> **2** Love is the state in which man sees things most widely different from what they are. The force of illusion reaches its zenith here, as likewise the sweetening and transfiguring power. When a man is in love he endures more than at any other time; he submits to everything. [*The Antichrist* Aphorism 23]

> **3** In revenge and love woman is more barbarous than man. [*Beyond Good and Evil* pt 4]

> **4** In every ascetic morality man worships a part of himself as God and for that he needs to diabolize the other part. [*Human, All Too Human* 137]

> **5** I fear animals regard man as a creature ... which has in a highly dangerous fashion lost its healthy animal reason – as the mad animal. [*Joyous Science* 224]

> **6** Morality is the herd instinct in the individual. [*Joyous Science*]

> **7** For art to exist ... a certain physiological precondition is indispensable: *intoxication*. [*Twilight of the Idols*, 'Expeditions of an Untimely Man' 8]

> **8** The most dangerous follower is he whose defection would destroy the whole party: that is to say, the best follower. [*Wanderer and His Shadow* 290]

> **9** Only the most acute and active animals are capable of boredom. – A theme for a great poet would be *God's boredom* on the seventh day of creation. [*Wanderer and his Shadow*]

NIN Anaïs 1903–1977
French-born US novelist and diarist.

> Life shrinks or expands in proportion to one's courage. [*Diary* June 1941]

NIXON Richard 1913–1994
US Republican president.

> There can be no whitewash at the White House. [Television speech on Watergate 30 Apr 1973]

37th US president Richard Milhous Nixon, the only president ever to resign from office. During his presidency Nixon began the gradual withdrawal of US troops from Vietnam and improved relations with the Eastern bloc. He resigned 9 Aug 1974, over his involvement in the Watergate scandal.

NORMAN Barry 1933–
English film critic.

> Perhaps at fourteen every boy should be in love with some ideal woman to put on a pedestal and worship. As he grows up, of course, he will put her on a pedestal the better to view her legs. [*Listener* 1978]

NORTON Caroline 1808–1877
English poet.

> **1** I do not love thee! – no! I do not love thee! / And yet when thou art absent I am sad. ['I do Not Love Thee']

> **2** And all our calm is in that balm – / Not lost but gone before. ['Not Lost but Gone Before']

NOVELLO Ivor 1893–1951
Welsh actor, composer and dramatist.

> And Her Mother Came Too. [Song title]

NOYES Alfred 1880–1958
English poet.

> Go down to Kew in lilac-time (it isn't far from London!) ['Barrel Organ']

NYE Bill 1850–1896
US humorist.

> I have been told that Wagner's music is better than it sounds. [Quoted in Mark Twain *Autobiography*]

OAKESHOTT Michael 1901–1990
English philosopher and political theorist.

> **1** Anyone who has had a glimpse of the range and subtlety of the thought of Plato or of a Hegel will long ago have despaired of becoming a philosopher. [*Experience and its Modes* ch 1]

> **2** Nearly always a philosopher hides a secret ambition, foreign to philosophy, and often it is that of the preacher. [*Experience and its Modes* ch 1]

OATES Joyce Carol 1938–
US author.

> Our enemy is by tradition our savior, in preventing us from superficiality. [Quoted in 'Master Race', in *Partisan Review 50th Anniversary Edition*]

OATES Lawrence 1880–1912
English Antarctic explorer.

> I am just going outside and may be some time. [Last words, quoted in R F Scott's *Diary* 16–17 Mar 1912]

O'BRIEN Edna 1936–
Irish novelist.

> To Crystal, hair was the most important thing on earth. She would never get married because you couldn't wear curlers in bed. [*Winter's Tales*, 'Come into the Drawing Room, Doris']

O'CASEY Sean 1884–1964
Irish dramatist.

> **1** The whole worl's in a state o' chassis! [*Juno and the Paycock*]

> **2** There's no reason to bring religion into it. I think we ought to have as great a regard for religion as we can, so as to keep it out of as many things as possible. [*Plough and the Stars*]

ODETS Clifford 1906–1963
US dramatist.

> Go out and fight so life shouldn't be printed on dollar bills. [*Awake and Sing*]

OLIVIER Laurence 1907–1989
English actor and director.

> What is acting but lying and what is good acting but convincing lying? [*Autobiography*]

English actor and director Laurence Olivier, a major figure of 20th-century English theatre. During a career that lasted nearly 60 years he proved himself a powerful and versatile actor, excelling in both Shakespearean and modern roles. He was one of the first classical actors to make a successful transition to film, appearing in romantic classics such as *Wuthering Heights* 1939 and *Rebecca* 1940, and in highly acclaimed film versions of Shakespeare's *Henry V* 1945 and *Richard III* 1955.

O'NEILL Eugene 1888–1953
US dramatist.

1 For de little stealin' dey gits you in jail soon or late. For de big stealin' dey makes you Emperor and puts you in de Hall o' Fame when you croaks. [*Emperor Jones*]

2 Our lives are merely strange dark interludes in the electric display of God the Father. [*Strange Interlude*]

3 The Iceman Cometh. [Play title]

4 A Long Day's Journey into Night. [Play title]

OPIE John 1761–1807
English artist.

I mix them with my brains, sir. [When asked with what he mixed his colours]

OPPENHEIMER Martin 1930–
German-born US sociologist.

Today's city is the most vulnerable social structure ever conceived by man. [*Urban Guerrilla* ch 7]

ORBACH Susie 1946–
US psychotherapist and writer.

Fat Is a Feminist Issue. [Book title]

ORCZY Emmusca, Baroness 1865–1947
Hungarian-born English novelist.

We seek him here, we seek him there, / Those Frenchies seek him everywhere. / Is he in heaven? Is he in hell? / That demmed, elusive Pimpernel? [*Scarlet Pimpernel*]

ORTEGA Y GASSET José 1883–1955
Spanish philosopher and critic.

1 Being an artist means ceasing to take seriously that very serious person we are when we are not an artist. [*Dehumanization of Art*, 'Doomed to Irony']

2 The poet begins where the man ends. The man's lot is to live his human life, the poet's to invent what is nonexistent. [*Dehumanization of Art*]

3 By speaking, by thinking, we undertake to clarify things, and that forces us to exacerbate them, dislocate them, schematize them. Every concept is in itself an exaggeration. ['In Search of Goethe from Within', *Partisan Review* Dec 1949]

4 We live at a time when man believes himself fabulously capable of creation, but he does not know what to create. [*Revolt of the Masses* ch 4]

5 Civilization is nothing else than the attempt to reduce force to being the *ultima ratio*. [*Revolt of the Masses* ch 8]

6 War is not an instinct but an invention. [*Revolt of the Masses*, epilogue]

ORTON Joe 1933–1967
English dramatist.

1 Every luxury was lavished on you – atheism, breast-feeding, circumcision. [*Loot* I]

2 Reading isn't an occupation we encourage among police officers. We try to keep the paper work down to a minimum. [*Loot* II]

ORWELL George 1903–1950
English author.

1 Four legs good, two legs bad. [*Animal Farm* ch 3]

4 All animals are equal but some animals are more equal than others. [*Animal Farm* ch 10]

3 One cannot really be a Catholic and grown up. ['Manuscript Notebook', *Collected Essays, Journalism and Letters of George Orwell* vol 4]

4 BIG BROTHER IS WATCHING YOU. [*Nineteen Eighty-Four* pt I, ch 1]

5 War is peace. Freedom is slavery. Ignorance is strength. [*Nineteen Eighty-Four* pt I, ch 1]

6 Freedom is the freedom to say that two plus two make four. If that is granted, all else follows. [*Nineteen Eighty-Four* pt 1, ch 7]

7 Doublethink means the power of holding two contradictory beliefs in one's mind simultaneously, and accepting both of them. [*Nineteen Eighty-Four* pt 2, ch 9]

8 If you want a picture of the future, imagine a boot stamping on a human face – for ever. [*Nineteen Eighty-Four* pt III, ch 3]

9 It is only because miners sweat their guts out that superior persons can remain superior. [*Road to Wigan Pier*]

10 To see what is in front of one's nose needs a constant struggle. [*Tribune* 22 Mar 1946]

11 Keep the Aspidistra Flying. [Title of novel]

OSBORNE John 1929–1995
English dramatist.

1 Don't clap too hard – it's a very old building. [*The Entertainer*]

2 They spend their time mostly looking forward to the past. [*Look Back in Anger* II.i]

O'SHAUGHNESSY Arthur 1844–1881
English poet.

We are the music makers, / We are the dreamers of dreams, ... / We are the movers and shakers / Of the world for ever, it seems. ['We are the Music Makers']

OSLER William 1849–1919
Canadian physician.

1 One finger in the throat and one in the rectum makes a good diagnostician. [*Aphorisms from his Bedside Teachings*]

2 One of the first duties of the physician is to educate the masses not to take medicine. [*Aphorisms from his Bedside Teachings*]

OVID 43 BC–AD 17
Roman poet.

1 Every lover is a warrior, and Cupid has his camps. [*Amores* bk 1 no 9]

2 Far from us be the omen! [*Amores*]

3 There are as many pangs in love as shells upon the shore. [*Ars Amatoria* bk 2]

4 I see and approve better things, but follow worse. [*Metamorphoses*]

5 Time the devourer of all things. [*Metamorphoses*]

6 I have laughed at the foolish man who feigned to love and fell like a fowler into his own snare. [*Remediorum Amoris* 501]

OWEN Wilfred 1893–1918
English poet.

It is pock-marked like the body of foulest disease, and its odour is the breath of cancer...No Man's Land under snow is like the face of the moon, chaotic, crater-ridden, uninhabitable, awful, the abode of madness. [Letter 19 Jan 1917]

OZ Amos 1939–
Israeli writer.

He formulated his remarks as if the very existence of two distinct sexes was a disorder which multiplied agony in the world, a disorder whose results people must do everything in their power to mitigate. [*My Michael*]

PAGLIA Camille 1947–
US writer and critic.

We need a new kind of feminism, one that stresses personal responsibility and is open to art and sex in all their dark, unconsoling mysteries. [*Sex, Art, and American Culture*, Introduction]

PAINE Thomas 1737–1809
English left-wing political writer.

1 The sublime and the ridiculous are often so nearly related, that it is difficult to class them separately. [*Age of Reason*]

2 These are the times that try men's souls. [*American Crisis*]

3 The final event to himself has been, that as he rose like a rocket, he fell like the stick. [Of Edmund Burke, *Letter to the Addressers on the late Proclamation*]

4 My country is the world, and my religion is to do good. [*Rights of Man*]

PALMER Vance 1885–1959
Australian poet and writer.

It is the business of thought to define things to find the boundaries; thought, indeed, is a ceaseless process of definition. It is the business of Art to give things shape. ['On Boundaries']

PALMERSTON Henry, Lord 1784–1865
British prime minister.

'Die, my dear Doctor, that's the last thing I shall do!' [Last words, attributed]

PANKHURST Emmeline 1858–1928
English suffragette.

Is not a woman's life, is not her health, are not her limbs more valuable than panes of glass? There is no doubt of that, but most important of all, does not the breaking of glass produce more effect upon the Government? [Speech 16 Feb 1912]

PARETO Vilfredo 1848–1923
Italian economist and political philosopher.

Give me fruitful error any time, full of seeds, bursting with its own corrections. You can keep your sterile truth for yourself. [*Mind and Society*]

PARKER Dorothy 1893–1967
US writer and wit.

1 Scratch a lover, and find a foe. ['Ballade of a Great Weariness']

2 Oh, life is a glorious cycle of song, / A medley of extemporanea; / And love is a thing that can never go wrong; / And I am Marie of Roumania. ['Comment']

3 Woman lives but in her lord; / Count to ten, and man is bored. / With this the gist and sum of it, / What earthly good can come of it? ['General Review of the Sex Situation']

4 Four be the things I'd been better without: / Love, curiosity, freckles, and doubt. ['Inventory']

5 One more drink and I'd have been under the host. [Quoted in H Teichmann *George S. Kaufman*]

6 Men seldom make passes / At girls who wear glasses. ['News Item']

7 The affair between Margot Asquith and Margot Asquith will live as one of the prettiest love stories in all literature. [Review of Margot Asquith's *Lay Sermons*, New Yorker 1927]

8 Why is it no one ever sent me yet / One perfect limousine, do you suppose? / Ah no, it's always just my luck to get / One perfect rose. ['One Perfect Rose']

9 There's a hell of a distance between wise-cracking and wit. Wit has truth in it; wise-cracking is simply callisthenics with words. [*Paris Review* Summer 1956]

10 Sorrow is tranquillity remembered in emotion. ['Sentiment']

11 Lady, Lady, should you meet, / One whose ways are all discreet, / One who murmurs that his wife / Is the lodestar of his life, / One who keeps assuring you / That he never was untrue, / Never loved another one ... / Lady, lady, better run. ['Social Note']

12 This is what I know: / Lovers' oaths are thin as rain; / Love's a harbinger of pain – / Would it were not so! ['Somebody's Song']

13 By the time you say you're his, / Shivering and sighing / And he vows his passion is / Infinite, undying – / Lady, make a note of this: / One of you is lying. ['Unfortunate Coincidence']

14 You know, she speaks eighteen languages. And she can't say 'No' in any of them. [Attributed remark 1967]

15 Love is like quicksilver in the hand. Leave the fingers open and it stays. Clutch it, and it darts away. [Attributed remark]

16 It serves me right for putting all my eggs in one bastard. [On entering hospital for an abortion]

PARKINSON C Northcote 1909–
English writer and historian.

Work expands so as to fill the time available for its completion. [*Parkinson's Law*]

PASCAL Blaise 1623–1662
French philosopher and mathematician.

1 The eternal silence of these infinite spaces terrifies me. [*Pensées*]

2 The heart has its reasons which reason knows nothing of. [*Pensées*]

3 If Cleopatra's nose had been shorter, the whole face of the earth would have changed. [*Pensées*]

4 That is what faith is: God perceived by the heart, not by the reason. [*Pensées* 424]

PASTERNAK Boris 1890–1960
Russian poet and novelist.

1 Most people experience love, without noticing that there is anything remarkable about it. [*Dr Zhivago* pt 2 ch 13]

2 To live life to the end is not a childish task. [*Doctor Zhivago*]

PATER Walter 1839–1894
English scholar, essayist and art critic.

To burn always with this hard, gem-like flame, to maintain this ecstasy, is success in life. [*Studies in the History of the Renaissance*]

PATMORE Coventry 1823–1896
English poet.

A Woman is a foreign land, / Of which, though there he settle young, / A man will ne'er quite understand / The customs, politics and tongue. [*Angel in the House* bk 2, ch 9, Prelude 2]

PATTON George Smith 1885–1945
US general.

There's one thing you men can say when it's all over and you're home once more. You can thank God that twenty years from now when you're sitting by the fireside with your grandson on your knee, and he asks you what you did in the war, you won't have to shift him to the other knee, cough and say, 'I shovelled shit in Louisiana'. [Speech to US 5th Army prior to D-Day landings 6 June 1944]

PAUL St c. 3 BC–68 AD
Christian missionary, apostle, martyr and saint.

> What would I have made of you, had I found you alive? [While weeping at Virgil's tomb, quoted in Ross Leckie *Bluff Your Way In the Classics*]

PAVLOVA Anna 1885–1931
Russian ballerina.

> An artist should know all about love and learn to live without it. [Attributed remark]

PAYN James 1830–1898
English writer and editor.

> I had never had a piece of toast / Particularly long and wide, / But fell upon the sanded floor, / And always on the buttered side. [*Chambers's Journal*]

PAYNE J H 1791–1852
US actor and dramatist.

> Mid pleasures and palaces though we may roam, / Be it ever so humble, there's no place like home; ... / Home, home, sweet, sweet home! / There's no place like home! there's no place like home! ['Home, Sweet Home']

PAZ Octavio 1914–
Mexican poet and essayist.

> 1 We are condemned to kill time: Thus we die little by little. [*Cuento de los Jardines*]

> 2 Love is an attempt at penetrating another being, but it can only succeed if the surrender is mutual. [*Labyrinth of Solitude* ch 1]

> 3 Wisdom lies neither in fixity nor in change, but in the dialectic between the two. [*The Times* 8 June 1989]

PEACOCK Thomas Love 1785–1866
English satirical novelist and poet.

> 1 But though first love's impassioned blindness / Has passed away in colder light, / I still have thought of you with kindness, / And shall do till our last good-night. ['Love and Age']

> 2 Marriage may often be a stormy lake, but celibacy is almost always a muddy horsepond. [*Melincourt*]

> 3 Sir, I have quarrelled with my wife; and a man who has quarrelled with his wife is absolved from all duty to his country. [*Nightmare Abbey*]

> 4 The mountain sheep are sweeter, / But the valley sheep are fatter; / We therefore deemed it meeter / To carry off the latter. ['War-Song of Dinas Vawr']

PEELE George 1558–1597
English dramatist.

> 1 His golden locks time hath to silver turn'd; / O time too swift, O swiftness never ceasing! ['Farewell to Arms']

> 2 What thing is love for (well I wot) love is a thing. / It is a prick, it is a sting, / It is a pretty, pretty thing; / It is a fire, it is a coal / Whose flame creeps in at every hole. [*Hunting of Cupid*]

PÉGUY Charles 1873–1914
French publisher and poet.

> He who does not bellow the truth when he knows the truth makes himself the accomplice of liars and forgers. [*Lettre du Provincial* 21 Dec 1899]

PEIRCE Charles Sanders 1839–1914
US philosopher.

> He [William James] is so concrete, so living; I, a mere table of contents, so abstract, a very snarl of twine. [Quoted in J Passmore *Hundred Years of Philosophy*]

PENN William 1644–1718
English Quaker.

> 1 It is a reproach to religion and government to suffer so much poverty and excess. [*Reflexions and Maxims* pt 1, no. 52]

2 Men are generally more careful of the breed of their horses and dogs than of their children. [*Reflexions and Maxims* pt 1, no. 85]

3 Let the people think they govern and they will be governed. [*Some Fruits of Solitude*]

4 They have a right to censure that have a heart to help. [*Some Fruits of Solitude*]

5 They that love beyond the world cannot be separated by it. Death is but crossing the world, as friends do the seas; they live in one another still. [*Some Fruits of Solitude*]

PEPYS Samuel 1633–1703
English diarist.

1 And so to bed. [*Diary* 20 Apr 1660]

2 But Lord! to see the absurd nature of Englishmen, that cannot forbear laughing and jeering at everything that looks strange. [*Diary* 27 Nov 1662]

3 My wife, who, poor wretch, is troubled with her lonely life. [*Diary* 19 Dec 1662]

4 Strange to see how a good dinner and feasting reconciles everybody. [*Diary* 9 Nov 1665]

5 Strange to say what delight we married people have to see these poor fools decoyed into our condition. [*Diary* 25 Dec 1665]

6 But it is pretty to see what money will do. [*Diary* 21 Mar 1667]

PERELMAN S J 1904–1979
US humorist.

Love is not the dying moan of a distant violin – it is the triumphant twang of a bedspring. [Attributed remark]

PERKINS Anthony 1932–1992
US film actor.

I have learned more about love, selflessness, and human understanding in this great adventure in the world of AIDS than I ever did in the cut-throat, competitive world in which I spent my life. [Statement published posthumously, *Independent on Sunday* 20 Sept 1992]

PERSE Saint-Jean 1887–1975
French poet and diplomat.

It is enough for the poet to be the bad conscience of his time. I am sure there must be others. [Letter Dec 1941]

PÉTAIN Henri, Marshal 1856–1951
French marshal and politician.

1 They shall not get past. [On the German army at Verdun 1916]

A portrait of the English diarist Samuel Pepys (1666) by John Hayls, National Portrait Gallery, London. The private diaries of Pepys, who was an energetic public servant, express a relish for life and its full range of experiences. His account of the last great plague epidemic 1665 and of the Fire of London 1666 are particularly valuable as social history.

2 To make a union with Great Britain would be a fusion with a corpse. [In response to Churchill's proposal of an Anglo-French union 1940]

PETER Laurence 1910–1990
Canadian writer and teacher.

1 The Peter Principle: In a Hierarchy Every Employee Tends to Rise to His Level of Incompetence. [*Peter Principle*]

2 Work is accomplished by those employees who have not yet reached their level of incompetence. [*Peter Principle*]

PETRARCH 1304–1374
Italian poet.

To be able to say how much you love is to love but little. [*To Laura in Death* poem 16]

PETRONIUS *Arbiter* D. C. AD 65
Roman author.

Beware of the dog. [*Satyricon*]

PHELPS Edward 1822–1900
US lawyer and diplomat.

The man who makes no mistakes does not usually make anything. [Speech 1899]

PHILIP Duke of Edinburgh 1921–
Prince of the UK, husband of Elizabeth II.

When a man opens the car door for his wife, it's either a new car or a new wife. [Quoted in *Observer* 6 March 1988]

PHILLIPS Wendell 1811–1884
US reformer.

1 Every man meets his Waterloo at last. [Lecture at Brooklyn 1859]

2 One, on God's side, is a majority. [Lecture at Brooklyn 1859]

PICABIA Francis 1878–1953
French painter and poet.

All beliefs are bald ideas. [*Jésus-Christ Rastaquoère* ch 1]

Pioneering Spanish artist Pablo Picasso, who had a great influence on the development of 20th century art.

PICASSO Pablo 1881–1973
Spanish artist.

1 Through art we express our conception of what nature is not. [*The Arts* May 1923, 'Picasso Speaks']

2 I paint objects as I think them, not as I see them. [Quoted in J Golding *Cubism*]

3 People who try to explain pictures are usually barking up the wrong tree. [Quoted in D Ashton *Picasso on Art*, 'Two statements by Picasso']

PINDAR C. 552 BC–442 BC
Greek poet.

A shadow in a dream is Man. [*Pythian* VIII]

PIRSIG Robert 1928–
US writer.

> Zen and the Art of Motorcycle Maintenance. [Book title]

PISAN Christine de 1364–1430
French poet and historian.

> Just as women's bodies are softer than men's, so their understanding is sharper. [*City of Ladies*]

PITKIN Walter 1878–1953
US writer.

> Life Begins at Forty. [Book title]

PITT William *the Elder* 1708–1778
British Whig prime minister.

> **1** The atrocious crime of being a young man ... I shall neither attempt to palliate nor deny. [Speech in House of Commons 27 Jan 1741]
>
> **2** I invoke the genius of the Constitution! [Speech, House of Lords 18 Nov 1777]
>
> **3** Our watchword is security. [Attributed remark]
>
> **4** The parks are the lungs of London. [Attributed remark]

PITT William *the Younger* 1759–1806
British Tory prime minister.

> **1** Roll up that map; it will not be wanted these ten years. [Referring to map of Europe, hearing of Napoleon's victory at Austerlitz 1805, in Stanhope's *Life of the Rt Hon William Pitt*]
>
> **2** Necessity is the plea for every infringement of human freedom. It is the argument of tyrants; it is the creed of slaves. [Speech in House of Commons 18 Nov 1783]

PLATH Sylvia 1932–1963
US poet and novelist.

> **1** A living doll, everywhere you look. / It can sew, it can cook, / It can talk, talk, talk. ... / My boy, it's your last resort. / Will you marry it, marry it, marry it. ['Applicant']
>
> **2** Widow. The word consumes itself. [*Crossing the Water*, 'Widow']

> **3** Dying, / Is an art, like everything else. / I do it exceptionally well. ['Lady Lazarus']

PLATO 429–347 BC
Greek philosopher.

> Every man is a poet when he is in love. [*Symposium*]

PLAUTUS Titus Maccius 254–184 BC
Roman poet and playwright.

> The boastful soldier. [Play title]

PLINY the Elder c. 23–79
Roman naturalist and writer.

> **1** The only certainty is that nothing is certain. [*Historia Naturalis* II. 7]
>
> **2** There is always something new out of Africa. [*Historia Naturalis* II. 8]
>
> **3** There's truth in wine. [*Historia Naturalis* II. 14]
>
> **4** Attic wit. [*Historia Naturalis* II. 31]

PLUMER Hubert 1857–1932
British general in World War I.

> Gentlemen, we may not make history tomorrow, but we shall certainly change the geography. [Remark to his staff before the Battle of Messines 1917 in which mines were extensively employed]

POE Edgar Allan 1809–1849
US writer and poet.

> **1** I was a child and she was a child, / In this kingdom by the sea; / But we loved with a love which was more than love / I and my Annabel Lee. ['Annabel Lee']
>
> **2** All that we see or seem/ Is but a dream within a dream. [*Dream within a Dream*]
>
> **3** To vilify a great man is the readiest way in which a little man can himself attain greatness. [*Marginalia*]
>
> **3** Quoth the Raven, 'Nevermore' [*The Raven*]

4 Helen, thy beauty is to me / Like those Nicean barks of yore, / That gently, o'er a perfumed sea, / The weary, wayworn wanderer bore / To his own native shore. / On desperate seas long wont to roam, / Thy hyacinth hair, thy classic face, / Thy Naiad airs have brought me home / To the glory that was Greece / And the grandeur that was Rome. ['To Helen']

5 Thou wast all that to me, love, / For which my soul did pine: / A green isle in the sea, love, / A fountain and a shrine. ['To One in Paradise']

French politician Georges Pompidou. A close adviser to General de Gaulle, Georges Pompidou played a leading role in the drafting of the new constitution 1958–59 and in the difficult negotiations over independence for Algeria 1961. His term as prime minister was brought to an end by the student riots of 1968, and he became president the following year.

POLO Marco 1254–1324
Venetian traveller and writer.

I have not told half of what I saw. [Last words]

POMPADOUR Madame de 1721–1764
Mistress of Louis XV of France.

After us the deluge. [Quoted in Madame du Hausset *Mémoires*]

POMPIDOU Georges 1911–1974
French president.

A statesman is a politician who places himself at the service of the nation. A politician is a statesman who places the nation at his service. [*Observer* Dec 1973]

PONSONBY Arthur 1871–1946
British politician and author.

When war is declared, Truth is the first casualty. [*Falsehood in Wartime*, epigraph]

POPE Alexander 1688–1744
English poet and satirist.

1 Or where the pictures for the page atone, / And Quarles is sav'd by beauties not his own. [*Dunciad* bk 1]

2 Poetic Justice, with her lifted scale, / Where, in nice balance, truth with gold she weighs, / And solid pudding against empty praise. [*Dunciad* bk 1]

3 And gentle dullness ever loves a joke. [*Dunciad* bk 2]

4 The Right Divine of Kings to govern wrong. [*Dunciad* bk 4]

5 Stretch'd on the rack of a too easy chair. [*Dunciad* bk 4]

6 Thy hand, great Anarch! lets the curtain fall, / And universal darkness buries all. [*Dunciad* bk 4]

7 Is there no bright reversion in the sky, / For those who greatly think, or bravely die? [*Elegy to the Memory of an Unfortunate Lady*]

8 What beck'ning ghost, along the moon-light shade / Invites my steps, and points to yonder glade? [*Elegy to the Memory of an Unfortunate Lady*]

9 Love, free as air, at sight of human ties, / Spreads his light wings, and in a moment flies. ['*Eloisa to Abelard*']

10 Oh happy state! when souls each other draw, / When love is liberty, and nature, law: / All then is full, possessing, and possessed, / No craving void left aching in the breast. ['*Eloisa to Abelard*']

11 Do good by stealth, and blush to find it fame. [*Epilogue 1*]

12 Yes, I am proud; I must be proud to see / Men not afraid of God, afraid of me. [*Epilogue*]

13 As yet a child, nor yet a fool to fame, / I lisped in numbers, for the numbers came. [*Epistle to Dr. Arbuthnot*]

14 Damn with faint praise, assent with civil leer, / And, without sneering, teach the rest to sneer; / Willing to wound, and yet afraid to strike, / Just hint a fault, and hesitate dislike. [*Epistle to Dr. Arbuthnot*]

15 Destroy his fib or sophistry – in vain! / The creature's at his dirty work again. [*Epistle to Dr. Arbuthnot*]

16 Let Sporus tremble. — A. What? that thing of silk, / Sporus, that mere white curd of ass's milk? / Satire or sense, alas! can Sporus feel? / Who breaks a butterfly upon a wheel? [*Epistle to Dr. Arbuthnot*]

17 So well-bred spaniels civilly delight / In mumbling of the game they dare not bite. [*Epistle to Dr. Arbuthnot*]

18 This long disease, my life. [*Epistle to Dr. Arbuthnot*]

19 This painted child of dirt, that stinks and stings. [*Epistle to Dr. Arbuthnot*]

20 Wit that can creep, and pride that licks the dust. [*Epistle to Dr. Arbuthnot*]

21 Nature and Nature's laws lay hid in night: / God said, *Let Newton be*! and all was light. [Epitaph intended for Sir Isaac Newton]

22 For fools rush in where angels fear to tread. [*Essay on Criticism*]

23 Let such teach others who themselves excel, / And censure freely who have written well. [*Essay on Criticism*]

24 A little learning is a dangerous thing; / Drink deep, or taste not the Pierian spring: / There shallow draughts intoxicate the brain, / And drinking largely sobers us again. [*Essay on Criticism*]

25 To err is human, to forgive, divine. [*Essay on Criticism*]

26 True ease in writing comes from art, not chance, / As those move easiest who have learned to dance. [*Essay on Criticism*]

27 True wit is nature to advantage dressed, / What oft was thought, but ne'er so well expressed. [*Essay on Criticism*]

28 Die of a rose in aromatic pain? [*Essay on Man 1*]

29 Expatiate free o'er all this scene of man; / A mighty maze! but not without a plan. [*Essay on Man 1*]

30 Hope springs eternal in the human breast; / Man never is, but always to be blessed. [*Essay on Man 1*]

31 In pride, in reas'ning pride, our error lies; / All quit their sphere and rush into the skies! / Pride still is aiming at the bless'd abodes, / Men would be angels, angels would be gods. [*Essay on Man 1*]

32 Know then thyself, presume not God to scan, / The proper study of mankind is man. [*Essay on Man 2*]

33 For forms of government let fools contest; / Whate'er is best administered is best. [*Essay on Man* 3]

34 An honest man's the noblest work of God. [*Essay on Man* 3]

35 If parts allure thee, think how Bacon shined, / The wisest, brightest, meanest of mankind. [*Essay on Man* 4]

36 Do good by stealth, and blush to find it fame. [*Imitations of Horace*]

37 When men grow virtuous in their old age, they only make a sacrifice to God of the devil's leavings. [*Miscellany* (with Jonathan Swift)]

38 She who ne'er answers till a husband cools, / Or, if she rules him, never shows she rules; / Charms by accepting, by submitting, sways, / Yet has her humor most, when she obeys. [*Moral Essays*, 'Epistle II, To Mrs M Blount']

39 Has she no faults then (Envy says), Sir? / Yes, she has one, I must aver; / When all the world conspires to praise her, / The woman's deaf, and does not hear. ['On a Certain Lady at Court']

40 I am his Highness' dog at Kew; / Pray tell me, sir, whose dog are you? ['On the Collar of a Dog which I gave to his Royal Highness']

41 What dire offence from am'rous causes springs, / What mighty contests rise from trivial things! [*Rape of the Lock* 1]

42 If to her share some female errors fall, / Look on her face, and you'll forget'em all. [*Rape of the Lock* 2]

43 Here thou, great Anna! whom three realms obey, / Dost sometimes counsel take – and sometimes tea. [*Rape of the Lock* 3]

44 Ev'n copious Dryden wanted, or forgot, The last and greatest art, the art to blot. [*To Augustus*]

45 The mob of gentlemen who wrote with ease. [*To Augustus*]

46 Party-spirit, which at best is but the madness of many for the gain of a few. [Letter 27 Aug 1714]

47 'Blessed is the man who expects nothing, for he shall never be disappointed', was the ninth beatitude which a man of wit (who, like a man of wit, was a long time in gaol) added to the eighth. [Letter 23 Sept 1725]

48 Bathos, the art of sinking in Poetry. [Title]

POPPER Karl 1902–1994
Austrian philosopher of science.

1 Every solution of a problem raises new unsolved problems. [*Conjectures and Refutations*]

2 In our infinite ignorance we are all equal. [*Conjectures and Refutations*]

3 More people are killed out of righteous stupidity than out of wickedness. [*Conjectures and Refutations*]

4 We may become the makers of our fate when we have ceased to pose as its prophets. [*Open Society and its Enemies*, introduction]

PORRITT Jonathon 1950–
English environmental campaigner.

Green consumerism is a target for exploitation. There's a lot of green froth on top, but murkiness lurks underneath. [Speech at a Friends of the Earth Conference 1989]

PORTER Cole 1893–1964
US composer and lyricist.

1 But I'm always true to you, darlin', in my fashion, / Yes, I'm always true to you, darlin', in my way. ['Always True to You in my Fashion']

2 In olden days a glimpse of stocking / Was looked on as something shocking / Now, heaven knows, / Anything goes. ['Anything Goes']

3 When you're near there's such an air of spring about it; / I can hear a lark somewhere begin to sing about it; / There's no love song finer, / But how strange the change from major to minor / Every time we say goodbye. ['Every Time We Say Goodbye']

4 I get no kick from champagne, / Mere alcohol doesn't thrill me at all / So tell me why should it be true / That I get a kick out of you? ['I Get a Kick Out of You']

5 Birds do it, bees do it, / Even educated fleas do it. / Let's do it, let's fall in love. ['Let's Do It' (1954 version)]

6 Night and day, you are the one, / Only you beneath the moon and under the sun. ['Night and Day']

7 I've Got You Under My Skin. [Song title]

PORTER Katherine Anne 1890–1980
US writer.

Love is purely a creation of the human imagination ... the most important example of how the imagination continually outruns the creature it inhabits. [Quoted in *Contemporary Novelists* 1976]

POST Emily 1873–1960
US writer.

1 To the old saying that man built the house but woman made of it a 'home' might be added the modern supplement that woman accepted cooking as a chore but man has made of it a recreation. [*Etiquette* ch 34]

2 To do *exactly as your neighbors do* is the only sensible rule. [*Etiquette* ch 33]

POTTER Beatrix 1866–1943
English writer and illustrator.

1 It is said that the effect of eating too much lettuce is 'soporific'. [*Tale of the Flopsy Bunnies*]

2 Once upon a time there were four little Rabbits, and their names were – Flopsy, Mopsy, Cottontail, and Peter. [*Tale of Peter Rabbit*]

POTTER Dennis 1935–1994
English playwright.

1 The trouble with words is that you never know whose mouths they have been in. [Remark]

2 You cannot make a pair of croak-voiced Daleks appear benevolent even if you dress one of them in an Armani suit and call the other Marmaduke. [Remark on the BBC management. August 1993]

POTTER Stephen 1900–1969
English writer.

1 A good general rule is to state that the bouquet is better than the taste, and vice versa. [*One-Upmanship* ch 14]

Classic British children's author and illustrator Beatrix Potter. She stands at the door of the Cumbrian farm she bought in 1905 with the revenue from her books. The tales of Tom Kitten, Jemima Puddleduck, and Samuel Whiskers were written and set here.

2 The Theory and Practice of Gamesmanship or The Art of Winning Games Without Actually Cheating. [Book title]

POUND Ezra 1885–1972
US poet.

1 One of the pleasures of middle age is to *find out* that one was right, and that one was much righter than one knew at say 17 *or* 23. [*ABC of Reading* ch 2]

2 Real education must ultimately be limited to one who insists on knowing, the rest is mere sheep-herding. [*ABC of Reading* ch 8]

3 Winter is icummen in, / Lhude sing Goddamm, / Raineth drop and staineth slop, / And how the wind doth ramm! / Sing: Goddamm. ['Ancient Music']

4 And even I can remember / A day when the historians left blanks in their writings, / I mean for things they didn't know. [*Draft of Cantos* XXX]

5 The modern artist must live by craft and violence. His gods are violent gods ... . Those artists, so called, whose work does not show this strife, are uninteresting. [*Egoist* Feb 1914]

6 Great literature is simply language charged with meaning to the utmost possible degree. [*How to Read*]

POWELL Anthony 1905–
English novelist.

1 He fell in love with himself at first sight and it is a passion to which he has always remained faithful. [*Acceptance World*]

2 Books Do Furnish a Room. [Title of novel]

3 A Dance to the Music of Time. [Title of novel sequence]

POWELL Enoch 1912–
British Conservative politician.

1 All political lives, unless they are cut off in midstream at a happy juncture, end in failure, because that is the nature of politics and of human affairs. [*Joseph Chamberlain*, epilogue]

2 As I look ahead, I am filled with foreboding. Like the Roman, I seem to see 'the River Tiber foaming with much blood'. [Speech at Conservative Political Centre, Birmingham 20 Apr 1968]

PRÉVERT Jacques 1900–1977
French poet.

When truth is no longer free, freedom is no longer real: the truths of the police are the truths of today. [*Spectacle*, 'Intermède']

PRIESTLEY J B 1894–1984
English novelist and playwright.

1 God can stand being told by Professor Ayer and Marghanita Laski that He doesn't exist. [*Listener* 1 July 1965]

2 It is hard to tell where the MCC ends and the Church of England begins. [*New Statesman* 20 July 1962]

3 Already we Viewers, when not viewing, have begun to whisper to one another that the more we elaborate our means of communication, the less we communicate. ['Writer in a Changing Society']

PRINGLE William LIVED 18TH/19TH CENTURY
English naval captain.

The Navy, Sir, yesterday lost one of its greatest ornaments, by Nelson's marriage. It is a national loss, that such an officer should marry; had it not been for that circumstance, I forsee that Nelson would become the greatest man in the Service. [Remark to a fellow officer, 12 March 1787, the day after Nelson's marriage and 15 years before the Battle of Trafalgar.]

PRIOR Matthew 1664–1721
English poet and diplomat.

1 I court others in verse: but I love thee in prose: / And they have my whimsies, but thou hast my heart. ['Better Answer']

2 Be to her virtues very kind; / Be to her faults a little blind; / Let all her ways be unconfin'd; / And clap your padlock on her mind. [English Padlock]

3 Cur'd yesterday of my disease, / I died last night of my physician. ['Remedy Worse than the Disease']

PROTAGORAS BORN C. 485 BC
Greek sophist.

Man is the measure of all things. [Quoted in Plato Theaetetus]

PROUDHON Pierre-Joseph 1809–1865
French anarchist.

Property is theft. [What is Property?]

PROUST Marcel 1871–1922
French novelist and critic.

1 In his younger days a man dreams of possessing the heart of the woman whom he loves; later, the feeling that he possesses a woman's heart may be enough to make him fall in love with her. [Remembrance of Things Past, vol 1, bk 1 Swann's Way]

2 People often say that, by pointing out to a man the faults of his mistress, you succeed only in strengthening his attachment to her, because he does not believe you: yet how much more if he does. [Remembrance of Things Past, vol 1, bk 1, Swann's Way]

3 As soon as one is unhappy one becomes moral. [Remembrance of Things Past, vol 1, bk 2, Within a Budding Grove]

4 Like everybody who is not in love, he imagined that one chose the person whom one loved after endless deliberations and on the strength of various qualities and advantages.

[Remembrance of Things Past, vol 2, bk 2, Cities of the Plain]

5 It is seldom indeed that one parts on good terms, because if one were on good terms one would not part. [Remembrance of Things Past, vol 3, bk 2, The Fugitive]

6 Happiness is salutary for the body but sorrow develops the powers of the spirit. [Remembrance of Things Past, vol 3, bk 3, Time Regained]

7 A work of art that contains theories is like an object on which the price tag has been left [Remembrance of Things Past, vol 3, bk 3, Time Regained]

PROUTY Olive Higgins 1882–1974
US novelist.

She drew in her breath sharply as if he had touched a nerve. 'O Jerry,' she said when she could trust her voice. 'Don't let's ask for the moon! We have the stars!' [Now Voyager ch 29]

PURVES Libby 1950–
English broadcaster and writer.

Had we but world enough and time, / This note would be a Valentine. / Since married life is what we have, / It's just to remind you to bring home / The haddock and the Sanilav. [Quoted in Woman's Hour Book of Humour, 'Just a Housewife?']

PUSHKIN Aleksandr 1799–1837
Russian poet and writer.

1 From early youth his dedication / Was to a single occupation; / He knew one torment, one delight / Through empty day and idle night; / The science of the tender passion. [Eugene Onegin ch 1]

2 A woman's love for us increases / The less we love her, sooth to say– / She stoops, she falls, her struggling ceases; / Caught fast, she cannot get away. [Eugene Onegin ch 4]

3 Habit is Heaven's own redress: it takes the place of happiness. [Eugene Onegin]

4 I loved you once, and in my soul maybe / Love is not altogether dead to-day. / But you shall not be troubled more by me / I would not sadden you in any way. / I loved you silently and hopelessly, / Worn now with jealousy and now with shame; / I loved so truly and so tenderly, – / God grant some other's love may be the same! ['I Loved You Once']

PUTNAM Israel 1718–1790
US revolutionary soldier.

Men, you are all marksmen – don't one of you fire until you see the whites of their eyes. [Order at the Battle of Bunker Hill 1775]

PUZO Mario 1920–
US novelist.

He's a businessman. ... I'll make him an offer he can't refuse. [*The Godfather* ch 1]

QUASIMODO Salvatore 1901–1968
Italian poet.

Poetry is the revelation of a feeling that the poet believes to be interior and personal [but] which the reader recognizes as his own. [Speech 1960]

1 Physicians of all men are most happy; what good success soever they have, the world proclaimeth, and what faults they commit, the earth covereth. [*Hieroglyphics of the Life of Man*]

2 My soul, sit thou a patient looker-on; / Judge not the play before the play is done: / Her plot hath many changes; every day / Speaks a new scene; the last act crowns the play. ['Respice Finem']

RABELAIS François 1495–1553
French satirist, monk, and physician.

1 Do what thou wilt. [*Gargantua* I. 42]

2 I go to seek a great perhaps. [Attributed remark on his deathbed]

3 Ring down the curtain, the farce is over. [Attributed remark on his deathbed]

RABIN Yitzhak 1922–
Israeli Labour prime minister.

The government of Israel has decided to recognize the PLO as the representative of the Palestinian people. [On signing peace agreement with PLO, Sept 1993]

RACINE Jean 1639–1699
French dramatist.

1 I loved you when you were inconstant. What should I have done if you had been faithful? [*Andromaque* IV. v]

2 It is the goddess Venus herself fastened on her prey. [*Phèdre* I. iii]

3 No money, no Swiss. [*Les Plaideurs* I. i]

RAINBOROWE Thomas D. 1648–
English soldier and poet.

Now what is love? I pray thee, tell. / It is that fountain and that well, / Where pleasure and repentance dwell. ['Description of Love']

RAINE Craig 1944–
British poet and critic.

The task of the artist at any time is uncompromisingly simple – to dis-cover what has not yet been done, and to do it. [*Guardian* 19 Aug 1988]

RALEIGH or *Ralegh* Walter c. 1552–1618
English courtier, navigator, and writer.

1 But true love is a durable fire, / In the mind ever burning, / Never sick, never old, never dead, / From itself never turning. ['As You Came from the Holy Land']

2 There is nothing exempt from the peril of mutation; the earth, the heavens, and whole world is thereunto subject. [*Cabinet Council* ch 24]

3 O eloquent, just, and mighty Death! [*History of the World* bk 5, ch 6]

4 Fain would I climb, yet fear I to fall. [Line written on a window-pane. Queen Elizabeth I wrote under it 'If thy heart fails thee, climb not at all.']

5 If all the world and love were young, / And truth in every shepherd's tongue, / These pretty pleasures might me move / To live with thee, and be thy love. ['Nymph's Reply to the Shepherd']

6 Give me my scallop-shell of quiet, / My staff of faith to walk upon, / My scrip of joy, immortal diet, / My bottle of salvation, / My gown of glory, hope's true gage, / And thus I'll take my pilgrimage. ['Passionate Man's Pilgrimage']

7 So the heart be right, it is no matter which way the head lies. [When asked which way he preferred to lay his head on the block, quoted in W Stebbing *Sir Walter Raleigh*]

8 Even such is time, which takes in trust / Our youth, our joys, and all we have, / And pays us but with age and dust, / Who in the dark and silent grave, / When we have wandered all our ways, / Shuts up the story of our days. [Lines written the night before his death]

RALEIGH Walter 1861–1922
English scholar.

1 In Examinations those who do not wish to know ask questions of those who cannot tell. ['Some Thoughts on Examinations']

2 An anthology is like all the plums and orange peel picked out of a cake. [*Letter to Mrs Robert Bridges* 15 Jan 1915]

RANSOME Arthur 1884–1967
English journalist and writer.

1 BETTER DROWNED THAN DUFFERS IF NOT DUFFERS WONT DROWN. [*Swallows and Amazons*]

2 Grab a chance and you won't be sorry for a might-have-been. [*We Didn't Mean to Go to Sea* ch 2]

RAPHAEL Frederic 1931–
English writer, screenwriter, and critic.

What adultery was to the nineteenth century novel, espionage is to today's. The sincerity of defection is common to both. [*Times Literary Supplement* 3 Apr 1987]

RATTIGAN Terence 1911–1977
English dramatist.

Do you know what 'le vice Anglais' – the English vice – really is? Not flagellation, not pederasty – whatever the French believe it to be. It's our refusal to admit our emotions. We think they demean us, I suppose. [*In Praise of Love* II]

RAY Man 1890–1976
US photographer.

It is marvelous that we are / the only species that creates / gratuitous forms. / To create is divine, to reproduce / is human. [*Objets de mon affection*, 'Originals Graphic Multiples']

REAGAN Ronald 1911–
US Republican president.

1 You know, by the time you reach my age, you've made plenty of mistakes if you've lived your life properly. [*Observer* 1987]

2 Politics is supposed to be the second oldest profession. I have come to realize that it bears a very close resemblance to the first. [At a conference in Los Angeles 2 Mar 1977]

REGER Max 1873–1916
German composer and pianist.

I am sitting in the smallest room of my house. I have your review before me. In a moment it will be behind me. [Letter to critic in response to review in *Münchener Neueste Nachrichten* 7 Feb 1906]

REINHARDT Ad 1913–1967
US artist.

Art is too serious to be taken seriously. [Quoted in Lippard, *Ad Reinhardt* pt 1]

REMARQUE Erich Maria 1898–1970
German novelist and soldier.

All Quiet on the Western Front. [Book title]

REUBEN David 1933–
US psychiatrist and author.

Everything You Always Wanted to Know about Sex, but Were Afraid to Ask. [Book title]

REYNOLDS Burt 1936–
US film actor.

When an actor marries an actress they both fight for the mirror. [*Guardian* 12 Mar 1988]

REYNOLDS Joshua 1723–1792
English portrait painter.

1 If you have great talents, industry will improve them: if you have but moderate abilities, industry will supply their deficiency. [Discourse to Students of the Royal Academy 11 Dec 1769]

Self-portrait of the eminent English portrait painter Sir Joshua Reynolds. The Neoclassical idealizing principles of art set forth in his *Discourses* were vehemently disputed by William Blake.

2 A mere copier of nature can never produce anything great. [Discourse to Students of the Royal Academy 14 Dec 1770]

RHODES Cecil 1853–1902
UK-born South African statesman.

So little done, so much to do. [On the day he died]

RHYS Jean 1894–1979
Dominican-born English novelist.

A room is a place where you hide from the wolves outside and that's all any room is. [*Good Morning, Midnight*]

RICCI Ruggiero 1918–
US violinist.

A specialist is someone who does everything else worse. [*Daily Telegraph* 25 May 1990]

RICE Grantland 1880–1954
US sports journalist.

For when the One Great Scorer comes to mark against your name, / He writes – not that you won or lost – but how you played the Game. ['Alumnus Football']

RICH Adrienne 1929–
US poet.

The connections between and among women are the most feared, the most problematic, and the most potentially transforming force on the planet. [*Chrysalis* no. 7, 1979]

RICHELIEU Armand, Cardinal 1585–1642
French cardinal and politician.

Nothing is as dangerous for the state as those who would govern kingdoms with maxims found in books. [*Political Testament*]

RIDGE William Pett 1857–1930
English writer.

He took her up in his arms in the way of a bachelor who in his time has had amateur experience of the carrying of nieces. [*Lost Property* pt 1, ch 8]

RILKE Rainer Maria 1875–1926
German poet.

1 A good marriage is that in which each appoints the other guardian of his solitude. [*Letters*]

2 Ideally, a painter (and, generally, an artist) should not become conscious of his insights; ... all his progress should enter so swiftly into the work that he is unable to recognise them in the moment of transition. [Letter to his wife 21 Oct 1907]

3 Just as the creative artist is not allowed to choose, so is he not allowed to turn his back on anything: a single refusal, and he is cast out of the state of grace and becomes sinful all the way through. [Letter to his wife 23 Oct 1907]

ROBERTSON Sir William 1860–1933
British general in World War I.

'Orace, you're for 'ome! [To General Smith-Dorrien, when relieving him of his command]

ROBIN Leo 1899–1984
US songwriter.

Diamonds Are a Girl's Best Friend. [Song title]

ROCHEFOUCAULD François, Duc de la 1613–1680
French writer.

1 The height of cleverness is to be able to conceal cleverness. [*Maxims*]

2 Hypocrisy is homage paid by vice to virtue. [*Maxims*]

3 In the misfortune of our best friends, we find something which is not displeasing to us. [*Maxims*]

4 There are very few people who are not ashamed of having been in love when they no longer love each other. [*Maxims* 71]

5 There is no disguise which can for long conceal love where it exists or simulate it where it does not. [*Maxims* 71]

6 The intellect is always fooled by the heart. [*Maxims* 102]

7 The pleasure of love is in loving; and we are much happier in the passion we feel than in that which we inspire. [*Maxims* 259]

8 There is hardly a man clever enough to recognize the full extent of the evil he does. [*Maxims* 312]

9 Lovers never get tired of each other, because they are always talking about themselves. [*Maxims* 312]

ROCHESTER John, Earl of 1647–1680
English poet and courtier.

1 A merry monarch, scandalous and poor. [Satire on King Charles II]

2 Here lies a great and mighty king / Whose promise none relies on; / He never said a foolish thing, / Nor ever did a wise one. ['The King's Epitaph']

RODDENBERRY Gene 1921–1991
US film producer.

These are the voyages of the starship Enterprise. Its five-year mission: to explore strange new worlds, to seek out new life and new civilizations, to boldly go where no man has gone before. [Introduction to television series *Star Trek*]

ROETHKE Theodore 1908–1963
US poet.

1 All lovers live by longing, and endure: / Summon a vision and declare it pure. [*Four for Sir John Davies* IV 'The Vigil']

2 Love begets love. The torment is my joy. ['Motion' II]

ROGERS Richard 1933–
British architect.

'Form follows profit' is the aesthetic principle of our times. [*The Times* 13 Feb 1991]

ROGERS Samuel 1763–1855
English poet.

It doesn't much signify whom one marries, for one is sure to find next morning that it was someone else. [Quoted in A Dyce *Table Talk of Samuel Rogers*]

ROGERS Will 1879–1935
US humorist.

1 Everything is funny as long as it is happening to Somebody Else. [*Illiterate Digest*, 'Warning to Jokers']

2 You know everybody is ignorant, only on different subjects. [*New York Times* 31 Aug 1924]

3 You can't say civilization don't advance, however, for in every war they kill you in a new way. [*New York Times* 23 Dec 1929]

4 I don't make jokes – I just watch the government and report the facts. [*Saturday Review* 25 Aug 1962]

ROLAND Madame 1754–1793
French intellectual and political figure.

O liberty! O liberty! what crimes are committed in thy name! [Remark on seeing a statue of Liberty as she was taken to the scaffold]

ROLF Ida 1896–1979
US biochemist and physical therapist.

Form and function are a unity, two sides of one coin. In order to enhance function, appropriate form must exist or be created. [*Rolfing*, Preface]

ROMAINS Jules 1885–1972
French novelist, playwright, and poet.

Every man who feels well is a sick man neglecting himself. [*Knock, or the Triumph of Medicine*]

ROOSEVELT Eleanor 1884–1962
US social worker, lecturer, and First Lady.

No one can make you feel inferior without your consent. [*Catholic Digest*]

ROOSEVELT Franklin D 1882–1945
US Democratic president.

1 I pledge you – I pledge myself – to a new deal for the American people. [Speech 1932]

2 In the field of world policy I would dedicate this Nation to the policy of the good neighbour. [Inaugural address 4 Mar 1933]

3 Let me assert my firm belief that the only thing we have to fear is fear itself – nameless, unreasoning, unjustified terror which paralyses needed efforts to convert retreat into advance. [Inaugural address 4 Mar 1933]

4 We must be the great arsenal of democracy. [Speech 1940]

ROOSEVELT Theodore 1858–1919
US Republican president.

1 I wish to preach, not the doctrine of ignoble ease, but the doctrine of the strenuous life. [Speech 1899]

2 There is a homely old adage which runs: 'Speak softly and carry a big stick; you will go far.' [Speech at Chicago 3 Apr 1903]

3 A man who is good enough to shed his blood for the country is good enough to be given a square deal afterwards. More than that no man is entitled to, and less than that no man shall have. [Speech at the Lincoln Monument, Springfield, Illinois 4 June 1903]

4 The men with the muck-rakes are often indispensable to the well-being of society; but only if they know when to stop raking the muck. [Speech in Washington 14 Apr 1906]

5 A hyphenated American is not an American at all. This is just as true of the man who puts 'native' before the hyphen as of the man who puts German or Irish or English or French before the hyphen. [Speech in New York 12 Oct 1915]

ROOTES Lord 1894–1964
English car manufacturer.

No other manmade device since the shields and lances of the ancient knights fulfils a man's ego like an automobile. [Quoted in 'Who Said That?', BBC TV, 14 Jan 1958]

ROSA Salvator 1615–1673
Italian Baroque painter, poet, and musician.

> Be silent, unless what you have to say is better than silence. [Motto on self-portrait *c*. 1645]

ROSEBERY Archibald, Lord 1847–1929
British Liberal politician.

> **1** It is beginning to be hinted that we are a nation of amateurs. [Address 1900]

> **2** I must plough my furrow alone. [Speech 1901]

ROSENBERG Harold 1906–1978
US art critic and writer.

> **1** The purpose of education is to keep a culture from being drowned in senseless repetitions, each of which claims to offer a new insight. [*Partisan Review* Summer 1972, 'Cultural Situation Today']

> **2** Whoever undertakes to create soon finds himself engaged in creating himself. Self-transformation and the transformation of others have constituted the radical interest of our century. [*Tradition of the New*, Preface]

ROSENSTEIN Harriet 1932–
US writer.

> Destiny is something men select; women achieve it only by default or stupendous suffering. [*Ms* July 1974]

ROSSETTI Christina 1830–1894
English poet.

> **1** My heart is like a singing bird. ['A Birthday']

> **2** Better by far you should forget and smile / Than that you should remember and be sad. ['Remember']

> **3** Remember me when I am gone away, / Gone far away into the silent land; / When you can no more hold me by the hand, / Nor I half turn to go, yet turning stay. ['Remember']

> **4** When I am dead, my dearest, / Sing no sad songs for me. [*Song*]

> **5** Does the road wind up-hill all the way? / Yes, to the very end. ['Up-Hill']

ROSSETTI Dante Gabriel 1828–1882
English poet and painter.

> **1** I have been here before, / But when or how I cannot tell: / I know the grass beyond the door, / The sweet keen smell, / The sighing sound, the lights around the shore. ['Sudden Light']

> **2** My name is Might-have-been; / I am also called No-more, Too-late, Farewell. ['A Superscription']

Poet and painter Dante Gabriel Rossetti was a central figure in the Pre-Raphaelite movement.

ROSTAND Jean 1894–1977
French biologist and writer.

> **1** A married couple are well suited when both partners usually feel the need for a quarrel at the same time. [*Marriage*]

2 Never feel remorse for what you have thought about your wife; she has thought much worse things about you. [*Marriage*]

3 My pessimism goes to the point of suspecting the sincerity of the pessimists. [*Journal of a Character*]

4 It may offend us to hear our own thoughts expressed by others; we are not sure enough of their souls. [*Thoughts of a Biologist*]

5 The nobility of a human being is strictly independent of that of his convictions. [*Thoughts of a Biologist*]

6 Renown? I've already got more of it than those I respect, and will never have as much as those for whom I feel contempt. [*Thoughts of a Biologist*]

7 There are certain errors of such ingenuity that one could regret their not ranking among the achievements of the human mind. [*Thoughts of a Biologist*]

8 To be adult is to be alone. [*Thoughts of a Biologist*]

ROTH Philip 1933–
US novelist.

1 Memories of the past are not memories of facts but memories of your imaginings of the facts. [*The Facts*, opening letter to Zuckerman]

2 Because to be bad, Mother, that's the real struggle: to be bad – and enjoy it! That's what makes men of us boys, Mother. LET'S PUT THE ID BACK IN YID! [*Portnoy's Complaint*]

ROURKE Constance 1885–1941
US writer.

In comedy, reconcilement with life comes at the point when to the tragic sense only an inalienable difference or dissension with life appears. [*American Humor* ch 8]

ROUSSEAU Jean-Jacques 1712–1778
French philosopher and writer.

1 We are born, so to speak, twice over; born into existence, and born into life; born a human being, and born a man. [*Emile* bk 4]

2 Censorship may be useful for the preservation of morality, but can never be so for its restoration. [*Social Contract*]

3 Man is born free, and everywhere he is in chains. [*Social Contract*]

4 Nations, like men, are teachable only in their youth; with age they become incorrigible. [*Social Contract*]

ROUTH Martin Joseph 1755–1854
English scholar.

You will find it a very good practice always to verify your references, sir! [Quoted in J W Burgon *Memoir of Dr. Routh*]

ROWE Nicholas 1674–1718
English poet and dramatist.

1 Death is the privilege of human nature, / And life without it were not worth our taking. [*Fair Penitent* V. i]

2 Is this that haughty, gallant, gay Lothario? [*The Fair Penitent* V. i]

ROWLAND Helen 1876–1950
US writer.

1 A husband is what is left of a lover, after the nerve has been extracted. [*Guide to Men*]

2 Somehow a bachelor never quite gets over the idea that he is a thing of beauty and a boy forever. [*Guide to Men*]

3 The hardest task of a girl's life is to prove to a man that his intentions are serious. [*Reflections of a Bachelor Girl*]

4 It is easier to keep half a dozen lovers guessing than to keep one lover after he has stopped guessing. [*Reflections of a Bachelor Girl*]

5 It takes a woman twenty years to make a man of her son, and another woman twenty minutes to make a fool of him. [*Reflections of a Bachelor Girl*]

6 When you see what some girls marry, you realize how they must hate to work for a living. [*Reflections of a Bachelor Girl*]

RUDNER Rita 1956–
US comedienne.

1 My boyfriend and I broke up. He wanted to get married, and I didn't want him to. [Quoted in *Ms* 1984]

2 Men who have a pierced ear are better prepared for marriage – they've experienced pain and bought jewellery. [Remark, on television 5 Dec 1989]

RUNYON Damon 1884–1946
US journalist and writer.

1 I always claim the mission workers came out too early to catch any sinners on this part of Broadway. At such an hour the sinners are still in bed resting up from their sinning of the night before, so they will be in good shape for more sinning a little later on. ['Idyll of Miss Sarah Brown']

2 'My boy,' he says, 'always try to rub up against money, for if you rub up against money long enough, some of it may rub off on you.' ['Very Honorable Guy']

RUSHDIE Salman 1948–
Indian-born British writer.

One of the extraordinary things about human events is that the unthinkable becomes thinkable. [*Guardian* 8 Nov 1990]

RUSKIN John 1819–1900
English art critic and social critic.

1 I don't like married women; I like sybils and children and vestals. [Quoted in J Hodges *Heart of the Writer*]

2 I believe the right question to ask, respecting all ornament, is simply this: Was it done with enjoyment – was the carver happy while he was about it? ['Lamp of Life']

3 Life without industry is guilt, and industry without art is brutality. [*Lectures on Art* 3 'The Relation of Art to Morals' 23 Feb 1870]

4 When we build, let us think that we build for ever. [*Seven Lamps of Architecture*]

5 To make your children *capable of honesty* is the beginning of education. [*Time and Tide*]

6 Government and co-operation are in all things the laws of life; anarchy and competition the laws of death. [*Unto this Last*]

7 I ... never expected to hear a coxcomb ask two hundred guineas for flinging a pot of paint in the public's face. [Comment on Whistler's *Nocturne in Black and Gold*]

RUSSELL Bertrand, Lord 1872–1970
English philosopher and mathematician.

1 Three passions, simple but overwhelmingly strong, have governed my life: the longing for love, the search for knowledge, and unbearable pity for the suffering of mankind. [*Autobiography* Prologue]

2 Drunkenness ... is temporary suicide. [*Conquest of Happiness* ch 2]

3 Boredom is ... a vital problem for the moralist, since at least half the sins of mankind are caused by the fear of it. [*Conquest of Happiness* ch 4]

4 If I were a medical man, I should prescribe a holiday to any patient who considered his work important. [*Conquest of Happiness* ch. 5]

5 If all our happiness is bound up entirely in our personal circumstances it is difficult not to demand of life more than it has to give. [*Conquest of Happiness* ch 10]

English philosopher and mathematician Bertrand Russell (right) meeting United Nations secretary general U Thant in London 1962. During a long, wide-ranging intellectual career Russell wrote numerous books on philosophy, education, morals, and religion. A life-long campaigner on a range of social issues, he was imprisoned in 1961 at the age of 89 for taking part in a nuclear disarmament demonstration in London.

6 A sense of duty is useful in work, but offensive in personal relations. People wish to be liked, not to be endured with patient resignation. [*Conquest of Happiness* ch 10]

7 To be able to fill leisure intelligently is the last product of civilization, and at present very few people have reached this level. [*Conquest of Happiness* ch 14]

8 When the intensity of emotional conviction subsides, a man who is in the habit of reasoning will search for logical grounds in favour of the belief which he finds in himself. [*Free Man's Worship* ch 2]

9 Aristotle's metaphysics, roughly speaking, may be described as Plato diluted by commonsense. He is difficult because Plato and commonsense do not mix easily. [*History of Western Philosophy* ch 19]

10 Hegel filled the universe with copulating contradictions. [*History of Western Philosophy* ch 22]

11 Marriage is for women the commonest mode of livelihood, and the total amount of undesired sex endured by women is probably greater in marriage than in prostitution. [*Marriage and Morals*]

12 The psychology of adultery has been falsified by conventional morals, which assume, in monogamous countries, that attraction to one person cannot coexist with a serious affection for another. Everybody knows that this is untrue. [*Marriage and Morals*]

13 To fear love is to fear life, and those who fear life are already three parts dead. [*Marriage and Morals*]

14 Most people would sooner die than think: in fact they do so. [Quoted in *Observer* 12 July 1925]

15 The infliction of cruelty with a good conscience is a delight to moralists. That is why they invented Hell. ['On the Value of Scepticism']

16 Man is a credulous animal, and must believe something; in the absence of good grounds for belief, he will be satisfied with bad ones. [*Unpopular Essays*, 'Outline of Intellectual Rubbish']

RUSSELL John 1795–1883
English 'sporting parson'.

1 If peace cannot be maintained with honour, it is no longer peace. [Speech 1853]

2 Two mothers-in-law. [On being asked what he considered to be an appropriate punishment for bigamy.]

RUSSELL Willy 1947–
English dramatist and writer.

The main purpose of marriage is rearing children and when that's done you should be free to renew your option – about twenty years seems like a reasonable term to me. [*Guardian* 20 Oct 1987]

RUTHERFORD Ernest 1871–1937
New Zealand physicist.

All science is either physics or stamp collecting. [Quoted in J B Birks *Rutherford at Manchester*]

RYLE Gilbert 1900–1976
English philosopher.

The dogma of the Ghost in the Machine. [*Concept of Mind* ch 1]

SAARINEN Eero 1910–1961
Finnish-born US architect.

> Always design a thing by considering it in its larger context – a chair in a room, a room in a house, a house in an environment, an environment in a city plan. [*Time* July 1956]

SAGAN Françoise 1935–
French writer.

> 1 Every little girl knows about love. It is only her capacity to suffer because of it that increases. [*Daily Express* 1957]

> 2 Marriage? It's like asparagus eaten with vinaigrette or hollandaise, a matter of taste but of no importance. [*Guardian* 21 June 1988]

> 3 To jealousy, nothing is more frightful than laughter. [*The Masquerade* ch 9]

> 4 At seventeen, you tend to go in for unhappy love affairs. [*Responses*]

SAINT-EXUPÉRY Antoine de 1900–1944
French writer and aviator.

> 1 What was my body to me? A kind of flunkey in my service. Let but my anger wax hot, my love grow exalted, my hatred collect in me, and that boasted solidarity between me and my body was gone. [*Flight to Arras* ch 19]

> 2 Charity never humiliated him who profited from it, nor ever bound him by the chains of gratitude, since it was not to him but to God that the gift was made. [*Flight to Arras* ch 23]

> 3 One can be a brother only *in* something. Where there is no tie that binds men, men are not united but merely lined up. [*Flight to Arras* ch 23]

> 4 Grown-ups never understand anything for themselves, and it is tiresome for children to be always and forever explaining things to them. [*Little Prince* ch 1]

> 5 Life has taught us that love does not consist in gazing at each other but in looking together in the same direction. [*Wind, Sand and Stars* ch 8]

SAKI 1870–1916
Burmese-born English writer.

> 1 But, good gracious, you've got to educate him first. You can't expect a boy to be depraved until he's been to a good school. ['Baker's Dozen']

> 2 'The man is a common murderer.' 'A common murderer, possibly, but a very uncommon cook.' ['Blind Spot']

> 3 A little inaccuracy sometimes saves tons of explanation. ['Comments of Moung Ka']

> 4 Waldo is one of those people who would be enormously improved by death. ['Feast of Nemesis']

> 5 Children with Hyacinth's temperament don't know better as they grow older; they merely know more. ['Hyacinth']

> 6 The people of Crete unfortunately make more history than they can consume locally. ['Jesting of Arlington Stringham']

> 7 All decent people live beyond their incomes nowadays, and those who aren't respectable live beyond other peoples'. A few gifted individuals manage to do both. ['Match-Maker']

> 8 He's simply got the instinct for being unhappy highly developed. ['Match-Maker']

9 Every reformation must have its victims. You can't expect the fatted calf to share the enthusiasm of the angels over the prodigal's return. ['Reginald on the Academy']

10 The cook was a good cook, as cooks go; and as cooks go she went. ['Reginald on Besetting Sins']

11 People may say what they like about the decay of Christianity; the religious system that produced green Chartreuse can never really die. ['Reginald on Christmas Presents']

12 I always say beauty is only sin deep. ['Reginald's Choir Treat']

13 A woman whose dresses are made in Paris and whose marriage has been made in Heaven might be equally biased for and against free imports. [*Unbearable Bassington* ch 9]

SALINGER J D 1919–
US writer.

I keep picturing all these little kids in this big field...[If] they don't look where they're going I have to come out from somewhere and catch them. That's all I'd do all day. I'd just be the catcher in the rye and all. [*Catcher in the Rye*]

SALLUST 86–34 BC
Roman historian.

With punic (Carthaginian) faith. [*Jugurtha*]

SAMUEL Lord 1870–1983
English Liberal statesman.

1 It takes two to make a marriage a success and only one a failure. [*Book of Quotations*]

2 A library is thought in cold storage. [*Book of Quotations*]

SAMUELSON Paul 1915–
US economist and journalist.

Man does not live by GNP alone. [*Economics* 1948]

SAND George 1804–1876
French novelist.

1 The beauty that addresses itself to the eyes is only the spell of the moment; the eye of the body is not always that of the soul. [*Handsome Lawrence* ch 1]

2 Liszt said to me today that God alone deserves to be loved. It may be true, but when one has loved a man it is very different to love God. [*Intimate Journal*]

3 We cannot tear out a single page of our life, but we can throw the whole book in the fire. [*Mauprat*]

4 What constitutes adultery is not the hour which a woman gives her lover, but the night which she afterwards spends with her husband. [Attributed remark]

SANDBURG Carl 1878–1967
US poet.

1 I am an idealist. I don't know where I'm going but I'm on the way. [*Incidentals*]

2 Shame is the feeling you have when you agree with the woman who loves you that you are the man she thinks you are. [*Incidentals*]

3 Sometime they'll give a war and nobody will come. [*The People*]

4 Poetry is the opening and closing of a door, leaving those who look through to guess about what is seen during a moment. ['Poetry Considered']

5 Slang is a language that rolls up its sleeves, spits on its hands and goes to work. [*New York Times* 13 Feb 1959]

6 Papa loved mamma / Mamma loved men / Mamma's in the graveyard / Papa's in the pen. ['Papa loved Mamma']

SANTAYANA George 1863–1952
Spanish-born US philosopher and poet.

1 Chaos is a name for any order that produces confusion in our minds. [*Dominations and Powers* bk 1, pt 1, ch 1]

2 The primary use of conversation is to satisfy the urge to talk. [*Last Puritan* 385]

3 Character is the basis of happiness and happiness the sanction of character. [*Life of Reason*]

4 Fanaticism consists in redoubling your effort when you have forgotten your aim. [*Life of Reason*]

5 It takes patience to appreciate domestic bliss; volatile spirits prefer unhappiness. [*Life of Reason*]

6 Those who cannot remember the past are condemned to repeat it. [*Life of Reason*]

7 The effort of art is to keep what is interesting in existence, to recreate it in the eternal. [*Life of Reason*, 'Reason in Art' ch 8]

8 The body is an instrument, the mind its function, the witness and reward of its operation. [*The Life of Reason*, 'Reason in Common Sense' ch 9]

9 That fear first created the gods is perhaps as true as anything so brief could be on so great a subject. [*Life of Reason*, 'Reason in Religion' ch 3]

SARGENT John Singer 1856–1925
US portrait painter.

Every time I paint a portrait I lose a friend. [Quoted in N Bentley and E Esar *Treasury of Humorous Quotations*]

SARTRE Jean-Paul 1905–1980
French philosopher, dramatist, and novelist.

1 I am condemned to be free. [*Being and Nothingness*]

2 To eat is to appropriate by destruction. [*Being and Nothingness*, 'Doing and Having' 3]

3 Hell is other people. [*Closed Doors* ch 5]

4 Communism I like, but communist intellectuals are savages. [Quoted in *Observer* 25 Mar 1956]

5 One is still what one is going to cease to be and already what one is going to become. One lives one's death, one dies one's life. [*Saint Genet: Actor and Martyr* bk 2]

6 I confused things with their names: that is belief. [*The Words*]

SASSOON Siegfried 1886–1967
English poet and novelist.

1 Does it matter? – losing your sight? ... / There's such splendid work for the blind; / And people will always be kind, / As you sit on the terrace remembering / And turning your face to the light. ['Does it Matter']

2 Soldiers are dreamers; when the guns begin / They think of firelit homes, clean beds, and wives. ['Dreamers' 1918]

3 Everyone suddenly burst out singing. ['Everyone Sang']

4 If I were fierce and bald and short of breath, / I'd live with scarlet majors at the Base, / And speed glum heroes up the line to death. [On General Haig, 'Base Details']

SAVAGE Richard D. 1743–
English poet.

No tenth transmitter of a foolish face. ['The Bastard']

SAYERS Dorothy L 1893–1957
English writer.

1 I admit it is better fun to punt than to be punted, and that a desire to have all the fun is nine-tenths of the law of chivalry. [*Gaudy Night* ch 14]

2 As I grow older and older, / And totter towards the tomb, / I find that I care less and less / Who goes to bed with whom. ['That's Why I Never Read Modern Novels']

English writer Dorothy L Sayers, author of tasteful and stylish mystery stories featuring the detective Lord Peter Wimsey.

SCARGILL Arthur 1938–
British leader of the NUM.

Only a fool wants a confrontation and only a fool wants a strike. [Quoted in *Observer* 6 Nov 1977]

SCHILLER Friedrich von 1759–1805
German dramatist, poet, and historian.

1 What is life without the radiance of love? [*Death of Wallenstein* IV. xii]

2 Against stupidity the gods themselves struggle in vain. [*Maid of Orleans*]

SCHNABEL Artur 1882–1951
Austrian pianist and composer.

The notes I handle no better than many pianists. But the pauses between the notes – ah, that is where the art resides! [*Chicago Daily News* 11 June 1958]

SCHNITZLER Arthur 1862–1931
Austrian dramatist.

Women always want to be our last love, and we their first. [Quoted in F Ungar (ed) *Practical Wisdom*]

SCHOPENHAUER Arthur 1788–1860
German philosopher.

1 Belief is like love; it cannot be compelled. [*Essays and Aphorisms*]

2 Buying books would be a good thing if one could also buy the time to read them in. [*Essays and Aphorisms*]

3 Every parting is a foretaste of death, and every reunion a foretaste of the resurrection. [*Essays and Aphorisms*]

4 To marry is to halve your rights and double your duties. [*World as Will and Idea*]

SCHUMACHER E F 1911–1977
German economist.

Small Is Beautiful. [Book title]

SCHWARZKOPF H Norman *Stormin' Norman* 1934–
US general.

He is neither a strategist, nor is he schooled in the operational art, nor is he a tactician, nor is he a general, nor is he a soldier. Other than that, he is a great military man. [On his adversary, Iraq's Saddam Hussein, March 1991]

SCHWEITZER Albert 1875–1965
French missionary surgeon.

'Reverence for Life'. [*My Life and Thought* ch 13]

SCOTT Hazel 1920–1981
US entertainer.

There's a time when you have to explain to your children why they're born, and it's a marvelous thing if you know the reason by then. [Quoted in *Ms* Nov 1974]

SCOTT Robert Falcon *Scott of the Antarctic* 1868–1912
English explorer.

> Great God! this is an awful place.
> [On the South Pole, in diary 17 Jan 1912]

SCOTT Walter 1771–1832
Scottish novelist and poet.

> 1 Come fill up my cup, come fill up my can, / Come saddle your horses, and call up your men; / Come open the West Port, and let me gang free, / And it's room for the bonnets of Bonny Dundee!
> ['Bonnie Dundee']

> 2 But answer came there none.
> [*Bridal of Triermain*]

> 3 Look not thou on beauty's charming, / Sit thou still when kings are arming, / Taste not when the wine-cup glistens, / Speak not when the people listens, / Stop thine ear against the singer, / From the red gold keep thy finger; / Vacant heart and hand, and eye, / Easy live and quiet die. [*Bride of Lammermoor*]

> 4 The hour is come, but not the man. [*Heart of Midlothian*]

> 5 And love is loveliest when embalm'd in tears. [*Lady of the Lake* canto IV]

> 6 Yet seem'd that tone, and gesture bland, / Less used to sue than to command. [*Lady of the Lake*]

> 7 The way was long, the wind was cold, / The Minstrel was infirm and old. [*Lay of the Last Minstrel* introduction]

> 8 Breathes there the man, with soul so dead, / Who never to himself hath said, / This is my own, my native land! [*Lay of the Last Minstrel* VI. 1]

> 9 O Caledonia! stern and wild, / Meet nurse for a poetic child! [*Lay of the Last Minstrel* VI. 2]

> 10 O, young Lochinvar is come out of the west, / Through all the wide Border his steed was the best. [*Marmion* V. 12]

> 11 So faithful in love, and so dauntless in war, / There never was knight like the young Lochinvar. [*Marmion* V. 12]

> 12 My castles are my King's alone, / From turret to foundation-stone – / The hand of Douglas is his own. [*Marmion* VI. 13]

> 13 'And dar'st thou then / To beard the lion in his den, / The Douglas in his hall? [*Marmion* VI. 14]

> 14 O what a tangled web we weave, / When first we practise to deceive! [*Marmion* VI. 17]

> 15 O Woman! in our hours of ease, / Uncertain, coy, and hard to please, ... / When pain and anguish wring the brow, / A ministering angel thou! [*Marmion* VI. 30]

> 16 My heart's in the Highlands, my heart is not here, / My heart's in the Highlands a-chasing the deer; / A-chasing the wild deer, and following the roe, / My heart's in the Highlands wherever I go. [*Waverley*]

SCRUTON Roger 1944–
English philosopher and social critic.

> 1 Hospitality is the only form of gift that imposes itself as an obligation. [*Meaning of Conservatism*]

> 2 The spirit of reform has been too much concerned with private 'rights', and not enough concerned with the public order that makes them possible. [*Meaning of Conservatism*]

SEATTLE Chief *c.* 1784–1866
Native American chief.

> What is man without the beasts? If all the beasts were gone, man would die from a great loneliness of spirit. [Reputed letter, 1854, to President Franklin Pierce, shown 1992 to have been largely a forgery, created 1971 by TV scriptwriter Ted Perry]

SEDLEY Charles 1639–1701
English courtier and poet.

> Love still has something of the sea / From whence his mother rose. ['Love Still Has Something']

SEEGER Alan 1888–1916
US poet.

> I have a rendezvous with Death / At some disputed barricade. ['I Have a Rendezvous with Death']

SEGAL Erich 1937–
US novelist.

> Love means never having to say you're sorry. [*Love Story* ch 13]

SELDEN John 1584–1654
English jurist and historian.

> **1** Old friends are best. King James used to call for his old shoes; they were easiest for his feet. [*Table Talk*, 'Friends']

> **2** 'Tis not the drinking that is to be blamed, but the excess. [*Table Talk*, 'Humility']

> **3** Ignorance of the law excuses no man; not that all men know the law, but because 'tis an excuse every man will plead, and no man can tell how to confute him. [*Table Talk*, 'Law']

> **4** Marriage is a desperate thing: the frogs in Aesop were extreme wise; they had a great mind to some water, but they would not leap into the well, because they could not get out again. [*Table Talk*, 'Marriage']

> **5** Marriage is nothing but a civil contract. [*Table Talk*, 'Marriage']

> **6** Philosophy is nothing but discretion. [*Table Talk*, 'Philosophy']

> **7** Pleasure is nothing else but the intermission of pain. [*Table Talk*, 'Pleasure']

SELLAR AND YEATMAN Sellar W C 1898–1951 and Yeatman R J 1898–1968
English writers.

> **1** The Roman Conquest was, however, a *Good Thing*, since the Britons were only natives at the time. [*1066 and All That* ch 1]

> **2** The utterly memorable Struggle between the Cavaliers (Wrong but Wromantic) and the Roundheads (Right but Repulsive). [*1066 and All That* ch 35]

> **3** Gladstone ... spent his declining years trying to guess the answer to the Irish Question; unfortunately whenever he was getting warm, the Irish secretly changed the Question. [*1066 and All That* ch 57]

SEWARD Thomas 1708–1790
English cleric.

> Seven wealthy towns contend for Homer dead, / Through which the living Homer begg'd his bread. ['On Homer']

SHADWELL Thomas 1642–1692
English dramatist and poet.

> **1** 'Tis the way of all flesh. [*The Sullen Lovers*]

> **2** And wit's the noblest frailty of the mind. [*True Widow* II. i]

> **3** The haste of a fool is the slowest thing in the world. [*True Widow* III. i]

> **4** Every man loves what he is good at. [*True Widow* V. i]

SHAKESPEARE William 1564–1616
English dramatist and poet.

> **1** It were all one / That I should love a bright particular star / And think to wed it, he is so above me. [*All's Well That Ends Well* I. i]

> **2** My friends were poor but honest. [*All's Well That Ends Well* I. iii 203]

> **3** Praising what is lost / Makes the remembrance dear. [*All's Well That Ends Well* V. iii 19]

4 Let Rome in Tiber melt, and the wide arch / Of the rang'd empire fall! Here is my space. / Kingdoms are clay. [*Antony and Cleopatra* I. i 33]

5 On the sudden / A Roman thought hath struck him. [*Anthony and Cleopatra* I. i 90]

6 In Nature's infinite book of secrecy / A little I can read. [*Antony and Cleopatra* I. ii 11]

7 Eternity was in our lips and eyes. [*Antony and Cleopatra* I. iii 35]

8 Though age from folly could not give me freedom, / It does from childishness. [*Anthony and Cleopatra* I. iii 57]

9 At the last, best. [*Anthony and Cleopatra* I. iii 61]

10 Give me to drink mandragora ... / That I might sleep out this great gap of time / My Antony is away. [*Antony and Cleopatra* I. v 4]

11 Where's my serpent of old Nile? [*Antony and Cleopatra* I. v 25]

12 My salad days, / When I was green in judgment. [*Antony and Cleopatra* I. v 73]

13 I do not much dislike the matter, but / The manner of his speech. [*Antony and Cleopatra* II. ii 117]

14 No worse a husband than the best of men. [*Antony and Cleopatra* II. ii 135]

15 The barge she sat in, like a burnish'd throne, / Burn'd on the water; the poop was beaten gold, / Purple the sails, and so perfumed, that / The winds were love-sick with them, the oars were silver, / Which to the tune of flutes kept stroke, and made / The water which they beat to follow faster, / As amorous of their strokes. [*Antony and Cleopatra* II. ii 199]

16 Age cannot wither her, nor custom stale / Her infinite variety. [*Antony and Cleopatra* II. ii 243]

17 Music, moody food / Of us that trade in love. [*Antony and Cleopatra* II. v 1]

18 I laugh'd him out of patience; and that night / I laugh'd him into patience. [*Antony and Cleopatra* II. v 19]

19 Give to a gracious message / A host of tongues. [*Antony and Cleopatra* II. v 86]

20 We have kiss'd away / Kingdoms and provinces. [*Antony and Cleopatra* III. viii]

21 Let's have one other gaudy night. [*Antony and Cleopatra* III. xi 182]

22 O infinite virtue! com'st thou smiling from / The world's great snare uncaught? [*Antony and Cleopatra* IV. viii 17]

23 Unarm, Eros; the long day's task is done, / And we must sleep. [*Antony and Cleopatra* IV. xii 35]

24 I am dying, Egypt, dying. [*Antony and Cleopatra* IV. xiii 18]

25 A Roman by a Roman / Valiantly vanquished. [*Antony and Cleopatra* IV. xiii 57]

26 O! see my women, / The crown o' the earth doth melt. My lord! / O! wither'd is the garland of the war, / The soldier's pole is fall'n; young boys and girls / Are level now with men; the odds is gone, / And there is nothing left remarkable / Beneath the visiting moon. [*Antony and Cleopatra* IV. xiii 62]

27 No more, but e'en a woman and commanded / By such poor passion as the maid that milks / And does the meanest chares. [*Antony and Cleopatra* IV. xiii 73]

28 What's brave, what's noble, / Let's do it after the high Roman fashion, / And make death proud to take us. [*Antony and Cleopatra* IV. xiii 86]

29 His delights / Were dolphin-like, they show'd his back above / The element they liv'd in. [*Antony and Cleopatra* V. ii 88]

30 I have / Immortal longings in me. [*Antony and Cleopatra* V. ii 282]

31 A lass unparallel'd. [*Antony and Cleopatra* V. ii 318]

32 Sweet are the uses of adversity, ... / And this our life, exempt from public haunt, / Finds tongues in trees, books in the running brooks, / Sermons in stones, and good in everything. [*As You Like It* II. i 12]

33 Sweep on, you fat and greasy citizens! [*As You Like It* II. i 55]

34 If thou rememb'rest not the slightest folly / That ever love did make thee run into, / Thou hast not lov'd. [*As You Like It* II. iv]

35 Under the greenwood tree / Who loves to lie with me. [*As You Like It* II. v 1]

36 I can suck melancholy out of a song as a weasel sucks eggs. [*As You Like It* II. v 12]

37 A motley fool. [*As You Like It* II. vii 13]

38 All the world's a stage, / And all the men and women merely players: / They have their exits and their entrances; / And one man in his time plays many parts, / His acts being seven ages. [*As You Like It* II. vii 139]

39 Last scene of all, / That ends this strange eventful history, / Is second childishness, and mere oblivion, / Sans teeth, sans eyes, sans taste, sans everything. [*As You Like It* II. vii 163]

40 Blow, blow, thou winter wind, / Thou art not so unkind / As man's ingratitude. [*As You Like It* II. vii 174]

41 Most friendship is feigning, most loving mere folly. [*As You Like It* II. vii 181]

42 I do desire we may be better strangers. [*As You Like It* III. ii 276]

43 For now I am in a holiday humour. [*As You Like It* IV. i 70]

44 Men have died from time to time, and worms have eaten them, but not for love. [*As You Like It* IV. i 110]

45 Men are April when they woo, December when they wed: maids are May when they are maids, but the sky changes when they are wives. [*As You Like It* IV. i 153]

46 The horn, the horn, the lusty horn / Is not a thing to laugh to scorn. [*As You Like It* IV. ii 17]

47 No sooner met, but they looked; no sooner looked but they loved; no sooner loved but they sighed; no sooner sighed but they asked one another the reason; no sooner knew the reason but they sought the remedy. [*As You Like It* V. ii]

48 It was a lover and his lass. [*As You Like It* V. iii 18]

49 An ill-favoured thing, sir, but mine own. [*As You Like It* V. iv 60]

50 The retort courteous ... the quip modest ... the reply churlish ... the reproof valiant ... the countercheck quarrelsome ... the lie circumstantial ... the lie direct. [*As You Like It* V. iv 96]

51 Your 'if' is the only peacemaker; much virtue in 'if'. [*As You Like It* V. iv 108]

52 Hark! hark! the lark at heaven's gate sings. [*Cymbeline* II. iii 22]

53 Great griefs, I see, medicine the less. [*Cymbeline* IV. ii 243]

54 Fear no more the heat o' the sun, / Nor the furious winter's rages; / Thou thy worldly task hast done, / Home art gone and ta'en thy wages: / Golden lads and girls all must, / As chimney-sweepers, come to dust. [*Cymbeline* IV. ii 258]

55 Quiet consummation have; / And renowned be thy grave! [*Cymbeline* IV. ii 280]

56 You come most carefully upon your hour. [*Hamlet* I. i 6]

57 For this relief much thanks; 'tis bitter cold, / And I am sick at heart. [*Hamlet* I. i 8]

58 This post-haste and romage in the land. [*Hamlet* I. i 107]

59 And then it started like a guilty thing / Upon a fearful summons. [*Hamlet* I. i 148]

60 Some say that ever 'gainst that season comes / Wherein our Saviour's birth is celebrated, / The bird of dawning singeth all night long. [*Hamlet* I. i 158]

61 But, look, the morn, in russet mantle clad, / Walks o'er the dew of yon high eastward hill. [*Hamlet* I. i 166]

62 A little more than kin, and less than kind. [*Hamlet* I. ii 65]

63 But I have that within which passeth show; / These but the trappings and the suits of woe. [*Hamlet* I. ii 85]

64 O! that this too too solid flesh would melt, / Thaw, and resolve itself into a dew. [*Hamlet* I. ii 129]

65 A truant disposition, good my lord. [*Hamlet* I. ii 169]

66 Thrift, thrift, Horatio! the funeral bak'd meats / Did coldly furnish forth the marriage tables. [*Hamlet* I. ii 180]

67 He was a man, take him for all in all, / I shall not look upon his like again. [*Hamlet* I. ii 187]

68 A countenance more in sorrow than in anger. [*Hamlet* I. ii 231]

69 And keep you in the rear of your affection. [*Hamlet* I. iii 34]

70 Do not, as some ungracious pastors do, / Show me the steep and thorny way to heaven, / Whiles, like a puff'd and reckless libertine, / Himself the primrose path of dalliance treads. [*Hamlet* I. iii 47]

71 The friends thou hast, and their adoption tried, / Grapple them to thy soul with hoops of steel. [*Hamlet* I. iii 62]

72 Give every man thine ear, but few thy voice. [*Hamlet* I. iii 68]

73 Costly thy habit as thy purse can buy, / But not express'd in fancy, rich, not gaudy; / For the apparel oft proclaims the man. [*Hamlet* I. iii 70]

74 Neither a borrower, nor a lender be; / For loan oft loses both itself and friend, / And borrowing dulls the edge of husbandry. [*Hamlet* I. iii 75]

75 It is a nipping and an eager air. [*Hamlet* I. iv 1]

76 Though I am native here, / And to the manner born, – it is a custom / More honour'd in the breach than the observance. [*Hamlet* I. iv 14]

77 Something is rotten in the state of Denmark. [*Hamlet* I. iv 90]

78 Meet it is I set it down, / That one may smile, and smile, and be a villain. [*Hamlet* I. v 107]

79 There are more things in heaven and earth, Horatio, / Than are dreamt of in your philosophy. [*Hamlet* I. v 166]

80 To put an antic disposition on. [*Hamlet* I. v 172]

81 The time is out of joint; O cursed spite, / That ever I was born to set it right! [*Hamlet* I. v 188]

82 Brevity is the soul of wit. [*Hamlet* II. i 90]

83 More matter with less art. [*Hamlet* II. i 95]

84 That he is mad, 'tis true; 'tis true 'tis pity; / And pity 'tis 'tis true. [*Hamlet* II. ii 97]

85 Doubt thou the stars are fire; / Doubt that the sun doth move; / Doubt truth to be a liar; / But never doubt I love. [*Hamlet* II. ii 115]

86 Though this be madness, yet there is method in it. [*Hamlet* II. ii 211]

87 There is nothing either good or bad, but thinking makes it so. [*Hamlet* II. ii 259]

88 I could be bounded in a nutshell, and count myself a king of infinite space, were it not that I have bad dreams. [*Hamlet* II. ii 263]

89 Beggar that I am, I am poor even in thanks. [*Hamlet* II. ii 286]

90 I am but mad north-north-west. [*Hamlet* II. ii 405]

91 The play, I remember, pleased not the million; 'twas caviare to the general. [*Hamlet* II. ii 465]

92 Use every man after his desert, and who should 'scape whipping? [*Hamlet* II. ii 561]

93 What's Hecuba to him or he to Hecuba / That he should weep for her? [*Hamlet* II. ii 593]

94 A dull and muddy-mettled rascal. [*Hamlet* II. ii 602]

95 The play's the thing / Wherein I'll catch the conscience of the king. [*Hamlet* II. ii 641]

96 Whereto serves mercy / But to confront the visage of offence? [*Hamlet* II. iii 46]

97 To be, or not to be: that is the question: / Whether 'tis nobler in the mind to suffer / The slings and arrows of outrageous fortune, / Or to take arms against a sea of troubles, / And by opposing end them? [*Hamlet* III. i 56]

98 'Tis a consummation / Devoutly to be wish'd. [*Hamlet* III i 63]

99 The undiscover'd country from whose bourn / No traveller returns. [*Hamlet* III. i 79]

100 Thus conscience doth make cowards of us all. [*Hamlet* III. i 83]

101 With this regard their currents turn awry, / And lose the name of action. [*Hamlet* III. i 87]

102 Get thee to a nunnery. [*Hamlet* III. i 124]

103 Let the doors be shut upon him, that he may play the fool nowhere but in's own house. [*Hamlet* III. i 137]

104 O! what a noble mind is here o'erthrown: / The courtier's, soldier's, scholar's, eye, tongue, sword. [*Hamlet* III. i 159]

105 Speak the speech, I pray you, as I pronounced it to you, trippingly on the tongue. [*Hamlet* III. ii 1]

106 Suit the action to the word, the word to the action. [*Hamlet* III. ii 20]

107 A man that fortune's buffets and rewards / Hast ta'en with equal thanks. [*Hamlet* III. ii 72]

108 The lady doth protest too much, methinks. [*Hamlet* III. ii 242]

109 They fool me to the top of my bent. [*Hamlet* III. ii 408]

110 'Tis now the very witching time of night. [*Hamlet* III. ii 413]

111 Let me be cruel, not unnatural; / I will speak daggers to her, but use none. [*Hamlet* III. ii 420]

112 How now! a rat? Dead, for a ducat, dead! [*Hamlet* III. iv 23]

113 A king of shreds and patches. [*Hamlet* III. iv 102]

114 Assume a virtue, if you have it not. [*Hamlet* III. iv 160]

115 I must be cruel, only to be kind. [*Hamlet* III. iv 178]

116 For 'tis the sport to have the enginer / Hoist with his own petar. [*Hamlet* III. iv 206]

117 How all occasions do inform against me, / And spur my dull revenge! [*Hamlet* IV. iii 32]

118 Rightly to be great / Is not to stir without great argument, / But greatly to find quarrel in a straw / When honour's at the stake. [*Hamlet* IV. iv 53]

119 How should I your true love know / From another one? / By his cockle hat and staff, / And his sandal shoon. [*Hamlet* IV. v 23]

120 When sorrows come, they come not single spies, / But in battalions. [*Hamlet* IV. v 78]

121 There's such divinity doth hedge a king, / That treason can but peep to what it would. [*Hamlet* IV. v 123]

122 You must wear your rue with a difference. [*Hamlet* IV. v 181]

123 For bonny sweet Robin is all my joy. [*Hamlet* IV. v 186]

124 And where the offence is let the great axe fall. [*Hamlet* IV. v 218]

125 Alas! poor Yorick. I knew him, Horatio; a fellow of infinite jest, of most excellent fancy. [*Hamlet* V. i 201]

126 Imperious Caesar, dead, and turn'd to clay, / Might stop a hole to keep the wind away. [*Hamlet* V. i 235]

127 There's a divinity that shapes our ends, / Rough-hew them how we will. [*Hamlet* V. ii 10]

128 It did me yeoman's service. [*Hamlet* V. ii 36]

129 Not a whit, we defy augury; there's a special providence in the fall of a sparrow. If it be now, 'tis not to come; if it be not to come, it will be now; if it be not now, yet it will come: the readiness is all. [*Hamlet* V. ii 232]

130 A hit, a very palpable hit. [*Hamlet* V. ii 295]

131 This fell sergeant, death, / Is strict in his arrest. [*Hamlet* V. ii 350]

132 If thou didst ever hold me in thy heart, / Absent thee from felicity awhile. [*Hamlet* V. ii 360]

133 The rest is silence. [*Hamlet* V. ii 372]

134 If all the year were playing holidays, / To sport would be as tedious as to work; / But when they seldom come, they wish'd for come. [*1 Henry IV* I. ii 226]

135 There live not three good men unhanged in England, and one of them is fat and grows old. [*1 Henry IV* II. iv 146]

136 Instinct is a great matter, I was a coward on instinct. [*1 Henry IV* II. iv 304]

137 I am as vigilant as a cat to steal cream. [*1 Henry IV* IV. ii 64]

138 Rebellion lay in his way, and he found it. [*1 Henry IV* V. i 28]

139 Two stars keep not their motion in one sphere. [*1 Henry IV* V. iv 65]

140 Ill-weav'd ambition, how much art thou shrunk! / When that this body did contain a spirit, / A kingdom for it was too small a bound. [*1 Henry IV* V. iv 88]

141 I could have better spar'd a better man. [*1 Henry IV* V. iv 104]

142 The better part of valour is discretion. [*1 Henry IV* V. iv 120]

143 Rumour is a pipe / Blown by surmises, jealousies, conjectures, / And of so easy and so plain a stop / That the blunt monster with uncounted heads, / The still-discordant wavering multitude, / Can play upon it. [*2 Henry IV* Induction 15]

144 Yet the first bringer of unwelcome news / Hath but a losing office. [*2 Henry IV* I. i 100]

145 I am not only witty in myself, but the cause that wit is in other men. [*2 Henry IV* I. ii 9]

146 It is the disease of not listening, the malady of not marking, that I am troubled withal. [*2 Henry IV* I. ii 139]

147 You that are old consider not the capacities of us that are young. [*2 Henry IV* I. ii 198]

148 I do now remember the poor creature, small beer. [*2 Henry IV* II. ii 12]

149 Let the end try the man. [*2 Henry IV* II. ii 52]

150 Uneasy lies the head that wears a crown. [*2 Henry IV* III. i 31]

151 A soldier is better accommodated than with a wife. [*2 Henry IV* III. ii 73]

152 We have heard the chimes at midnight. [*2 Henry IV* III. ii 231]

153 I care not; a man can die but once; we owe God a death. [*2 Henry IV* III. ii 253]

154 Commit / The oldest sins the newest kind of ways. [*2 Henry IV* IV. v 124]

155 How ill white hairs become a fool and jester! [*2 Henry IV* V. v 53]

156 They sell the pasture now to buy the horse. [*Henry V* II. chorus 5]

157 Once more unto the breach, dear friends, once more. [*Henry V* III. i 1]

158 Follow your spirit; and, upon this charge / Cry 'God for Harry! England and Saint George!' [*Henry V* III. i 33]

159 A little touch of Harry in the night. [*Henry V* IV. chorus 47]

160 Every subject's duty is the king's; but every subject's soul is his own. [*Henry V* IV. ii 189]

161 O God of battles! steel my soldiers hearts; / Possess them not with fear. [*Henry V* IV. ii 309]

162 If we are mark'd to die, we are enow / To do our country loss; and if to live, / The fewer men, the greater share of honour. [*Henry V* IV. iii 20]

163 We would not die in that man's company / That fears his fellowship to die with us. [*Henry V* IV. iii 38]

164 We few, we happy few, we band of brothers. [*Henry V* IV. iii 60]

165 She's beautiful and therefore to be woo'd; / She is a woman, therefore to be won. [*1 Henry VI* V. iii 78]

166 Live we how we can, yet die we must. [*2 Henry VI* V. ii 28]

167 When he falls, he falls like Lucifer, / Never to hope again. [*Henry VIII* III. ii 372]

168 I charge thee, fling away ambition: / By that sin fell the angels. [*Henry VIII* III. ii 441]

169 Men's evil manners live in brass; their virtues / We write in water. [*Henry VIII* IV. ii 45]

170 Beware the Ides of March. [*Julius Caesar* I. i 18]

171 Ye gods, it doth amaze me, / A man of such a feeble temper should / So get the start of the majestic world, / And bear the palm alone. [*Julius Caesar* I. ii 128]

172 Men at some time are masters of their fates: / The fault, dear Brutus, is not in our stars, / But in ourselves, that we are underlings. [*Julius Caesar* I. ii 138]

173 Let me have men about me that are fat; / Sleek-headed men and such as sleep o' nights; / Yond' Cassius has a lean and hungry look; / He thinks too much: such men are dangerous. [*Julius Caesar* I. ii 191]

174 He reads much; / He is a great observer, and he looks / Quite through the deeds of men. [*Julius Caesar* I. ii 200]

175 For mine own part, it was Greek to me. [*Julius Caesar* I. ii 288]

176 But men may construe things after their own fashion, / Clean from the purpose of the things themselves. [*Julius Caesar* I. iii 34]

177 It is the bright day that brings forth the adder; / And that craves wary walking. [*Julius Caesar* II. i 14]

178 That lowliness is young ambition's ladder, / Whereto the climber-upward turns his face. [*Julius Caesar* II. i 22]

179 Cowards die many times before their deaths / The valiant never taste of death but once. [*Julius Caesar* II. ii 30]

180 But I am constant, as the northern star, / Of whose true-fix'd and resting quality / There is no fellow in the firmament. [*Julius Caesar* III. i 60]

181 Et tu, Brute! [*Julius Caesar* III. i 77]

182 O mighty Caesar! dost thou lie so low? [*Julius Caesar* III. i 148]

183 The choice and master spirits of this age. [*Julius Caesar* III. i 163]

184 Thou art the ruins of the noblest man / That ever lived in the tide of times. [*Julius Caesar* III. i 256]

185 Not that I loved Caesar less, but that I loved Rome more. [*Julius Caesar* III. ii 22]

186 Friends, Romans, countrymen, lend me your ears; / I come to bury Caesar, not to praise him. [*Julius Caesar* III. ii 79]

187 For Brutus is an honourable man; / So are they all, all honourable men. [*Julius Caesar* III. ii 88]

188 When that the poor have cried, Caesar hath wept; / Ambition should be made of sterner stuff. [*Julius Caesar* III. ii 97]

189 If you have tears, prepare to shed them now. [*Julius Caesar* III. ii 174]

190 This was the most unkindest cut of all. [*Julius Caesar* III. ii 188]

191 Tear him for his bad verses. [*Julius Caesar* III. iii 34]

192 When love begins to sicken and decay, / It useth an enforced ceremony. / There are no tricks in plain and simple faith. [*Julius Caesar* IV. ii 20]

193 Do not presume too much upon my love; / I may do that I shall be sorry for. [*Julius Caesar* IV. iii 63]

194 A friend should bear his friend's infirmities. [*Julius Caesar* IV. iii 85]

195 There is a tide in the affairs of men, / Which, taken at the flood, leads on to fortune. [*Julius Caesar* IV. iii 217]

196 O! that a man might know / The end of this day's business, ere it come; / But it sufficeth that the day will end, / And then the end is known. [*Julius Caesar* V. i 123]

197 This was the noblest Roman of them all. [*Julius Caesar* V. v 68]

198 Mad world! Mad kings! Mad composition! [*King John* II. i 561]

199 That smooth-fac'd gentleman, tickling Commodity, / Commodity, the bias of the world. [*King John* II. i 573]

200 To gild refined gold, to paint the lily, / To throw a perfume on the violet, ... / Is wasteful and ridiculous excess. [*King John* IV. ii 11]

201 How oft the sight of means to do ill deeds / Makes ill deeds done! [*King John* IV. ii 219]

202 We have seen the best of our time: machinations, hollowness, treachery, and all ruinous disorders, follow us disquietly to our graves. [*King Lear* I. i 125]

203 We make guilty of our disasters the sun, the moon, and the stars; as if we were villains by necessity, fools by heavenly compulsion. [*King Lear* I. ii 134]

204 Have more than thou showest, / Speak less than thou knowest, / Lend less than thou owest. [*King Lear* I. iv 132]

205 How sharper than a serpent's tooth it is / To have a thankless child! [*King Lear* I. iv 312]

206 Here I stand, your slave, / A poor, infirm, weak, and despis'd old man. [*King Lear* III. ii 19]

207 There was never yet fair woman but she made mouths in a glass. [*King Lear* III. ii 35]

208 O! that way madness lies; let me shun that. [*King Lear* III. iv 21]

209 Unaccommodated man is no more but such a poor, bare, forked animal as thou art. [*King Lear* III. iv 109]

210 The prince of darkness is a gentleman. [*King Lear* III. iv 148]

211 I am tied to the stake, and I must stand the course. [*King Lear* III. vii 54]

212 As flies to wanton boys, are we to the gods; / They kill us for their sport. [*King Lear* IV. i 36]

213 Ay, every inch a king. [*King Lear* IV. vi 110]

214 When we are born we cry that we are come / To this great stage of fools. [*King Lear* IV. vi 187]

215 I am a very foolish, fond old man, / Fourscore and upward, not an hour more or less; / And, to deal plainly, / I fear I am not in my perfect mind. [*King Lear* IV. vii 60]

216 Men must endure / Their going hence, even as their coming hither: / Ripeness is all. [*King Lear* V. ii 9]

217 The gods are just, and of our pleasant vices / Make instruments to plague us. [*King Lear* V. iii 172]

218 The wheel is come full circle. [*King Lear* V. iii 176]

219 Her voice was ever soft, / Gentle, and low, an excellent thing in woman. [*King Lear* V. iii 274]

220 Love, whose month is ever May, / Spied a blossom passing fair, / Playing in the wanton air. [*Love's Labour's Lost* IV. iii 102]

221 Subtle as Sphinx; as sweet and musical / As bright Apollo's lute, strung with his hair; / And when Love speaks, the voice of all the gods / Makes heaven drowsy with the harmony. [*Love's Labour's Lost* IV. iii 342]

222 They have been at a great feast of languages, and stolen the scraps. [*Love's Labour's Lost* V. i 39]

223 In the posteriors of this day; which the rude multitude call the afternoon. [*Love's Labour's Lost* V. i 96]

224 In russet yeas and honest kersey noes. [*Love's Labour's Lost* V. ii 414]

225 A world-without-end bargain. [*Love's Labour's Lost* V. ii 705]

226 A jest's prosperity lies in the ear / Of him that hears it, never in the tongue / Of him that makes it. [*Love's Labour's Lost* V. ii 869]

227 Cuckoo, cuckoo; O, word of fear, / Unpleasing to a married ear! [*Love's Labour's Lost* V. ii 909]

228 When shall we three meet again / In thunder, lightning, or in rain? [*Macbeth* I. i 1]

229 Fair is foul, and foul is fair: / Hover through the fog and filthy air. [*Macbeth* I. i 11]

230 So well thy words become thee as thy wounds; / They smack of honour both. [*Macbeth* I. ii 44]

231 So foul and fair a day I have not seen. [*Macbeth* I. iii 38]

232 If you can look into the seeds of time, / And say which grain will grow and which will not. [*Macbeth* I. iii 58]

233 And oftentimes, to win us to our harm, / The instruments of darkness tell us truths; / Win us with honest trifles, to betray's / In deepest consequence. [*Macbeth* I. iii 123]

234 Present fears / Are less than horrible imaginings. [*Macbeth* I. iii 137]

235 If chance will have me king, why, chance may crown me, / Without my stir. [*Macbeth* I. iii 143]

236 Come what come may, / Time and the hour runs through the roughest day. [*Macbeth* I. iii 146]

237 Nothing in his life / Became him like the leaving it. [*Macbeth* I. iv 7]

238 There's no art / To find the mind's construction in the face; / He was a gentleman on whom I built / An absolute trust. [*Macbeth* I. iv 12]

239 Yet do I fear thy nature; / It is too full o' the milk of human kindness / To catch the nearest way. [*Macbeth* I. v 17]

240 This castle hath a pleasant seat; the air / Nimbly and sweetly recommends itself / Unto our gentle senses. [*Macbeth* I. vi 1]

241 If it were done when 'tis done, then 'twere well / It were done quickly. [*Macbeth* I. vii 1]

242 I dare do all that may become a man; / Who dares do more is none. [*Macbeth* I. vii 46]

243 But screw your courage to the sticking-place, / And we'll not fail. [*Macbeth* I. vii 54]

244 Is this a dagger which I see before me, / The handle toward my hand? [*Macbeth* II. i 33]

245 The attempt and not the deed, / Confounds us. [*Macbeth* II. ii 12]

246 Sleep that knits up the ravel-l'd sleave of care. [*Macbeth* II. ii 38]

247 Infirm of purpose! ... / The sleeping and the dead / Are but as pictures; 'tis the eye of childhood / That fears a painted devil. [*Macbeth* II. ii 52]

248 The primrose way to the ever-lasting bonfire. [*Macbeth* II. iii 22]

249 In the great hand of God I stand. [*Macbeth* II. iii 137]

250 I must become a borrower of the night / For a dark hour or twain. [*Macbeth* III. i 27]

251 To be thus is nothing; / But to be safely thus. [*Macbeth* III. i 48]

252 Things without all remedy / Should be without regard: what's done is done. [*Macbeth* III. ii 11]

253 We have scotch'd the snake, not killed it. [*Macbeth* III. ii 13]

254 Things bad begun make strong themselves by ill. [*Macbeth* III. ii 55]

255 But now I am cabin'd, cribb'd, confin'd, bound in / To saucy doubts and fears. [*Macbeth* III. iv 24]

256 Stand not upon the order of your going. / But go at once. [*Macbeth* III. iv 119]

257 I am in blood / Stepp'd in so far that, should I wade no more, / Returning were as tedious as go o'er. [*Macbeth* III. iv 136]

258 You lack the season of all natures, sleep. [*Macbeth* III. iv 141]

259 Double, double toil and trouble; / Fire burn, and cauldron bubble. [*Macbeth* IV. i 10]

260 By the pricking of my thumbs, / Something wicked this way comes. [*Macbeth* IV. i 44]

261 A deed without a name. [*Macbeth* IV. i 49]

262 But yet I'll make assurance double sure. [*Macbeth* IV. i 83]

263 What! will the line stretch out to the crack of doom? [*Macbeth* IV. i 117]

264 Out, damned spot! [*Macbeth* IV. v 38]

265 All the perfumes of Arabia will not sweeten this little hand. [*Macbeth* V. i 56]

266 Throw physic to the dogs; I'll none of it. [*Macbeth* V. ii 37]

267 I have lived long enough: my way of life / Is fall'n into the sear, the yellow leaf; / And that which should accompany old age, / As honour, love, obedience, troops of friends, / I must not look to have. [*Macbeth* V. iii 22]

268 To-morrow, and to-morrow, and to-morrow, / Creeps in this petty pace from day to day, / To the last syllable of recorded time; / And all our yesterdays have lighted fools / The way to dusty death. Out, out, brief candle! / Life's but a walking shadow, a poor player, / That struts and frets his hour upon the stage, / And then is heard no more; it is a tale / Told by an idiot, full of sound and fury, / Signifying nothing. [*Macbeth* V. v 19]

269 Blow, wind! come, wrack! / At least we'll die with harness on our back. [*Macbeth* V. v 51]

270 'Tis one thing to be tempted, Escalus, / Another thing to fall. [*Measure for Measure* II. i 17]

271 This will last out a night in Russia, / When nights are longest there. [*Measure for Measure* II. i 144]

272 O! it is excellent / To have a giant's strength, but it is tyrannous / To use it like a giant. [*Measure for Measure* II. ii 107]

273 Man, proud man, / Drest in a little brief authority, / Most ignorant of what he's most assur'd, / His glassy essence, like an angry ape, / Plays such fantastic tricks before high heaven, / As make the angels weep. [*Measure for Measure* II. ii 117]

274 Be absolute for death; either death or life / Shall thereby be the sweeter. [*Measure for Measure* III. i 5]

275 The poor beetle, that we tread upon, / In corporal sufferance finds a pang as great / As when a giant dies. [*Measure for Measure* III. i 77]

276 The hand that made you fair hath made you good. [*Measure for Measure* III. i 182]

277 There, at the moated grange, resides this dejected Mariana. [*Measure for Measure* III. i 279]

278 Take, O take those lips away, / That so sweetly were forsworn. [*Measure for Measure* IV. i 1]

279 A man whose blood / Is very snow-broth. [*Measure for Measure* IV. i 57]

280 I am a kind of burr; I shall stick. [*Measure for Measure* IV. iii 193]

281 Haste still pays haste, and leisure answers leisure; / Like doth quit like, and Measure still for Measure. [*Measure for Measure* V. i 411]

282 Fish not, with this melancholy bait, / For this fool gudgeon, this opinion. [*Merchant of Venice* I. i 101]

283 God made him, and therefore let him pass for a man. [*Merchant of Venice* I. ii 59]

284 I dote on his very absence. [*Merchant of Venice* I. ii 118]

285 How like a fawning publican he looks! / I hate him for he is a Christian. [*Merchant of Venice* I. iii 42]

286 The devil can cite Scripture for his purpose. [*Merchant of Venice* I. iii 99]

287 I like not fair terms and a villain's mind. [*Merchant of Venice* I. iii 180]

288 But love is blind, and lovers cannot see / The pretty follies that themselves commit. [*Merchant of Venice* II. 36]

289 My daughter! O my ducats! O my daughter! / Fled with a Christian! O my Christian ducats! [*Merchant of Venice* II. viii 15]

290 Let none presume / To wear an undeserved dignity. [*Merchant of Venice* II. ix 39]

291 I would not have given it for a wilderness of monkeys. [*Merchant of Venice* III. i 127]

292 He makes a swan-like end / Fading in music. [*Merchant of Venice* III. ii 44]

293 Tell me where is fancy bred, / Or in the heart or in the head? [*Merchant of Venice* III. ii 63]

294 A harmless necessary cat. [*Merchant of Venice* IV. i 55]

295 The quality of mercy is not strain'd, / It droppeth as the gentle rain from heaven / Upon the place beneath: it is twice bless'd; / It blesseth him that gives and him that takes. [*Merchant of Venice* IV. i 184]

296 A Daniel come to judgment! [*Merchant of Venice* IV. i 223]

297 How far that little candle throws his beams! / So shines a good deed in a naughty world. [*Merchant of Venice* V. i 90]

298 Let me give light, but let me be not light: / For a light wife doth make a heavy husband. [*Merchant of Venice* V. i 129]

299 I will make a Star-Chamber matter of it. [*Merry Wives of Windsor* I. i 1]

300 Here will be an old abusing of God's patience, and the king's English. [*Merry Wives of Windsor* I. iv 5]

301 Why, then the world's mine oyster. [*Merry Wives of Windsor* II. ii 2]

302 Marry, this is the short and the long of it. [*Merry Wives of Windsor* II. ii 62]

303 The course of true love never did run smooth. [*Midsummer Night's Dream* I. i 134]

304 Love looks not with the eyes, but with the mind, / And therefore is wing'd Cupid painted blind. [*Midsummer Night's Dream* I. i 234]

305 A part to tear a cat in, to make all split. [*Midsummer Night's Dream* I. ii 32]

306 I'll speak in a monstrous little voice. [*Midsummer Night's Dream* I. ii 55]

307 I will aggravate my voice so that I will roar you as gently as any sucking dove; I will roar you as 'twere any nightingale. [*Midsummer Night's Dream* I. ii 84]

308 I'll put a girdle round about the earth / In forty minutes. [*Midsummer Night's Dream* II. i 175]

309 Bless thee, Bottom! bless thee! thou art translated. [*Midsummer Night's Dream* III. i 124]

310 Lord, what fools these mortals be! [*Midsummer Night's Dream* III. ii 115]

311 Jack shall have Jill; / Nought shall go ill; / The man shall have his mare again, / And all shall be well. [*Midsummer Night's Dream* III. ii 461]

312 The eye of man hath not heard, the ear of man hath not seen, man's hand is not able to taste, his tongue to conceive, nor his heart to report, what my dream was. [*Midsummer Night's Dream* IV. i 218]

313 The lunatic, the lover, and the poet, / Are of imagination all compact. [*Midsummer Night's Dream* V. i 7]

314 And, as imagination bodies forth / The forms of things unknown, the poet's pen / Turns them to shapes, and gives to airy nothing / A local habitation and a name. / Such tricks hath strong imagination, / That, if it would but apprehend some joy, / It comprehends some bringer of that joy; / Or in the night, imagining some fear, / How easy is a bush suppos'd a bear! [*Midsummer Night's Dream* V. i 14]

315 The best in this kind are but shadows, and the worst are no worse, if imagination amend them. [*Midsummer Night's Dream* V. i 215]

316 A victory is twice itself when the achiever brings home full numbers. [*Much Ado About Nothing* I. i 8]

317 He is a very valiant trencherman. [*Much Ado About Nothing* I. i 52]

318 Benedick the married man.
[*Much Ado About Nothing* I. i 278]

319 There was a star danced, and under that was I born. [*Much Ado About Nothing* I. ii 351]

320 Sigh no more, ladies, sigh no more, / Men were deceivers ever. [*Much Ado About Nothing* I. iii 65]

321 Speak low, if you speak love. [*Much Ado About Nothing* II. i 104]

322 Friendship is constant in all other things / Save in the office and affairs of love: / Therefore all hearts in love use their own tongues; / Let every eye negotiate for itself / And trust no agent. [*Much Ado About Nothing* II. i 184]

323 Would it not grieve a woman to be over-mastered with a piece of valiant dust? [*Much Ado About Nothing* II. i 64]

324 Paper bullets of the brain. [*Much Ado About Nothing* II. iii 261]

325 The world must be peopled. When I said I would die a bachelor, I did not think I should live till I were married. [*Much Ado About Nothing* II. iii 262]

326 The most peaceable way for you, if you do take a thief, is, to let him show himself what he is and steal out of your company. [*Much Ado About Nothing* III. iii 61]

327 For there was never yet philosopher / That could endure the toothache patiently. [*Much Ado About Nothing* V. i 35]

328 In a false quarrel there is no true valour. [*Much Ado About Nothing* V. i 121]

329 What though care killed a cat, thou hast mettle enough in thee to kill care. [*Much Ado About Nothing* V. i 135]

330 A fellow almost damn'd in a fair wife. [*Othello* I. i 21]

331 The beast with two backs. [*Othello* I. i 117]

332 She lov'd me for the dangers I had pass'd, / And I lov'd her that she did pity them. [*Othello* I. iii 167]

333 To mourn a mischief that is past and gone / Is the next way to draw new mischief on. [*Othello* I. iii 204]

334 The robb'd that smiles steals something from the thief. [*Othello* I. iii 208]

335 Put money in thy purse. [*Othello* I. iii 345]

336 Base men being in love have then a nobility in their natures more than is native to them. [*Othello* II. i]

337 If it were now to die, / 'Twere now to be most happy, for I fear / My soul hath her content so absolute / That not another comfort like to this / Succeeds in unknown fate. [*Othello* II. i 192]

338 A slipper and subtle knave, a finder-out of occasions. [*Othello* II. i 247]

339 I have very poor and unhappy brains for drinking: / I could well wish courtesy would invent some other custom of entertainment. [*Othello* II. iii 34]

340 Reputation, reputation, reputation! O! I have lost my reputation. I have lost the immortal part of myself, and what remains is bestial. [*Othello* II. iii 264]

341 Good name in man or woman, dear my lord, / Is the immediate jewel of their souls; / Who steals my purse steals trash; 'tis something, / nothing; / 'Twas mine, 'tis his, and has been slave to thousands; / But he that filches from me my good name / Robs me of that which not enriches him, / And makes me poor indeed. [*Othello* III. iii 155]

342 O! beware, my lord, of jealousy; / It is the green-ey'd monster which doth mock / The meat it feeds on. [*Othello* III. iii 165]

343 For I am declin'd / Into the vale of years. [*Othello* III. iii 265]

344 O curse of marriage, / That we can call these delicate creatures ours, / and not their appetites! I had rather be a toad / And live upon the vapour of a dungeon, / Than keep a corner in the thing I love / For others' uses. [*Othello* III. iii 268]

345 O, she will sing the savageness out of a bear. [*Othello* IV. i 198]

346 Sing willow, willow, willow: / Sing all a green willow must be my garland. [*Othello* IV. iii 48]

347 He hath a daily beauty in his life / That makes me ugly. [*Othello* V. i 19]

348 It is the cause, it is the cause, my soul. [*Othello* V. ii 1]

349 O ill-star'd wench! / Pale as thy smock! [*Othello* V. ii 271]

350 I have done the state some service, and they know 't; / No more of that. I pray you, in your letters, / When you shall these unlucky deeds relate, / Speak of me as I am; nothing extenuate, / Nor set down aught in malice: then, must you speak / Of one that lov'd not wisely but too well; / Of one not easily jealous, but, being wrought, / Perplex'd in the extreme. [*Othello* V. ii 338]

351 I kiss'd thee ere I kill'd thee. [*Othello* V. ii 357]

352 Few love to hear the sins they love to act. [*Pericles* I. i 92]

353 Old John of Gaunt, time-honour'd Lancaster. [*Richard II* I. i 1]

354 We were not born to sue, but to command. [*Richard II* I. i 196]

355 There is no virtue like necessity. [*Richard II* I. iii 278]

356 This royal throne of kings, this scepter'd isle, / This earth of majesty, this seat of Mars, / This other Eden, demi-Paradise, / This fortress built by Nature for herself / Against infection and the hand of war, / This happy breed of men, this little world, / This precious stone set in the silver sea, ... / This blessed plot, this earth, this realm, this England. [*Richard II* II. i 40]

357 Grace me no grace, nor uncle me no uncle. [*Richard II* II. iii 87]

358 Things past redress are now with me past care. [*Richard II* II. iii 171]

359 Not all the water in the rough rude sea / Can wash the balm from an anointed king. [*Richard II* III. ii 54]

360 How sour sweet music is, / When time is broke, and no proportion kept! [*Richard II* V. i 42]

361 Now is the winter of our discontent / Made glorious summer by this sun of York. [*Richard III* I. i 1]

362 Since every Jack became a gentleman / There's many a gentle person made a Jack. [*Richard III* I. iii 72]

363 I am not in the giving vein today. [*Richard III* IV. ii 115]

364 An honest tale speeds best being plainly told. [*Richard III* IV. ii 359]

365 A horse! a horse! my kingdom for a horse! [*Richard III* V. iv 7]

366 A pair of star-crossed lovers. [*Romeo and Juliet* Prologue]

367 Saint-seducing gold. [*Romeo and Juliet* I. i 220]

368 O Romeo, Romeo! wherefore art thou Romeo? [*Romeo and Juliet* II. ii 33]

369 What's in a name? that which we call a rose / By any other name would smell as sweet. [*Romeo and Juliet* II. ii 43]

370 With love's light wings did I o'er perch these walls; / For stony limits cannot hold love out, / And what love can do that dares love attempt. [*Romeo and Juliet* II. ii 66]

371 This bud of love, by summer's ripening breath, / May prove a beauteous flower when next we meet. [*Romeo and Juliet* II. ii 121]

372 My bounty is as boundless as the sea, / My love as deep; the more I give to thee, / The more I have, for both are infinite. [*Romeo and Juliet* II. ii 133]

373 Love goes toward love, as schoolboys from their books; / But love from love, toward school with heavy looks. [*Romeo and Juliet* II. ii 156]

374 Wisely and slow; they stumble that run fast. [*Romeo and Juliet* II. iii 94]

375 I am the very pink of courtesy. [*Romeo and Juliet* II. iv 63]

376 Two may keep counsel, putting one away. [*Romeo and Juliet* II. iv 211]

377 A plague o' both your houses! [*Romeo and Juliet* III. i 112]

378 Hang up philosophy! / Unless philosophy can make a Juliet. [*Romeo and Juliet* III. iii 56]

379 One writ with me in sour misfortune's book. [*Romeo and Juliet* V. iii 82]

380 No profit grows where is no pleasure ta'en; / In brief, sir, study what you most affect. [*Taming of the Shrew* I. i 39]

381 There's small choice in rotten apples [*Taming of the Shrew* I. i 137]

382 I must dance barefoot on her wedding day, / And, for your love to her, lead apes in hell. [*Taming of the Shrew* II. i]

383 This is the way to kill a wife with kindness. [*Taming of the Shrew* IV. i]

384 Thy husband is thy lord, thy life, thy keeper, / Thy head, thy sovereign; one that cares for thee, / And for thy maintenance commits his body / To painful labour both by sea and land. [*Taming of the Shrew* V. ii]

385 He hath no drowning mark upon him; his complexion is perfect gallows. [*Tempest* I. i 33]

386 What seest thou else / In the dark backward and abysm of time? [*Tempest* I. ii 49]

387 My library / Was dukedom large enough. [*Tempest* I. ii 109]

388 You taught me language; and my profit on't / Is, I know how to curse. [*Tempest* I. ii 363]

389 Full fathom five thy father lies; / Of his bones are coral made: / Those are pearls that were his eyes: / Nothing of him that doth fade, / But doth suffer a sea-change / Into something rich and strange. [*Tempest* I. ii 394]

390 They'll take suggestion as a cat laps milk. [*Tempest* II. i 296]

391 A very ancient and fish-like smell. [*Tempest* II. ii 27]

392 The isle is full of noises, / Sounds and sweet airs, that give delight, and hurt not. [*Tempest* III. ii 147]

393 We are such stuff / As dreams are made on, and our little life / Is rounded with a sleep. [*Tempest* IV. i 156]

394 Deeper than did ever plummet sound, / I'll drown my book. [*Tempest* V. i 56]

395 O brave new world, / That has such people in 't. [*Tempest* V. i 183]

396 'Tis not enough to help the feeble up, / But to support him after. [*Timon of Athens* I. i 108]

397 He that loves to be flattered is worthy o' the flatterer. [*Timon of Athens* I. i 233]

398 Nothing emboldens sin so much as mercy. [*Timon of Athens* III. v 3]

399 My long sickness / Of health and living now begins to mend, / And nothing brings me all things. [*Timon of Athens* V. i 191]

400 She is a woman, therefore may be woo'd; / She is a woman, therefore may be won. [*Titus Andronicus* II. i 82]

401 Take but degree away, untune that string, / And, hark! what discord follows. [*Troilus and Cressida* I. iii 109]

402 Mongrel beef-witted lord. [*Troilus and Cressida* II. i 14]

403 To be wise, and love, / Exceeds man's might. [*Troilus and Cressida* III. ii]

404 Time hath, my lord, a wallet at his back, / Wherein he puts alms for oblivion. [*Troilus and Cressida* III. iii 145]

405 If music be the food of love, play on; / Give me excess of it, that, surfeiting, / The appetite may sicken, and so die. / That strain again! it had a dying fall. [*Twelfth Night* I. i 1]

406 Many a good hanging prevents a bad marriage. [*Twelfth Night* I. v 20]

407 O! you are sick of self-love, Malvolio. [*Twelfth Night* I. v 96]

408 O mistress mine! where are you roaming? / O! stay and hear; your true love's coming, / That can sing both high and low. / Trip no further, pretty sweeting; / Journeys end in lovers meeting, / Every wise man's son doth know. / What is love? 'tis not hereafter; / Present mirth hath present laughter; / What's to come is still unsure: / In delay there lies no plenty; / Then come kiss me, sweet and twenty, / Youth's a stuff will not endure. [*Twelfth Night* II. iii 42]

409 He does it with a better grace, but I do it more natural. [*Twelfth Night* II. iii 91]

410 Dost thou think, because thou art virtuous, there shall be no more cakes and ale? [*Twelfth Night* II. iii 124]

411 Come away, come away, death, / And in sad cypress let me be laid. [*Twelfth Night* II. iv 51]

412 She never told her love, / But let concealment, like a worm i' th' bud, / Feed on her damask cheek. [*Twelfth Night* II. iv 112]

413 She sat like patience on a monument, / Smiling at grief. [*Twelfth Night* II. iv 116]

414 Some men are born great, some achieve greatness, and some have greatness thrust upon them. [*Twelfth Night* II. v 158]

415 Love sought is good, but giv'n unsought is better. [*Twelfth Night* III. i 170]

416 Why, this is very midsummer madness. [*Twelfth Night* III. iv 62]

417 Still you keep o' the windy side of the law. [*Twelfth Night* III. iv 183]

418 In nature there's no blemish but the mind; / None can be call'd deform'd but the unkind. [*Twelfth Night* III. iv 403]

419 Leave thy vain bibble-babble. [*Twelfth Night* IV. ii 106]

420 And thus the whirligig of time brings in his revenges. [*Twelfth Night* V. i 388]

421 When that I was and a little tiny boy, / With hey, ho, the wind and the rain; / A foolish thing was but a toy, / For the rain it raineth every day. [*Twelfth Night* V. i 401]

422 Home-keeping youth have ever homely wits. [*Two Gentlemen of Verona* I. i 2]

423 O! how this spring of love resembleth / The uncertain glory of an April day. [*Two Gentlemen of Verona* I. iii 84]

424 Who is Silvia? what is she, / That all our swains commend her? [*Two Gentlemen of Verona* IV. ii 40]

425 Hunting he lov'd, but love he laugh'd to scorn. [*Venus and Adonis* l. 4]

426 Love comforteth like sunshine after rain. [*Venus and Adonis* l. 799]

427 Two lads that thought there was no more behind / But such a day to-morrow as to-day, / And to be boy eternal. [*Winter's Tale* I. ii 63]

428 A sad tale's best for winter. [*Winter's Tale* II. i 24]

429 Exit, pursued by a bear. [*Winter's Tale* III. iii (stage direction)]

430 A snapper-up of unconsidered trifles. [*Winter's Tale* IV. ii 26]

431 Jog on, jog on the foot-path way, / And merrily hent the stile-a: / A merry heart goes all the day, / Your sad tires in a mile-a. [*Winter's Tale* IV. ii 133]

432 I love a ballad in print, ... for then we are sure they are true. [*Winter's Tale* IV. iii 262]

433 Shall I compare thee to a summer's day? / Thou art more lovely and more temperate: / Rough winds do shake the darling buds of May, / And summer's lease hath all too short a date. [Sonnet 18]

434 Full many a glorious morning have I seen / Flatter the mountain-tops with sovereign eye. [Sonnet 33]

435 Suns of the world may stain when heaven's sun staineth. [Sonnet 33]

436 What is your substance, whereof are you made, / That millions of strange shadows on you tend? [Sonnet 53]

437 Not marble, nor the gilded monuments / Of princes, shall out-live this powerful rhyme. [Sonnet 55]

438 Like as the waves make towards the pebbled shore, / So do our minutes hasten to their end. [Sonnet 60]

439 Time doth transfix the flourish set on youth / And delves the parallels in beauty's brow. [Sonnet 60]

440 No longer mourn for me when I am dead / Than you shall hear the surly sullen bell / Give warning to the world that I am fled. [Sonnet 71]

441 That time of year thou mayst in me behold / When yellow leaves, or none, or few, do hang / Upon those boughs which shake against the cold, / Bare ruin'd choirs, where late the sweet birds sang. [Sonnet 73]

442 Farewell! thou art too dear for my possessing, / And like enough thou know'st thy estimate. [Sonnet 87]

443 Thus have I had thee, as a dream doth flatter, / In sleep a king, but, waking, no such matter. [Sonnet 87]

444 Lilies that fester smell far worse than weeds. [Sonnet 94]

445 To me, fair friend, you never can be old. [Sonnet 104]

446 Let me not to the marriage of true minds / Admit impediments. Love is not love / Which alters when it alteration finds, / Or bends with the remover to remove. / O, no! it is an ever-fixèd mark, / That looks on tempests and is never shaken. [Sonnet 116]

447 And ruined love, when it is built anew, / Grows fairer than at first, more strong, far greater. [Sonnet 119]

448 My mistress' eyes are nothing like the sun. [Sonnet 130]

449 Good friend, for Jesu's sake forbear / To dig the dust enclosed here. / Blest be the man that spares these stones, / And curst be he that moves my bones. [Epitaph on Shakespeare's grave in Stratford-upon-Avon church]

SHAMIR Yitzhak 1915–
Polish-born Israeli right-wing politician.

Our image has undergone a change from David fighting Goliath to being Goliath. [On Israel, *Observer* Jan 1989]

SHARMAN Helen 1963–
First Briton in space.

> Space is out of this world. [Speech May 1991]

SHAW George Bernard 1856–1950
Irish dramatist.

1 There is only one religion, though there are a hundred versions of it. [*Arms and the Man*, preface]

2 You can always tell an old soldier by the inside of his holsters and cartridge boxes. The young ones carry pistols and cartridges: the old ones, grub. [*Arms and the Man* I]

3 When a stupid man is doing something he is ashamed of, he always declares that it is his duty. [*Caesar and Cleopatra*]

4 Do you think that the things people make fools of themselves about are any less real and true than the things they behave sensibly about? [*Candida* I]

5 We have no more right to consume happiness without producing it than to consume wealth without producing it. [*Candida* I]

6 The worst sin towards our fellow creatures is not to hate them, but to be indifferent to them: that's the essence of inhumanity. [*Devil's Disciple* II]

7 The British soldier can stand up to anything except the British War Office. [*Devil's Disciple* III]

8 A life spent in making mistakes is not only more honourable but more useful than a life spent doing nothing. [*Doctor's Dilemma*, 'The Technical Problem', Preface 1911]

9 Home life as we understand it is no more natural to us than a cage is natural to a cockatoo. [*Getting Married*, Preface]

10 What God hath joined together no man ever shall put asunder: God will take care of that. [*Getting Married*]

Caricature of dramatist George Bernard Shaw by Bernard Partridge, dated 1925. A dramatist of ideas, Shaw merged didacticism with entertainment in plays such as *Widowers' Houses* 1892, which attacks slum landlords, and *Mrs Warren's Profession* 1893, which deals with prostitution.

11 The captain is in his bunk, drinking bottled ditchwater; and the crew is gambling in the forecastle. She will strike and sink and split. Do you think the laws of God will be suspended in favour of England because you were born in it? [*Heartbreak House* III]

12 A man who has no office to go to – I don't care who he is – is a trial of which you can have no conception. [*Irrational Knot* ch 18]

13 The more a man knows, and the further he travels, the more likely he is to marry a country girl afterwards. [*John Bull's Other Island* II]

14 What really flatters a man is that you think him worth flattering. [*John Bull's Other Island* IV]

15 A lifetime of happiness: No man alive could bear it: it would be hell on earth. [*Man and Superman* I]

16 The more things a man is ashamed of, the more respectable he is. [*Man and Superman* I]

17 The true artist will let his wife starve, his children go barefoot, his mother drudge for his living at seventy, sooner than work at anything but his art. [*Man and Superman* I]

18 You think that you are Ann's suitor; that you are the pursuer and she the pursued ... Fool: it is you who are the pursued, the marked down quarry, the destined prey. [*Man and Superman* II]

19 An Englishman thinks he is moral when he is only uncomfortable. [*Man and Superman* III]

20 There are two tragedies in life. One is not to get your heart's desire. The other is to get it. [*Man and Superman* IV]

21 In Heaven an angel is nobody in particular. [*Man and Superman*, 'Maxims for Revolutionists: Greatness']

22 Marriage is popular because it combines the maximum of temptation with the maximum of opportunity. [*Man and Superman*, 'Maxims: Marriage']

23 Do not do unto others as you would they should do unto you. Their tastes may not be the same. [*Maxims for Revolutionists*]

24 Home is the girl's prison and the woman's workhouse. [*Maxims for Revolutionists*]

25 Anarchism is a game at which the Police can beat you. [*Misalliance*]

26 I don't believe in circumstances. The people who get on in this world are the people who get up and look for the circumstances they want, and, if they can't find them, make them. [*Mrs. Warren's Profession* II]

27 The only way for a woman to provide for herself decently is for her to be good to some man that can afford to be good to her. [*Mrs Warren's Profession* II]

28 The fickleness of the women I love is only equalled by the infernal constancy of the women who love me. [*The Philanderer*]

29 How can what an Englishman believes be heresy? It is a contradiction in terms. [*St Joan* IV]

30 Must then a Christ perish in torment in every age to save those that have no imagination? [*St Joan*, epilogue]

31 Assassination is the extreme form of censorship. [*Shewing-Up of Blanco Posnet*, 'Rejected Statement pt 1', Preface]

32 Like fingerprints, all marriages are different. [Quoted in C Pulling *They Were Singing* ch 5]

33 Great art is never produced for its own sake. It is too difficult to be worth the effort. [*Three Plays by Brieux*, Preface]

SHAWN Ted 1891–1972
US dancer and choreographer.

Dance is the only art of which we ourselves are the stuff of which it is made. [*Time* July 1955]

SHELLEY Percy Bysshe 1792–1822
English lyric poet.

1 He hath awakened from the dream of life. [*Adonais* 39]

2 The quick Dreams, / The passion-winged Ministers of thought. [*Adonais* 9]

3 From the contagion of the world's slow stain / He is secure, and now can never mourn / A heart grown cold, a head grown grey in vain. [*Adonais* 40]

4 He is a portion of the loveliness / Which once he made more lovely. [*Adonais* 43]

5 Life, like a dome of many-coloured glass, / Stains the white radiance of Eternity. [*Adonais* 52]

6 That orbed maiden, with white fire laiden,/ Whom mortals call the Moon. [*The Cloud*]

7 Poets are the unacknowledged legislators of the world. [*Defence of Poetry*]

8 I never was attached to that great sect, / Whose doctrine is, that each one should select / Out of the crowd a mistress or a friend, / And all the rest, though fair and wise, commend / To cold oblivion. [*Epipsychidion*]

9 Let there be light! said Liberty, / And like sunrise from the sea, / Athens arose! [*Hellas*]

10 I met Murder in the way – / He had a mask like Castlereagh. [*Mask of Anarchy*]

11 O wild West Wind, thou breath of Autumn's being, / Thou, from whose unseen presence the leaves dead / Are driven, like ghosts from an enchanter fleeing. [*Ode to the West Wind*]

12 What is Love? It is that powerful attraction towards all that we conceive, or fear, or hope beyond ourselves. ['On Love', quoted in D L Clark *Shelley's Prose*]

13 My name is Ozymandias, king of kings: / Look on my works, ye Mighty, and despair! ['Ozymandias']

14 All love is sweet, / Given or returned. Common as light is love, / And its familiar voice wearies not ever. ... / They who inspire it most

are fortunate, / As I am now; but those who feel it most / Are happier still. [*Prometheus Unbound* II. v]

15 Rarely, rarely, comest thou, / Spirit of Delight! ['Song']

16 Hail to thee, blithe spirit! / Bird thou never wert, / That from Heaven, or near it, / Pourest thy full heart / In profuse strains of unpremeditated art. ['To a Skylark']

SHENSTONE William 1714–1763
English poet and essayist.

Laws are generally found to be nets of such a texture, as the little creep through, the great break through, and the middle-sized are alone entangled in. [*Essays*, 'On Politics']

SHERIDAN Philip 1831–1888
US general.

The only good Indian is a dead Indian. [Attributed remark, at Fort Cobb Jan 1869]

SHERIDAN Richard Brinsley 1751–1816
Irish dramatist and politician.

1 Not a translation – only taken from the French. [*The Critic* I]

2 When a heroine goes mad she always goes into white satin. [*The Critic* III]

3 The Right Honourable gentleman is indebted to his memory for his jests, and to his imagination for his facts. [Speech in reply to Mr Dundas, quoted in T Moore *Life of Sheridan*]

4 'Tis safest in matrimony to begin with a little aversion. [*The Rivals* I. ii]

5 No caparisons, miss, if you please. Caparisons don't become a young woman. [*The Rivals* IV]

6 Our ancestors are very good kind of folks; but they are the last people I should choose to have a visiting acquaintance with. [*The Rivals* IV]

Portrait of the Irish dramatist and statesman Richard Brinsley Sheridan by Joshua Reynolds. After achieving success in the theatre, writing and producing a number of polished satirical plays, Sheridan went on to pursue a career in politics which culminated in his appointment to the office of secretary of the treasury 1783.

7 Thro' all the drama–whether damned or not– / Love gilds the scene, and women guide the plot. [*The Rivals*]

8 Here's to the maiden of bashful fifteen; / Here's to the widow of fifty; / Here's to the flaunting, extravagant queen; / And here's to the housewife that's thrifty. [*School for Scandal*]

SHERMAN William 1820–1891
US Union general in the American Civil War.

There is many a boy here to-day who looks on war as all glory, but, boys, it is all hell. [*Speech* 1880]

SHIRLEY James 1596–1666
English dramatist.

The glories of our blood and state / Are shadows, not substantial things. [*Contention of Ajax and Ulysses* I]

SHOSTAKOVICH Dmitry 1906–1975
Soviet composer.

A Soviet composer's reply to just criticism. [Epigraph to his fifth symphony]

SICA Vittorio de 1901–1974
Italian film director and actor.

Moral indignation is in most cases 2% moral, 48% indignation and 50% envy. [Quoted in *Observer* 17 Dec 1961]

SIDNEY Philip 1554–1586
English poet and soldier.

1 Who shoots at the mid-day sun, though he be sure he shall never hit the mark; yet as sure he is he shall shoot higher than who aims but at a bush. [*Arcadia* II]

2 My true love hath my heart and I have his, / By just exchange one for the other giv'n. [*Arcadia* III]

3 'Fool!' said my Muse to me, 'look in thy heart, and write.' [*Astrophel and Stella* Sonnet 1]

4 With how sad steps, O Moon, thou climb'st the skies! / How silently, and with how wan a face! [*Astrophel and Stella* Sonnet 31]

5 Leave me, O Love, which reacheth but to dust. [*Astrophel and Stella* Sonnet 110]

6 With a tale forsooth he cometh unto you, with a tale which holdeth children from play, and old men from the chimney corner. [*Defence of Poesy*]

7 Thy necessity is yet greater than mine. [On giving his water-bottle to a critically wounded soldier at the Battle of Zutphen 1586]

Sir Philip Sidney used to be idealized as the epitome of Renaissance nobility. Sidney's distinction lies in the passionate individuality of his poetry, particularly the *Astrophel and Stella* sonnet sequence, and in the network of stories in *Arcadia*, written for his sister and foreshadowing the development of the English novel.

SIÈYES Emmanuel Joseph 1748–1836
French statesman.

> I survived. [Answer on being asked what he had done during the French Revolution]

SILLITOE Alan 1928–
English novelist.

> The Loneliness of the Long-Distance Runner. [Book title]

SIMON Neil 1927–
US dramatist.

> Twelve years doesn't mean you're a *happy* couple. It just means you're a *long* couple. [*Odd Couple* I]

SIMONIDES OF CEOS 556–468 BC
Greek lyric poet.

> Go, tell the Spartans, thou who passest by, / That here obedient to their laws we lie. [*Epigrams*]

SINGER Isaac Bashevis 1904–1991
Polish-born US writer.

> Sometimes love is stronger than man's convictions. [Quoted in *New York Times Magazine* 26 Nov 1978]

SITWELL Osbert 1892–1969
English writer and poet.

> The British Bourgeoisie / Is not born, / And does not die, / But, if it is ill, / It has a frightened look in its eyes. ['At the House of Mrs Kinfoot']

SKINNER Cornelia Otis 1901–1979
US writer and actress.

> If it is true that we have sprung from the ape, there are occasions when my own spring appears not to have been very far. [*Ape in Me*, title essay]

SLIM William, Viscount 1891–1970
British field marshal in World War II.

> In a battle nothing is ever as good or as bad as the first reports of excited men would have it. [*Unofficial History*]

SMART Elizabeth 1913–1986
US poet.

> By Grand Central Station I Sat Down and Wept. [Book title]

SMEDLEY Francis Edward 1818–1864
English novelist.

> All's fair in love and war. [*Frank Farleigh* ch 50]

SMILES Samuel 1812–1904
Scottish writer.

> 1 The shortest way to do many things is to do only one thing at once. [*Self Help*]

2 A place for everything, and everything in its place. [*Thrift*]

SMITH Adam 1723–1790
Scottish economist.

1 The propensity to truck, barter and exchange one thing for another ... is common to all men, and is to be found in no other race of animals. [*Wealth of Nations* vol 1, bk 1, ch 2]

2 To found a great empire for the sole purpose of raising up a people of customers, may at first sight appear a project fit only for a nation of shopkeepers. It is, however, a project altogether unfit for a nation of shopkeepers; but extremely fit for a nation that is governed by shopkeepers. [*Wealth of Nations* vol 2, bk 4, ch 7]

SMITH F E 1872–1930
British politician and lawyer.

1 We have the highest authority for believing that the meek shall inherit the Earth; though I have never found any particular corroboration of this aphorism in the records of Somerset House. ['Marquess Curzon']

2 The world continues to offer glittering prizes to those who have stout hearts and sharp swords. [Rectorial Address, Glasgow University 1923]

SMITH Lillian 1897–1966
US writer.

To believe in something not yet proved ... is the only way we can leave the future open. Man, surrounded by facts, permitting himself no surmise, no intuitive flash, no great hypothesis, no risk, is a locked cell. Ignorance cannot seal the mind and imagination more surely. [*The Journey* ch 15]

SMITH Logan Pearsall 1865–1946
US-born British writer.

1 People say that life is the thing, but I prefer reading. [*Afterthoughts*]

2 There are few sorrows, however poignant, in which a good income is of no avail. [*Afterthoughts*]

3 There are two things to aim at in life: first, to get what you want; and, after that, to enjoy it. Only the wisest of mankind achieve the second. [*Afterthoughts*]

4 A best-seller is the gilded tomb of a mediocre talent. [*Afterthoughts*, 'Art and Letters']

5 Married women are kept women, and they are beginning to find out. [*Afterthoughts*, 'Other people']

6 Only among people who think no evil can Evil monstrously flourish. [*Afterthoughts*, 'Other People']

SMITH Stevie 1902–1971
English poet and novelist.

1 He told his life story to Mrs Courtly / Who was a widow. 'Let us get married shortly', / He said. 'I am no longer passionate, / But we can have some conversation before it is too late.' ['Autumn']

2 Marriage I think / For women / Is the best of opiates. / It kills the thoughts / That think about the thoughts, / It is the best of opiates. ['Marriage I Think ']

3 I was much too far out all my life / And not waving but drowning. ['Not Waving but Drowning']

SMITH Sydney 1771–1845
English journalist, clergyman and wit.

1 Poverty is no disgrace to a man, but it is confoundedly inconvenient. [*His Wit and Wisdom*]

2 As the French say, there are three sexes – men, women, and clergymen. [Quoted in Lady Holland *Memoirs*]

3 He has occasional flashes of silence, that make his conversation perfectly delightful. [Of J B Macaulay, quoted in Lady Holland *Memoirs*]

4 How can a bishop marry? How can he flirt? The most he can say is, 'I will meet you in the vestry after service.' [Quoted in Lady Holland *Memoirs*]

5 It requires a surgical operation to get a joke well into a Scotch understanding. Their only idea of wit ... is laughing immoderately at stated intervals. [Quoted in Lady Holland *Memoirs*]

6 My definition of marriage ... it resembles a pair of shears, so joined that they cannot be separated; often moving in opposite directions, yet always punishing anyone who comes between them. [Quoted in Lady Holland *Memoirs*]

7 Not body enough to cover his mind decently with; his intellect is improperly exposed. [Quoted in Lady Holland *Memoirs*]

8 You find people ready enough to do the Samaritan, without the oil and twopence. [Quoted in Lady Holland *Memoirs*]

9 A Curate – there is something which excites compassion in the very name of a Curate!!! [*Persecuting Bishops*]

10 I am just going to pray for you at St. Paul's, but with no very lively hope of success. [Quoted in H Pearson *The Smith of Smiths*]

11 I never read a book before reviewing it; it prejudices a man so. [Quoted in H Pearson *The Smith of Smiths*]

12 My idea of heaven is, eating *pâté de foie gras* to the sound of trumpets. [Quoted in H Pearson *The Smith of Smiths*]

13 What a pity it is that we have no amusements in England but vice and religion! [Quoted in H Pearson *The Smith of Smiths*]

14 I have no relish for the country; it is a kind of healthy grave. [Letter to Miss G Harcourt 1838]

15 What bishops like best in their clergy is a dropping-down-deadness of manner. [First Letter to Archdeacon Singleton]

16 Going to marry her! Going to marry her! impossible!...There is enough of her to furnish wives for a whole parish... You might people a colony with her; or give an assembly with her; or perhaps take your morning walks around her, always providing there were frequent resting places, and you are in rude health... Or you might read the Riot Act and disperse her; in short, you might do anything with her but marry her. [On hearing of the prospective marriage of an acquaintance to an extremely large widow twice his age]

SMOOT George 1945–
US astrophysicist.

We now have direct evidence of the birth of the Universe and its evolution ... ripples in space-time laid down earlier than the first billionth of a second. If you're religious its like seeing God. [Attributed remark 1992]

SOCRATES *c.* 469 BC–399 BC
Athenian philosopher.

1 Nothing can harm a good man, either in life or after death. [Quoted in Plato *Apology* 42]

2 Crito, we owe a cock to Aesculapius; pay it, therefore, and do not neglect it. [Last words, quoted in Plato *Phaedo*]

SOLON *c.* 640–*c.* 558 BC
Greek lawgiver, merchant, and poet.

Call no man happy till he dies, he is at best but fortunate. [Quoted in Herodotus Histories]

SOLZHENITSYN Alexander 1918–
Russian novelist, US citizen from 1974.

1 You only have power over people as long as you don't take *everything* away from them. But when you've robbed a man of *everything*

Russian novelist Alexander Solzhenitsyn. In the 1960s and 1970s, Solzhenitsyn's novels laid bare many of the darker aspects of life in Stalinist Russia and increasingly expressed his conviction that the Soviet system was morally and spiritually void. His autobiography *The Oak and the Calf* appeared 1975, the year after he had become a US citizen, and became available in translation 1980.

he's no longer in your power – he's free again. [*First Circle*]

2 The salvation of mankind lies only in making everything the concern of all. [Nobel lecture 1970]

SONTAG Susan 1933–
US critic, novelist, and screenwriter.

1 Interpretation is the revenge of the intellect upon art. [*Against Interpretation*]

2 Much of modern art is devoted to lowering the threshold of what is terrible. By getting us used to what, formerly, we could not bear to see or hear, because it was too shocking, painful, or embarrassing, art changes morals. [*On Photography*, 'America, Seen Through Photographs, Darkly']

3 Existence is no more than the precarious attainment of relevance in an intensely mobile flux of past, present, and future. [*Styles of radical Will*, "Thinking Against Oneself': Reflections on Cioran']

SOPHOCLES c. 496–405 BC
Athenian dramatist.

1 None loves the messenger who brings bad news. [*Antigone*]

2 They are not wise, then, who stand forth to buffet against Love; for Love rules the gods as he will, and me. [*Antigone* 441]

3 Wonders are many, and none is more wonderful than man. [*Antigone*]

4 Children are a mother's anchors of life. [Quoted in F Kinchin Smith and T W Melluish *Teach Yourself Greek*]

SOUTHEY Robert 1774–1843
English poet and author.

1 'And everybody praised the Duke, / Who this great fight did win.' / 'But what good came of it at last?' / Quoth little Peterkin. / 'Why that I cannot tell,' said he, / 'But 'twas a famous victory.' ['Battle of Blenheim']

2 Curses are like young chickens, they always come home to roost. [*The Curse of Kehama*, motto]

3 From his brimstone bed, at break of day / A walking the Devil is gone, / To look at his little snug farm of the World, / And see how his stock went on. ['Devil's Walk' i]

4 Show me a man who cares no more for one place than another, and I will show you in that same person one who loves nothing but himself. Beware of those who are homeless by choice. [*The Doctor* ch 34]

5 Live as long as you may, the first twenty years are the longest half of your life. [*The Doctor* ch 130]

6 No stir in the air, no stir in the sea, / The ship was still as she could be. ['Inchcape Rock']

7 In the days of my youth I remembered my God! / And He hath not forgotten my age. ['Old Man's Comforts']

SPARK Dame Muriel 1918–
Scottish novelist.

1 The one certain way for a woman to hold a man is to leave him for religion. [*Comforters* ch 1]

2 'I am putting old heads on your young shoulders ... and all my pupils are the crème de la crème.' [*Prime of Miss Jean Brodie*]

SPEIGHT Johnny 1920–
English TV scriptwriter.

You silly moo. [Alf Garnett's favourite attribution for his wife, in the TV series *Till Death Us Do Part*]

SPENCER Herbert 1820–1903
English philosopher.

1 Science is organized knowledge. [*Education*]

2 The Republican form of Government is the highest form of government; but because of this it requires the highest type of human nature – a type nowhere, at present existing. [*Essays*, 'The Americans']

3 The ultimate result of shielding men from the effects of folly, is to fill the world with fools. [*Essays*, 'State Tamperings with Money and Banks']

4 This survival of the fittest. [*Principles of Biology*]

5 A living thing is distinguished from a dead thing by the multiplicity of the changes at any moment

Scottish novelist Muriel Spark. Her novels, which are witty, finely structured satires, blend fantasy and sharply observed realism to express essentially spiritual themes. She has also written biographies and poetry.

taking place in it. [*Principles of Biology* pt 1, ch 4]

6 Progress ... is not an accident, but a necessity....It is part of nature. [*Social Statics* 1, ch 2]

7 Education has for its object the formation of character. [*Social Statics* 2, ch 17]

8 No one can be perfectly free till all are free; no one can be perfectly moral till all are moral; no one can be perfectly happy till all are happy. [*Social Statics* 4, ch 30]

SPENGLER Oswald 1880–1936
German philosopher.

Christian theology is the grandmother of Bolshevism. [*Hour of Decision*]

SPENSER Edmund c. 1552–1599
English poet.

1 Most glorious Lord of life, that on this day / Didst make thy triumph over death and sin: / And, having harrow'd hell, didst bring / Captivity thence captive, us to win. [*Amoretti* sonnet 68]

2 The woods shall to me answer and my echo ring. [*Epithalamion* l. 18]

3 Fierce wars and faithful loves shall moralize my song. [*Faerie Queene* I. 1]

4 A gentle knight was pricking on the plain. [*Faerie Queene* I. 1]

5 Sleep after toil, port after stormy seas, / Ease after war, death after life does greatly please. [*Faerie Queene* I. 9]

6 O goodly usage of those antique times, / In which the sword was servant unto right. [*Faerie Queene* III. 1]

7 Dan Chaucer, well of English undefiled. [*Faerie Queene* IV. 2]

8 O sacred hunger of ambitious minds. [*Faerie Queene* V. 12]

9 Sweet Thames, run softly, till I end my song. [*Prothalamion*]

10 To be wise and eke to love, / Is granted scarce to God above. [*Shepherd's Calendar*, 'March']

SPIELBERG Steven 1947–
US director, writer, and producer.

1 Close Encounters of the Third Kind. [Film title]

2 I wanted the water to mean shark. The horizon to mean shark. I wanted the shark's presence to be felt everywhere. [On his film *Jaws*]

SPINOZA Benedict 1632–1677
Dutch philosopher.

1 Whatsoever is, is in God. [*Ethics* I. xv]

2 Virtue is nothing else but action in accordance with the laws of one's own nature. [*Ethics* IV. xviii]

3 All things excellent are as difficult as they are rare. [*Ethics* V. xlii]

4 We feel and know that we are eternal. [*Ethics*]

SPONG Bishop John 1931–
US cleric.

I learned early in life that you get places by having the right enemies. [*Guardian* 20 July 1988]

SPOONER William 1844–1930
Warden of New College, Oxford.

Kinquering Congs their titles take. [Announcing the hymn in New College Chapel 1879]

SPRING-RICE Cecil 1859–1918
English poet.

I vow to thee, my country – all earthly things above – / Entire and whole and perfect, the service of my love. ['Last Poem']

SQUIRE J C 1884–1958
English journalist.

It did not last: the Devil howling 'Ho! / Let Einstein be!' restored the status quo. [*Poems*]

STAËL Madame de 1766–1817
French writer.

1 Love is the whole history of a woman's life, it is but an episode in a man's. ['On the Influence of the Passions']

2 Love is above the laws, above the opinion of men; it is the truth, the flame, the pure element, the primary idea of the moral world. [*Zulma, and Other Tales*]

3 Speech happens not to be his language. [On being asked what she talked about with her new lover]

STANLEY Henry Morton 1841–1904
Welsh-born US explorer and journalist.

> Dr Livingstone, I presume? [On meeting David Livingstone at Lake Tanganyika Nov 1871, in *How I Found Livingstone*]

STARK Freya 1893–1993
English traveller, mountaineer, and writer.

> The great and almost only comfort about being a woman is that one can always pretend to be more stupid than one is, and no one is surprised. [*Valley of the Assassins*]

STEELE Richard 1672–1729
Irish essayist and dramatist.

> **1** The insupportable labour of doing nothing. [*Tatler*]
>
> **2** It is to be noted that when any part of this paper appears dull, there is a design in it. [*Tatler*]
>
> **3** These ladies of irresistible modesty are those who make virtue unamiable. [*Tatler*]
>
> **4** To love her is a liberal education. [*Tatler*]

STEFFENS Lincoln 1866–1936
US journalist.

> I have seen the future; and it works. [Of the newly formed Soviet Union, in letter to Marie Howe 3 Apr 1919]

STEIN Gertrude 1874–1946
US writer.

> **1** Anyone who marries three girls from St Louis hasn't learned much. [Of Ernest Hemingway, in J R Mellow *Charmed Circle: Gertrude Stein and Company*]
>
> **2** A rose is a rose is a rose, is a rose. [*Sacred Emily*]
>
> **3** You are all a lost generation. [Quoted in Ernest Hemingway *The Sun Also Rises*]

STEINBECK John 1902–1968
US novelist.

> I know this – a man got to do what he got to do. [*Grapes of Wrath*]

STEINEM Gloria 1934–
US feminist and journalist.

> **1** We are becoming the men we wanted to marry. [*Ms* July/August 1982]
>
> **2** The authority of any governing institution must stop at its citizen's skin. ['Night Thoughts of a Media-Watcher', *Ms* Nov 1981]
>
> **3** Pornography is about dominance. Erotica is about mutuality. [*Outrageous Acts and Everyday Rebellions*]

US novelist John Steinbeck in 1968. As a young man, Steinbeck worked for some years as a casual labourer and some of his finest fiction is based on his encounters with the migrant workers of California's farming valleys. His critical reputation declined in the early 1960s, although novels such as *The Grapes of Wrath* 1939 won him the Nobel Prize for Literature 1962.

4 A woman without a man is like a fish without a bicycle. [Attributed remark]

5 I can't mate in captivity. [On being asked why she has never married. Attributed remark.]

STEINER George 1929–
French-born US critic and novelist.

The immense majority of human biographies are a gray transit between domestic spasm and oblivion. [*In Bluebeard's Castle* ch 1]

STENDHAL 1783–1842
French novelist.

1 Love has always been the most important business in my life, I should say the only one. [*Life of Henry Brulard*]

2 Beauty is only the promise of happiness. [*On Love*]

3 One can acquire everything in solitude except character. [*On Love*]

STEPHEN J K 1859–1892
English poet.

1 Two voices are there: one is of the deep; / And one is of an old half-witted sheep / Which bleats articulate monotony, / And Wordsworth, both are thine. [*Lapsus Calami*, Sonnet]

2 When the Rudyards cease from kipling / And the Haggards ride no more. [*Lapsus Calami*, Sonnet 'To R. K.']

STERN Richard G 1928–
US writer and educator.

When love gets to be important to someone, it means that he hasn't been able to manage something else. Falling in love seems to me an almost sure sign of failure. Except for the very few who have a talent for it. [*Golk* ch 2]

STERNE Laurence 1713–1768
Irish writer.

1 They order, said I, this matter better in France. [*Sentimental Journey*, opening words]

2 I saw the iron enter into his soul! [*Sentimental Journey*, 'The Captive']

3 There are worse occupations in this world than feeling a woman's pulse. [*Sentimental Journey*, 'The Pulse']

4 Love, an' please your Honour, is exactly like war, in this, that a soldier, though he has escaped three weeks complete o' Saturday night, may, nevertheless, be shot through his heart on Sunday morning. [*Tristram Shandy*]

5 A man should know something of his own country, too, before he goes abroad. [*Tristram Shandy*]

6 My brother Toby, quoth she, is going to be married to Mrs Wadman. Then he will never, quoth my father, lie *diagonally* in his bed again as long as he lives. [*Tristram Shandy*]

7 The nonsense of the old women (of both sexes). [*Tristram Shandy*]

8 Said my mother, 'what is all this story about?' – 'A Cock and a Bull,' said Yorick. [*Tristram Shandy*]

9 'Tis known by the name of perseverance in a good cause, – and of obstinacy in a bad one. [*Tristram Shandy*]

STEVAS Norman St John 1929–
British Conservative politician.

I mustn't go on singling out names. One must not be a name dropper, as Her Majesty remarked to me yesterday. [Speech, Museum of the Year luncheon, 20 June 1979]

STEVENS Wallace 1879–1955
US poet.

1 If sex were all, then every trembling hand / Could make us squeak, like dolls, the wished-for words. ['Le Monocle de Mon Oncle']

2 I do not know which to prefer, / The beauty of inflections / Or the beauty of innuendoes, / The blackbird whistling / Or just after. ['Thirteen Ways of Looking at a Blackbird']

STEVENSON Adlai 1900–1965
US Democrat politician.

1 An editor is one who separates the wheat from the chaff and prints the chaff. [*Stevenson Wit*]

2 I suppose flattery hurts no one, that is, if he doesn't inhale. [TV broadcast 30 Mar 1952]

3 There is no evil in the atom; only in men's souls. [Speech at Hartford Connecticut 18 Sept 1952]

4 In America any boy may become President and I suppose it's just one of the risks he takes! [Speech in Indianapolis 26 Sept 1952]

5 My definition of a free society is a society where it is safe to be unpopular. [Speech in Detroit 7 Oct 1952]

6 I have been thinking that I would make a proposition to my Republican friends ... that if they will stop telling lies about the Democrats, we will stop telling the truth about them. [Speech during 1952 presidential campaign]

STEVENSON Robert Louis 1850–1894
Scottish writer.

1 Everyone lives by selling something, whatever be his right to it. [*Across the Plains*, 'Beggars' 3]

4 Here lies one who meant well, tried a little, failed much: surely that may be his epitaph, of which he need not be ashamed. [*Across the Plains*, 'Christmas Sermon']

3 A mortified appetite is never a wise companion. [*Across the Plains*, 'Christmas Sermon']

4 To make our idea of morality centre on forbidden acts is to defile the imagination and to introduce into our judgments of our fellow-men a secret element of gusto. [*Across the Plains*, 'Christmas Sermon']

5 A child should always say what's true, / And speak when he is spoken to, / And behave mannerly at table: / At least as far as he is able. [*Child's Garden of Verses*, 'Whole Duty of Children']

6 I've a grand memory for forgetting. [*Kidnapped*]

7 I will make you brooches and toys for your delight / Of bird-song at morning and star-shine at night. [*Songs of Travel*, 'Youth and Love']

8 For my part, I travel not to go anywhere, but to go. I travel for travel's sake. The great affair is to move. [*Travels with a Donkey*]

9 Fifteen men on the dead man's chest / Yo-ho-ho, and a bottle of rum! [*Treasure Island*]

10 Go, little book, and wish to all / Flowers in the garden, meat in the hall, / A bin of wine, a spice of wit, / A house with lawns enclosing it, / A living river by the door, / A nightingale in the sycamore! [*Underwoods*, 'Envoy']

11 Under the wide and starry sky / Dig the grave and let me lie. / Glad did I live and gladly die, / And I laid me down with a will. / This be the verse you grave for me: / 'Here he lies where he longed to be; / Home is the sailor, home from sea, / And the hunter home from the hill.' [*Underwoods*, 'Requiem']

12 The cruellest lies are often told in silence. [*Virginibus Puerisque* I]

13 Even if we take matrimony at its lowest, even if we regard it as no more than a sort of friendship recognised by the police. [*Virginibus Puerisque* I]

14 In marriage, a man becomes slack and selfish, and undergoes a fatty degeneration of his moral being. [*Virginibus Puerisque* I]

15 A little amateur painting in water-colour shows the innocent and quiet mind. [*Virginibus Puerisque* I]

16 Marriage is a step so grave and decisive that it attracts light-headed, variable men by its very awfulness. [*Virginibus Puerisque* I]

17 No woman should marry a tee-totaller, or a man who does not smoke. [*Virginibus Puerisque* I]

18 Times are changed with him who marries; there are no more bypath meadows, where you may innocently linger, but the road lies long and straight and dusty to the grave. [*Virginibus Puerisque* I]

19 To marry is to domesticate the Recording Angel. Once you are married, there is nothing left for you, not even suicide, but to be good. [*Virginibus Puerisque* I]

20 By the time a man gets well into the seventies his continued existence is a mere miracle. [*Virginibus Puerisque* V]

STILLS Stephen 1945–
Canadian rock musician.

> There are three things men can do with women: love them, suffer for them or turn them into literature. [Attributed remark]

STONE Lucy 1818–1893
US suffragette and writer.

> In education, in marriage, in religion, in everything, disappointment is the lot of women. It shall be the business of my life to deepen this disappointment in every woman's heart until she bows down to it no longer. [Speech Oct 1855]

STOPPARD Tom 1937–
Czechoslovak-born British dramatist.

> **1** A lady, if surprised by melancholy, might go to bed with a chap, once; or a thousand times, if consumed by passion. But twice, Wagner, *twice* ... a lady might think she'd been taken for a tart. [*Night and Day* I]

Stravinsky Russian composer Igor Stravinsky, lived in Paris from 1920, moved to the USA in 1939, and in 1945 took US citizenship.

2 The bad end unhappily, the good unluckily. That is what tragedy means. [*Rosencrantz and Guildenstern Are Dead* II]

3 Eternity's a terrible thought. I mean, where's it all going to end? [*Rosencrantz and Guildenstern Are Dead* II]

4 Life is a gamble, at terrible odds – if it was a bet, you wouldn't take it. [*Rosencrantz and Guildenstern Are Dead* III]

STOWE Harriet Beecher 1811–1896
US suffragist, abolitionist, and author.

'Do you know who made you?' 'Nobody, as I knows on,' said the child, with a short laugh. ... 'I 'spect I grow'd.' [*Uncle Tom's Cabin*]

STRAVINSKY Igor 1882–1971
Russian born composer.

Work brings inspiration, if inspiration is not discernible at the beginning. [*Chronicle of My Life*]

STREISAND Barbra 1942–
US singer and film actress.

The moral immune system of this country has been weakened and attacked, and the AIDS virus is the perfect metaphor for it. [*Guardian* 26 Nov 1992]

STRINDBERG August 1849–1912
Swedish dramatist and novelist.

Now things are so ill arranged that some people are born monogamous, that is, faithful, which is not a virtue but a quality, while others are born polygamous, that is, unfaithful. If these two opposites come together the result is great misery. [*Getting Married* Preface]

SUCKLING John 1609–1642
English poet and dramatist.

1 Why so pale and wan, fond lover? / Prithee, why so pale? / Will, when looking well can't move her, / Looking ill prevail? [*Aglaura*, 'Song']

2 Her feet beneath her petticoat, / Like little mice, stole in and out, / As if they fear'd the light. ['A Ballad Upon a Wedding' viii]

3 The Prince of Darkness is a gentleman. [*The Goblins* III]

4 Out upon it, I have loved / Three whole days together; / And am like to love three more, / If it prove fair weather. ['Poem with the Answer']

SUETONIUS c. AD 75–160
Roman historian.

1 He so improved the city that he justly boasted that he found it brick and left it marble. [*Lives of the Caesars*, 'Augustus']

2 Make haste slowly. [*Lives of the Caesars*, 'Augustus']

3 Hail, Emperor, those who are about to die salute thee. [*Lives of the Caesars*, 'Claudius']

4 So many men, so many opinions. [*Phormio*]

SURTEES R S 1803–1864
English novelist.

1 More people are flattered into virtue than bullied out of vice. [*Analysis of the Hunting Field*]

2 'Unting is all that's worth living for ... it's the sport of kings, the image of war without its guilt, and only five-and-twenty per cent of its danger. [*Handley Cross* ch 7]

3 It ar'n't that I loves the fox less, but that I loves the 'ound more. [*Handley Cross* ch 16]

4 Con-found all presents wot eat! [*Handley Cross* ch 37]

5 Hellish dark, and smells of cheese! [*Handley Cross* ch 50]

6 Three things I never lends – my 'oss, my wife, and my name. [*Hillingdon Hall* ch 33]

7 Better be killed than frightened to death. [*Mr Facey Romford's Hounds* ch 32]

8 He was a gentleman who was generally spoken of as having nothing a-year, paid quarterly. [*Mr Sponge's Sporting Tour*]

SWAFFER Hannen 1879–1962
English journalist.

Freedom of the press in Britain means freedom to print such of the proprietor's prejudices as the advertisers don't object to. [Quoted in Tom Driberg *Swaff*]

SWIFT Jonathan 1667–1745
Irish satirist and Anglican cleric.

1 Satire is a sort of glass, wherein beholders do generally discover everybody's face but their own. [*Battle of the Books*]

2 Whoever could make two ears of corn or two blades of grass to grow upon a spot of ground where only one grew before, would deserve better of mankind, and do more essential service to his country than the whole race of politicians put together. [*Gulliver's Travels*, 'Voyage to Brobdingnag']

3 He had been eight years upon a project for extracting sun-beams out of cucumbers. [*Gulliver's Travels*, 'Voyage to Laputa']

4 Proper words in proper places, make the true definition of a style. [*Letter to a Young Clergyman* 1720]

5 I shall be like that tree, I shall die at the top. [Quoted in Walter Scott *Memoirs of Swift*]

6 We have just enough religion to make us hate, but not enough to make us love one another. [*Miscellany* (with Alexander Pope)]

7 Philosophy, the lumber of the schools. ['Ode to Sir W. Temple']

8 Yet malice never was his aim; / He lash'd the vice, but spared the name. [*On the Death of Dr. Swift*]

9 So geographers, in Afric-maps, / With savage-pictures fill their gaps; / And o'er unhabitable downs / Place elephants for want of towns. ['On Poetry']

10 Bachelor's fare; bread and cheese, and kisses. [*Polite Conversation*, 'Dialogue 1']

11 Few are qualified to shine in company; but it is in most men's power to be agreeable. [*Thoughts on Various Subjects*]

12 I have almost done with harridans, and shall soon become old enough to fall in love with girls of fourteen. [Letter to Alexander Pope, Sept 1725]

13 Where fierce indignation can no longer tear the heart. [Epitaph]

SWINBURNE Algernon Charles 1837–1909
English poet.

1 Bright with names that men remember, loud with names that men forget. ['Eton: An Ode']

2 Stretched out on the spoils that his own hand spread. / As a god self-slain on his own strange altar, / Death lies dead. ['A Forsaken Garden']

3 From too much love of living, / From hope and fear set free, / We thank with brief thanksgiving / Whatever gods may be / That no man lives forever, / That dead men rise up never; / That even the weariest river / Winds somewhere safe to sea. [*Garden of Proserpine*]

4 Thou hast conquered, O pale Galilean; the world has grown grey from Thy breath. ['Hymn to Proserpine']

5 To have known love, how bitter a thing it is. ['Laus Veneris']

6 If love were what the rose is, / And I were like the leaf, / Our life would grow together / In sad or singing weather. ['Match']

7 If you were queen of pleasure, / And I were king of pain, / We'd hunt down love together, / Pluck out his flying feather, / And teach his feet a measure, / And find his mouth a rein. ['Match']

SWOPE Herbert B 1882–1958
US journalist.

I cannot give you the formula for success, but I can give you the formula for failure, which is –: Try to please everybody. [Speech 20 Dec 1950]

SYMONS Arthur 1865–1945
Welsh poet and critic.

And I would have, now love is over, / An end to all, an end: / I cannot, having been your lover, / Stoop to become your friend! ['After Love']

SYRUS Publilius LIVED 1ST CENTURY BC
Roman writer.

1 He gives twice who gives soon. [Proverbial, attributed to Syrus]

2 Necessity has no law. [Proverbial, attributed to Syrus]

SZASZ Thomas 1920–
Hungarian-born US psychiatrist.

1 A child becomes an adult when he realizes that he has a right not only to be right but also to be wrong. ['Childhood']

2 The stupid neither forgive nor forget; the naïve forgive and forget; the wise forgive but do not forget. ['Personal Conduct']

3 Formerly, when religion was strong and science weak, men mistook magic for medicine; now, when science is strong and religion weak, men mistake medicine for magic. ['Science and Scientism']

4 Every act of conscious learning requires the willingness to suffer an injury to one's self-esteem. [*Second Sin*, 'Education']

5 In the animal kingdom, the rule is, eat or be eaten; in the human kingdom, define or be defined. [*Second Sin*, 'Language']

TACITUS Publius c. AD 55–c. 117
Roman historian.

1 It is human nature to hate the man whom you have injured. [*Agricola*]

2 When they make a desolation they call it peace. [*Agricola*]

TAGORE Rabindranath 1861–1941
Bengali Indian writer.

1 The butterfly counts not months but moments, and has time enough. [*Fireflies*]

2 He who wants to do good knocks at the gate; he who loves finds the door open. ['Stray Birds']

TANFIELD Elizabeth c. 1565–1628
Wife of the Viscount of Falkland.

Love made me poet, / And this I writ; / My heart did do it, / And not my wit. [Epitaph for her husband, in the parish church of Burford]

TARKINGTON Booth 1869–1946
US novelist.

Arguments only confirm people in their own opinions. [*Looking Forward to the Great Adventure*]

TAYLOR Bert Leston 1866–1921
US humorist.

A bore is a man who, when you ask him how he is, tells you. [*The So-Called Human Race* 163]

TAYLOR Elizabeth 1932–
English-born US actress.

Some of my best leading men have been dogs and horses. [*The Times* 18 Feb 1981]

TAYLOR Jeremy 1613–1667
English theologian.

1 Curiosity is the direct incontinency of the spirit. [*Rule and Exercises of Holy Living* ch 2, 5]

2 He that loves not his wife and children feeds a lioness at home and broods a nest of sorrows. [*Sermons*, 'Married Love']

TENNYSON Alfred, Lord 1809–1892
English poet.

1 The noblest answer unto such, / Is kindly silence when they brawl. ['After-Thought']

2 The peace of God came into my life before the altar when I married her. [On his marriage to Emily Sellwood, in *Alfred Lord Tennyson: A Memoir by his Son* pt 1]

3 Cleave ever to the sunnier side of doubt. ['Ancient Sage']

4 Bare-footed came the beggar maid / Before the king Cophetua. ['Beggar Maid']

5 Break, break, break, / On thy cold gray stones, O Sea! ['Break, Break, Break']

6 For men may come and men may go, / But I go on for ever. ['The Brook']

7 'Forward, the Light Brigade!' / Was there a man dismay'd? ['Charge of the Light Brigade']

8 Half a league, half a league, / Half a league onward. ['Charge of the Light Brigade']

9 Into the jaws of Death, / Into the mouth of Hell. ['Charge of the Light Brigade']

10 Some one had blunder'd. ['Charge of the Light Brigade']

11 Their's not to make reply, / Their's not to reason why, / Their's but to do and die: / Into the valley of Death / Rode the six hundred. ['Charge of the Light Brigade']

Alfred, Lord Tennyson, photographed in 1888.

12 I hope to see my Pilot face to face / When I have crost the bar. ['Crossing the Bar']

13 Sunset and evening star, / And one clear call for me! / And may there be no moaning of the bar, / When I put out to sea. ['Crossing the Bar']

14 And on her lover's arm she leant, / And round her waist she felt it fold, / And far across the hills they went / In that new world which is the old. [*Day Dream,* 'Departure']

15 Read my little fable: / He that runs may read. ['The Flower']

16 Clothed in white samite, mystic, wonderful. [*Idylls of the King,* 'Coming of Arthur']

17 From the great deep to the great deep he goes. [*Idylls of the King,* 'Coming of Arthur']

18 We needs must love the highest when we see it. [*Idylls of the King,* 'Guinevere']

19 Our hoard is little, but our hearts are great. [*Idylls of the King,* 'Marriage of Geraint']

20 It is the little rift within the lute, / That by and by will make the music mute. [*Idylls of the King,* 'Merlin and Vivien']

21 Man dreams of fame while woman wakes to love. [*Idylls of the King,* 'Merlin and Vivien']

22 And slowly answer'd Arthur from the barge: / 'The old order changeth, yielding place to new, / And God fulfils himself in many ways. [*Idylls of the King,* 'Passing of Arthur']

23 If thou shouldst never see my face again, / Pray for my soul. More things are wrought by prayer / Than this world dreams of. [*Idylls of the King,* 'Passing of Arthur']

24 The whole round earth is every way / Bound by gold chains about the feet of God. [*Idylls of the King,* 'Passing of Arthur']

25 Our little systems have their day; / They have their day and cease to be. [*In Memoriam* prologue]

26 I hold it true, whate'er befall; / I feel it, when I sorrow most; / 'Tis better to have loved and lost / Than never to have loved at all. [*In Memoriam* 27]

27 Nature, red in tooth and claw. [*In Memoriam* 56]

28 So many worlds, so much to do, / So little done, such things to be. [*In Memoriam* 73]

29 Their meetings made December / Their every parting was to die. [*In Memoriam* 97]

30 Ring out, wild bells, to the wild sky. / Ring out the old, ring in the new. [*In Memoriam* 106]

31 Kind hearts are more than coronets, / And simple faith than Norman blood. ['Lady Clara Vere de Vere']

32 The fairy tales of science, and the long result of Time. ['Locksley Hall']

33 He will hold thee, when his passion shall have spent its novel force. / Something better than his dog, a little dearer than his horse. ['Locksley Hall']

34 In the Spring a young man's fancy lightly turns to thoughts of love. ['Locksley Hall']

35 'Courage!' he said, and pointed toward the land. ['The Lotos-Eaters']

36 A land / In which it seemed always afternoon. ['Lotos-Eaters']

37 Come into the garden, Maud, / For the black bat, night, has flown. [*Maud*]

38 O that 'twere possible / After long grief and pain / To find the arms of my true love again! [*Maud* pt 2]

39 It is better to fight for the good, than to rail at the ill; / I have felt with my native land, I am one with my kind, / I embrace the purpose of God, and the doom assign'd. [*Maud* pt 3]

40 For I'm to be Queen o' the May, mother, I'm to be Queen o' the May.

41 ['The May Queen']**1** O you chorus of indolent reviewers. ['Milton. Hendecasyllabics']

42 And is there any moral shut / Within the bosom of the rose? ['Moral']

43 Dosnt thou marry for munny, but gos where munny is! ['Northern Farmer. New Style']

44 Alone and warming his five wits, / The white owl in the belfry sits. ['The Owl']

45 With prudes for proctors, dowagers for deans, / And sweet girl-graduates in their golden hair. [*The Princess*, prologue]

46 The splendour falls on castle walls / And snowy summits old in story. [*The Princess* 4]

47 Tears, idle tears, I know not what they mean, / Tears from the depth of some divine despair. [*The Princess* 4]

48 Man for the field and woman for the hearth: / Man for the sword and for the needle she: / Man with the head and woman with the heart: / Man to command and woman to obey: / All else confusion. [*The Princess* 5]

49 The woman is so hard / Upon the woman. [*The Princess* 6]

50 Now sleeps the crimson petal, now the white; / Nor waves the cypress in the palace walk; / Nor winks the gold fin in the porphyry font: / The fire-fly wakens: waken thou with me. [*The Princess* 7]

51 At Flores in the Azores Sir Richard Grenville lay, / And a pinnace, like a fluttered bird, came flying from far away: / 'Spanish ships of war at sea! we have sighted fifty-three!' ['The Revenge']

52 'I have fought for Queen and Faith like a valiant man and true; / I have only done my duty as a man is bound to do: / With a joyful spirit I Sir Richard Grenville die!' / And he fell upon their decks, and he died. ['The Revenge']

53 The woods decay, the woods decay and fall, / The vapours weep their burthen to the ground, / Man comes and tills the field and lies beneath, / And after many a summer dies the swan. [*Tithonus*]

54 It little profits that an idle king, / By this still hearth, among these barren crags, / Match'd with an aged wife, I mete and dole / Unequal laws unto a savage race. [*Ulysses* l. 1]

55 I will drink / Life to the lees: all times I have enjoy'd / Greatly, have suffer'd greatly, both with those / That loved me, and alone. [*Ulysses* l. 6]

56 Much have I seen and known; cities of men / And manners, climates, councils, governments, / Myself not least, but honour'd of them all; / And drunk delight of battle with my peers, / Far on the ringing plains of windy Troy. / I am a part of all that I have met; / Yet all experience is an arch wherethro' / Gleams that untravell'd world, whose margin fades / For ever and for ever when I move. / How dull it is to pause, to make an end, / To rust unburnish'd, not to shine in use! [*Ulysses* l. 12]

57 Tho' much is taken, much abides; and tho' / We are not now that strength which in old days / Moved earth and heaven; that which we are, we are; / One equal temper of heroic hearts, / Made weak by time and fate, but strong in will / To strive, to seek, to find, and not to yield. [*Ulysses* l. 44]

58 Old age hath yet his honour and his toil; / Death closes all: but something ere the end, of noble note, may yet be done. [*Ulysses* l. 50]

TERENCE 190–159 BC
Roman dramatist.

1 Lovers' quarrels are the renewal of love. [*Andria* 555]

2 Fortune favours the brave. [*Phormio*]

3 Many men, so many opinions. [*Phormio*]

TERESA Mother 1910–
Albanian-born Roman Catholic missionary nun.

1 We ourselves feel that what we are doing is just a drop in the ocean. But if that drop was not in the ocean, I think the ocean would be

less because of that missing drop. I do not agree with the big way of doing things. [*Gift for God*, 'Carriers of Christ's Love']

2 Jesus said love one another. He didn't say love the whole world. [Quoted in *Observer* 2 March 1980]

THACKERAY William Makepeace
1811–1863
English novelist and essayist.

1 He who meanly admires mean things is a Snob. [*Book of Snobs*]

2 'Tis not the dying for a faith that's so hard – every man of every nation has done that – 'tis the living up to it that is difficult. [*History of Henry Esmond* bk 1, ch 6]

3 'Tis strange what a man may do, and a woman yet think him an angel. [*History of Henry Esmond* bk 1, ch 7]

4 Yes, I am a fatal man, Madame Fribsbi. To inspire hopeless passion is my destiny. [*Pendennis* ch 23]

5 Remember, it is as easy to marry a rich woman as a poor woman. [*Pendennis* ch 28]

6 This I set down as a positive truth. A woman with fair opportunities and without a positive hump, may marry whom she likes. [*Vanity Fair* ch 4]

7 Whenever he met a great man he grovelled before him, and my-lorded him as only a free-born Briton can do. [*Vanity Fair* ch 13]

8 We love being in love, that's the truth on't. [*Vanity Fair* ch 15]

THATCHER Margaret 1925–
British Conservative prime minister.

1 I am extraordinarily patient, provided I get my own way in the end. [*Observer* 4 Apr 1989]

2 There is no such thing as Society. There are individual men and women, and there are families. [*Woman's Own* 31 Oct 1987]

Conservative politician and former prime minister Margaret Thatcher, whose brand of Conservatism and European policy eventually provoked a crisis in her party and government. The 1990 leadership challenge led to her resignation as prime minister, an office she had held since 1979, and her replacement as leader of the conservative Party, a post she had held for nearly 16 years.

3 To those waiting with bated breath for that favourite media catch-phrase, the U-turn, I have only one thing to say. You turn if you want to. The lady's not for turning. [Speech to the Conservative Party Conference 1980]

4 No one would remember the Good Samaritan if he'd only had good intentions. He had money as well. [Television interview 6 Jan 1986]

THEOPHRASTUS c. 372–287 BC
Greek philosopher.

Men marry, indeed, so as to get a manager for the house; to solace weariness, to banish solitude; but a faithful slave is a far better manager, more submissive to the master, more observant of his ways, than a wife who thinks she proves herself mistress if she acts in opposition to her husband, that is, if she does what pleases her, not what she is commanded. [*On Marriage*]

THEROUX Paul 1941–
US novelist and travel writer.

Extensive travelling induces a feeling of encapsulation, and travel, so broadening at first, contracts the mind. [*Great American Railway*]

THOMAS Caitlin 1913–1994
Widow of the poet Dylan Thomas.

I wouldn't have married him if he had not got the genius. He was too unattractive as a man. [On her marriage to Dylan Thomas]

THOMAS Dylan 1914–1953
Welsh poet.

1 Do not go gentle into that good night, / Rage, rage against the dying of the light. ['Do Not Go Gentle into That Good Night']

2 Now as I was young and easy under the apple boughs / About the lilting house and happy as the grass was green. ['Fern Hill']

3 Mrs Ogmore-Pritchard: And before you let the sun in, mind it wipes its shoes. [*Under Milk Wood*]

4 You're thinking, you're no better than you should be, / Polly, and that's good enough for me. Oh, isn't life a terrible thing, thank God? [*Under Milk Wood*]

THOMAS Lewis 1913–
US physician and educator.

1 It hurts the spirit, somehow, to read the word *environments*, when the plural means that there are so many alternatives there to be sorted through, as in a market, and voted on. [*Lives of a Cell*, 'Natural Man']

Welsh poet Dylan Thomas. Thomas had a fine speaking voice and his BBC broadcasts of his poems and short stories, particularly the warm and intimate recollections of his childhood in Wales, were very popular and made him one of the best known British poets of the 1940s and 1950s.

2 We are built to make mistakes, coded for error. [*Medusa and the Snail* 'To Err is Human']

THOMPSON Francis 1859–1907
English poet.

1 And human love needs human meriting: / How hast thou merited – / Of all man's clotted clay the dingiest clot? ['Hound of Heaven']

2 The angels keep their ancient places; / Turn but a stone, and start a wing! / 'Tis ye, 'tis your estrangèd faces, / That miss the many-splendoured thing. ['Kingdom of God']

3 Spring is come home with her world-wandering feet. / And all things are made young with young desires. ['Ode to Easter']

THOMPSON Hunter S 1939–
US writer and journalist.

Fear and Loathing in Las Vegas. [Title of two articles in *Rolling Stone* Nov 1972]

THOMPSON William Hepworth 1810–1886
English scholar.

We are none of us infallible – not even the youngest of us. [Remark]

THOMSON James 1700–1748
Scottish poet.

1 When Britain first, at heaven's command, / Arose from out the azure main, / This was the charter of the land, / And guardian angels sung this strain: / 'Rule, Britannia, rule the waves; / Britons never will be slaves.' [*Alfred: a Masque*]

2 Delightful task! to rear the tender thought, / To teach the young idea how to shoot. [*The Seasons*, 'Spring']

THOREAU Henry David 1817–1862
US author and naturalist.

1 There is no remedy for love but to love more. [*Journal* 25 July 1839]

2 Some circumstantial evidence is very strong, as when you find a trout in the milk. [*Miscellanies*]

3 The mass of men lead lives of quiet desperation. [*Walden*, 'Economy']

4 Every man is the builder of a temple, called his body, to the god he worships ... . We are all sculptors and painters, and our material is our own flesh and blood and bones. [*Walden*, 'Higher Laws']

5 The three-o'-clock in the morning courage, which Bonaparte thought was the rarest. [*Walden*, 'Sounds']

6 Simplify, simplify. [*Walden*, 'Where I Lived, and What I Lived For']

7 It takes two to speak the truth, – one to speak, and another to hear. [*Week on the Concord and Merrimack Rivers*]

8 Not that the story need be long, but it will take a long while to make it short. [Letter to Mr B. 16 Nov 1857]

THURBER James 1894–1961
US humorist.

1 Art – the one achievement of Man which has made the long trip up from all fours seem well advised. [*Forum and Century* June 1939]

2 Her own mother lived the latter years of her life in the horrible suspicion that electricity was dripping invisibly all over the house. [*My Life and Hard Times*]

3 It takes that *je ne sais quoi* which we call sophistication for a woman to be magnificent in a drawing-room when her faculties have departed but she herself has not yet gone home. [*New Yorker* 2 Aug 1930]

4 It's a naïve domestic Burgundy without any breeding, but I think you'll be amused by its presumption. [Cartoon caption in *New Yorker* 27 Mar 1937]

5 Well, if I called the wrong number, why did you answer the phone? [Cartoon caption in *New Yorker* 5 June 1937]

THURLOW Edward 1731–1806
English lawyer.

1 Corporations have neither bodies to be punished, nor souls to be condemned, they therefore do as they like. [Quoted in Poynder *Literary Extracts*]

2 Did you ever expect a corporation to have a conscience, when it has no soul to be damned, and nobody to be kicked? [Attributed remark]

TOCQUEVILLE Alexis de 1805–1859
French politician and political scientist.

1 Americans are so enamored of equality that they would rather be equal in slavery than unequal in freedom. [*Democracy in America*]

2 Democratic institutions generally give men a lofty notion of their country and themselves. [*Democracy in America*]

3 When I refuse to obey an unjust law, I do not contest the right of the majority to command, but I simply appeal from the sovereignty of the people to the sovereignty of mankind. [*Democracy in America*]

Russian novelist Count Leo Tolstoy wrote his greatest novels, *War and Peace* and *Anna Karenina*, while living on his estate at Yasnaya Polyana. Between 1857 and 1861 he fostered an interest in educational reforms on two trips to western Europe, establishing a school for peasants on his return to the estate.

TOLSTOY Leo 1828–1910
Russian novelist.

> 1 All happy families resemble each other, but each unhappy family is unhappy in its own way. [*Anna Karenina*]
>
> 2 To love one person for a whole lifetime is like saying that one candle will burn a whole life. [*Kreutzer Sonata* ch 2]
>
> 3 All, everything that I understand, I understand only because I love. [*War and Peace* bk 7 ch 16]

TOMLIN Lily 1939–
US actress.

> If love is the answer, could you rephrase the question? [Attributed remark]

TOOKE John Horne 1736–1812
English clergyman and politician.

> With all my heart. Whose wife shall it be? [In reply to a suggestion that he take a wife]

TOSCANINI Arturo 1867–1957
Italian conductor.

> 1 When I was young, I kissed my first woman, and smoked my first cigarette on the same day. Believe me, never since have I wasted any more time on tobacco. [Attributed remark 1957]
>
> 2 Can't you read? The score demands *con amore*, and what are you doing? You are playing it like married men! [Attributed remark, during rehearsal with an Austrian orchestra]

TOWNSEND Sue 1946–
English humorous novelist.

> The Secret Diary of Adrian Mole Aged 13¾. [Book title]

TOYNBEE Arnold 1889–1975
English historian.

> Civilization is a movement and not a condition, a voyage and not a harbour. [*The Reader's Digest* Oct 1958]

TRAPIDO Barbara 1941–
South-African-born British novelist.

> It was one of those weddings where the bride's and groom's families stand out like opposing football teams, wearing their colours. All the decent hats were, thank God, on our side. [*Brother of the More Famous Jack*]

TREE Herbert Beerbohm 1853–1917
English actor and theatre manager.

> He is an old bore. Even the grave yawns for him. [Of Israel Zangwill, quoted in Max Beerbohm *Herbert Beerbohm Tree*]

TRENCH Herbert 1865–1923
Irish poet and dramatist.

> Come, let us make love deathless, you and I. ['To Arolilia']

TRINDER Tommy 1909–1989
English entertainer.

> Overpaid, overfed, oversexed, and over here. [Of US troops in Britain during World War II, in *Sunday Times* 4 Jan 1976]

TROLLOPE Anthony 1815–1882
English novelist.

> 1 Three hours a day will produce as much as a man ought to write. [*Autobiography*]
>
> 2 Among these Mr Quiverful, the rector of Puddingdale, whose wife still continued to present him from year to year with fresh pledges of her love. [*Barchester Towers* ch 7]
>
> 3 It's dogged as does it. It ain't thinking about it. [*Last Chronicles of Barset*]
>
> 4 Nothing reopens the springs of love so fully as absence, and no absence so thoroughly as that which must be endless. [*Last Chronicle of Barset* ch 67]
>
> 5 I doubt whether any girl would be satisfied with her lover's mind if she knew the whole of it. [*Small House at Allington* ch 4]

6 Love is like any other luxury. You have no right to it unless you can afford it. [*Way We Live Now* ch 84]

7 Of course I draw from life – but I always pulp my acquaintance before serving them up. You would never recognize a pig in a sausage. [Remark]

TROTSKY Leon 1879–1940
Russian revolutionary.

1 The depth and the strength of a human character are defined by its moral reserves. People reveal themselves completely only when they are thrown out of the customary conditions of their life, for only then do they have to fall back on their reserves. [*Diary in Exile* 5 April 1935]

2 Old age is the most unexpected of all things that happen to a man. [*Diary in Exile*]

3 Go where you belong from now on – into the dustbin of history! [Addressing the Mensheviks in *History of the Russian Revolution*]

4 Any contemporary of ours who wants peace and comfort before anything has chosen a bad time to be born. [Quoted in *Observer* 26 March 1933]

TRUDEAU Pierre 1919–
Canadian Liberal prime minister.

The state has no place in the bedrooms of the nation. [On the decriminalization of homosexuality, 1969]

TRUFFAUT François 1932–1984
French film director.

In love women are professionals, men are amateurs. [Remark 1979]

TRUMAN Harry S 1884–1972
US Democratic president.

1 It's a recession when your neighbour loses his job; it's a depression when you lose yours. [*Observer* 13 Apr 1958]

2 The buck stops here. [Sign on his presidential desk]

Russian revolutionary Leon Trotsky in Aug 1940, a few weeks before his assassination. Trotsky had been one of the leaders of the Bolshevik revolution but was forced into exile 1929 by Stalin, who was systematically ridding himself of real or imagined threats to his position. When Trotsky continued to condemn Stalin's policies and methods, Stalin ordered his assassination.

TUCKER Sophie 1884–1966
Russian born US singer and entertainer.

From birth to 18 a girl needs good parents. From 18 to 35, she needs good looks. From 35 to 55, good personality. From 55 on, she needs good cash. I'm saving my money. [Quoted in M Freedland *Sophie*]

TURNER Lana 1920–
US film actress.

A successful man is one who makes more money than his wife can spend. A successful woman is one who can find such a man. [Attributed remark 1980]

TWAIN Mark 1835–1910
US writer.

1 There was things which he stretched, but mainly he told the truth. [*Adventures of Huckleberry Finn* ch 1]

2 The statements was interesting, but tough. [*Adventures of Huckleberry Finn* ch 17]

3 There are three kinds of lies: lies, damned lies, and statistics. [*Autobiography*]

4 Are you going to hang him *anyhow* – and try him afterward? [*Innocents at Home*]

5 The man who is a pessimist before 48 knows too much; if he is an optimist after it, he knows too little. [*Notebook* ch 33, Dec 1902]

6 There was never yet an uninteresting life. Such a thing is an impossibility. Inside of the dullest exterior there is a drama, a comedy, and a tragedy. [*Refuge of the Derelicts* ch 4]

7 The cross of the Legion of Honour has been conferred upon me. However, few escape that distinction. [*Tramp Abroad* ch 8]

8 A classic – something that everybody wants to have read and nobody wants to read. [Quoting Professor Caleb Winchester in a speech at the Nineteenth Century Club, New York City, 20 Nov 1900]

TYNAN Kenneth 1927–1980
English theatre critic and author.

A good drama critic is one who perceives what is happening in the theatre of his time. A great drama critic also perceives what is *not* happening. [*Tynan Right and Left*]

UNAMUNO Miguel de 1864–1936
Spanish writer of Basque origin.

1 The chiefest sanctity of a temple is that it is a place to which men go to weep in common. [*Tragic Sense of Life*, 'Man of Flesh and Bone']

2 The only way to give finality to the world is to give it consciousness. [*Tragic Sense of Life* ch 7]

3 There are pretences which are very sincere, and marriage is their school. [*Two Mothers*]

UPDIKE John 1932–
US writer and critic.

1 If men do not keep on speaking terms with children, they cease to be men, and become merely machines for eating and for earning money. [*Assorted Prose*, 'Foreword for Younger Readers']

2 A healthy male adult bore consumes each year one and a half times his own weight in other people's patience. ['Confessions of a Wild Bore']

3 Neutrinos, they are very small. / They have no charge and have no mass / And do not interact at all. ['Cosmic Gall']

4 Among the repulsions of atheism for me has been its drastic uninterestingness as an intellectual position. Where was the ingenuity, the ambiguity, the humanity ... of saying that the universe just happened to happen and that when we're dead we're dead? [*Self-Consciousness: Memoirs* ch 4]

5 Existence itself does not feel horrible; it feels like an ecstasy, rather, which we have only to be still to experience. [*Self-Consciousness: Memoirs* ch 6]

6 The yearning for an afterlife is the opposite of selfish; it is love and praise for the world that we are privileged, in this complex interval of light, to witness and experience. [*Self-Consciousness: Memoirs* ch 6]

USTINOV Peter 1921–
English actor, writer, and director.

1 Contrary to general belief, I do not believe that friends are necessarily the people you like best, they are merely the people who got there first. [*Dear Me*]

2 Unfortunately, the balance of nature decrees that a super-abundance of dreams is paid for by a growing potential for nightmares. [On the USA, *Independent* 25 Feb 1989]

3 Laughter would be bereaved if snobbery died. [Quoted in *Observer* 13 Mar 1955]

4 A diplomat these days is nothing but a head-waiter who's allowed to sit down occasionally. [*Romanoff and Juliet*]

English actor, dramatist, and director Peter Ustinov is easily recognized by his mellifluous, drawling voice and shambling manner. He has appeared in many films, almost always in light or comic roles, and has written many plays, as well as novels and an autobiography that gives full range to his skill as a raconteur.

VALÉRY Paul 1871–1945
French poet and mathematician.

1 A poem is never finished; it's always an accident that puts a stop to it – i.e. gives it to the public. [Littérature]

2 God made everything out of the void, but the void shows through. [Mauvaises pensées et autres]

3 Politics is the art of preventing people from taking part in affairs which properly concern them. [Tel Quel 2, 'Rhumbs']

VANBRUGH John 1664–1726
English architect and dramatist.

1 Love, like fortune, turns upon a wheel, and is very much given to rising and falling. [False Friends I. i]

2 Once a woman has given you her heart you can never get rid of the rest of her. [Relapse II.i]

VANDERBILT William Henry 1821–1885
US financier and railway promoter.

The public be damned! [Reply when asked if the public should be consulted about luxury trains, New York Times 25 August 1918]

VAN DER POST Laurens 1906–
South African writer.

1 Of all man's inborn dispositions there is none more heroic than the love in him. Everything else accepts defeat and dies, but love will fight no-love every inch of the way. [Flamingo Feather ch 7]

2 Organized religion is making Christianity political, rather than

South African writer Laurens van der Post. Throughout his work – novels, essays, travel books, and autobiographies – he has expressed his concern that modern man needs to regain a harmony between the unconscious, feminine element of the psyche and the conscious, masculine element. He has applied this search for psychic harmony to race (he was forced to leave South Africa for running an anti-apartheid periodical) and also to ecology, becoming a close advisor to Prince Charles.

making politics Christian. [Observer 9 Nov 1986]

VAN DOREN Carl 1885–1950
US man of letters.

A classic is a book that doesn't have to be written again. [Quoted by James Thurber in Bermudian Nov 1950]

VAN GOGH Vincent 1853–1890
Dutch artist.

> It is not the language of painters but the language of nature one should listen to ... . The feeling for the things themselves, for reality, is more important than the feeling for pictures. [Letter to his brother Theo 21 July 1882]

VARGAS LLOSA Mario 1936–
Peruvian novelist.

> Eroticism has its own moral justification because it says that pleasure is enough for me; it is a statement of the individual's sovereignty. [*International Herald Tribune* 23 Oct 1990]

VAUGHAN Henry 1622–1695
Welsh poet and physician.

> **1** And in those weaker glories spy / Some shadows of eternity. ['The Retreat']

> **2** Happy those early days, when I / Shin'd in my angel-infancy. ['The Retreat']

> **3** They are all gone into the world of light, / And I alone sit lingering here.
> [*Silex Scintillans*, 'They Are All Gone']

> **4** I saw Eternity the other night, / Like a great ring of pure and endless light. [*Silex Scintillans*, 'The World']

VAUVENARGUES Marquis de 1715–1747
French moralist.

> Most people grow old within a small circle of ideas, which they have not discovered for themselves. There are perhaps fewer wrong-minded people than thoughtless. [*Réflexions et Maximes* no. 238]

VEBLEN Thorstein 1857–1929
US social critic.

> Conspicuous consumption of valuable goods is a means of reputability to the gentleman of leisure. [*Theory of the Leisure Class*]

VEGETIUS 4TH–5TH CENTURY AD
Roman military writer.

> Let him who desires peace, prepare for war. [*De Re Militare*]

VICTORIA 1819–1901
Queen of Great Britain and Ireland.

> **1** We are not amused. [*Notebooks of a Spinster Lady* 2 Jan 1900]

> **2** He speaks to Me as if I was a public meeting. [*Remark about her prime minister Gladstone*]

VIDAL Gore 1925–
US writer and critic.

> **1** It is the spirit of the age to believe that any fact, no matter how suspect, is superior to any imaginative exercise, no matter how true. [*Encounter* Dec 1967]

> **2** A triumph of the embalmer's art. [Describing Ronald Reagan, *Observer* 26 Apr 1981]

> **3** Democracy is supposed to give you the feeling of choice, like Painkiller X and Painkiller Y. But they're both just aspirin. [Interview in *Observer* 7 Feb 1982]

> **4** There is something about a bureaucrat that does not like a poem. [*Sex, Death and Money*, preface]

> **5** I can understand companionship. I can understand bought sex in the afternoon. I cannot understand the love affair. [Quoted in *Sunday Times* 1973]

VIDOR King 1895–1982
US film director.

> Take it from me, marriage isn't a word ... it's a *sentence*! [*The Crowd* 1928 film]

VILLIERS George 1627–1687
English courtier and author.

> **1** What the devil does the plot signify, except to bring in fine things? [*The Rehearsal* III. i]

2 Ay, now the plot thickens very much upon us. [*The Rehearsal* III. ii]

VILLON François 1431–1465
French poet.

But where are the snows of yesteryear? ['Ballade des dames du temps jadis']

VIORST Judith 1931–
US writer.

Love is much nicer to be in than an automobile accident, a tight girdle, a higher tax bracket or a holding pattern over Philadelphia. [*Redbook*, 'What IS This Thing Called Love?']

VIRGIL 70–19 BC
Roman poet.

1 Arms and the man I sing. [*Aeneid* I]

2 A mind conscious of right. [*Aeneid* I]

3 Tears in the nature of thing. [*Aeneid* I]

4 A woman is always fickle and changeful. [*Aeneid* IV]

5 Easy is the descent to Avernus! [*Aeneid* VI]

6 Hence, hence, ... uninitiated! [*Aeneid* VI]

7 Roman, this is your task – these your arts – to hold sway over the nations and to impose the law of peace, to spare the humbled and to quell the proud! [*Aeneid* VI]

8 Everyone is dragged on by their favourite pleasure. [*Eclogues* I]

9 Love conquers all things; let us too surrender to Love. [*Eclogues* X]

10 Meanwhile, Time is flying – flying, never to return. [*Georgics*]

VIZINCZEY Stephen 1933–
Hungarian novelist and critic.

Consistency is a virtue for trains: what we want from a philosopher is insights, whether he comes by them consistently or not. [*Sunday Telegraph* 21 April 1974]

VOLTAIRE François 1694–1778
French writer.

1 If we do not find anything pleasant, at least we shall find something new. [*Candide* ch 17]

2 In this country [England] it is thought well to kill an admiral from time to time to encourage the others. [*Candide* ch 23]

3 'That is well said,' replied Candide, 'but we must cultivate our garden.' [*Candide* ch 30]

4 If God did not exist, it would be necessary to invent him. [*Épîtres*]

5 It is said that God is always for the big battalions. [Letter to A M le Riche 6 Feb 1770]

VONNEGUT Kurt, Jr. 1922–
US writer.

God grant me the serenity to accept the things I cannot change, courage to change the things I can, and wisdom always to tell the difference. [*Slaughterhouse Five*]

WAGNER Richard 1813–1883
German opera composer.

Where the speech of men stops short, then the art of music begins. [*Happy Evening*]

WAITE Terry 1939–
Envoy to the Archbishop of Canterbury.

Politics come from man. Mercy, compassion and justice come from God. [Quoted in *Observer* 13 Jan 1985]

WALLACE Edgar 1875–1932
English writer of thrillers.

What is a highbrow? He is a man who has found something more interesting than women. [*New York Times* 24 Jan 1932]

WALLACE George 1919–
US politician.

Segregation now, segregation tomorrow and segregation forever! [Inaugural speech as Governor of Alabama Jan 1963]

WALLACE Henry 1888–1965
US editor and public official.

The century on which we are entering – the century which will come out of this war – can be and must be the century of the common man. [Speech 8 May 1942]

WALLER Edmund 1606–1687
English poet.

1 Go, lovely Rose! / Tell her, that wastes her time and me, / That now she knows, / When I resemble her to thee, / How sweet and fair she seems to be. ['Go, Lovely Rose!']

German opera composer Richard Wagner. Wagner's conception of 'music drama' led him to abolish many aspects of the classical structure of opera and to introduce new devices, for example, recurring musical themes (leitmotifs) which mark the presence of characters or dramatic themes. In Bayreuth, Bavaria, he created his own theatre, the Festspielhaus, where he could ensure the unity of music, drama, and setting that he considered essential.

2 It is not that I love you less / Than when before your feet I lay: / But, to prevent the sad increase / Of hopeless love, I keep away. In vain, alas! for every thing / Which I have known belong to you, / Your form does to my fancy bring / And makes my old wounds bleed anew. ['Self-Banished']

WALPOLE Horace, Lord 1717–1797
English novelist, letter writer, and politician.

1 The balance of power. [Speech in House of Commons 1741]

2 Our supreme governors, the mob. [Letter to Horace Mann 1743]

3 My Lord Denbigh is going to marry a fortune, I forget her name; my Lord Gower asked him how long the honey-moon would last? He replied, 'Don't tell me of the honey-moon; it is harvest moon with me.' [Letter to George Montagu, 19 May 1756]

4 Everybody talks of the constitution, but all sides forget that the constitution is extremely well, and would do very well, if they would but let it alone. [Letter to Sir Horace Mann 18–19 Jan 1770]

5 This world is a comedy to those that think, a tragedy to those that feel. [Letter to the Countess of Upper Ossory 1776]

6 Prognostics do not always prove prophecies, – at least the wisest prophets make sure of the event first. [Letter to Thomas Walpole 19 Feb 1785]

WALPOLE Robert, Lord 1676–1745
British prime minister.

1 My Lord Bath, you and I are now two as insignificant men as any in England. [Quoted in W. King *Literary Anecdotes*]

2 They now *ring* the bells, but they will soon *wring* their hands. [Remark when war against Spain was declared 1739.]

WALSH William 1663–1708
English poet.

1 A lover forsaken / A new love may get, / But a neck when once broken / Can never be set. ['Despairing Lover']

2 Of all the plagues a lover bears, / Sure rivals are the worst. ['Song']

WALTON Izaak 1593–1683
English author.

1 I am, Sir, a Brother of the Angle. [*Compleat Angler* ch 1]

2 I love such mirth as does not make friends ashamed to look upon one another next morning. [*Compleat Angler* ch 5]

3 Look to your health; and if you have it, praise God, and value it next to a good conscience. [*Compleat Angler* ch 21]

4 The great Secretary of Nature and all learning, Sir Francis Bacon. [*Life of Herbert*]

WARD Artemus 1834–1867
US humorist and writer.

1 My pollertics, like my religion, bein of a exceedin accommodatin character. [*Artemus Ward His Book*, 'The Crisis']

2 The ground flew up and hit me in the hed. [*Artemus Ward His Book*, 'Thrilling Scenes in Dixie']

3 I am happiest when I am idle. I could live for months without performing any kind of labour, and at the expiration of that time I should feel fresh and vigorous enough to go right on in the same way for numerous more months. [*Pyrotechny* III]

4 Why care for grammar as long as we are good? [*Pyrotechny* V]

5 Let us all be happy, and live within our means, even if we have to borrer the money to do it with. [*Science and Natural History*]

WARHOL Andy 1928–1987
US Pop artist and filmmaker.

1 In the future everyone will be famous for 15 minutes. [*Exposures*]

2 Being born is like being kidnapped. And then sold into slavery. [*From A to B and Back Again* ch 6]

WASHINGTON George 1732–1799
First US president.

Father, I cannot tell a lie. [Attributed remark]

George Washington. Having turned an ill-assorted militia into an army that finally defeated the British, General Washington became the first president of the USA 1789–97. As president he helped to build a strong central government, establishing a national bank and a federal judiciary, and sought to remain neutral despite the development of political parties.

WATKYNS Rowland c. 1616–1664
English poet.

> For every marriage then is best in tune, / When that the wife is May, the husband June. ['To the most Courteous and Fair Gentlewoman, Mrs Elinor Williams']

WATTS Isaac 1674–1748
English Nonconformist writer of hymns.

> **1** How doth the little busy bee / Improve each shining hour. [*Divine Songs for Children*, 'Against Idleness and Mischief']

2 In works of labour, or of skill, / I would be busy too; / For Satan finds some mischief still / For idle hands to do. [*Divine Songs for Children*, 'Against Idleness and Mischief']

3 Let dogs delight to bark and bite, / For God hath made them so. [*Divine Songs for Children*, 'Against Quarrelling']

4 'Tis the voice of the sluggard; I heard him complain, / 'You have wak'd me too soon, I must slumber again'. [*Moral Songs*, 'The Sluggard']

WAUGH Evelyn 1903–1966
English novelist.

1 Any who have heard that sound will shrink at the recollection of it; it is the sound of English county families baying for broken glass. [*Decline and Fall*, 'Prelude']

2 I expect you'll be becoming a schoolmaster, sir. That's what most of the gentlemen does, sir, that gets sent down for indecent behaviour. [*Decline and Fall*, 'Prelude']

3 'But you married?' 'Yes, mum. but it was in the war, and he was very drunk.' [*Decline and Fall* pt 2 ch 5]

4 Any one who has been to an English public school will always feel comparatively at home in prison. [*Decline and Fall* pt 3, ch 4]

5 Manners are especially the need of the plain. The pretty can get away with anything. [*Observer* 15 Apr 1962]

6 Mr Salter's side of the conversation was limited to expressions of assent. When Lord Copper was right, he said, 'Definitely, Lord Copper'; when he was wrong, 'Up to a point'. [*Scoop*]

7 Brideshead Revisited. [Title of novel]

WAVELL 1st Earl 1883–1950
English soldier.

> It is like a cigar. If it goes out, you can light it again but it never tastes quite the same. [Definition of love. Attributed remark.]

WAYNE John 1907–1979
US film actor.

1 I'm fifty-three years old and six feet four. I've had three wives, five children and three grandchildren. I love good whiskey. I still don't understand women, and I don't think there is any man who does. [Remark 1960]

2 They have a right to work wherever they want to – as long as they have dinner ready when you get home. [On liberated women. Attributed remark]

WEBB Beatrice 1858–1943
English socialist and writer.

If I ever felt inclined to be timid as I was going into a room full of people, I would say to myself, 'You're the cleverest member of one of the cleverest families in the cleverest class of the cleverest nation in the world, why should you be frightened?'. [Quoted in Bertrand Russell *Autobiography*]

WEBER Max 1864–1920
German sociologist.

The idea of duty in one's calling prowls about in our life like the ghost of dead religious beliefs. [*The Protestant Ethic*]

WEBSTER John c. 1580–1625
English dramatist.

1 Women like that part which, like the lamprey, / Hath never a bone in't. ... / I mean the tongue; variety of courtship; / What cannot a neat knave with a smooth tale / Make a woman believe? [*Duchess of Malfi* I. i]

2 Is not old wine wholesomest, old pippins toothsomest, old wood burn brightest, old linen wash whitest? Old soldiers, sweethearts are surest, and old lovers are soundest. [*Westward Hoe* II. ii]

WEIL Simone 1909–1943
French philosopher and mystic.

1 An atheist may be simply one whose faith and love are concentrated on the impersonal aspects of God. [Quoted by W H Auden, *A Certain World*, 'God']

2 The real stumbling-block of totalitarian regimes is not the spiritual need of men for freedom of thought; it is men's inability to stand the physical and nervous strain of a permanent state of excitement, except during a few years of their youth. ['Cold War Policy in 1939']

3 All sins are attempts to fill voids. [*Gravity and Grace*]

4 The most important part of teaching = to teach what it is to *know*. [*London Notebook*]

5 Charity. To love human beings in so far as they are nothing. That is to love them as God does. ['New York Notebook']

6 Nothing can have as its destination anything other than its origin. The contrary idea, the idea of progress, is poison. ['New York Notebook']

7 To write the lives of the great in separating them from their works necessarily ends by above all stressing their pettiness, because it is in their work that they have put the best of themselves. ['Otto Rühle: Karl Marx' in *La Critique Sociale* March 1934]

8 In the Church, considered as a social organism, the mysteries invariably degenerate into beliefs. [Quoted in McLellan, *Simone Weil: Utopian Pessimist* ch 9]

9 Evil is neither suffering nor sin ... it is something common to them both. ... Sin makes us suffer and suffering makes us evil, and this indissoluble complex of suffering and sin is the evil in which we are submerged against our will, and to our horror. ['Some Thoughts on the Love of God' Oct 1940–May 1942]

10 God's mercy is manifest in affliction as in joy. [*Waiting on God*]

WELCH Raquel 1940–
US actress.

Being a sex symbol was rather like being a convict. [Quoted in *Observer* 25 Feb 1979]

WELDON Fay 1931–
English novelist and TV screenwriter.

Men are so romantic, don't you think? They look for a perfect partner when what they should be looking for is perfect love. [Quoted in *Sunday Times* 6 Sept 1987]

WELLES Orson 1915–1985
US actor and film and theatre director.

This is the biggest electric train set any boy ever had! [Of the RKO studio, quoted in P Noble *The Fabulous Orson Welles*]

WELLS H G 1866–1946
English writer.

1 Miss Madeleine Philips was making it very manifest to Captain Douglas that she herself was a career; that a lover with any other career in view need not – as the advertisements say – apply. [*Bealby* pt 5, ch 5]

2 If Max gets to Heaven he won't last long. He will be chucked out for trying to pull off a merger between Heaven and Hell ... after having secured a controlling interest in key subsidiary companies in both places, of course. [Of Max Beaverbrook, quoted in A J P Taylor *Beaverbrook*]

3 After all, the rosy love-making and marrying and Epithalamy are no more than the dawn of things ... Try as we may to stay those delightful moments they fade and pass remorselessly ... We go on – we grow. At least we age. [*Love and Mr Lewisham*]

Orson Welles as Harry Lime in *The Third Man* 1949. By his mid-twenties Welles had established himself as an outstanding director, writer, and actor with his first film *Citizen Kane*, an influential film widely accepted as a classic. As an actor he appeared most memorably – though briefly – in Carol Reed's *The Third Man*.

4 Human history becomes more and more a race between education and catastrophe. [*Outline of History*]

5 I sometimes think that if Adam and Eve had been merely engaged, she would not have talked with the serpent; and the world had been saved an infinity of misery. [*Select Conversations with an Uncle*]

6 Bricklayers kick their wives to death, and dukes betray theirs; but it is among the small clerks and shopkeepers nowadays that it comes most often to the cutting of throats. [*Short Stories*, 'Purple Pileus']

7 In England we have come to rely upon a comfortable time-lag of fifty years or a century intervening between the perception that something ought to be done and a serious attempt to do it. [*Work, Wealth and Happiness of Mankind*]

8 It is possible to believe that all the human mind has accomplished is but the dream before the awakening. [Lecture, the Royal Institute, London, 24 Jan 1902]

9 The Shape of Things to Come. [Book title]

10 The War that Will End War. [Book title]

WESLEY John 1703–1791
English Methodist preacher.

Beware you be not swallowed up in books! An ounce of love is worth a pound of knowledge. [Quoted in R Southey *Life of Wesley* ch 16]

WEST Mae 1892–1980
US vaudeville, stage, and film actress.

1 A man in the house is worth two in the street. [As Ruby Carter in *Belle of the Nineties*]

2 Give a man a free hand and he'll try to put it all over you. [As Frisco Doll in *Klondike Annie*]

3 Too many girls follow the line of least resistance – but a good line is hard to resist. [As Frisco Doll in *Klondike Annie*]

4 Brains are an asset to the woman in love who's smart enough to hide 'em. [Quoted in J Weintraub *Peel Me a Grape*]

5 Don't marry a man to reform him – that's what reform schools are for. [Quoted in J Weintraub *Peel Me a Grape*]

6 Gentlemen may prefer blondes – but who says that blondes prefer gentlemen? [Quoted in J Weintraub *Peel Me a Grape*]

7 Is that a gun in your pocket, or are you just glad to see me? [Quoted in J Weintraub *Peel Me a Grape*]

8 It's not the men in my life that counts – it's the life in my men. [Quoted in J Weintraub *Peel Me a Grape*]

9 Love is the only industry which can't operate on a five-day week. [Quoted in J Weintraub *Peel Me a Grape*]

11 Love thy neighbour – and if he happens to be tall, debonair and devastating, it will be that much easier. [Quoted in J Weintraub *Peel Me a Grape*]

12 Marriage is a great institution. No family should be without it. [Quoted in J Weintraub *Peel Me a Grape*]

13 Men admire devotion in their wives – beauty in other women. [Quoted in J Weintraub *Peel Me a Grape*]

14 Opportunity knocks for every man, but you have to give a woman a ring. [Quoted in J Weintraub *Peel Me a Grape*]

15 Some women pick men to marry – and others pick them to pieces. [Quoted in J Weintraub *Peel Me a Grape*]

16 A woman in love can't be reasonable – or she probably wouldn't be in love. [Quoted in J Weintraub *Peel Me a Grape*]

WEST Rebecca 1892–1983
English journalist, novelist, and feminist.

1 Journalism – an ability to meet the challenge of filling the space. [*New York Herald Tribune* 22 Apr 1956]

2 There is no such thing as conversation. It is an illusion. There are intersecting monologues, that is all. [*There Is No Conversation*, 'The Harsh Voice' 1]

3 Peculiar mathematics ... apply to many cases of desertion. A woman who loses her husband or her lover seems to lose more by his absence than she ever gained by his presence. [*Times Literary Supplement* 26 July 1974]

WHARTON Edith 1862–1937
US novelist.

1 An unalterable and unquestioned law of the musical world required that the German text of French operas sung by Swedish artists should be translated into Italian for the clearer understanding of English-speaking audiences. [*Age of Innocence*]

2 Mrs. Ballinger is one of the ladies who pursue Culture in bands, as though it were dangerous to meet it alone. [*Xingu*]

WHATELY Richard 1787–1863
English churchman.

1 Happiness is no laughing matter. [*Apophthegms*]

2 It is a folly to expect men to do all that they may reasonably be expected to do. [*Apophthegms*]

WHITE E B 1899–1985
US writer and editor.

1 One of the most time-consuming things is to have an enemy. [*Essays of E. B. White*, 'A Report in January']

2 Commuters give the city its tidal restlessness; natives give it solidity and continuity; but the settlers give it passion. ['Here is New York', in *Holiday* April 1949]

3 Democracy is the recurrent suspicion that more than half of the people are right more than half of the time. [*New Yorker* 3 July 1944]

WHITE Patrick 1912–1990
Australian writer.

Inspiration descends only in flashes, to clothe circumstances; it is not stored up in a barrel, like salt herrings, to be doled out. [*Voss*]

WHITE T H 1906–1964
English writer.

The Once and Future King. [Title of novel]

WHITEHEAD Alfred North 1861–1947
English philosopher and mathematician.

1 Unfortunately, life is an offensive, directed against the repetitious mechanism of the Universe. [*Adventures of Ideas* ch 5]

2 Intelligence is quickness to apprehend as distinct from ability, which is capacity to act wisely on the thing apprehended. [*Dialogues* 15 Dec 1939]

3 Civilization advances by extending the number of important operations which we can perform without thinking about them. [*Introduction to Mathematics*]

4 Philosophy is the product of wonder. [*Nature and Life* ch 1]

WHITEHEAD William 1715–1785
English poet and dramatist.

Yes, I'm in love, I feel it now / And Caelia has undone me; / And yet I swear I can't tell how / The pleasing plague stole on me. ['Je ne sçay quoi song']

WHITEHORN Katharine 1926–
English writer and journalist.

My brother cuts the time it takes to read a newspaper by skipping everything in the future tense; and it's amazing what he doesn't miss. ['Never-Never Land']

WHITMAN Walt 1819–1892
US poet.

1 The institution of the dear love of comrades. ['I Hear it was Charged against Me']

2 Out of the cradle endlessly rocking, / Out of the mocking-bird's throat, the musical shuttle, / A reminiscence sing. ['Out of the Cradle Endlessly Rocking']

3 Behold, I do not give lectures or a little charity, / When I give I give myself. ['Song of Myself']

4 Do I contradict myself? Very well then I contradict myself (I am large, I contain multitudes). ['Song of Myself']

5 I celebrate myself, and sing myself. ['Song of Myself']

6 The look of the bay mare shames silliness out of me. ['Song of Myself']

WHITTON Charlotte 1896–1975
Canadian writer and politician.

Whatever women do they must do twice as well as men to be thought half as good. Luckily, this is not difficult. [*Canada Month* June 1963]

WHURR Cornelius LIVED C. 1835–1855
English poet.

What lasting joys the man attend / Who has a polished female friend. ['Accomplished Female Friend']

WILDE Oscar 1856–1900
Irish writer.

1 I never saw a man who looked / With such a wistful eye / Upon that little tent of blue / Which prisoners call the sky. [*Ballad of Reading Gaol*]

2 Yet each man kills the thing he loves, ... / The coward does it with a kiss, / The brave man with a sword! [*Ballad of Reading Gaol*]

3 When you really want love, you will find it waiting for you. [*De Profundis*]

4 All women become like their mothers. That is their tragedy. No man does. That's his. [*Importance of Being Earnest* I]

5 The amount of women in London who flirt with their own husbands is perfectly scandalous. It looks so bad. It is simply washing one's clean linen in public. [*Importance of Being Earnest* I]

6 In married life three is company and two none. [*Importance of Being Earnest* I]

7 The chapter on the Fall of the Rupee you may omit. It is somewhat too sensational. [*Importance of Being Earnest* II]

8 On an occasion of this kind it becomes more than a moral duty to speak one's mind. It becomes a pleasure. [*Importance of Being Earnest* II]

9 No woman should ever be quite accurate about her age. It looks so calculating. [*Importance of Being Earnest* IV]

10 Experience is the name every one gives to their mistakes. [*Lady Windermere's Fan*]

11 A man who knows the price of everything and the value of nothing. [*Lady Windermere's Fan*, definition of a cynic]

12 It is only shallow people who do not judge by appearances. The true mystery of the world is the visible, not the invisible. [*Picture of Dorian Gray*]

13 A man cannot be too careful in the choice of his enemies. [*Picture of Dorian Gray*]

14 The only way to get rid of a temptation is to yield to it. [*Picture of Dorian Gray*]

15 There is a luxury in self-reproach. When we blame ourselves we feel no one else has a right to blame us. [*Picture of Dorian Gray*]

16 There is no such thing as a moral or an immoral book. Books are well written, or badly written. [*Picture of Dorian Gray*]

17 There is only one thing in the world worse than being talked about, and that is not being talked about. [*Picture of Dorian Gray*]

18 Those who are faithful know only the trivial side of love: it is the faithless who know love's tragedies. [*Picture of Dorian Gray*]

19 When a woman marries again it is because she detested her first husband. When a man marries again, it is because he adored his first wife. Women try their luck; men risk theirs. [*Picture of Dorian Gray*]

20 A thing is not necessarily true because a man dies for it. [*Sebastian Melmoth*]

21 The public .... degrade the classics into authorities. They use them as bludgeons for preventing the free expression of Beauty in new forms. ['Soul of Man under Socialism', *Fortnightly Review* Feb 1891]

22 I have found that all ugly things are made by those who strive to make something beautiful, and that all beautiful things are made by those who strive to make something useful. [*Value of Art in Modern Life*]

23 One should never trust a woman who tells one her real age. A woman who would tell one that, would tell one anything. [*Woman of No Importance*]

24 Twenty years of romance make a woman look like a ruin; but twenty years of marriage make her something like a public building. [*Woman of No Importance* I]

25 Men always want to be a woman's first love. That is their clumsy vanity. We women have a more subtle instinct about things. What we like is to be a man's last romance. [*Woman of No Importance* II]

26 I have nothing to declare except my genius. [Remark at the New York Customs House]

WILDER Billy 1906–
US film director.

I've met a lot of hardboiled eggs in my time, but you're twenty minutes. [*Ace in the Hole*]

WILDER Thornton 1897–1975
US dramatist and novelist.

1 Marriage is a bribe to make a housekeeper think she's a householder. [*Merchant of Yonkers*]

2 The fights are the best part of married life. The rest is merely so-so. [*Merchant of Yonkers* II]

3 A man looks pretty small at a wedding, George. All those good women standing shoulder to shoulder, making sure that the knot's tied in a mighty public way. [*Our Town* II]

4 Most everybody in the world climbs into their graves married. [*Our Town* II]

5 The comic spirit is given to us in order that we may analyze, weigh, and clarify things in us which nettle us, or which we are outgrowing, or trying to reshape. [Interview in Cowley *Writers at Work*, 1st Series]

WILKES John 1727–1797
British Radical politician.

The chapter of accidents is the longest chapter in the book. [Attributed remark]

WILLANS AND SEARLE Geoffrey Willans 1911–1958 and Ronald Searle 1920–
English writer and cartoonist.

The only good things about skool are the boys wizz who are noble brave fearless etc. although you hav various swots, bulies, cissies, milksops, greedy guts and oiks with whom i am forced to mingle hemhem. [*Down With Skool*]

WILLIAM III 1650–1702
King of Great Britain and Ireland.

> **1** I will die in the last ditch. [Quoted in Hume *History of Great Britain*]
>
> **2** Every bullet has its billet. [Quoted in John Wesley *Journal* 6 June 1765]

WILLIAMS Kenneth 1926–1987
British actor.

> I am not conceited. It is just that I have a fondness for the good things in life and I happen to be one of them. [In a TV interview]

WILLIAMS Tennessee 1914–1983
US dramatist.

> **1** It is almost as if you were frantically constructing another world while the world that you live in dissolves beneath your feet, and that your survival depends on completing this construction at least one second before the old habitation collapses. [*Camino Real*, Author's Foreword]
>
> **2** We're all of us guinea pigs in the laboratory of God. Humanity is just a work in progress. [*Camino Real*]
>
> **3** In memory everything seems to happen to music. [*The Glass Menagerie* 1]

WILLIAMS William Carlos 1883–1963
US poet.

> Liquor and love / rescue the cloudy sense / banish its despair / give it a home. ['World Narrowed to a Point']

WILLIAMSON Marianne 1953–
US benefactor.

> God is definitely out of the closet. [Quoted in *Vanity Fair* June 1991]

WILMOT John, Earl of Rochester 1647–1680
English poet.

> Love ... / That cordial drop heaven in our cup has thrown / To make the nauseous draught of life go down. ['Letter from Artemisia in the Town to Chloe in the Country']

WILSON Sandy 1924–
English songwriter.

> **1** We've got to have / We plot to have / For it's so dreary not to have / That certain thing called the Boy Friend. [*The Boyfriend*]
>
> **2** It's never too late to have a fling, / For Autumn is just as nice as Spring, / And it's never too late to fall in love. ['It's Never too Late to Fall in Love']

WILSON Woodrow 1856–1924
US Democratic president.

> **1** Democracy is not so much a form of government as a set of principles. [*Atlantic Monthly* March 1901]
>
> **2** The world must be made safe for democracy. [Address to Congress 2 Apr 1917]

WINTERS Shelley 1922–
US film actress.

> In Hollywood all marriages are happy. It's trying to live together afterwards that causes the problems. [Attributed remark]

WISTER Owen 1860–1938
US novelist.

> When you call me that, smile! [*The Virginian*]

WITHER George 1588–1667
English poet and pamphleteer.

> **1** Shall I, wasting in despair, / Die because a woman's fair? ['Sonnet']
>
> **2** If she love me, this believe, / I will die ere she shall grieve; / If she slight me when I woo; / I can scorn and let her go; / For if she be not for me, / What care I for whom she be? ['Lover's Resolution']

WITTGENSTEIN Ludwig 1889–1951
Austrian philosopher.

1 Philosophy ... is a fight against the fascination which forms of expression exert upon us. [*Blue Book*]

2 If a lion could talk, we could not understand him. [*Philosophical Investigations*]

3 It is not *how* things are in the world that is mystical, but *that* it exists. [*Tractatus Logico-Philosophicus*]

4 The limits of my language mean the limits of my world. [*Tractatus Logico-Philosophicus*]

5 The world is everything that is the case. [*Tractatus Logico-Philosophicus*]

WODEHOUSE P G 1881–1975
English novelist.

1 Chumps always makes the best husbands. When you marry, Sally, grab a chump. Tap his forehead first, and if it rings solid, don't hesitate. All the unhappy marriages come from the husbands having brains. [*Adventures of Sally*]

2 What good are brains to a man? They only unsettle him. [*Adventures of Sally*]

3 He spoke with a certain what-is-it in his voice, and I could see that, if not actually disgruntled, he was far from being gruntled. [*Code of the Woosters*]

4 It is no use telling me that there are bad aunts and good aunts. At the core, they are all alike. Sooner or later, out pops the cloven hoof. [*Code of the Woosters*]

5 Slice him where you like, a hell-hound is always a hellhound. [*Code of the Woosters*]

6 The Right Hon. was a tubby little chap who looked as if he had been poured into his clothes and had forgotten to say 'When!'. ['Jeeves and the Impending Doom']

Austrian-born philosopher Ludwig Wittgenstein who had a profound influence on the development of 20th-century British and American philosophy. Though his early and late philosophies differ radically, they are both based on a concern with the relationship between language, thought, and reality.

7 I was in rare fettle and the heart had touched a new high. I don't know anything that braces one up like finding you haven't got to get married after all. [*Jeeves in the Offing*]

8 Judges, as a class, display, in the matter of arranging alimony, that reckless generosity that is found only in men who are giving away someone else's cash. [*Louder and Funnier*]

9 Like so many substantial Americans, he had married young and kept on marrying, springing from blonde to blonde like the chamois of the Alps leaping from crag to crag. [Quoted in Richard Usborne *Wodehouse at Work to the End* ch 2]

WOLFE Charles 1791–1823
Irish curate.

> **1** Not a drum was heard, not a funeral note, / As his corse to the rampart we hurried. ['Burial of Sir John Moore at Corunna']

> **2** We carved not a line, and we raised not a stone – / But we left him alone with his glory. ['Burial of Sir John Moore at Corunna']

WOLFE Humbert 1886–1940
English poet.

> You cannot hope to bribe or twist, thank God! the British journalist. / But, seeing what the man will do unbribed, there's no occasion to. ['Over the Fire']

WOLFE Thomas 1900–1939
US novelist.

> There is no spectacle on earth more appealing than that of a beautiful woman in the act of cooking dinner for someone she loves. [*Web and the Rock*]

WOLLSTONECRAFT Mary 1759–1797
English feminist and writer.

> **1** The *divine right* of husbands, like the divine right of kings, may, it is hoped, in this enlightened age, be contested without danger. [*Vindication of the Rights of Woman* ch 3]

> **2** I do not wish them [women] to have power over men; but over themselves. [*Vindication of the Rights of Woman* ch 4]

WOLSEY Thomas c. 1475–1530
English cleric and politician.

> **1** Father Abbot, I am come to lay my bones amongst you. [Quoted in G Cavendish *Negotiations of Thomas Wolsey*]

> **2** Had I but served God as diligently as I have served the king, he would not have given me over in my gray hairs. [Quoted in G Cavendish *Negotiations of Thomas Wolsey*]

WOOLF Virginia 1882–1941
English novelist and critic.

> **1** The poet gives us his essence, but prose takes the mould of the body and mind entire. [*Captain's Death Bed* 'Reading']

> **2** We are nauseated by the sight of trivial personalities decomposing in the eternity of print. [*Common Reader*, 'The Modern Essay']

> **3** I don't believe in ageing. I believe in forever altering one's aspect to the sun. Hence my optimism. [*Diary of Virginia Woolf* vol 4, 2 Oct 1932]

> **4** Rigid, the skeleton of habit alone upholds the human frame. [*Mrs Dalloway*]

Novelist and essayist Virginia Woolf, one of the major English writers of the 20th century. She developed an experimental fiction, using her 'stream of consciousness' technique to capture the subtle, ceaseless flow of everyday experience. In several influential essays she argued that women had to develop their own form of fiction.

5 It is in our idleness, in our dreams, that the submerged truth sometimes comes to the top. [*Room of One's Own*]

6 Women have served all these centuries as looking-glasses possessing the magic and delicious power of reflecting the figure of a man at twice its natural size. [*Room of One's Own*]

WOOLLCOTT Alexander 1887–1943
US theatre critic and literary figure.

1 A broker is a man who takes your fortune and runs it into a shoestring. [Quoted in S H Adams *Alexander Woollcott*]

2 All the things I really like to do are either illegal, immoral, or fattening. [Quoted in R E Drennan *Wit's End*]

WORDSWORTH Elizabeth 1840–1932
Principal of Lady Margaret Hall, Oxford.

If all the good people were clever, / And all clever people were good, / The world would be nicer than ever / We thought that it possibly could. / But somehow, 'tis seldom or never / The two hit it off as they should; / The good are so harsh to the clever, / The clever so rude to the good! [*St Christopher and Other Poems*]

WORDSWORTH William 1770–1850
English Romantic poet.

1 For oft, when on my couch I lie / In vacant or in pensive mood, / They flash upon that inward eye / Which is the bliss of solitude; / And then my heart with pleasure fills, / And dances with the daffodils. ['Daffodils']

2 I wandered lonely as a cloud / That floats on high o'er vales and hills, / When all at once I saw a crowd, / A host, of golden daffodils; / Beside the lake, beneath the trees, / Fluttering and dancing in the breeze. ['Daffodils']

3 Never to blend our pleasure or our pride / With sorrow of the meanest thing that feels. ['Hart-leap Well']

4 I have learned / To look on nature not as in the hour / Of thoughtless youth; but hearing often-times / The still, sad music of humanity, / Nor harsh nor grating, though of ample power / To chasten and subdue. And I have felt / A presence that disturbs me with the joy / Of elevated thoughts; a sense sublime / Of something far more deeply interfused, / Whose dwelling is the light of setting suns, / And the round ocean and the living air, / And the blue sky, and in the mind of man. ['Lines Composed a Few Miles above Tintern Abbey']

5 That best portion of a good man's life, / His little, nameless, unremembered acts / Of kindness and of love. ['Lines Composed a Few Miles above Tintern Abbey']

6 And much it grieved my heart to think / What man has made of man. ['Lines Written in Early Spring']

7 There is a comfort in the strength of love; / 'Twill make a thing endurable, which else / Would overset the brain, or break the heart. ['Michael']

8 Milton! thou shouldst be living at this hour: / England hath need of thee; she is a fen / Of stagnant waters. ['Milton! Thou Shouldst Be Living at This Hour']

9 My heart leaps up when I behold / A rainbow in the sky. ['My Heart Leaps Up']

10 Nuns fret not at their convent's narrow room; / And hermits are contented with their cells. ['Nuns Fret Not']

11 There was a time when meadow, grove, and stream, / The earth, and every common sight, / To me did seem / Apparelled in celestial light, / The glory and the freshness of a dream. / It is not now as it hath been of yore; – / Turn whereso'er I may, / By night or day, / The things which I have seen I now can see no more. [*Ode. Intimations of Immortality* i]

12   The rainbow comes and goes, / And lovely is the rose, / The moon doth with delight / Look round her when the heavens are bare, / Waters on a starry night / Are beautiful and fair; / The sunshine is a glorious birth: / But yet I know, where'er I go, / That there hath passed away a glory from the earth. [*Ode. Intimations of Immortality* ii]

13   Whither is fled the visionary gleam? / Where is it now, the glory and the dream? [*Ode. Intimations of Immortality* iv]

14   Our birth is but a sleep and a forgetting: / The Soul that rises with us, our life's Star, / Hath had elsewhere its setting, / And cometh from afar: / Not in entire forgetfulness, / And not in utter nakedness, / But trailing clouds of glory do we come / From God, who is our home: / Heaven lies about us in our infancy! / Shades of the prison-house begin to close / Upon the growing boy, / But he beholds the light, and whence it flows, / He sees it in his joy; / The youth, who daily farther from the east / Must travel, still is Nature's priest, / And by the vision splendid / Is on his way attended; / At length the man perceives it die away, / And fade into the light of common day. [*Ode. Intimations of Immortality* v]

15   Though nothing can bring back the hour / Of splendour in the grass, of glory in the flower; / We will grieve not, rather find / Strength in what remains behind. [*Ode. Intimations of Immortality* ix]

16   Thanks to the human heart by which we live, / Thanks to its tenderness, its joys, and fears, / To me the meanest flower that blows can give / Thoughts that do often lie too deep for tears. [*Ode. Intimations of Immortality* xi]

17   Once did she hold the gorgeous East in fee, / And was the safeguard of the West. ['On the Extinction of the Venetian Republic']

18   Where the statue stood / Of Newton, with his prism and silent face, / The marble index of a mind for ever / Voyaging through strange seas of thought alone. [*Prelude* III. 61]

19   Sweet Spenser, moving through his clouded heaven / With the moon's beauty and the moon's soft pace. [*Prelude* III. 280]

20   Bliss was it in that dawn to be alive, / But to be young was very heaven! [*Prelude* XI]

21   I thought of Chatterton, the marvellous boy, / The sleepless soul, that perished in his pride. ['Resolution and Independence']

22   She dwelt among the untrodden ways / Beside the springs of Dove, / A maid whom there were none to praise / And very few to love: / A violet by a mossy stone / Half hidden from the eye! / Fair as a star, when only one / Is shining in the sky. / She lived unknown, and few could know / When Lucy ceased to be; / But she is in her grave, and, oh, / The difference to me! ['She Dwelt Among the Untrodden Ways']

23   A slumber did my spirit seal; / I had no human fears: / She seemed a thing that could not feel / The touch of earthly years. ['A Slumber Did My Spirit Seal']

24   Behold her, single in the field, / Yon solitary Highland lass! ['Solitary Reaper']

25   Perhaps the plaintive numbers flow / For old, unhappy, far-off things, / And battles long ago. ['Solitary Reaper']

26   She gave me eyes, she gave me ears; / And humble cares, and delicate fears; / A heart, the fountain of sweet tears; / And love, and thought, and joy. ['Sparrow's Nest']

27 One impulse from a vernal wood / May teach you more of man, / Of moral evil and of good, / Than all the sages can. ['Tables Turned']

28 Two Voices are there; one is of the sea, / One of the mountains; each a mighty Voice. ['Thought of a Briton on the Subjugation of Switzerland']

29 O Cuckoo! Shall I call thee bird, / Or but a wandering voice? ['To the Cuckoo']

30 The world is too much with us; late and soon, / Getting and spending, we lay waste our powers. ['The World is Too Much with Us']

31 Plain living and high thinking are no more. ['Written in London. O Friend! I know Not']

WOTTON Henry 1568–1639
English poet and diplomat.

1 How happy is he born and taught / That serveth not another's will; / Whose armour is his honest thought / And simple truth his utmost skill! ['Character of a Happy Life']

2 Lord of himself, though not of lands, / And having nothing, yet hath all. ['Character of a Happy Life']

3 He first deceas'd; she for a little tri'd / To live without him: lik'd it not, and di'd. ['Death of Sir Albertus Moreton's Wife']

4 You meaner beauties of the night, / That poorly satisfy our eyes, / More by your number, than your light; / You common people of the skies, / What are you when the moon shall rise? ['On His Mistress, the Queen of Bohemia']

5 An ambassador is an honest man sent to lie abroad for the good of his country. [Written in the Album of Christopher Fleckmore]

WRIGHT Frank Lloyd 1869–1959
US architect.

The physician can bury his mistakes, but the architect can only advise his clients to plant vines. [*New York Times Magazine*]

WYATT Thomas c. 1503–1542
English poet.

They flee from me, that sometime did me seek. ['Remembrance']

WYATT Woodrow 1919–
English politician.

A man falls in love through his eyes, a woman through her ears. [*To the Point*]

US architect Frank Lloyd Wright . The originality of his work stands out in city buildings like the Guggenheim Museum in New York 1959. He condemned the growing congestion of cities and encouraged closeness to nature.

WYCHERLEY William 1640–1716
English dramatist.

> The woman that marries to love better will be as much mistaken as the wencher that marries to live better. Marrying to increase love is like gaming to become rich; you only lose what little stock you had before. [*Country Wife* IV]

XENOPHON c. 430–354 BC
Greek historian, philosopher, and soldier.

> The sea! the sea! [The cry of the Greek mercenaries on reaching safety at the Black Sea, after escaping from the Battle of Cunaxa, 401 BC; *Anabasis* IV. vii]

YANKWICH Judge Leon R 1888–1975
US judge.

There are no illegitimate children – only illegitimate parents. [Decision in Southern District of California court, June 1928, quoting columnist O O McIntyre]

YEATS W B 1865–1939
Irish poet and dramatist.

1 A pity beyond all telling, / Is hid in the heart of love. [*Countess Kathleen*]

2 Down by the salley gardens my love and I did meet; / She passed the salley gardens with little snow-white feet. / She bid me take love easy, as the leaves grow on the tree; / But I, being young and foolish, with her would not agree. ['Down by the Salley Gardens']

3 All changed, changed utterly: / A terrible beauty is born. ['Easter 1916']

4 When I play on my fiddle in Dooney / Folk dance like a wave of the sea. ['Fiddler of Dooney']

5 I have spread my dreams under your feet; / Tread softly, because you tread on my dreams. ['He Wishes for the Cloths of Heaven']

6 Nor law, nor duty bade me fight, / Nor public men, nor cheering crowds, / A lonely impulse of delight / Drove to this tumult in the clouds; / I balanced all, brought all to mind, / The years to come seemed waste of breath, / A waste of breath the years behind / In balance with this life, this death. ['Irish Airman Foresees His Death']

7 Like a long-legged fly upon the stream / His mind moves upon silence. ['Long-Legged Fly']

8 Hearts are not had as a gift but hearts are earned / By those that are not entirely beautiful. ['Prayer for my Daughter']

9 Cast a cold eye / On life, on death. / Horseman pass by! ['Under Ben Bulben']

10 When you are old and gray and full of sleep, / And nodding by the fire, take down this book, / And slowly read, and dream of the soft look / Your eyes had once, and of their shadows deep. ['When you are Old']

YELLEN Jack 1892–
US lyricist.

I'm the Last of the Red-Hot Mamas. [Song title]

YOUNG Edward 1683–1765
English poet and dramatist.

1 You are so witty, profligate, and thin, / At once we think thee Milton, Death, and Sin. ['Epigram on Voltaire']

2 Be wise with speed; / A fool at forty is a fool indeed. [*Love of Fame*]

3 Procrastination is the thief of time. [*Night Thoughts*]

4 Life is the desert, life the solitude; / Death joins us to the great majority. [*The Revenge*]

Z

ZANGWILL Israel 1864–1926
English writer.

1 America is God's Crucible, the great Melting-Pot where all the races of Europe are melting and reforming! ... God is making the American. [*The Melting Pot*]

2 The only true love is love at first sight; second sight dispels it. [Attributed remark]

ZANUCK Darryl F 1902–1979
Hollywood film producer.

For God's sake don't say yes until I've finished talking. [Quoted in Philip French *The Movie Moguls*]

ZAPPA Frank 1940–1993
US rock musician, bandleader, and composer.

1 Rock journalism is people who can't write interviewing people who can't talk for people who can't read. [Quoted in L Botts *Loose Talk*]

2 It isn't necessary to imagine the world ending in fire or ice – there are two other possibilities: one is paperwork, and the other is nostalgia [*Real Frank Zappa Book* ch 9]

ZEMECKIS Robert 1952–
US film director.

Back to the Future. [Film title]

ZIA UL-HAQ Mohammed 1924–1988
Pakistani general and president.

If the Court sentences the blighter to hang, then the blighter will hang. [Of the death sentence imposed on former president Zulfikar Ali Bhutto 1979]

French novelist and social reformer Émile Zola. Zola's reforming zeal took him from naturalistic novels to the defence of Capt Dreyfus in *J'accuse*/*I Accuse* 1898, the famous open letter to the president.

ZOLA Émile 1804–1902
French novelist and social reformer.

I accuse. [Heading of an open letter to the President of the Republic concerning the Dreyfus case 1898]

not necessarily improve with a.: Hall, Peter
not of an a., but for all time: Jonson 5
Every a. has a keyhole to which: McCarthy, Mary 2
pleasures of middle a.: Pound 1
a. from folly could not: Shakespeare 8
A. cannot wither her: Shakespeare 16
Old a. hath yet his honour: Tennyson 58
Old a. is the most unexpected: Trotsky 2
At least we a.: Wells 3
ageing
don't believe in a.: Woolf 3
Agnes
St. A.' Eve: Keats 3
agriculture
taxes must, at last, fall upon a.: Gibbon 2
AIDS
learned more ... in the world of A.: Perkins
air
a nipping and an eager a.: Shakespeare 75
Alamein
Before A. we never had a victory: Churchill, Winston 9
albatross
I shot the A.: Coleridge, Samuel Taylor 1
Albert
A. married beneath him: Coward 9
alcohol
A. is like love: Chandler 3
ale
Good a., the true and proper drink: Borrow 3
England talked of a.: Chesterton 17
alimony
A. is the curse of the writing classes: Mailer 4
matter of arranging a.: Wodehouse 8
alive
had I found you a.: Paul
Bliss was in it that dawn to be a.: Wordsworth, William 20
all
to have his a. neglected: Johnson, Samuel 15
alone
eats a. chokes a.: Arab proverb
A. on a wide wide sea: Coleridge, Samuel Taylor 5
never less a.: Gibbon 7
travels the fastest who travels a.: Kipling 46
Alpha
I am A. and Omega: Bible 139
alter
dare not a. these things: Austin
am
I a. that I a.: Bible 16
Amazon
She was an A.: Blanch
ambassador
a. is an honest man: Wotton 5
ambition
All a.s are lawful except: Conrad 6
Ill-weav'd a.: Shakespeare 140
fling away a.: Shakespeare 168
lowliness is young a.'s ladder: Shakespeare 178
A. should be made: Shakespeare 188
ambitious
hunger of a. minds: Spenser 8
America
God bless A.: Berlin, Irving 2

nothing wrong with A. that cannot: Clinton
O my A.! my new-found-land: Donne 8
impresses me most about A.: Edward VIII 1
A.'s present need is not heroics: Harding
A. is God's Crucible: Zangwill 1
American
Good A.s: Appleton 1
business of the A. people is business: Coolidge 2
A. system of rugged individualism: Hoover 2
A. professors like their literature clear: Lewis, Sinclair
new deal for the A. people: Roosevelt, Franklin D 1
A hyphenated A.: Roosevelt, Theodore 5
A.s are so enamored of equality: Tocqueville 1
like so many substantial A.s: Wodehouse 9
amour
ravishing thing ... an A.: Behn 1
amuse
talent to a.: Coward 2
amused
We are not a.: Victoria 1
analogies
A. decide nothing: Freud, Sigmund 7
anarchism
A. is a game: Shaw 25
anarchist
trying to set up a small a. community: Bennett, Alan 3
anatomy
A. is destiny: Freud, Sigmund 3
ancestor
Our a.s are: Sheridan, Richard Brinsley 6
ancient
It is an a. Mariner: Coleridge, Samuel Taylor 2
angel
on the side of the a.s: Disraeli 18
Make friends with the a.s: Francis de Sales, St
If an a. ... his philosophy: Lichtenberg 2
Bright-harnest A.s sit: Milton 28
A ministering a. thou: Scott, Walter 15
In Heaven an a. is nobody: Shaw 21
a.s keep their ancient places: Thompson, Francis 2
anger
A. makes dull men: Elizabeth I 5
A. is one of the sinews: Fuller, Thomas 1
A. is a short madness: Horace 3
angry
was never an A. Young Man: Amis 2
When a., count ten: Jefferson 1
animal
wisdom and experience to a.s: Bardot 3
All a.s are equal but: Orwell 2
In the a. kingdom, the rule: Szasz 5
Anna
Here thou, great A.: Pope 43
answer
But a. came there none: Scott, Walter 2
noblest a. unto such: Tennyson 1
ant
Go to the a., thou sluggard: Bible 41
antagonism
a. is based on love: Miller, Henry 1
anthology
An a. is like: Raleigh 2

Antony
My A. is away: Shakespeare 10

antic
put an a. disposition on: Shakespeare 80

antiquities
A. are history defaced: Bacon 3

anxiety
first experience of a.: Freud, Sigmund 5

anything
A. goes: Porter, Cole 2

apathy
a. of human beings: Keller

ape
true that we have sprung from the a.: Skinner

apology
stiff a. is a second insult: Chesterton 3

appearance
Keep up a.s: Churchill, Charles 3
shallow ... not judge by a.s: Wilde 12

appetite
mortified a. is never a wise: Stevenson, Robert Louis 3

apple
a. of an eye: Common Prayer, Book of 16

April
A. is the cruellest month: Eliot, T S 2
A. of your youth: Herbert, Edward, Lord
Men are A. when they woo: Shakespeare 45

Aprille
A. with his shoures sote: Chaucer 4

archaeologist
An a. is the best husband: Christie

archbishop
A. — A Christian ecclesiastic of a rank: Mencken 4

architect
a. can only advise: Wright

architecture
A. comprises two ideas: Behrens
rise and fall of English a.: Betjeman 5
A., of all the arts: Dimnet
a. must ease: Erskine
A. is the art ... waste space: Johnson, Philip

argument
A knock-down a.: Dryden 12
A.s only confirm: Tarkington

aristocracy
An a. in a republic: Mitford

Aristotle
follow the counsel of A.: Ascham
This man (A.) is ... an example: Averroës 2

arm
the everlasting a.s: Bible 21
took her up in his a.s: Ridge
on her lover's a. she leant: Tennyson 14
a.s of my true love again: Tennyson 38
A.s and the man I sing: Virgil 1

armies
ignorant a. clash by night: Arnold, Matthew 4

army
British A. always fights uphill: Horrocks 1
The A. had been fought to a standstill: Ludendorff

arrow
a.s in the hand of a giant: Common Prayer, Book of 37
shot an a. into the air: Longfellow 1

art
A. is an experience: Anderson, Lindsay
first mistake of A.: Bangs
A. is not a *brassière*: Barnes, Julian 1
A. is meant to disturb: Braque 2
The history of a.: Butler, Samuel 12
Without freedom, no a.: Camus 1
Economics and a. are strangers: Cather 1
sombre enemy of good a.: Connolly, Cyril 3
aspires ... to the condition of a.: Conrad, Joseph 4
deny that a. can be taught: Courbet
man devotes himself to a.: Dürer
A. is a jealous mistress: Emerson 4
Nature is inside a.: Frye
A. is either a plagiarism: Gauguin
A. is the accomplice of love: Gourmont 1
A. is so wonderfully irrational: Grass 1
a. ... adventure of the mind: Ionesco 2
the madness of a.: James, Henry 8
Irresponsibility ... pleasure of all a.: Kael
free society a. is not a weapon: Kennedy, John F 9
A., that great undogmatized: Key, Ellen 2
clever, but is it A.: Kipling 6
A. is the objectification of feeling: Langer
A. must be parochial: Moore, George 2
A. is the final cunning: Murdoch 1
To speak of morals in a.: Nathan
For a. to exist: Nietzsche 7
business of A. to give things shape: Palmer
Through a. we express: Picasso 1
last and greatest a., the a. to blot: Pope 44
A work of a. contains: Proust 7
A. is too serious: Reinhardt
The effort of a.: Santayana 7
More matter with less a.: Shakespeare 83
Great a. is never produced: Shaw 33
Much of modern a.: Sontag 2
A. — the one achievement: Thurber 1

artist
task of the a. now: Beckett 1
truthful ... great a., knows how difficult: Cather 4
a. will be judged: Connolly, Cyril 6
a. ... becomes historical: De Kooning
What is an a.: Fellini
No a. is ahead of his time: Graham, Martha
a. now has a very important job: Hockney
Portrait of the A.: Joyce 5
a. means never to look away: Kurosawa
What an a. dies with me: Nero
Being an a. means: Ortega y Gasset 1
a. should know all about love: Pavlova
modern a. must live by craft: Pound 5
task of the a. at any time: Raine
creative a. is not allowed: Rilke 3
The true a. will let his wife starve: Shaw 17

ashamed
more things a man is a. of: Shaw 16
need not be a.: Stevenson, Robert Louis 2

aspidistra
Keep the A. Flying: Orwell 11

Asquith
affair between Margot A. and Margot A.: Parker 7

assassination
  A. — an accident of my trade: Alfonso XIII
  A. ... extreme form of censorship: Shaw 31
assent
  can get a. to almost any: Chapman
assess
  cannot a. in terms of cash: Betjeman 3
Assyrian
  The A. came down: Byron, George, Lord 17
ate
  If ever I a. a good supper: Anstey 2
atheism
  Among the repulsions of a.: Updike 4
atheist
  no a.s in foxholes: Cummings, William
    Thomas
  An a. may be simply: Weil 1
Athens
  A. arose: Shelley 9
atom
  unleashed power of the a.: Einstein 7
attacking
  situation excellent. I am a.: Foch 1
attempt
  a. and not the deed: Shakespeare 245
Auburn
  Sweet A.: Goldsmith 4
aunt
  bad a.s and good a.s: Wodehouse 4
Australia
  Visitors to A. rarely fail: Baker, Sidney John
Austria
  Don John of A.: Chesterton 7
author
  a. of peace and lover: Common Prayer, Book
    of 4
  Choose an a. as you choose: Dillon 2
  glory of every people arises from its a.s:
    Johnson, Samuel 2
authority
  a., whether secular or religious: Ayer 2
  defer to the a. of the bootmaker: Bakunin
  I don't like a.: Benson 2
  A. poisons everybody: Lenin 1
  a. of any governing institution: Steinem 2
autobiography
  Every a. is concerned: Auden 4
  a. is an obituary in serial: Crisp 4
autocrat
  I shall be an a.: Catherine II
automobile
  fulfils a man's ego like an a.: Rootes
autumnal
  I have seen in one A. face: Donne 5
avarice
  A., the spur of industry: Hume 3
Avernus
  Easy is the descent to A.: Virgil 5
awake
  A., arise, or be for ever fall'n: Milton 40
axe
  let the great a. fall: Shakespeare 124

babies
  Other people's b.: Herbert, A P 6
Babylon
  By the waters of B.: Common Prayer, Book of
    38

Bach
  human things divine; such is B.: Casals 1
  B. almost persuades: Fry, Roger
bachelor
  b. never quite gets over: Rowland 2
  When I said I would die a b.: Shakespeare
    325
  B.'s fare: Swift 10
back
  Will you no come b.: Hogg 1
  Will ye no come b. again: Nairne 1
  B. to the Future: Zemeckis
Bacon
  think how B. shined: Pope 35
  of Nature and all learning, Sir Francis B.:
    Walton 4
bad
  to be b. ... real struggle: Roth 2
  b. end unhappily: Stoppard 2
Baker Street
  The B. irregulars: Doyle 9
ballad
  love a b. in print: Shakespeare 432
ballot
  b. is stronger than the bullet: Lincoln 2
bank
  What's breaking into a b.: Brecht 4
  The Man Who Broke The B. at Monte Carlo:
    Gilbert, Fred
  tyrannize over his b. balance: Keynes 3
Bankhead
  Tallulah B. barged down the Nile: Brown,
    John Mason
barge
  The b. she sat in: Shakespeare 15
Barkis
  B. is willin': Dickens 9
bathos
  B., ... sinking in poetry: Pope 48
battle
  B.'s magnificently stern: Byron, George,
    Lord 9
  O God of b.s: Shakespeare 161
  In a b. nothing is ever: Slim
bauble
  Take away these b.s: Cromwell 3
be
  preferable to b. than not: Cioran 2
  To b., or not to b.: Shakespeare 97
beaches
  We shall fight on the b.: Churchill, Winston 5
bear
  savage as a b. with a sore head: Marryat 1
  I am a B. of Very Little Brain: Milne 5
beast
  What is man without the b.s: Seattle
  The b. with two backs: Shakespeare 331
beastie
  Wee, sleekit, cow'rin, tim'rous b.: Burns,
    Robert 16
beaurocrat
  b. does not like a poem: Vidal 4
beauteous
  I love all b. things: Bridges 1
beautiful
  Against the b. and the clever: Greene,
    Graham 2
  use the word 'b.' to denote: Moore, G E
  b. and therefore to be woo'd: Shakespeare 165

beauty
B. soon grows familiar to the lover:
Addison 3
You can only perceive real b.: Aimée
B. is one of the rare: Anouilh 3
as many kinds of b. as: Baudelaire 1
no absolute standard of b.: Galbraith 4
thing of b. is a joy: Keats 2
B. is truth: Keats 10
loveliest things of b. God has ever showed:
Masefield 1
B. is an ecstasy: Maugham 2
b. is only sin deep: Saki 12
b. that addresses itself: Sand 1
Look not thou on b.'s charming: Scott, Walter
3
daily b. in his life: Shakespeare 347
B. is the only promise: Stendhal 2
beaver
a b. sixty-eight feet long: Juster
bed
And so to b.: Pepys 1
bedfellow
tricks with his b.: Erasmus
bedroom
doesn't matter what you do in the b.:
Campbell, Mrs Patrick 1
bee
little busy b. / Improve each shining hour:
Watts 1
beer
Life isn't all b. and skittles: Hughes
beetle
poor b., that we tread upon: Shakespeare 275
before
I have been here b.: Rossetti, Dante Gabriel 1
beggar
B. that I am: Shakespeare 89
Bare-footed came the b. maid: Tennyson 4
beginning
In the b. God created: Bible 1
In the b. was the Word: Bible 111
I am ... the b. and the ending: Bible 139
b., a muddle and an end: Larkin 3
behind
led his regiment from b.: Gilbert, W S 3
being
smell of b.: Artaud 2
decision that defines a b.: Cioran 3
B. is a fiction: Dowell
who would lose ... intellectual b.: Milton 45
Think only what concerns thee and thy b.:
Milton 62
Belgium
B's capital had gather'd then: Byron, George,
Lord 7
Belial
sons of B. had a glorious time: Dryden 3
sons / Of B., flown: Milton 41
belief
remaining faithful to one's b.s: Baldwin,
James 5
B. like any other moving body: Butler, Samuel
15
B. consists in accepting: Emerson 5
All b.s are bald ideas: Picabia
b. which he finds in himself: Russell,
Bertrand, Lord 8

that is b.: Sartre 6
B. is like love: Schopenhauer 1
mysteries ... degenerate into b.s: Weil 8
believe
loss to know how much to b.: Irving 2
I don't b.: Jung 2
if one b.s then miracles occur: Miller,
Henry 2
To b. in something not yet proved: Smith,
Lillian
believed
sometimes I've b.: Carroll 14
believer
Devout b.s are safeguarded: Freud,
Sigmund 4
believing
b. in our own lives: Grass 2
bell
'Twould ring the b.s of heaven: Hodgson 1
belt
b. without hitting below: Asquith, Margot 1
bemused
We are b. and crazed creatures: Laing 2
Benedick
B. the married man: Shakespeare 318
benevolence
b. of mankind does most good: Bagehot 3
render unto the wife due b.: Bible 121
benighted
armies of the b.: Forster 8
Berliner
Ich bin ein B.: Kennedy, John F 8
Bermuda
Where the remote B.s ride: Marvell 1
Bernard Shaw
B. is greatly improved: Eliot 6
berry
have made a better b.: Butler, William
beseech
b. you, in the bowels: Cromwell 2
best-seller
A b. is: Smith, Logan Pearsall 4
betray
All a man can b.: Conrad 8
betrayal
ecstasy of b.: Genet 1
better
no b. than you should: Beaumont and
Fletcher 1
B. to be despised: Burke, Edmund 5
I am getting b. and b.: Coué
far, far b. thing I do: Dickens 29
see and approve b. things: Ovid 4
I'd been b. without: Parker 4
no b. than you should be, / Polly: Thomas,
Dylan 4
bibble-babble
Leave thy vain b.: Shakespeare 419
bicycle
b. made for two: Dacre
big
b. man has no time: Fitzgerald, F Scott 4
Billy
B., in one of his nice new sashes: Graham,
Harry 2
biographies
majority of human b.: Steiner

biography
B. should be written by: Balfour 2
The Art of B.: Bentley 1
Read ... nothing but b.: Disraeli 1

bird
Mountain and brilliant b.: Campbell, David
Gordon
God gives every b. his worm: James, P D
we are a nest of singing b.s: Johnson, Samuel
20
B.s do it, bees do it: Porter, Cole 5
The b. of dawning: Shakespeare 60

Birkenhead
Lord B. is very clever: Asquith, Margot 2

Birmingham
night we went to B.: Chesterton 16

birth
The act of b.: Freud, Sigmund 5
b. is but a sleep and a forgetting:
Wordsworth, William 14

bisexuality
B. immediately doubles your chances:
Allen 9

bishop
How can a b. marry: Smith, Sydney 4
What b.s like best in their clergy: Smith,
Sydney 15

blackbird
The b. whistling: Stevens 2

blame
No b. should attach to telling the truth:
Brookner 1

bless
except thou b. me: Bible 12
The Lord b. thee: Bible 19
God b. the King: Byrom
God b. us every one Dickens 7
dying, b. the hand: Dryden 23

blessed
b. be the name of the Lord: Bible 34
B. are the meek: Bible 78
more b. to give than to receive: Bible 116
b. them unaware: Coleridge, Samuel Taylor 6

blind
If the b. lead the b.: Bible 91
splendid work for the b.: Sassoon 1

block
the old b. itself: Burke, Edmund 25

blonde
It was a b.: Chandler 1
who says that b.s prefer gentlemen: West,
Mae 6

blood
B. and iron: Bismarck 2
River Tiber foaming with much b.: Powell,
Enoch 2
in b. / Stepp'd in so far: Shakespeare 257
whose b. / Is very snow-broth: Shakespeare
279

blunder'd
Some one had b.: Tennyson 10

boat
messing about in b.s: Grahame 1
They sank my b.: Kennedy, John F 2
slow b. to China: Loesser 2

bodies
b. would not seem so filthy: Lichtenberg 3

body
human b. is an energy system: Brown,
Norman
Gin a b. meet a b.: Burns, Robert 4
B., remember: Cavafy
woman watches her b. uneasily: Cohen 3
b. is the church: De Sade
b. of a weak and feeble: Elizabeth I 4
difficult to live with one's b.: Lawrence 15
What was my b. to me: Saint-Exupéry 1
The b. is an instrument: Santayana 8
a temple, called his b.: Thoreau 4

boet
I hate all B.s and Bainters: George I

bomb
No country without an atom b.: De Gaulle 4

bone
come to lay my b.s amongst you: Wolsey 1

book
cannot review a bad b.: Auden 5
Some b.s are undeservedly: Auden 6
Some b.s are to be tasted: Bacon 35
B.s must follow sciences: Bacon 42
do not throw this b. about: Belloc 1
his b.s were read: Belloc 17
lard their lean b.s: Burton, Robert 2
If my b.s had been any worse: Chandler 5
with b.s as with young girls: Feuerbach
only b.s that influence: Forster 9
b. that is shut is but a block: Fuller,
Thomas 6
b. is never a masterpiece: Goncourt
All good b.s are alike: Hemingway 1
Another damned, thick, square b.: Henry,
William
A bad b. is as much of a labour: Huxley,
Aldous 10
he who destroys a good b.: Milton 4
B.s are not absolutely dead: Milton 5
A good b. is the precious life-blood: Milton 6
Deep versed in b.s and shallow in himself:
Milton 70
contact with reality ... surrounded by his b.s:
Mitterand
B.s Do Furnish a Room: Powell, Anthony 2
govern kingdoms with maxims found in b.s:
Richelieu
Buying b.s would be a good thing:
Schopenhauer 2
I'll drown my b.: Shakespeare 394
never read a b. before: Smith, Sydney 11
Go, little b., and wish: Stevenson, Robert
Louis 10
no such thing as a moral or an immoral b.:
Wilde 16

book-learned
Those b. fools: Drinkwater 1

bookseller
he once shot a b.: Campbell, Thomas 2
b.s are generous liberal-minded: Johnson,
Samuel 11

boot
B., saddle, to horse: Browning, Robert 4

bore
B. ... talks when you wish: Bierce 2

bore *(cont.)*
b. is a man who: Taylor, Bert Leston
He is an old b.: Tree
A healthy male adult b.: Updike 2
bored
he b. for England: Muggeridge 2
boredom
effect of b. on a large scale: Inge 1
acute and active animals are capable of b.: Nietzsche 9
B. ... problem for the moralist: Russell, Bertrand, Lord 3
born
man that is b.: Conrad 3
thing that I was b. to do: Daniel 2
to be b. he must first die: Gurdjieff 2
b., so to speak, twice: Rousseau 1
b. to set it right: Shakespeare 81
b. is like being kidnapped: Warhol 2
borrow
B. fivers off everyone you meet: Branson
borrower
Neither a b., nor a lender: Shakespeare 74
borrowing
b. as this ... accounted plagiarism: Milton 14
Boston
B. man is the east wind: Appleton 2
And this is good old B.: Bossidy
Bottom
Bless thee, B.: Shakespeare 309
boundary
there is a secret b.: Akhmatova
bountiful
My Lady B.: Farquhar 1
bounty
My b. is as boundless: Shakespeare 372
bouquet
b. is better than the taste: Potter, Stephen 1
bourgeois
How beastly the b. is: Lawrence 3
Bourgeoisie
The Discreet Charm of the B.: Buñuel 3
The British B. / Is not born: Sitwell
bow
drew a b. at a venture: Bible 32
boxing
B. is just show business: Bruno
boy
b. stood on the burning deck: Hemans 1
It's b.; only b: Kipling 44
b.s in the back room: Loesser 1
b. playing on the sea-shore: Newton
Perhaps at fourteen every b.: Norman
boy friend
certain thing called the B.: Wilson, Sandy 1
boy-friend
girl whose b. starts: Auden 15
boyfriend
My b. and I broke up: Rudner 1
brain
I mix them with my b.s: Opie
B.s are an asset to the woman: West, Mae 4
What good are b.s to a man: Wodehouse 2
brain-washing
right is pre-empted ... b.: Greer 5
branch
Cut is the b.: Marlowe 5

brandy
hero must drink b.: Johnson, Samuel 31
brave
How sleep the b.: Collins, William 1
Toll for the b.: Cowper 3
None but the b.: Dryden 9
Some have been thought b.: English proverb
B. men, and worthy patriots: Milton 24
breach
Once more unto the b.: Shakespeare 157
bread
doth not live by b. only: Bible 20
Cast thy b. upon the water: Bible 59
b. to strengthen man's heart: Common Prayer, Book of 29
Loaf of B. beneath the bough: Fitzgerald, Edward 3
that b. should be so dear: Hood 7
Honest b. is very well: Jerrold 1
break
B., b., b. ... O Sea: Tennyson 5
breast
Between her b.s is my home: Lawrence 8
bred
B. en bawn in a brier-patch: Harris 2
bride
b.'s attitude towards her betrothed: Muir
Brideshead
B. Revisited: Waugh 7
bridesmaid
Why am I always the b.: Leigh 2
bright
All things b. and beautiful: Alexander, Cecil Frances
b. day that brings forth: Shakespeare 177
brightness
B. falls from the air: Nashe
brilliant
less b. pen than mine: Beerbohm 3
Britain
make B. a fit country for heroes: Lloyd George 3
Britannia
Rule, B.: Thomson 1
British
B. have the distinction: Attlee 2
B. love permanence more: Casson
B. public ... fits of morality: Macaulay 13
British Honduras
If the world had any ends B.: Huxley, Aldous 2
Briton
as only a free-born B. can: Thackeray 7
broker
A b. is a man: Woollcott 1
bronx
The b.? No thonx: Nash 4
brooches
make you b.: Stevenson, Robert Louis 7
brother
Am I my b.'s keeper: Bible 8
my b., forever, hail: Catullus 5
want to be the white man's b.: King, Martin Luther 1
BIG B. IS WATCHING YOU: Orwell 4
can be a b. only: Saint-Exupéry 3
we band of b.s: Shakespeare 164
I am, Sir, a B. of the Angle: Walton 1

cherub
Fall'n C., to be weak: Milton 36
chest
Fifteen men on the dead man's c.: Stevenson, Robert Louis 9
chicken
Some c.! Some neck: Churchill, Winston 17
Chief Justice
The C. was rich, quiet and famous: Macaulay 4
child
Whenever a c. lies: Adler, Alfred
event in the life of a c.: Bachelard 1
When I was a c.: Bible 126
pleasure in deceiving a c.: Canetti 3
old Adam in this C.: Common Prayer, Book of 1
To have a thankless c.: Shakespeare 205
c. should always say what's true: Stevenson, Robert Louis 5
c. becomes an adult when: Szasz 1
childbirth
Death and taxes and c.: Mitchell 1
childhood
The c. shows the man: Milton 69
children
started life as c.: Amis 1
C.'s talent to endure: Angelou 2
C. sweeten labours: Bacon 29
C. ... listening to their elders: Baldwin, James 4
violations committed by c. on c.: Bowen, Elizabeth 2
estranged from the world of c.: Campbell, Beatrix
arrows ... are the young c.: Common Prayer, Book of 37
c. produce adults: De Vries 4
just because they are one's c.: García Márquez
c. are the makers of men: Montessori 1
more careful of the breed of their horses ... c.: Penn 2
explain to your c. why they're born: Scott, Hazel
C. are a mother's anchors: Sophocles 4
If men do not keep on speaking terms with c.: Updike 1
no illegitimate c.: Yankwich
child-wife
It's only my c.: Dickens 14
China
slow boat to C.: Loesser 2
chip
c. off the old 'block': Burke, Edmund 25
chivalry
The age of c. is gone: Burke, Edmund 4
Cervantes smiled Spain's c. away: Byron, George, Lord 36
have all the fun ... law of c.: Sayers 1
choice
c. and master spirits: Shakespeare 183
small c. in rotten apples: Shakespeare 381
choosing
Pleas'd me long c., and beginning late: Milton 63
Christian
to form C. men: Arnold, Thomas
Teaching a C. how he ought to live: Basil

C. religion doubted: Butler, Samuel 18
souls of C. people: Chesterton 1
C. religion ... cannot be believed: Hume 3
anarchist and the C. ... common origin: Nietzsche 1
hate him for he is a C.: Shakespeare 285
C. theology is: Spengler
Christianity
His C. was muscular: Disraeli 2
C. has done a great deal: France 1
takes a great deal of C.: Kipling 30
decay of C.: Saki 11
organized religion is making C. political: Van Der Post 2
Christmas
I'm dreaming of a white C.: Berlin, Irving 4
C. ... dreadful, if you're single: Cope 4
And all this at C. time: Dietrich
church
abhorrent to the c. ... human being: Joyce 4
get me to the c. on time: Lerner 2
churchman
As for the British c.: Blythe
cigar
a good c. is a smoke: Kipling 3
It is like a c.: Wavell
cinema
the sky of the c.: Berger 1
c. both gives life and takes: Godard 2
circumstance
C.s do that: Brookner 3
I don't believe in c.s: Shaw 26
citizen
good c. who has not the quality: Aquinas 2
c. of the world: Bacon 20
A c. of no mean city: Bible 117
Healthy c.s are the greatest asset: Churchill, Winston 18
you fat and greasy c.s: Shakespeare 33
city
A rose-red c.: Burgon
He so improved the c.: Caesar, Augustus 1
remedy to life ... the big c.: Camus 4
not be known, live in a c.: Colton 2
huge c. which the West had built: Forster 7
c. ... is a human zoo: Morris, Desmond 1
chief function of the c.: Mumford 2
c. is the most vulnerable: Oppenheimer
He so improved the c.: Suetonius 1
Commuters give the c.: White, E B 2
City of Emeralds
road to C. is paved: Baum, L Frank
civil
how c. to folk he ne'er saw: Anstey 1
civilization
C. and profits: Coolidge 1
C. is a process: Freud, Sigmund 1
missionaries of c.: Hegel
c. ... given up believing in the devil: Knox, Ronald Arbuthnot 2
beings do not carry c. in their genes: Mead
C. ... arteriosclerosis of culture: Miller, Henry 10
C. is nothing else than: Ortega y Gasset 5
can't say c. don't advance: Rogers, Will 3
C. is a movement: Toynbee
C. advances by: Whitehead, Alfred North 3

clap
Don't c. too hard: Osborne 1

claret
C. is the liquor for boys: Johnson, Samuel 31

class
lower c., I am in it: Debs

classes
Mankind ... two great c.s: Beerbohm 4
upper c. ... upper hand: Coward 8

classic
Definition of a c.: Bennett, Alan 4
A c. is a book: Calvino 2
A c. — something that: Twain 8
c. ... doesn't have to be written again: Van Doren
degrade the c.s into authorities: Wilde 21

clear
On a c. day (you can see forever): Lerner 4

Cleopatra
If C.'s nose had been shorter: Pascal 3

clerk
A C. ther was of Oxenford: Chaucer 1

clever
let who will be c.: Kingsley, Charles 1

cleverness
height of c.: Rochefoucauld 1

climb
Fain would I c.: Raleigh 4

Close
breathless hush in the C. tonight: Newbolt 5

clothes
liquefaction of her c.: Herrick 12
poured into his c.: Wodehouse 6

cloud
ariseth a little c.: Bible 29
not a man, but—a c. in trousers: Mayakovsky 1
I wandered lonely as a c.: Wordsworth, William 2

coaster
Dirty British c.: Masefield 2

coat
A c. of many colours: Bible 13

cocksure
wish I was as c. of anything: Melbourne 1

college
This great C.: Housman 14

colourless
C. green ideas sleep: Chomsky 2

comedies
All c.s are ended by: Byron 28

comedy
C. is a tragedy: Carter, Angela 2
All I need to make a c.: Chaplin 2
C. is an escape: Fry, Christopher 4
In c., reconcilement with life: Rourke

comfort
I tell you naught for your c.: Chesterton 2
not, carrion c., Despair: Hopkins 1

comic
c. spirit is given: Wilder, Thornton 5

command
not born to sue, but to c.: Shakespeare 354

committee
c. is an animal with four back legs: Le Carré

commodity
C., the bias of the world: Shakespeare 199

common
He nothing c. did or mean: Marvell 7

Commons
The C. ... wise and masterly inactivity: Mackintosh 2

commonsense
C. ... widely distributed: Descartes 1

communication
Evil c.s corrupt good manners: Menander 1

communism
C. is Soviet power plus: Lenin 3
C. is a hammer: Mao Zedong 1
C. I like: Sartre 4

company
Few are qualified to shine in c.: Swift 11

complain
c. about the tune: Bevan 3

complainer
loudest c.s for the public: Burke, Edmund 1

composer
first requirement for a c.: Honegger

composition
Read over your c.s: Johnson, Samuel 29

compromise
c. is the art: Erhard

comrade
dear love of c.s: Whitman 1

concealment
let c. ... Feed on her: Shakespeare 412

conceited
never any pity for c.: Eliot, George 5
I am not c.: Williams, Kenneth

conference
c. a ready man: Bacon 34

confidence
C. in an unfaithful man: Bible 52
c. and security ... can be measured: King, Florence 2

conflict
Never in the field of human c.: Churchill, Winston 7

conformist
honors its live c.s and its dead troublemakers: McLaughlin

conformity
C. is the jailer of freedom: Kennedy 4

confuse
to c. the minds of others: Disraeli 10

confusion
offer ... my own c.: Kerouac
C. ... order which is not understood: Miller, Henry 5

connect
Only c.: Forster 4

conquered
I came, I saw, I c.: Caesar, Julius 1

conscience
C. is thoroughly well-bred: Butler, Samuel 6
c. is the curse: Faulkner 3
Freedom of c. entails: Focault 2
will not cut my c.: Hellman 2
C.: self-esteem with a halo: Layton
doesn't abide by majority rule ... c.: Lee, Harper
c. is not the vessel of eternal verities: Lippman 2
sufficient c. to bother him: Lloyd George 1

My c. is taken captive by God's word: Luther
3
C. ... someone may be looking: Mencken 6
c. doth make cowards: Shakespeare 100
conscious
our less c. thoughts: Butler, Samuel 17
Between the c. and the unconscious: Kabir 1
consciousness
history of c. starts: Brodsky 1
if c. is common: Camus 3
C. is much more than the thorn: Cioran 4
consequence
Logical c.s are the scarecrows: Huxley,
Thomas Henry 3
conservation
C. ... before recreation: Charles, Prince of
Wales 2
consistency
A foolish c.: Emerson 12
C. is contrary to nature: Huxley, Aldous 5
constant
c., as the northen star: Shakespeare 180
constitution
invoke the genius of the C.: Pitt, William *the*
Elder 2
Everybody talks of the c.: Walpole, Horace,
Lord 4
consumer
In a c. society: Illich
consummation
a c. / Devoutly to be wish'd: Shakespeare 98
consumption
Conspicuous c. of valuable goods: Veblen
contemporary
Any c. of ours: Trotsky 4
contract
verbal c. isn't worth: Goldwyn 3
contradict
Do I c. myself: Whitman 4
controlled
c. by rather than to control: Heraclitus 3
conversation
when you stick on c.'s burrs: Holmes, Oliver
Wendell 5
Your ignorance cramps my c.: Hope 3
primary use of c.: Santayana 2
Mr Salter's side of the c.: Waugh 6
no such thing as c.: West, Rebecca 2
conviction
C. is the conscience of intellect: De Chamfort
cook
common murderer ... uncommon c.: Saki 2
c. was a good c.: Saki 10
cookery
C. is become an art: Burton, Robert 3
cooking
woman accepted c. as a chore: Post 1
beautiful woman ... c. dinner: Wolfe, Thomas
copy
cats c. the Mona Lisa: Armstrong 2
cord
No c. nor cable can so forcibly: Burton,
Robert 9
corn
Whoever could make two ears of c.: Swift 2
Cornish
twenty thousand C. men: Hawker

corporation
C.s have neither bodies: Thurlow 1
ever expect a c. to have a conscience:
Thurlow 2
corpse
c.s and chloride of lime: Hay
corruption
first sign of c. in a society: Bernanos 3
C. ... symptom of constitutional liberty:
Gibbon 3
cosmos
c. is about the smallest hole: Chesterton 12
counsel
Two may keep c.: Shakespeare 376
counsellor
multitude of c.s: Bible 45
country
my c. is a disgrace: Anacharsis
c. built more on people: Ben-Gurion 1
I died for my c.: Booth
leave his c. as good: Cobbett 1
I loathe the c.: Congreve 11
Was this c. settled: Cook
God made the c.: Cowper 7
Our c., right or wrong: Decatur
great c. worthy of the name: De Gaulle 7
When I am in the c.: Hazlitt 6
to die for one's c.: Horace 11
ask not what your c. can do for you:
Kennedy, John F 5
The c. in town: Martial
My c. is the world: Paine 4
undiscover'd c. from whose bourn:
Shakespeare 99
no relish for the c.: Smith, Sydney 14
I vow to thee, my c.: Spring-Rice
should know something of his own c.: Sterne
5
couple
doesn't mean you're a *happy* c.: Simon
courage
no man can be sure of his c.: Anouilh 4
C. is not simply *one* of the virtues: Lewis, C S
6
wary of ready-made ideas about c.: Mauriac
screw your c. to the sticking-place:
Shakespeare 243
'C.!' he said: Tennyson 35
three-o'-clock in the morning c.: Thoreau 5
courtesy
Grace of God is in C.: Belloc 11
very pink of c.: Shakespeare 375
courtship
C. to marriage, is: Congreve 8
coward
C.s die many times: Shakespeare 179
cowardice
C., as distinguished from panic: Hemingway
3
coxcomb
Never expected to hear a c.: Ruskin 7
cradle
Out of the c. endlessly rocking: Whitman 2
create
not desired to c.: Belloc 12
does not know what to c.: Ortega y Gasset 4
To c. is divine, to reproduce: Ray
Whoever undertakes to c.: Rosenberg 2

created
Male and female c. he them: Bible 3
creation
Beauteous, bright c.: Caedmon
creativity
Whatever c. is: Aldiss
True c. often starts: Koestler 1
creature
The c.'s at his dirty work again: Pope 15
remember the small c.: Shakespeare 148
credulity
little c. helps one through life: Gaskell 3
creetur
'I am a lone lorn c.': Dickens 8
Crete
people of C. unfortunately: Saki 6
cricket
C. to us ... more than play: Blunden 2
c. existed long before I was born: Bradman
C. — conception of eternity: Mancroft
Crillon
Hang yourself, brave C.: Henri IV
crisis
When is a c. reached: Kapuscinski
in Chinese the word c.: Kennedy 3
cannot be a c. next week: Kissinger 2
critic
c.s ... failed in literature: Disraeli 7
good c. is he: France 2
scepticism ... attribute of a good c.: Lowell, James Russell 1
A good drama c. is one: Tynan
criticism
Soviet composer's reply to just c.: Shostakovich
criticize
What the public c.s in you, cultivate: Cocteau 5
crowd
c. will always save Barabbas: Cocteau 4
Far from the madding c.'s ignoble strife: Gray 7
I hate the profane c.: Horace 10
talk with c.s and keep your virtue: Kipling 14
crown
can't have the c. of thorns and: Bevan 1
labour this c. of thorns: Bryan
the glory of my c.: Elizabeth I 3
sweet fruition of an earthly c.: Marlowe 14
head that wears a c.: Shakespeare 150
crucify
c. mankind upon a cross: Bryan
cruel
must be c., only to be kind: Shakespeare 115
cuckoo
C., c.; O, word of fear: Shakespeare 227
O C.! Shall I see: Wordsworth, William 29
culture
c. are the true apostles: Arnold, Matthew 2
C., the acquainting ourselves: Arnold, Matthew 9
cup
Come, fill the C.: Fitzgerald, Edward 2
curate
I was a pale young c. then: Gilbert, W S 30
compassion in the very name of a C.: Smith, Sydney 9

curiosity
C. is the direct incontinency: Taylor, Jeremy 1
curiouser
'C. and c.': Carroll 1
current affairs
misleading guide to c.: Keynes 4
curse
C. God, and die: Bible 35
C.s are like chickens: Southey 2
curtain
iron c. has descended: Churchill, Winston 19
down the c., the farce is over: Rabelais 3
curtsey
C. while you think: Carroll 10
custom
C. reconciles us: Burke, Edmund 2
What times, what c.s: Cicero 4
C. ... guide of human life: Hume 2
c. / More honour'd in the breach: Shakespeare 76
cut
most unkindest c. of all: Shakespeare 190
cynic
C. ... sees things as they are: Bierce 3
cynicism
C. ... saying the truth: Hellman 1
Czech
The C.s voted for the jungle: Forman

d
I never use a big, big D.: Gilbert, W S 9
D. is a very weak-minded: Haig
daffodil
Fair d.s, we weep to see: Herrick 3
dances with the d.s: Wordsworth, William 1
dagger
I will speak d.s to her: Shakespeare 111
Is this a d. which I see: Shakespeare 244
Daisy
D., D.: Dacre
damn
Frankly, my dear, I don't give a d.: Howard
My dear, I don't give a d.: Mitchell 2
D. with faint praise: Pope 14
dance
On with the d: Byron, George, Lord 8
will you join the d.: Carroll 7
d. in the old dame yet: Marquis 6
A D. to the Music of Time: Powell, Anthony 3
must d. barefoot: Shakespeare 382
D. is the only art of which: Shawn
dancing
prove anything by d.: Astaire
d. is love's proper exercise: Davies, John
Daniel
A D. come to judgement: Shakespeare 296
Dante
D., who loved well: Browning, Robert 17
dappled
Glory be to God for d. things: Hopkins 5
dare
I d. do all that may become: Shakespeare 242
dark
a great leap in the d.: Hobbes 1
O d., d., d., amid the blaze of noon: Milton 71
Hellish d., and smells of cheese: Surtees 5

darkness
in d. have seen a great light: Bible 68
Lighten our d., we beseech: Common Prayer,
Book of 6
Talks of d. at noon-day: Cowper 6
To sit in d. here: Milton 47
universal d. buries all: Pope 6
prince of d. is a gentleman: Shakespeare 210
the instruments of d.: Shakespeare 233
Prince of D. is a gentleman: Suckling 3
daughter
d.'s my d. all her life: Craik
d. and my mother, my pupil and my teacher:
Lewis, C S 2
My d.! O my ducats: Shakespeare 289
Davy
Sir Humphrey D. / Abominated gravy:
Bentley 4
day
Sufficient unto the d.: Bible 86
Every d. in every way: Coué
knell of parting d.: Gray 2
Seize the d.: Horace 7
single d. is enough: Klee 1
that d. shall men come forth: Koran 6
On a clear d. (you can see forever): Lerner 4
idle singer of an empty d.: Morris, William 2
So foul and fair a d.: Shakespeare 231
Happy those early d.s: Vaughan 2
dead
do not mourn me d.: Ballou
deal to be said / For being d.: Bentley 2
d. don't die: Lawrence 16
d. shall not have died in vain: Lincoln 7
No longer mourn for me when I am d.:
Shakespeare 440
deaf
Surely the Holy One is not d.: Kabir 4
dear
My D. One is mine: Auden 16
D. 338171: Coward 10
thou art too d. for my: Shakespeare 442
death
The chief problem about d.: Allen 13
the stroke of d.: Bacon 14
fear d. as children fear: Bacon 15
D. has so many doors: Beaumont and
Fletcher 2
D. is the dark backing: Bellow
man's d. makes everything: Berger 2
in their d. they were not divided: Bible 26
shadow of d. ... light: Bible 68
last enemy ... is d.: Bible 128
O d., where is thy sting: Bible 130
name that sat on him was D.: Bible 140
friend and enemy is but D.: Brooke 5
d. is the cure of all diseases: Browne, Thomas
8
'Not D., but Love': Browning, Elizabeth
Barrett 1
D., the poor man's dearest friend: Burns,
Robert 10
midst of life we are in d.: Common Prayer,
Book of 2
D. be not proud: Donne 11
Fear of d. throws me: Dunbar
danger of violent d.: Hobbes 3

disappointed by that stroke of d.: Johnson,
Samuel 45
Where is d.'s sting: Lyte 2
in a d. so noble: Milton 73
D. is but crossing the world: Penn 5
eloquent, just, and mighty D.: Raleigh 3
D. is the privilege: Rowe 1
I have a rendezvous with D.: Seeger
This fell sergeant, d.: Shakespeare 131
we owe God a d.: Shakespeare 153
Be absolute for d.: Shakespeare 274
Come away, d.: Shakespeare 411
Into the jaws of D.: Tennyson 9
Into the valley of D.: Tennyson 11
In balance with this life, this d.: Yeats 6
debt
A New Way to Pay Old D.s: Massinger 2
decay
castle or building not in d.: Bacon 28
deceive
d. a woman by pretence of love: La Bruyère 2
December
Their meetings made D.: Tennyson 29
decision
monologue is not a d.: Attlee 3
realistic d. ... something bad: McCarthy, Mary
1
deed
A d. without a name: Shakespeare 261
deep
singularly d. young man: Gilbert, W S 27
From the great d. to the great d.: Tennyson 17
deer
I was a stricken d.: Cowper 13
defeat
In d. unbeatable: Churchill, Winston 1
In d.: defiance: Churchill, Winston 8
defence
The only d. is in offence: Baldwin, Stanley 2
defended
What God abandoned, these d.: Housman 1
degree
Take but d. away: Shakespeare 401
delight
d. ... misfortunes and pains of others: Burke,
Edmund 3
His d.s / Were dolphin-like: Shakespeare 29
rarely, comest thou, / Spirit of D.: Shelley 15
deluge
After us the d.: Pompadour
democracy
D. means government by: Attlee 4
D. is the fig leaf of elitism: King, Florence 1
D. ... opportunity to be everyone's slave:
Kraus 2
modern d. is a tyranny: Mailer 3
D. ... theory that the common people:
Mencken 9
capacity for justice makes d.: Niebuhr 1
great arsenal of d.: Roosevelt, Franklin D 4
D. is supposed to give you: Vidal 3
D. is the recurrent suspicion: White, E B 3
D. is not so much a form: Wilson,
Woodrow 1
must be made safe for d.: Wilson,
Woodrow 2
democratic
D. institutions generally give: Tocqueville 2

distress
All pray in their d.: Blake 8
ditch
I will die in the last d.: William III 1
divided
If a house be d.: Bible 100
divinity
d. that shapes our ends: Shakespeare 127
divorce
take a vacation or get a d.: Allen 11
D. and suicide: Alvarez
D. is a system whereby: Deighton
think d. a panacea: Dix
only good thing about d.: Luce 3
do
will of the child to d.: Faulkner 2
I can d. no other: Luther 3
D. what thou wilt: Rabelais 1
little done, so much to d.: Rhodes
D. not d. unto others as: Shaw 23
a man got to d.: Steinbeck
doctrine
d. is something you kill for: Benn
Dodger
'The artful D.': Dickens 23
dog
every d. has his day: Borrow 4
great pleasure of a d.: Butler, Samuel 10
grin like a d.: Common Prayer, Book of 24
when a man bites a d.: Dana
The d. it was that died: Goldsmith 6
If you call a d. Hervey: Johnson, Samuel 13
your heart to a d. to tear: Kipling 33
Beware of the d.: Petronius
I am his Highness' d. at Kew: Pope 40
Something better than his d.: Tennyson 33
Let d.s delight to bark and bite: Watts 3
dogged
d. as does it: Trollope 3
doing
find out what everyone is d.: Herbert, A P 3
doll
A living d., everywhere you look: Plath 1
dollar
The almighty d.: Irving 3
life shouldn't be painted on d. bills: Odets
domestic
to appreciate d. bliss: Santayana 5
done
Whatever have you ... gone and d.: Gilbert,
W S 2
If it were d.: Shakespeare 241
ought to be d. ... attempt to do: Wells 7
doom
stretch out to the crack of d.: Shakespeare 263
Doon
Ye banks and braes o' bonny D.: Burns,
Robert 19
Dooney
play on my fiddle in D.: Yeats 4
door
Let the d.s be shut upon him: Shakespeare
103
double
D., d. toil and trouble: Shakespeare 259
double-bed
peace of the d.: Campbell, Mrs Patrick 2

doublethink
D. means: Orwell 7
doubt
shall end in d.s: Bacon 1
saucy d.s and fears: Shakespeare 255
sunnier side of d.: Tennyson 3
Doubting-Castle
castle, called D.: Bunyan 1
Douglas
hand of D. is his own: Scott, Walter 12
The D. in his hall: Scott, Walter 13
Dove
Beside the springs of D.: Wordsworth,
William 22
down
He that is d. needs fear: Bunyan 2
Dr. Fell
I do not love you D.: Brown, Thomas
dream
d.s to sell: Beddoes
old men shall d. d.s: Bible 77
who make our d.s come true: Hoffer 3
no more impossible d.s: Jackson, Jesse
I have a d.: King, Martin Luther 7
If you can d.: Kipling 12
Dreamer of d.s, born out of my due time:
Morris, William 1
d. within a d.: Poe 2
were it not that I have bad d.s: Shakespeare
88
such stuff / As d.s are made on: Shakespeare
393
The quick D.s: Shelley 2
abundance of d.s is paid for: Ustinov 2
spread my d.s under your feet: Yeats 5
dreaming
City with her d. spires: Arnold, Matthew 19
dreamt
d. that I dwelt: Bunn
dressed
all d. up and no place: Burt
drink
five reasons we should d.: Aldrich
reason why I don't d.: Astor 1
strong d. is raging: Bible 51
She drove me to d.: Fields, W C 1
D. not the third glass: Herbert, George 3
D. to me only: Jonson 4
One more d. and: Parker 5
d. / Life to the Lees: Tennyson 55
drinking
not the d. that is to be blamed: Selden 2
poor and unhappy brains for d.: Shakespeare
339
drive
no man will admit he can't ... d.: Moss
driving
like the d. of Jehu: Bible 33
drop
just a d. in the ocean: Teresa 1
drowned
BETTER D. THAN DUFFERS: Ransome 1
drowning
no d. mark upon him: Shakespeare 385
drum
Not a d. was heard: Wolfe, Charles 1

drunkenness
d. ... valid human experience: James,
William 7
D. ... is temporary suicide: Russell, Bertrand,
Lord 2
duck
I just forgot to d.: Dempsey
I turn to d.s: Harvey
duke
A fully-equipped d. costs: Lloyd George 2
The D. returned from the wars today:
Marlborough
Duke of Plaza Toro
Nobleman, / The D.: Gilbert, W S 5
dull
How d. it is to pause: Tennyson 56
Dundee
bonnets of Bonny D.: Scott, Walter 1
dusk
d. with a light behind her: Gilbert, W S 32
dust
For d. thou art: Bible 7
shall the d. return to the earth: Bible 60
What of vile d.?: Chesterton 14
fear in a handful of d.: Eliot, T S 3
troubles of our proud and angry d.: Housman
4
As chimney-sweepers, come to d.:
Shakespeare 54
Dutch
my dear old D.: Chevalier, Albert
duty
every man's d.: Cobbett 1
task becomes a d. from the moment:
Hammarskjöld 1
England expects every man will do his d.:
Nelson 3
sense of d. is useful in work: Russell,
Bertrand, Lord 6
stupid man ... declares that it is his d.: Shaw
3
idea of d. in one's calling: Weber
dying
an unconscionable time d.: Charles II 1
D., / Is an art: Plath 3
I am d., Egypt, d.: Shakespeare 24

ear
hath e.s to hear, let him: Bible 101
lend me your e.s: Shakespeare 186
earth
e. is all the home I have: Aytoun, William
Edmondstoune
new heaven and a new e.: Bible 141
conquest of the e.: Conrad 1
e. and her sister planets: Daly
e. only has so much: Elton
Spaceship E.: Fuller, R Buckminster
But did thee feel the e. move: Hemingway 2
e. itself is a kind of manned spaceship:
Humphrey 2
E. is here so kind: Jerrold 2
into your mouth what the e. has grown:
Lappé
put a girdle round the e.: Shakespeare 308
whole round e. is every way: Tennyson 24
hath passed away a glory from the e.:
Wordsworth, William 12

east
E. bow'd low before: Arnold, Matthew 11
E. is E., and West: Kipling 2
Fool ... tried to hustle the E.: Kipling 29
Once did she hold the gorgeous E.:
Wordsworth, William 17
East End
look the E. in the face: Elizabeth, the *Queen
Mother*
Eastern
uncivilized E. instincts: Kipling 30
eat
To e. is to appropriate: Sartre 2
ecology
left doesn't have a monopoly on e.: Le Pen
Eden
garden eastward in E.: Bible 4
Through E. took their solitary way: Milton 67
editor
An e. is one: Stevenson, Adlai 1
educate
got to e. ... to be depraved: Saki 1
education
E. ... discloses to the wise: Bierce 4
close to great minds ... best kind of e.: Buchan
1
complete and generous e.: Milton 25
E. costs money, but: Moser
e. must ultimately be limited: Pound 2
The purpose of e.: Rosenberg 1
E. has for its object: Spencer 7
egg
putting all my e.s in one bastard: Parker 16
met a lot of hardboiled e.s: Wilder, Billy
ego
e. is just imagination: Hoffa
egotism
e. is a protection: Freud, Sigmund 6
Einstein
howling 'Ho! / Let E. be: Squire
electricity
e. was dripping invisibly: Thurber 2
electronic
new e. interdependence recreates the world:
McLuhan 1
elephant
An E.'s Child: Kipling 17
Elginbrodde
Here lie I, Martin E.: Macdonald
eloquence
finest e. is that which gets things done: Lloyd
George 4
Elvis
without E., you're nothing: Madonna 2
embalmer
triumph of the e.'s art: Vidal 2
emperor
Hail, E.: Suetonius 3
empire
Great Britain has lost an e.: Acheson 2
Westward the course of e.: Berkeley 1
day of E.s has come: Chamberlain, Joseph
liquidation of the British E.: Churchill,
Winston 16
An e. founded by war: Montesquieu
To found a great e.: Smith, Adam 2
encounter
Close E.s of the Third Kind: Spielberg 1

end
e. justifies the means: Bernanos 3
It is the e. that crowns us: Herrick 5
wills the e. wills also: Kant 2
free way of life proposes e.s: Kennedy, Robert
Keep right on to the e.: Lauder 1
Let the e. try the man: Shakespeare 149
e. of this day's business: Shakespeare 196
He makes a swan-like e.: Shakespeare 292

endure
if ye can e. patiently: Koran 4

enemies
by having the right e.: Spong
careful in the choice of his e.: Wilde 13

enemy
last e. that shall be destroyed: Bible 128
be just to our e.: Campbell, Thomas 2
e. is by tradition our savior: Oates, Joyce
Carol
time-consuming ... to have an e.: White,
E B 1

England
We have in E. a particular bashfulness:
Addison 14
Walk upon E.'s mountains green: Blake 15
E., home and beauty: Braham
E. is the mother of Parliaments: Bright 1
corner of a foreign field ... forever E.:
Brooke 6
I am in E., everywhere: Browne, Thomas 2
Oh, to be in E.: Browning, Robert 10
E. is a paradise for women: Burton, Robert 5
we are the people of E.: Chesterton 18
E. with all thy faults: Cowper 9
Slaves cannot breathe in E.: Cowper 10
E., Home, and Beauty: Dickens 17
E. to be the workshop of the world:
Disraeli 14
stately homes of E.: Hemans 2
open my legs and think of E.: Hillingdon
E. is a nation of shopkeepers: Napoléon 4
not three good men unhanged in E.:
Shakespeare 135
this earth, this realm, this E.: Shakespeare 356
E. but vice and religion: Smith, Sydney 13
In ... [E.] it is thought well to kill: Voltaire 2

English
E. may not like music: Beecham 2
rolling E. drunkard made: Chesterton 15
The E. have undertaken: Hegel
Take of E. earth as much: Kipling 4
E. have hot water bottles: Mikes 1
the E. vice: Rattigan

Englishman
born an E. and remained: Behan 1
not that the E. can't feel: Forster 2
He remains an E.: Gilbert, W S 8
thorough an E. as ever coveted: Kingsley,
Charles 2
E. ... forms an orderly queue of one: Mikes 2
E. thinks he is moral only: Shaw 19
How can what an E. believes be heresy: Shaw
29

Englishmen
Mad dogs and E.: Coward 3
the absurd nature of the E.: Pepys 2

Englishwomen
E.'s shoes look: Halsey

enslaved
never be e. by machinery: Čapek

Enterprise
voyages of the starship E.: Roddenberry

enough
'Tis not e.: Shakespeare 396

enthusiasm
e. moves the world: Balfour 3

environment
to read the word e.s: Thomas, Lewis 1

envy
E. never makes holiday: Bacon 8
dullard's e. of brilliant men: Beerbohm 5

epoch
e. when ladies apparently rolled: Huxley,
Aldous 12

equal
all men are created e.: Lincoln 6

equality
E. may be perhaps a right: Balzac 1
never be e. in the servants' hall: Barrie 1
majestic e. of the law: France 3

eroticism
E. has its own moral: Vargas Llosa

err
To e. is human: Pope 25

error
one thing to show a man that he is in e.:
Locke 1
Give me fruitful e. any time: Pareto
certain e.s of such ingenuity: Rostand 7

esthete
e. ... relation to beauty: Kraus 3

eternal
E. Passion: Arnold, Matthew 12
E. spirit of the chainless mind: Byron, George,
Lord 41
to be boy e.: Shakespeare 427
feel and know that we are e.: Spinoza 4

eternity
E.! thou pleasing, dreadful thought: Addison
7
E. was in our lips and eyes: Shakespeare 7
E.'s a terrible thought: Stoppard 3
Some shadows of e.: Vaughan 1
I saw E. the other night: Vaughan 4

Ethiopian
Can the E. change his skin: Bible 76

Eureka
E.! I have found it: Archimedes 1

Europe
process of making E. explosive: Liddell Hart

Eve
When E. upon the first of Men: Hood 6

evening
Some enchanted e.: Hammerstein 2

evensonge
belles ringeth to e.: Hawes

event
An e. has happened: Burke, Edmund 21
force of e.s wakens: Hoagland
things about human e.s: Rushdie

ever
I go on for e.: Tennyson 6

everlasting
Underneath are the e. arms: Bible 21

evidence
Circumstancial e. ... convincing: Doyle 2

faithful
better to be unfaithful than f.: Bardot 2
f. to thee, Cynara! in my fashion: Dowson 2
if you had been f.: Racine 1
f. know only the trivial: Wilde 18

Falklands
The F. thing was a fight: Borges 2

fall
he f.s like Lucifer: Shakespeare 167

fame
F. is like a river: Bacon 30
F. is the spur: Milton 19
F. is no plant that grows: Milton 20

families
Old f. last not three oaks: Browne, Thomas 12
two f. ... Haves and the Have-nots: Cervantes 4
happy f. resemble each other: Tolstoy 1

family
f. with its narrow privacy: Leach

famous
Let us now praise f. men: Apocrypha 2
awoke ... and found myself f.: Byron, George, Lord 40
f. for 15 minutes: Warhol 1

fanatic
F.s have their dreams: Keats 5

fanaticism
F. consists: Santayana 4

fancy
Tell me where is f. bred: Shakespeare 293

fantasies
exchange of two f.: Chamfort

far
too f. out all my life: Smith, Stevie 3

farmer
F. will never be happy again: Herbert, A P 1

fashion
F.! ... knaves and fools may use: Churchill, Charles 5
construe things after their own f.: Shakespeare 176

fast
allowed on the night of the f.: Koran 1

fat
O f. white woman: Cornford, Frances
F. Is a Feminist Issue: Orbach
men about me that are f.: Shakespeare 173

fatal
most f. complaint of all: Hilton

fate
when f. summons: Dryden 17
F., then, is a name: Emerson 3
I am the master of my f.: Henley 3
become the makers of our f.: Popper 4
masters of their f.s: Shakespeare 172

father
Full fathom five thy f. lies: Shakespeare 389

fault
no one without a f.: Hazlitt 1

fear
hate so long as they f.: Cicero 5
continual f. and danger: Hobbes 3
'f.' is my substance: Kafka 1
only thing we have to f. is f.: Roosevelt, Franklin D 3
f. first created the gods: Santayana 9
Present f.s / Are less: Shakespeare 234

feel
What we f. and think: Huxley, Aldous 9

feeling
Great f.s will often: Eliot, George 4

feet
And did those f.: Blake 15
f. beneath her petticoat: Suckling 2

female
f. of the species is more deadly: Kipling 7
If to her share some f. errors fall: Pope 42
who has a polished f. friend: Whurr

feminism
need a new kind of f.: Paglia

feminist
All f. arguments: Dworkin
became a f. as an alternative: Kempton

fetishist
no unhappier creature than a f.: Kraus 1

fiction
work of f. should be ... journey: Burgess

fierce
If I were f.: Sassoon 4

fight
'Let's f. till six: Carroll 12
We shall f. on the beaches: Churchill, Winston 5
don't want to f., but, by jingo: Hunt
not yet begun to f.: Jones
Nor law, nor duty bade me f.: Yeats 6

film
f. lives, becomes alive: Cimino
f. is a petrified fountain of thought: Cocteau 1

finger
The Moving F. writes: Fitzgerald, Edward 6
One f. in the throat: Osler 1

first
nothing ... for the f. time: Cornford, Francis
doing something for the f. time: Ffrangcon-Davies

fish
F. not, with this: Shakespeare 282

fishing
Fly f. may be: Johnson, Samuel 54

fish-knives
Phone for the f., Norman: Betjeman 1

Flanders
poppies grow / In F. fields: McCrae

flatter
what really f.s a man: Shaw 14

flattered
He that loves to be f.: Shakespeare 397

flattereth
more favour than he that f.: Bible 54

flattery
f. hurts no one: Stevenson, Adlai 2

flaunt
got it, f. it: Brooks, Mel

flea
Great f.s have little f.s: Morgan

flee
They f. from me: Wyatt, Thomas

flesh
in my f. shall I see God: Bible 37
twain shall be one f.: Bible 94
f. is weak: Bible 97
All f. is as grass: Bible 136
I wants to make your f. creep: Dickens 25
'Tis the way of all f.: Shadwell 1

flesh *(cont.)*
that this too too solid f. would melt:
    Shakespeare 64
Flores
At F. in the Azores: Tennyson 51
flower
f.s of the forest: Elliot
f.s that bloom in the spring: Gilbert, W S 16
many a f. is born to blush unseen: Gray 6
flux
All is f.: Heraclitus 1
fly
Like a long-legged f.: Yeats 7
folk song
trouble with a f.: Lambert
follower
The most dangerous f.: Nietzsche 8
folly
rememb'rest not the slightest f.: Shakespeare
    34
effects of f.: Spencer 3
food
F. comes first, then morals: Brecht 5
F. probably has a very great influence:
    Lichtenberg 1
fool
f. returneth to his folly: Bible 53
f. hath said in his heart: Common Prayer,
    Book of 14
I am two f.s, I know: Donne 19
f. all the people some of the time: Lincoln 3
learned f. is more foolish: Molière
f.s rush in where angels: Pope 22
haste of a f. is the slowest: Shadwell 3
A motley f.: Shakespeare 37
f. me to the top of my bent: Shakespeare 109
f.s by heavenly compulsion: Shakespeare 203
great stage of f.s: Shakespeare 214
things people make f.s of themselves about:
    Shaw 4
'F.!' said my Muse to me: Sidney 3
foolish
No man was more f.: Johnson, Samuel 40
force
F. is not a remedy: Bright 2
use of f. alone: Burke, Edmund 19
May the f. be with you: Lucas
Who overcomes / By f.: Milton 43
forefather
Think of your f.s!: Adams, John Quincy
rude f.s of the hamlet sleep: Gray 3
forget
do not thou f. me: Astley
never forgive but I always f.: Balfour 1
better in one's work to f.: Carducci
Better by far ... f. and smile: Rossetti,
    Christina 2
forgive
never f. but I always forget: Balfour 1
God may f. you: Elizabeth I 2
stupid neither f. nor forget: Szasz 2
form
His f. had not yet lost: Milton 42
F. follows profit: Rogers, Richard
F. and function are a unity: Rolf
fortune
so many men of large f.: Austen 3

hostages to f.: Bacon 25
f.'s buffets and rewards: Shakespeare 107
F. favours the brave: Terence 2
forward
never turned his back ... breast f.: Browning,
    Robert 24
those behind cried 'F.!': Macaulay 10
looking f. to the past: Osborne 2
fox
f. knows many things: Archilochus
arn't that I loves the f. less: Surtees 3
France
F. has lost a battle: De Gaulle 6
If I am not F.: De Gaulle 8
Fair stood the wind for F.: Drayton 3
this matter better in F.: Sterne 1
free
Was he f.: Auden 19
None who have always been f.: Buck 3
better to be in chains than to be f.: Kafka 3
wish that all men ... be f.: Lincoln 4
Man is born f.: Rousseau 3
condemned to be f.: Sartre 1
No one can be perfectly f.: Spencer, Herbert 8
definition of a f. society: Stevenson, Adlai 5
freedom
F. is not something ... can be given: Baldwin,
    James 3
F. is the by-product: Bevan 2
F. is when one hears the bell: Bidault 1
A people that loves f.: Bolívar
Without f., no art: Camus 1
few men talked of f.: Chesterton 17
f. of expression for people we despise:
    Chomsky 1
f. ... is no more than: Cioran 1
But what is f.: Coleridge, Hartley 1
Perfect f. is reserved: Collingwood
not fully sane ... spirit of f.: Cooley
unless f. is universal: Hill, Christopher
F. is the most contagious virus: Humphrey 1
freest ... unconscious of f.: Lawrence 10
In giving f. to the slave: Lincoln 5
f. for the one who thinks differently:
    Luxemburg
no one can be at peace unless he has his f.:
    Malcolm X 2
f. and equality are mutually exclusive: Mann
None can love f. heartily, but good: Milton 75
F. is slavery: Orwell 5
F. is the f. to say: Orwell 6
French
Every F. soldier carries: Naploéon 1
only taken from the F.: Sheridan, Richard
    Brinsley 1
friend
A f. in power: Adams, Henry Brooks 2
One f. in a lifetime: Adams, Henry Brooks 3
f. that sticketh closer: Bible 50
Who's your fat f.: Brummell
save me from the candid f.: Canning 1
How to Win F.s and Influence People:
    Carnegie
fly from your f.'s forehead: Chinese proverb
To find a f. ... close one eye: Douglas,
    Norman 1
not have a f. in the world: Hazlitt 1

F.s ... apology for relations: Kingsmill
with a little help from my f.s: Lennon and
  McCartney 4
misfortune of our best f.s: Rochefoucauld 3
Old f.s are best: Selden 1
My f.s were poor but honest: Shakespeare 2
The f.s thou hast: Shakespeare 71
F.s, Romans, countrymen: Shakespeare 186
f. should bear his f.'s: Shakespeare 194
not believe that f.s are necessarily: Ustinov 1

friendship
little f. in the world: Bacon 17
F. is Love without its wings: Byron, George,
  Lord 37
swear an eternal f.: Canning 2
F. ... commerce between equals: Goldsmith 7
keep his f. in constant repair: Johnson,
  Samuel 18
Most f. is feigning: Shakespeare 41
F. is constant in all other: Shakespeare 322

frost
f. performs its secret ministry: Coleridge,
  Samuel Taylor 14

fruit
By their f.s ye shall know: Bible 87
Man's first disobedience, and the f.: Milton 31

funeral
should be jolly at my f.: Mountbatten

funny
Everything is f. as long as: Rogers, Will 1

future
If you want a picture of the f.: Orwell 8
seen the f.; and it works: Steffens

gain
To g. that which is worth having: Devlin
  (McAliskey)

Galilean
Thou hast conquered, O G.: Julian
Thou hast conquered, O pale G.:
  Swinburne 4

Galilee
blue wave rolls nightly on deep G.: Byron,
  George, Lord 17

gallantry
What men call g.: Byron, George, Lord 19

Gallipoli
the landing at G.: Mackenzie 1

gambling
G. is a great leveller: Gogol

game
G.s People Play: Berne
how you played the G.: Rice

gamesmanship
Theory and Practice of G.: Potter, Stephen 2

garden
I value my g.: Addison 16
God Almighty first planted a g.: Bacon 19
g. eastward in Eden: Bible 4
A g. inclosed is my sister: Bible 66
A g. is a lovesome thing: Brown, T E
God the first g. made: Cowley 1
Glory of the G.: Kipling 10
Come into the g., Maud: Tennyson 37
must cultivate our g.: Voltaire 3
Down by the salley g.s: Yeats 2

gas
All is g. and gaiters: Dickens 21

gaudy
Let's have one another g. night: Shakespeare
  21

Gaunt
Old John of G.: Shakespeare 353

gazelle
I never nurs'd a dear g.: Moore, Thomas 3

Geldof
wish I had been Bob G.: Charles, Prince of
  Wales 1

general
bite some other of my g.s: George II

generation
Every g. revolts: Mumford 1
You are all a lost g.: Stein 3

genius
function of g.: Aragon
known no man of g. who: Beerbohm 1
Only an organizing g.: Bevan 5
G. is only a great aptitude: Buffon 2
'G.' (which means): Carlyle, Thomas 2
G. is of no country: Churchill, Charles 6
G. is one per cent: Edison
G. is the talent of a dead man: Goncourt
G. only thrives in the dark: Huxley,
  Aldous 14
concentration of talent and g.: Kennedy, John
  F 1
G. does what it must: Meredith, Owen
love, that is the soul of g.: Mozart
nothing to declare except my g.: Wilde 26

gentleman
not quite a g.: Ashford 1
g., though spoiled: Brome
say the g. is somewhat simple: Middleton

gentlemen
G., include me out: Goldwyn 2

gentlemen-rankers
G. out on the spree: Kipling 9

geographer
So g.s, in Afric-maps: Swift 9

George
G. the Third / Ought never: Bentley 5
G. — don't do that: Grenfell
G. the First was always reckoned: Landor 1

German
Don't let's be beastly to the G.s: Coward 1

ghost
What beck'ning g.: Pope 8
dogma of the G. in the Machine: Ryle

Gilpin
John G. was: Cowper 1

Gipper
Win this one for the G.: Gipp

girdeth
Let not him that g.: Bible 31

girl
young g.s plan for whom: Gilman 3
If you were the only g.: Grossmith
When I'm not near the g. I love: Harburg
prevent g.s from being g.s: Hope 1
gentleman said a g. with brains: Loos
I like the g.s who do: Miller, Max
hardest task of a g.'s life: Rowland 3
From birth to 18 a g. needs: Tucker
g.s follow the line of least resistance: West,
  Mae 3

give
such as I have g. I thee: Bible 115
more blessed to g. than: Bible 116
He g.s twice who g.s soon: Syrus 1
When I g. I g. myself: Whitman 3

giver
God loveth a cheerful g.: Bible 131

giving
not in the g. vein to-day: Shakespeare 363

Gladstone
G. ... spent his declining years: Sellar and Yeatman 3

glasses
seldom make passes / At girls who wear g.: Parker 6

gleam
Whither is fled the visionary g.: Wordsworth, William 13

gloat
I g.! Hear me g.: Kipling 39

glories
The g. of our blood and state: Shirley

glory
g. of Europe is extinguished: Burke, Edmund 4
paths of g. lead but to the grave: Gray 5
quickly the g. of the world passes: Kempis 1
left him alone with his g.: Wolfe, Charles 2

GNP
Man does not live by G. alone: Samuelson

go
g. at once: Shakespeare 256

goal
g. was scored ... by the hand of God: Maradona

god
the voice of G.: Alcuin
Lord G. made them all: Alexander, Cecil Frances
If only G. would give: Allen 8
nearer the Church the further from G.: Andrewes
On, to the City of G.: Arnold, Matthew 14
G. has been replaced: Baraka 2
in my flesh shall I see G.: Bible 37
Now, G. be thanked: Brooke 4
G.'s in his heaven: Browning, Robert 20
G. is our hope: Common Prayer, Book of 22
proof of G.'s omnipotence: De Vries 3
G. is subtle: Einstein 4
He [G.] does not play dice: Einstein 5
Those who marry G.: Greene, Graham 1
My G. and King: Herbert, George, 1
May the g.s grant you all: Homer
charged with the grandeur of G.: Hopkins 2
G. is beginning to resemble: Huxley, Julius
honest G. is the noblest work of man: Ingersoll 1
G. of our fathers: Kipling 34
G. / Must think ... odd: Knox, Ronald Arbuthnot 1
G. in the passions: Lichtenberg 5
mills of G. grind slowly: Longfellow 6
Better authentic mammon than a bogus g.: MacNeice 1
He for G. only, she for G. in him: Milton 56

G. perceived by the heart: Pascal 4
One, on G.'s side: Phillips 2
G. can stand being told: Priestley 1
As flies ... to the g.s: Shakespeare 212
In the great hand of G.: Shakespeare 249
What G. hath joined together: Shaw 10
I remembered G.: Southey 7
Whatsoever is, is in G.: Spinoza 1
G. fulfils himself in many ways: Tennyson 22
If G. did not exist: Voltaire 4
G. is always for the big battalions: Voltaire 5
G. is definitely out of the closet: Williamson
Had I but served G. as diligently: Wolsey 2

gold
cured only with g.: Cortés
travell'd in the realms of g.: Keats 19
To gild refined g.: Shakespeare 200
Saint-seducing g.: Shakespeare 367

goldfish
wouldn't mind turning into a vermillion g.: Matisse 1

Goliath
from David fighting G. to G.: Shamir

good
Content thyself to be obscurely g.: Addison 6
God saw that it was g.: Bible 2
g. of the people is the chief law: Cicero 1
The highest g.: Cicero 2
Take the g. the gods provide: Dryden 8
Nothing is so g.: Eliot, George 9
luxury of doing g: Goldsmith 13
G., but not religious-good: Hardy 7
never had it so g.: Macmillan 2
why not ask — 'How much g': Miller, Henry 3
Do g. by stealth: Pope 11, 36
man loves what he is g. at: Shadwell 4
nothing either g. or bad: Shakespeare 87
better to fight for the g.: Tennyson 39
If all the g. people were clever: Wordsworth, Elizabeth

goodbye
G. to All That: Graves 5
Every time we say g.: Porter, Cole 3

gout
that old enemy the g.: Hood 5

govern
How can you g. a country: De Gaulle 2
to g. ... to choose: De Gaulle 5
dead people g. our lives: Gurdjieff 1
No man is good enough to g. ... without: Lincoln 1
He that would g. others: Massinger 1
Let the people think they g.: Penn 3

government
g. is not theirs: Galbraith 3
see the g. get out of war: Heller 1
Fancy giving money to the G.: Herbert, A P 9
lack of honour in g.: Hoover 1
not the function of our G.: Jackson, Robert
No g. ought to be without censors: Jefferson 4
important thing for G.: Keynes 1
country has the g. it deserves: Maistre
For forms of g. let fools contest: Pope 33

308

grace
 G. does not abolish nature: Aquinas 3
 G. is given of God: Clough 1
 G. under pressure: Hemingway 5
 enough that, through Thy G.: Kipling 28
 G. me no g.: Shakespeare 357
 He does it with a better g.: Shakespeare 409
grammar
 Why care for g.: Ward 4
grammarian
 Idly inquisitive tribe of g.s: Antiphanes
grand
 It's g., and you canna expect: Barrie 3
Grand Central Station
 By G. I Sat Down and Wept: Smart
grapeshot
 A whiff of g.: Carlyle, Thomas 6
grass
 g. withereth, and the flower: Bible 136
 When you destroy a blade of g.: Bottomley,
   Gordon
grave
 The g.'s a fine and private place: Marvell 10
 renowned be thy g.: Shakespeare 55
great
 g. actions speak g. minds: Beaumont and
   Fletcher 8
 G. men are the guide-posts: Burke,
   Edmund 13
 To compare / G. things with small:
   Milton 51
 To vilify a g. man: Poe 3
 Rightly to be g.: Shakespeare 118
 Some men are born g.: Shakespeare 414
 To write the lives of the g.: Weil 7
Great Britain
 G. has lost an empire: Acheson 2
 To make a union with G.: Pétain 2
greatness
 nature of all g.: Burke, Edmund 14
Greece
 sprinkled isles, / Lily ... 'G.': Browning,
   Robert 6
 The isles of G.: Byron, George, Lord 29
 that G. might still be free: Byron, George,
   Lord 30
greediness
 G. closed Paradise: Innocent III
Greek
 it was G. to me: Shakespeare 175
green
 G. grow the rashes: Burns, Robert 8
 How G. Was My Valley: Llewellyn
 g. thought in a g. shade: Marvell 2
 G. consumerism is a target: Porritt
Greenfield
 Dora G. left her husband: Murdoch 2
Grenville
 I Sir Richard G. die: Tennyson 52
ground
 g. flew up and hit: Ward 2
grow
 We go on—we g.. At least we age: Wells 3
grown-up
 G.s never understand: Saint-Exupéry 4
growth
 G. ... only evidence of life: Newman, John
   Henry 1

guard
 G.s die but do not surrender: Cambronne
 who will g. the g.s: Juvenal 2
guiding-star
 g. of a brave nation: Motley 1
guilt
 dwell on g. and misery: Austen 5
guilty
 started like a g. thing: Shakespeare 59
gun
 can only defend ourselves with g.s: Goebbels
 G.s will make us powerful: Goering
 loaded g., how can you have God: Kabir 2
 Is that a g. in your pocket: West, Mae 7
Gunga Din
 better man than I am, G.: Kipling 11

habit
 H. is Heaven's own redress: Pushkin 3
 Costly thy h. as thy purse: Shakespeare 73
 skeleton of h. alone: Woolf 4
hack
 Do not h. me: Monmouth
hair
 To Crystal, h. was the most important:
   O'Brien
 ill white h.s become a fool: Shakespeare 155
half
 The h. was not told me: Bible 28
hamburger
 Why have h. out: Newman, Paul
hand
 little h.s were made to take: Belloc 2
 h. will be against every man: Bible 9
 If you want to win her h.: Braisted
 keep my h.s from picking: Common Prayer,
   Book of 3
 Licence my roving h.s: Donne 6
 If someone puts his h. on you: Malcolm X 1
 Come, knit h.s, and beat the ground: Milton
   10
 fatal h.s / No second stroke intend: Milton 50
 Thy h., great Anarch: Pope 6
 will not sweeten this little h.: Shakespeare 265
 h. that made you fair: Shakespeare 276
 will soon *wring* their h.s: Walpole, Robert,
   Lord 2
hang
 Are you going to h. him *anyhow*: Twain 4
 the blighter will h.: Zia ul-Haq
happiness
 greatest h. of the greatest number: Bentham 2
 h. that comes with innocence: Buñuel 2
 possess only the h. we ... understand:
   Maeterlinck
 H. is salutary: Proust 6
 If all our h. is bound up: Russell, Bertrand,
   Lord 5
 Character is the basis of h.: Santayana 3
 right to consume h.: Shaw 5
 A lifetime of h.: Shaw 15
 H. is no laughing matter: Whately 1
happy
 To be h. is: Benjamin 1
 H., thrice h. and more: Horace 8
 Thrice h. he ... read in Nature's mystic book:
   Marvell 12

happiness *(cont.)*
Ask yourself whether you are h., and you
cease: Mill 1
Call no man h. till he dies: Solon
How h. is he born and taught: Wotton 1
hard
It's been a h. day's night: Lennon and
McCartney 2
harm
Nothing can h. a good man: Socrates 1
harmless
h. as doves: Bible 88
harmony
from heavenly h.: Dryden 21
harp
h. that once: Moore, Thomas 2
harridan
I have almost done with h.s: Swift 12
Harry
Cry 'God for H.': Shakespeare 158
little touch of H. in the night:
Shakespeare 159
haste
Make h. slowly: Augustus
Make h. slowly: Suetonius
hate
I h., I love: Catullus 4
h. so long as they fear: Cicero 5
can scarcely h. anyone that we know:
Hazlitt 5
next to love the sweetest thing is h.:
Longfellow 7
h. the man whom you have injured:
Tacitus 1
hatred
h. is by far the longest pleasure: Byron,
George, Lord 35
haunted
'tis h., holy ground: Byron, George, Lord 4
have
the H.s and the Have-nots: Cervantes 4
To h. and to hold: Common Prayer, Book of
42
head
That one small h. could carry: Goldsmith 2
h. is bloody, but unbowed: Henley 1
If you can keep your h.: Kipling 13
health
Look to your h.: Walton 3
hear
hath ears to h., let him: Bible 101
heard
'You ain't h. nuttin' yet: Jolson
heart
same h. beats: Arnold, Matthew 1
Where your treasure is ... h. be: Bible 82
finite h.s that yearn: Browning, Robert 25
My h.'s in the Highlands: Burns, Robert 11
His h. was one of those: Byron, George,
Lord 1
h. is on me sleeve: Chesterton 9
h. to pity, and a hand to bless: Churchill,
Charles 4
h. ... love it would conceal: Coleridge, Samuel
Taylor 18
h. runs away with his head: Colman 2
strings ... in the human h.: Dickens 3

Unto a broken h.: Dickinson, Emily 3
H.s just as pure and fair: Gilbert, W S 13
'Give ... not your h. away: Housman 7
h. aches and a drowsy numbness: Keats 14
holiness of the h.'s affections: Keats 22
Two h.s that beat as one: Lovell
The H. Is a Lonely Hunter: McCullers 2
My h. is a lonely hunter: McLeod
h. that has truly loved: Moore, Thomas 1
The h. has its reasons: Pascal 2
So the h. be right: Raleigh 7
My h. is like a singing bird: Rossetti,
Christina 1
ever hold me in thy h.: Shakespeare 132
A merry h. goes all the day: Shakespeare 431
My true love hath my h.: Sidney 2
but our h.s are great: Tennyson 19
Kind h.s are more than coronets:
Tennyson 31
Thanks to the human h.: Wordsworth,
William 16
H.s are not had as a gift: Yeats 8
heaven
new h. and a new earth: Bible 141
h.s declare the glory of God: Common Prayer,
Book of 17
starry h.s above: Kant 1
ever-moving spheres of h.: Marlowe 4
more things in h. and earth: Shakespeare 79
My idea of h.: Smith, Sydney 12
merger between H. and Hell: Wells 2
Hecuba
What's H. to him: Shakespeare 93
Hegel
H. filled the universe: Russell, Bertrand, Lord
10
Helen
H., thy beauty: Poe 5
hell
to get out of h.: Artaud 3
H. ... is to love no more: Bernanos 1
safest road to H. is the gradual: Lewis, C S 4
this is h., nor am I out of it: Marlowe 2
Better to reign in h. than serve: Milton 39
H. is other people: Sartre 3
hellhound
h. is always a h.: Wodehouse 5
help
with a little h. from my friends: Lennon and
McCartney 4
hence
H., h. ... uninitiated: Virgil 6
hero
No man is a h. to his valet: Cornuel
Every h. becomes a bore: Emerson 16
See the conquering h. comes: Lee, Nathaniel
heroes
land that is in need of h.: Brecht 1
heroine
When a h. goes mad: Sheridan, Richard
Brinsley 2
Hesperus
It was the schooner H.: Longfellow 9
hewer
H.s of wood: Bible 22
highbrow
What is a h.: Wallace, Edgar

Highlands
My heart's in the H.: Burns, Robert 11
My heart's in the H.: Scott, Walter 16
hill
eyes unto the h.s: Common Prayer, Book of 33
Over the h.s and far away: Gay 3
hippopotamus
I shoot the H.: Belloc 3
historian
God cannot alter the past, h.s can: Butler, Samuel 5
h. must have some conception: Forster 1
H.s repeat each other: Guedalla 2
h., essentially, wants more documents: James, Henry 4
h.s left blanks: Pound 4
history
H. An account, mostly false: Bierce 5
great dust-heap called 'h.': Birrell
H. portrays: Canetti 1
h. of the world is but: Carlyle, Thomas 4
H. will absolve me: Castro 1
H. teaches us: Eban
properly no h.: Emerson 9
H. is bunk: Ford, Henry 2
materials for h.: Gibbon 1
H. repeats itself: Guedalla 2
do not learn very much from ... h.: Huxley, Aldous 4
h. is on our side: Khrushchev 3
we may not make h. tomorrow: Plumer
into the dustbin of h.: Trotsky 3
Human h. becomes more and more: Wells 4
history-book
Happy the people ... blank in h.s: Carlyle, Thomas 3
hit
A h., a very palpable h.: Shakespeare 130
hoist
H. with his own petar: Shakespeare 116
holiday
prescribe a h. to any patient: Russell, Bertrand, Lord 4
I am in h. humour: Shakespeare 43
If all the year were playing h.s: Shakespeare 134
Holmes
Sherlock H. remarked: Doyle 11
holy
'tis haunted, h. ground: Byron, George, Lord 4
H. Deadlock: Herbert, A P 10
home
H. of lost causes: Arnold, Matthew 6
Keep the h. fires burning: Ford, Lena Gilbert
H. is the place: Frost 3
What's the good of a h.: Grossmith and Weedon 1
Pleasure never is at h.: Keats 6
There's no place like h.: Payne
H. life as we understand: Shaw 9
H. is the girl's prison: Shaw 24
Homer
if worthy H. nods: Horace 1
contend for H. dead: Seward
homosexuality
If h. were the normal way: Bryant

honest
A few h. men: Cromwell 1
h. man's the noblest work of God: Pope 34
honesty
H. is a good thing but: Marquis 2
make your children *capable of h*.: Ruskin 5
honey
h. still for tea: Brooke 2
How a bear likes h.: Milne 4
honour
h. is a private station: Addison 6
louder he talked of his h.: Emerson 6
only h. remains: Francis I
Lov'd I not h. more: Lovelace 2
When h.'s at the stake: Shakespeare 118
cross of the Legion of H.: Twain 7
hope
H. is a good breakfast: Bacon 7
H. deferred maketh the heart: Bible 47
All h. abandon ye who enter: Dante Alighieri 2
triumph of h. over experience: Johnson, Samuel 26
H. springs eternal: Pope 30
horn
The h., the h.: Shakespeare 46
Horne
Godolphin H. was nobly born: Belloc 4
horror
'The h.!': Conrad, Joseph 2
horse
h. is simply a h.: Avicenna
Boot, saddle to h.: Browning, Robert 4
They Shoot H.s Don't They: McCoy
cannot ride two h.s ... no right in the circus: Maxton
my kingdom for a h.: Shakespeare 365
hospitality
H. is the only form of gift: Scruton 1
hour
This was their finest h.: Churchill, Winston 6
h. is come, but not the man: Scott, Walter 4
come most carefully upon your h.: Shakespeare 56
house
If a h. be divided: Bible 100
a man's h. is his castle: Coke
doorkeeper in the h. of my God: Common Prayer, Book of 25
The h. where I was born: Hood 3
h. ... but a playroom: Ibsen 1
h. that has got over all its troubles: Jerome, Jerome K 5
nothing in your h.s ... not know to be useful: Morris, William 3
household
keep a h. in oneness of mind: Homer
housekeeper
I am a marvellous h.: Gabor, Zsa Zsa 6
housekeeping
h. cares bring with them: Desbordes-Valmore
housework
no need to do any h.: Crisp 3
human
H. nature is so well disposed: Austen 1
predatory h. hands: Ellis
all h. life is there: James, Henry 6

infallible
We are none of us i.: Thompson, William
Hepworth
inferior
No one can make you feel i.: Roosevelt,
Eleanor
influenza
call it i. if you like: Bennett, Arnold 2
inhumanity
Man's i. to man: Burns, Robert 9
injustice
I. anywhere is a threat: King, Martin
Luther 5
innocence
our business to lose i.: Bowen, Elizabeth 4
insight
moment's i. is sometimes worth: Holmes,
Oliver Wendell 4
insignificant
as i. men as any in England: Walpole, Robert,
Lord 1
inspiration
Work brings i.: Stravinsky
I. descends only in flashes: White, Patrick
instinct
good animal, true to your i.s: Lawrence 11
I. is a great matter: Shakespeare 136
intellect
i. is always fooled by the heart:
Rochefoucauld 6
i. is improperly exposed: Smith, Sydney 7
intellectual
word 'Intellectual' suggests: Auden 14
Treason of the I.s: Benda
i. is someone whose mind: Camus 5
intelligence
i. is powerless: Crisp 5
underestimating the i. of the great masses:
Mencken 3
I. is quickness: Whitehead, Alfred North 2
intelligent
i. are to the intelligentsia: Baldwin, Stanley 4
intercourse
Sexual i. began: Larkin 1
interest
common i. always will prevail: Dryden 7
interested
i. in everything ... well done: Cochran
interpretation
I. is the revenge: Sontag 1
interviewed
When you i. the Pope: Castro 3
intimacy
In human i.: Akhmatova
invasion
the long-promised i.: Churchill, Winston 13
invisible
an i. man: Ellison
Ireland
I. is the old sow: Joyce 3
Irish
I. and the Jews have a psychosis: Behan 5
iron
I have tamed men of i.: Alva
two i.s in the fire: Beaumont and Fletcher 4
i. curtain has descended: Churchill, Winston
19

Ishmael
Call me I.: Melville
island
what a snug little I.: Dennis 3
Israel
State of I. ... peace: Arafat
issue
happy i. ... afflictions: Common Prayer, Book
of 11
Italy
I. a paradise for horses: Burton, Robert 5

Jabberwock
Beware the J.: Carroll 9
Jack
'Have you news of my boy J.': Kipling 27
J. shall have Jill: Shakespeare 311
Since every J. became a gentleman:
Shakespeare 362
Jade
Holla, ye pampered J.s of Asia: Marlowe 15
jam
j. to-morrow and j. yesterday: Carroll 13
James
work of Henry J.: Guedalla 1
He [William J.] is so concrete: Peirce
jaw-jaw
j. is always better: Churchill, Winston 20
jealousy
all j. to the bride: Barrie 7
negative judgement ... smacks of j.:
Baudrillard 1
j. is cruel as the grave: Bible 64
J. ... alone against smiling enemies: Bowen,
Elizabeth 3
j. of husbands ... never faithful: Crisp 6
To j., nothing is more frightful: Sagan 3
beware, my lord, of j.: Shakespeare 342
Jerusalem
pray for the peace of J.: Common Prayer,
Book of 35
jest
j.'s prosperity lies in the ear: Shakespeare 226
Jesu
friend, for J.'s sake forbear: Shakespeare 449
Jew
Irish and the J.s have a psychosis: Behan 5
J.s will come from everywhere: Ben-Gurion 1
jewellery
Don't ever wear artistic j.: Colette 1
just rattle your j.: Lennon 2
job
It's just a j.: Ali 1
I was looking for a j.: Morrissey 1
jog
J. on, j. on: Shakespeare 431
John
King J. was not a good man: Milne 1
Johnny
O marry me, J.: Auden 11
Little J. Head-in-Air: Hoffman 3
Johnson
no arguing with J.: Goldsmith 9
Why, Dr. J.: Goldsmith 10
joke
j. with a double meaning: Barker
A j.'s a very serious thing: Churchill, Charles
2

joke *(cont.)*
  gentle dullness ever loves a j.: Pope 3
  don't make j.s ... watch the government:
    Rogers, Will 4
Jonson
  J. knew the critic's part: Collins, William 2
Josephine
  Not tonight, J.: Napoléon 5
journalism
  J. — an ability: West, Rebecca 1
  Rock j. is: Zappa 1
journalist
  J.s say a thing: Bennett, Arnold 7
  cannot hope to bribe ... British j.: Wolfe,
    Humbert
journey
  Long Day's J. into Night: O'Neill 4
joy
  j. cometh in the morning: Common Prayer,
    Book of 19
  J. ruled the day: Dryden 22
  j.s of the chase: Gordon 2
  vain deluding j.s: Milton 15
judge
  'I'll be j., I'll be jury: Carroll 2
  J. not the play before: Davies, John 2
  a j. should be looked upon: Leon
  J. not the play before: Quarles 2
  J.s, as a class: Wodehouse 8
judgement
  When I was green in j.: Shakespeare 12
Jumblies
  lands where the J. live: Lear 2
justice
  The price of j.: Bennett, Arnold 4
  J. is truth in action: Disraeli 16
  j. ... seen to be done: Hewart
  what stings is j.: Mencken 10
  capacity for j. makes democracy possible:
    Niebuhr 1
  Poetic J., with her lifted scale: Pope 2

kangaroo
  Old Man K.: Kipling 21
Kansas
  K. had better stop raising: Lease
Keats
  Who killed John K.: Byron, George, Lord 39
Kew
  Go down to K. in lilac-time: Noyes
kick
  I get a k. out of you: Porter, Cole 4
kill
  not k.; but need'st not strive: Clough 3
  k. a wife with kindness: Shakespeare 383
  each man k.s the thing he loves: Wilde 2
killed
  Better be k. than frightened: Surtees 7
killing
  k. of a criminal can be: Benjamin 2
kin
  little more than k.: Shakespeare 62
kind
  fellow-feeling makes one wond'rous k.:
    Garrick 2
kindled
  K. he was, and blasted: Byron, George, Lord
    11

kindness
  tak a cup o' k. yet: Burns, Robert 3
  When k. has left people: Cather 2
  k. and lies are worth: Greene, Graham 3
king
  The k. never dies: Blackstone 1
  the k. can do no wrong: Blackstone 3
  God bless the K.: Edward VIII 2
  my duties as K.: Edward VIII 2
  only five K.s left: Farouk
  K. of glory, K. of peace: Herbert, George 8
  Right Divine of K.s to govern wrong: Pope 4
  Here lies a great and mighty k.: Rochester 2
  A k. of shreds and patches: Shakespeare 113
  such divinity doth hedge a k.:
    Shakespeare 121
  every inch a k.: Shakespeare 213
  The Once and Future K.: White, T H
King
  chief defect of Henry K.: Belloc 5
kinquering
  K. congs their titles take: Spooner
kiss
  K. till the cows: Beaumont and Fletcher 9
  Let him k. me with: Bible 61
  K. me a thousand times: Catullus
  must not k. and tell: Congreve 4
  come let us k. and part: Drayton 2
  promised k. of springtime: Hammerstein 1
  What is a k.: Herrick 6
  K. me, Hardy: Nelson 4
kiss'd
  We have k. away: Shakespeare 20
  I k. thee ere I kill'd thee: Shakespeare 351
kissing
  K. don't last: cookery do: Meredith, George 4
knight
  a verray parfit gentil k.: Chaucer 2
  what can ail thee, K. at arms: Keats 7
  gentle k. was pricking: Spenser 4
know
  no man truly k.s another: Browne, Thomas 6
  more a man k.s: Shaw 13
knowing
  proud of k. something: Nabokov 2
knowledge
  taken all k. to be: Bacon 43
  words without k.: Bible 39
  k. is bought in the market: Clough 1
  province of k. to speak: Holmes, Oliver
    Wendell 3
Kubla Khan
  In Xanadu did K.: Coleridge, Samuel Taylor
    16

labor
  l. ... employer of capital: George, Henry
labour
  Honest l. bears a lovely face: Dekker 1
  insupportable l. of doing nothing: Steele 1
labourer
  l. is worthy of his hire: Bible 107
Labour Party
  to become a left-winger in the L.: Nellist
lad
  l.s that will die in their glory: Housman 10
  Two l.s that thought: Shakespeare 427

lady
There is a l. sweet and kind: Ford, Thomas
L., L., should you meet: Parker 11
l. doth protest too much: Shakespeare 108
l., if surprised by melancholy: Stoppard 1

lamb
Little L., who made thee: Blake 11

lamp
l.s are going out all over Europe: Grey

lamp-post
leaning on a l.: Formby

land
L. of Hope and Glory: Benson 1
l. flowing with milk and honey: Bible 15
l. of lost content: Housman 12
seen the promised l.: King, Martin Luther 10
Into the l. of my dreams: King, Stoddard
L. of our birth, we pledge: Kipling 5
my own, my native l.: Scott, Walter 8
A l. ... seemed always afternoon:
   Tennyson 36

language
L. is the dress of thought: Johnson, Samuel 44
great feast of l.s: Shakespeare 222
You taught me l.: Shakespeare 388
not the l. of painters but the l. of nature: Van
   Gogh
limits of my l. mean: Wittgenstein 4

lapidary
l. instructions a man is: Johnson, Samuel 24

large
l. as life, and twice: Carroll 15

lark
l. at heaven's gate: Shakespeare 52

lass
A l. unparallel'd: Shakespeare 31
Yon solitary Highland l.: Wordsworth,
   William 24

lassie
What can a young l. do: Burns, Robert 17
I Love a L.: Lauder 3

last
At the l., best: Shakespeare 9

Las Vegas
Fear and Loathing in L.: Thompson, Hunter

Latin
Small L., and less Greek: Jonson 6

laugh
if I l. at any mortal thing: Byron, George,
   Lord 31

laughed
when he l.: Auden 7

Laura
if L. had been Petarch's wife: Byron, George,
   Lord 27

law
L. is a bottomless pit: Arbuthnot
windward of the l.: Churchill, Charles 1
'the l. is a ass': Dickens 24
fair play of the British criminal l.: Doyle 7
repeal of bad or obnoxious l.s: Grant
The Common L. of England: Herbert, A P 8
part which l.s or kings can cause: Johnson,
   Samuel 50
till the fear of the L. Joyce 2
The army of unalterable l.: Meredith, George
   2

l.s of life: Ruskin 6
Ignorance of the l. excuses no man: Selden 3
windy side o' the l.: Shakespeare 417
L.s are generally found: Shenstone
Unequal l.s unto a savage race: Tennyson 54
refuse to obey an unjust l.: Tocqueville 3

lay
L. your sleeping head: Auden 12

leader
final test of a l.: Lippman 1

league
Half a l. onward: Tennyson 8

leal
To the land o' the l.: Nairne 3

Lear
pleasant to know Mr. L.: Lear 1

learning
Much l., doth make thee mad: Bible 118
little l. is a dangerous thing: Pope 24
act of conscious l.: Szasz 4

Lee
I and my Annabel L.: Poe 1

leg
Four l.s good: Orwell 1

leisure
To be able to fill l. intelligently: Russell,
   Bertrand, Lord 7

lend
Three things I never l.s: Surtees 6

leopard
change ... or the l. his spots: Bible 76

less
l. in this than meets the eye: Bankhead 2

lettuce
eating too much l. is 'soporific': Potter, Beatrix
   1

leveller
l.s wish to level down: Johnson, Samuel 23

lexicographer
L. ... harmless drudge: Johnson, Samuel 4

liar
best l. is he: Butler, Samuel 21

liberal
l. ...tells other people what to do: Baraka 1
L.s offer a mixture: Macmillan 4

liberty
L. is l.: Berlin, Sir Isiah 2
L., too, must be limited: Burke, Edmund 24
L.'s in every blow: Burns, Robert 13
holy name of l. or democracy: Gandhi,
   Mahatma 2
play not with my l.: Godolphin
give me l., or give me death: Henry,
   Patrick 2
tree of l. must be refreshed: Jefferson 3
isn't true that l. is precious: Lenin 2
l. ... must be thus far limited: Mill 5
O l.! what crimes: Roland

Liberty-Hall
This is L., gentlemen: Goldsmith 11

library
l. is thought in cold storage: Samuel 2
My l. / Was dukedom large enough:
   Shakespeare 387

lie
A l. would have no sense: Adler, Alfred
mixture of a l.: Bacon 40

live

had six months to l.: Asimov
Man doth not l. by bread: Bible 20
Everything that l.s, / L.s not alone: Blake 5
To l. is like love: Butler, Samuel 11
should l. our lives as though: Carter,
  Jimmy 2
Let us l., my Lesbia: Catullus 2
don't actually l. longer: Freud, Clement
Bid me to l.: Herrick 8
means by which we l.: King, Martin Luther 3
l. together as brothers: King, Martin Luther 9

lived

I have l. long enough: Shakespeare 267

lives

l. ... strange dark interludes: O'Neill 2
l. of quiet desperation: Thoreau 3

living

Wasted his substance with riotous l.: Bible 109
l. and ceasing to live ... imaginary: Breton,
  André 1
The long habit of l.: Browne, Thomas 10
l. thing is distinguished: Spencer 5
too much love of l.: Swinburne 3
Plain l. and high thinking: Wordsworth,
  William 31

Livingstone

Dr L., I presume: Stanley

Lochinvar

L. is come out of the west: Scott, Walter 10
never was knight like the young L.: Scott,
  Walter 11

Lolita

L., light of my life: Nabokov 3

London

people of L. ... would say to Hitler: Churchill,
  Winston 15
This is a L. particular: Dickens 4
When a man is tired of L.: Johnson, Samuel
  36
MPs never see the L. that exists beyond:
  Livingstone, Ken

loneliness

L. of the Long-Distance Runner: Sillitoe

lonely

I sit beside my l. fire: Aíde

long

not l., the weeping and the laughter: Dowson
  3
A l. shot, Watson: Doyle 8

longing

Immortal l.s in me: Shakespeare 30

look

l. of love alarms: Blake 18
shall not l. upon his like again: Shakespeare
  67

lord

The L. gave ... blessed be the name: Bible 34
L. is my shepherd: Common Prayer, Book of
  18
see the works of the L.: Common Prayer,
  Book of 30
fear of the L. ... wisdom: Common Prayer,
  Book of 31
L. shall preserve: Common Prayer, Book of 34
Except the L. build: Common Prayer, Book of
  36

The L. survives the rainbow of His will:
  Lowell, Robert 2
Mongrel beef-witted l.: Shakespeare 402
glorious L. of life: Spenser 1
L. of himself: Wotton 2

Lord Ronald

L. ... flung himself: Leacock 2

lost

All is not l.: Milton 35
Praising what is l.: Shakespeare 3

lot

l. is fallen unto me: Common Prayer, Book of
  15

Lothario

that haughty, gallant, gay L.: Rowe 2

louse

between a l. and a flea: Johnson, Samuel 42

lov'd

till we l.? were we not wean'd: Donne 10
Thou hast not l.: Shakespeare 34
She lov'd me for the dangers: Shakespeare
  332

love

When l.'s well-tim'd: Addison 4
l. is bitter: Aiken
To l. is to suffer: Allen 6
where l. isn't allowed: Angelou 1
l. ... life, its enemy: Anouilh 2
l. you till the ocean: Auden 1
thought that l. would last: Auden 8
We must l. one another: Auden 17
O tell me the truth about l.: Auden 18
L. and do what you will: Augustine of
  Hippo 3
likes to be crossed in l.: Austen 14
where there is no l.: Bacon 18
L. can find entrance: Bacon 23
Nuptual l. maketh mankind: Bacon 24
L. is just a system: Barnes, Julian 3
L. ... the delightful interval: Barrymore
most power to hurt us that we l.: Beaumont,
  Francis
Women who l. the same man: Beerbohm 6
somebody to l. you: Behan 6
L. ceases to be a pleasure: Behn 2
At twenty a man is rash in l.: Bennett, Arnold
  1
falling in l. is wonderful: Berlin, Irving 1
I am sick of l.: Bible 62
Rise up, my l.: Bible 63
l. is strong as death: Bible 64
waters cannot quench l.: Bible 65
Greater l. hath no man: Bible 114
L. seeketh not itself to please: Blake 6
L., the human form divine: Blake 7
L. that never told can be: Blake 16
the wilder shores of l.: Blanch
When l. is done: Bourdillon
Absence and letters ... forcing ground of l.:
  Brenan 1
think that the most important thing ... is l.:
  Brenan 4
Ends all our month-long l.: Bridges 2
So sweet l. seemed that April morn: Bridges 4
My l. for Linton ... for Heathcliff: Brontë,
  Emily 3
'Not Death, but L.': Browning, Elizabeth
  Barrett 1

love *(cont.)*

How do I l. thee: Browning, Elizabeth Barrett 2

l. thee with a l.: Browning, Elizabeth Barrett 3

Such ever was l.'s way: Browning, Robert 9

O lyric L., half angel: Browning, Robert 22

To see her was to l. her: Burns, Robert 1

L. indeed ... united provinces: Burton, Robert 6

hold so fast, as l. can: Burton, Robert 9

All l. at first: Butler, Samuel 1

what a mischievous devil l. is: Butler, Samuel 9

His l. was passion's essence: Byron, George, Lord 11

never wrote ... till I was in l.: Byron, George, Lord 16

In her first passion woman l.s: Byron, George, Lord 25

l. and marriage rarely can: Byron, George, Lord 26

L. and marriage ... horse and carriage: Cahn

L. and all his pleasures are but toys: Campion 2

they / Conquer l., that run away: Carew

lay aside a long-cherished l.: Catullus 3

I hate, I l.: Catullus 4

L. and War are the same: Cervantes 3

L. ... exchange of two fantasies: Chamfort

What is l.? 'tis nature's: Chatterton

L. is noght oold as whan: Chaucer 5

Servant in l.: Chaucer 6

L. is he that alle thing may bind: Chaucer 11

l. gushed from my heart: Coleridge, Samuel Taylor 6

All are but ministers of L.: Coleridge, Samuel Taylor 17

well-nourished l.: Colette 2

recreation it is to be in l.: Colman 1

L. and a cottage: Colman and Garrick

hardly ever tire of l. or rhyme: Cope 7

L., l. ... failing that, alcohol: Cope 8

with life's cares, l. yet: Crabbe

L., thou art absolute sole Lord: Crashaw 1

L. is a sickness full of woes: Daniel 1

l. that moves the sun: Dante Alighieri 3

L. is the whole history: De Staël 1

L. is above the laws: De Staël 2

all we know of L.: Dickinson, Emily 2

To men l. is an incident: Diderot 1

l. robs ... of their wit: Diderot 4

magic of first l.: Disraeli 3

Come live with me, and be my l.: Donne 2

hold your tongue and let me l.: Donne 3

L. built on beauty, soon: Donne 4

The right true end of l.: Donne 7

Only our l. hath no decay: Donne 14

L., all alike, no season knows: Donne 17

Sweetest l., I do not go: Donne 18

L. that dare not speak its name: Douglas, Alfred

My l.'s a noble madness: Dryden 11

l.'s the noblest frailty: Dryden 16

rul'd ... L. the night: Dryden 22

Give all to l.: Emerson 13

I l., and know not why: Ephelia

rheumatism and true l.: Eschenbach

L. distills desire: Euripedes 2

L. and scandal: Fielding 3

What is commonly called l.: Fielding 5

icy blasts that blow on l.: Flaubert

L.'s tongue is in the eyes: Fletcher, Phineas 1

L. is like linen: Fletcher, Phineas 2

L.'s pleasure lasts but a moment: Florian

L. is the tyrant: Ford, John 2

tale without l.: France 4

defenceless against suffering ... we l.: Freud, Sigmund 2

All that matters is l. and work: Freud, Sigmund 8

L. is an irresistible desire: Frost 2

Try thinking of l., or something: Fry, Christopher 2

l. is sufficient unto l.: Gibran 3

make not a bond of l.: Gibran 4

When l. beckons to you: Gibran 5

special quality of l.: Gide 1

l. ...between tyrants and slaves: Goldsmith 7

l. is maister wher he wile: Gower

In l. as in sport: Graves 1

L. is a universal migraine: Graves 4

If only it were possible to l.: Greene, Graham 6

Ah! what is l.: Greene, Robert

L. is the drug: Greer 1

l.—all the wretched cant: Greer 2

great l. is never returned: Hammarskjöld 4

I wish I were in l. again: Hart

L. is a fanclub: Henri, Adrian

L. is swift of foot: Herbert, George 4

L. bade me welcome: Herbert, George 7

L. is a circle: Herrick 7

when I was in l. with you: Housman 8

rather live and l. where death is king: Ingersoll 3

L. is not to be purchased: Jerome, St

L. is like the measles: Jerome, Jerome K 3

l. that has weathered: Jerome, Jerome K 4

L.'s like the measles: Jerrold 5

L. is the wisdom of the fool: Johnson, Samuel 9

l. rules ... no will to power: Jung 8

L. in a hut: Keats 9

For ever wilt thou l.: Keats 11

let the warm L. in: Keats 18

against the reasons of my L.: Keats 29

no deep disappointment ... not deep l.: King, Martin Luther 4

To l. for the sake of being loved: Lamartine

I L. a Lassie: Lauder 3

All You Need Is L.: Lennon and McCartney 5

one of the miracles of l.: Lewis, C S 1

L. in my bosom like a bee: Lodge, Thomas

nothing holier ... first consciousness of l.: Longfellow 3

nothing in this world so sweet as l.: Longfellow 7

L. is more than gold: Lydgate

leaving only l. remedyless: Lyly 2

You made me l. you: McCarthy, Joseph 1

Even making l. can be a duty: Mailer 2

joy of l. is too short: Mallory, Sir Thomas

l. in sincerity the fellow-creatures: Marcus 1

Come live with me and be my l.:
   Marlowe 11
tragedy of l. is indifference: Maugham 12
L. is the only dirty trick: Maugham 13
Marriage is law, and l. is instinct: Maupassant
L. ...: no arboured paradise: Mayakovsky 2
l. boat has crashed: Mayakovsky 3
L. is the delusion that: Mencken 7
l. ... state of perpetual anesthesia:
   Mencken 12
L. is based on a view of women: Mencken 15
whom I l. is hard to catch: Meredith,
   George 1
L. is not all: Millay 3
Hail, wedded L.: Milton 59
So dear I l. him: Milton 65
L.-quarrels oft in pleasing concord end:
   Milton 72
L. is nothing else but: Montaigne 3
L. is enough: Morris, William 4
L. is the state in which: Nietzsche 2
I do not l. thee: Norton 1
are as many pangs in l.: Ovid 3
foolish man who feigned to l.: Ovid 6
L. is like quicksilver: Parker 15
Most people experience l.: Pasternak 1
L. is an attempt: Paz 2
first l.'s impassioned blindness: Peacock 1
What thing is l.: Peele 2
L. is not the dying moan: Perelman
to say how much you l.: Petrarch
wast all that to me, l.: Poe 6
L., free as air: Pope 9
let's fall in l.: Porter, Cole 5
L. is purely a creation: Porter, Katherine Anne
fell in l. with himself: Powell, Anthony 1
Like everybody who is not in l.: Proust 4
Now what is l.: Rainborowe
true l. is a durable fire: Raleigh 1
If all the world and l.: Raleigh 5
ashamed of having been in l.:
   Rochefoucauld 4
no disguise ... long conceal l.:
   Rochefoucauld 5
pleasure of l. is in loving: Rochefoucauld 7
L. begets l.: Roethke 2
To fear l. is to fear life: Russell, Bertrand,
   Lord 13
little girl knows about l.: Sagan 1
L. does not consist in gazing:
   Saint-Exupéry 5
radiance of l.: Schiller 1
l. is loveliest when: Scott, Walter 5
L. still has something of the sea: Sedley
L. means never having to say: Segal
but not for l.: Shakespeare 44
never doubt I l.: Shakespeare 85
How should I your true l. know: Shakespeare
   119
When l. begins to sicken: Shakespeare 192
Do not presume too much upon my l.:
   Shakespeare 193
L., whose month is ever May:
   Shakespeare 220
when L. speaks: Shakespeare 221
But l. is blind: Shakespeare 288
true l. never did run smooth:
   Shakespeare 303

L. looks not with the eyes: Shakespeare 304
With L.'s light wings: Shakespeare 370
This bud of l.: Shakespeare 371
L. goes toward l.: Shakespeare 373
L. sought is good: Shakespeare 415
spring of l. resembleth: Shakespeare 423
l. he laughed to scorn: Shakespeare 425
L. comforteth like sunshine: Shakespeare 426
L. is not l. / Which alters: Shakespeare 446
ruined l., when it is built anew:
   Shakespeare 447
What is L.: Shelley 12
All l. is sweet: Shelley 14
L. gilds the scene: Sheridan, Richard
   Brinsley 7
Leave me, O L.: Sidney 5
l. is stronger than: Singer
All's fair in l. and war: Smedley
L. rules the gods: Sophocles 2
To l. her is: Steele 4
L. has always been the most important:
   Stendhal 1
When l. gets to be important: Stern
L., an' please your Honour: Sterne 4
To have known l.: Swinburne 5
If l. were what the rose is: Swinburne 6
now l. is over: Symons
who l.s finds the door open: Tagore 2
L. made me poet: Tanfield
needs must l. the highest: Tennyson 18
We l. being in l.: Thackeray 8
human l. needs human meriting: Thompson,
   Francis 1
no remedy for l.: Thoreau 1
To l. one person for a whole lifetime:
   Tolstoy 2
understand only because I l.: Tolstoy 3
If l. is the answer: Tomlin
let us make l. deathless: Trench
L. is like any other luxury: Trollope 6
In l. women are professionals: Truffaut
L., like fortune: Vanbrugh 1
none more heroic than the l.: Van Der Post 1
cannot understand the l. affair: Vidal 5
L. is much nicer to be in than: Viorst
L. conquers all things: Virgil 9
It is not that I l. you less: Waller 2
ounce of l. is worth: Wesley
L. is the only industry: West, Mae 9
Yes, I'm in l.: Whitehead, William
When you really want l.: Wilde 3
L. ... / That cordial drop: Wilmot
never too late to fall in l.: Wilson, Sandy 2
If she l. me: Wither 2
comfort in the strength of l.: Wordsworth,
   William 7
man falls in l. through his eyes: Wyatt,
   Woodrow
The only true l.: Zangwill 2
loved
   I l. thee once: Aytoun, Robert
   We l., sir: Browning, Robert 7
   We that had l. him: Browning, Robert 15
   better to have l. and lost: Butler, Samuel 23
   better to be left than never ... l.: Congreve 9
   Twice or thrice had I l. thee: Donne 1
   l. but not brought up: Gudmundsdottir
   better to have l. a short man: Kington

man *(cont.)*
two civilizers of m.: Disraeli 19
m. will not merely endure: Faulkner 4
M. is neither the oldest: Foucault 1
M. is the only animal: Fromm
m. has been up against Nature: Gabor, Dennis
never hated a m. enough: Gabor, Zsa Zsa 4
m. ... is *so* in the way: Gaskell 1
to keep a m.: Hall, Jerry
m. can be destroyed but not defeated:
    Hemingway 6
to love a m. for his virtue: Holmes, John
    Oliver
ought a m. to be ... 'himself': Ibsen 5
Many people ... repelled by m.: Inge 3
m. may build himself a throne: Inge 5
M., biologically considered: James, William 1
greatest m. you had ... seen. Johnson, Samuel
    55
m. of infinite-resource-and-sagacity:
    Kipling 19
Give m. time and he will spoil: Leacock 3
world began without m.: Lévi-Strauss
M. is to be found in reason: Lichtenberg 5
The four stages of m. are: Linkletter
no more time arguing what a good m. should
    be: Marcus 4
M. acts it out. He is the act: Miller, Henry 9
animals regard m. as: Nietzsche 5
A shadow in a dream is M.: Pindar
M. is the measure: Protagoras
Every m. who feels well: Romains
A m. who is good enough: Roosevelt,
    Theodore 3
M. is a credulous animal: Russell, Bertrand,
    Lord 16, 17
Use every m. after his desert: Shakespeare 92
could have better spar'd a better m.:
    Shakespeare 141
m. of such feeble temper: Shakespeare 171
Unaccommodated m.: Shakespeare 209
M., proud m.: Shakespeare 273
let him pass for a m.: Shakespeare 283
none is more wonderful than m.: Sophocles 3
M. dreams of fame while woman:
    Tennyson 21
M. for the field: Tennyson 48
strange what a m. may do: Thackeray 3
m. in the house is worth: West, Mae 1
Give a m. a free hand: West, Mae 2
What m. has made of m.: Wordsworth,
    William 6
Mandalay
the road to M.: Kipling 24
mankind
M. will not be reasoned: Blackstone 2
propensity of m. towards the marvellous:
    Hume 1
No great improvements in the lot of m.: Mill 2
If all m. minus one: Mill 3
proper study of m. is man: Pope 32
salvation of m.: Solzhenitsyn 2
manner
m.s are especially: Waugh 5
manoeuvre
no room for m.: Horrocks 2
map
Roll up that m.: Pitt, William *the Younger* 1

Marathon
mountains look on M.: Byron, George,
    Lord 30
March
Beware the Ides of M.: Shakespeare 170
Mariana
this dejected M.: Shakespeare 277
mariner
It is an ancient M.: Coleridge, Samuel
    Taylor 2
market
m. ... not the invention of capitalism:
    Gorbachev 3
marriage
For the first year of m: Allen 15
M., to women as to men: Anthony 2
appropriate age for m.: Aristotle 3
Happiness in m.: Austen 10
m. had always been her object: Austen 13
more for a m. than a ministry: Bagehot 2
In m. you are chained: Bardot 1
M. ... finest arts of insincerity: Baum, Vicki
every m. is different: Berger 4
M., n ... master, a mistress and two slaves:
    Bierce 7
Moses had a mixed m.: Botha
think of m. as a train: Bowen, Elizabeth 5
M. ... advanced form of warfare: Bradbury 1
distrust ... definition of m.: Bradbury 2
In a happy m.: Brenan 2
M. is an arrangement by which: Brenan 3
friendships ... invalidated by m.: Butler,
    Samuel 22
merry as a m. bell: Byron, George, Lord 6
love and m. rarely can: Byron, George,
    Lord 26
Love and m. ... horse and carriage: Cahn
m. ... before the battle: Carlyle, Jane 3
What is m. but prostituion: Carter, Angela 1
M. is a noose: Cervantes 5
Servant in love, and lord in m.: Chaucer 6
Medieval m.s were entirely: Clark
most happy m.: Coleridge, Samuel Taylor 19
M. belongs to society: Coleridge, Samuel
    Taylor 21
not against hasty m.s: Collins, Wilkie
Though m. makes man and wife: Congreve 1
Courtship to m., is: Congreve 8
M. is a wonderful invention: Connolly, Billy
m. is but for a little while: Crisp 7
M. is to courtship: De Vries 1
The value of m.: De Vries 4
no disparity in m. like: Dickens 15
Society requires that he ... by m.: Dickens 19
woman dictates before m.: Eliot, George 3
m. an open question: Emerson 15
Never say that m.: Euripedes 1
rob a lady ... by way of m.: Fielding 4
Most m.s don't add two people: Fleming
joys of m. are the heaven on earth: Ford, John
    1
eyes wide open before m.: Franklin 2
haven't known many open m.s: Gabor, Zsa
    Zsa 1
M. is a lot like the army: Garner
Whether the m. is true or false: Giraudoux 2
M.s would in general be happy: Johnson,
    Samuel 27

marriage *(cont.)*

M. has many pains: Johnson, Samuel 49

m. is immoral without love: Key, Ellen 1

house of m. ... room for an interpreter: Kunitz

M. is *fun*: Larkin 2

M. is a triumph of habit over hate: Levant 1

no more lovely ... than a good m.: Luther 1

Both my m.s were failures: Mahler

four stages to a m.: Mailer 1

early m.s of silly children: Martineau 2

m. without conflicts ... inconceivable: Maurois 1

successful m. is an edifice: Maurois 2

M. ... necessary evil: Menander 2

M. is like a cage: Montaigne 4

m. ... not a public conveyance: Murdoch 4

realistic deterrent to m.: Nicholson

M. may often be a stormy lake: Peacock 2

good m. is that in which: Rilke 1

M. is for women: Russell, Bertrand, Lord 11

main purpose of m.: Russell, Willy

M. ... matter of taste: Sagan 2

two to make a m. a success: Samuel 1

M. is a desperate thing: Selden 4

M. ... civil contract: Selden 5

curse of m.: Shakespeare 344

hanging prevents a bad m.: Shakespeare 406

M. is popular because: Shaw 22

all m.s are different: Shaw 32

M., I think / For women: Smith, Stevie 2

My definition of m.: Smith, Sydney 6

In m., a man becomes: Stevenson, Robert Louis 14

M. is a step so grave: Stevenson, Robert Louis 16

pretences which are very sincere ... m.: Unamuno 2

m. ... a *sentence*: Vidor

every m. then is best in tune: Watkyns

M. is a great institution: West, Mae 11

M. is a bribe: Wilder, Thornton 1

In Hollywood all m.s are happy: Winters

married

I m. beneath me: Astor 2

not being m. before: Austen 16

he that is m. careth: Bible 123

Reader, I m. him: Brontë, Charlotte

He is dreadfully m.: Browne, Charles Farrar

never m., and that's his hell: Burton, Robert 4

m. to a single life: Crashaw 2

Ven you're a m. man, Samivel: Dickens 27

m. past redemption: Dryden 18

don't sleep with m. men: Ekland

happiness in the m. estate: Fuller, Thomas 3

he has m.. Then he's finished: Gabor, Zsa Zsa 3

if ever we had been m.: Gay 1

sum which two m. people owe: Goethe 1

You, that are going to be m.: Goldsmith 8

honest man who m.: Goldsmith 16

When a woman gets m.: Gorky

m. impossible men: Graves 3

m. men of forty: Hardy 3

young man m. is a young man marred: Kipling 40

distasteful ... new-m. couple: Lamb,

Charles 2

I'm getting m. in the morning: Lerner 2

I've been m. six months: Linklater 1

never having been m. or ... written: Linklater 2

m. – to be the more together: MacNeice 4

No m. man's ever made up his mind till: Maugham 6

No man is genuinely happy, m., who has: Mencken 13

If m. life were all that it might be expected: Mill 7

what delight we m. people: Pepys 5

Since m. life is what we have: Purves

m. couple are well suited when: Rostand 1

peace of God ... I m. her: Tennyson 2

wouldn't have m. him if: Thomas, Caitlin

playing it like m. men: Toscanini 2

'But you m.': Waugh 3

m. life ... three is company: Wilde 6

fights ... best part of m. life: Wilder, Thornton 2

climbs into their graves m.: Wilder, Thornton 4

haven't got to get m.: Wodehouse 7

marries

No man is in love when he m.: Burney 1

doesn't much signify whom one m.: Rogers, Samuel

with him who m.: Stevenson, Robert Louis 18

When a woman m. again: Wilde 19

woman that m. to love: Wycherley

marry

taken in when they m.: Austen 4

when a man should m.: Bacon 26

No man should m. until: Balzac 3

Never m. a man who hates: Bennett, Jill

better to m. than to burn: Bible 122

m. for purely selfish reasons: Brookner 4

to live single or to m.: Burton, Robert 11

positive engagement to m.: Carlyle, Jane 2

excited about nothing – and then m. him: Cher

m. ... any man with a good estate: Congreve 2

proper time to m.: Cowper 4

Every woman should m.: Disraeli 6

They that m. ancient people: Fuller, Thomas 4

that m. where they do not love: Fuller, Thomas 5

M. your son when you will: Herbert, George 6

I'll m. a landlord's daughter: Lamb, Charles 1

The men that women m.: Longfellow 4

must love those whom they do not m.: Martineau 1

When you see what some girls m.: Rowland 6

To m. is to halve: Schopenhauer 4

Going to m. her: Smith, Sydney 16

No woman should m. a teetotaller: Stevenson, Robert Louis 17

m. is to domesticate: Stevenson, Robert Louis 19

Dosnt thou m. for munny: Tennyson 43
Men m., indeed, so as to get: Theophrastus
Don't m. a man to reform him: West, Mae 5
marry'd
    m. in haste, we may repent: Congreve 7
marrying
    M. for love: Allen 10
Martha
    M. was cumbered: Bible 108
masses
    back the m. against the classes: Gladstone
master
    He needs a m.: Diogenes 1
matches
    m. are made in heaven: Burton, Robert 7
mate
    can't m. in captivity: Steinem 5
mathematician
    God is a m.: Dirac
mathematics
    Peculiar m. ... apply to many: West,
        Rebecca 3
Matilda
    M. told such Dreadful Lies: Belloc 10
matrimonial
    difference in m. affairs: Austen 15
    In all m. associations: Ford, Ford Madox
    M. devotion: Gilbert, W S 19
matrimony
    think m. a duty: Austen 6
    argument in favour of m.: Austen 19
    matters of religion and m.: Chesterfield 8
    not be joined in holy M.: Common Prayer,
        Book of 41
    more of love than m.: Goldsmith 17
    critical period in m.: Herbert, A P 2
    M. and murder: Mortimer
    'Tis safest in m.: Sheridan, Richard Brinsley 4
    if we take m. at its lowest: Stevenson, Robert
        Louis 13
Maxim Gun
    got / The M., and they have not: Belloc 14
May
    month of M. / Is comen: Chaucer 9
MCC
    hard to tell where the M. ends: Priestley 2
meadow
    M.s trim with daisies pied: Milton 1
mean
    sight of m.s to do ill deeds: Shakespeare 201
    live within our m.s: Ward 5
meaning
    The m. doesn't matter: Gilbert, W S 26
measure
    M. still for M.: Shakespeare 281
meat
    Some hae m., and canna eat: Burns,
        Robert 14
Meccah
    some to M. turn to pray: Flecker 1
medicine
    m. worse than the malady: Beaumont and
        Fletcher 6
    griefs, I see, m. the less: Shakespeare 53
    mistake m. for magic: Szasz 3
mediocre
    Some men are born m.: Heller 2

mediocrity
    M. knows nothing higher: Doyle 12
medium
    The m. is the message: McLuhan 4
meek
    Blessed are the m.: Bible 78
meet
    When shall we three m. again: Shakespeare
        228
melodies
    Heard m. are sweet: Keats 12
memorial
    m. more enduring than brass: Horace 12
memories
    Our m. are card indexes: Connolly, Cyril 10
    false m. and true ones: Dali 5
    M. of the past are not m.: Roth 1
memory
    m. shows to each man: Benjamin 3
    Our m. is our coherence: Buñuel 1
    indebted to his m. for his jests: Sheridan,
        Richard Brinsley 3
    grand m. for forgetting: Stevenson, Robert
        Louis 6
men
    believe m. were the answer: Barnes, Julian 2
    when m. and mountains meet: Blake 9
    m. in women do require: Blake 10
    To tax and to please ... not given to m.:
        Burke, Edmund 15
    sorts and conditions of m.: Common Prayer,
        Book of 10
    many kinds of awful m.: Cope 2
    Bloody m. are like bloody buses: Cope 3
    not as other m.: Dewey
    cannot learn m. from books: Disraeli 12
    M. are but children: Dryden 10
    Beware of m. who cry: Ephron 1
    love m. like some ... food and wine: Greer 4
    M. must work, and women: Kingsley, Mary
        Henrietta
    M.! The only animal ... to fear: Lawrence 5
    The m. that women marry: Longfellow 4
    Whatever you do, you lose a lot of m.:
        Mangin
    M. exist for the sake of one another:
        Marcus 3
    O shame to m.: Milton 48
    M. who have a pierced ear: Rudner 2
    M. were deceivers ever: Shakespeare 320
    Base m. being in love: Shakespeare 336
    becoming the m. we wanted to marry:
        Steinem 1
    Some of my best leading m.: Taylor, Elizabeth
    M. are so romantic: Weldon
    not the m. in my life that counts: West, Mae 8
    M. admire devotion in their wives: West, Mae
        12
    Some women pick m. to marry: West, Mae 14
mercy
    M. has a human heart: Blake 7
    To M., Pity, Peace, and Love: Blake 8
    M. I asked, m. I found: Camden
    M. and truth are met: Common Prayer, Book
        of 26
    quality of m. is not strain'd: Shakespeare 295
    Nothing emboldens sin so much as m.:
        Shakespeare 398

mercy *(cont.)*
  M., compassion and justice come from God: Waite
  God's m. is manifest: Weil 10
merit
  silence that accepts m.: Emerson 7
merriment
  source of innocent m.: Gilbert, W S 23
mess
  Don't m. with me: Campbell, Kim
  In every m. I finds: Dibdin 2
messenger
  m. who brings bad news: Sophocles 1
messiah
  M. Is a ... apostle of Allah: Koran 2
method
  You know my m.s, Watson: Doyle 6
meum
  distinctions of *m.* and *tuum*: Lamb, Charles 7
Mexico
  Poor M., so far from God: Díaz
mice
  best laid schemes of m. and men: Burns, Robert 15
middle
  people who stay in the m. of the road: Bevan 4
midnight
  cease upon the m. with no pain: Keats 15
  embalmer of the still m.: Keats 21
  heard the chimes at m.: Shakespeare 152
mighty
  How the m. are fallen: Bible 27
military
  Other than that ... great m. man: Schwarzkopf
milk
  full o' the m. of human kindness: Shakespeare 239
mill
  m.s of God grind slowly: Longfellow 6
miller
  m. sees not all the water: Burton, Robert 8
Milton
  M. ... was a genius: Johnson, Samuel 38
  M.! thou shouldst be living: Wordsworth, William 8
  we think thee M., Death, and Sin: Young 1
mince
  dined on m., and slices of quince: Lear 4
mind
  My m. is not a bed: Agate
  Our m.s are like those maps: Boyd
  not enough to have a good m.: Descartes 3
  My M. to Me a Kingdom: Dyer
  There is no female m.: Gilman 2
  human m. is like an umbrella: Gropius
  There are no chaste m.s: Hoffer 6
  Little m.s are interested: Hubbard 2
  concentrates his m.: Johnson, Samuel 32
  sound m. in a sound body: Juvenal 4
  lose myself in other men's m.s: Lamb, Charles 5
  To know the *m.* of a woman: Lawrence 17
  waking m. ... least serviceable in the arts: Miller, Henry 11
  The m. is its own place: Milton 38
  calm of m. all passion spent: Milton 74

clap your padlock on her m.: Prior 2
noble m. here is o'erthrown: Shakespeare 104
I am not in my perfect m.: Shakespeare 215
satisfied with her lover's m.: Trollope 5
A m. conscious of right: Virgil 2
all the human m. has accomplished: Wells 8
to speak one's m.: Wilde 8
miner
  only because m.s sweat: Orwell 9
minority
  m. is always right: Ibsen 2
minstrel
  A wandering m.: Gilbert, W S 25
  The M. was infirm and old: Scott, Walter 7
minute
  take care of the m.s: Chesterfield 2
  our m.s hasten to their end: Shakespeare 438
miracle
  M.s do not happen: Arnold, Matthew 10
mirth
  public mischief in your m.: Cowper 8
  M., admit me of thy crew: Milton 2
  I love such m. as: Walton 2
mischief
  To mourn a m.: Shakespeare 333
misery
  dwell on guilt and m.: Austen 5
misfortune
  in sour m.'s book: Shakespeare 379
mislead
  One to m. the public: Asquith, Herbert, Earl of 2
miss
  A m. for pleasure: Gay 8
Miss Dombey
  I positively adore M.: Dickens 16
mission
  man's highest m. on earth: Dali 4
Miss T
  whatever M. eats: De La Mare 4
mistake
  M.s ... of a sacred nature: Dali 3
  M.s are a fact of life: Giovanni
  The man who makes no m.s: Phelps
  m.s if you've lived ... properly: Reagan 1
  life spent in making m.s: Shaw 8
  built to make m.s: Thomas, Lewis 2
mistress
  to a man the faults of his m.: Proust 2
  O m. mine: Shakespeare 408
  My m.' eyes are nothing like: Shakespeare 448
Mizpah
  M.; for he said: Bible 11
mob
  supreme governors, the m.: Walpole, Horace, Lord 2
model
  m. of a modern Major-General: Gilbert, W S 28
Model T
  can have the M. in any colour: Ford, Henry 1
moderation
  astonished at my own m.: Clive 1
  m. even in excess: Disraeli 13
modest
  good deal to be m. about: Churchill, Winston 2

modesty
ladies of irresistible m.: Steele 3

mom
M. and Pop were just a couple of kids: Holiday

moment
m.s when you feel free: Brookner 3
who seizes the right m.: Goethe 2

monarch
m. of all I survey: Cowper 15
m.s must obey: Dryden 17
merry m., scandalous and poor: Rochester 1

money
M. is better than poverty: Allen 14
Making m. ain't nothing: Armstrong 1
except for large sums of m.: Ayckbourn 2
M. is like muck: Bacon 32
M. ... exactly like sex: Baldwin, James 1
M. speaks sense ... all nations: Behn 6
M. gives me pleasure: Belloc 13
m. is the root of all evil: Bible 134
most important thing ... is m.: Brenan 4
m. has a power above: Butler, Samuel 4
M. doesn't not talk: Dylan 2
M. is the sinews of love: Farquhar 6
m. is the most chilling: Flaubert
Put not your trust in m.: Holmes, Oliver Wendell 1
M. can't buy me love: Lennon and McCartney 1
enough m. ... unless I buy something: Mason
M. is like a sixth sense: Maugham 8
M. ... better class of enemy: Milligan
pretty to see what m. will do: Pepys 6
rub up against m.: Runyon 2
Put m. in thy purse: Shakespeare 335

mongrel
M. beef-witted lord: Shakespeare 402

monkey
for a wilderness of m.s: Shakespeare 291

monogamous
some people are born m.: Strindberg

monogamy
looking for m.: Ephron 2

Montreal
Oh God! Oh M: Butler, Samuel 16

monument
If you see his m. look around:

moo
You silly m.: Speight

moon
'Don't let's ask for the m.: Prouty
Whom mortals call the M.: Shelley 6
sad steps, O M., thou climb'st: Sidney 4
it is harvest m. with me: Walpole, Horace, Lord 3

moral
a matter of m. imperative: Geldof 2
pretend that we're basically m.: Hands
teach the m.s of a whore: Johnson, Samuel 22
m. law within me: Kant 1
Mankind's true m. test: Kundera
as one is unhappy one becomes m.: Proust 3
m. immune system of this country: Streisand
is there any m. shut: Tennyson 42

moralist
cruelty ... delight to m.s: Russell, Bertrand, Lord 15

morality
No m. can be founded: Ayer 1
M. is the herd instinct: Nietzsche 6
our idea of m.: Stevenson, Robert Louis 4

morn
m., in russet mantle clad: Shakespeare 61

mornin'
it's nice to get up in the m.: Lauder 2

morning
hate to get up in the m.: Berlin, Irving 3
Never glad confident m. again: Browning, Robert 14
joy cometh in the m.: Common Prayer, Book of 19
M. in the Bowl of Night: Fitzgerald, Edward
many a glorious m. I have seen: Shakespeare 434

Morocco
M. is like a tree: Hassan II

morrow
And now good m.: Donne 9

mortal
what fools these m.s be: Shakespeare 310

mother
M. is the dead heart of the family: Greer 3
She was no different from other m.s: Jacobson
And Her M. Came Too: Novello

mother-in-law
marvellous place to drop one's m.: Foch 2
savage contemplates his m.: Frazer
m. died ... funeral expenses: Jerome, Jerome K 6
Two m.s: Russell, John 2

mountain
M. and brilliant bird: Campbell, David Gordon
M.s will be in labour: Horace 2

mourn
one m.s alone: Berger 4

mouth
m. of very babes: Common Prayer, Book of 12

moved
The day he m. out: Cope 5

movie
m. is never any better than: Hecht
demand for extraordinary m.s: James, Clive

Mr. Micawber
I will never desert M.: Dickens 11

Mr Quiverful
M., the rector of Puddingdale: Trollope 2

Mrs Ballinger
M. is one of the ladies: Wharton 2

Mrs Courtly
told his life story to M.: Smith, Stevie 1

Mr. Selwyn
If M. calls again: Fox

Mrs Ogmore-Pritchard
M.: And before you let the sun in: Thomas, Dylan 3

Mrs Wadman
to be married to M.: Sterne 6

Mr Toad
intelligent M.: Grahame 2

muck
when to stop raking the m.: Roosevelt, Theodore 4

munny
Dosnt thou marry for m.: Tennyson 43

murder
I met M. in the way: Shelley 10

muscle
function of a m.: Da Vinci

music
M., the greatest good: Addison 11
English may not like m.: Beecham 2
how potent cheap m. is: Coward 6
We are the m. makers: O'Shaughnessy
M., moody food: Shakespeare 17
How sour sweet m. is: Shakespeare 360
If m. be the food of love: Shakespeare 405
then the art of m. begins: Wagner
everything seems to happen to m.: Williams, Tennessee 3

musical
law of the m. world: Wharton 1

musick
M. has charms to sooth: Congreve 5

mutation
nothing exempt from the peril of m.: Raleigh 2

mystery
Behold, I shew you a m.: Bible 129

name
n. liveth for evermore: Apocrypha 3
In the n. of human nature: Burke, Edmund 22
glory and the nothing of a n.: Byron, George, Lord 14
n., at which the world: Johnson, Samuel 51
whose n. was writ in water: Keats 30
My n. is Might-have-been: Rossetti, Dante Gabriel 2
Good n. in man or woman: Shakespeare 341
What's in a n.: Shakespeare 369
must not be a n. dropper: Stevas
Bright with n.s that men remember: Swinburne 1

nation
let fierce contending n.s know: Addison 8
what our N. stands for: Betjeman 2
N.s, like men, have their infancy: Bolingbroke
day of small n.s has passed: Chamberlain, Joseph
this n. will rise up: King, Martin Luther 8
new n., conceived in liberty: Lincoln 6
a n. of amateurs: Roseberry 1
N.s, like men, are teachable: Rousseau 4

nationalism
N. is a silly cock: Aldington
n., when hate for people: De Gaulle 1
N. is an infantile sickness: Einstein 1

nature
not man the less, but N. more: Byron, George, Lord 13
drive out n. with a pitchfork: Horace 5
In n. there are neither rewards: Ingersoll 2
unravelling n. like an old jumper: Kemp
law of n. which love alone: Laclos
N. I loved, and next to N., Art: Landor 2
N. does not make jumps: Linnaeus
happy he ... read in N.'s mystic book: Marvell 12

Whom universal N. did lament: Milton 18
mere copier of n.: Reynolds, Joshua 2
N.'s infinite book: Shakespeare 6
In n. there's no blemish but: Shakespeare 418
N., red in tooth and claw: Tennyson 27
look on n. not as in the hour: Wordsworth, William 4

naval
Don't talk to me about n. tradition: Churchill, Winston 3

necessity
N. is the plea: Pitt, William *the Younger* 2
no virtue like n.: Shakespeare 355
Thy n. is yet greater than mine: Sidney 7
N. has no law: Syrus 2

negative
n. judgement ... more satisfaction: Baudrillard 1

Negro
To be a N. in this country: Baldwin, James 7

neighbor
do *exactly as your* n.s do: Post 2

neighbour
make sport for our n.s: Austen 17
love thy n. as thyself: Bible 95
our n.'s house is on fire: Burke, Edmund 11
Love thy n. — and if he: West, Mae 10

Nelly
Let not poor N. starve: Charles II 2

Nelson
keep the N. touch: Newbolt 3
N.'s marriage: Pringle

neutrino
N.s, they are very small: Updike 3

news
bringer of unwelcome n.: Shakespeare 144

newspaper
only truths to be relied on in a n.: Jefferson 5
A good n., I suppose: Miller, Arthur 3
cuts the time it takes to read a n.: Whitehorn

Newton
God said, *Let N. be*: Pope 21
statue stood / Of N.: Wordsworth, William 18

New York
N. is my Lourdes: Behan 4

nice
'N. but nubbly': Kipling 20

nickname
A n. is the heaviest stone: Hazlitt 4

night
what of the n.: Bible 70
drowned with us in endless n.: Herrick 2
honey'd middle of the n.: Keats 4
N. hath a thousand eyes: Lyly 3
N. and day, you are the one: Porter, Cole 6
borrower of the n.: Shakespeare 250
Do not go gentle into that good n.: Thomas, Dylan 1
meaner beauties of the n.: Wotton 4

nightingale
O n., that on yon bloomy spray: Milton 76

no
The everlasting n.: Carlyle, Thomas 9
she can't say 'N.': Parker 14

Noah
N. he often said: Chesterton 19

nobility
idea of n. in our heads: Lichtenberg 4
n. of a human being: Rostand 5

noise
N. A stench in the ear: Bierce 8
those that made such a n.: Edwards, Jonathan
The isle is full of n.s: Shakespeare 392

No Man's Land
N. under snow: Owen

north
N. alone is silent and at peace: Leacock 3

nose
see what is in front of one's n.: Orwell 10

nostalgia
N. for the gutter: Augier

note
N.s ... necessary evils: Johnson, Samuel 47
pauses between the n.s: Schnabel

nothing
N. can be created out of n.: Lucretius 2
n. a-year, paid quarterly: Surtees 8

novel
reason for existence of a n.: James, Henry 7
to the nineteenth century n.: Raphael

novelty
public will always clamour for ... n.: Hood 1

number
I lisped in n.s: Pope 13
If I called the wrong n.: Thurber 5
Perhaps the plaintive n.s flow: Wordsworth,
William 25

nun
N.s fret not: Wordsworth, William 10

nunnery
Get thee to a n.: Shakespeare 102

nurse
always keep a-hold of N.: Belloc 7

nut
N.s: McAuliffe

oat
O.s ... in Scotland supports: Johnson,
Samuel 5

obit
I read the o.s in The Times: Douglas-Home

oblivion
certain o. at that point: Bannister

observation
Let o. with extensive view: Johnson,
Samuel 52

occasion
all o.s do inform against me:
Shakespeare 117

occupation
worse o.s in this world: Sterne 3

Odyssey
surge and thunder of the O: Lang

offence
confront the visage of o.: Shakespeare 96

offer
o. he can't refuse: Puzo

office
When we got into o.: Kennedy, John F 7
man who has no o.: Shaw 12

old
o. age is always fifteen years older: Baruch 1
O. and well stricken: Bible 10
Grow o. along with me: Browning, Robert 21

'You are o., Father William: Carroll 3
man is as o. as he's feeling: Collins, Mortimer
Most people grow o. within: De
Vauvenargues
I grow o.: Eliot, T S 1
You that are o.: Shakespeare 147
friend, you never can be o.: Shakespeare 445
o. heads on young shoulders: Spark 2
When you are o.: Yeats 10

older
As i grow o.: Sayers 2

ole
if you knows of a better 'o.: Bairnsfather

Oliver Twist
O. has asked for more: Dickens 22

omen
Far from us be the o.: Ovid 2

one
O. is still: Sartre 5

opinion
never had a humble o.: Baez
upon the difference of an o.: Browne, Thomas
4
Variety of o. is necessary: Feyerabend
They that approve a private o.: Hobbes 2
never so good or so bad as their o.s:
Mackintosh 1
the o. we are endeavouring to stifle: Mill 4
So many men, so many o.s: Suetonius 4
Many men, so many o.s: Terence 3

opponent
ascribe to an o. motives: Barrie 12

opportunities
can present people with o.: Lehmann

opportunity
A man must make his o.: Bacon 4
O. makes a thief: Bacon 44

opposition
duty of an O.: Churchill, Randolph 1

oppression
never again ... o. of one by another: Mandela

optimist
The o. proclaims: Cabell
o. ... never had much experience: Marquis 4

Orace
O., you're for 'ome: Robertson

orchestra
golden rules for an o.: Beecham 1
o. play as they like: Beecham 3

orgy
o. looks particularly alluring: Muggeridge 1

original
most o. in a man's nature: Cohen 1

outside
I am just going o.: Oates, Lawrence

overpaid
O., overfed, oversexed and over here: Trinder

owl
O. and the Pussy-Cat: Lear 3
white o. in the belfry sits: Tennyson 44

owner
Down went the o.s: Gilbert, W S 1

Ozymandias
My name is O.: Shelley 13

paddle
every man p. his own canoe: Marryat 3

pain
P.s of love be sweeter: Dryden 24
Of all p.s, the greatest p.: Granville
p. of loving you: Lawrence 13

paint
I p. objects as I think them: Picasso 2
p. a portrait I lose a friend: Sargent

painted
paltry, foolish p. things: Drayton 1

painter
gain has never made a p.: Allston
Ideally, a p.: Rilke 2

painting
amateur p. in water-colour: Stevenson, Robert
Louis 15

pale
Why so p. and wan: Suckling 1

papa
P. loved mamma: Sandburg 6

Papacy
P. is not other than the Ghost: Hobbes 4

paper
any part of this p. appears dull: Steele 2

paradise
To live in P. alone: Marvell 6
A P. within thee, happier far: Milton 66

parent
p.s obey their children: Edward VIII 1
tangled web do p.s weave: Nash 2

Paris
P. is a movable feast: Hemingway 4
P. is well worth a mass: Henri IV 2

park
p.s are the lungs of London: Pitt, William *the Younger* 4

Parliament
England is the mother of P.s: Bright 1

parliamentarian
only safe pleasure for a p.: Critchley

parrot
This p. is no more: Cleese

parson
p. knows enough who knows: Cowper 14

part
only p. to meet again: Gay 7
seldom indeed that one p.s on good terms:
Proust 5
p. to tear a cat in: Shakespeare 305

parted
P. are those who are singing today: Bowen,
Edward Ernest
When we two p.: Byron, George, Lord 43

parties
one of the two p. would be in office ... other
in prison: Bukharin

parting
P. is all we know of heaven: Dickinson, Emily
1
In every p.: Eliot, George 8
Every p. is a foretaste of death: Schopenhauer
3
Their every p. was to die: Tennyson 29

party
Stick to your p.: Disraeli 4
No p. has a monopoly over ... right:
Gorbachev 1
best number for a dinner p.: Gulbenkian
P. loyalty lowers the greatest: La Bruyère 3

party-spirit
P., which at best is but: Pope 46

passed
So he p. over, and all the trumpets:
Bunyan 7

passion
What is p.: Boorman
Infinite p., and the pain: Browning,
Robert 25
no such thing as a life of p.: Byron, George,
Lord 44
When the glowing of p.'s over: Centilevre 1
one p., the p. for happiness: Diderot 3
desolate and sick of an old p.: Dowson 1
P., though a bad regulator: Emerson 2
inferno of his p.s: Jung 4
science of the tender p.: Pushkin 1
Three p.s ... governed my life: Russell,
Bertrand, Lord 1
To inspire hopeless p. is my destiny:
Thackeray 4

past
rather absurd about the p.: Beerbohm 2
two kept house, the P. and I: Hardy 4
The p. is a foreign country: Hartley
looking forward to the p.: Osborne 2
They shall not get p.: Pétain 1
cannot remember the past are condemned:
Santayana 6

pasture
To-morrow to fresh woods, and p.s new:
Milton 23
sell the p. now to buy: Shakespeare 156

path
beaten p. to his door: Emerson 18
p.s lead to a woman's love: Fletcher, John
primrose p. of dalliance: Shakespeare 70

patience
P. A minor form of despair: Bierce 9
p., p. everywhere like a fog: Greene,
Graham 5
I laugh'd him out of p.: Shakespeare 18
like p. on a monument: Shakespeare 413

patient
Beware the future of a p. man: Dryden 2
p., provided I get my own way: Thatcher 1

patriotism
P. is a lively sense: Aldington
p. is not enough: Cavell
P. is when love of your own: De Gaulle 1
P. is the last refuge: Johnson, Samuel 28

patron
P. Commonly a wretch: Johnson, Samuel 6
Is not a P., my Lord: Johnson, Samuel 17

payment
p. of half twenty shillings: Burke,
Edmund 16

peace
no p. ,.. unto the wicked: Bible 72
P. to him that is far: Bible 74
p.; when there is no p.: Bible 75
into the way of p.: Bible 104
depart in p.: Bible 105
makes a solitude, and calls it p.: Byron,
George, Lord 2
P. with honour ... p. for our time:
Chamberlain, Neville 2

In p.: goodwill: Churchill, Winston 8
easier to make war than to make p.:
  Clemenceau
p. which the earth cannot: Common Prayer,
  Book of 7
P. cannot be kept by force: Einstein 2
not p. at any price: Jerrold 4
Give P. a Chance: Lennon 3
P. is indivisible: Litvinov
can't separate p. from freedom: Malcolm X 2
If p. cannot be maintained: Russell, John 1
desolation they call it p.: Tacitus 2
him who desires p., prepare for war: Vegetius

pearl
p.s before swine: Bible 85

pebble
not the only p. on the beach: Braisted

pedantry
P. is the dotage of knowledge: Jackson,
  Holbrook

pelican
a wondrous bird is the p.: Merritt

pen
p.s dwell on guilt and misery: Austen 5
less brilliant p. than mine: Beerbohm 3

pennies
P. from heaven: Burke, Johnny

people
A stiff-necked p.: Bible 18
thy p. shall be my p.: Bible 25
The p. are the masters: Burke, Edmund 20
p. p. have for friends: Gilman 1
P. who like this sort of thing: Lincoln 9

perfection
pursuit of p.: Arnold, Matthew 3

perhaps
The grand P.: Browning, Robert 2
I go to see a great p.: Rabelais 2

peril
Through p.s both of wind: Butler, Samuel 3
no p. in the fight: Corneille

persecution
P. is a bad and indirect: Browne, Thomas 7
P. produced its natural effect: Macaulay 6

Persepolis
ride in triumph through P.: Marlowe 12

perseverance
p. in a good cause: Sterne 9

person
no more a p.: Auden 10
don't love qualities, we love p.s: Maritain

personalities
sight of trivial p.: Woolf 2

pessimism
P., when you get used to it: Bennett,
  Arnold 5
My p. goes to the point: Rostand 3

pessimist
p. before 48: Twain 5

Petrarch
if Laura had been P.'s wife: Byron, George,
  Lord 27

Peter
to see Shock-headed P.: Hoffman 1
The P. Principle: Peter 1

pew
Talk about p.s and steeples: Chesterton 1

Phil
fidgety P., / He won't sit still: Hoffman 2

Philadelphia
I would rather be living in P.: Fields, W C 3

philanthropist
one of those wise p.s: Jerrold 6

philosopher
tried ... to be a p.: Edwards, Oliver
p. hides a secret ambition: Oakeshott 2
never yet a p.: Shakespeare 327
what we want from a p. is insights: Vizinczey

philosophy
P. is the friend and milk-sister: Averroës 1
A little p. inclineth: Bacon 11
think freely about political p.: Comte
mere touch of cold p.: Keats 8
How charming is divine p.: Milton 12
P. is nothing but discretion: Selden 6
Hang up p.: Shakespeare 378
P., the lumber of the schools: Swift 7
P. is the product of wonder: Whitehead,
  Alfred North 4
P. ... is a fight against: Wittgenstein 1

photography
P. is truth: Godard 3

physic
Throw p. to the dogs: Shakespeare 266

physician
P., heal thyself: Bible 106
One of the first duties of the p.: Osler 2
I died last night of my p.: Prior 3
P.s of all men: Quarles 1

picture
p. that produces a moral impression: De
  Goncourt 1
P.s are for entertainment: Goldwyn 1
People who try to explain p.s: Picasso 3
p.s for the page atone: Pope 1

piffle
are as p. before the wind: Ashford 2

pilgrim
To be a p.: Bunyan 8

pilgrimage
I'll take my p.: Raleigh 6

pilot
hope to see my P. face to face: Tennyson 12

Pimpernel
That demmed, elusive P.: Orczy

pink
The very p. of perfection: Goldsmith 12
very p. of courtesy: Shakespeare 375

pious
In p. times: Dryden 5

piper
Wi' a hundred p.s an' a': Nairne 2

pitch
toucheth pitch shall be defiled: Apocrypha 1

pitee
For p. renneth sone: Chaucer 7

pith
all the p. is in the postscript: Hazlitt 2

pity
man without p. is mad: Bond
A heart to p.: Churchill, Charles 4
p. beyond all telling: Yeats 1

place
p., not to live, but to die in: Browne, Thomas
  3

place *(cont.)*
    this is an awful p.: Scott, Robert Falcon
    A p. for everything: Smiles 2
    cares more for one p.: Southey 4
plague
    p. o' both your houses: Shakespeare 377
plan
    but not without a p.: Pope 29
planet
    one look at this p.: Burroughs, William
platitude
    A p. is simply a truth: Baldwin, Stanley 1
Plato
    subtlety of the thought of P.: Oakeshott 1
    P. and commonsense do not mix: Russell,
      Bertrand, Lord 9
play
    Judge not the p. before: Davies, John 2
    p. up! and p. the game: Newbolt 4
    Judge not the p. before: Quarles 2
    The p., I remember: Shakespeare 91
    The p.'s the thing: Shakespeare 95
pleasant
    improper; so many p. things are: Gaskell 2
    If we do not find anything p.: Voltaire 1
pleas'd
    He more had p. us: Addison 10
pleasure
    understand the p.s of the other: Austen 2
    P.'s a sin: Byron, George, Lord 20
    No man tastes p.s truly: Chesterfield 6
    paucity of human p.s: Johnson, Samuel 8
    p. ... not enough to form a bond: Laclos
    P. ... intermission of pain: Selden 7
    No profit grows where is no p.: Shakespeare
      380
    If you were queen of p.: Swinburne 7
    dragged on by their favourite p.: Virgil 8
    Never to blend our p. with: Wordsworth,
      William 3
plenty
    here is God's p.: Dryden 15
PLO
    recognize the P.: Rabin
plot
    regards p.s ... life no help: Compton-Burnett
    What the devil does the p.: Villiers 1
    now the p. thickens: Villiers 2
plough
    We p. the fields, and scatter: Campbell, Jane
      Montgomery
    I must p. my furrow alone: Roseberry 2
ploughing
    Is my team p.: Housman 11
pocket
    want to put me in your p.: Lawrence 9
poem
    like to be married to a p.: Keats 27
    A p. is never finished: Valéry 1
poet
    p.'s hope: Auden 2
    All p.s are mad: Burton, Robert 1
    For a man to become a p.: Byron, George,
      Lord 15
    tragedy for a p.: Cocteau 6
    ever yet a great p., without: Coleridge,
      Samuel Taylor 11

    madness ... should posess a p.'s brain:
      Drayton 4
    the first p.s had: Drayton 5
    P.s should never marry: Gonne
    among the English P.s: Keats 26
    p. begins where the man ends: Ortega y
      Gasset 2
    enough for the p. to be: Perse
    Every man is a p. when: Plato
    P.s ... unacknowledged legislators: Shelley 7
    Love made me p.: Tanfield
    p. gives us his essence: Woolf 1
poetry
    The Fleshly School of P.: Buchanan
    She that with p. is won: Butler, Samuel 2
    p. = the best words: Coleridge, Samuel Taylor
      22
    P. is what is lost: Frost 8
    P. is a way of taking life: Frost 9
    P. should be great and unobtrusive: Keats 24
    If p. comes not as naturally: Keats 25
    civilization advances, p. ... declines: Macaulay
      12
    Writing a book of p. is like: Marquis 5
    P. is the revelation: Quasimodo
    P. is the opening: Sandburg 4
poison
    strongest p. ever known: Blake 3
policeman
    I'm a secret p.: Behan 2
    terrorist and the p.: Conrad 5
    The p.'s lot is not a happy one: Gilbert,
      W S 29
policy
    My (foreign) p.: Bevin
    In the field of world p.: Roosevelt, Franklin D
      2
political
    by nature is a p. animal: Aristotle 2
    saddest life is that of a p. aspirant:
      Mencken 2
    All p. lives: Powell, Enoch 1
politician
    p. never believes what he says: De Gaulle 3
    A p. is a statesman who: Pompidou
politics
    P. as a practice: Adams, Henry Brooks 1
    P. is just like ...bad woman: Batt
    P. is not an exact science: Bismarck 1
    Magnanimity in p.: Burke, Edmund 18
    not the language of p.: Disraeli 17
    P. is not the art: Galbraith 5
    P. is the art of acquiring: Gandhi, Indira
    Without alienation ... no p.: Miller, Arthur 2
    P. is supposed to be: Reagan 2
    P. is the art of preventing: Valéry 3
    P. come from man: Waite
pollertics
    My p., like my religion: Ward 1
Polly
    P. put the kettle on: Dickens 2
polygamous
    Hogamous, higamous / Man is p.: James,
      William 3
poor
    The p. always ye have: Bible 113
    every desire a p. man has: Céline 1

sex *(cont.)*
  If s. were all: Stevens 1
  Being a s. symbol: Welch
sexes
  two distinct s. was a disorder: Oz
  three s. — men, women, and clergymen:
    Smith, Sydney 2
sexton
  The s. toll'd the bell: Hood 2
shadow
  in the s. of death, to guide: Bible 104
  Follow a s., it still flies you: Jonson 3
  best in this kind are but s.s: Shakespeare 315
  millions of strange s.s on you tend:
    Shakespeare 436
Shakespeare
  honour to S.: Jonson 1
shame
  S. is the feeling: Sandburg 2
shape
  S. of Things to Come: Wells 9
shark
  s.'s presence to be felt everywhere:
    Spielberg 2
she
  S. who must be obeyed: Haggard
  S. who ne'er answers: Pope 38
sheep
  hungry s. look up, and are not fed:
    Milton 22
  their loves, or else their s.: Milton 29
  mountain s. are sweeter: Peacock 4
Shelley
  did you once see S. plain: Browning,
    Robert 16
shepherd
  Lord is my s.: Common Prayer, Book of 18
shillin'
  S. a day, / Bloomin good pay: Kipling 36
ship
  something wrong with our bloody s.s: Beatty
  Whither, O splendid s.: Bridges 3
  It was so old a s.: Flecker 3
  Heart of oak are our s.s: Garrick 1
  And the s.s shall go abroad: Kipling 22
  S.s that pass in the night: Longfellow 8
  s. was still as: Southey 6
shock
  short, sharp s.: Gilbert, W S 15
shoot
  Who s.s at the mid-day sun: Sidney 1
  teach the young idea how to s.: Thomson 2
short
  s. and the long of it: Shakespeare 302
shortest
  s. way to do many things: Smiles 1
shot
  s. heard round the world: Emerson 1
show business
  no business like s.: Berlin, Irving 6
showest
  Have more than thou s.: Shakespeare 204
sickness
  My long s.: Shakespeare 399
silence
  S. is the virtue of fools: Bacon 9
  applause of s. is the only kind: Jarry

eternal s. of these infinite spaces: Pascal 1
The rest is s.: Shakespeare 133
occasional flashes of s.: Smith, Sydney 3
lies are often told in s.: Stevenson 12
silent
  Ah, he is s.: Hardy 8
  Be s., unless what you have to say: Rosa
silliness
  shames s. out of me: Whitman 6
silver
  for a handful of s. he left us: Browning,
    Robert 13
Silvia
  Who is S.: Shakespeare 424
simple
  Keep it s.: Bergman
simplicity
  O holy s.: Huss
simplify
  S., s.: Thoreau 6
sin
  hide from us our favourite s.: Amiel 1
  wages of s. is death: Bible 119
  s. ye do by two and two: Kipling 42
  there is no s. but ignorance: Marlowe 9
  Commit / The oldest s.s: Shakespeare 154
  Few love to hear the s.s: Shakespeare 352
  worst s. towards our fellow creatures: Shaw
    6
  All s.s are attempts: Weil 3
sing
  Swans s. before they die: Coleridge, Samuel
    Taylor 13
  s. the Lord's song: Common Prayer, Book of
    39
  He knew / Himself to s.: Milton 17
  s. the savageness out of a bear:
    Shakespeare 345
  S. willow, willow, willow: Shakespeare 346
singing
  S. lieder is like putting: Baker, Janet
  suddenly burst out s.: Sassoon 3
single
  Christmas ... dreadful, if you're s.: Cope 4
sinner
  s.s are still in bed: Runyon 1
siren
  Blest pair of S.s ... Voice and Verse: Milton 8
sister
  his s.s and his cousins and his aunts: Gilbert,
    W S 7
sixty four
  When I'm s.: Lennon and McCartney 3
skin
  A thick s.: Adenauer
  Got You Under My Skin: Porter, Cole 7
skool
  only good things about s.: Willans
sky
  no bright reversion in the s.: Pope 7
  Under the wide and starry s.: Stevenson 11
  Which prisoners call the s.: Wilde 1
slang
  S. is a language: Sandburg 5
slave
  would have made him a s.: Burke,
    Edmund 16

s. of capitalist society: Connolly, James

The moment the s. resolves: Gandhi, Mahatma 3

In giving freedom to the s.: Lincoln 5

Here I stand, your s.: Shakespeare 206

slavery
cannot be classified as s.: Churchill, Winston 4

sleep
Let a little s.: Bible 42

S. is sweet to the labouring man: Bunyan 6

Oh S.! it is a gentle thing: Coleridge, Samuel Taylor 7

What hath night to do with s.: Milton 9

And we must s.: Shakespeare 23

S. that knits: Shakespeare 246

season of all natures, s.: Shakespeare 258

In s. a king, but, waking: Shakespeare 443

S. after toil: Spenser 5

slipper
A s. and a subtle knave: Shakespeare 338

slough
name of the s. was Despond: Bunyan 4

Slough
friendly bombs, and fall on S.: Betjeman 4

sluggard
'Tis the voice of the s.: Watts 4

slug-horn
Dauntless the s. to my lips: Browning, Robert 5

slumber
Golden s.s kiss your eyes: Dekker 2

s. did my spirit steal: Wordsworth, William 23

small
S. Is Beautiful: Schumacher 1

smell
very ancient and fish-like s.: Shakespeare 391

smile
s. I could feel in my hip pocket: Chandler 2

s., and be a villain: Shakespeare 78

The robb'd that s.: Shakespeare 334

When you call me that, s.: Wister

smiled
Until she s. on me: Coleridge, Hartley 2

snake
scotch'd the s., not killed: Shakespeare 253

snapper-up
s. of unconsidered trifles: Shakespeare 430

Snark
If your S. be a Boojum: Carroll 17

snob
admires mean things is a S.: Thackeray 1

snobbery
if s. died: Ustinov 3

snor
even like th way you s.: Cope 6

snoring
had to stop her s.: Graham, Harry 3

snow
where are the s.s of yesteryear: Villon

social
s. offenders who might well: Gilbert, W S 18

socialist
flourishing s. culture in our land: Mao Zedong 2

society
Man seeketh in s.: Bacon 5

The s. is ended: Berlin, Irving 5

In the affluent s.: Galbraith 2

upward to the Great S.: Johnson, Lyndon Baines 4

protected an individual ... protected s.: Kaunda 1

no such thing as S.: Thatcher 2

soldier
The boastful s.: Plautus

S.s are dreamers: Sassoon 2

s. is better accommodated: Shakespeare 151

tell an old s. by: Shaw 2

The British s. can stand up: Shaw 7

Old s.s, sweethearts are surest: Webster 2

solitude
To this delicious s.: Marvell 5

protects the s. of the other: Rilke 2

solution
Every s. ... raises new unsolved: Popper 1

somebodee
When every one is s.: Gilbert, W S 6

somebody
Let's stop s.: Herbert, A P 4

someday
S. I'll find you: Coward 7

somer
In a s. seson: Langland 2

Somerset House
records of S.: Smith, F E 1

something
S. will come of this: Dickens 1

son
A wise s. maketh: Bible 44

s. till he gets him a wife: Craik

S.s of Mary seldom bother: Kipling 38

twenty years to make a man of her s.: Rowland 5

song
cage the singer but not the s.: Belafonte

The s. is ended: Berlin, Irving 5

What s. the Syrens sang: Browne, Thomas 13

improvisation of human ... s. unfinished: McCullers 1

Sing no sad s.s for me: Rossetti, Christina 4

suck melancholy out of a s.: Shakespeare 36

sophistication
s. for a woman to be: Thurber 3

sorrow
bring down my grey hairs with s.: Bible 14

Man of s.s: Bible 73

S. is tranquillity: Parker 10

more in s. than in anger: Shakespeare 68

When s.s come: Shakespeare 120

few s.s ... which a good income: Smith, Logan Pearsall 2

sorry
never saw a wild thing / S. for itself: Lawrence 7

sought
They s. it with thimbles: Carroll 18

soul
Why shrinks the s.: Addison 7

exact measure of his own s.: Béart

gain the whole world ...lose his own s.: Bible 93

No coward s. is mine: Brontë, Emily 1

awkward thing to play with s.s: Browning, Robert 12

soul *(cont.)*

advise you of your s.'s health: Catherine of Aragon

real dark night of the s.: Fitzgerald, F Scott 2

every two s.s are absolutely different: Gibran 2

s. of indefatigable Industry: Hayley

my unconquerable s.: Henley 2

I am the captain of my s.: Henley 3

ye contented with your s.s: Kipling 15

Two s.s with but a single thought: Lovell

saw the iron enter unto his s.: Sterne 2

sound

secret s. ... inside you: Kabir 3

persistent s. ... war drums: Koestler 3

S.'s. the clarion: Mordaunt

Any who have heard that s.: Waugh 1

soup

S. of the evening: Carroll 6

sour

s. grapes and ashes: Ashford 3

south

beaker full of the warm S.: Keats 16

sower

The s. went forth sowing: Bourne

space

S. isn't remote at all: Hoyle

For tribal man s. ... uncontrollable mystery: McLuhan 2

S. is out of this world: Sharman

spaniel

So well-bred s.s civilly delight: Pope 17

spareth

s. the rod hateth his son: Bible 48

sparrer-grass

Hit look lak s.: Harris 3

Spartan

Go, tell the S.s: Simonides

speak

Always be ready to s. your mind: Blake 12

S. low, if you s. love: Shakespeare 321

S. of me as I am: Shakespeare 350

He s.s to Me as if: Victoria 2

specialism

his s. is omniscience: Doyle 5

specialist

definition of a s.: Mayo

A s. is someone: Ricci

spectator

I live in the world rather as a s.: Addison 12

speech

S. happens not to be: De Staël 3

S. is the small change of silence: Meredith, George 5

The manner of his s.: Shakespeare 13

Speak the s.: Shakespeare 105

speeches

From all the easy s.: Chesterton 11

speed

safety is in our s.: Emerson 11

Spenser

Sweet S., moving through: Wordsworth, William 19

spider

said a s. to a fly: Howitt

spinster

When you're a s. of forty: Cope 1

spirit

s. shall return unto God: Bible 60

s. indeed is willing, but: Bible 97

perfecting of our s.: Lichtenberg 6

S. of Delight: Shelley 15

Hail to thee, blithe s.: Shelley 16

spiritual

Millions of s. creatures walk the earth: Milton 58

splendour

s. falls on castle walls: Tennyson 46

split

When I s. an infinitive: Chandler 6

spoil

Nothing was made by God for man to s.: Locke 2

s.s that his own hand spread: Swinburne 2

spoke

s. among your wheels Beaumont and Fletcher 7

spoon

S. feeding in the long run: Forster 5

ate with a runcible s.: Lear 4

sport

Detested s.: Cowper 12

S. that wrinkled Care derides: Milton 3

Sporus

Let S. tremble: Pope 16

spot

Out, damned s.: Shakespeare 264

spring

S. should vanish with the Rose: Fitzgerald, Edward 8

Sweet s., full: Herbert, George 10

In the S. a young man's fancy: Tennyson 34

S. is come home: Thompson, Francis 3

spur

Let the boy win his s.s: Edward III

stage

your daughter on the s.: Coward 4

All the world's a s.: Shakespeare 38

stand

firm place on which to s.: Archimedes 2

who will s. on either hand: Macaulay 9

must s. the course: Shakespeare 211

star

s.s in their courses fought: Bible 23

Go, and catch a falling s.: Donne 13

Hitch your wagon to a s.: Emerson 17

Bright s., would were steadfast: Keats 1

love a bright particular s.: Shakespeare 1

Two s.s keep not their motion: Shakespeare 139

There was a s. danced: Shakespeare 319

Star-Chamber

I will make a S. matter of it: Shakespeare 299

star-spangled

'Tis the s. banner: Key, Francis Scott

state

Nothing doth more hurt in a s.: Bacon 13

s. without the means ... change: Burke, Edmund 9

ruin or to rule the s.: Dryden 6

S.s, like men, have: Landor 3

I am the S.: Louis XIV 1

worth of a S., in the long run: Mill 6

Oh happy s.: Pope 10

superstition *(cont.)*
S. is the religion of feeble minds: Burke,
Edmund 10

support
May He s. us all the day: Newman, John
Henry 2
to s. him after: Shakespeare 396

sure
make assurance double s.: Shakespeare 262

surrealism
S. is destructive: Dali 2

surrender
Give me the man who will s.: Barbellion
Guards die but do not s.: Cambronne
We shall never s.: Churchill, Winston 5

survival
s. of the fittest: Spencer 4

survived
She s. whatever happened: Auden 13
I s.: Sièyes

suspect
makes a man s. much: Bacon 39

suspicion
S.s amongst thoughts: Bacon 38

Sussex
S. by the sea: Kipling 41

swan
Sweet S. of Avon: Jonson 7
after many a summer dies the s.: Tennyson 53

swindle
truly great s.s are: Henry, O 2

Swiss
No money, no S.: Racine 3

sword
beat their s.s into plowshares: Bible 67
take the s. shall perish with the s.: Bible 98
a s. between the sexes: Lewis, C S 3

system
Our little s.s have their day: Tennyson 25

tail
Brother, thy t. hangs down: Kipling 35

tale
t. speeds best being plainly told: Shakespeare
364
With a t. forsooth he cometh: Sidney 6

talent
no substitute for t.: Huxley, Aldous 11
That one t. which is death to hide: Milton 26
t.s, industry will improve: Reynolds,
Joshua 1

talk
t. six times ... single lady: Byron, George,
Lord 34
wished him to t. on for ever: Hazlitt 3

talked
believed they t. of me: Farquhar 3
worse than being t. about: Wilde 17

talking
don't say yes until I've finished t.: Zanuck

tank
Don't mess with me, I got t.s: Campbell, Kim

Tar-baby
T. ain't sayin' nuthin': Harris 1

Tarquin
great house of T.: Macaulay 8

Tarzan
Me T., you Jane: Burroughs, Edgar Rice

task
done my t., let others do: Corday

Tasmanian
T.s, who never committed adultery:
Maugham 1

taxes
no new t.: Bush
death and t.: Franklin 6

teach
T. me, my God and King: Herbert, George 5
t. others who themselves excel: Pope 23

teaching
most important part of t.: Weil 4

tear
If you have t.s: Shakespeare 189
T.s, idle t.s: Tennyson 47
T.s in the nature of thing: Virgil 3

technology
sufficiently advanced t.: Clarke

television
T. has brought back murder: Hitchcock

temple
chiefest sanctity of a t.: Unamuno 1

temptation
oughtn't to yield to t.: Hope 4
way to get rid of a t.: Wilde 14

tempted
one thing to be t.: Shakespeare 270

tent
better to have him inside the t.: Johnson,
Lyndon Baines 1

terror
T. ... concept of the truth: Baudrillard 2
no t. untempered by some great moral:
Godard 1

terrorist
t. and the policeman: Conrad 5

Thames
Sweet T., run softly: Spenser 9

Thatcher
If Margaret T. wins: Kinnock 1

thee
I die / As often as from t. I go: Donne 15

there
Because it's t.: Mallory, George Leigh

thief
if you do take a t.: Shakespeare 326

think
t., therefore I am: Descartes 2
Some people would sooner die than t.:
Russell, Bertrand, Lord 14
He t.s too much: Shakespeare 173

thirty
Women over t. are at their best: Belmondo

thou
Whither t. goest: Bible 25
T. wast all that to me: Poe 6

thought
Every t. derives: Cioran 5
T. is the child of action: Disraeli 12
business of t. to define: Palmer
our own t.s expressed by others: Rostand 4

thoughtlessness
t. is the weapon of the male: Connolly,
Cyril 9

threescore
t. years and ten: Common Prayer, Book of 27

thrift
T., t., Horatio: Shakespeare 66
thrush
That's the wise t.: Browning, Robert 11
thumb
By the pricking of my t.s: Shakespeare 260
thunder
they steal my t.: Dennis 2
thus
To be t. is nothing: Shakespeare 251
thyself
Know t.: Anonymous
tide
t. in the affairs of men: Shakespeare 195
tiger
t.s of wrath are wiser: Blake 14
T.! T.! burning bright: Blake 19
time
T., which is the author: Bacon 2
'That passed the t.': Beckett 2
T. is a great teacher: Berlioz
t. to be born and a t. to die: Bible 57
What t.s, what customs: Cicero 4
t. is money: Franklin 1
Old T. is still a-flying: Herrick 10
be not coy, but use your t.: Herrick 11
T., you old gypsy: Hodgson 2
As t. goes by: Hupfeld
T. will not be ours for ever: Jonson 8
t. is running out: Koestler 2
T., ... strengthens friendship, weakens love: La Bruyère 1
A good t. coming: Mackay
mark of our t. is its revulsion against: McLuhan 3
T. was away and somewhere else: MacNeice 2
can't make pure clay of t.'s mud: Malamud
T.'s wingèd chariot: Marvell 9
T. for a little something: Milne 6
T. will run back, and fetch: Milton 30
With thee conversing I forget all t.: Milton 57
T. the devourer: Ovid 5
the t.s that try men's souls: Paine 2
O t. too swift: Peele 1
A Dance to the Music of T.: Powell, Anthony 3
Even such is t.: Raleigh 8
seen the best of our t.: Shakespeare 202
look into the seeds of t.: Shakespeare 232
T. and the hour runs through: Shakespeare 236
dark backward and abysm of t.: Shakespeare 386
T. hath, my lord, a wallet: Shakespeare 404
whirligig of t. brings in: Shakespeare 420
T. doth transfix the flourish: Shakespeare 439
usage of those antique t.s: Spenser 6
long result of T.: Tennyson 32
Meanwhile, T. is flying: Virgil 10
There was a t.: Wordsworth, William 11
time-lag
comfortable t. of fifty years: Wells 7
timid
If I ever felt inclined to be t.: Webb
tobacco
wasted any more time on t.: Toscanini 1

today
here t. and gone tomorrow: Behn 3
together
must indeed all hang t.: Franklin 4
t. for 25 years: Herbert, A P 5
toil
Horny-handed sons of t.: Kearney
to-morrow
T., and t., and t.: Shakespeare 268
tone
seem'd that t., and gesture bland: Scott, Walter 6
tongue
t.s of men and of angels: Bible 124
A host of t.s: Shakespeare 19
tool
Without t.s he is nothing: Carlyle, Thomas 8
Give us the t.s: Churchill, Winston 14
toothpaste
t. is out of the tube: Haldeman
torch
hand on the t. of life: Lucretius 1
torment
how many t.s lie: Cibber
Tory
wise T. and a wise Whig: Johnson, Samuel 53
totalitarian
stumbling-block of t. regimes: Weil 2
tough
When the going gets t.: Kennedy, Joseph P
town
never go down to the end of the t.: Milne 2
trade
No nation was ever ruined by t.: Franklin 3
There isn't any t.: Herbert, A P 7
tragedie
go litel myn t.: Chaucer 12
tragedies
All t. are finished by: Byron 28
two t. in life: Shaw 20
tragedy
A perfect T.: Addison 13
T. is restful: Anouilh 1
trail
long t. a-winding: King, Stoddard
train
biggest electric t. set: Welles
translation
T.s (like wives): Campbell, Roy
He is T.'s thief that addeth more: Marvell 8
travel
two classes of t.: Benchley 3
I t. light: Fry, Christopher 1
I t. for t.'s sake: Stevenson, Robert Louis 8
traveller
real t.s are only those who leave: Baudelaire 2
'Is there anybody there?' said the t.: De La Mare 3
travelling
T. is the ruin of all happiness: Burney 2
t. induces a feeling: Theroux
treason
The T. of the Intellectuals: Benda
love the t.: Daniel 3
T. doth never prosper: Harington
If this be t., make the most: Henry, Patrick 1
treasure
Where your t. is: Bible 82

tree
t. of the knowledge of good and evil: Bible 5
spare the beechen t.: Campbell, Thomas 1
I like t.s because: Cather, Willa 3
when t.s were green: Clare
It is not growing like a t.: Jonson 2
never see / A poem as lovely as a t.: Kilmer
all the t.s that grow so fair: Kipling 43
Standing ... at the trunk of the t.: Klee 2
in a t. did end their race: Marvell 3
Crown'd from some single herb or t.: Marvell 4
Under the greenwood t.: Shakespeare 35
like that t. ... die at the top: Swift 5

Trelawny
And shall T. die: Hawker

trial
only a t. if I recognize: Kafka 2

triumph
meet with T. and Disaster: Kipling 12

trivial
mighty contests rise from t. things: Pope 41

trouble
pack up your t.s: Asaf
Man is born unto t.: Bible 36

trousers
never put on one's best t.: Ibsen 3

trowel
lays it on with a t.: Congreve 3

truant
A t. disposition, good my lord: Shakespeare 65

truck
propensity to t., barter and exchange: Smith, Adam 1

true
said t. things, but called: Browning, Robert 1
What I tell you three times is t.: Carroll 16
what he wishes to be t.: Demosthenes
t. to you, darlin', in my fashion: Porter, Cole 1
not necessarily t. because a man dies: Wilde 20

trust
put not your t. in princes: Common Prayer, Book of 40

truth
The t. which makes men free: Agar
T. is not only violated by falsehood: Amiel 2
t. universally acknowledged: Austen 9
no original t.: Bachelard 2
listening to these murmurs ... hears the t.: Bachelard 3
What is t.? said jesting Pilate: Bacon 41
Terror ... concept of the t.: Baudrillard 2
T. is the cry of all: Berkeley 2
no t. in him: Bible 112
T. exists; only lies: Braque 1
great is t., & shall prevail: Brooks, Thomas
enemies of the t.: Browne, Thomas 5
T. is within ourselves: Browning, Robert 18
t. is so seldom: Cornforth
desires that hide the t.: Depardieu
whatever remains ... must be the t.: Doyle 10
T. never damages a cause: Gandhi, Mahatma 4
Everyone has experienced that t.: Gibran 1

T. from his lips prevail'd: Goldsmith 5
t. through a series of errors: Huxley, Aldous 6
Irrationally held t.s: Huxley, Thomas Henry 1
customary fate of new t.s: Huxley, Thomas Henry 2
best policy to speak the t.: Jerome, Jerome K 1
to put him in posession of the t.: Locke 1
ocean of t. lay all undiscovered: Newton
who does not bellow the t.: Péguy
When t. is no longer free: Prévert
takes two to speak the t.: Thoreau 7
mainly he told the t.: Twain 1
submerged t. sometimes comes: Woolf 5

truthful
stupid believe that to be t. is easy: Cather 4

tunnel
light at the end of the t. ... train: Lowell, Robert 3
That t. will collapse: Morrissey 2

turn
T. on, tune in and drop out: Leary
You t. if you want to: Thatcher 3

turtle
The t. lives 'twixt plated decks: Nash 1

Tuscany
even the ranks of T.: Macaulay 11

twenty
T. years a child: Irish proverb

Tyrawley
T. and I have been dead: Chesterfield 10

ugliness
U. ... most reliable stimulants: Montherlant 2

ugly
all u. things are made: Wilde 22

Ulster
U. will fight: Churchill, Randolph 2

umble
We are so very 'u.: Dickens 12

unbeliever
O ye U.s: Koran 7

uncertainty
little u. is good: Kissinger 3

unconscious
The u. is the ocean: Calvino 1
images of the u.: Jung 3

understand
This rage to u.: Buñuel 2
u. only because I love: Tolstoy 3

understanding
Look with your u.: Bach
not, by knowing ... obtain an u.: Feynman

undesirable
I knows an u. character: Fry, Christopher 3

undone
have left u. those things: Common Prayer, Book of 8

unhappiness
loyalty we all feel to u.: Greene, Graham 4

unhappy
in mourning for my life, I'm u.: Chekov 1

union
secret of a succesful u.: Ayckbourn 1
value and beauty of a perfect u.: Galsworthy

unity
when people talk about u.: Jenkins

war *(cont.)*
magnificent, but it is not w.: Bosquet
In w. there is no second: Bradley
W. always finds a way: Brecht 2
W. is like love, it always: Brecht 3
In w. ... no winners: Chamberlain, Neville 1
In w.: resolution: Churchill, Winston 8
Let w.s yield to peace: Cicero 3
never was a good w.: Franklin 5
gave a w. & Nobody came: Ginsberg
W.'s annals will cloud: Hardy 5
essence of w. is violence: Macaulay 3
moderation in w. is imbecility: Macaulay 3
W. is not an instinct: Ortega y Gassett 6
W. is peace: Orwell 5
asks you what you did in the w.: Patton
When w. is declared, Truth: Ponsonby
give a w. and nobody will come: Sandburg 3
looks on w. as all glory, but: Sherman
Fierce w.s and faithful loves: Spenser 3
W. that Will End W.: Wells 10

Waring
What's become of W: Browning, Robert 26

wasted
W. his substance: Bible 109

watch
The Lord w. between me and thee: Bible 11

watchman
W., what of the night: Bible 70

watchword
Our w. is security: Pitt, William *the Elder* 4

water
Many w.s cannot quench love: Bible 65
W., w., everywhere: Coleridge, Samuel Taylor 4
w.s are ever flowing: Heraclitus 4
name was writ in w.: Keats 30
Not all the w. in the rough rude sea: Shakespeare 359

Waterloo
Every man meets his W.: Phillips 1

Watson
Mr W., come here: Bell

weak
The w. have one weapon: Bidault 2
Like all w. men: Maugham 7
to be w. is miserable: Milton 36

weaknesses
Once we know our w.: Lichtenberg 3

wealth
w. accumulates, and men decay: Goldsmith 3

wear
better to w. out: Cumberland

weather
the w. the cuckoo likes: Hardy 9
If it prove fair w.: Suckling 4

web
what a tangled w. we weave: Scott, Walter 14

Webster
W. was much possessed: Eliot, T S 5

wedding
day after that w. night: Colette 3
Tomorrow is our w. day: Cowper 2
happy a thing were a w.: Flatman
one of those w.s where: Trapido
man looks pretty small at a w.: Wilder, Thornton 3

wedlock
w.'s the devil: Byron, George, Lord 38

weep
w. the more because I w. in vain: Gray 9

well-written
A w. life is almost as rare: Carlyle, Thomas 1

west
Go W., young man: Greeley

Westminster Abbey
shall have gained a peerage, or W.: Nelson 1

westward
W. the course of empire: Berkeley 1

wheel
w. is come full circle: Shakespeare 218

Whig
caught the W.s bathing: Disraeli 15

whisper
There's a w. down the field: Kipling 23
stealthily withdrawing w. (Satan): Koran 5

whistle
W. and she'll come: Beaumont and Fletcher 10
w. and I'll come to you: Burns, Robert 18
joly w. wel y-wet: Chaucer 8

white
The so-called w. races: Forster 6
Take up the W. Man's burden: Kipling 45
see the w.s of their eyes: Putnam

whitewash
no w. at the White House: Nixon

whore
'Tis Pity She's a W.: Ford, John 3

wicked
no peace ... unto the w.: Bible 72
No one ... extremely w. suddenly: Juvenal 1

wickedness
Hated w. that hinders loving: Browning, Robert 17
men ... capable of every w.: Conrad 7

widow
When w.s exclaim loudly: Fielding 1
Do like other w.s: Gay 4
you, my dear, will be my w.: Guitry 2
W. The word consumes: Plath 2

wife
My w. was an immature woman: Allen 3
something was wrong with my first w.: Allen 4
My w. got the house: Allen 12
owes his success to his first w.: Backus
loving w. is better than: Barrie 13
Giving honour unto the w.: Bible 137
If ever w. was happy in a man: Bradstreet
w. not only edited his works: Brooks, Van Wyck
bitterest creature under heaven is the w.: Buck 2
w. ... trying to turn him into: Chesterton 13
dwindle into a w.: Congreve 13
W., spouse, my dear, joy: Congreve 14
away from his w. for seven years: Darling
Here lies my w.: Dryden 25
One w. is too much: Gay 5
a w. for breed: Gay 8
I chose my w.: Goldsmith 15
The trouble with my w.: Gorer
man steals your w., no better revenge: Guitry 1

woman (*cont.*)
A w.'s whole history: Irving 1
a w.'s preaching: Johnson, Samuel 21
life with an amiable w.: Johnson, Samuel 30
in a post-chaise with a pretty w.: Johnson, Samuel 33
In every w.'s heart: Jong
stages in a w.'s life: Kelly
w. is only a w.: Kipling 3
silliest w. can manage a clever man: Kipling 32
w. unsatisfied must have luxuries: Lawrence 4
mental relation with a w.: Lawrence 17
Why can't a w. be more like a man: Lerner 3
the sort of w. who lives for others: Lewis, C S 5
another w. to make a man appreciate his wife: Luce 2
w. exists for the sake of man: Luther 2
w. will always sacrifice herself: Maugham 3
w. does not want her love affairs talked about: Maurois 3
W. will be the last thing civilized: Meredith, George 3
no legal slaves – except for the w.: Mill 8
w. is made for man: Montherlant 1
Is not a w.'s life: Pankhurst
W. lives but in her lord: Parker 3
A W. is a foreign land: Patmore
The w.'s deaf, and does not hear: Pope 39
the heart of the w. whom he loves: Proust 1
A w.'s love for us increases: Pushkin 2
A w. whose dresses: Saki 13
W.! in our hours of ease: Scott, Walter 15
No more, but e'en a w.: Shakespeare 27
never yet fair w. but: Shakespeare 207
Would it not grieve a w.: Shakespeare 323
w., therefore may be woo'd: Shakespeare 400
w. to provide for herself: Shaw 27
way for a w. to hold a man: Spark 1
comfort about being a w.: Stark
w. without a man: Steinem 4
w. is so hard / Upon the w.: Tennyson 49
w. with fair opportunities: Thackeray 6
Once a w. has given you her heart: Vanbrugh 2
w. is always fickle: Virgil 4
have to give a w. a ring: West, Mae 13
A w. in love can't be reasonable: West, Mae 15
w. who lives for others: Whitehorn 2
No w. should ever be quite accurate: Wilde 9
never trust a w. who: Wilde 23
want to be a w.'s first love: Wilde 25
Die because a w.'s fair: Wither 1
womb
if God had wanted us to think just with our w.s: Luce 1
women
W. over thirty: Belmondo
w. in men require: Blake 10
Good w. always think: Brookner 2
money or your life; w. require: Butler, Samuel 26
Alas! the love of w.: Byron, George, Lord 24
tide in the affairs of w.: Byron, George, Lord 33

w. are angels, yet wedlock's: Byron, George, Lord 38
man of sense only trifles with them [w.]: Chesterfield 4
to save [w.] from nature: Dior
worship w. they'll forgive: Durrell
not denyin' the w. are foolish: Eliot, George 2
The happiest w.: Eliot, George 6
proper function of w.: Eliot, George 7
Faithful w. are all alike: Giraudoux 1
If men knew how w. pass the time: Henry, O 1
W.'s liberation is: Kent
sick of the hired w.: Kipling 25
Some w.'ll stay in a man's memory: Kipling 26
Monstrous Regiment of W.: Knox, John
W. ... to behave like men: Mackenzie 2
Because w. can do nothing except love: Maugham 10
Just as w.'s bodies: Pisan
between and among w.: Rich
don't like married w.: Ruskin 1
W. always want: Schnitzler
O! see my w.: Shakespeare 26
fickleness of the w. I love: Shaw 28
w. guide the plot: Sheridan, Richard Brinsley 7
Married w. are kept w.: Smith, Logan Pearsall 5
old w. (of both sexes): Sterne 7
three things men can do with w.: Stills
disappointment is the lot of w.: Stone
I still don't understand w.: Wayne 1
W. like that part: Webster 1
Whatever w. do: Whitton
All w. become like their mothers: Wilde 4
amount of w. in London: Wilde 5
do not wish them [w.] to have power over men: Wollstonecraft 2
W. have served all these centuries: Woolf 6
womman
She was a worthy w. al hir lyve: Chaucer 3
wonder
W.s are many: Sophocles 3
wood
I am for the w.s against the world: Blunden 1
We'll to the w.s no more: Housman 3
w.s shall to me answer: Spenser 2
w.s decay and fall: Tennyson 53
impulse from a vernal w.: Wordsworth, William 27
woodshed
something nasty in the w.: Gibbons 3
word
w.s without knowledge: Bible 39
In the beginning was the W.: Bible 111
For each there is a w.: Campbell, David Gordon
my w.s are my own: Charles II 3
w.s once spoke: Dillon 1
stroke people with w.s: Fitzgerald, F Scott 3
W.s ... most powerful drug: Kipling 47
The trouble with w.s: Potter, Dennis
w.s become thee as thy wounds: Shakespeare 230
Proper w.s in proper places: Swift 4